*Educational
Patterns in
Contemporary
Societies*

Educational

Patterns in

Contemporary

Societies

I. N. THUT

Professor of Education
The University of Connecticut

DON ADAMS

Associate Professor of Education
Syracuse University

McGraw-Hill Book Company
New York   San Francisco
Toronto   London

Educational Patterns in Contemporary Societies

Library of Congress Catalog Card Number: 63-23538

64556

FOUNDATIONS IN EDUCATION
Harold Benjamin, *Consulting Editor*

Preface

A cliché of ancient vintage states that to study education well is to study it comparatively. This bit of sage advice is enjoying new respectability of late as peoples are coming to realize that education is a matter of universal concern and that the variety of means invented and employed to cope with it make for interesting as well as rewarding study. Comparative education accordingly is a field of growing scholarly activity. The educational provincialism once cultivated behind arbitrarily drawn national boundaries is diminishing slowly in the face of increased knowledge of other educational patterns. This trend, however, has not yet progressed far enough to neutralize the tenacity with which many people—teachers as well as laymen—still cling to inherited biases for "their" school system. Perhaps each of us always should nurture such a bias; but the fact remains that as more people have become involved in the study of educational institutions and programs in other national settings, an awareness of the utility of such study has increased in direct proportion. To paraphrase Parkinson's law, the growth of interest seemingly feeds on expanded information and broader insights.

But arguing for the timeliness of a book is not a becoming occupation for its authors. The question of real importance is "For whom is the book written?" This book has been prepared specifically to help advanced and graduate students in education, primarily teachers and administrators engaged in elementary and secondary education, to acquire a knowledge of educational systems func-

tioning in other cultural settings. It is assumed that such students have had little if any previous acquaintance with schools outside their own country or time. This, therefore, is an introductory textbook. Its content is planned to orient such students to this field of study and to afford them a more fruitful understanding of the nature of education in general and of their role as teachers in their unique local situations in particular.

The authors acknowledge with gratitude the help they received from students and colleagues, especially as the manuscript was taking shape. Often the value of such help was neither recognized nor appreciated at the time, either by those who gave it or those who received it. The authors are fully aware, however, that special thanks are due several distinguished scholars in this field for their suggestions and criticism. Among them are Prof. Harold R. W. Benjamin, whose knowledge and authority are widely known and respected; Prof. H. H. Benjamin, who read the entire manuscript with a critical eye to its historical accuracy and was particularly helpful in the chapter on Spain; and Prof. Archibald W. Anderson, who also read the manuscript in its late stage of development under what were for him rather difficult circumstances. Among others who were consulted with reference to specific sections or chapters, the authors are indebted to Prof. Hobert Burns, who clarified several matters relating to Latin America; Prof. Mamoru Oshiba, who gave many suggestions regarding

vii

Japanese education; Prof. Sun Kang-tseng, whose friendly criticism hopefully compensates at least in part for our lack of knowledge of the Chinese language and whose homeland is the only country treated which has not been visited by one or the other author; and Prof. David Scanlon, whose extensive knowledge of Middle Africa contributed substantially to Chapter 15.

Lastly the "patience and forbearance" so commonly attributed to the wives and children of authors have special meaning in this case. Of course good wives should have these qualities anyway, but their observance tested during prolonged periods of undone household chores and abandoned holiday jaunts has been nonetheless appreciated. The junior author feels especially beholden to his wife for assistance in library research and editing. Her tasks were often tedious and her reward, at least in monetary value, was indeed slight.

I. N. Thut
Don Adams

Contents

List of Figures

List of Tables

CHAPTER 1

The Comparative Study of Education

Interest in the comparative study of education has reached significant heights since World War II. In part, this interest reflects a breaking down of the narrow provincialism fostered behind national boundaries in years gone by and, in part, the rise of aggressive internationalism in nations or groups of nations determined not to be outdone in any area of endeavor in the race for world leadership. Beyond these factors, however, there also is a growing uneasiness over the great economic, social, and cultural differences among the several groupings of the world's populations. Such differences have existed for a long time; but modern forms of communication and the unprecedented intermingling of peoples induced of late by economic and political interests have aroused expectations in the less favored areas that no longer can be denied. Both the late-developing peoples and those disposed to help them have come to look upon education as a major instrument for transforming the culture or upgrading the social system. As a consequence, the study of educational programs and agencies by which other peoples seek the fulfillment of their highest aspirations is becoming the object of scholarly attention in many places. Perhaps it is this desire to know as much as possible about all educational activities everywhere that best characterizes the study of comparative education today.

The recent introduction of comparative studies in a number of colleges and universities and the substantial expansion of existing programs in others have created the impression that this is a new field of interest. This is an illusion, however. In Asia, China was regarded as the center of learning for nearly two thousand years. The rulers of Japan, Korea, and somewhat later, the kingdoms of South Asia sent their learned men to China to borrow from that ancient culture. They brought back the Chinese language, a knowledge of the educational system, and the wisdom of Confucius and other sages. Curricula based on the Confucian canon of classical works provided the major part of the formal education of upper-class boys in all East Asia until well into the nineteenth century.

Comparative studies were initiated under substantially different circumstances in the West. Education in the West, after the Age of Darkness, was not so much borrowed as exported as an aid to conquest. It was provided by the Roman Catholic Church which for centuries claimed the exclusive right to maintain schools. The Church, then as now, was an international institution with highly centralized, hierarchical administrative control. It operated in the field of education without direct competition from either religious or secular agencies, and church schools offered a singularly uniform curriculum and pattern of institutional forms. Under these conditions, scholars had neither a strong motive nor a promising opportunity to engage in comparative studies.

After the Reformation, the Church's monopoly in education was no longer permitted. Many of the independent sovereignties that emerged from the turmoil of the religious wars embraced a Protestant faith. New ecclesiastical systems were organized on national lines, and the educational institutions that went over to these new systems soon lost their international character. Some of the German states, in particular, pioneered the development of national systems of education. During this period of rapid development, numerous national differences appeared. In some states, education forged ahead and in time aroused the admiration, and sometimes the envy, of states which had been less aggressive.

Through a series of singular circumstances, the educational system which came to attract the widest attention, early in the nineteenth century, was that of Prussia. While her leadership had not been outstandingly enlightened or liberal, she had adopted, in the eighteenth century, both a program of compulsory military training and a policy of universal education. The combined effects of these two policies contributed substantially to her subsequent achievement of military superiority, amply supported by a strong economy and an efficient organization. Prussia's rise to power quite understandably aroused the envy of her competitors. Foreign educators and statesmen came in considerable number to observe at firsthand the educational institutions and programs that had helped her achieve such a brilliant success in such an incredibly short time. The reports of these visitors, published in the first half of the nineteenth century, constitute the first significant body of literature in comparative education.[1]

Although it was not the earliest comparative study of education reported by

historians, the Report on the State of Public Instruction in Prussia by Victor Cousin to the French government in 1831 is typical of those published during this period. Cousin had been commissioned to undertake his study by a government that was seriously attempting to reorganize its institutional forms to achieve a higher level of social development. At about the same time the several American states, which had but recently ventured on the road to self-government, also were looking around for promising institutional forms and practices that could be adapted to their particular needs. The Cousin report was circulated widely in America; and New York ultimately imitated, in the University of the State of New York, important features of the administrative system developed by the French.

Not all Americans were willing to depend upon secondhand reports. Henry Barnard was only one of several Americans who traveled to Europe before 1860 to visit schools and consult with educational leaders. He reported his observations, first, in the *American Journal of Education* and, later, as the first United States Commissioner of Education, in the *Annual Reports of the Commissioner of Education*. In 1854 some of these, together with selected reports submitted by others, were published under the title of *National Education in Europe*.[2] In his preface, Barnard gave some indication of the extent to which leading American educators had been active in the field of comparative education at that time. He wrote that he had been able to add freely to his own observations and study of documents

[1] George F. Kneller, "Comparative Education," *Encyclopedia of Educational Research*, 3d ed., Macmillan, New York, 1960, pp. 316–322.

[2] Henry Barnard, *National Education in Europe*, 2d ed., Case, Tiffany, Hartford, Conn., 1854.

... from the elaborate and valuable reports of Prof. Calvin E. Stowe, D.D., to the Legislature of Ohio, in 1837, of President Alexander Dallas Bache, L.L.D., to the trustees of the Girard College of Orphans in Philadelphia, in 1839, of Hon. Horace Mann, L.L.D., to the Massachusetts Board of Education in 1846....[3]

This was by no means a complete list of the studies published by Americans before 1854, not even by those who had observed European schools at firsthand.

Although the War between the States brought an end to this first period of American interest in European education, scholarly activity was renewed later in the century. Then the focus of attention was the curricular and methodological reforms being pressed by liberal educators abroad. It was during this later period that American education received its generous infusion of Froebelian and Herbartian theories and practices. The establishment of kindergartens and normal schools was an institutional manifestation of this infusion.

Meanwhile several European governments were also taking a closer look at their neighbors' schools. England was particularly active in this respect in the latter half of the nineteenth century. The reports of several of her leading educators, including Matthew Arnold,[4] are still important contributions to the literature of comparative education.

Perhaps the greatest of all educational hunting expeditions in this period was conducted by the Japanese government. Having rejected the classical Chinese learning, the Japanese sought fresh wisdom in the West. Brigades of bright young men were sent to Germany, England, France, and the United States of America to acquire the knowledge needed to industrialize the Japanese economy and modernize the military machine. The Japanese educational system was reconstructed along Western lines, new schools were introduced, and scholars from the West were offered high positions in the universities and the government. The benefits Japan derived from this vast program of borrowing are still something of a marvel to students of comparative education; and its phenomenal results afford hope to those engaged in helping underdeveloped nations today.

The purpose of comparative studies

Early comparative studies were clearly a search for institutional forms and practices that could be transplanted from one culture to another. Indeed, some of the American reports recommended the adoption of the Prussian system without delay; but the state legislators, fortunately, were not easily persuaded. Perhaps those practical men sensed intuitively that such outright borrowing is fraught with much danger. This fact has become painfully apparent in the rather pitiful imitation of the French *lycée* in parts of Southeast Asia and the Near East and in the fumbling attempts to imitate American comprehensive high schools in East Asia. Perhaps the classic examples of educational institutions lacking cultural and even linguistic roots were those imposed on certain African colonies by their European rulers.

But not all comparative studies have

[3] *Ibid.*, p. 3.
[4] See especially *Schools Inquiry Commission,* H.M. Stationery Office, London, 1868, vol. I.

3

been hunting expeditions. At least a few were motivated by a desire to compile a catalog of all existing institutional forms and arrangements together with their salient features. Such studies have described, among other traits, the legal bases on which the educational activities rest, the administrative powers by which specified activities are put into operation, the facts brought to light by periodic pupil enumerations, the types of institutions and the courses offered, and the functions of the several divisions and levels of the systems observed. Usually, however, little attention has been given to the unique ends the arrangements and procedures noted are intended to serve.

Obviously, there is much to be gained from an encyclopedic collection of information on education around the world. Information of this type is needed for understanding the conditions under which educational programs operate and how they vary. It is also necessary for identifying weaknesses and strengths and anticipating specific problems that will be encountered if identified needs are to be satisfied. But studies which are accumulations of facts merely emphasize material considerations, such as operational economy and administrative efficiency, and neglect questions relating to the human aspects. Evidence that some students of comparative education become lost in a maze of factual information may be found in the observation voiced now and then that one system is as good as any other and that the differences are due merely to the exigencies of social evolution. Needless to say, more fruitful concepts are gained from studies that seek to discover functional relationships between the aspirations of people as individuals and the

means employed by those in authority to bring direction and order into their common life. While it is customary for comparative studies to focus upon the latter and, therefore, to compare one national system of education with another, it is only after a nation's goals and values have been brought into view that existing political controls, institutional arrangements, and instructional practices can be observed in their proper perspective or even judged in a fair and understanding manner.

Different societies, quite naturally, have different ends in view. Furthermore, every formal program of education has been brought into existence through a deliberate effort to realize some specific, consciously held value or social ideal. People who establish a system of education, no matter how primitive, have a reason for doing so; and their selection of a given type of institution, curriculum, or practice is never merely the chance product of an indifferent process of evolution.

This does not mean that deliberate choices are always the wisest ones possible. A better informed judgment or a more sophisticated point of view might lead to different choices. The ability to make intelligent decisions depends upon both the adequacy of the end in view and the appropriateness of the means selected to achieve it. Thus a comparative study of education should not be limited merely to learning all there is to know about other systems of education; its primary aim should be to develop the ability, based on a knowledge of ends as well as means, to exercise intelligent leadership in the educational enterprise in which the student himself is employed. A talent for creative, constructive educational statesmanship is called for, a talent that grows with the ability to identify that which is lacking and to suggest ways in which needs may be met. For this the educational statesman must learn to see local problems in a perspective far broader than that afforded by the local situation alone and to utilize experiences acquired outside as well as inside the local scene.

A comparative study of education can do much to develop the talent for constructive leadership. Such study may extend the student's intellectual equipment by supplying him information about the aspirations, ideas, and experiences of others. As such knowledge is acquired, local facilities and practices can be evaluated in the light of standards much more broadly based than those which the supporting group affords. And from a knowledge of alternatives and their consequences, new ideas may spring forth to show the way to more effective arrangements and practices. In brief, a comparative study of education, properly pursued, should enable the student to function more intelligently within his sphere of responsibility, whatever or wherever that sphere may be. Such benefits are not automatic, however, but are derived in fullest measure when they are deliberately sought.

It is this latter prospect that has made the comparative study of education especially attractive to educational planners in the newly developing countries. Since World War II dozens of new nations and nationality groups have achieved either self-governing status or complete independence. In a manner reminiscent of the American states during their first decades of independence, these new nations are faced with the necessity of replacing institutions and processes of control imposed by their

former rulers with others more compatible with the aspirations of a sovereign people. With populations frequently numbering in the millions, mostly illiterate and often ignorant of even the most elementary aspects of modern science, technology, and the more highly developed social processes, these nations now aspire to achieve mass education and universal literacy in a single generation. Their problems are made doubly difficult by their lack not only of trained, native leaders, but also of the economic and cultural resources necessary to support such a formidable transformation.

In this dilemma, many of the new nations, encouraged by offers of foreign aid, are sending their potential leaders abroad for the desired training. This course has the advantage of placing highly developed programs of education and institutions at the disposal of the culture-seeking students. As a training program for leadership within their native environments, however, it may leave some things to be desired. The programs and institutions with which a majority of such students come into contact are almost without exception dependent upon a highly industrialized economy for their support. Neither the institutional forms nor the curricular content can be effectively transplanted to newly developing environments. What such students need, in addition to a general education, is a comparative study that points out the relation of educational means to cultural ends; they need to try to identify the ends that have highest immediate priority in their home country and to survey current practices in order to discover those which appear especially promising in reference to those particular ends. Such studies, competently directed, can do

5

much to develop the student's ability to predict the consequences of particular educational innovations, and thereby prepare him to exercise constructive leadership in national planning. It may be far more vital for the future educational leader to be able to predict the consequences of introducing free, compulsory education or coeducation in his nation than for him to master the higher branches of mathematics or to peruse the literature of a strange and highly sophisticated people.

Types of comparative studies

The variety and amount of factual information encountered in a comparative study of education can quickly become unmanageable unless a conscious effort is made to supply order. To deal with this problem, leaders in the field have suggested a number of approaches. These consist, in the main, of listing the major features of various educational systems, logically arranged, that offer suitable bases for making comparisons.

One might, of course, base a comparison of several systems on any selected feature or combination of features. The American studies prior to the War between the States, for example, concentrated on the types of schools found abroad and the subjects offered in each type. Little significance was attached to the social philosophies that had motivated the several nations to establish those particular types and not some others. Nor were questions raised as to how appropriately such schools and curricula would fit into the social environment on this side of the Atlantic. Some recent studies seem to venerate administrative efficiency and operational economy above all else, and have directed attention almost exclusively to the legal and fiscal aspects of the several systems reviewed. These studies sometimes have seemed to equate quality of education with the degree of centralized administrative control that has been achieved or with the per pupil cost of providing a given level of literacy throughout the school population. Of late, a number of students have given considerable attention to the amount of technical and scientific content offered in competing national systems of education and the proportions of the total school populations exposed to such instruction. For the moment, at least, all other requirements for adequate living under modern conditions appear insignificant to these students.

More sophisticated students of comparative education feel that studies narrowly focused on one or two selected features of schools and their management are not adequate. A new approach in which an educational system is viewed as part of the cultural setting in which it is found has led to anthropological and sociological studies. Many of these have attempted to identify and describe the forces that determine the character of primitive societies and their education, and how such forces differ from those found in more advanced societies. As yet, there have been very few scholarly attempts to compare different cultures or even to make nonspeculative studies of a single culture. A notable exception is the attractively written study of Japan entitled *The Chrysanthemum and the Sword*.[5] However, the trenchant criticisms of the easy generalizations the author draws from rather scanty

[5] Ruth Benedict, *The Chrysanthemum and the Sword*, Houghton Mifflin, Boston, 1946.

data point to a need for truly interdisciplinary approaches if such studies are to achieve acceptable validity.

More modest studies have been content to identify the cultural roots of each system of education discussed. These have sought to relate various characteristics of education to the unique "national character," a term identified by one writer as

> ...a kind of fixed mental constitution that guarantees a common purpose and a common effort from the whole group. It is a kind of large-scale sentiment and is the result of the qualities needed by the whole group, for the attainment of the group ideal....[6]

Whereas this definition implies a philosophical commitment, a conscious effort to achieve a commonly held ideal, another writer is inclined to generalize from traits unconsciously exhibited by individual nationals. For example,

> The Englishman more than any other national believes that an ounce of practice is worth a pound of theory and that bridges must not be crossed until they are reached, for you never can tell.[7]

According to this view a student of comparative education would need to become a kind of anthropologist or social psychologist as well as a professional educator. Nevertheless, it is implied that the national character as identified may be used to explain distinctive features of the national system of education, and

sometimes to predict probable trends of future development.

Other students of comparative education find a single sweeping generalization setting forth the national character of a nation or people too vague to be useful for comparative purposes. Such persons, therefore, attempt to identify components of the group image that may be described in more specific terms. Certain social, religious, political, economic, and even geographic factors have been used for this purpose, as, for example, the seven factors listed below.

1. Sense of national unity

2. General economic situation

3. Basic beliefs and traditions, including religious and cultural heritage

4. Status of progressive educational thought

5. Language problems

6. Political backgrounds: communism, democracy

7. Attitude toward international cooperation and understanding [8]

It is assumed that each of these factors, and others, may have had a unique impact upon the character of the educational system that has emerged, and that a knowledge of the contributing factors will help the student understand that particular system.

Among the large number of scholars who emphasize the importance of understanding the cultural backgrounds of educational institutions and practices, there are differences as to which factors contribute most significantly. One of the most frequently stressed factors is the historical tradition out of which the

[6] Vernon Mallinson, *An Introduction to the Study of Comparative Education,* Heinemann, London, 1957, p. 4.

[7] I. L. Kandel, *Comparative Education,* Houghton Mifflin, Boston, 1933, p. 25.

[8] From John Francis Cramer and George Stephenson Browne, *Contemporary Education,* Harcourt, Brace, New York, 1956, p. 5.

education system emerged. Indeed, one writer has stated that comparative education "...may be considered a continuation of the study of the history of education into the present."[9] Another group of scholars is inclined to stress the influence of the dominant philosophical commitment. One of these wrote that

> ...men who have been brought up and educated in countries where Platonic ideologies or at least systems of philosophy affiliated to them are powerful and persuasive...will tend to think "naturally" that human beings are classified into at least three types and that heredity matters a great deal....[10]

Still another group is inclined to believe that the determining factors are sociological and even anthropological. This group, employing the techniques of the sociologist, is likely to look for narrower, more definitive aspects of society as possible determinants of educational forms and practices. The family, the community, and the language are examined for their social meaning; individual villages are put under a microscope in the hope that a variety of microcosmic studies will lead to an understanding of the macrocosm.[11] This group, perhaps more than any other, has pioneered in the use of techniques designed to quantify relationships be-

tween education and specific cultural factors. Tentative explorations, using statistical techniques, have been made of the correlation between literacy and per capita income, the degree of urbanization, infant mortality, and the like. While these attempts, understandably, have been cautious, more sophisticated statistical methods may prove to be highly useful in future studies.

From this rather hasty review, it may be seen that studies of comparative education fall into one of two general categories. In the first category are studies, broad in scope, designed to acquaint the novice with the field and to provide factual information essential to understanding the most widely accepted generalizations current among scholars today. What the student needs at this stage is a system of organization that will help him to gather information, usually from secondary sources, and use it in the development of general principles to guide his future work. The second category consists of studies by more sophisticated scholars seeking new information through original research. These studies may call for experimental designs and the rigorous use of the research methods of social scientists. They require a prior acquaintance with the general area of study and are usually narrowly focused upon a specific feature, relationship, or social unit.

The present study belongs in the first category. While no claim is made that the best approach has been found, the bases for comparing educational systems suggested in the section that follows will afford not merely an orderly introduction to the field but will, hopefully, lead the student into areas that invite investigation on a more sophisticated level. The approach here sug-

[9] I. L. Kandel, "The Methodology of Comparative Education," *International Review of Education*, vol. V, no. 3, p. 273, 1959.

[10] Joseph A. Lauwerys, "The Philosophical Approach to Comparative Education," *International Review of Education*, vol. V, no. 3, p. 293, 1959.

[11] C. Arnold Anderson, "The Utility of Societal Typologies in Comparative Education," *Comparative Education Review*, vol. 3, no. 1, p. 21, June, 1959.

gested assumes that the supporting culture has a determining influence on the education carried on within it; that the theoretical commitments of a people give form and direction to their institutions; and that such commitments, particularly those relating to the nature of man and his methods of acquiring knowledge, spell out not only the place within the social system to which each individual is to be assigned, but also the way he is to be prepared to play his designated role. It follows that special attention need be given to such commitments when studying a given system of education or when comparing it with other systems.

Features for comparison

Since the dominant social commitment of a group plays the determining role in education, introductory studies in comparative education must begin with an inquiry into the social philosophies of the supporting groups. The primary question to be kept in mind is what the educating society hopes to achieve through its educational activities. In other words, what is the social role of the school? A second question asks what forms of administrative controls are thought necessary to make sure that the educational system will play the role it has been assigned. A third question, one with which descriptive studies sometimes have dealt exclusively, asks the nature and number of institutional types and instructional programs that are employed to achieve the ends sought. It is here that students sometimes have become lost in a mass of detailed information when they have lacked a sense of direction to help them determine what is important. Finally, a comparative study conducted in this time of rising expectations and rapid developments among peoples everywhere should ask what types of opportunities, and how many opportunities, are provided for what classes of individuals. These four questions are focal points in the following discussion of educational patterns, and each constitutes a basis for making comparisons.

Social role

Every individual, group, community, society, or nation that undertakes a program of formal education does so deliberately and for a specific reason. The reason is derived from a common faith by which the individuals concerned are committed to a particular way of meeting situations that call for decisions and group action. When individuals are so committed, they have a basis for developing an internally harmonious and compatible community life; and the form of their commitment, whether a simple principle of procedure or an elaborate statement of assumptions and their logical derivatives, may be considered their social philosophy. The social commitment spells out how decisions affecting the welfare of all are to be made and who is to make them. The resulting political arrangements are designed to place the decision-making powers in what are judged to be the proper hands; and the resulting rules and procedures, the social customs and laws, regulate the relations of individuals with individuals. Thus governments, social institutions, customs, and the standards of justice and morality everywhere reflect the pervasive influence of the prevailing social philosophies.

When people are convinced they have

9

come by a way of life which is of incomparable worth, they seek means to transmit it to their young. It is precisely this desire that has given rise to formal education. It is no accident that the bodies of beliefs and systems of knowledge that constitute the content of education are referred to variously as the social or the cultural heritage. Obviously, the more extensive the body of knowledge to be transmitted and the more numerous the individuals who are to receive it, the more extensive and complex will be the educational enterprise. Curricula and methodologies are never developed apart from a prior social commitment; and the student of comparative education must be attentive always to such underlying commitments before he undertakes a study of the more readily identified, superficial appearances of institutional forms and instructional practices.

The suggestion that a comparative study of education should seek to develop philosophical insights may come as an unexpected reversal of recent trends. Since the opening decades of the present century, students of education, particularly in the United States, have preferred to focus attention, first, upon the institutional and administrative aspects of operating systems, and, lately, upon the sociological and anthropological forces that are assumed to be at work in the supporting environments. This development came about largely because the speculative philosophies of the eighteenth and nineteenth centuries had proved unsatisfactory guides for correcting widely admitted educational deficiencies. Many leading educators therefore abandoned theoretical speculation in favor of a scientific method. What was overlooked is the fact that

scientific methods also represent particular philosophical commitments, for scientific inquiries are in reality attempts to discover, bit by bit, pieces of information which may point toward a more effective way of life. When all philosophy is viewed as a many-pronged search for knowledge by which men seek to achieve a good life, the several systems of philosophy variously known as idealism, realism, pragmatism, empiricism, materialism, existentialism, etc., including scientific methods, must be looked upon as competing theories of inquiry. The aspect of such inquiry which focuses most directly upon defining and improving the relations of man with man is what is meant here by social philosophy; and it is of particular importance in determining the social role of the school.

A number of social philosophies influence the affairs of men today. By what names these are called, or how they are grouped, varies according to the purpose for which their study is undertaken. In many cases the names and categories employed are meaningless, if not actually misleading, to all but the few who are philosophers by profession. For the less specialized needs of the larger number of students, a method of identification that permits the classification of social systems by more readily recognized characteristics is greatly to be desired. Fortunately, a system consisting of only three gross categories is available.[12] According to this system there are societies in which it is believed that knowledge of the good is "received" from a supernatural source. In others it is believed that such knowl-

[12] I. N. Thut, *The Story of Education: Philosophical and Historical Foundations*, McGraw-Hill, New York, 1957.

10

edge is "discovered" in nature or in processes of the natural universe. In still others it is held that knowledge is "constructed" in an intellectual process based on the everyday experiences of ordinary men. In each case, those who are expected to know what is good are accorded special privileges and educational opportunities commensurate with the importance of the social role they are to play in adult life. Where such roles are substantially different, the educational opportunities are made to differ accordingly.

Included in the first category above are societies whose members believe they have received, or are continuing to receive, knowledge of the good in some miraculous manner from a source that lies outside the world of everyday experience. Related to this view is the belief that men, lacking the direct benefits of received knowledge, are no more capable of achieving the Good Life than are the beasts of the field and jungle. The lack of received knowledge, so it is said, accounts for the differences between primitive and civilized societies; and the status of the former can be raised only by bringing to them the necessary knowledge from the outside. According to this view, the more advanced peoples today also lived in a state of ignorance and were disposed to work for evil ends before they received knowledge of a better way of life. The discerning student will note, however, that assigning to a supernatural agent or realm the status of source does not in itself explain how knowledge from that source is made available to man. The varying accounts given to explain this mystery afford some bases for the different social organizations and institutional forms, including education, found

among societies of this category today.

One of the more widely encountered educational systems of this category is maintained by the Jews. The Jewish tradition is based on revelation, literally the miraculous revealing of knowledge originating with God, to the people He has chosen to receive it. His chosen agents through whom successive gifts of knowledge have been delivered are known as prophets. Biblical accounts tell of the revelations delivered through the agencies of Moses, Isaiah, Hosea, and other major and minor prophets. Because the utilization of these revelations does not call for a highly structured social organization, or a hierarchical system of control, the Jews have lived for centuries as scattered families and congregations, each of which can be self-sufficient and independent of the others. This is possible because each has a copy of the revelation by which God wants individual Jews to direct their personal affairs. The necessary educational function is fulfilled by teaching boys and girls, especially boys, to read the Books of Moses and other sacred literature and to take the directions for living contained therein as their daily guide. It is this acceptance of a special revelation as their guide that has set Jews off as unique people wherever they are found. It explains both the existence of Hebrew schools wherever a number of Jews live together and the instruction given in the home by Jewish parents, particularly when families live in isolation.

Societies having a different explanation of revelation have developed other types of social organizations and educational agencies. The educational problems of emerging Arabic nations can no more be understood apart from a knowledge of the Moslem religion than can those of Israel be understood without a knowledge of the Jewish faith. Students of comparative education tend to overlook, however, that many aspects of Christian nations are also derived from a commitment to a revealed body of knowledge. Herein lies the origin of the belief widely held among Western peoples that sovereignty resides in the head of state and is to be exercised by the people only if it has been delegated to them from above. In the following chapter a brief account will be given to show how the social and educational history of Europe is in large measure the story of the conflict between those who held that God had delegated sovereignty and the authority to interpret His will to the head of the Roman Catholic Church and those who supported the claims of divine appointment and authority asserted by emperors and kings. The rise of the absolute monarchies indicated a victory for the latter group; and their governments, literally the machinery by which the will of God was to be put into practice among men, were developed to make sure that control in all aspects of national life would be centered in the person whom God had put upon the throne.

In certain states today, the church is still recognized as the spokesman for God and is accepted as the supreme power by the head of state and the people. In such states, notably Spain, the church may enjoy certain veto rights in civil affairs, priority in education, and a monopoly in religion. Civil as well as ecclesiastical institutions may reflect dependence upon policy made by the religious authority; and education is engaged in not merely to promote such policy, but also to justify by theo-

logical argument the existing lines of direction and control. Evidence of this type of philosophical commitment is found in the existence of an established church and the inclusion of a prescribed form of religious instruction in the official system of education. When minority groups committed to a revealed body of knowledge find themselves in a society where other beliefs are taught in the schools, they are likely to undertake the education of their own children in a system of separate or parochial schools. But nations strongly committed to an official religious establishment usually have not allowed such deviation.

The twentieth century has seen two outstanding examples of large, highly developed societies claiming to be directed by knowledge revealed to them by a supernatural power through the agency of a divinely appointed leader or king. Prior to World War II the Emperor of Japan quite openly was regarded as the Son of Heaven. In a later chapter the impact of this belief on the Japanese social policies and institutions, particularly education, will be described. According to the "leader principle" advocated by the National Socialist Party in Germany, knowledge of what is good was revealed to the leader by the mystical spirit of Germania, the eternal, organic, living unity which encompassed the souls of all racially pure Germans no matter when or where they may have lived. The government, education, and even the traditional religion of Germany were transformed by the Nazis as they took over complete control of the state.

In the second major category are societies committed to social philosophies which assume that knowledge of the good can be "discovered" from data derived by observing the objects and processes in the natural universe itself. This is the premise put forward by Aristotle, and his description of the inductive and deductive aspects of the discovery process later incited several philosophical revolutions in Europe against entrenched forms of social control based on the authority of "received" knowledge. Such revolutions were led, first, by the scholastics and, later, by the rationalists. The latter produced the eighteenth- and nineteenth-century political revolutions which tumbled several absolute monarchies, with their supporting educational and ecclesiastical institutions, and drastically reduced by means of constitutional controls the powers of king and church in many other states.

While there are differences in the methods by which knowledge of the good is said to be discovered, and these have led to corresponding differences in the social organizations of various groups, each of these methods teaches that the discovery process is strictly a natural phenomenon. The discovery of knowledge therefore may prosper in direct ratio to the amount of effort expended in promoting the search. Furthermore, the method of discovery can be taught, and proficiency in its use can be developed. Education therefore is looked upon as a matter of great social importance and is usually provided at public expense even though only a small portion of the population may be thought capable of benefiting from it. The educational system of France, with its great emphasis upon the intensive training of those thought to be intellectually talented, is an example. This system, too, will be examined in some detail in a later chapter.

While the French philosophical commitment since the revolution has entailed a rational method for discovering knowledge, and the French have sought to direct national affairs in the light of policy formulated by their "best minds," another world power—the Union of Socialist Soviet Republics—claims that direction of its social endeavors is provided by knowledge discovered in a "scientific" method of inquiry. The philosophical commitment operating in the Soviet Union is known as dialectical materialism, a method of inquiry radically different from the scientific method developed by Francis Bacon, Isaac Newton, and their successors in the scientific movement familiar to the twentieth-century student of philosophy and education. Since the social philosophy and education of the U.S.S.R. also will be described later it is not necessary to devote further space to them here. Nor is it desirable to review at this time other philosophical systems which, though they are classified as methods for discovering knowledge of the good and are much discussed in academic circles, are not as directly responsible for the education found in modern states as are rationalism and dialectical materialism.[13] The conclusion is inescapable, however, that knowledge said to have been discovered tends to be regarded as authoritative and infallible just as is knowledge said to have been revealed. Those individuals thought to have a special talent for discovering knowledge therefore also tend to be elevated to the status of a ruling elite requiring a unique and usually separate education, to be accorded special privileges, and to be empowered to cast the controlling vote

[13] Those interested in pursuing such systems may refer to *ibid.*, part III, including the bibliography.

on policies affecting the good of all. Social institutions, particularly the schools, found in societies in this category very often defer to what is identified, perhaps only vaguely, as the intellectual aristocracy.

There is, of course, still a third category of nations and lesser social groups, according to our system of classification. Peoples in this category do not claim to have access to knowledge that is either complete or infallible, whatever its alleged source or the manner in which it is acquired. That is to say, men who are by their very nature less than God never can know the good as God knows it; and for that reason the institutions and arrangements they fashion always fall short of perfection and constantly require modification, adjustment, and even replacement.

To say that all men are finite, however, does not mean that all men are identical or have the same knowledge. What an individual presumes to know is necessarily colored by his personal experiences, aspirations, and prejudices. Nor can the judgments of one man arbitrarily be taken to have a higher degree of validity in all matters than those of another. In societies of this category, authority is said to reside with the people themselves; and they both create and control the institutions by which they carry on their common endeavors.

When such a community designs its social arrangements, special provisions are made to facilitate communication between its members and to encourage wide participation in decision-making activities. It is believed that all will benefit from a pooling of diverse experiences and opinions. Knowledge may be pooled, however, only if individual members are guaranteed freedom of belief,

of speech, of assembly, and the free use of the media of communication. Individuals will engage in the decision-making processes only if they can participate as equals. Hence, the decision-making role is shared by all and no class of individuals or special interest group is allowed to force its will upon the total group.

It is not difficult today to identify a number of nations whose citizens aspire to have political control exercised through the active participation of all their peoples in the decision-making processes. To achieve this the general cultural level must be high. Programs of universal education are provided. Individual schools in systems of this type generally are accessible to persons from any segment of society. They are articulated to form a unitary system within which the learner may move freely from level to level and from subject area to subject area in search of his optimal development. Instructional programs provide appropriate training in the processes of self-government as well as in the more conventional academic disciplines. In this respect the social role of education is to enable the people to retain their sovereignty and to make the exercise of their powers both efficient and personally rewarding.

In this brief review of the social role of education it has been suggested that schools are expected to function quite differently in groups that differ with respect to their philosophical commitments. Groups that believe knowledge of the good is accessible only to certain individuals or special segments of society generally seek to segregate such persons from the general population at an early age. They are accorded the status of an elite and are shown deference in many ways. Special schools are provided in which every effort is made to cultivate their avowed leadership talents. If schools are provided for the masses, they are likely to be separate and to provide only the minimal facilities necessary to assure the level of economic efficiency and political subordination desired by those in control. The role of the schools for the masses in such societies is to fit the individual for his predetermined place in a social system which he has not helped to create and over which he has little or no control.

In contrast to the above, societies in which it is believed that knowledge is derived from the experiences and insights of individuals in all segments of the population, seek to minimize social differences resulting from wealth or other forms of inherited status. Schools are expected to encourage social mobility and to cultivate special talent wherever it may be found. Children are not segregated on a class basis but are entered in a common school system within which each may find the facilities and services needed to achieve the Good Life as it comes to be viewed by him.

Power structure and administrative organization

The decisive role played by philosophical commitments in shaping social institutions and practices is nowhere more evident than in the forms of administrative control employed by societies in their educational systems. Wherever it is believed that access to knowledge of what is good for the society as a whole is more readily available to one segment of the people than to the rest, arrangements are adopted by which decisions affecting all will be made by that seg-

ment and no other. It matters very little whether the knowledge needed to govern wisely is said to be received or discovered, for in either case administrative controls are concentrated in a single, central agency, and policies made there are directed through a hierarchical chain of command to the subordinate administrative levels.

Administrative arrangements in societies committed to the theory that knowledge is received from a supernatural source generally are structured to utilize the leadership of an official state church. The clergy are represented on the major governing bodies and have special, if not final, authority in all matters touching upon matters of belief. In education an official ecclesiastical body generally has the authority either to prepare the textbooks used in the schools or to review them, with powers of veto. The authority of the clergy is extended in some places, notably Spain, to include the approval of persons appointed as teachers, and their recall if they are judged to have deviated from the official doctrine. The central agency for educational administration, with the advice of the ecclesiastical authority, may, by means of licenses, control the privilege of establishing private schools; it may also be responsible for inspecting all schools in operation, both public and private, and for prescribing the content of instruction. In extreme cases, the central government even determines who may gather together for religious as well as for civil purposes and under what circumstances they may do so.

The situation is not significantly different in societies committed to a communistic philosophy. Although knowledge is believed to be discovered by employing a special dialectic, the process

15

of discovery is said to be too complicated to be used by any persons other than a selected group of experts. The election machinery, hardened by tradition, generally prevents persons from being appointed to policy-making and policy-executing posts who have not qualified as members of the expert class, in this case the Communist Party. Here, again, control is exercised by a central agency which directs its authority downward, through administrative channels, to the lower levels. The Party organization and its functioning are designed specifically to identify and train the leaders and to make their control, through the machinery of government, effective at all levels and in all matters.

Where knowledge is said to be discovered in a rational process, as in France, the administrative arrangements are designed to place control in the hands of an intellectual elite. French administrative practice is based on a highly centralized type of control, perhaps more highly centralized than in any other nation not under a totalitarian form of government. This centralized structure makes it possible to concentrate the policy-making functions on the national level and to execute such policy uniformly through subordinate administrative departments in all parts of the nation. It is very important to the French that the policy-making functions, as well as the higher administrative posts, are in the hands of persons with the proper intellectual qualifications. Their secondary and higher educational institutions have been specifically designed to afford such training to selected students; and the civil service system, as well as the election machinery, has been designed to favor those

who have made a good record in these schools.

In contrast to the highly centralized systems employed by societies of the two categories above, Switzerland and the United States provide examples of decentralized systems of administrative control. This is so because their social philosophies call for the policy-making and policy-executing functions to be located as close as possible to the people affected by them. The decentralized arrangements, particularly evident in the administration of public education, make it possible for those individuals who are directly concerned to participate in the decision-making process. It is no accident that neither Switzerland nor the United States has a national ministry of education, or that relatively little financial support for public education comes from national sources. States and local communities in both countries enjoy a status and autonomy not found among the political subdivisions of other nations. Decentralization of administrative authority, it would be found, indicates the presence of a social philosophy that attributes dignity to all individuals and values their active participation in the decision-making functions of government and other aspects of their common life. Such commitments understandably have produced unique forms of educational administration and control.

Educational institutions

Philosophical commitments that differentiate between leaders and followers on a class basis also call for separate educational institutions to serve the specialized needs of the two groups. The differences between leaders and followers generally are thought to be so fundamental that they cannot be mitigated by education. A fundamental task of education, it is said, is to identify and separate the born leader from the follower and to prepare each for his proper social role.

Schools designed to serve the leader class, often referred to as "secondary" schools, were developed long before formal education for the masses was thought necessary. Furthermore, at the time schools for leaders were introduced the philosophical commitment was to a body of knowledge said to have been revealed. Hence, these early schools were designed to give the future leaders access to the literary works in which the cultural heritage was recorded. Education for leadership acquired a literary character, and since the heritage of Western Europe was recorded in Latin, the leader class continued to be instructed in Latin long after other languages had been accepted as the media of communication. Indeed, the ability, or lack of ability, to read Latin became the mark of the individual's social rank. A parallel situation developed in East Asia where classical Chinese, also far removed from the vernacular of the people, remained for many centuries the official language of government. In both cases schools were used deliberately to create superficial differences between those designated to become leaders and those who were to remain without a voice in the councils of state and church.

Although literary instruction was provided at the outset to the leaders only, changes in the philosophical commitments of certain European states called for some reading instruction to be given all people. When this occurred, the masses were not instructed in Latin, but only in their mother tongues. Separate schools established for the masses generally came to be known as vernacular reading schools, elementary schools, or the people's schools. As nations became interested in raising the cultural level of their peoples, largely for competitive reasons, the vernacular schools came under public control and support. Attendance was made compulsory except for those who were able to secure schooling through private means. For the latter, the Latin schools were preferred; and these schools remained highly selective by virtue of tuitions and other discriminatory practices. Because a knowledge of Latin was a prerequisite for study in the universities, pupils attending vernacular schools were ordinarily excluded from higher studies and the social advantages such studies afforded. Thus, in Europe two independent systems of schools came to stand side by side, each isolated from the other by the languages they employed for instruction.

Educational systems in contemporary societies very often bear unmistakable evidence of having evolved from a two-class pattern. The degree to which the earlier distinctions between the education for leaders and that for the masses still persist can serve as a clue to the philosophical commitments operative in the supporting societies. Similar inferences may be drawn from the existence, or nonexistence, of facilities for teaching the practical arts and whether such instruction is articulated in any way with either the vernacular schools or those that prepare for admission to higher studies. It also may be revealing to inquire if instruction in health and

17

physical education is more in evidence in the vernacular schools than in the others; and if such instruction is related in any way to the national program for military preparedness.

Educational opportunities

The type and variety of educational institutions provided by a society have a direct bearing on the opportunities made available to its members. With further reference to physical education, students in the select schools in some societies not so long ago could engage freely in sports and recreational activities under school sponsorship, while pupils in the vernacular schools were drilled in precision calisthenics and other forms of mass exercises reminiscent of the training of military recruits. One form of instruction was intended to develop self-reliance and independence of action; the other counteracted individualism to secure obedience and regimentation. The philosophical issue involved was whether the individual pupil is a subject who exists to serve the state or whether the state has been created to serve the individual. Authoritarian societies have asserted the former, and democratic groups the latter.

The commitments particular societies have made on this issue have had far-reaching effects on education. They have determined not only the number and types of schools available, but also the programs of instruction offered in each type, and who may benefit from them. Admissions practices are especially subject to influence from the dominating philosophical attitudes. Where the state seeks to dominate the minds of its subjects, children either are forbidden to attend any schools not approved by the state, or they are required to attend

schools maintained by the state. The only exceptions are children whose parents are known to be philosophically and politically reliable. Opportunity to dissent is nonexistent insofar as education can make it so. The wishes of the state also take precedence in determining how many will be allowed to enter the various programs and schools. Teacher training institutions, for example, are given a quota based on an estimate of the number of teaching positions that will need to be filled several years hence. Competitive admissions examinations are administered, and only the number of applicants desired are accepted, regardless of the qualifications of other candidates. The determining policy clearly is to serve the needs of the state, and not to help individuals rise above their inherited status, even though the elevation of the general welfare may be the ultimate goal. Admissions standards are raised or lowered in response to public policy, and existing schools are expanded and new schools built, not in response to popular demand, but at the discretion of the persons in power. One may venture the opinion that the nature and significance of state-administered admissions practices, particularly competitive examinations, have not received the attention they merit from students of comparative education.

Other restrictions on the individual's opportunity to acquire an education of his choice have been exerted at times in a more arbitrary and categorical manner than that posed by competitive examinations. Girls, for example, were not admitted to many schools and programs open to boys. In parts of Europe and Asia, particularly, the exclusion of girls from the schools that prepared students for admission to the universities prevented women from entering many professions, including, in some cases, teaching in secondary schools.

Similar restrictions exist where an established church is permitted to use the schools to propagate its sectarian doctrines. Parents holding dissenting views often take their children out of school as soon as the minimum requirements of compulsory attendance are met. Less subtle restrictions are imposed where tuition fees are charged by those schools which, in effect, control admission to the universities and higher technical schools. Preparatory training in tuition schools is necessary because the vernacular schools, which are the only ones that are free, do not offer the foreign language instruction required to qualify for admission to the higher institutions. Furthermore, admission to the preparatory schools sometimes can be gained only by attending special primary classes which also charge tuitions. Thus children who are not able to enter a tuition school at the outset find it increasingly more difficult to do so at a later time. Indeed, the educational choices that determine the child's future must be made when he is five or six years of age, and certainly before twelve. Such choices, obviously, are made more often by the parent than the child; and educational opportunity therefore is more dependent on the economic ability and social position of the parents than on the personal aspirations and actual potentials of the child.

Among social groups whose institutions and arrangements are looked upon as agencies to help the individual achieve personal development, schools take on the characteristics of service agencies. They are made accessible to the widest possible number of children. The programs of instruction are many and varied. Transfer from one program or level of instruction to another is made relatively easy on the theory that as the pupil matures, his interests and aptitudes may change. This consideration has led to the development of comprehensive schools which house a variety of programs under one roof—in marked contrast to systems whose schools offer only one program and thereby force the early segregation of children. Competitive examinations are less frequently used as admissions devices than are other evidences of ability. Entrance requirements for the various programs are likely to be defined in specific terms, and all who can qualify are admitted without strict regard to official estimates of future needs for persons so trained. Furthermore, whenever the demand for training exceeds the available facilities, additional facilities are produced by voluntary if not by public effort. Segregation, whether on the basis of sex, religion, social class, or educational interest, is minimized. The objective throughout is to help individuals help themselves through education.

There is considerable evidence today that educational programs in many places are being expanded and revised to afford a greater measure of individual opportunity and self-determination. The phenomenal increase in adult education programs throughout the world since World War II is a case in point. Another line of development is bringing about greatly increased opportunities for industrial, technical, and vocational training for those who do not aspire to study at a university. From such expansion, a middle class is likely to emerge in societies where only two classes of citizens, a higher and a lower, have had any real significance. New schools are rising which stand between the terminal vernacular schools and the select preparatory schools. These promise to provide transfer points that will help to articulate horizontally as well as vertically all educational institutions to form a single national system. A hasty, but likely, generalization might be that such national educational systems will inevitably raise the general economic and cultural level of the supporting society, for a variety of institutions and programs, each articulated with the others, will enable the child to acquire the knowledge, skills, and social development needed to rise above the economic and social level of his parents.

Recapitulating briefly, an introductory study in the area of comparative education is likely to be rewarding to the degree that it sheds light on a very few questions, sharply defined at the outset. Among the questions to be asked regarding each society studied are the following: Who is expected to make the decisions affecting the general welfare? By what type of knowledge are such persons to be guided and how is it acquired? By what political arrangement is the authority to make decisions placed in the hands of those thought best qualified to exercise it? How are these authority-exercising individuals identified and placed in power? Who is in control of education and through what administrative channels is their control made effective? What types and varieties of educational opportunities are made available? Who may take advantage of those opportunities? And who decides what kind of education, and how much, a given child will be allowed to receive?

These are discriminating questions.

The answers they evoke are not intended to foster prejudice or to encourage arbitrary value judgments based on external standards. Rather it is hoped that they will help students become better prepared to project in terms of their own commitments new and improved procedures wherever needed. The educational patterns reviewed in the following chapters will, therefore, be described with particular attention to (1) the social role of the schools; (2) the organizations for administering the educational programs; (3) the institutional arrangements; and (4) the variety and extent of educational opportunities afforded.

Sources of useful information

Some sources of information to which a student of comparative education may refer deal with the schools of a single nation or treat one specific aspect of education only. Specialized sources of this nature used in this book are cited in footnotes or listed at the end of the chapter to which they apply.

There are, however, a number of general sources which treat the subject of comparative education in such encyclopedic fashion that they have become standard reference tools. These are not listed in the end-of-chapter references. They include encyclopedias, surveys, yearbooks, bulletin series, books, monographs, and periodicals that the student will consult as a matter of course when investigating a specific topic.

It is impossible to give a complete list of these general sources, but the following items are shelved in many libraries. The student is urged to make an inventory of his local resources at the outset. The following bibliography can serve not merely as a checklist, but also as an indication of the categories of sources in which considerable additional material may be available.

References

Historical sources

Barnard, Henry: *National Education in Europe,* 2d ed., Case, Tiffany, Hartford, Conn., 1854.

de Bary, William Theodore (ed.): *Sources of Chinese Tradition,* Columbia, New York, 1960.

————: *Sources of Indian Tradition,* Columbia, New York, 1958.

————: *Sources of Japanese Tradition,* Columbia, New York, 1958.

Good, H. G.: *A History of Western Education,* 2d ed., Macmillan, New York, 1960. Especially chaps. 13–15.

Kandel, I. L.: *Comparative Education,* Houghton Mifflin, Boston, 1933. For the period between World War I and World War II.

Monroe, Paul (ed.): *A Cyclopaedia of Education,* 5 vols., Macmillan, New York, 1911.

Poole, Reginald Lane: *Medieval Thought and Learning,* rev. ed., Macmillan, New York, 1920.

Rashdall, Hastings: *The Universities of Europe in the Middle Ages,* 3 vols., Oxford, Fair Lawn, N.J., 1936.

Reisner, Edward H.: *The Evolution of the Common School,* Macmillan, New York, 1932.

————: *Nationalism and Education since 1789,* Macmillan, New York, 1922.

Woodward, William Harrison: *Studies in Education during the Age of the Renaissance,* Cambridge, New York, 1924.

U.S. Commissioner of Education: *Annual Report,* 1870. The early *Reports,* *Circulars of Information,* and *Bulletins* contain numerous accounts of education in Europe and other parts of the world as described by prominent American scholars.

Encyclopedias, handbooks, and surveys

The Australian Encyclopaedia, 10 vols., Michigan State University Press, East Lansing, Mich., 1958. See vol. III.

Chambers, M. M.: *The Universities of the World outside the U.S.A.,* American Council on Education, Washington, D.C., 1950.

Encyclopedia Americana, 30 vols., Americana Corporation, New York. Current edition.

Encyclopaedia Britannica, Encyclopaedia Britannica, Inc., Chicago. Current edition. Earlier editions have historical value.

Encyclopaedia Canadiana, 10 vols., The Canadian Co., Ltd., Ottawa, 1960. See vol. III.

Europa: The Encyclopedia of Europe, Europa Publications, Ltd., London. Latest editions.

Heath, Kathryn G.: *Ministries of Education,* U.S. Office of Education, 1961.

King, Margaret L., and George Male: "A Compilation of Data on the Educational Systems of Western Europe," *Studies in Comparative Education,* U.S. Office of Education, 1961.

Lexikon der Padagogik, 3 vols., A. Francke Verlag, Bern, 1950. See vol. III.

Sasnett, M. T.: *Educational Systems of the World,* University of Southern California Press, Los Angeles, 1952.

UNESCO. *World Survey of Education,* vol. I, *Handbook of Educational Organization and Statistics,* 1955; vol. II, *Primary Education,* 1958; vol. III, *Secondary Education,* 1961; vol. IV, *Higher Education* (in preparation), Paris.

————: *Basic Facts and Figures: International Statistics Relating to Education, Culture, and Mass Communication,* Paris, 1960.

Yearbooks

The Educational Yearbook, International Institute of Teachers College, Columbia University, New York. Published annually from 1924 through 1944.
International Yearbook of Education, International Bureau of Education, Geneva, and UNESCO, Paris. Available in the United States from Columbia, New York. Published annually since 1933 except 1940–1945.
Yearbook of Education, World, Tarrytown-on-Hudson, N.Y. Since 1953. Issues for 1932–1941 and 1947–1952 were published in London.

Yearbooks and summaries of official actions are published by a number of governments and other agencies, including the following.
Canada Year Book, Dominion Bureau of Statistics, Information Services Division, Ottawa.
Gordon-Brown, A. (ed.): *The Year Book and Guide to East Africa,* Robert Hale, Ltd., London.
————: *The Year Book and Guide to South Africa,* Robert Hale, Ltd., London.
Wood, G. E. (ed.): *The New Zealand Official Yearbook.* Compiled in the Census and Statistics Department, R. E. Owen, Government Printer, Wellington, New Zealand.

Books and monographs

Benjamin, Harold: *Under Their Own Command: Observations on the Nature of a People's Education for War and Peace,* Macmillan, New York, 1947.
Cramer, John Francis, and George Ste-

phenson Browne: *Contemporary Education,* Harcourt, Brace & World, New York, 1956.
Field, G. Lowell: *Governments in Modern Society,* McGraw-Hill, New York, 1951.
Hans, Nicholas A.: *Comparative Education,* Routledge, London, 1951.
Hawgood, John A.: *Modern Constitutions since 1787,* Macmillan, London, 1939.
Kandel, I. L.: *The New Era in Education: A Comparative Study,* Houghton Mifflin, Boston, 1955.
Kerr, Anthony: *Schools of Europe,* Bowes, London, 1960.
King, Edmund J.: *Other Schools and Ours,* rev. ed., Holt, New York, 1963.
————: *World Perspectives in Education,* Bobbs-Merrill, Indianapolis, 1962.
Lowell, A. Lawrence: *Governments and Parties in Continental Europe,* 2 vols., Harvard, Cambridge, Mass., 1896.
Mallinson, Vernon: *An Introduction to the Study of Comparative Education,* Macmillan, New York, 1957.
Meyer, Adolph E.: *The Development of Education in the Twentieth Century,* 2d ed., Prentice-Hall, Englewood Cliffs, N.J., 1949.
Moehlman, Arthur H. (ed.): *Comparative Education,* Dryden, New York, 1953.
Reller, Theodore, and Edgar L. Morphet: *Comparative Educational Administration,* Prentice-Hall, Englewood Cliffs, N.J., 1962.
Ulich, Robert: *The Education of Nations,* Harvard, Cambridge, Mass., 1961.
Wit, Daniel: *Comparative Political Institutions,* Holt, New York, 1953.

Bulletin series

UNESCO: *Educational Abstracts,* Education Clearing House, Paris. Published periodically since 1949.
————: *Monographs on Fundamental*

Education, Education Clearing House, Paris, 1949–1956.

——: *Problems in Education,* Paris. First published in 1950.

——: *Studies in Compulsory Education,* Paris. First published in 1951.

U.S. Office of Education: Bulletin series.

——: *Information on Education around the World* series.

——: *Studies in Comparative Education* series.

Periodicals

Bulletin of the International Bureau of Education, UNESCO, Paris, International Bureau of Education, Geneva.

Comparative Education Review. Official organ of the Comparative Education Society, Kent State University, Kent, Ohio.

Comparative Studies in Society and History, Mounton, The Hague.

Foreign Education Digest. Mimeographed. Mrs. Sophie W. Downs, 1650 Oxford Street, Berkeley 9, Calif.

International Journal of Adult and Youth Education (formerly Fundamental and Adult Education), Division of Educational Information and Materials, UNESCO, Paris.

International Review of Education, Martinus Nijhoff, The Hague.

Overseas: The Magazine for Educational Exchange, The Institute of International Education, New York.

Overseas Education: A Journal of Educational Experiment and Research in Tropical and Sub-tropical Areas, London.

The Times Educational Supplement, London.

PART I

Representative Western Patterns

CHAPTER 2

European Education

in the Fifteenth Century

Modern systems of education derived from Western Europe have important common features. Their universities and certain secondary schools are articulated to offer continuous, coordinated programs of instruction for a relatively small segment of the school population. Latin is the prestige language even where large numbers of the present generation of students neglect it. The curricula give evidence of having received a generous infusion of the liberal, humanistic disciplines zealously cultivated by European scholars at the close of the Middle Ages. The internal organization of the universities has evolved from the original faculties of theology, law, and medicine; and the administrative officers charged with keeping the institutions running are generally designated by titles derived from the same ancient sources. Thus whether the modern systems are located in Europe, in North America, in South America, or in one of the later colonial areas, these and other similarities that come to light on further study betray a common ancestor.

To find an explanation for the similarities, one must turn back to the time when Western Europe was dominated by a single social institution. This precedes the era of colonial expansion, for Europe was divided politically, linguistically, and religiously before the great colonizing nations—Belgium, England, France, Germany, Holland, Italy, Portugal, Spain—began to extend their political systems and social institutions abroad. The divisive social forces which were to bring these nations into existence were stirring even in the Middle Ages; and except for the unifying influences exerted by the Roman section of the Christian church, Western Europe might have splintered into sovereign states long before the sixteenth century. But the foundations of European education had been laid before the splintering occurred. They had been laid by the Church which, prior to the sixteenth century, reached into every corner of the Continent, preaching, teaching, baptizing, marrying, burying, supervising the making of contracts, and recording in its institutional Latin these and other significant events in the lives of the inhabitants. It is to fifteenth-century Europe that one must turn, therefore, to discover the common ancestor of the so-called Western systems of education.

Historical development

The Roman Christians, of course, did not invent schools, nor did they introduce them to the European continent. Credit for these accomplishments is shared by priests of the pagan civilizations in the Middle East and the pre-Christian civil populations of Greece and Rome. Pagan Rome already had a well-developed system of schools when the first small, disconnected Christian congregations were springing up. Included in that system were the schools of the *litterator,* which provided children instruction in reading and writing and training in the civic virtues that made for competent, loyal membership in the community. Beyond these pri-

27

mary institutions there were several forms of organized instruction which specialized in cultivating traits becoming to the orator, accomplishments sought by the sons of the socially ambitious and nurtured through the meticulous study of grammar, literature, the sciences, mathematics, and music. The best known among these forms of instruction were referred to as schools of oratory or rhetoric, and they were looked upon as valuable training schools for future leaders especially in the realms of economics and politics. Finally, there existed numerous rather loosely associated groups of adults who were motivated by intellectual curiosity and the drive for self-improvement as distinguished from more directly practical considerations. Such persons met more or less regularly to explore topics of interest in the manner of philosophers. Several groups which attracted able members and became distinguished for their well-formed and consistent points of view have been called schools of philosophy. Usually these were formed around a distinguished scholar whose leadership brought about contributions that are of interest to philosophers to this day.

While primary education in Rome remained the responsibility of the family and the local neighborhood, the schools of oratory and philosophy attracted public interest and some support. Roman politicians were masters of the art of winning political support by spending the people's money, and some, particularly several of the early emperors, endowed chairs of philosophy and oratory by drawing upon the public treasury. Such endowments were granted to selected cities to enable them to persuade distinguished scholars to establish

schools in their midst. Several schools established in this manner became famous and a few of the teachers were so distinguished that they were accorded many of the privileges of the senatorial class. But in spite of all this encouragement, the practical bent of the Roman character turned scholarly efforts in the direction of law, medicine, and architecture rather than toward literature and philosophy. Indeed, the latter disciplines were perverted from their original purpose of conducting free inquiry into the meaning of political life in the ancient and free city-state, and were employed to provide adulation and approval of the policies put forth by a Nero or a Caligula. In short, the philosophers and writers subsidized by the Imperium all too often merely pandered to their political master.

It was during this period of a rather high state of institutional development that Christianity appeared in the Roman Empire. In contrast to the philosophical and scientific methods of inquiry cultivated in the higher circles of Roman society, early Christian teachings proclaimed that the Good Life was to be won by complete and unquestioning acceptance of a body of revealed knowledge. Scholarly activity that might arouse doubts was vigorously opposed. From an educational point of view, early Christians deliberately encouraged the destruction of the Roman schools through a policy of avoidance and neglect. This policy was made official in A.D. 401 when the Council of Carthage forbade the Christian clergy to read pagan literature, and in A.D. 529 when Emperor Justinian published an edict ordering the closing of the pagan schools. It was this calculated neglect of the schools and scholarly inquiry, more than the destruction of libraries and the burning of books, that brought on the Dark Ages, a period extending roughly from A.D. 500 to 1000.

Meanwhile, the Christians had been developing an administrative organization to promote their cause. At first individual Christians in a given locality had drawn together into communities or congregations for mutual encouragement and support. These centers soon became nuclei around which missionary activities were organized. For such purposes the congregations assigned special duties to those members thought best qualified to fulfill them, and in this manner a class of clergy came to be distinguished from the laity. By the third century a distinct hierarchy had emerged in which bishops enjoyed a dignity and authority not shared by the lesser clergy. Then further distinctions arose among the bishops "according to the position of their cities and with particular consideration for the apostolic foundation of certain congregations."[1] In the fourth century, Emperor Constantine found it useful to employ the political strength inherent in this administrative organization to promote his own imperial ambitions. To gather control into his own hands he first accorded the clergy corporate status and extended to the individual members numerous benefits and privileges previously reserved to officials of the imperial government. The hierarchy then was permitted to develop further, a process that resulted in concentrating control in fewer hands. Finally, Christianity was made an official religion of the Empire and the Christian Church was given

legal status and protection under the authority of the emperor. This had the effect of erecting a sort of "universal [catholic] Christian church" with the emperor at its head.[2]

Early in the fourth century Constantine moved the capital of the Roman Empire to Constantinople, and with it went the central administrative control of the Christian Church. To facilitate the administration of ecclesiastical affairs, as distinguished from more strictly civil matters, the five patriarchal seats —Alexandria, Antioch, Constantinople, Jerusalem, and Rome—were made subordinate or departmental capitals for the geographic regions in which they were located. This subdivision of ecclesiastical control had important consequences, for as the power of the imperial government declined, the "bishop of Rome," Pope Leo III, took steps, late in the eighth century, to create a new civil authority in Western Europe which would be politically as well as ecclesiastically independent of Constantinople. This decisive step was proclaimed to the world, at the beginning of the ninth century, when Charlemagne the king of the Franks was invited to Rome to be crowned emperor of a new "Holy Roman Empire" to encompass that portion of the original empire that had been ecclesiastically subordinate to the patriarchical capital of Rome.

It is said by some historians that the Pope had hoped by this act to establish the supremacy of ecclesiastical authority over civil powers. If so, he did not succeed, for Charlemagne immediately asserted his independence. Indeed, a struggle for supremacy ensued which was carried on by succeeding popes and emperors until the Holy Roman Empire

[1] Jakob Burckhardt, *The Age of Constantine the Great*, translated by Moses Hadas, Pantheon, New York, 1949, p. 126.

[2] *Ibid.*, pp. 306–311.

was dissolved one thousand years later. Nevertheless, in educational matters the Roman Catholic Church quickly became the controlling agency. Even Charlemagne acknowledged this arrangement. After noting the illiteracy and ignorance of occupants of even the highest offices, he charged the bishops with responsibility for correcting the situation. The resulting educational activities, beginning around A.D. 826, ultimately helped lift the cloak of darkness from medieval Europe.

Reference will be made in later chapters to the substantial role played by Irish monks in this effort to reestablish schools in Europe. Christianity did not reach the more distant parts of the British Isles until the processes of decay were already well under way on the Continent. Because of the vigor of these new Christian outposts, together with their remote location, many of the Irish monasteries escaped the destructive fanaticism that raged elsewhere in the Empire. When the Carolingians gave evidence of an awakening interest in learning, more than a thousand missionaries, among them Alcuin, swarmed out of these Irish nests to bring remnants of the ancient literary heritage to Britain and Northern Europe. But a continent which for centuries had shunned books, the literary arts, and formal schooling as a religious obligation could not be returned to a state of enlightenment in a single generation or even a century. The most the Church was able to do in its new role of educator was to establish training schools for its clergy.

The literary heritage supplied by the Irish missionaries had been made fully compatible with their version of Christian doctrine. The Church, which re-

garded itself as the custodian of a revealed truth, incorporated the Irish contributions without particular difficulty, and sought to preserve that body of knowledge and transmit it from generation to generation. Parts of this heritage had been assembled before the time of Charlemagne by a succession of church leaders, now frequently designated as "church fathers," and by councils of bishops and other high church dignitaries. A major portion of the religious documents, including the Bible, had been cast into vernacular Latin prior to the sixth century. Not only was the Vulgate Bible made the accepted book of revealed knowledge, but the vernacular (or vulgar) form of Latin was also used by the Roman clergy in preaching and teaching. Thus when the Church established schools in response to Charlemagne's instructions, it did so at the outset to teach the clergy to read, and occasionally to write, the church Latin, and the schools became known as Latin schools.

Two types of Latin schools appeared almost from the beginning of the Church's venture into formal education. One was developed by the individual bishops to train the younger clergy recruited to fill the needs of their respective dioceses. These schools were made part of the regular diocesan administrative system over which the bishop presided, and they became known as bishop's schools or cathedral schools. The second type was developed by the cloistered religious orders, also to train newly recruited members. These became known as cloister or monastery schools. Because the religious orders prior to the twelfth century generally lived in seclusion, the cloister schools made very little impression on the outside world. Their chief educational contribution, apart from occasionally undertaking to provide some instruction to *externi* or persons who were not committed to life in the cloister, was to preserve and reproduce by hand the limited number of manuscripts that had survived the bonfires of the fifth century or had been produced by Christian authors in the succeeding centuries. While most of these were in church Latin, occasional manuscripts were in the older languages and a few were on nonreligious subjects. The libraries of several monasteries, notably at St. Gall, gave important assistance to the Renaissance scholars in their efforts to recover the works of pagan writers.

Meanwhile, because of a growing interest in education, new schools sprang up in some of the larger parishes in imitation of the cathedral schools. Large parishes, as well as cathedrals, were generally served by a considerable number of clergy, all of whom were known as "canons." The canons of the cathedral were organized for administrative purposes into a "chapter," whereas those of a parish formed a "college" presided over by a "dean." The church in a parish large enough to boast a college of canons, therefore, became known as a "collegiate" church. Hence, there came, in time, to be collegiate schools as well as cathedral and monastic schools, each maintained by the local clergy for the training of clerics and each offering the same Latin curriculum.

Soon, however, other schools were established by gift or legacy placed in trust with the Church with instructions that an education similar to that provided the clergy should be made available to persons, particularly poor boys, not necessarily intending to enter re-

ligious life. Poor boys of promise, the sons of the nobility, and other lay persons thus found educational opportunities opening to them which formerly had been reserved to the clergy. Known as "foundation" schools because of the method of their support, such schools generally offered the full course of instruction found in other Latin schools—Latin grammar, rhetoric, and a little logic or dialectic. These three branches of study formed the famous "trivium."

Occasional parish priests, whose regular duties included training the choir and teaching the children the Creed and the Lord's Prayer, offered a little instruction in Latin grammar, possibly in the hope that some promising boys would be stimulated to study for the priesthood at a regular Latin school. From such efforts "parish" and "choir" schools developed. The practice also arose for wealthy persons to leave sums of money with the Church to employ a priest to say prayers in the family chapel for members of the family who had died. Sometimes these bequests were given with the stipulation that the priest should take on the additional duties of instructing young boys of the neighborhood. From these beginnings arose "chantry" schools. Finally, the development of trade and industry by the medieval guilds, and the accompanying rise of commercial cities in which the guild activities were sheltered, brought about a middle class which developed distinct cultural aspirations. In due time, municipal governments, usually controlled by members of the middle class, were persuaded to sponsor schools for the sons of the local inhabitants. At first these "municipal" schools merely imitated the forms and curricula of the cathedral and parish schools, but with the passing of time they made significant concessions to the expanding secular interests of the inhabitants, or burghers, even to offering instruction in the local dialect.[3]

It is apparent from this account that a variety of schools existed in Europe as the Middle Ages drew to a close. In all of them the Church exercised control, chiefly by authorizing their establishment and by supplying members of the clergy as teachers. The instruction offered in the parish and chantry schools was designed, in the main, for the laity. The method of instruction consisted of having pupils repeat after the teacher, word for word, the Latin versions of the Creed and the Lord's Prayer until these had been memorized. A more sophisticated form of instruction was found in the Latin schools. "The first duty of each of these schools was the same: Instruction in all the areas of knowledge, and development of each competency which the clerical calling required. . . ." Of first importance were ". . . singing, reading, writing, together with a knowledge of the language of the Church (*grammaticus*) and the calculation of the holy days (*computus*). . . ." But as the clergy came to be consulted on other than strictly religious matters, their needs in the areas of the arts and sciences grew constantly greater. Hence, the scope of the curriculum tended to expand "to include all of the seven liberal arts which the textbooks of Alcuin and his successors" had helped to render into acceptable form.[4]

The creation of the office of the *mag-ister scholarum* prior to the twelfth century had considerable influence in shaping the later forms of administrative control. As educational activities at the various seats of learning increased, their direction had been made the special responsibility of a trusted member of the local chapter or college. Known first as the *magister scholarum,* the canon so designated at the cathedral chapter ultimately became known as the *scholasticus;* and to his other duties were added that of giving general supervision to all schools in the diocese. Thereafter the heads of the individual schools were designated as *rector scholarum,* or simply *scholarium.* But the authority of the *scholasticus* as the responsible agent in all educational matters throughout the diocese remained intact. The office of *scholasticus* acquired a high place in the administrative hierarchy, and from it developed the monopoly exercised by the Church over all educational activity. Without the *licentia docendi s. scholas regendi,* a license obtainable only from the *scholasticus,* nobody was permitted to teach any subject in any place. Somewhat later, as new forms of knowledge not given in revelation came to be sought by the people, ecclesiastical control of education became the source of much unrest, especially in the municipalities.[5]

As long as the Christian tradition was based on a specific body of beliefs said to have been revealed, the individual Christian had no alternative but to accept those beliefs literally and as an act of faith. The medieval schools clearly fostered such unquestioning acceptance. Medieval man lived by faith and found no need to cultivate intellectual powers to help him interpret what had been revealed in the beginning and had

[3] Friedrich Paulsen, *Geschichte des Gelehrten Unterrichts,* Verlag von Veit, Leipzig, 1919, vol. I, pp. 15–21.

[4] *Ibid.,* pp. 14–15. Translations by I. N. Thut.

[5] *Ibid.,* p. 16.

been preserved for him by the Church. Thus when a report gained wide circulation that, according to Christian revelation, the second coming of Jesus would take place in the year A.D. 1000, it too was accepted on faith and a great wave of frenzied expectation swept over Western Europe. The failure of this prediction to materialize caused many persons to entertain doubts about other facets of their faith; and when the Crusades and contact with the Moors in Spain brought such persons a knowledge of the culture of the East, a change in the intellectual climate of Western Europe known as the Renaissance soon was under way.

One of the first fruits of the Renaissance that affected the institutional pattern of European education is known as "scholasticism." The name was derived from the fact that the movement originated with the schoolmen, beginning in the eleventh and twelfth centuries. The schools at that time still were oriented to the requirements of the clergy, and matters of belief still occupied the major attention of scholars. But now the recovery of portions of the Aristotelian logic from Eastern sources excited schoolmen, particularly among the schools of Paris, with the prospect that theological studies could employ the techniques of the logician. Exploratory efforts were reassuring; and Parisian teachers were soon substituting methods of rational inquiry, employing the deductive techniques of Aristotle, for the strictly memorizing activities which had previously been used in the schools. Many of the cathedral, collegiate, cloister, and parallel schools now began to place first emphasis upon training students in the use of the logical processes with the expectation that these

would be employed as tools of research in later stages of their education. Theological studies proper were postponed until after the necessary literary and reasoning skills had been developed. The Latin schools thus became "preparatory" schools, and in centers where more mature scholars carried on rational inquiries to discover new truth, universities arose.

The first university corporation, in the modern sense, was probably organized by the schoolmen of Paris around the close of the twelfth century. It was a corporation of masters all of whom were members of the Paris clergy, chiefly canons of Notre Dame and St. Geneviève. A corporate structure was adopted because it was useful in preventing persons who had not been admitted into the company of approved masters from giving lectures or engaging in disputations. Similarly, as a corporation the university was able to establish and enforce admissions standards whereby persons unprepared to hear the lectures and disputations were excluded. As members of the clergy, most of the masters were under the discipline of the bishop of Paris, but the canons of St. Genevieve were not.[6] This exception thus afforded some freedom of inquiry from the very beginning. Academic freedom advanced still further when the university corporation was granted autonomous status by the pope. Although students continued to receive the *licentia docendi* from the local chancellor, only those recommended by the corporation were eligible.[7]

Many new universities were founded

[6] Frederick Eby and Charles Flinn Arrowood, *History and Philosophy of Education, Ancient and Medieval*, Prentice-Hall, Englewood Cliffs, N.J., 1950, p. 777.
[7] *Ibid.*, pp. 778–779.

in the thirteenth century, and most imitated the pattern developed by the University of Paris. However, at Bologna a corporation was formed by lay persons, mostly noblemen and other men of wealth, who were desirous of studying law. At Salerno, a famous health resort, a corporation was formed to promote the study of medicine. Thus the three traditional university faculties of theology, law, and medicine originated independently and at about the same time. In 1224, Emperor Frederick II, jealous of the prestige of the Church, chartered the University of Naples and thereby set a precedent for later foundations by royal rather than ecclesiastical charter. But for many years the university corporations continued to look to Rome for their authority to teach and to award degrees. On the other hand, local authorities, municipal as well as state, were the source of economic benefits and legal privileges enjoyed by students and masters alike as members of the clergy.

Although the earliest university corporations consisted of only one faculty, later corporations aspired to offer instruction in each of the three recognized fields of scholarship—law, theology, and medicine. Their hopes did not always meet with success, however, particularly with respect to the faculty of medicine. Then as the Renaissance progressed, and the humanists recovered more Greek and Roman manuscripts, the perusal of this pagan literature was made the special responsibility of a fourth faculty, the faculty of arts.

Fifteenth-century education

With the rise of universities, the outline of a genuine system of education
34

had appeared in Europe. The several faculties provided professional studies in the scholastic tradition. Open to students from all parts of Europe, they conducted their lectures and disputations in the one language of communication common to all educated Europeans, the Latin of the Church. This circumstance made it necessary for students to be prepared linguistically if they were to take part in the activities of the community of scholars and to consult the sources on which their study depended. Schools of the cathedral, cloister, college, and chapter, therefore, gradually confined their efforts to giving students the necessary proficiency in Latin, and left to the universities the responsibility for imparting the knowledge required to engage in the "learned" professions. Between the Latin schools and the universities a relationship evolved that made for the ready accommodation of students no matter what their mother tongue or place of origin. The subjects pursued, the methods of instruction employed, the levels of achievement demanded, and the steps of progression through which each student was expected to move were gradually worked out in practice and established in tradition. In modern terms, the schools became articulated.

Social role

In the fifteenth century the Church found that other forces were rising to challenge her monopoly in education. First among these were the market towns and commercial centers which an expanding economy had been developing into more or less independent and often self-governing municipalities. These were supplied, of course, with the usual religious establishments and offices of the Church, including schools. But the outlook and aspirations of the inhabitants of the cities were different from those of the feudal aristocracy, on the one hand, and the land-bound peasantry, on the other. The educational establishments of the Church had been developed to function under the static conditions of a feudal society. The city populations were demanding instruction oriented to the daily needs of a middle class, of a society resting upon a money economy rather than an agricultural economy. Earlier the rising aspirations of the burghers had led to the establishment of municipal Latin schools; now the development of a middle class called for the introduction of vernacular schools, schools in which the more immediate literary needs of the tradesman could be met.

To understand the social and intellectual forces at work among the people during the fifteenth century, it will be helpful to remember that at the beginning of the century there were only a limited number of books in existence. They were handwritten manuscripts, and their circulation was restricted not only by their scarcity, but also because few persons other than the clergy could read. Most of the books were on religious subjects and were kept in the libraries of the cloisters, of the schools, and of persons of position. But by the end of the century, there were more than a thousand printers at work turning out books and pamphlets. In just fifty years after the invention of the printing press in 1438, some thirty thousand titles had been put into print, and of these at least nine million copies had been distributed.

In a parallel development, the fifteenth-century European witnessed the expansion of his physical world to include the continents of Africa and the Americas. His concept of the universe was drastically reshaped, and the authenticity of the revealed truths taught by his clergy were further challenged. In 1453 Constantinople, long regarded as the capital of Christendom, fell to the Turks. This event sent Eastern scholars fleeing to the West carrying their books and their foreign learning with them. Alternate intellectual bases and supplementary systems of reasoning thus came to stand side by side with those which had been derived from Aristotle by the scholastics, and the world of Christian scholars began to show signs of a new individualism and independence of thought. Similarly, the Ptolemaic and Aristotelian scientific theories were coming under attack both inside and outside the Church.

By the end of the fifteenth century medieval man was dead and a new type of man was rising who was impatient to explore the intellectual and physical horizons in every direction. New religions, new sciences, new literary languages, new governments, and new modes of thought and action were the direct and visible results. And although new political and educational institutions also appeared, particularly in Northern Italy, their effect was not wholly felt until the following century, and for that reason will be described in subsequent chapters.

In spite of these developments, the social role of education changed only slightly in the fifteenth century. As agencies of the traditional social system the schools continued to be used to maintain the weakening power structure inherited from the age of faith, the so-called "medieval system." The dominating feature of that system was its hierarchical structure, with power concentrated at the top in the hands of a single agent held to be responsible not to man, but to God. The person who sat in the place of highest authority, it was asserted, had been placed there by divine will and thus deserved the unquestioning obedience and support of all who had been assigned lesser stations by the same power. The schools were expected to justify and transmit the system of religious beliefs on which that power structure rested. Even the scholastic theology afforded such support; and theological studies had continued to occupy a central place in the schools under scholastic direction. Humanism and its accompanying tendency toward secular interests could not yet affect education in a significant way, although the ancient languages were finding a place in the Latin schools, and pagan authors were coming to be read. Educational objectives continued to be centered upon the religious heritage of Rome and on winning a good life in the hereafter. Although the seeds of reform were being planted, the philosophical revolution had not progressed far enough to bring forth the various forms of social revolution that were to break out all over Europe in the next and succeeding centuries.

Power structure and administrative organization

The neat arrangement of authority one might expect in a monolithic, hierarchical power structure, such as the Holy Roman Empire was intended to provide, was not much in evidence in the fifteenth century. The lines of authority were confused—and had been more or less from the days of Charlemagne—by the conflicting claims put forth by the successive popes and emperors as to which had been divinely appointed to sit in the place of highest authority.

In Figure 1 the major lines of political power are shown as they existed in the fifteenth century. It should be re-

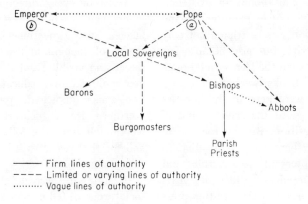

——— Firm lines of authority
- - - - Limited or varying lines of authority
·········· Vague lines of authority

Figure 1. Lines of Social Control in Fifteenth-century Europe
a. Pope Leo III proclaimed the "Holy Roman Empire" in A.D. 800 and invited Charlemagne to become the emperor.
b. Charlemagne refused to be subordinate to the pope thereby setting off the struggle for supremacy waged by popes and emperors for centuries.

membered that the domains of the Holy Roman Empire and of the Roman Catholic Church were to have been coterminous and to have included all Europe under the ecclesiastical domination of Rome. Within this vast realm civil matters were to have been the responsibility of the emperor, and ecclesiastical affairs the exclusive province of the pope. However, it was soon obvious that unless one conceded superiority to the other, the system was actually two-headed.

A further source of conflict arose from the fact that the emperors failed to gain control over all Western Europe. Important political units, notably Spain, France, and England, were able to remain free, and thus to challenge the imperial authority. Indeed, the Empire was essentially a German institution, although territories in Western Europe sometimes became connected with it through inheritance, military conquest, or diplomacy. On several occasions nobles of the Western regions made strong bids for the imperial crown, and Charles V of Spain actually succeeded in this ambition early in the sixteenth century, owing largely to his Austrian ancestry.

Especially significant for the present purpose, however, is the fact that the papal claim to supremacy had been asserted with more than usual success from the twelfth to the fourteenth centuries. Pope Innocent had actually exercised civil as well as ecclesiastical control over

... the Italian states, the Spanish peninsula, the Scandinavian states, Hungary, Bohemia, Poland, Servia, Bosnia, Bulgaria, and the Christian state of Syria.[8]

[8] *Encyclopaedia Britannica*, "Popery," 14th ed., vol. XVII, p. 203.

Kings were even deposed on the orders of Rome. It was not until Philip the Fair of France, backed by his States-General, marched on Rome and humbled one of Innocent's successors, Boniface VIII, that this long period of papal domination was temporarily brought to an end.

Philip's overt action against the papacy also indicated a decline in the power and influence of the Empire. By this time the prestige and power of local sovereigns, such as Philip, had risen to the point that various aggressive political units entertaining national ambitions had to be reckoned with. Thus the conflicting claims of authority put forth by popes, emperors, and now also kings, created a most confusing power structure as the fifteenth century drew to a close; and schools as well as individuals were becoming increasingly uncertain which master they were expected to serve.

From the above account it is obvious that the lines of authority indicated in Figure 1 are an oversimplification of the actual situation. The two older power structures, the Church and the Empire, are shown standing side by side with overlapping claims of jurisdiction. One might dominate the other, depending upon which enjoyed the more aggressive leadership at the moment. The potential importance of the local sovereigns or heads of state is apparent, for neither of the two major contenders could enforce his authority without their cooperation. At the same time, pope and emperor, as well as king, each claimed authority on the basis of divine appointment. Conflicting claims, therefore, did not in themselves indicate a turning away from the medieval preoccupation with religious matters, for each claimant found it necessary to lend support to institutionalized religion to maintain his power structure, and each looked to the schools to provide religious arguments to bolster his assertions of divine appointment.

The conflict of authority reached explosive proportions as the fifteenth century drew to a close. It centered, ultimately, on the question of appointments to ecclesiastical office. From the beginning of the Empire, emperors had sought not only to dictate the appointment of bishops and other high ecclesiastical dignitaries, but the election of popes as well. Popes in their turn attempted to control the election of the emperors. Both interfered openly in the confusing struggles for succession to lesser titles and positions, a struggle induced in part by the devious rules of hereditary succession and the vagaries of the laws of legitimacy prevalent among the aristocracy of that day. Meanwhile, the higher ecclesiastical offices had taken on special importance as a consequence of the extensive landholdings the Church had acquired over the years. Such lands generally were attached as benefices or foundations to subsidize specific ecclesiastical offices. Thus many bishops enjoyed not merely the dignities and privileges of a prince of the Church, but the power and wealth of a prince of the realm as well. By appointing cooperative bishops, popes were able to interfere in the administration of civil affairs within a sovereign state or even in the Empire. These were matters in which kings and emperors thought they should have primary if not exclusive jurisdiction.

In educational administration, the rise of scholasticism in the thirteenth and fourteenth centuries had not changed appreciably the hierarchical form of the inherited power structure. The scholastics were students of theology primarily; and as educators they were interested in training their successors in the proper use of their preferred method of inquiry, the deductive logic. Although leading scholars devoted considerable effort to reviewing the extensive body of religious beliefs inherited from the preceding age of faith, little interest was generated in the problems of the comman man and his practical needs. The ecclesiastical domination of the social structure, so much in evidence in their day, went unchallenged. Indeed, their theological studies afforded impressive new arguments to bolster the existing administrative arrangements. As members of the ecclesiastical hierarchy they found it quite reasonable, and in keeping with God's will, that temporal powers should be subordinate to the Church and that the clergy should enjoy numerous privileges and great prestige among all social classes and in all walks of life. In brief, "clericalism" was justified on the grounds that the intellectual processes involved in acquiring knowledge of the good exceed the powers of ordinary men, and that laymen, including kings, must have ready access to the counsel of the trained specialists, the clergy, in all matters involving the determination of policy. Under the leadership of the scholastics the role of the scholars acquired considerable importance, and the schools, and education in general, increased in number and influence.

It has been noted that by the beginning of the fifteenth century schools were being sponsored by a variety of agencies in addition to the religious orders and the Church. Among such sponsors were kings and lesser nobles, a few

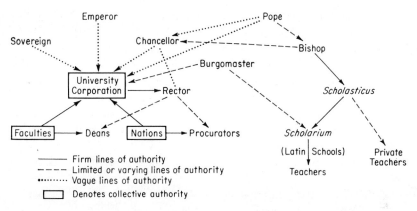

Figure 2. Lines of Educational Authority in Fifteenth-century Europe

Italian city-states, foundations,[9] local parishes, municipalities, and even guilds. It was the custom for such schools to collect tuition fees from all pupils, except the very poor and those committed to religious life. At the outset all such fees seem to have reverted to the *scholasticus*. He, in turn, employed and paid the regular teachers, paid whatever other expenses were incurred in operating the schools, and retained in his treasury the excess revenues earned. In due time the inevitable question of the disposition of these funds, as well as other matters relating to the operation of the schools, brought school sponsors into conflict with the *scholasticus*. In the ensuing struggles, particularly those waged by German municipal authorities, the educational monopoly enjoyed by the Church gradually weakened.[10]

In Figure 2 the numerous Latin schools, as well as those offering instruction in the vernacular, are shown under the administrative control of the *scholasticus*. The universities, however, had already won their independence from local control. This outcome was inevitable because the masters were generally the equals, and often the superiors, of the *scholasticus* in the clerical hierarchy. Also, as members of the local chapter or of a college of canons, as at Paris, some of the masters were subject to the discipline of the local bishop but others not. Furthermore, a university's privileges— those of teaching, holding examinations, and recommending candidates for degrees—almost without exception were derived from the pope. The university's status as a corporation, on the other hand, was usually acquired by charter from the king or, as in the case of Naples and Prague, from the emperor. Finally, the special privileges which masters and students alike claimed as members of the clergy, such as the right to solicit food and money from the local people, exemption from taxes and public service including military duty, and the jurisdiction of civil courts, were granted by the local authorities. The anomalous status of the universities therefore had become quite apparent early in their history, and the masters were quick to play municipality against municipality, bishop against king, and pope against each of these to promote their own free-

[9] Foundation funds designated for educational purposes usually were administered by the *scholasticus*.

[10] Paulsen, *op. cit.*, vol. I, p. 20.

dom of operation. Quite understandably, the ideal of academic freedom held high by universities today owes much to the vociferous masters of the fifteenth and even earlier centuries. Today most European universities are under the administrative control of either the state or a municipality, but they carry on their academic pursuits with very little direct interference from any outside agencies.

Among the universities, internal administrative controls developed along two distinct lines. At Bologna the university corporation had been formed by students desiring a knowledge of law. These were, for the most part, mature men of noble birth who anticipated assuming heavy administrative responsibilities as the heirs to power in their native states. They were men of means and accustomed to having their own way. Hence they, the students, formed a corporation, hired and fired their teachers, set the curriculum, defined the rules of procedure, policed the academic community, and negotiated with the authorities of the Church, the state, and the municipality for such privileges and guarantees as they believed were needed. In Paris, however, the corporation had been formed by members of the clergy desiring to pursue the study of theology in a more orderly manner and on a higher level than the Latin schools provided. As members of the clergy they were accustomed to discipline by superiors who, at least among the French clergy, were usually elected locally. Their corporation was formed by the masters to afford themselves protection and to prevent unauthorized persons from lecturing on matters bordering on heresy. Thus at Paris the masters set the curriculum, made contracts with the

authorities, approved the teachers, admitted students, and governed the university community.

The large measure of authority and independence enjoyed by the students at Bologna is still in evidence in universities whose antecedents were located south of the Alps, while the pattern developed at Paris is more widely seen in those which evolved from sources north of the Alps. In general, universities in Northern Europe were formed around one of the three faculties, law, theology, or medicine. The faculty of theology at Paris developed the basic administrative pattern. The masters who constituted its membership elected one of their fellows, who was given the title of "dean," to assume administrative responsibilities for the faculty as a whole. The reputation of the Paris faculty spread quickly and soon students gathered from regions far removed from Paris. Both masters and students tended to cluster in groups, according to their national origin, to share living quarters and a common kitchen. This gave rise to the "nations," the remote ancestors of modern dormitories and fraternities, and more directly of the residential colleges of Oxford and Cambridge. Social life centered around the nations; and each developed a form of self-government headed by an elected official named the *procurator*.

Since both masters and students belonged to nations, the nations came to occupy an important place in the university community and they ultimately constituted the basic units for the regulation of affairs affecting the university as a whole. An administrative officer, called the "rector," was elected to represent the university as a whole. His election, in time, came to call for a university-wide celebration with food and drink provided by the successful candidate—a circumstance which may account for the fact that the rector's term of office to this day is limited in some European universities to one year. The rector generally was a wealthy student, one who not only could afford the financial burdens of his office, but who also might have influence in high places which he could use in behalf of the university. But as the university communities expanded to include two, three, and finally four faculties, and the number of students and masters multiplied, the politically conscious scholars resorted to the practice of asking some influential person not directly connected with the university to speak for it before the civil and ecclesiastical authorities. This official came to be known as the "chancellor." [11]

The administration of municipal schools presented some special problems. In the smaller cities and villages, such schools evolved from parish or chantry schools, and the regular lines of ecclesiastical authority applied. As city life developed, a need for more education became apparent. Thereupon the inhabitants went to their municipal governments with requests that the city councils provide the funds and employ the desired teachers. At first, such pressures merely opened up more places in the existing schools, but by the fourteenth century, the city governments were functioning as school patrons and were providing funds and negotiating with the *scholasticus* for teachers for their schools. Schoolmasters secured in this manner soon came to be looked

[11] The chancellor in English universities was an exception, as will be shown in Chap. 6.

upon as municipal employees, and were often assigned part-time clerical and other public duties under the direction of the city councils. By the fifteenth century, therefore, teachers assigned to municipal schools were subject not only to the discipline of the *scholasticus,* but frequently were also supervised and directed in the performance of their teaching functions by the municipal council. Councils came to demand forms of instruction and services not ordinarily expected of a teacher of a parish or chantry school, such as the teaching of arithmetic, modern languages, and even Latin. Among the German states and in the Low Countries municipal schools frequently rivaled the cathedral and foundation schools as preparatory institutions for the universities, and some ultimately rivaled the universities with respect to instruction in the liberal arts. The municipal governments, therefore, must also be considered part of the administrative system by which fifteenth-century education was controlled.

Educational institutions

A list of the various educational institutions offering instruction in the fifteenth century would contain a surprisingly large number of types, as Figure 3 indicates. However, each type that enjoyed official status and boasted a formal program of studies, was expected to help the pupil master the church Latin and prepare him for study in one of the university faculties. Differences among Latin schools therefore were derived largely from differences in the manner in which they were supported, rather than from differences in their ultimate goals. A few Latin schools, specifically those operated by the more progressive municipalities and an occasional parish school, offered instruction in the vernacular, as well as in Latin, and in such immediately useful subjects as contemporary foreign languages. Outside of the Latin and vernacular schools, private instruction was offered by an array of individuals, each of whom set his own course and charged whatever the traffic would bear. The subjects most frequently taught by such persons included reading in the vernacular, writing, arithmetic, and keeping accounts. To operate legitimately, such teachers needed to be licensed by the *scholasticus* and to pay a tithe of the fees collected into his treasury. Private studies of this nature were pursued for the purpose of securing immediately profitable employment and were not generally considered part of the regular system of education.

Among the Latin schools it was gen-

erally understood that by age fifteen a boy should have learned to read and write Latin and have mastered the elements of Christian doctrine and a few rules of the scholastic logic. These were considered enough to prepare him for university studies. The fifteenth-century university afforded a more congenial atmosphere for boys in their teens than does the modern university. A protective regimen and discipline not unlike that of the cloister looked after their physical and social needs. Students, like their masters, were regarded as members of the clergy, and they lived together in hostels or resident halls, each of which constituted a little community of scholars that was presided over by a master. The academic side of the university also was quite hospitable, for each faculty administered its own admissions procedures. By the fifteenth century, stu-

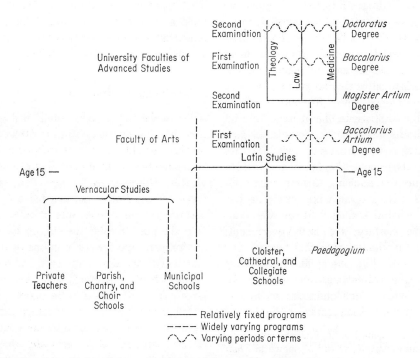

Figure 3. Educational Institutions in Fifteenth-century Europe

dents entering the universities generally sought admission to the faculty of arts first. This enabled them to perfect their command of Latin, possibly to develop some proficiency in Greek, and to attend lectures on the arts. Boys not prepared to take up these studies were not sent home, but were accommodated in a lower division known as the *paedagogium*, which was in fact a Latin school operated by the university.

At this time the arts curriculum was defined in terms of a specific number and kind of lectures and disputations which the student must hear and in which he must take part. After two or three years the student was permitted to take his first examination. If successful, he was awarded the *baccalarius artium* degree; and thereafter was required to assist in teaching the younger students, particularly those in the *paedagogium*. After another two years of study, he became eligible for the second examination. If successful, he was awarded the degree of *magister artium,* and was expected, and sometimes required, to serve several years as a master in an arts faculty. Thereafter he was eligible to study in one of the advanced faculties, where the courses were also divided into two distinct levels; the first led to the bachelor's degree in the field of specialization and the second to the doctor's degree. Unlike modern university students, the fifteenth-century scholar frequently collected degrees in more than one professional area.

Although degrees seem not to have been required for appointment to various offices, municipal authorities increasingly demanded that the teachers assigned to their Latin schools should possess them, particularly the master of arts degree. Consequently, some municipal schools were able to offer instruction substantially superior to that of other Latin schools, and sometimes even parallel to that of the lower division of the arts faculty at a university. Such municipal schools developed a proud tradition and a few later formed the nuclei for universities.

Educational opportunities

As long as the nobility and clergy exercised social control, formal schooling for other fifteenth-century social classes was very limited. Authority in civil affairs was usually inherited or assigned by the crown to trusted associates. Ecclesiastical appointments were also made from a list of candidates who claimed eligibility either by birth, by education and faithful service, or by a combination of these and other factors. In either branch the highly centralized social structure and the hierarchical administrative organization did not require a large number of persons trained in the arts of government. The Latin schools and universities were thought to be admirably suited to train the sons of the ruling class and other selected youths to fill responsible places in either church or state. The ruling class was satisfied with the existing state of affairs, and its members did not expect the schools to press for social reforms or to raise the social or cultural level of the masses.

The great mass of mankind had exceedingly limited powers of self-determination or social responsibility. Few owned anything of worth in their own names. Many were serfs on the great estates without freedom of movement or the hope of escape to employment for real wages. Nearly all had been baptized by the Church in their infancy and were willing to conform, even though only passively, to whatever was required of them by tradition and the disposition of their local priests. The oral ministrations of the Church were their major source of information and guidance. A knowledge of the literary arts was not thought necessary, or even beneficial, to their prescribed way of life. Nearly all lived out their lives in total ignorance of the alphabet and every other "mystery" then associated by the masses with formal schooling.

A rising middle class, however, was setting new educational wheels in motion. Resting on a guild system of industrial production and commerce, this class was beginning to feel an urgent need for the literary skills useful in developing the arts of production and promoting trade in a regulated and orderly manner. Production records needed to be kept, contracts needed to be recorded, and communication lines needed to be established beyond the boundaries of the local community and the reaches of the local dialects.

The first venture into the field of education by the guilds resulted in an apprentice training system. This was nothing more than an arrangement, ultimately standardized in practice and regulated by the guild and municipal officials, whereby a boy agreed to work at a nominal wage for a master craftsman for a fixed number of years, usually seven. In return he was to receive instruction in the knowledge and skills that constituted "the secrets of the trade," and which he in turn agreed not to teach to another except as provided under the rules of the apprenticeship system. Many fifteenth-century craftsmen, however, were beginning to feel the need for additional training in read-

ing, writing, arithmetic, and sometimes in foreign languages. Furthermore, their commercial activities increasingly were bringing them into contact with members of the ruling class. Special legal guarantees needed to be secured from the crown and privileges extracted to enable them to carry on their work. These matters called for equivalent education, and as a result the guilds and municipalities became patrons of Latin as well as vernacular schools.

Finally, the invention of printing in the middle of the century and the resulting rapid increase in the number of books and pamphlets, as well as the extension of the list of subjects on which a vernacular literature became available, greatly increased the demand for reading instruction from persons not interested in attending Latin schools. The need for instruction in reading the vernacular seems to have developed separately from that of writing it, or of acquiring mastery of arithmetic. As a general rule instruction in these matters was given privately, and usually by different teachers. It was not uncommon, even several centuries later, for persons to be able to read their mother tongue, but not to write it, or to do even simple sums. However, the contracts for apprenticeship training increasingly called for some instruction in reading and writing, and sometimes arithmetic, so that masters came to feel the need for collective action. A rapid development of vernacular schools under guild and municipal sponsorship was the result.

A list of the educational opportunities enjoyed by various classes of the fifteenth-century youths therefore would include the following. For the great mass of peasant and unskilled working-class children little was available aside from the instruction a local priest might offer boys in his choir. Youths of more fortunate circumstances found opportunities in apprenticeship training. Sons of the increasingly affluent guild and commercial families could find places in the municipal schools or in the older Latin schools. And, finally, sons of the nobility and the older families of wealth could choose freely from among the municipal as well as the older Latin schools, and could expect to progress to a university to study for a profession or high position in church or state.

Although the schools did not discriminate overtly on a class basis, tuition fees beginning at the first levels of instruction often presented a formidable barrier. Only one avenue lay open to poor boys who aspired to an education. It consisted of life commitment to the service of the Church either in the priesthood or in a religious order. Either road opened the available educational facilities to the candidate without limit except as dictated by the student's own interests and ability and the demands of his superiors.

From an educational viewpoint fifteenth-century Europe was a man's world. Girls generally were not enrolled in the regular vernacular programs and were specifically excluded from the Latin schools and universities. Only in exceptional cases were arrangements made for them to be instructed privately, exceptions which obviously occurred only in higher-class families. Nor did the schools afford the male student much variety. Latin schools pointed their students toward the three learned professions. Vernacular instruction was intended to be immediately useful. The philosophical outlook was narrowly restricted on all levels of instruction. The

intellectual ferment from which world-shaking social, economic, political, and technical developments shortly were to arise had not yet become obvious in the schools and universities.

Subsequent developments

Although scholasticism retained its hold on the schools and universities through most of the fifteenth century, there were signs that a change was on its way. In 1382 Wycliffe had produced an English translation of the Bible from sources older than the Vulgate. A reform movement, known as Lollardism, had followed which inspired intellectual and social unrest in far places. Thus John Huss, a Bohemian priest, had challenged the theological doctrines of the Church and had criticized the behavior of his fellow priests. Cloistered religious orders in the northern regions of the Alps which were economically and socially self-sufficient and geographically isolated from Rome, encouraged an independence of mind not generally found among the clergy in the more populous regions. New intellectual and other cultural interests were appearing among persons closely identified with the stream of social activity in the growing cities.

This movement, known as the Renaissance, started in Italy and progressed slowly northward. Its presence was felt in many schools of Europe, in some even before the fifteenth century. It brought them a different literature, new languages, and a new point of view that expanded and transformed in a limited way the offerings of the arts faculties. Classical Latin and Greek gradually made their way into the universities, and as they did so the spirit of the Renaissance also introduced them into the

Latin preparatory schools. Thus, as the fifteenth century progressed students on both levels increasingly were perusing literary works long neglected by the scholars of the medieval period. These classical sources added fuel to the spirit of unrest brewing in the scattered intellectual centers mentioned above, and soon new educational developments were to rise from them that would alter rather drastically the neatly articulated system of schools developed by the scholastics.

Of the two major educational movements generated during the later phases of the Renaissance, the Protestant Reformation was the first to produce widespread educational consequences. Although Protestantism generally is regarded as a development of the sixteenth century, numerous reform efforts came much earlier. In addition to the Lollards and Hussites, the Waldenses and Albigenses had become active in scattered regions of Northern Italy, France, Spain, and Switzerland, some as early as the twelfth century. In France, and especially in Spain, the Inquisition was invoked in the fifteenth century to crush these and other reputed heresies, a development that may have held back educational changes in those regions for many years. As the fifteenth century drew to a close, Luther and Zwingli were engaged in their respective studies from which more thoroughgoing and lasting reforms were to follow. John Calvin was to follow them by only a few years. These three ultimately carried with them much of Europe north and west of the Alps; and since each insisted upon accepting literally that which the New Testament recorded as revealed and final knowledge, vernacular reading schools were established on a massive

scale in each Protestant area. The educational systems of England, Germany, the Netherlands, the Scandinavian states, Switzerland, and other Protestant countries are derived in substantial part from these pioneering efforts in mass education and will be discussed, at least briefly, in following chapters.

The second major educational development originating in the later stages of the Renaissance was brought about by humanists. They, too, rejected much of the medieval philosophical outlook and objected particularly to the exercise of authority by persons who had no claim to power other than a line of royal ancestors. Unlike the religious reformers, however, the humanists looked for knowledge of the Good Life within the realm of human affairs by employing man's natural endowments alone. Humanism thus fostered a secular outlook; and in the centers of scholarly activity a new concern appeared which focused upon the improvement of life in this world. The early humanists were persuaded by their study of the recovered Greek and Roman classics that the ancient authors already had possessed knowledge of the best way of life possible for mankind. They became exceedingly active in promoting the study of the classical languages and literature. Schools originally developed and operated by scholastics were taken over and reformed by humanists. Curricula were revised by substituting classical Latin for the church Latin, and classical Greek was added as a second, and superior, language of scholarship. Works on religious subjects were neglected and the writings of pagan authors such as Cicero, Vergil, Homer, and Aristotle, were substituted for them. The intellectual man became the educational ideal, an objective which is very much in evidence to this day in European preparatory schools and universities. These humanistic developments also will be noted in later chapters.

Although humanism, like the Reformation, was making itself felt in certain parts of Europe during the closing years of the fifteenth century, it achieved a significant place in the education and social life of the various peoples at different times. Generally, the periods of greatest influence were attained after the fifteenth century. But in spite of the educational activity aroused, neither the Reformation nor humanism may be regarded as a first cause in the development of the modern European systems of education. Each in its own way helped to extend and redirect educational institutions and practices already in use in many parts of Europe during the fifteenth and even earlier centuries.

References

Brinton, Clarence Crane: *Ideas and Men: The Story of Western Thought,* Prentice-Hall, Englewood Cliffs, N.J., 1950.

Burckhardt, Jakob: *The Age of Constantine the Great,* translated by Moses Hadas, Pantheon, New York, 1949.

————: *The Civilization of the Renaissance,* translated by S. G. C. Middlemore, Phaidon, London, 1945.

Castiglione, Count Baldassare: *The Book of the Courtier,* translated by L. E. Opdycke, Scribner, New York, 1903.

Eby, Frederick, and Charles Flinn Arrowood: *The History and Philosophy of Education, Ancient and Medieval,* Prentice-Hall, Englewood Cliffs, N.J., 1940.

Ferguson, Wallace K.: *The Renaissance in Historical Thought,* Houghton Mifflin, Boston, 1948.

————: *A Survey of European Civilization,* Houghton Mifflin, Boston, 1939.

Graves, Frank Pierrepont: *A History of Education,* 3 vols., Macmillan, New York, 1931.

Haskins, Charles Homer: *The Rise of Universities,* Cornell, Ithaca, N.Y., 1957.

————: *Studies in Medieval Culture,* Oxford, Fair Lawn, N.J., 1929.

Monroe, Paul: *A Text-book in the History of Education,* Macmillan, New York, 1908.

Moore, Ernest Carroll: *The Story of Instruction: The Church, the Renaissance, and the Reformation,* Macmillan, New York, 1938.

Paulsen, Friedrich: *Geschichte des Gelehrten Unterrichts,* vol. I, Verlag von Veit, Leipzig, 1919; vol. II, Walter de Gruyter & Co., Leipzig, 1921.

Pico della Mirandola, Giovanni: "Oration on the Dignity of Man," in C. Cassiere and Others (eds.), *The Renaissance Philosophy of Man,* The University of Chicago Press, Chicago, 1948, pp. 213–254.

Randall, John Herman, Jr.: *The Making of the Modern Mind,* rev. ed., Houghton Mifflin, Boston, 1940.

Rashdall, Hastings: *The Universities of Europe in the Middle Ages,* 3 vols., Oxford, Fair Lawn, N.J., 1936.

Sabine, George H.: *A History of Political Theory,* rev. ed., Holt, New York, 1955.

Symonds, John Addington: *Renaissance in Italy,* vol. II, *The Revival of Learning;* vols. VI, VII, *The Catholic Reaction,* Smith, Elder, London, 1898.

Tawney, Richard Henry: *Religion and the Rise of Capitalism: A Historical Study,* Harcourt, Brace, New York, 1926.

Watson, Foster: *The Old Grammar Schools,* Cambridge, New York, 1916.

CHAPTER 3

Spanish Education:
Imposing a Foreign Culture

The standard indexes and other guides to the literature on comparative education do not list many items under Spain. Nor is much to be gained by looking for entries such as Portugal or even Latin America, for the Spanish antecedents of the education found in these and other parts of the ancient Spanish domains are usually mentioned only fleetingly. With particular reference to Central and Latin America, schools and other cultural institutions either evolved from, or were imposed upon, a pattern that was transplanted from the Spanish peninsula in the sixteenth and seventeenth centuries. In that period Spain acquired a far-flung empire as a result of the venturesome spirit of her sailors and the aggressive policies of her agents at the Vatican. But the Church extracted a price for her blessings, for the Spanish government had to promise to subordinate itself eternally to the spiritual leadership of Rome, and to propagate the Catholic religion and ecclesiastical institutions throughout the newly acquired territories. It was in fulfillment of the latter condition that the Spanish educational pattern was transported to the colonies.

The effects of the compact made between "the Catholic Sovereigns" and the Vatican during the last years of the fifteenth century have been very much in evidence in the Spanish world ever since. Even today spokesmen for the Franco government declare that education must be used to counteract the secular trends promoted by the Liberals and to reestablish "the ancient Spanish tradi-

tion." The most important elements of that tradition, as presently conceived, are "Christianity; Graeco-Roman culture; Spanish humanism as found in its language, literature, and history; and the more recent developments in science and mathematics."[1] Christianity in this instance is meant to include Roman Catholicism only. The reference to Graeco-Roman culture implies philosophical, social, and other cultural dispositions channeled to the Western world from ancient Greece through the Roman Empire. Elements of humanistic scholarship received favorable attention in the sixteenth century. The purpose of the present account is to describe the educational consequences of the Spanish tradition, as it attained its peak in the sixteenth and seventeenth centuries, and to note the varied reception it has enjoyed from the Spanish people in the succeeding years.

Historical development

Spain came within the orbit of Greek and Roman affairs long before the rise of the Roman Empire. Her climate and fertile lands invited colonization, and her harbors on the Mediterranean nurtured the growth of cities which soon matched in wealth and splendor the best the homelands could boast. The colonials in Spain were proud of their Greek and Roman antecedents and eagerly imported the cultural and social institu-

[1] Patrick J. McCormick, *History of Education,* Catholic Education Press, Washington, D.C., 1950, pp. 605–606.

tions which bound them to the mainlands. Their cities became famous for their schools and the cultivation of learning; and when Christianity gained the ascendancy within the Empire the Spanish people embraced the new religion and accepted its institutional forms. In brief, Spain considered herself one of the foremost exemplars of all that the Empire stood for and claimed her full share of the glory for having made it possible. The Spanish people still count that as one of the brightest periods in their long history.

The decline of the Roman Empire exposed the Christian inhabitants of the Spanish peninsula to successive waves of invaders. First to come had been the Vandals, then the Visigoths, and finally, in A.D. 711, the Moors who remained masters of most of the peninsula well into the twelfth century. Indeed, a political map of the peninsula early in the eleventh century bears no trace of the modern states of Spain and Portugal. A line running from Oporto on the Atlantic to Barcelona on the Mediterranean would separate, in a rough way, the southern two-thirds under Moslem rule from the areas to the north claimed by the kingdoms of León and Castile, of Navarre, of Aragon, and the county of Barcelona. Indeed, from the ninth to the eleventh century the few remaining Christian kingdoms were tributaries of the mighty Caliph of Córdoba, bringing not only their riches for his treasury, but also their petty disputes for his arbitration.

Into their vast outpost in Europe the Moslem people transplanted the rich culture acquired from the Greeks and enriched by their own genius as well as by the intellectual gifts brought by their traders from the East. To this was added a substantial infusion of Jewish wisdom, intellectual integrity, and thirst for learning. By contrast with the intellectual poverty of the rest of Europe, the Moorish cities of Córdoba, Granada, Seville, Toledo, and others became centers of artistic beauty and intellectual vigor. The defenders of the Christian faith residing in the north therefore had good reason to fear the presence of these nonbelievers in lands which but a few centuries earlier had been under the rule of Christian emperors. For this reason the Roman Church, through its devoted subordinates installed as ruling sovereigns here and there, waged a continuous campaign to drive the unbelievers from the continent. However, that objective was not reached before this extensive repository of Arabic and Hebraic literature had made substantial contributions to a revival of learning which began among the Christians around the eleventh century.

The task of building a united Spanish nation out of many Moslem and Christian political segments was begun, and in great measure completed, under the brilliant, and sometimes ruthless, leadership of the two "Catholic Sovereigns," Isabella and Ferdinand. In 1469 their marriage brought together the kingdoms of Castile and Aragon, although each continued to rule independently of the other. Together, they united the Christians in a crusade of liberation. They steadily extended Christian sovereignty southward, and in 1492 finally forced Granada, the last Moslem stronghold, to yield to their overwhelming power. Twenty years later all of the peninsula save Portugal was united under a Spanish sovereign; and in 1519 the King of Spain was elected Emperor Charles V of the Holy Roman Empire.

During this period of political consolidation, Spain's territorial possessions were being extended in such areas as Mexico, Peru, and parts of Africa. For nearly a century Spanish power was superior to that of any other European state. This day of glory was brought to an end in 1588 by the defeat of the Spanish Armada—a humiliating blow from which the nation's political and military power never recovered. Hence, it is to the joint reigns of Isabella and Ferdinand that one must look for the beginnings of modern Spain and the foundations of her distinctive cultural and social institutions, including education.

Attainment of national status

Prior to the reigns of Isabella and Ferdinand, sovereigns of Spanish states were limited in the exercise of their authority by the nobles and even the commoners. Nobles of a given state usually formed a council, known as the Cortes, by which the whims of the sovereign were mitigated and their own ambitions enhanced. In time such councils admitted representatives of the principal cities, a number of which enjoyed a form of corporate independence with powers of self-government. Thus the nobles, on the one hand, and the commoners from the cities, on the other, had become conscious of their political importance and had taken to the field on more than one occasion to enforce their claims against sovereign, prelate, or even against each other. Isabella and Ferdinand therefore had not inherited undisputed control of established, integrated power structures; rather, they were merely the most powerful figures among the nominal heads of a variety of fac-

tions and political units. They achieved their many triumphs, both military and political, by paying strict attention, at the outset, to the dignity of their subjects and by sharing the good fortunes of their many ventures with the people as a whole. Their long reigns did much to bring these diverse peoples and factions together to form a single, enduring national group.

From the present point of view, however, three specific developments during the reigns of Isabella and Ferdinand made lasting impressions upon Spanish thought and social practices. *First* among these is the high degree of popular support they won for the crown at the expense of the lesser nobility, the city governments, and even the ecclesiastical hierarchy emanating from Rome. This success was not only the fruit of shrewd political maneuvering at home, but also of intrigue and ruthless machinations on the diplomatic front.[2]

During much of the fifteenth century, the first temporal objective of the Roman Catholic Church was to drive the Moslems out of Europe. This was a continuation of the spirit which had called forth the Crusades, and many Spanish noblemen were members of the crusading military orders, notably the Knights Templars and the Orders of St. James and of Calatrava.[3] Thus when Ferdinand invited the noblemen to join him in a "holy" war against the remaining Moslem stronghold in Granada, they

[2] A popular anecdote tells of a complaint from the king of France that Ferdinand had deceived him twice. In reply Ferdinand is said to have boasted: "The king of France lies. I have deceived him ten times."

[3] William H. Prescott, *History of the Reign of Ferdinand and Isabella, The Catholic*, Lippincott, Philadelphia, 1868, vol. I, p. 209.

were glad to accept his leadership. Similarly, Roman Catholic prelates, both inside and outside of Spain, welcomed this new effort in behalf of the Church and urged their subordinates to support it. When the military campaign against Granada brought victory, Ferdinand and his loyal queen and partner emerged as the foremost defenders of the faith in their time. A grateful Church and the orders of nobles readily granted them political advantages formerly denied any sovereign in Spain and ecclesiastical privileges usually reserved to prelates. Not the least among the latter was the right to claim the loyalty and obedience of their subjects as matters of religious duty. This was a long step in the establishment of the doctrine of the divine right of Christian kings later explicitly asserted by sovereigns in the northern states of Europe.

A *second* development of great importance was brought about primarily by the devout but resolute Isabella. While the Queen had gained the open admiration of the Church both at home and in Rome, she was nevertheless unbending in her insistence that only Spaniards should hold ecclesiastical office in her domain. At this time when the Pope was entrenching the power of the Vatican by making expedient appointments of Italian prelates to high office in other states, Isabella won from Pope Sixtus IV "the right of nominating to higher dignities of the church," [4] both for herself and her successors. Fortunately for her successors and the Church, she used this privilege to make certain that the offices were filled by men of good character and pious disposition. As a consequence the Spanish clergy, unlike those in the northern states, did not suffer the

[4] *Ibid.*, vol. III, p. 436.

reformers' condemnations in the next century. Nor was the privilege of nomination relinquished by the heirs of Isabella and her royal consort. It was again asserted in no uncertain terms by Philip II in his rejection of claims of supremacy put forward by Pope Pius V and has been retained by heads of the Spanish state to this day.

A further privilege which the pope granted the Spanish sovereigns and their successors was the tercia,[5] or two-ninths of the tithes of Castile; this was granted in 1493 so that they would hurry to his aid in the face of an impending invasion of Rome by the French. It was in addition to an earlier grant of a tenth of the ecclesiastical rents of the entire realm which had been given to help wage the war against the Moors and to make sure that Spain would continue to support the Vatican against future enemies. Thus, Isabella and Ferdinand initiated the close ecclesiastical and political ties that have become traditional between the rulers of Spain and the Vatican.

The *third* development has had a prolonged effect on education in Spain. It also had religious roots and grew out of the fact that the campaign against Granada did not produce the decisive defeat for which the devout had hoped. The peace was a negotiated one, and the terms agreed upon contained the promise of full civil and religious liberties for the vanquished. However, these generous terms were disavowed by Ferdinand, with the approval of the militant clergy and under strong pressure from the Queen's confessor, Cardinal Ximenes. As soon as the Moslem remnants laid down their arms, they were confronted

[5] William H. Prescott, *History of the Reign of Philip II,* Lippincott, Philadelphia, 1868, vol. III, p. 441.

by a royal decree in which they were given the alternative of accepting Christian baptism or exile. Many Moslems chose to remain. But the Cardinal was not satisfied with the public professions of persons who were being forced to the baptismal font. He called for more convincing evidence and took the lead in enforcing stronger measures. Soon the Moslem centers of learning and places of worship were being destroyed. Huge piles of books, some on religious topics but many priceless copies of Greek and Arabic works on philosophy and science, were burned in the public squares of the cities.[6]

When the cultural as well as religious evidence of the Moslem faith had been destroyed, and those who had worshiped Allah had been reduced to a state of extreme humiliation, the crusading Christians turned their fanatical zeal upon another body of non-Christians and their culture, the Jews. Many Jewish families had lived in Spain for several generations and some had risen to positions of influence and wealth. The instrument invoked to carry out their extermination was the Inquisition. Almost immediately it was also turned against Moslems and even Christians who suffered the charge of heresy.

Originally, the Inquisition had been established by Pope Innocent III to combat the Albigensian heresies. Known as the Holy Office, the papal order had authorized the sovereigns of Roman Catholic states to employ their civil powers to arrest, to try, and to punish persons under their rule who were suspected of deviating from the religious doctrines of the Church. Since the inquisitors were responsible immediately

to the sovereigns, and the crimes of the accused were represented as the most heinous of all because they endangered the souls of men and not merely their bodies and possessions, no punishment was considered too harsh. The condemned generally were burned and their property seized to pay the fees of the judges and other costs incurred in the trial process. The royal treasury took what was left. Hence, judge and executioner alike had powerful reasons to prefer that the verdict should go against the accused, and the number of acquittals was negligible.

The Inquisition was popular with the Christians as long as it was directed against Moslems and Jews only. Its administration was assigned to the Dominicans; and Cardinal Ximenes, as the Queen's confessor and the highest-ranking prelate in Spain, made certain that they carried out their work with vigor. Isabella had been instrumental in securing his elevation to high office; and in return, he gave the support of the entire Spanish hierarchy to the enhancement of the powers of the sovereigns. A union of church and state was established which has remained unusually close ever since.

Establishment of schools

Modern apologists of Spanish culture are likely to compare the science, literature, and education in the Spanish peninsula at this time with the ignorance and superstition that still prevailed in the rest of Europe. What is overlooked is the fact that most of the cultural achievements in Spain were attained under Moslem rule and in an atmosphere of free inquiry that had brought Moslem, Jewish, and Christian scholars and

[6] Prescott, *History of the Reign of Ferdinand and Isabella,* vol. II, p. 448.

teachers together as equals. Religious doctrine was neither the arbiter nor the end of scholarship, and the benefits of learning were available to all. That these advantages were not spread evenly throughout the population merely indicated a defect that was shared by Christian lands in even greater measure.

These Moslem achievements had been preceded, of course, by a period during which the Graeco-Roman tradition became deeply rooted in the Spanish peninsula. Pagan schools and learning had come from Greece and Rome long before the rise of Christianity, and the colonists cultivated the transplanted institutions with enthusiasm. Some of their schools were famous throughout the Empire, and their scholars included a few of the most distinguished of that time. Nevertheless, scholarship and education in Spain suffered the same slow death by neglect at the hands of the Christians that had brought on the Dark Ages elsewhere. Hence, when the Moors invaded Spain their scholars encountered surprisingly little competition; and the cultural level in the few Christian strongholds that remained in the north was low in comparison with that which was attained under Moslem rule.

It is quite evident that when the Roman Catholic leaders marshaled their forces to resist the Moslem invasion, they already looked upon the Graeco-Roman era in a more kindly light than had their Christian predecessors of the fifth and sixth centuries. The pagan aspects of that era were forgiven and the crusade against the Moslems sometimes seemed to be a campaign of cultural liberation as well as a religious war. The Christian kingdoms in the north were like staging areas for the anticipated crusades. As schools became part of the ecclesiastical equipment with which to wage war against disbelief, bishops and abbots established Latin schools among the Spanish Christians. These were augmented by universities, beginning in the thirteenth century. But even these more sophisticated Christian institutions could not match the Moslem centers of learning either in number or brilliance. The most enduring and far-reaching cultural accomplishment during this period of consolidation and preparation for war was the subordination of the small, independent kingdoms to the unifying leadership of Rome. Thus the spiritual, intellectual, and even social changes brought to the southern portions of the peninsula in the ensuing period of Christian resurgence were not Spanish in origin. In this sense the beginnings of the modern era in Spanish history had a distinctly colonial flavor.

Spanish education

Modern Spain dates from the latter half of the fifteenth century. As previously stated, the marriage of Isabella and Ferdinand in 1469 united the kingdoms of Castile and Aragon and formed the nucleus of the Christian forces which gradually overcame Moslem political and cultural domination. The spiritual leadership behind their campaign was provided by the Roman Catholic Church; and as political control was extended southward, the ecclesiastical institutions of Rome moved in behind the lines to effect control over the native populations. These occupying forces were not slow in destroying the visible evidence of Moslem religion and culture—libraries and schools as well as numerous religious edifices.

In a few places formerly occupied by

Moslem centers of learning, the occupying Christians established universities after the model of Paris and her daughters at Oxford and in other northern cities. The one at Salamanca was especially favored and soon became one of the foremost universities of Europe. Cardinal Ximenes personally founded a new university at Alcala which, like Paris, was devoted to the education of the clergy.[7] The program of studies, however, seems to have been conceived on a broader scale than usual, for there were fourteen chairs "appropriate to grammar, rhetoric, and the ancient classics." [8] The staff was made up of the most renowned scholars the Cardinal could bring together and is said to have been especially alert and productive, possibly because each appointment was reviewed, subject to termination or renewal, every four years.

Schools of a lower order necessarily preceded the universities. Latin schools similar to those in the Christian kingdoms were established in the principal ecclesiastical centers formed in the newly liberated regions. As elsewhere, the Latin schools functioned not merely as training schools to raise up a new generation of clergy, but also as preparatory schools for the universities. The institutional pattern typical of education in fifteenth-century Europe therefore also prevailed in sixteenth-century Spain, with exceptions that will be noted later.

Social role

The program of studies introduced at Alcala had a humanistic flavor not readily found in other parts of Europe in that period. This might have been due

[7] *Ibid.*, vol. III, p. 315.
[8] *Ibid.*, p. 318.

to the fact that political events in Spain drew the attention of all European Christendom and lured militant scholars as well as crusading warriors to the campaign against the Moslems. In any event, elements of the new learning that was taking root in Northern Italy and the Low Countries also found their way to Spain. New teachers and scholars were needed in large numbers, and among the recruits were at least some who entertained enthusiasm for the new learning. Furthermore, the opportunity to found schools and universities *de novo* was an open invitation to introduce new programs and types of organization.

This early humanism was more concerned with the recovery of Greek and Roman thought than with the production of new ideas and improved solutions to the problems of men. It was not only popular among the more literate segments of the conquered peoples, but also appealed to the descendants of the ancient colonists who longed for a return to the Graeco-Roman tradition. This stage of humanistic interest was concerned with literary forms and the cultivation of grace and artistry in every area of human endeavor. Its measure of excellence was beauty as opposed to usefulness or even humanitarianism. Hence, culture and scholarship came to be identified with a segment of society which could remove itself from the sweat and soil of labor—precisely those individuals who had gained the greatest measure of wealth and status within the emerging Spanish Empire. They became its ruling class, and education came to be looked upon as their exclusive property. As the Spanish Empire prospered, the Spanish elite quickly became the most powerful group in Europe, and their cultural attainments and social aspirations were admired and imitated by the ruling classes everywhere.

The social role of the Spanish schools, therefore, was clearly defined. They were to function as agencies of a conquering force committed to the establishment of the Roman Catholic religion among a large population whose religious orientation had been non-Christian. Their cultural roots were planted in the Graeco-Roman tradition, and their intellectual ideal was the cultivation of literary and artistic pursuits rather than the study of the sciences and philosophy which had made the Moslem schools distinguished. Finally, the Spanish schools focused upon the elevation of a small privileged class to the status of a perpetual ruling elite, which by its outward appearances could be distinguished from those it had been appointed to rule. To this small group the Spanish philosophical commitments entrusted the responsibility for making all decisions affecting the national welfare; and

education was supposed to make that group capable of fulfilling its responsibilities in keeping with the Christian, Graeco-Roman, humanistic traditions as these came to be interpreted by the Spanish scholars.

Power structure and administrative organization

The close union of church and state established in the fifteenth century made Roman Catholicism the official and exclusive religion of Spain, but gave the crown the right to make nominations to high ecclesiastical offices. By this arrangement the Church could control what was to be taught in the schools, but the crown could determine who was to administer them. Nevertheless, education was looked upon as the privilege and responsibility of the Church, not of the state.

Figure 4 indicates the administrative relationships that existed between the

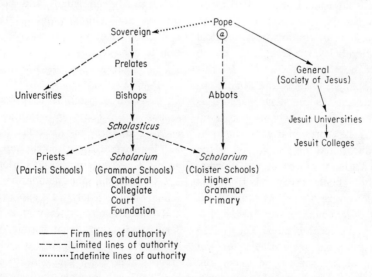

Figure 4. Lines of Educational Authority in Sixteenth-century Spain

a. Spanish prelates were nominated by the sovereign and installed by the pope. The Society of Jesus, however, was responsible only to the pope.

crown and the Church for educational purposes. Latin schools were established and operated by bishops and abbots to raise up a literate native clergy. In this sense they were under the complete control of the Roman Catholic Church and reflected the theological and intellectual interests of the particular ecclesiastic in charge. This accounted for the introduction of humanistic elements here and there. However, since the higher offices of the Church were filled by native personnel on the nomination of the crown, Spanish civil and educational administrative practices differed from those in other parts of Europe at that time and were singularly effective in imposing a prescribed culture upon the subdued population. The transmission of the culture was achieved, both in Spain and in the colonies, by controlling the education of those who were to become the future leaders. The leaders, in turn, transmitted it to the people through the channels afforded them in their positions of ecclesiastical and civil control.

It also should be evident from Figure 4 that the lines of administrative control in education below the level of the crown followed those of the Church. In this respect, Spanish bishops and abbots enjoyed authority in the same measure as their counterparts elsewhere. The *scholasticus* as the representative of the bishop for educational matters served as the chief educational officer in the diocese. The only schools exempted from his jurisdiction were those maintained by religious orders not subject to the discipline of the local bishop. The palace school established by Isabella for the education of her sons came under the supervision of a higher prelate, and the interest she displayed in its operation inspired other nobles to establish simi-

lar institutions for the instruction of members of their families.

The religious orders seem to have been especially favored as sponsors of preparatory schools as compared with the Church and municipalities. Cloister schools appeared in somewhat larger ratio to the other types than was the case in the German states or Northern Italy. In 1534 Ignatius de Loyola organized a new order known as the Society of Jesus which had considerable effect upon Spanish education both at home and in the colonies. Its structure was different from the other orders in that it was under the complete control of the head of the order, the general, who was elected for life and recognized no authority in the ecclesiastical hierarchy other than the pope. In this respect the members of the order were not subject to the discipline of the regular hierarchy, and, indeed, have sometimes been its severest critics. The Society defined its role as that of supplying trained, competent, and dedicated leaders for church and state, and launched a vigorous program of education to achieve this end.

The Society of Jesus was approved by Pope Paul III in 1540. It immediately set about establishing preparatory schools and colleges and training teachers to staff these institutions. A revised and improved plan of instruction known as the Ratio Studiorum was adopted in 1599 which became mandatory in all schools of the Society. Its superior form and effective methodology won for the Jesuit institutions great popularity, and leading families in Spain, as well as in other states, were soon enrolling their sons in Jesuit schools in preference to others. Indeed, the extent to which Jesuit schools provided educational opportunities to boys not destined for careers in the Church may have been one of the reasons why guild and municipal schools were not so popular in Spain as they were in Germany, the Low Countries, and Northern Italy.

Spain acquired her colonial possessions during this period of widespread approval of Jesuit education. Her claims to the new territories were affirmed by the pope; and by mutual agreement the ecclesiastical and civil arrangements that had been established at home were extended to the colonies. Jesuit priests accompanied the royal expeditions wherever they penetrated. If a permanent settlement was made they remained to build a church and establish a school. Soon a fully developed system of ecclesiastical institutions, including schools and universities, was developed under the protection and authority of the crown exercised through the agency of the Council for Indies.

The Jesuits' days of unrestricted activity were numbered, however. Their zeal to fill high offices in both church and state with persons educated in their discipline, and the manner in which they operated outside the channels of regular ecclesiastical authority soon brought them into conflict with the administrative officers of both the Church and the crown. Particularly offensive to the crown was their ability to circumvent the historic right of nomination. The conflict became so bitter that the Jesuits were banned from Spain and all her possessions in 1767, and the Society was suppressed by the pope in 1773.[9]

In view of the extensive role the Society had come to play in Spanish education during the preceding two hundred years, its suppression meant that the nation lost the services of a majority of her best trained teachers and had to close many schools. Nevertheless, the administrative arrangements for education were simplified. Some Jesuit schools were taken over by other orders, and teaching again became a responsibility of the regular clergy. Exceptions, of course, were the schools of exempted religious orders and the universities. The latter in particular enjoyed whatever autonomy their royal or municipal charters afforded them, and the personal dispositions of their rectors and chancellors would allow.

Educational institutions

Christian schools during the reign of Isabella and Ferdinand were typical of those in other parts of Europe in the fifteenth century.[10] Parish priests instructed children in the Creed and the Lord's Prayer and prepared them for their first communion. Some assistance in these matters was provided by several religious orders, particularly those committed to missionary work among the inhabitants of the newly acquired territories. Developing a literate population was not an objective, however, and vernacular reading schools did not materialize as they did elsewhere in the sixteenth and seventeenth centuries. Spanish culture as a consequence did not develop out of indigenous elements, but from the changes effected in a transplanted culture as it was transmitted from generation to generation by converted Spanish teachers.

The Church maintained the conventional Latin schools in Spain, and supplied members of the clergy as teach-

[9] The Society was reestablished in 1814.

[10] See Fig. 3., p. 42.

57

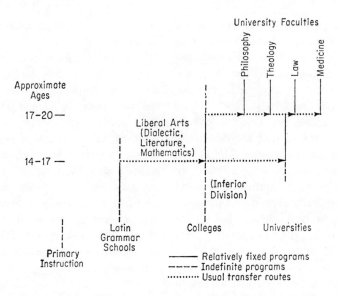

University Faculties

Philosophy Theology Law Medicine

Approximate
Ages

17-20 —

Liberal Arts
(Dialectic,
Literature,
Mathematics)

14-17 —

(Inferior
Division)

Latin   Colleges   Universities
Grammar
Primary   Schools   ——— Relatively fixed programs
Instruction   ———— Indefinite programs
                              ·········· Usual transfer routes

Figure 5. Educational Institutions in Sixteenth-century Spain

ers for similar schools maintained by other sponsors. Secular agencies were not so active as sponsors, however, as they were in places where commerce and industry were the basis of the economy. Like the universities, the newly formed Latin schools were affected by the humanistic influences at work in neighboring states. Attention was given to classical Latin and Greek and the works of secular writers; the first lecture delivered at Alcala, the university founded by Cardinal Ximenes, was on Aristotle's *Ethics*. The erudition and industry of the scholars was demonstrated by the preparation, and ultimate publication in printed form, of the famous *Complutensian Polyglot,* the first complete Bible prepared from the various original sources. That the love of learning and respect for scholarship had not penetrated deeply outside the small company of scholars, however, is indicated by the fact that a few years later the university librarian sold as waste paper all the original source manuscripts

which had been gathered together at such great expense! [11]

The institutional organization also anticipated later developments brought about by the humanists, particularly in Germany. Unlike the fifteenth-century Latin schools which had sent their students to the universities around age fifteen, Spanish schools tended to add the liberal arts to the preparatory studies in grammar and, therefore, to retain the students until a later age. The Jesuit colleges were of this type, and the Ratio Studiorum referred to the *studia inferiora* which afforded instruction in classical Latin and Greek, and the higher studies which were called the liberal arts but emphasized training in the scholastic dialectic and philosophy. Figure 5 shows that the upper section of the colleges thus duplicated the instruction offered by the liberal arts faculties in the universities. Graduates of the complete or higher colleges, there-

[11] Prescott, *History of the Reign of Ferdinand and Isabella,* vol. III, p. 325.

fore, could be admitted directly to the professional faculties. At the same time, the upper divisions of university faculties of arts were extended upward to constitute faculties of philosophy; and from this development preparation for teaching in the arts faculties acquired status equivalent to that of preparation for a career in medicine, law, or theology. Later, secondary school teachers in Spain were also required to prepare in a university faculty of philosophy, a regulation that is operative even today.

Spanish education in the sixteenth and seventeenth centuries thus consisted of three levels of instruction. Grammar schools and the inferior division of the colleges enrolled boys to about age fifteen or sixteen, by which time they were to become competent in Latin and Greek and acquire familiarity with the more elementary literary works in these languages. Colleges provided an additional three or four years of study in the liberal arts, and some were authorized to award degrees. Universities offered parallel instruction in the liberal arts as well as advanced professional work in philosophy, law, theology, and medicine. Among these three levels of institutions there was considerable overlapping of instruction. Most universities, for example, continued to offer the entire program of liberal arts studies; and colleges generally included an inferior division or grammar school or had close working arrangements with independently operated grammar schools. Similarly, universities maintained connections with colleges in their vicinity, particularly those without authority to award degrees. Thus in Salamanca there were twenty-six colleges in addition to the university, four of which were of higher and twenty-two of inferior type. Lesser

numbers were to be found around the other universities.[12]

Educational opportunities

Christian scholars in Spain were sorely pressed to match the level of learning and the quality of education which they were endeavoring to replace. Perhaps the stimulation of this competition, together with the zeal of the crusading clergy, accounted for the substantial efforts that were made during the sixteenth century. Also, some Spanish scholars had acquired enough of the humanistic spirit to be willing to delve into whatever Arabic literature had escaped the bonfires of the previous century. They made some significant additions to the growing collection of recovered Greek and Roman manuscripts, and several became leading humanists. It was during this period that Spanish universities acquired their reputation as centers of learning. Studies in medicine and civil law prospered briefly in almost the same measure as those in philosophy and theology. Spanish names decorated the lists of scholars in every known department of science. It should be noted, however, that their method of inquiry was borrowed from that used in philosophy and letters, and bore no resemblance to the laboratory techniques of a later era.

But this period of intellectual vigor was short-lived. As the conquering nobility and clergy came to feel more secure in their assertion of authority over the subdued peoples, they began to use less humane methods of control. The Inquisition was invoked. Soon

[12] Paul Monroe (ed.), *A Cyclopaedia of Education*, Macmillan, New York, 1914, vol. 5, p. 380.

Christian scholars felt the lash of the inquisitors' whip just as readily as did Jewish merchants or Moslem landlords. Freedom of inquiry was lost in the seventeenth century, and many brilliant scholars found it necessary to flee. The closing of the Jesuit schools in 1767 deprived Spain of a large part of her educational facilities. Partly as a result of the Inquisition, the literary and fine arts have until recent decades been looked upon as the only safe domains for creative talents.

The sixteenth century seems to have marked the high point in Spanish education both with respect to the range of educational opportunities and the number of schools. Some reports indicate that at first students of the higher social classes flocked to the universities by the thousands and that grammar schools and colleges were generally available in the populous areas. As the Inquisition and the accompanying destructive forces made their way even among Christian families, the number of students became progressively smaller. The masses had no opportunities for formal education. As long as they accepted the ministrations of the Roman Catholic Church and remained submissive to the ruling aristocracy, their cultural and social arrangements were left undisturbed. The nation thus slumbered through the last half of the seventeenth century and all of the eighteenth in a feudalism presided over by the hierarchy working in closest cooperation with the ruling house.

Subsequent developments

Spain was aroused from her feudal slumbers by the thunder of Napoleon's armies crossing her borders. By this time the ruling class had become so weak that it offered little effective resistance to the invasion. The French army quickly overran the Spanish homeland and Napoleon's brother Joseph was set up as the head of state in 1808. The new regime attempted to introduce Napoleonic political reforms, but the Spanish people refused to be shaken out of their established ways. A resistance movement was born which ultimately played a part in the general military action that brought an end to the Napoleonic dream of a world empire. The immediate effect in Spain was to reestablish the traditional union of the Church and the royal family. However, enough intellectual and social ferment had been started in the interlude to prevent a complete return to the previous state of affairs. As elsewhere in Europe, French intellectualism had left its potent seeds in Spanish centers of learning. Spanish scholarship which for several centuries had restricted itself to literature and art was now to turn slowly to new philosophical and social interests as well.

By the early part of the nineteenth century various strata of Spanish society were developing secular interests that set them at odds with the ruling clique. The fact that it was the people and not the government who had defied Napoleon weakened the popular support for the monarchy. A constitution had been written and adopted by the Cortes even while Napoleon's brother was in power. Although it was nullified in the restoration, this document remained in the minds of a growing segment of the Spanish people as a statement of their highest political and social expectations. Land reforms and the liberation of the peasantry from subordination by the hereditary aristocracy were demanded. Increasing numbers of the people called for a voice in government and for the establishment of a constitutional monarchy. Significantly, the Constitution of 1812 had reasserted Roman Catholicism as the official, and exclusive, religion of Spain.[13] But in spite of this concession to tradition, the document aimed obvious threats at the abuses of the ruling clique, including the threat to confiscate the excessive properties of the Church. Although the clergy had previously tended to side with the peasants in their demands for more just treatment, the hierarchy now joined unequivocally with the wealthy landowners and commercial families.[14]

As the nineteenth century progressed, both sides adopted uncompromising positions. The monarchy was retained, but the relative influence of the liberals and the Church on government fluctuated periodically as they struggled for supremacy. In this struggle, control of education became a prime objective.

The beginnings of public education

The Constitution of 1812 had provided for the establishment of universal education under state control. Although Ferdinand VII had sworn to support it, he and his royal and ecclesiastical colleagues opposed its implementation at every turn. A law passed in 1825, under pressure from the liberals, called for the establishment of a system of primary schools. It also was fruitless, owing to neglect and the general state

of unrest. Continuing pressures resulted in the appointment of a study commission in 1834; and finally a general act for education was passed in 1857. Under this law the crown assumed control of popular education by establishing a department of education in the Ministry of the Interior. The director of education was to be assisted by a staff of inspectors, also appointed by the crown, and an advisory council. Children were ordered to attend school between the ages of six and twelve, although the crown assumed little responsibility for providing qualified teachers or the physical facilities, and the law was not enforced. Religious orders retained their status as school sponsors and enjoyed all the privileges and benefits extended to municipalities and other political subdivisions in the field of education.

The law of 1857 did establish machinery for the support of education by local agencies. Both provinces and municipalities were required to organize school boards on which the local government officials, the clergy, and the citizens were represented. These boards were supposed to establish public schools or make arrangements with private agencies to provide instruction. They were also authorized to license teachers, and the provinces were instructed to establish normal schools to train them. However, the development of an effective system of education was hampered by official indifference, the absence of financial support, and the domination of the provincial and local school boards by the clergy. Not until 1900 was any appreciable support forthcoming from the national government. As a consequence 63 per cent of the population was illiterate even at this late date.

[13] Charles Edward Chapman, *A History of Spain,* Macmillan, New York, 1918, p. 494.

[14] Gerald Brenan, *The Spanish Labyrinth,* Cambridge, New York, 1950, pp. 45–46.

As long as education remained under the control of the Church, the children of the masses received only oral instruction in the Creed, the catechism, and a few simple manual skills. Upper-class boys attended grammar schools and colleges in which the courses of study differed little from those of the sixteenth century. A few of the more progressive schools, those attended by boys in poorer circumstances, experimented with various kinds of technical training. Generally, however, science, mathematics, political economy, and secular history were considered too controversial for anyone but trained theologians. Against this reactionary stand, the liberal forces continued to advocate greater freedom of inquiry, the elimination of illiteracy, and the development of "secular" state schools. Secularism did not mean the elimination of religious instruction, or even the admission of non-Catholic doctrines, but merely the sponsorship of schools by the government. Even in the brief periods when a few secular schools were in operation, parents sometimes complained that in the state schools the children passed half their time saying the rosary and learning sacred history, but never learned to read.[15] The ultimate outcome of clerical efforts to stem the liberal trends was a catechism, also used in the state schools, which taught that liberalism was a sin.

In the midst of this long struggle between the Church and the liberals for control of education, Francisco Giner became the leader of a group of intellectuals whose interest in education led them far beyond the realms of politics and the clash of sectarian doctrines. In 1876 Giner and his colleagues established the Institution Libre de Ensenanza as a private university. They soon added, at Giner's suggestion, preparatory and elementary classes. As a result of the attention given to the full development of the young, and the influence in public life exerted both by the teachers and former pupils in succeeding years, the Institution has been called "the true nursery of contemporary Spain." [16]

By the beginning of the twentieth century the Church had largely lost its hold on the people by allying itself with the wealthy. Some turned to socialism or anarchism, others to republicanism. The crown still claimed absolute power but obviously was unable to exercise it. In this period of uncertainty various strong men close to the crown virtually ran the government. In 1923, General Primo de Rivera, with the support of the army, became prime minister in name, and dictator in the true Spanish tradition which attributes to every general the ambition "to save his country by becoming her ruler." [17] Because he attempted to retain the support of the Church, the monarchy, the army, and the people all at the same time, all elements became dissatisfied, and the king seized upon a spurious incident as an opportunity to dismiss him. The people were not willing to see power restored to the king, and shortly thereafter he was forced to abdicate and the Second Spanish Republic was born.

The new government was based on principles long advocated by liberal Spaniards. Freedom of religion was pro-

[15] *Ibid.*, p. 51.

[16] Salvador de Madariaga, *Spain: A Modern History*, rev. ed., Frederick A. Praeger, Inc., New York, 1958, p. 79.

[17] *Ibid.*, p. 342.

claimed; clerical controls were ended; schools were placed under state control and extended, in theory, to provide free education for all children; and government was made responsible to the will of the people through the introduction of free elections. However, the diverse groups which had united to form the republic soon ran into difficulties as factionalism reappeared. The historically reactionary Church, the army, and the wealthy aristocracy were drawn together by the oppressive measures taken against them by the new government. Civil war broke out in 1936 in what was initially a struggle between the Spanish groups of the Left and those of the Right. The Left counted republicans, socialists, communists, and anarchists in its ranks, and represented the majority of the intellectuals and the workers, particularly those engaged in industry. The Right included both conservatives and reactionaries, and represented the Church, the wealthy, the army, and a number of intellectuals. Initially only Spaniards were involved, but the issue was soon complicated by the intervention of outside powers. Russia sent aid to the Left; Italy and Germany provided very substantial support for the Right. In 1937, Francisco Franco organized a government of the Right, and by 1939 had led his forces to victory and established the present government.

Education under Franco

In the absence of an official statement of the social objectives of the Franco government, they must be inferred from scattered statements and the actions of its leaders. The government clearly was not of the people, for it seized power by force. Its supporting elements are coordinated politically through the Falange, a political party of which Franco is the head. All other political parties or movements are outlawed. The party leadership and the government have stated repeatedly their dedication to the "restoration of the ancient Spanish tradition," a tradition which as previously indicated consists of "Christianity, Graeco-Roman culture, and Spanish humanism as found in its language, literature, and history." The Falangists, however, include those elements of the population who have most to gain from a strong and growing economy. Thus Franco has extended the above objectives by adding that his government would seek ". . . to establish an economic regime overriding the interests of individual group or class . . . to multiply wealth in the service of the state. . . ." [18] To accomplish this goal, he has added the study of science and mathematics as a fourth element; and the cultivation of the ancient tradition, as augmented, has been made the prime responsibility of the schools. While secondary schools and universities now are adding technical and scientific studies, religion remains a required subject on each level of education. The preamble to the Primary Education Act of 1945 states that the primary schools "must provide first and foremost a Catholic education." [19]

Popular opinion and the wishes of the people have little weight in the new order. With all political activity outlawed, except that of the Falangists, and the government maintained in office by military force, Spain has many of the external aspects of the ancient mon-

[18] *Ibid.*, pp. 555–556.
[19] UNESCO, *World Survey of Education: Primary Education,* Paris, 1958, p. 908.

archy. Indeed, the Succession Bill of 1947 reads in part as follows:

Article 1. Spain, as a political unit, is a Catholic and Social State, which, in accordance with her tradition, declares herself constituted into a Realm.

Article 2. The post of Head of the State belongs to the Leader of Spain and of the Crusade and Commander-in-Chief of the Forces, D. Francisco Franco Bahamonde.

This bill also specifies in Article 6:

The Head of State may at any time propose to the Cortes the nomination of the person who he considers should be called upon in due course to succeed him, under the title of King or Regent, having the qualifications demanded by this Law; and he may likewise submit to the Cortes, for approval, the withdrawal of any person he may have proposed, even if such a person shall have already been accepted by the Cortes.

Should the post of Head of State become vacant without a successor having been named, a Regency Council consisting of "the President of the Cortes, the prelate of highest hierarchical rank being a Councillor of the Realm"; and the highest ranking military officer, shall act as Head of State until the person the Council may nominate shall have been approved by the Cortes and established in office.

In 1953 Franco signed a concordat with the Vatican making official a relationship that had existed in practice from the time his government first assumed power. Under the terms of this document, the Head of State is given a voice in ecclesiastical affairs which, in effect, makes him the chief administrative officer of the Spanish branch of

the Roman Catholic Church. Thus, the ecclesiastical privileges first enjoyed by Ferdinand and Isabella have been restored. In return, Roman Catholicism has been proclaimed the official and protected religion of Spain, the members of the Roman Catholic clergy have been granted judicial immunity, and the hierarchy may review appointments to all public offices, with the privilege of rejecting any that do not meet its approval. The Church similarly has resumed its former control over education, including that provided in state schools. Not only must teachers be acceptable to the Church, but the curriculum and the content of specific courses must pass its inspection and meet its tests of orthodoxy, social and political as well as theological.

The absolute powers of the Head of State are evident in the control exercised over the Cortes, the nominal legislative branch of government and the historical descendant of the form of popular government that existed prior to the reign of Isabella and Ferdinand. The membership, consisting of approximately five hundred, is carefully controlled. A sizable number of the members are appointed by the Head of State; others are members ex officio, including clergy. Together these constitute a substantial majority. No member may introduce a bill, although a group of fifty members may request the permanent commission to give consideration to a specific matter of concern with a view to recommending to the Head of State that some action might be desirable.[20] But the Cortes may not initiate legislation; it is limited

[20] House Committee on Foreign Affairs, U.S. Congress, *Report of the Special Mission to Germany and Certain Other Countries,* Apr. 7, 1952, p. 79.

to approving legislation proposed by the Head of State.

The elaborate arrangements by which the Falangists maintain themselves in power suggest that the so-called Spanish tradition still is not part of the indigenous culture and that those in power are fearful that any relaxation in the control of education will allow the people to return to their true nature. Although the people accept authority in politics and religion, they continue to transmit to their children a tradition of separatism and individualism. In private life these traits have caused Spaniards to be labeled provincial. In national life they have been demonstrated in the strength and spirit with which cities and provinces have resisted proclamations of central authority, in the inability of diverse groups to compromise and voluntarily to work together, and in the tendency of citizens of particular areas to think of themselves first as Basques or Catalans, and only second as Spaniards. In spite of Franco's strong dictatorship the traits of separatism and individualism are still evident in Spain and, supplemented by economic pressures, account in part for a growing uneasiness which has been particularly apparent since 1956.

The Ministry of Education

The Education Act of 1857 had provided for provincial and local boards of education which became in effect the chief sponsors of public schools. Because of the clerical influence in these boards, and the fear that such schools would weaken the control of the religious orders, public education was not allowed to flourish. Not until 1900 was a separate ministry of public instruction cre-

ated. The liberal forces which brought this about were also able to launch an ambitious program to build schools, train teachers, and develop a core of public school teachers as civil servants with salaries paid out of the national treasury. Modern curricula were introduced and freedom of religious beliefs encouraged by excluding religious instruction from the public schools. The reaction from the hierarchy was swift and in the case of the leading educational reformer, Francesco Ferrer, tragic. Nevertheless, the liberal forces were able to sustain themselves and slowly to build the outlines of a national system of education.

New public secondary schools called *institutos* were government-sponsored, and offered a full program of studies leading to the bachelor's degree. In this respect they were the equivalent of the higher colleges developed in Spain in the sixteenth century, with added studies in mathematics, science, and the modern languages. Meanwhile, the colleges, or *colegios,* operated by the religious orders remained conservative in philosophy and curriculum, and their students were generally required to attend an *instituto* before entering a university.[21] All these were, of course, schools for boys. Girls were still instructed in separate schools operated mostly by convents.

The Franco government reversed the trend toward secular schools and freedom of conscience which had gained considerable momentum among the people of the Left. Today, educational policies of the government are administered by a Minister of National Education who is appointed by the Head of State. Educational policy reflects fully the objectives of the forces of the Falange.

[21] Monroe, *op. cit.,* p. 382.

In keeping with the "ancient tradition" they are committed to restore the Church, whose highest offices are filled on the nomination of the Head of State, to a status which will give it a controlling voice not merely in the Ministry, but also in every subdivision, from the university districts down to the smallest municipalities. Furthermore, religious schools receive public support in equal measure with public schools; and agencies of the Church have first priority in selecting school locations. The public agencies then are required to take up what is left and to provide instruction to those who are not served by private agencies.

As indicated in Figure 6, the work of the Ministry is divided among a number of directorates, such as (1) higher education, (2) secondary education, (3) primary education, (4) vocational and technical education, (5) industrial education, and (6) fine arts. Obviously, certain problems of articulation are inherent in this arrangement. The Directorate for Primary Education, for example, is responsible for building, staffing, and financing all public elementary schools throughout the nation. Its authority also extends in some measure to all private elementary schools. The Directorate for Secondary Education operates in a corresponding manner with respect to all secondary schools. Hence, in a given municipality the coordination of elementary and secondary instruction is complicated by the vertical lines of authority which extend to the Ministry level in each case; and the two types of schools operate with little reference to each other. The same independence of operation is evident in vocational and technical schools and industrial schools.

As in many other countries that provide public education through a national ministry of education, the officials in the Spanish Ministry usually are not educators by training or profession. Rather, they are administrators, lawyers, or accountants, and their assignment to the Ministry of National Education rather than to the Ministry of Agriculture, Naval Affairs, or some other branch of government is usually due to political accident rather than to strong personal preference. For this reason, a National Council of Education consisting of educators and other professionally trained leaders was established in 1952 to confer with Ministry officials. This Council has advisory powers only; recommendations to the Ministry involving a change in basic policy must be referred to the Head of State who will decide whether or not the change, or any modification thereof, will be authorized. Recent reports suggest, however, that the Ministry gradually is being given some freedom to formulate and carry out policies.

Since each Directorate General is responsible for all aspects of instruction within its assigned area, each has its parallel staffs of administrators and inspectors. While the inspectors are attached to and in most cases seem to operate from the national level, the administrative staff generally functions on three levels: national, intermediate, and local.[22] The literature refers to two types of intermediate administrative units. These are the provinces, numbering about fifty, and the twelve university regions or districts organized around the twelve universities. University districts are utilized chiefly by the Directorates of Secondary Education and of

[22] UNESCO, *op. cit.*, pp. 910–915.

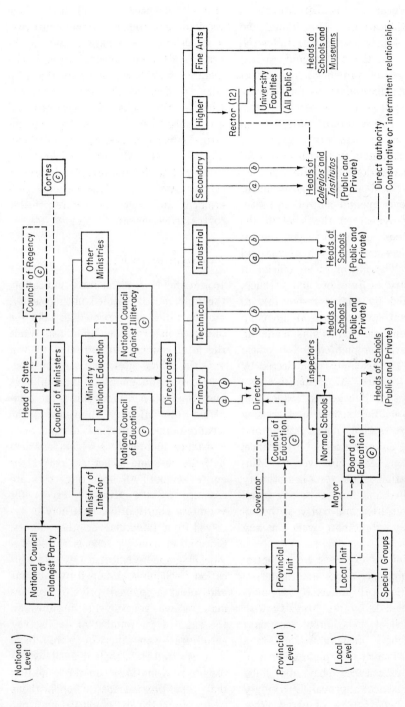

Figure 6. Lines of Educational Authority in Modern Spain

a. Departmental staff for administration.
b. Departmental staff for inspection.
c. Roman Catholic Church officially represented.

Higher Education. The Directorates of Primary Education, of Vocational and Technical Education, and of Industrial Education, on the other hand, appear to employ the provincial regions as their intermediate divisions for administration as well as some supervisory functions. The Directorate of Fine Arts, in contrast, appears to operate directly from the national level with only negligible cooperation from intermediate and even local units of government.

Local governmental controls and services are provided on the level of the municipalities. Municipal government typically is exercised by a mayor and a council. The mayor is an official of the Ministry of Interior, and as such, is appointed by and is responsible to the national government. Membership of the municipal councils is made up in large part of appointed and ex officio members. The remainder are elected by "heads of families." Municipalities have specific responsibilities in education, such as providing school sites, raising money for school construction and equipment, enforcing school attendance, and collecting taxes. However, the Ministry of National Education has primary responsibility and final authority in all areas of education and can veto the actions of any subordinate agency at any time.

The Ministry exercises tight control over teaching personnel and materials of instruction. All university appointments are made by the Ministry with the approval of the Church. Secondary school teachers must be trained in a university faculty of philosophy and letters or of science. They, too, must have ecclesiastical approval. Elementary school teachers may be prepared either in public normal schools or in training schools operated by religious agencies.

But all who wish to teach in a school receiving government support must pass a qualifying examination and be licensed. All appointments to public elementary schools are made by the Ministry, subject to the approval of the Church. Textbooks are prescribed and are furnished by the Ministry; and instruction is supervised by inspectors employed by the Ministry. All teachers, save a few in nonsubsidized private schools, are paid by the national government and therefore are responsible to that government.

Extension of facilities

In the field of elementary education, the form most neglected until recently, municipalities are expected to take the initiative in providing buildings. While the local councils are expected to provide the school sites, pay the construction costs, and maintain the buildings and grounds when the facilities are completed, the Ministry supplements the local resources on the basis of need. Such assistance apparently is seldom less than half the cost and sometimes covers the entire amount. All operating costs are assumed by the Ministry, except for voluntary contributions that may be received from individuals or other sources. Since all elementary schools "must provide first and foremost a Catholic education," schools maintained by religious and other approved private agencies may receive government subsidies on the basis of the number of pupils they enroll free who otherwise would have to attend public schools. Schools which receive full subsidies, on the condition that they provide instruction without cost, apparently are supported on a par with the municipal schools.

The Ministry, through the Directorate for Primary Education, has assumed responsibility for training elementary school teachers. Two normal schools, one for men and one for women, are called for in each province. There were 106 normal schools in 1954–1955, with 25,213 students enrolled.[23] At this rate, universal instruction on the elementary level should be possible in the foreseeable future.

The Ministry's use of public teacher training institutions for inservice education is also worthy of notice. In cooperation with the provincial offices of inspection, these institutions have become centers where information and suggestions for teachers are disseminated, where experimental work for the improvement of teaching methods is carried on, where demonstrations are given, and where short, inservice courses and professional conferences are held. Since 1957, the routine school inspections have been supplemented by meetings with the municipal councils of education "to study the educational problems of the municipality and adopt the necessary means for the improvement of teaching." Furthermore, provision is made to hold conferences of all the teachers of a given zone to study problems of general interest "independently of the advice given to each teacher by his inspector."[24] This implies that, as the professional competency of the primary teachers has improved, the Ministry has tended to relax its strong control.

Municipal governments also are called upon to assist in the development of facilities for technical, vocational, and industrial education. These are new fields and are therefore more directly

sponsored from the level of the Ministry than are the elementary schools. Furthermore, Spanish industry and the labor forces are organized on the basis of "syndicates" sponsored by the government. The syndicates are organized vertically on a national basis, with one syndicate for the managerial officials and workers in each industry. Their controlling officers are appointed by the Head of State. They have ex officio representation in the Cortes as well as in the provincial and municipal councils or boards. Naturally, each has a special interest in the training of workers for the industry it represents; and the several syndicates, through their appointed officers, have a voice in determining what schools are needed and where they are to be located.

It was inevitable that as technical, vocational, and industrial schools were introduced, it would be necessary to relate them to primary education. Arrangements have been made for the representatives of the three directorates to consult on the local levels as well as at the Ministry level. Also, several other Ministries such as Health and Agriculture, which are not directly active in public education, have become involved as the Ministry of National Education has extended its activities. Consequently their representatives are also consulted in matters of mutual concern; and arrangements have been made for cooperation where their interests overlap.

As in elementary education, the Directorates of Technical and Vocational Education and of Industrial Education develop the basic programs of instruction, including detailed courses of study and study materials. They are also responsible for training, appointing, and paying the teachers. Instruction is su-

[23] UNESCO, *International Yearbook of Education*, Paris, 1957, vol. XIX, p. 349.
[24] *Ibid.*, p. 346.

pervised by staffs of inspectors who are responsible, ultimately if not directly, to the respective Directors-General.

Facilities for secondary education have been significantly extended since this area of education was taken out of the hands of the university rectors. A separate Directorate for Secondary Education now operates from the Ministry level, although the twelve university districts are still the chief subordinate administrative units. Furthermore, the universities continue to influence the curricula and instruction through their administration of the baccalaureate examination, which must be passed to gain admission to a university.

The traditional secondary schools, known as *colegios* were sponsored by religious orders. As a consequence, scientific and technical education was long neglected, and the Spanish economy lagged. The vested interest of the Church in secondary education still is respected, and the *colegios* still enjoy the favor of those classes which can afford an education not specifically related to vocational training. But the economic goals of the Franco government call for a more extensive effort in the secondary school field. Accordingly, the Directorate for Secondary Education has been ordered to establish public secondary schools, known as *institutos,* at government expense. The traditional policy of allowing the Church to exercise prior rights, however, has hindered the establishment of *institutos* in the numbers required. At present they are being established only in populous areas which are not already served by *colegios.* While the *institutos* prepare for admission to the universities, the technical and scientific subjects they offer are attractive primarily to persons not

anticipating professional careers. They do, nevertheless, afford some social mobility in contrast to the rigid class structure which the *colegios* have helped to preserve. *Colegios* still outnumber *institutos,* but the trend seems to be turning in favor of the latter.

Although Spanish universities enjoyed an autonomy not experienced by other segments of the national system of education, the philosophical and social climate within which they operated did not stimulate them to exert much leadership. The curricula and modes of operation remained static and traditions became so deeply engrained that change had to come from external forces. The twelve universities of Spain are now public institutions. Each is being assigned a role in providing the personnel needed to accomplish the national goals. They receive their funds from the national government and are under the Directorate for Higher Education in the Ministry of National Education. While each university administers the funds appropriated to it, the programs of instruction and educational services are now planned at the national level. A university may not add a new area of study or establish a new professorship on its own authority. Such changes are determined by the Directorate, and any additions, deletions, or transfers are assigned where it is judged they will best serve the national interest. The lists of new areas of instruction and added professorships announced in recent years indicate the trend which national planning is taking.[25]

While the Directorate for Higher Education employs no inspectors, profes-

[25] For such lists see recent editions of UNESCO's *International Yearbook of Education.*

sors are appointed by the Ministry and, according to the Concordat of 1953, are subject to approval by the Church. A further measure of control over university education, and indirectly over secondary education, is exercised by reserving to the Ministry the right to award academic degrees. This is done in part to raise academic standards, particularly among the private institutions, but also to keep the educational activities of the Church under civil control. This practice also is popular in the former Spanish colonies in the Western Hemisphere.

Interest in the arts is traditional with the Spanish people, and the present regime has made the cultivation of special talent a matter of national concern. The Directorate for Fine Arts operating from the Ministry level not only has responsibility for preserving the many fine old buildings, museums, and works of art as part of the national heritage, but also is directed to search for new talent and to give it every encouragement. Accordingly, the Directorate maintains art schools, conservatories, and specialized schools for the development of literary, theatrical, and other artistic talents. Moreover, competitions and exhibits are sponsored to give the performing and creative artists public hearings. It is no exaggeration to say that artistic talent is one of the most pampered human resources in Spain today.

Extension of opportunities

Extreme social stratification in Spain until the present century had left a large segment of the population without schools. Franco, therefore, inherited an educational problem of major proportions; but unlike previous leaders of the

Right he committed his government to a program of national education. By a succession of laws and ministerial orders, the Franco Government has made it clear that all Spanish children are expected to attend school from the ages of six to twelve. This recently was ordered extended to age fourteen. An order, dated September 30, 1955, directed the municipalities to take a school census covering all children between the ages of two and fifteen and to check the list with the school attendance records.[26] Parents who refuse to send their children to school may be deprived of "family allowance, annual holidays with pay and other special allowances to which they are entitled." Nevertheless, certain children may be excused from attending —those who live more than two kilometers from the nearest school, for example. The Ministry seems determined to reduce the number of such exemptions, and since 1953 it has been committed to a ten-year plan to build at least one thousand new schools a year. Reports issued by the Ministry suggest that this goal is being met.

A national campaign against illiteracy has been launched and is being directed from the Ministry level by the National Board to Combat Illiteracy. "Moving" schools have been developed to reach people in the more remote areas or where substantial numbers of illiterates are found. Special training programs have been introduced to provide teachers for these schools. The provincial and, especially, the municipal councils have been ordered to take necessary action to eliminate illiteracy in their districts, with assurances of assistance from the National Board.

[26] UNESCO, *World Survey of Education: Primary Education,* p. 909.

Coupled with the campaign against illiteracy and the ambitious program of building and staffing public schools, the government is enlisting to the full the resources of private elementary schools. A child can fulfill the legal obligation to attend school by enrolling in any "recognized," "subsidized," or "public" elementary school. Recognized and subsidized schools are private schools that meet the standards set by the Directorate for Primary Education. Recognized schools may charge fees, whereas subsidized schools are free. Not all schools of a given type offer the full number of years of instruction prescribed, but since all schools use the same materials of instruction, follow virtually identical courses of study, and are supervised by the same staff of inspectors, transfers are relatively easy.

Because a large number of children begin their schooling in incomplete schools, the Ministry has broken the elementary program into two cycles, as indicated in Figure 7. The first cycle constitutes the basic program and is of four years' duration. All elementary schools must begin with the first year of this cycle and continue as far as their resources allow. Private schools generally cannot be approved unless they offer at least the first three years.

On completing the four-year cycle, pupils may continue in an elementary school for an additional two years or transfer to a secondary school. The transfer is controlled by a qualifying examination, and the number electing to write them is relatively small. However, the *instituto* because of its greater range of educational services and levels of instruction is gaining favor over the higher elementary schools, even among those who do not anticipate entering a

university. The promising aspect of this development is that growing numbers ultimately may find their way to academic and vocational secondary schools, and from there to the normal schools and universities.

Perhaps even more significant for children from the working classes are the new technical and industrial schools. Industrial schools may be entered, without examination, on the completion of the second cycle of elementary education. While this point marks the end of the compulsory-attendance age, and those who have made a satisfactory record are awarded the certificate of general primary studies and the right to vote, the economic and social advantages of further education are luring increasing numbers into programs that provide specialized training in manual skills and the technical operations demanded by the expanding economy. Training programs in these areas are graduated to provide increasing levels of competency. A few prepare students for the new technical schools, which are of university grade, and even for the scientific faculties of the universities. In the meantime, higher education is being extended into the technical and scientific fields at a surprising rate. And since higher education is supported by the national government, the cost of such study to the student is low.

Finally, educational opportunities are being extended to adults on a part-time or continuing basis on several levels. Foremost among the programs for adults are those designed to combat illiteracy. Basic elementary instruction is now available to persons who were denied an education in their youth. But secondary education also is made available in some places. Evening *institutos*

72

are being tried on an experimental basis, as are programs of industrial education for persons already employed. Even teacher education has been introduced on a part-time basis in an effort to accelerate the training of needed elementary school teachers.

Two aspects of the present program seem to restrict the full development of the national potential. The first is the barrier which separates the elementary school teacher from his colleagues in secondary schools. Elementary teachers are still trained in normal schools that have no organic connection with the universities and, indeed, are classed as a special form of secondary education. In contrast, secondary school teachers are required to secure their preparation in a university, usually the faculty of philosophy and letters. This dichotomy is the product of the historic two-class social system, and as long as it is perpetuated will add to the difficulties of

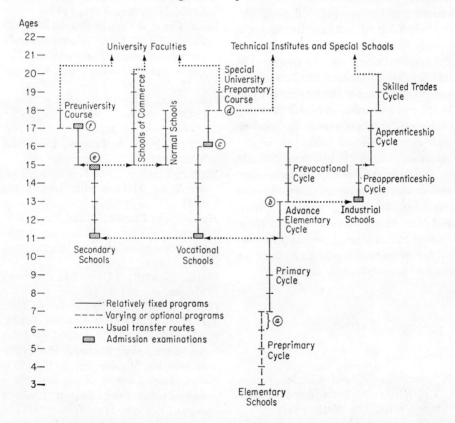

Figure 7. Educational Institutions in Modern Spain
a. The last year of the preprimary cycle, known as the *escuela da párvulos,* sometimes is listed as part of the primary cycle.
b. General primary school certificate.
c. Elementary vocational baccalaureate.
d. Higher vocational baccalaureate.
e. Elementary baccalaureate (preuniversity).
f. Higher baccalaureate (preuniversity).

children from the public elementary schools who wish to transfer to secondary schools. It also hardens the resistance of secondary school teachers to changes in the traditional classical content of the academic programs, particularly in the *colegios*.

The second obstacle is the control exercised by the government and the Roman Catholic clergy over the content of the educational programs and the teaching personnel on all levels. The existence of but one political party and the toleration of but one theology obviously impose formidable restraints on the creative talents of the people. The introduction of modern faculties of science to stand beside the faculties of philosophy in the universities will probably create new conflicts among the intellectual classes. Indeed, some basic disagreements have already been brought to light over the question of succession; and newspaper accounts have reported numerous arrests of professors, writers, and other intellectuals accused of propagating liberal ideas. It would seem that neither politics nor education faces an entirely peaceful future in Spain.

References

Books

Bertrand, Louis, and Charles Petrie: *The History of Spain*, Appleton-Century-Crofts, New York, 1937.

Brenan, Gerald: *The Spanish Labyrinth*, 2d ed., Cambridge, New York, 1950.

Castillejo, Jose: *Wars of Ideas in Spain*, J. Murray, London, 1937.

Chaguaceda, Rev. John Manuell: "Current Position of the Universities in Spain, 1939–1958," unpublished doctoral dissertation, Catholic University of America, Washington, D.C., 1958.

Cleugh, James: *Spain in the Modern World*, Knopf, New York, 1953.

Ferrer Guardia, Francisco: *The Origin and Ideas of the Modern School*, Putnam, New York, 1913.

Foltz, Charles, Jr.: *The Masquerade in Spain*, Houghton Mifflin, Boston, 1948.

Herr, Richard: *The Eighteenth Century Revolution in Spain*, Princeton, Princeton, N.J., 1958.

Hughes, Emmett John: *Report from Spain*, Holt, New York, 1947.

Lynn, Caro: *A College Professor of the Renaissance: Lucio Marineo Siculo among the Spanish Humanists*, The University of Chicago Press, Chicago, 1937.

Madariaga, Salvador de: *Spain*, Cape, London, 1942.

————: *Spain: A Modern History*, rev. ed., Frederick A. Praeger, Inc., New York, 1958.

Manuel, Frank E.: *The Politics of Modern Spain*, McGraw-Hill, New York, 1938.

McCormick, Patrick J., and Francis P. Cassidy: *History of Education*, Catholic Education Press, Washington, D.C., 1950.

Pattee, Richard: *This Is Spain*, Bruce, Milwaukee, 1951.

Peers, E. Allison: *Spain in Eclipse, 1937–1943*, Methuen, London, 1945.

Perz, John Raymond: *Secondary Education in Spain*, Catholic University of America, Washington, D.C., 1934.

Pfeffer, Leo: *Church, State and Freedom*, Beacon Press, Boston, 1953.

Prescott, William H.: *History of the Reign of Emperor Charles V*, 3 vols., Lippincott, Philadelpia, 1865, 1868.

————: *History of the Reign of Philip II*, 3 vols., Lippincott, Philadelphia, 1868.

————: *The Reign of Ferdinand and Isabella, The Catholic*, 3 vols., Lippincott, Philadelphia, 1868.

Reid, John Turner: *Modern Spain and Liberalism: A Study in Literary Contrasts,* Stanford, Stanford, Calif., 1937.

Trend, J. B.: *The Civilization of Spain,* Oxford, Fair Lawn, N.J., 1944.

———: *The Origins of Modern Spain,* Macmillan, New York, 1934.

Ugarte, Francisco: *Espana y su Civilizacion,* Odyssey, New York, 1952.

Pamphlets and periodicals

Carlson, Marjorie, and Robert Beck: "The Education of Spanish Youth," *Educational Forum,* vol. 43, pp. 29–49, November, 1948.

Diplomatic Information Service: *Education in Spain,* Spanish Embassy, Washington, D.C., 1963.

———: *Fifteen Years of Spanish Culture,* Spanish Embassy, Washington, D.C., 1954.

Ebaugh, Cameron D.: "Higher Education in Spain," *College and University,* vol. 25, pp. 110–133, October, 1949.

Ebenstein, William: *Church and State in Franco Spain,* Center of International Studies Research Monograph no. 8, Woodrow Wilson School of Public and International Affairs, Princeton, Princeton, N.J., 1960.

Grayson, W. H., Jr.: "Teacher Training in Spain," *Journal of Educational Sociology,* vol. 27, pp. 49–53, October, 1953.

Guldescu, S.: *Education in Spain Today,* Spanish Embassy, Washington, D.C., 1947.

Hoz, Victor Garcia: "The Education of Teachers in Spain," *Journal of Educational Research,* vol. 43, pp. 561–570, April, 1950.

———: "Spain," *Review of Educational Research,* vol. 32, pp. 347–351, June, 1962.

Ministry of Education: *Revista de Educacion,* Madrid. See especially vol. 32, no. 92, 1959.

Montgomery, Walter Alexander: *Educational Conditions in Spain,* Bureau of Education, U.S. Government Printing Office, 1919.

Reid, R. H.: "American on a World Educational Odyssey," *National Association of Secondary School Principals' Bulletin,* vol. 41, pp. 10–12, October, 1957.

"Report of the Special Study Mission to Germany and Certain Other Countries," Committee on Foreign Affairs, U.S. House of Representatives, 1952.

Roucek, J. S.: "Colleges and Universities in Spain Today," *Catholic Educational Review,* vol. 53, pp. 323–333, May, 1955.

U.S. Office of Education: "Educational Data: Spain," *Information on Education around the World,* Bulletin 34, November, 1959.

CHAPTER 4

German Education: Building a
National Feeling

The mere mention of German education today is likely to bring to mind visions of highly regimented schools within which discipline is strict and every activity is organized to the last detail. The image circulated abroad is of an educational system geared into a total national effort to achieve military supremacy; and at home the schools are credited with raising the nation from the ruins of defeat to the status of a great world empire within the span of two generations. This brilliant success story, in which the German schoolmaster is cast as the hero, made a strong impression abroad and by the end of the nineteenth century virtually every major government of the world had turned to education as an essential part of national policy. Some, notably the Scandinavian countries, Switzerland, and the United States, adopted important features of the German pattern outright. Others adopted German patterns only after extensive modifications.

However, it was not a German pattern of education that made this striking impression abroad, but that of Prussia, one of the several German states which continued to be independent through most of the past century. Indeed, the German nation which the present generation remembers as a united world power did not even exist prior to 1871. Before that time there had only been numerous more or less autonomous sovereign states, numbering as many as 300 at one time, whose borders and political loyalties kept shifting with the fortunes of war and diplomacy. In each a local variety of German was used as the language of communication. Evidence of these language differences may still be observed in the dialects found in Austria, the Low Countries, and Switzerland as well as in Germany itself. A single political system was put together out of these scattered pieces primarily through the vigorous, single-minded efforts of Prussia, and it appeared in the form of the German Empire. Just as the other states of the empire ultimately yielded to Prussia's political domination, so also did they yield to her example in education. It is to Prussia, then, that one must turn for the story of German education, and particularly to the period between the signing of the Treaty of Tilsit in 1807 and the formation of the German Empire in 1871.

Historical background

The Roman Empire never succeeded in gaining political control over that portion of the Germanic peoples who lived north of a line connecting the garrison outposts at Cologne, Mainz, Augsburg, Regensburg, and Vienna. Beyond this line the Teutonic tribes had continued to live in a relatively primitive manner without a common social organization or a uniform set of cultural traditions and commitments. Clovis, King of the Franks and head of the Merovingian dynasty, succeeded in bringing together important segments of these people and in laying the foundations for the empire over which Charlemagne later

76

was to rule. By the ninth century Frankish rule extended to the Elbe and included much of the territory now claimed by France and the Low Countries, as well as Western Germany.

Meanwhile, Clovis had opened the doors of his realm to St. Boniface and other missionaries who ultimately succeeded in bringing the Teutonic peoples within the Christian fold. With the new religion came the forms of religious instruction employed by the Christian clergy of that day.

Prior to the fifteenth century the heads of the numerous German states paid little attention to the cultural and social needs of their subjects. Feudalism provided the basic pattern of social organization, political control, and military strength. Consequently, the all-absorbing occupation of the heads of state had been the endless task of keeping their holdings intact and of enlarging them at the expense of their neighbors as opportunity afforded. In the meantime the Roman Church did what it could to introduce schools in the principal centers of population. Scattered communities of the religious orders maintained monastic schools. But since the educational interests of the Church did not extend beyond the training of its clergy, the general population was not well served until it learned to take matters into its own hands. Reference was made in Chapter 2 to the fact that the Germanic peoples had acquired a substantial number and variety of schools by 1500, all more or less directly under ecclesiastical supervision. Universities had been developed at Prague, Leipzig, and Tubingen, and in 1502, at Wittenberg. For various reasons the Germanic people had not developed the extreme fear of secular and pagan learning which

had prevailed in the south. Furthermore, the coastal regions, particularly at the mouths of great rivers, encouraged the development of trade. Villages at these places gradually became centers of handicraft and small industry. Soon laymen became aware of the value of the literary arts and requested the services of teachers. This lay interest led to the development of vernacular schools to teach reading, writing, and the keeping of accounts, and as trade expanded, the languages of other peoples. As local pride grew, municipality came to compete with municipality, and state with state, in the establishment of schools and the acquisition of other cultural adornments. Schools and universities multiplied rapidly during this time, especially those sponsored by municipal governments.

The municipal Latin schools soon became eager recipients of humanistic ideals and forms of learning. From their sponsorship of classical Latin and Greek studies, there emerged the distinctive type of secondary school known as the *Gymnasium,* which became so deeply rooted among the German peoples in the next centuries that it is the standard by which German secondary education is measured even today.

From the fifteenth to the nineteenth century

The humanistic studies had other effects on German life and education. The introduction of Greek enabled scholars to search the sources of Christian doctrines and to verify questioned interpretations. For many centuries the higher clergy had exercised a veritable monopoly in these matters, but as humanism spread, their claim to authority in matters of belief, as well as social practices, was challenged. Various reform movements appeared, such as those of the Waldenses in Italy and Switzerland, Wycliffe and the Lollards in England, the Albigenses in France and Spain, and the Hussites in Bohemia. Early in the sixteenth century a similar movement was started in Germany by Martin Luther. Immediately, the uneasy political atmosphere in which the German states had existed over the years was transformed into bitter conflict among the different religious factions.

Luther, an Augustinian monk and a respected teacher of theology, had been assigned to the newly formed university at Wittenberg. His academic preparation had included a fair portion of humanistic studies, particularly Greek grammar and literature. His close attention to the Greek version of the New Testament gospels persuaded him that the agents of the Roman Church had come to claim powers and authority not bestowed upon them by the Divine Founder. This position was welcomed by many people north of the Alps, who felt that the tithes and other fees demanded by the agents of the Church had become excessive. Beyond this, various kings and princes resented interference by the higher clergy in local political matters. Thus, in 1517, when Luther denounced the activities of Johann Tetzel, a Dominican monk who was offering absolution to those who gave freely to the fund to rebuild St. Peter's Church in Rome, a number of German princes and other prominent citizens came to Luther's support. In brief, the purely doctrinal issue which separated Luther from the official position of his superiors was almost immediately magnified to such proportions that a complete civil as well as ecclesiastical break

with Rome was unavoidable. Lutheran churches were formed in many states to replace the Roman Catholic Church; and in the transition, lands, endowments, buildings, and schools were transferred to new owners. The transformation was especially thorough in the northern states, such as Saxony, Hesse, Brandenburg, Prussia, and the Scandinavian countries. The unifying influence of this common religious commitment later afforded substantial assistance to Prussia and the Hohenzollerns in their drive to bring the other Lutheran states into the German Empire. However, some Roman Catholic states were included also.

The Hapsburgs in Austria, meanwhile, took a dim view of these Protestant developments. As the traditional heads of the Holy Roman Empire, they were expected to defend the Roman Church against its enemies, and in this capacity they employed every imperial resource to oppose the Reformation. They were successful to the extent that they held not only Austria, but also other south and east German states, principally Bavaria and most of Bohemia, within the Roman fold. But the religious situation became even more complicated when Germans residing in areas bordering on France and Switzerland joined the separate reform movements led by Calvin in Geneva and by Zwingli in Zurich. Although both were Protestants and therefore suffered at the hands of the Hapsburgs, some Lutheran rulers also regarded them as enemies.

As a consequence of these complicated religious conflicts the seventeenth century was a most unhappy one for the German people. From 1618 to 1648 military invasions, pillaging, and outright attempts at total destruction wracked almost every German community. Much of the havoc was brought on by the employment of mercenaries whose pay was, in part, the privilege of unlimited looting and plundering. The implied motive of these hostile raids by neighbor upon neighbor was the religious issue. But when it is remembered that only about forty out of three hundred separate German states survived to the time of the empire, some estimate can be made of the extent to which the larger states had expanded at the expense of the smaller ones.

Among the larger states, Austria and Prussia were the two chief competitors. Neither, however, seemed able to achieve the undisputed supremacy needed to unite all Germans under a single political authority, even as late as 1800. Thus when Napoleon began his campaign of military conquests his troops captured the divided German states one by one with astounding swiftness. In 1806 he consolidated part of his gains by putting a number of the northern and western states together in a loose association known as the Confederation of the Rhine. He hoped by this move to build a buffer between France and the Hapsburgs with their Holy Roman Empire. Strange as it may seem, this forced coordination of the states in the Confederation helped create a popular sentiment for unification. Furthermore, it exposed German intellectuals and the growing middle class to the liberal philosophical and political doctrines that had gained wide acceptance in France at the time of the Revolution. These ideas took root among the Germans and grew into a formidable movement that was to culminate in the unsuccessful German revolutions of 1848.

But the Napoleonic adventures in Eastern Europe bore other more immediate fruit. Moving with characteristic swiftness, Napoleon's army crushed Prussia and reduced Austria to an utterly helpless state. Although they were permitted to exist as independent political entities, they were stripped of extensive territories and burdened with debt. The impact upon Austria was so severe that the Holy Roman Empire, which for some time had been little more than an empty name, was officially dissolved.

Defeat also weighed heavy on Prussia which under Frederick the Great had become a major power. Her system of civil administration had been highly developed, her economy had prospered, her cultural institutions had flourished, and her army had become one of the most efficient military machines in Europe. Nevertheless, under Frederick's immediate successors, Prussian officialdom had grown fat and the army had become better adapted to the parade grounds than to the fields of battle. Consequently, the severe terms of the Treaty of Tilsit stung Prussian pride so deeply that, indirectly, they helped to unite the people in a gigantic effort to rebuild. The story of that effort and its brilliant success has been used by German leaders from Bismarck to Hitler to inspire their subjects to make extreme personal sacrifices to achieve certain glory for the state. The role of the Prussian educational system in that gigantic national effort will be told shortly.

The beginnings of public education

It will be recalled that Prussia, together with other German states, had encountered the Reformation in the sixteenth century. One of the most important educational effects that followed from the Protestant's emphasis upon the Bible as

79

the authority for all Christian beliefs had been the introduction of mass instruction in reading. Furthermore, the weary states finally agreed in 1555 to put an end to the religious conflicts by permitting the head of each state to choose the religion he wished to establish in his realm, and to require all his subjects to conform. This is known as the Peace of Augsburg. Protestant states meanwhile confiscated lands and other properties owned by the Roman Catholic Church, including schools. Many schools were immediately converted to Protestant purposes, particularly the training of ministers, teachers, and other leaders. As enthusiasm for the new religion grew, new schools were founded. Each state now wished to have at least one university, and the demand for preparatory instruction increased accordingly.

The Prussian choice of alternatives offered by the Treaty of Augsburg was Lutheranism. Local pastors received orders from their superiors to proceed with all possible speed to establish vernacular schools in each parish. In several neighboring states the crown came

to the aid of the new ecclesiastical establishments. The Duchy of Wurttenberg did so in 1559. In 1619 Weimar went even further by making education in the vernacular compulsory for all children between the ages of six and twelve. Several Catholic states found themselves under pressure from a restless population to provide schools. Some introduced exceptionally fine programs of education and Bavaria later took the lead in developing schools to serve the practical as well as the religious needs of the people.

Prussia did not follow the example of the other states until 1716. In that year the king ordered all children to attend the local parish schools unless their education was provided for in some other manner. This exception was made in deference to the wealthier classes who received private instruction, either at home or in small classes, until the boys were ready to enter a *Gymnasium*. Even at this early date, therefore, the pattern of a two-class system of education was apparent. In 1763 Frederick the Great sought to raise the quality of instruction in the vernacular schools by de-

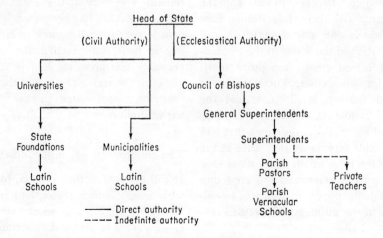

Figure 8. Lines of Educational Authority in Early Lutheran States

scribing the methods of instruction to be used and the subject matter to be taught.

The vernacular schools of this period were parish schools under ecclesiastical control and support. However, since Lutheranism was the established religion in Prussia, the Lutheran church was the state church and the Lutheran clergy were in effect agents of the state. Furthermore, whole villages were uniformly Lutheran, and any attempt to distinguish between a parish school and a village school would have been meaningless. Vernacular instruction was a function of the ecclesiastical branch of the state, and the quality of the schools was determined by the interest the church showed in its educational responsibilities.

By 1787 the government had become a bit uneasy about the church's apparent lack of vigor in educational affairs. Therefore, a special branch of the civil government known as the *Oberschulkollegium,* or high commission for schools, was established to provide leadership. This action was intended to place the schools under civil control, but Frederick William II, who was not in favor of such a change, succeeded to the throne just in time to fill the commission with high-ranking churchmen. Ecclesiastical control continued even though the Prussian civil code of 1794, the famous *Allgemeines Landrecht,* clearly stated that the state was to be superior to the church in educational matters. The state failed to gain control not merely because of the long tradition of ecclesiastical domination, but primarily because the royal government made no effort to provide financial support. Thus vernacular instruction continued to serve religious ends, and the quality of instruction varied in direct relation to the interest, ability, and resources of the local pastor.

Although secondary schools increasingly were municipal institutions, they, too, were closely associated with the church and were required to give religious instruction. The universities, although chartered by the crown, were required to serve the ends of the church by supplying a constant flow of recruits to the ranks of the clergy. And so matters stood with respect to Prussian education when Napoleon, on his march to Russia, swept away all the illusions of invincibility and cultural supremacy which had grown up after the brilliant reign of Frederick the Great.

Prussian education

The terms of the peace dictated by Napoleon not only deprived Prussia of vast territories, but also saddled her with a huge debt, limited her army to 42,000 men, and stationed French occupation troops on her soil. Obviously, the usual avenues for rebuilding a nation were closed. But now the fruits of the relatively extensive education provided by the *Gymnasien* and universities, which were nurtured by competition among the municipalities and states, began to appear. Writers and other intellectuals, among them Kleist and Fichte, began to call for a spiritual rearming. The German people were pictured as a unique people, an *Urvolk,* that was destined to build a new culture, a new empire to supersede that of ancient Rome, and ultimately to dominate the world. Fichte in particular preached the gospel of German nationalism. It is said that he delivered his famous "Addresses to the German People" in the Academy of

Science in Berlin even while French soldiers were on duty outside; and from such inspiration the Prussians developed a concept of national unity that was skillfully employed by the ruling class to arouse the fanatical patriotism for which the Prussian people became noted. The instrument fashioned by their government to achieve this end was a system of universal elementary education under civil control.

Social role

Although various kings before 1806 had admonished the church to be more vigorous in its educational efforts and to broaden its objectives, the clergy absorbed these royal proddings without much visible effect. But innovations not of official sponsorship had appeared in Prussia as well as in other German states. Some had demonstrated in dramatic fashion the value of education in raising the morale and social level of the people. Among these reforms were those of Francke, Basedow, and Salzmann. Each had been motivated on religious grounds to raise the level of the people; and each had developed schools that were substantial improvements over the usual parish or village schools, both with respect to methods and curricula.

The particular reform which now appealed to the Prussian rulers was the system of education developed by Johann Heinrich Pestalozzi in Switzerland. Pestalozzi, although deeply religious, believed that the guiding principles necessary to develop strong character and worthy life objectives could best be taught when they were developed inductively from the pupil's own sensory experiences. He therefore concentrated on determining which sensory experiences would serve this purpose best and in what order they should be presented. The resulting curriculum and methodology impressed the Prussian officials and they resolved to incorporate them in the Prussian state schools. But, first, it was necessary to establish civil control over the schools and, then, to develop an administrative agency to exercise control.

It should be noted that the Prussian school system was not an outgrowth of popular demand, but was conceived and imposed by royal decree. Frederick William III, by reputation a benevolent ruler, was quite certain in his own mind that he ruled by divine authority. Nevertheless, the circumstances imposed upon him by Napoleon made it expedient for him to draw closer to the people in an effort to rewin their loyalty and support. He appointed liberal men to head his government and was well rewarded by the economic and social improvements achieved by such men as vom Stein, von Hardenberg, and von Humboldt. In addition, their military experts invented the ingenious rotation system by which they circumvented the intent of the Treaty of Tilsit to limit the army to 42,000 men, and thereby enabled Prussia to contribute substantially to the ultimate defeat of Napoleon in 1814. But enlightened and liberal as the reform programs proved to be for some segments of society, odious features of the old feudalism remained for others. Thus the principle of divine right of kings never was renounced and, indeed, was reasserted during every period of reaction until World War I when the monarchy came to an end. While municipalities were given enough self-government to enable the commercial classes to build an economy that could support the reconstruction program, the rural areas remained under the autocratic control of the landed families.

These landowners, the *Junker* class, originally had been Teutonic knights of the early feudal days. They had been given estates in return for their services to persons of higher social status. On their estates the *Junkers* made and administered law, maintained order, settled disputes, and collected taxes. Landownership was highly restricted by custom and law, and serfs were bound for life on the estates on which they were born. Vom Stein attempted to free the serfs and to liberalize the landownership system, but the *Junkers* were able to defeat his efforts. The *Junkers,* thus, continued in power in the rural areas, and went on to gain a virtual monopoly of the officer grades in the army and the higher positions in the administrative bureaucracy. The *Junker* class and the royal house, therefore, afforded each other mutual support in opposing the recurring waves of liberalism that originated with the intellectual and commercial classes in the cities. Prussian education must be viewed in the light of the uses this alliance between the royal house and the *Junker* class made of it.[1]

Evidence of the arrogance with which the ruling class regarded the common people appeared at various times. Subdued at first, while the nation was rebuilding, it was flaunted before all the Germans by Frederick William IV

when he refused the crown of the constitutional monarchy proposed by the Frankfurt Assembly because "it came from the gutter" instead of the German princes. The following year, when the people rioted in the streets of Berlin and other cities, Frederick William and his *Junkers* almost yielded to the demands for a constitutional government. But the unswerving determination of the *Junkers* to keep control of the army prevailed, and the demands were quieted. Indeed, some have suggested that by 1848 the Prussian schools had done their work so well that the people had lost the ability to stage a successful revolt.

Frederick William was sufficiently shaken by these uprisings to give the people a constitution. It was an instrument of his own design, however, and did not reduce his fundamental powers. Although an elected legislative body, the *Landtag,* was established, it was given virtually no power to introduce legislation. Members of the upper chamber were hereditary or crown-appointed and those of the lower were named by an electoral body heavily weighted in favor of the *Junkers*. The army and the executive branch of government remained under the exclusive authority of the crown, as did the power to levy and collect certain taxes.

When Bismarck was called to head the government in 1862 there was no question in his mind about whom he represented or from what source he derived his authority. When the *Landtag* became frightened by his obvious moves to convert Prussia into a military state, and refused to approve his budget for the army, he merely ignored it and proceeded to govern as though there were no legislature. It later went on record as having approved the budget, and be-

[1] Lysbeth Walker Muncy, *The Junker in the Prussian Administration under William II, 1888–1914,* Brown University Press, Providence, R.I., 1944. See especially chap. I for an account of the origin of the *Junkers* and their role during the administration of Frederick William III.

stowed upon Bismarck its highest honors. From this point on, the crown, supported by the *Junkers* through their control of the army and the administrative bureaucracy, was able to use the schools and every other agency of government to build Prussia into the military machine that became the nucleus of the German Empire.

Power structure and administrative organization

As the eighteenth century drew to a close the crown had become increasingly interested in the educational activities of the church and other school patrons. The universities operated under royal charters and as a rule received grants from the royal treasury. Kings and other members of the royal family helped to found and maintain secondary schools. Even the experimental activities of Francke and others enjoyed royal commendation and support. Some of these, particularly the work of Hecker in Berlin, became the nuclei of the *Realschulen* which later enabled the Germans to take the lead in developing scientific and technical education. But prior to 1806 the only significant moves made by the crown to acquire control over education had been to establish the ineffective *Oberschulkollegium* and to insert the references to the rights of the state in educational matters into the *Allgemeines Landrecht.* Using this civil code as its authority, the crown had called upon the local communities, or *Gemeinden,* to support their schools through taxes. Also, school attendance was made compulsory; and the local school authorities were directed to provide suitable compensation for the teachers, but the crown offered no finan-

84

cial assistance to enable them to do so. School inspection was a responsibility of the clergy. The decision as to when children had fulfilled the legal requirements of compulsory school attendance also was made by the local pastors, and was usually equated with preparation for confirmation. This interpretation had considerable influence later in fixing the school-leaving age.

A royal commission appointed to study the educational situation at the turn of the century had reported that, in general, schools were available but that their quality left much to be desired. Teachers had to practice some trade to make a living. Hence, schools were likely to be housed in tailor shops or other types of workrooms where the teacher could carry on his trade while keeping one eye on the pupils. Attendance dropped off as the children became old enough to work. Girls were taught separately and generally received inferior instruction. In some industrial communities elementary vocational skills could be learned in private schools. Although it seems clear that Prussia could boast a literacy rate about as high as that of other states of that time, the military found it desirable to introduce "garrison" schools because many of the conscripts lacked sufficient skill in reading and writing to make good soldiers. The success of these schools was so startling that Frederick William began to fear that the soldiers might be learning too much, a concern that was voiced repeatedly by his successors as they viewed the system of education that took shape under the direction of their ministers.

As soon as the Prussian government could get on its feet following its humiliating encounter with Napoleon, it replaced the ineffective *Oberschulkolle-*

gium with a single national agency, the Ministry of Education. At first, this agency operated as a bureau in the Ministry of the Interior; but by 1817 its importance in the national effort had become so obvious that it was made a department in the Ministry of Religion, Education, and Public Health. Separate divisions established to look after elementary, secondary, and higher education contributed, from the outset, to the perpetuation of the class differences already observed between the vernacular schools, on one hand, and the *Gymnasien* and universities, on the other. This departmental arrangement is shown in Figure 9.

Although the Prussian universities were chartered by the crown after the Reformation, this in itself had not kept them from acting as self-governing corporations. They accepted support from the royal treasury and placed themselves under the protection of the crown. There was inevitably some surveillance, mild at first, of their activities and of individual professors. Now, however, the universities were made directly responsible to the Ministry of Education, a change which, as will be shown later, seriously restricted their freedom.

Secondary and elementary education were administered through subordinate levels in the Ministry of the Interior, namely, the provinces. The administrative head in each province, the *Oberpräsident,* and his advisory board or council were appointed by the crown on the recommendation of the Minister of the Interior. These officials were responsible for all aspects of provincial government; therefore, a subcommittee known as the *Schulkollegium* was created to look after educational matters.

Since the church, municipalities,

guilds, trade associations, and even individuals had been free to establish and operate schools, a variety of elementary and secondary schools had evolved. The *Schulkollegien,* which were expected to give most of their attention to secondary education, were directed to work for some standardization of instruction. Two procedures emerged from their efforts. The first called for the certification of teachers by the *Schulkollegien.* As their authority and freedom of action increased, they specified the program of studies prospective teachers were to pursue in the universities, and ultimately prepared and administered the examinations for certification. The second device called for a uniform examination to regulate admissions to the universities. Again, each *Schulkollegium* devised and administered the examination used within its province; but as time went on and the Ministry of Education reached ever more directly into the administration of education on all levels, both the certification of teachers and the administration of the *Reifeprüfung,* the admissions examination, were controlled on a national basis in accordance with the wishes of the crown.

The *Schulkollegien* were also responsible for training teachers for the elementary schools, but the central government played an active role and assumed some financial responsibility, including the cost of maintaining teachers' seminaries. Vernacular elementary schools were administered on a succession of levels subordinate to the provincial agencies, as shown in Figure 9. Immediately below the level of the province, was the *Regierungsbezirk,* or administrative district. Like the province, this unit of government was presided over by a president and council

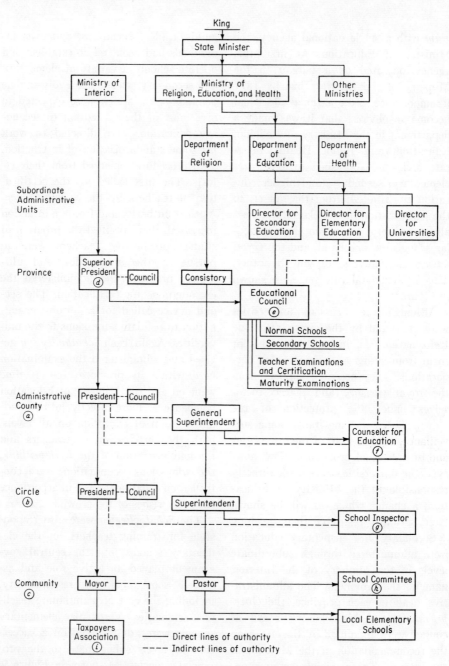

King

State Minister

| Ministry of Interior | Ministry of Religion, Education, and Health | Other Ministries |

Department of Religion

Department of Education

Department of Health

Subordinate Administrative Units

Director for Secondary Education

Director for Elementary Education

Director for Universities

Province

Superior President (d) — Council

Consistory

Educational Council (e)

Normal Schools

Secondary Schools

Teacher Examinations and Certification

Maturity Examinations

Administrative County (a)

President — Council

General Superintendent

Counselor for Education (f)

Circle (b)

President — Council

Superintendent

School Inspector (g)

Community (c)

Mayor

Pastor

School Committee (h)

Local Elementary Schools

Taxpayers Association (i)

——— Direct lines of authority
---- Indirect lines of authority

Figure 9. Lines of Educational Authority in Nineteenth-century Prussia

a. *Regierungsbezirk*
b. *Kreis*
c. *Gemeinde*
d. *Oberpräsident*
e. *Schulkollegium*

f. *Schulrat*
g. *Schulinspector*
h. *Schulvorstand*
i. *Schulverein*

appointed by the Minister of the Interior. Educational matters were delegated to a member of the council called the *Schulrat,* or counselor for schools. While the *Schulrat* directed the implementation of the official program of elementary education within his district, the actual establishment and operation of the schools were the responsibilities of still lower administrative units. These were the *Kreise* and the *Gemeinden,* respectively. The *Gemeinden* were the local school districts, generally encompassing the inhabitants of a small village or a single parish. The *Kreise* usually included a number of *Gemeinden* and corresponded to the territory over which a superintendent in the ecclesiastical hierarchy presided. The major educational function preformed on the level of the *Kreis,* or circle, was that of inspecting the elementary schools, a duty performed by the *Kreisschulinspector,* who almost invariably was a member of the clergy. Recommendations for the office of school inspector were made by the ecclesiastical authorities on the level of the province, but the appointments were made by the Minister of Education.

The establishment and maintenance of the individual schools were responsibilities of the *Gemeinden.* These matters were clearly spelled out in edicts and directives issued by the central government. In each *Gemeinde,* all persons owning land or maintaining a household within the district were required to belong to a school association, or a *Schulverein,* which levied and collected the taxes needed to support the local elementary schools. However, the operation of the schools, including the preparation of the budgets, was assigned to a special school committee in each dis-

trict. Such a committee was called a *Schulvorstand* in rural areas, and a *Schulkommission* or *Schuldeputation* in urban districts that maintained several schools. In such school committees, the local clergy enjoyed privileged status. Indeed, only the clergy were permitted to supervise the instructional programs, including the deportment of the teachers. Lay members were permitted to look after the buildings, equipment, and other "external" matters.

Clearly evident in the development of this administrative arrangement was the central government's intention of gradually substituting civil control for traditional ecclesiastical control. Public resistance was avoided by utilizing the existing parish and municipal schools and by continuing to use the services of the local clergy as school inspectors. At the beginning, the government limited its activities to increasing the number and quality of the schools; but after gaining acceptance as the final authority in educational matters, it gradually redirected the schools to serve national rather than religious ends. The single, most effective device used to achieve this transformation was the assumption of complete authority over the training, appointment, payment, and promotion of the teachers. Secondary school teachers, at least those appointed to the *Gymnasien,* were trained in state-controlled universities; elementary teachers in the state-operated teachers seminaries. As the government became more reactionary and autocratic, particularly under Bismarck, the curricula and operation of the teachers' seminaries were so minutely controlled that the elementary school teachers became not merely instruments for the regimentation of children, but also effective propaganda agents among their parents. As state institutions the *Gymnasien* and universities came under equally stringent controls. Municipalities lost their freedom to operate secondary schools, and many such schools were no longer permitted to be known as *Gymnasien*.[2]

Educational institutions

Educational experimentation had flourished in Prussia during the latter half of the eighteenth century. Some of this had been inspired by the earlier work of Francke at Halle. Francke's genius for identifying areas of need and then developing new institutional forms to serve them had produced a whole cluster of new schools ranging from charity schools for the children of the very poor to select boarding schools for the rich, and from classes at the most elementary level to a program of teacher education for students in the neighboring university. Even the university, the famous University of Halle, showed the effects of his creative genius by introducing instruction in science and by challenging the traditional teachings in the faculty of theology.

Francke's educational activities had grown out of his commitment to help his parishioners in whatever ways they needed assistance. He found among them a desperate need for knowledge and training in the practical aspects of life, and his activities played an important role in introducing into German education such subjects as modern languages, mineralogy, astronomy, mechanics, and other natural sciences, as well as activities designed to develop skills in glass blowing, copper engraving, and similar handicrafts. Such subjects became known as the *Realen* to distinguish them from the classical subjects. Another pastor in Halle, Christopher Semler, developed a school specifically designed to give young boys instruction in mathematical and mechanical subjects. His school became the forerunner of a type of institution known as the *Realschulen*. The *Realschule* movement was brought to a status of greater development in Berlin by John Hecker; and in 1810 the University of Berlin was established on the foundations provided by the collection of scientific and technical schools which had grown up there.

Although there were numerous other educational developments in Prussia and neighboring German states prior to 1800, the above list shows that the Prussian government did not need to limit itself to parish schools, Latin grammar schools, and classical universities to establish a system of public education as an instrument of national policy. Indeed, Prussian leaders felt that such traditional institutions would not serve the national needs as they understood them. Accordingly, a new plan of education was called for, and a young German teacher, J. W. Süvern, was commissioned to prepare it.

Süvern, who had been associated with Pestalozzi in Switzerland for several years, had been given an important post in the new Ministry of Education in 1809. His liberal tendencies were well known and the fact that he was selected to prepare the master plan for the entire nation indicates that the royal government was similarly disposed at the beginning of the reconstruction period.

[2] Friedrich Paulsen, *Geschichte des Gelehrten Unterrichts*, Walter de Gruyer, Berlin, 1921, vol. II, pp. 286–302.

After several years of study Süvern proposed that a unitary, completely integrated system of schools should be introduced which would eliminate the socially divisive effects of the existing class-structured institutions. Not including the universities, his plan called for three levels of education—elementary schools, middle schools, and *Gymnasien* —so articulated that pupils might progress from one level to the next without undue difficulty. By 1819, however, when the plan was finally considered by the government, the crown felt so secure that it no longer pretended to hold democratic sentiments, and the plan was rejected.

Elementary Schools. The resurgent royalists now moved rather quickly to develop a system of schools in which the children of the poor were to be segregated from those of the higher class throughout the entire period of instruction. Government officials had become interested in the teaching methods by which Pestolozzi was instructing poor children in Yverdun, and had been sending selected young men to study with him since 1809. On returning, some of these young men were placed in charge of teachers' seminaries which had arisen under private effort after the models provided by Francke and Hecker. Others were commissioned to establish new ones. Then all the teachers' seminaries were made state institutions and placed under the control of the Ministry. The curricula and training programs were standardized, and other steps were taken to make sure that the institutions would produce a new corps of teachers uniformly trained in a systematic methodology adapted from the Pestalozzian model. By 1826 the teachers' seminaries were turning out enough graduates to enable the Ministry of Education to introduce a further screening process. All teachers for the vernacular elementary schools now were required to be certified, and a state qualifying examination was introduced to evaluate the candidate's academic as well as pedagogical qualifications. To ensure an adequate supply of teachers, the number of seminaries was steadily increased until there were forty-six in 1840. The curriculum included some general education as well as pedagogical studies. The expectation was that the teachers would not only serve as instructors for the children, but also as up-grading influences in the community.

By controlling the training and certification of the teachers, the royal government acquired control of the vernacular schools without having to assume financial responsibility for them. Parish and village schools were forbidden to employ any but certified teachers. Where no suitable school buildings existed, the Ministry of Education, in cooperation with its sister Ministry for Religion, brought pressure upon the local authorities to provide them. Children were ordered to attend the vernacular schools for specified periods unless excused from doing so. Through these and similar measures, many issued as royal decrees, the enrollments in the vernacular elementary schools quickly increased until they included about 90 per cent of the compulsory school-age population. This widespread use of the vernacular elementary schools led to their being designated as *Volksschulen,* that is, schools for the people. However, they were not free schools, for parents were required to pay from 6 to 12

Pfennige per child per week, depending upon their ability to pay. The very poor were excused from such payments, with the local community, of course, carrying the burden.

The spirit in which the *Volksschulen* were received varied rather widely from place to place. In rural districts where parents and local authorities regarded children as necessary hands in the fields, compulsory schooling was looked upon as a state duty, literally the *Schulpflict*, and fell into the same category of inescapable duties as paying taxes and rendering compulsory military service. In the commercial cities, the schools were welcomed as a means to personal advancement. Considerable effort was made by the people in the cities to increase and extend the educational opportunities their schools provided, and several developments of educational significance resulted. Among these was the development of higher elementary schools. Although the local authorities were urged to provide them wherever the population warranted,[3] attendance was not compulsory. It appears that they were desired primarily by the higher levels of skilled laborers and small proprietors who wanted their children to have educational opportunities somewhat beyond those available in the regular elementary schools, but not necessarily on a par with the secondary schools. The higher elementary schools provided the most frequently used path to gain admission to the teachers' seminaries.

When viewed as a group of connecting institutions, the *Volksschulen,* the higher elementary schools, and the *Leh-*

[3] Henry Barnard, *National Education in Europe,* Case, Tiffany, Hartford, Conn., 1854, p. 104.

rerseminarien, or teachers' seminaries, constituted a closed system. This system, shown in Figure 10, was regarded as adequate for the masses, and no need was felt to provide opportunities for transfer to the parallel system consisting of the secondary and higher institutions. In contrast to the latter, the former group of schools was referred to as the "elementary" system. Neither the teachers nor the pupils were given instruction in the languages that would make transfer to the "secondary" system possible. In the "elementary" system the *Volksschulen* offered just those studies which the government thought would make the great mass of inhabitants efficient and devoted subjects. The teachers were selected, trained, and appointed to achieve precisely this end. When, in 1848–1849, the royalists discovered that they had allowed the teachers to learn too much, thereby enabling them to take the lead in the liberal revolution, the curricula, both in the seminaries and the elementary schools, were pruned of subject matter which might teach the common people to think on political and other social matters. The school discipline and deportment also were redesigned along military lines to instill discipline and to prepare boys for their future careers as soldiers.

Secondary Schools. Prior to 1800 upper-class families had provided for the education of their children privately. The introduction of the *Volksschulen* did not cause them to abandon these arrangements, but rather to strengthen them. Secondary education also had arisen in municipal or *Bürger* schools. Some of these offered instruction in the vernacular only including subjects of the *real* categories. Others offered the traditional Latin and Greek studies

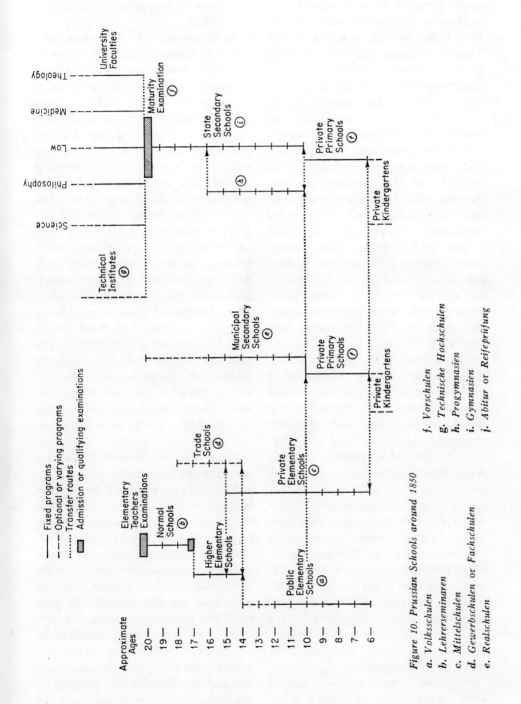

Figure 10. Prussian Schools around 1850

a. *Volksschulen*
b. *Lehrerseminaren*
c. *Mittelschulen*
d. *Gewerbschulen* or *Fachschulen*
e. *Realschulen*
f. *Vorschulen*
g. *Technische Hochschulen*
h. *Progymnasien*
i. *Gymnasien*
j. *Abitur* or *Reifeprüfung*

which prepared for admission to the universities. Some of the better ones offered both curricula, including modern foreign languages; and a few even boasted a program of higher studies duplicating that of the arts faculties at the universities. The universities, on their side, had been regulating their own admissions and had offered instruction on the preparatory level in a section known as the *Paedagogium*. At the beginning of the nineteenth century, therefore, the secondary school situation was reminiscent of that indicated in Figure 3, with each institution more or less free to develop its own curriculum in response to the demands of local patrons and students. This particularly was the case among the municipal or *Bürger* schools, which were more numerous among the Germanic peoples than elsewhere.

The reconstruction government lost little time in asserting more stringent controls over both the secondary schools and the universities. The universities now found themselves under the direct supervision of the Ministry of Education. By 1820 this included control of the philosophical orientation of instruction, and by 1850, the activities and behavior of individual professors. Many who refused to compromise their professional integrity were dismissed and a few were imprisoned. The government, which now was providing the funds, also took a dim view of the overlapping curricula of many secondary schools and universities. Equally objectionable, the secondary schools had no standardized program of studies; institutions, all of which called themselves *Gymnasien,* served quite different purposes, ranging from the preparation of students to enter a trade to helping them qualify for

admission to a professional faculty at a university.

In earlier efforts to bring some order into this confused situation, proposals had been made for a system of external examinations by which the products of the secondary schools could be measured and admissions to the universities made more uniform. At first these efforts had produced little, but as the government became more secure, a series of decrees were issued which ultimately achieved standardization. The first among these instituted an official *Reifeprüfung,* or maturity examination. It replaced an earlier type of examination known as the *Abiturientenprüfung* which had been introduced in 1788 as school-leaving examinations. Because the latter were administered by individual schools, they had failed to bring about the desired standardization of instruction. The Ministry, therefore, placed the maturity examinations in the hands of the provincial *Schulkollegien,* which were responsible to the Ministry. By spelling out the subject matter in which candidates were to be examined, the commissions were able to control what was taught in the individual schools.

A second decree ordered the universities to admit only those candidates who presented a certificate showing that they had passed the maturity examination. This ruling inevitably resulted in closing the preparatory departments which the universities had maintained. At the same time the secondary schools were restrained from offering university-level instruction. The maturity examinations now marked the border separating secondary education from higher education and provided the only gateway by which a student might pass from one level to the other.

The Ministry then focused its attention upon reforming the curriculum of the secondary schools. A plan of studies was outlined covering nine years. It included Latin as the principal subject, with Greek, German, and mathematics as the major supporting subjects. Religion, Hebrew, French, philosophy, and a little natural science were assigned a substantially lesser status. Many of these subjects, particularly the ancient languages, mathematics, and philosophy, were precisely those which students heretofore had pursued in the university arts faculties. Now that these were taken over by the secondary schools, the maturity certificate became in effect the equivalent of the bachelor of arts degree, and the transition from secondary school to university generally came at about age twenty. The maturity certificate now admitted the holder directly to the faculties of law, theology, and medicine. Furthermore, what had been the arts faculty was transformed into a graduate faculty, frequently called the faculty of philosophy, and was put on a par with the three older faculties.

In its efforts to achieve system and standardization in secondary education, the Ministry permitted only candidates who had attended a university to take the examinations for secondary school teachers. It also restricted admission to the maturity examinations to persons who had prepared at an accredited *Gymnasium*. The Ministry then took the harsh step of certifying a very select list of secondary schools as accredited *Gymnasien*—those which had been most exclusive with respect to admissions and which had focused most directly upon the classical-humanistic studies. Excluded were many municipal and even ecclesiastical schools, some of which

had developed effective programs in the *real* and other modern studies. Furthermore, the *Gymnasien* were brought under the guardianship of the Ministry so that, together with the Ministry-controlled universities, they constituted, after 1850, a closed, state-supported system of institutions which afforded the only avenue leading to secondary school teaching, the learned professions, the higher public offices, and the commissioned ranks of the military. By retaining high tuition fees in the *Gymnasien*, the ruling class made certain that only the sons of acceptable families could enter into positions of influence.

These changes had a depressing effect upon the vast majority of the secondary schools, which were not accredited. Those which had prepared for careers in commerce and industry now tended to concentrate upon these programs, and generally became known as *Realschulen*. Others, which came to be known as *Progymnasien*, duplicated the instruction in the lower classes of the *Gymnasien*, hoping to enable some students to transfer to a regular *Gymnasium* with advanced standing. The remaining secondary schools catered to the small proprietor and lower officeholder classes by offering instruction paralleling that in the *Volksschulen*, but since they were private, they were looked upon as more respectable in a social as well as an academic way. These became known as *Mittelschulen* and *höhere Bürgerschulen*. They generally offered a year or so of instruction beyond the upper limits of compulsory school attendance and made further pretenses to superiority by teaching one or more modern foreign languages in the upper grades. Understandably, some parents of children attending *Volksschulen* were willing to make substantial sacrifices to get them transferred to a *Mittelschule,* and opportunities for such transfer sometimes were provided in the lower grades.

While the *Volksschulen* and *Mittelschulen* ran parallel programs, the *Realschulen* as well as the *Gymnasien* and *Progymnasien* assumed that their pupils had received elementary training in reading, writing, arithmetic, and religion before they were presented for admission. Hence, the age of admission to these schools was nine or ten. Theoretically, a child could secure the necessary preparation in a *Volksschule* or *Mittelschule,* but practically all parents who wished to have their sons pursue the *Gymnasium* course started them in a more exclusive, private school known as a *Vorschule.* By entering them in such a school at age five or six, higher-class families were assured that their sons could complete their entire education without having contact with lower-class children at any point.

Technical and Vocational Schools. Interest in vocational and technical education also became apparent after 1800. As the first minister in the reconstruction government, vom Stein had looked upon scientific studies as an invaluable aid to economic and political development. With his active encouragement, von Humboldt established the University of Berlin and made it the model for higher education to promote scientific ends. Enjoying generous support from the royal treasury the University of Berlin quickly developed into the leading center for scientific research and instruction, and incited imitation both in Europe and America. Soon other Prussian cities followed Berlin's lead, and several of the existing universities became distinguished for their development of research techniques and the promotion of scientific studies. These older institutions, however, were by tradition oriented to scholarship for the sake of knowing, and gave little thought to the practical application of their discoveries, a tendency which led to the sharp distinction academicians make between the pure and the applied sciences even to this day. In Prussia, as elsewhere, industry and commerce were forced to develop special institutions committed to translating scientific knowledge into practical operations. Most of these were fostered, not by the Ministry of Education, but by other branches of government.

Among the first trade or industrial schools developed were the *Gewerbschulen,* each as a rule preparing boys to enter but a single trade or industry. The new institutions received boys from the *Volksschulen* and gave them a foundation of scientific knowledge before turning them over to the guilds for practical training. Thus apprenticeship training was not eliminated, but was shortened substantially.

A more theoretical type of vocational education was made available in *Fachschulen.* These were technical schools, each offering basic preparation for one field, or *Fach,* such as agriculture, architecture, forestry, mining, or the postal service.

Since the basic sciences upon which the several technical fields depended were often identical, more advanced schools were formed by combining several *Fachschulen.* In this manner *Polytechnicums* were established in various places. By mid-century, technical and scientific training was becoming so academic, and its foundations so theoretical, that in many respects it could stand on the same level as the instruction offered in the universities. In some of the more aggressive commercial and industrial centers, the municipal authorities took the lead in transforming their *Polytechnicums* into *technische Hochschulen,* or technical universities. In some neighboring German states, these institutions prepared teachers of mathematics and science for secondary schools, including the *Gymnasien,* but Prussia was slow to follow this example. Indeed, for a time Prussia even insisted upon the maturity certificate for admission to the technical universities, thereby making certain that the lower classes could not gain admission to the leader class by way of an unguarded door.

The two-class system of education represented by the *Vorschulen-Gymnasien-Universitäten,* on the one side, and the *Volksschulen-Lehrerseminaren,* on the other, obviously could be maintained only as long as the population was willing to remain neatly divided into an upper and a lower class. In general, bifurcated societies of this type have continued to exist only in agricultural economies where status is determined by landownership. These conditions prevailed in Prussia well into the eighteenth century, and even longer in the eastern provinces, the stronghold of the *Junkers.* But commerce and industry were making significant inroads by the middle of the nineteenth century. The numerous municipal secondary schools, as many as 400 prior to 1800, had been evidence of the growing social importance of the rising middle class; and the regulations of 1812 and 1834, depriving the vast majority of these schools of the privilege of sending their students on to the institutions of higher education, had been bitterly resented. By

1834 the proponents of the municipal schools secured official recognition of two additional types of secondary schools. One of these, continuing to be known as the *Realschule* type, was allowed to offer a six-year course without Latin. At the outset this was looked upon as a terminal program. The second type, however, was allowed to develop a nine-year program which included Latin, and paralleled the program of the *Gymnasien* in nearly every way except for the omission of instruction in Greek. Now as the higher technical schools developed and acquired status, these nine-year schools changed their name to *Realgymnasien* and began the long struggle to win the right to send their students to the higher technical schools.

Meanwhile the philosophical faculties in the universities also were expanding their programs to include more instruction in modern languages, mathematics, and the sciences. Friends of the *Realgymnasien* were quick to point out that a knowledge of the classical languages, particularly Greek, was not necessary to study these subjects, and requested that the maturity examinations be changed to admit students from *Realgymnasien* as well as those from the *Gymnasien.* However, the reactionary groups in control of the Ministry of Education at mid-century would have none of this, and in general were as contemptuous of the graduates of the *Realgymnasien* as of those of the *Realschulen.* This attitude gradually softened during the second half of the century.

Secondary education for girls has scarcely been mentioned for the simple reason that girls were expressly excluded from the *Gymnasien* and *Realschulen* as well as from the universities.

Indeed, the sexes were separated even in the *Volksschulen* except in places so small that only a mixed school could be maintained. As the nineteenth century progressed, special schools of the *Mittelschule* type were provided here and there for girls; and more advanced schools offering instruction in the scientific fields as well as in modern foreign languages were established. All of these were under local or private sponsorship, and each therefore reflected those aspects of secondary education which the sponsors thought would enhance the female personality and lend grace to the higher-class household. Such schools generally were known as *Mädchenschulen, Mädchensekundarschulen,* or *höhere Tochterschulen.* Not until the late years of the nineteenth century did they seek to duplicate the classical studies of the *Gymnasien* and to demand admission to the universities for their students. Prussia, however, was not among the first of the German states to yield to such persuasion.

In reviewing the Prussian schools, one must remember that most of the institutional forms used in Prussia were borrowed outright or adapted from forms developed elsewhere. Even the *Volksschulen,* for which Prussia received world renown, had been inspired by the Pestalozzian experiments in Switzerland; and the University of Berlin, which set a new mode in higher education, had been preceded by the private pioneering work of Francke and Hecker. The Prussian government did achieve complete coordination of education through the administrative authority of the Ministry of Education; but even in this aspect Prussia had been preceded by the government of France. Prussia set an educational pattern primarily because she

was the first European state to establish civil control over education. From 1850 on, all aspects of Prussian education were part of a national school system and under the effective control of the crown.

Educational opportunities

The opportunities afforded by an educational system are not necessarily determined by the number of institutional types and the variety of programs found in the system. Opportunities are more likely to depend upon how accessible the facilities are to all segments of the population and upon whose purposes, the individual's or the school's, are served. In Prussia the question of how much opportunity a given school afforded was related directly to whether or not the school offered instruction in Latin and whether or not its students could qualify to limit their active military duty to one year.

The study of Latin had acquired the status of a privilege during the times when the church was the principal educational agency. Later, Latin retained this privileged status in the community of scholars as the universities emerged, and it continued to be the primary language used in university studies to the nineteenth century. Therefore, the major emphasis in the maturity examinations introduced by the Prussian Ministry of Education in 1812 and 1834 was placed on Latin; and schools not permitted to send candidates to the examinations were not allowed to teach this subject. Latin studies, as offered in the accredited *Gymnasien,* became a status symbol. The right of municipal or other schools, either public or private, to offer Latin was pressed with considerable vigor by the middle classes, but was not clearly established until the end of the nineteenth century.

Meanwhile, the great mass of the Prussian people attended schools without Latin privileges. The *Volksschulen* were available virtually everywhere, and by 1871 illiteracy was no longer a problem among the recruits conscripted for military duty. Statistics based on military sources should not be interpreted too generously, however, for girls generally attended separate and somewhat inferior schools. Although the literacy rate in Prussia compared favorably with that in many non-Germanic states, it was not so high as that of several of her sister states which were not motivated by similar nationalistic ambitions.[4]

More significant evidence of the popular attitude toward the *Volksschulen* is found in the use of the term *Schulpflict* to designate the period of compulsory school attendance. Translated literally this term means a school obligation or duty, as distinguished from a privilege. This view is not surprising if one recalls the manner in which the state gradually diverted the schools from their original religious purposes and required them to serve the objectives of the ruling class. Even after the government had acquired sweeping authority in education it continued to require the people to establish and maintain *Volksschulen* without support from the royal treasury or a voice in their management.

As the nineteenth century progressed, the will of the royal government became ever more apparent in educational matters. Even the period of compulsory school attendance was determined without consulting the people. Since the vernacular schools had been established to serve religious ends, the ecclesiastical authorities decided that the purpose of the schools had been achieved when the children had been prepared for confirmation and had taken part in their first communion. Since confirmation generally took place at age twelve or thirteen, attendance at school came to be required by the government for all children between the ages of six and twelve. This was later extended to age fourteen; but prior to 1871 relatively few schools outside the larger cities offered the full eight-year course, and children enrolled in the *Volksschulen* almost invariably left as soon as they had been confirmed, regardless of age.

Rural children of twelve or thirteen or even younger had no difficulty finding employment as field workers. Expanding needs of the new industries created similar demands for young unskilled workers in the cities. As long as the *Volksschulen* represented the lowest status levels and children were required to attend them only if their parents could not enroll them in a higher status school, most children were glad to fulfill their "school duty" at an early age. The facts are that although about 90 per cent of the school-age population was enrolled in the *Volksschulen,* very few pupils continued their studies even in the trade and vocational schools when such became available. When some continuation schools were established in cities to help young workers upgrade their skill and earning power, a few enlightened municipalities required employers of boys under the age of sixteen to provide them opportunities

[4] Thomas Alexander, *The Prussian Elementary School,* Macmillan, New York, 1918, p. 43.

97

to attend such schools. These measures did not necessarily produce the hoped-for results, however, for the employers found it possible to employ children at the age of nine instead of twelve, as long as they attended school in the evenings and on Sundays.[5]

Children attending *Mittelschulen,* or even those who transferred from the *Volksschulen* to a higher elementary school, usually hoped to continue their studies beyond the legal school-leaving age. These schools charged a tuition fee slightly higher than that in the *Volksschulen,* and thus provided a measure of social distinction to those who were identified with them. The vocational and technical schools, as well as the teachers' seminaries, drew most of their students from these schools rather than from the *Volksschulen.* But as long as Latin was not offered, educational opportunities were definitely limited for those enrolled in the *Mittelschulen* and *Realschulen* as well as for those in the *Volksschulen.*

The second privilege dispensed by certain schools was the so-called *Einjährigerschein.* This was the much-coveted certificate entitling the holder to one year of military duty instead of the usual three. Discriminatory military privileges had originated in the times when most students were members of the clergy and therefore enjoyed exemption from military duty as well as other forms of state service. Exemptions had not created a particular problem as long as wars were waged by the aristocracy only and military service was regarded as a mark of social distinction. However, when universal military service was introduced in the eighteenth century the

suspicion grew that wealthy farmers and merchants were sending their sons to the municipal secondary schools to secure exemption from conscription. In Prussia this practice became so widespread that the government of Frederick William II instituted the *Abiturientenprüfung,* an examination for all students who were about to enter the *sekunda,* as the next to the last class in the Latin schools was called, to determine which were legitimately enrolled [6] and therefore entitled to the *Entlassungsschein,* or exemption certificate.

The reconstruction government was inclined to be less generous in dispensing military exemptions, however, particularly in view of the fact that Frederick William had allowed schools to conduct their own examinations and to award the certificates of exemption as they saw fit. A major purpose of the regulations of 1812 and 1834 instituting the maturity examinations, therefore, had been to close this academic door to suspected draft dodgers. Not only were steps taken to standardize the qualifying examinations, but all who qualified were still required to render military service for one year. However, the *Einjährigen,* or one-year recruits, could elect within limits both the time they chose to serve and the regiment to which they would be attached. And since only *Einjährigen* could become officers, this privilege became eagerly sought.

As in other matters, the reconstruction government was at first inclined to be liberal in dispensing the *Einjährigerscheine.* Initially distributed to all those who passed the special examination given at the close of the sixth year of

[5] Barnard, *op. cit.,* p. 97.

[6] Paulsen, *op. cit.,* vol. II, p. 96.

study in a secondary school, by mid-century it was limited to those who passed the regular maturity examination in one of the accredited *Gymnasien*. This harsh restrictive measure was bitterly resented by the more powerful segments of the middle classes, and by 1859 they succeeded in having their *Realgymnasien* officially recognized, and a modified form of the maturity examination introduced which also conveyed the privileges of the *Einjähriger*.

This close relationship between the privileges of the *Einjähriger* and study in a secondary school authorized to prepare for the maturity examinations indicates the extent to which the royal government and the *Junkers* employed education to serve their nationalistic ambitions. By controlling admissions to the maturity examinations they were able to perpetuate themselves in power and to keep the large majority of the population in a subordinate status. Thus, during the most reactionary period, only 115 *Gymnasien* screened and indoctrinated all who became doctors, lawyers, clergymen, administrative officials, professors, secondary school teachers, and officers of the army. For a time, admission even to the higher technical institutes and the *Fachschulen,* such as the one for forestry, was similarly restricted. As the nineteenth century progressed, however, the aspirations of the common people called for greater educational opportunities. Significantly, many of their efforts were focused merely upon acquiring the privileges of the *Einjähriger* and gaining admission to the maturity examinations, rather than upon the development of new programs. Subsequent German history may have been determined to some degree by this attitude.

Subsequent developments

In 1871 Prussia, under the crafty direction of Bismarck, brought about the union of German states which endured as the German Empire until 1918. Because Bismarck feared Austria and her ability to challenge Prussian domination he formed the empire without her. The king of Prussia became known as the "Emperor in Germany," and Prussia exercised the controlling voice in all imperial matters.

While the emperor, or *Kaiser,* asserted his authority as a divine right, he wisely allowed the several states to handle most internal matters, including education. Thus few highly centralized forms of control were developed, and as long as the emperor and his Prussian *Junkers* could control the military forces and have a free hand in foreign affairs, they seldom directed themselves to the daily activities of the people.

Education had reached a high level in each of the member states before the empire was formed. Common origins, language, and other cultural forces such as religion had influenced educational developments. Therefore, similar institutional forms, often bearing the same names, were found throughout the empire, and the earlier religious interest in vernacular instruction had produced a high state of literacy everywhere. The same interest had led to the establishment of some form of administrative agency, usually a ministry for religion and education, in each state which directed and controlled educational activities. In spite of the official policy of decentralized administration, however, certain educational problems affected all parts of the empire and therefore called for coordinated action. Training doctors to fill the needs of the imperial army and maintaining a uniform basis for admission to the officer corps are two examples. Since the Prussian tradition connected such problems with school-leaving examinations and attendance at official "maturity" schools, these also became matters for coordinated empire-wide action.

Several educational conferences were convened, late in the nineteenth century, from which the so-called school reforms of 1892 and 1901 were derived. They defined three parallel types of secondary schools, each with a nine-year course of study. Each was authorized to prepare candidates for new maturity examinations modified to fit the several purposes. However, the courses of study differed chiefly with respect to which languages were offered and how much time was given to mathematics and science. Thus the *Gymnasien* required both Latin and Greek; the *Realgymnasien*, Latin and two modern foreign languages; and the elongated *Realschulen*, now known as the *Oberrealschulen*, required modern languages only but with compensating emphasis on mathematics and science. These three types have been preserved in German secondary education to this day in the so-called "ancient-language," "modern-language," and "mathematical-scientific" curricula, as shown in Figure 11.

Finally, it was recognized that many more students were seeking admission to the nine-year schools than could expect to finish. To relieve overcrowding, and possibly to give some satisfaction to municipalities and other sponsoring agencies whose schools previously were left off the list of accredited institutions, an abbreviated form of each

of the three types was authorized to offer the first six years of the official courses of study. These abbreviated schools were known as *Progymnasien, Realprogymnasien,* and *Realschulen* or *höhere Bürgerschulen*. Students who finished the studies provided in these six-year schools could complete preparation for one of the maturity examinations by transferring with advanced standing to the appropriate nine-year school.

Although different types of maturity examinations were required to accommodate the three nine-year institutions, the examinations were declared to be of equal status. However, not all university faculties were willing to accept students who came without the traditional preparation in one or more of the ancient languages. Medical faculties, which were under the jurisdiction of the empire, refused to accept students from the *Oberrealschulen* because they felt a knowledge of Latin was necessary. Faculties of theology throughout the empire seem to have been most insistent on competency in both Latin and Greek, and to have accepted students from the *Gymnasien* only. Faculties of philosophy, on the other hand, seem to have accepted students from all three types of institutions, although those from the *Oberrealschulen* were allowed to study mathematics and science only. Nevertheless, this relaxation of standards made it possible for students from any of the nine-year schools to qualify for teaching assignments in secondary schools.

The years immediately preceding World War I also witnessed a substantial expansion of educational opportunities for women. By 1900, there were a few *Gymnasien* for girls as well as schools of a new type known as the

Lyzeums. The development of these institutions, coupled with a shortage of trained male teachers, persuaded the school officials to introduce a higher teachers' examination for women, and to certify those who passed for appointment in secondary schools. Ultimately a few universities, notably Munich, admitted women to certain lectures. In the more liberal states, girls were admitted to the maturity examinations and were accepted as regular students in certain faculties of the universities. In some places, however, women were admitted as auditors only.

The different attitudes taken by the several states with regard to the education of women suggest that similar variations existed in their attitudes to social-class differences. Indeed, before the empire was brought to an end, openly democratic trends were apparent in several states. In general, these developments provided for a common elementary education for all children, during their first years of schooling, in what was called a *Grundschule.* At the conclusion of this "foundation" education, provision was made for differentiated instruction in middle and secondary schools fully articulated with the *Grundschulen.* This type of integrated system, it may be recalled, had been suggested by Süvern in 1817. Similar trends toward integration appeared in secondary education in programs that combined the elements common to the first years of the *Gymnasien, Realgymnasien,* and *Oberrealschulen.* From such efforts there emerged a type of secondary school known as the *Reformgymnasium,* sometimes called a "comprehensive" school in Europe today. But the efforts toward integration and the elimination of class discrimination, on either the elementary

or the secondary level, were very limited. Particularly troublesome was the fact that the *Grundschulen* and even the *Mittelschulen* did not offer Latin; this deficiency, it was felt, made them unfit to prepare pupils for later association in the secondary schools with children who had had a more discriminating background. Similarly, very little was done to eliminate the financial barriers that kept children from working-class families out of the secondary schools.

The Weimar Republic

The defeat of Germany and her allies in World War I forced the termination of the monarchy, the expulsion of the royal family, and the end of *Junker* domination in internal affairs. The Weimar Constitution, approved in 1918, provided for a federation of the several states in the form of a republic. Education was to be a cooperative activity in which the federal government, the several states, and the municipalities shared responsibility and control. Liberal political forces, encouraged by the West, favored rather sweeping educational reforms. Thus the dual system of elementary schools was outlawed, the selective, private *Vorschulen* were abolished, and a four-year elementary education was introduced for all children in the *Grundschulen.* There was even some talk of a common education to the age of twelve, but this rather drastic proposal failed to win major support. Regulations were approved, however, relating to freedom of conscience and making religious education an optional subject, for both the teacher and the pupil. Public and private agencies were allowed to deal with the religious issue as they chose. Denominational schools, interdenominational schools, and secular schools were permitted. The Constitution provided further that education should be compulsory in full-time schools for all children from age six to fourteen; and on a part-time basis in continuation schools from age fourteen to eighteen unless the student was enrolled on a full-time basis.

In addition to establishing *Grundschulen* as the universal form of elementary schools, the Constitution militated against the discrimination formerly experienced by teachers in the elementary school system. The teachers' seminaries, which had in reality been higher vocational schools, were now reorganized as institutions of higher education. A maturity certificate was required for admission. Elementary teachers thereby acquired the privileges formerly reserved to the graduates of the secondary schools, including the right to study at a university. Indeed, in several states elementary teacher education became an integral part of the university program, although the usual practice was to enroll the students in universities for the academic part of their training and in separate but connected institutes for their pedagogical training.

Administrative control over education, both public and private, was relegated to the individual states. Nevertheless, there was strong feeling that some coordinated effort was required to provide a common loyalty to the national ideal. A federal agency was established to promote such coordination through consultation. At the outset, voluntary coordination was greeted with high hopes, for it was expected that the federal government would cooperate with the states and municipalities in providing financial support. When it became clear that the federal government could not

contribute funds for education, the individual states fell back on their own resources and each went its own way.

The one lasting administrative reform was that professionally trained state officials now replaced the local clergy as school inspectors. Because of their previous training and teaching experience the new school inspectors were able to promote cooperative efforts to bring about improvements from within. Coupled with this was a substantial relaxation of centralized control. In secondary education, particularly, local lay committees, guided by frequent conferences with the teachers and school inspectors, were encouraged to take the leadership. Hence many variations developed from community to community, not only in the programs of study, but also with respect to educational opportunities.

Two new types of secondary schools, the *Deutsche Oberschule* and the *Aufbauschule,* developed from such local efforts. They did not replace, but rather complemented the older *Oberrealschulen, Realgymnasien,* and *Gymnasien.* They reached further into the middle and lower social classes for their students and gave greater attention to the so-called "modern" subjects. The *Deutsche Oberschule* offered a nine-year program leading to a maturity examination. Initially, it offered instruction in German only, but when the universities refused to accept its students, the program was expanded to include two modern foreign languages. It differed very little from the *Oberrealschulen* except with respect to the amount of time given to languages.

The *Aufbauschulen* became especially popular in smaller communities which could afford only limited facilities for secondary education. Unlike the other types which admitted pupils from the *Grundschulen* after their third or fourth year, the *Aufbauschule* admitted pupils from the regular elementary and *Mittelschulen* at the end of the sixth year or at about age thirteen. Since these schools also prepared for a maturity examination, their six-year program placed great emphasis on foreign languages and other modern subjects.

A further liberal trend was noted in the various examinations that regulated progression from one level of study to the next. The two used most frequently were those which regulated admissions to the secondary schools from the *Grundschulen* and the maturity examinations which controlled admissions to the universities. Significantly, the examinations were taken out of the hands of the admitting institutions and placed in the hands of the preparing institutions. Thus, although the principal of a secondary school continued to determine how many pupils he would admit and what other qualifications he would require, the *Grundschule* teachers now decided if the applicants had the necessary academic ability and preparation. Similarly, the secondary schools and not the universities now decided upon both the content and the marking standards used in maturity examinations. As time went on considerable friction developed between the universities and secondary schools on this subject, with the latter accusing the former of being far too conservative and theoretical for the good of the nation.

The Nazi period

Liberal as the educational developments under the Weimar Republic appeared when compared with the situation during the empire, they were not genuinely popular with the people as a whole. Long accustomed to rigid controls and thoroughly indoctrinated in the *Volksschulen* as to their duty to the German nation, many of the working-class people were uncomfortable under the relaxed conditions provided by the republic. Furthermore, the people had not lost their fear of the *Junkers* or given up their belief that a powerful military machine was the foundation of a successful government. Even substantial segments of the teaching corps longed for the days of order and certainty which the empire had provided. Thus when Adolf Hitler went about organizing mobs of unemployed and discontented youths into militarylike units for the restoration of the ancient German traditions, the *Junkers,* royalists, wealthy commercial families, and many other segments of the old privileged classes quickly came to his assistance. They encountered little resistance from the working classes. In 1933 the Nazis took control in Germany and wiped out the Weimar achievements.

Under Nazi control, a centralized form of government was introduced for the first and only time in German history. The old state governments were almost completely eliminated. Education was made a national function, and a unified system of schools was introduced extending from the kindergartens through the universities. The twin doctrines of the superiority of the Aryan race and the mystical brotherhood of all persons of German blood called for the elimination of social class differences. Secondary schools were singled out as the training schools for leaders in the new order and the curricula were thoroughly reorganized to serve this end.

The Nazi educational program stressed the doctrines of race, German supremacy, and the need to punish those responsible for "the crime committed against the German people" by the Treaty of Versailles and the Weimar Constitution. Germans were indoctrinated in the need for total national mobilization and the infallibility of the Nazi leadership. German history and geography, with strong propagandistic overtones, became major school subjects. Latin and Greek were greatly restricted. English was made the chief foreign language. The school day was substantially reduced to provide time for various Nazi party activities. Physical education programs clearly anticipated military duty. In brief, education became a major instrument for converting Germany into a war machine. Within six years her armies were on the march.

After World War II

After 1945 Germany again found herself crushed militarily, crippled economically, and under foreign political control. The terms of the occupation agreement worked out by the four major Western powers called for four separate administrative regions. Elaborate efforts were made to eliminate Nazi power and ideology. A long reconstruction period was projected in order that the democratic tendencies, apparent in the Weimar period, might be nurtured and developed into a competent and successful political force.

The occupying powers proceeded to implement these objectives in their respective zones, each in its own way. From the outset each made a determined effort to rid the various public offices and positions of influence of any proven Nazis. Teachers were particularly suspect, in view of the lengths to

which the Nazis had gone to control the schools, and the recruiting of politically safe teachers became a task of major proportions. Schoolbooks needed to be rewritten, and new courses of study introduced. The extensive damage to school buildings created a housing problem; and the near-starvation diet of many children called for mass feeding programs which could only be provided by the occupying forces.

Almost immediately, differences between Russia and the Western occupation powers divided Germany into two parts, with separate governments arising in each. In East Germany the educational institutions, though continuing to bear the familiar German names, tend to resemble the Communist institutions described in Chapter 7. Meanwhile, the regions formerly governed by England, France, and the United States have been organized as the German Federal Republic and have developed a form of government based upon democratic principles. The following observations relate to this, the Western portion of postwar Germany.

In Western Germany, education has been returned to the several constituent states. As in the Weimar Republic there is no federal administrative agency for education, but the Permanent Conference of Ministers of Education serves as the medium for communication and mutual consultation among states. Matters agreed upon unanimously by this agency are urged by the member ministers upon their respective governments with a view to having them enacted as law. The federal government provides some financial aid to the states, particularly in the areas of science and technology.

In 1947 the Allied Control Council in its Directive No. 54 issued general

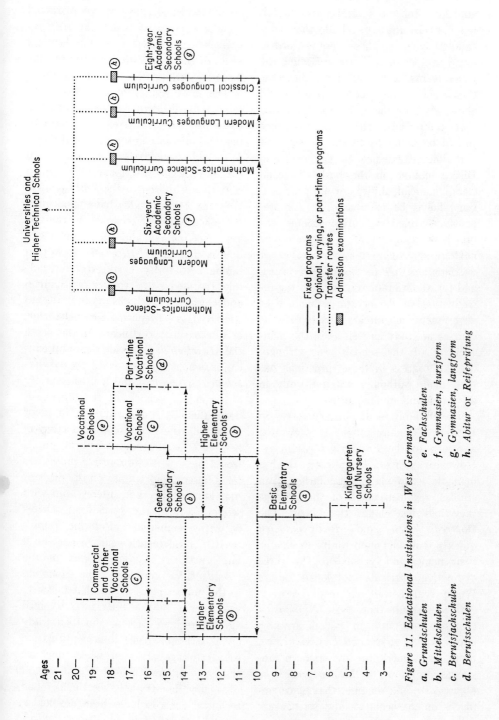

Figure 11. Educational Institutions in West Germany

a. *Grundschulen*

b. *Mittelschulen*

c. *Berufsfachschulen*

d. *Berufsschulen*

e. *Fachschulen*

f. *Gymnasien, kurzform*

g. *Gymnasien, langform*

h. *Abitur or Reifeprüfung*

105

guidelines for the several states to follow in their efforts to rebuild their educational systems. These were not orders but directions or goals toward which the governments were urged to move as their resources and public support would allow. Among these, it was proposed that compulsory full-time attendance should be extended to age fifteen, and part-time attendance to age eighteen. Discrimination on the basis of social class, financial ability, or future vocation should be eliminated. A comprehensive, unified system of schools was urged, with one level leading to the next rather than running parallel or overlapping. Free textbooks were urged, and the abolition of tuition fees; the introduction of democratic principles of government as integral parts of the courses of study as well as in the management of the schools was strongly urged. Progress in these directions has been made, although not uniformly in all states and municipalities.

The prohibition of military forces in Western Germany obviously prevented a return to the *Einjähriger* privileges. However, as Figure 11 indicates, the humanistic curricula, particularly Latin studies, regained much of the prestige they had lost under the Nazis. The *Oberrealschulen* and *Realgymnasien* quickly took this opportunity to change their names to *Gymnasien*. The three distinctive curricula developed before World War I were retained, however, with the result that those *Gymnasien* that featured Latin and Greek are now known as the *altsprachliche Gymnasien,* those featuring Latin and modern languages are known as the *neusprachliche Gymnasien,* and the ones that place emphasis on mathematics and science are called the *mathematischnaturwissenschaftliche Gymnasien.* Comprehensive

secondary schools have not yet attracted popular support, although the *Aufbauschulen* which offer only the last six years of the preparatory studies for the maturity examination are increasing.

The most significant development is related to the *Mittelschulen.* Formerly these had been relatively few in number, had offered no privileges, and therefore had been patronized by social classes only slightly above those which sent their children to the *Volksschulen.* Now the *Mittelschulen* have taken over the place formerly occupied by the six-year *Realschulen* and their pupils can qualify for the *Mittlere Reife,* a preliminary maturity certificate that admits the holder to a variety of technical and vocational schools as well as to special classes preparing for the *Abitur,* or full maturity certificate. In this sense the *Mittelschulen* provide a general education which connects with the *Grundschulen* at one end and a broad variety of secondary schools at the other. Indeed, there is some sentiment in favor of making the *Mittelschulen* a comprehensive school through which all pupils would pass, with appropriate provisions for differentiated studies on the basis of individual ability and interest, but with separation into the specialized schools occurring sometime after the pupil's twelfth or thirteenth year. At present, a large majority of the pupils in the *Grundschulen* continue their education in the "upper classes" of what formerly was known as the *Volksschulen,* until age fourteen or fifteen, and then study on a part-time basis in a continuation school to age eighteen while they are employed or are learning a trade.

Meanwhile trade, vocational, and technical schools have been developed, greatly expanded in number and kind, and articulated more directly with the elementary and middle schools. These schools are graded with respect to the preparation they require for admission and the level of competency for which they train. The lower schools also are directly connected with the trades and constitute an integral part of the apprenticeship training which is supervised in cooperation with the trade unions. A student may progress from a school on one level to another on a higher level; and the *Fachschulen,* or higher technical schools, sometimes send students to a university. This is becoming more frequent as adult classes, duplicating on a part-time basis the instruction in the *Gymnasien,* are introduced to enable interested persons to prepare for the maturity examinations.

The trend in West Germany to an integrated, unified educational system in each of the member states is marked by the return to the four-year *Grundschulen,* introduced in the Weimar Republic, which all children must attend, and the considerable progress that has been made to extend this period of common instruction to six years or even longer. The class differences formerly cultivated by the selective secondary schools have been substantially reduced by making admission easier and by extending many of their advantages to the *Mittel* and vocational schools. The *Gymnasien* no longer have a monopoly in preparing candidates for the *Abitur* or maturity examinations. Admission requirements for universities and other institutions of higher education have been relaxed, particularly with respect to the proficiency required in Latin. An element of mobility has been introduced into the educational system, and with it, a corresponding degree of social mobility. How long or how far this trend will continue remains to be seen.

References

Books

Alexander, Thomas: *The Prussian Elementary Schools,* Macmillan, New York, 1918.

———— and Beryl Parker: *The New Education in the German Republic,* John Day, New York, 1929.

Becker, Carl: *Secondary Education and Teacher Training in Germany,* Teachers College, Columbia University, New York, 1931.

Becker, H.: *German Youth: Bond or Free,* Oxford, Fair Lawn, N.J., 1946.

Engelmann, S. C.: *German Education and Re-education,* International Press, New York, 1945.

Fletcher, Arthur W.: *Education in Germany,* Heffer, Cambridge, England, 1934.

Good, H. G.: "National Trends in German Education," *A History of Western Education,* 2d ed., Macmillan, New York, 1960, chap. 14.

Heiden, K.: *A History of National Socialism,* Knopf, New York, 1935.

Huebener, Theodore: *The Schools of West Germany,* New York University Press, New York, 1962.

Hylla, Erich J., and Frederich O. Kegel: *Education in Germany,* Institute for Studies in International Education, Frankfurt-am-Main, 1958.

Kandel, I. L.: *The Making of Nazis,* Teachers College, Columbia University, New York, 1935.

Kneller, George F.: *The Educational Philosophy of National Socialism,* Yale, New Haven, Conn., 1941.

Learned, W. S.: *The Oberlehrer: A Study of the Social and Professional Evolution of the German Schoolmaster,* Harvard, Cambridge, Mass., 1914.

Lexis, W. H.: *A General View of the History and Organization of Public Education in the German Empire,* translated by G. J. Tamson, A. Ascher, Berlin, 1904.

Meyer, Adolph E.: *The Development of Education in the Twentieth Century,* 2d ed., Prentice-Hall, Englewood Cliffs, N.J., 1949, pp. 226–274.

Paulsen, Friedrich: *German Education: Past and Present,* translated by T. Lorenz, Scribner, New York, 1908.

———: *The German Universities,* translated by Edward Delavan Perry, Macmillan, New York, 1895.

———: *Geschichte des Gelehrten Unterrichts,* 2 vols., Verlag von Veit, Leipzig, 1919, vol. I; Walter de Gruyer, Berlin, 1921, vol. II.

Pilgert, Henry P.: *The West German Educational System,* U.S. High Commissioner for Germany, Frankfurt-am-Main, 1953.

Richter, W.: *Re-educating Germany,* The University of Chicago Press, Chicago, 1945.

Samuel, R. H., and Thomas R. Hinton: *Education and Society in Modern Germany,* Routledge, London, 1949.

Shirer, William L.: *The Rise and Fall of the Third Reich,* Simon and Schuster, New York, 1960.

Stahl, Walter (ed.): *Education for Democracy,* Frederick A. Praeger, Inc., New York, 1961.

Wells, Roger Hewes: *The States in West German Federalism,* Bookman Associates, New York, 1961.

Wilke, Reinhard: *The Volkshochschulen in the Federal Republic of Germany and West Berlin,* Association of German Universities, Frankfurt-am-Main, n.d.

Pamphlets and periodicals

Bodenman, Paul: *Education in the Soviet Zone of Germany,* U.S. Office of Education Bulletin 1959, no. 26, 1959.

———: "Secondary School Mathematics in the Federal Republic of Ger-

many," *The Mathematics Teacher,* vol. 52, pp. 465–470, October, 1959.

Conant, Grace Richards: "West German Education in Transition: German Textbooks and the Nazi Past," *Saturday Review,* vol. 46, no. 29, pp. 52–53, July 20, 1963.

Friedeberg, Ludwig von: "West Germany," *Review of Educational Research,* vol. 32, pp. 308–319, June, 1962.

Henderson, James L.; "Education in Modern Germany: An Appraisal," *Educational Forum,* vol. 21, pp. 315–326, March, 1957.

Hofman, Erich: "The Changing School in East Germany," *Comparative Education Review,* vol. 6, pp. 48–57, June, 1962.

Hofmann, Helmut: "School Psychology in Germany," *Comparative Education Review,* vol. 3, pp. 23–26, June, 1959.

Huebener, Theodore: "Proposed Reforms in the German Schools," *Comparative Education Review,* vol. 6, pp. 44–47, June, 1962.

———: "The Schools of West Germany," *Journal of Educational Sociology,* vol. 35, pp. 264–267, February, 1962.

Kirkpatrick, Ursula: "The *Rahmenplan* for West German School Reform," *Comparative Education Review,* vol. 4, pp. 18–25, June, 1960.

Lindergen, Aline: *Education in Germany,* U.S. Office of Education Bulletin 1938, no. 15, 1939.

———: *Germany Revisited: Education in the Federal Republic,* U.S. Office of Education Bulletin 1957, no. 12, 1957.

Plant, Richard: "West German Education in Transition: Schools at the Crossroads," *Saturday Review,* vol. 46, no. 29, pp. 49–51, 62–63, July 20, 1963.

Report of the Special Study Mission to Germany and Certain Other Countries, Committee on Foreign Affairs,

U.S. House of Representatives, 1952.

Ringkamp, Brother Henry: "Impressions of the German School System," *Journal of Secondary Education,* vol. 37, pp. 209–215, April, 1962.

Scanlon, David G.: "Some Comparative Reflections on German and Italian School Reforms," *Comparative Education Review,* vol. 4, pp. 31–34, June, 1960.

Smart, K. F.: "Education in East Germany," *Educational Forum,* vol. 25, pp. 463–471, May, 1961.

Snyder, Harold, and George Beauchamp: *An Experiment in International Cultural Relations,* American Council on Education, Washington, D.C., 1951.

Strevell, Wallace H.: "Centralized Control Handicaps German Schools Today," *The Nations Schools,* vol. 50, pp. 52–56, September, 1952.

CHAPTER 5

French Education: Developing an

Intellectual Elite

For many years French culture, education, and language were eagerly sought by peoples in many parts of the world. More recently this has been especially apparent among nations anxious to attain status in the eyes of Europeans. The reputation of France was established in philosophy, literature, art, and even in commerce and industry by the creative talents of citizens whose names are remembered with great respect. And while her empire has been all but liquidated, her language and her distinctive educational pattern are still in use on virtually every continent of the world.

France owes her beginnings as an integrated political unit to the colonizing efforts of ancient Rome. Her lands comprised the territory of the Gauls who succumbed to the military might of Julius Caesar. From that time she has been associated with Rome through language and religion and sometimes through politics. Medieval French was a corruption of the language brought by the occupying Roman soldiers and Christian missionaries. Early French laws and forms of social control, especially in the south, were provided by the Roman Empire. Ultimately, when the Eternal City no longer possessed the vigor to head an empire, Charlemagne, King of the Franks, kept the peace and protected the Christian Church in the West. The seat of his empire and the nearby provinces provided much of the geographic and human materials out of which the great French nation and empire later were built.

On the basis of language modern France is classed with Italy, Portugal, and Spain as a Latin country. In regard to religion, she has never renounced irrevocably her ties with the Roman Church; and from this connection she derived her early forms of education. Yet French education today differs markedly from that of other Latin countries, and one must turn to philosophy and politics to find the spark of creative genius which set France off both from her Roman antecedents and her modern contemporaries.

From the fifteenth to the twentieth century

Although the territorial limits of modern France had not been fixed by the fifteenth century, the Capetian dynasty which reigned until the Revolution had already been established on the throne. Furthermore, the House of Capet wore the crown with the blessing of Rome, and its first sons ascended to the throne with full confidence that they were, indeed, "the Lord's anointed." With the passing of time France became an absolute monarchy. But the seeds of revolution had been sown long before the excesses of the court of Louis XVI provoked the mobs of Paris to storm the Bastille in 1789.

The first of these troublesome seeds was encased in the ancient practice of election. It was a survival of the manner in which the warriors of Gaul had chosen the one to lead them in battle.[1] Hugh Capet, the first of the line, had been *elected* king. The principle of election

[1] Albert L. Guerard, *France: A Modern History,* The University of Michigan Press, Ann Arbor, Mich., 1959, p. 81.

110

also had been employed in the selection of priests and in the appointment of bishops and other high-ranking officials of the Church. However, under the later Capetians the practice had been circumvented by both bishop and king. Under the monarchy, succession to the throne came to be determined by inheritance, a practice that was also imposed to a degree in the Church. Nevertheless, the tradition of election did not die even in the times when the doctrine of the divine authority of kings was asserted most vigorously. It came to light again when the people rose against the monarchy in 1789 and elected rulers of their own choosing.

A second seed of revolt was sown by Philip the Fair at the close of the thirteenth century. In a bitter struggle with the pope for supremacy, Philip had reduced the papacy to a state of subordination and had even transferred it from Rome to Avignon where it remained for more than seventy years. During this "Babylonian captivity" the Roman Catholic Church was in effect a French institution. The French clergy, although maintaining spiritual ties with the Holy See, were appointed by the powers residing in France. Even several centuries after the papacy had returned to Rome, it was still the king and not the cardinal who determined the official attitude of the French section of the Church toward the rising Protestants and toward many matters that were usually left to the clergy in other lands. Indeed, this strong nationalistic trend in ecclesiastical matters, which historians call "Gallicanism," had been asserted in the Pragmatic Sanction of Bourges in 1438, the Concordat of Francis I in 1516, and the Declaration of the Clergy in 1682.[2] To-

day, it is said that France has remained nominally Roman Catholic because she already enjoyed the control over the Church which England was able to achieve only by making a complete break with Rome.[3]

Yet it should not be concluded that the king had an entirely free hand in matters of church and state. Although Louis XI in the third quarter of the fifteenth century laid the foundation for the absolute monarchy by radically centralizing political power, the Parliament refused to acknowledge his order to abolish the Pragmatic Sanction, thereby foreshadowing a disposition of the people to take even religious matters in their own hands whenever they felt themselves pressed too severely.

The third seed was a philosophical one which contained explosive political and social potential. Beginning as early as the twelfth century, the infant University of Paris had sheltered a rational method of inquiry with which the masters and their students challenged both the theology and the social doctrines of the medieval theocratic state. This new movement, known as scholasticism, opposed blind faith in a revealed truth with a better truth derived by reasoning deductively from accepted authority. Although this meant that reason must be confined within the boundaries of revelation, doctrines derived therefrom had to stand the test of a rigorous logical examination even when the verdict conflicted with the dogmas derived from the inherited religious traditions. In spite of these limitations, scholasticism succeeded in opening the minds of scholars to the possibilities of new forms of truth and to new sources of materials on which the rational process might feed

[2] *Ibid.*, p. 115.

[3] *Ibid.*, p. 144.

in its search for such truth. In due time humanism and the Reformation emerged. In the resulting resurgence of intellectual inquiry, one made a new path in the area of secular affairs and the other led men to define new bases for faith.

By the eighteenth century still a different philosophical system, one based upon inductive methods of inquiry and asserting the infallibility of the disciplined intellect, superseded the others as the guiding philosophy in French public as well as private life. From this philosophical disposition, fundamentally an intellectual outlook, the typical French pattern of education was derived. Thus, the beginnings of her native form of education appeared while France was ruled as an absolute monarchy.

The absolute monarchy

From the tenth to the eighteenth century the seat of social control among the French gradually shifted from Rome to Paris. This transfer had been deliberately sought by the Capetian kings, and their prolonged efforts ultimately produced the absolute monarchy. The monarchy rested on the doctrine that God ruled France through the person of the lawful sovereign, a doctrine which the people seemed willing to accept even while France as a nation continued to maintain spiritual ties with Rome. But it was the king who spoke on all matters affecting the common welfare and appointed officers of the Church as well as of the state. The Church was expected to endorse his nominations and to bless those who came to exercise power in the name of the crown.

This is not to say that the kings ruled without opposition, for the shadows of

the hereditary electors lingered among the nobility and the clergy. Although the Capetians ruled without calling upon the electors to determine the succession and often made appointments to high ecclesiastical offices without consulting the clergy, the common people continued to select their own parish priests, and the lesser clergy to elevate their own bishops.

Perhaps the major contribution made by the Capetian monarchs to the French educational pattern was the principle of centralized administrative control. To establish the absolute power of the crown they had first to destroy the power of the feudal barons and landed clergy. This was achieved, in part, by means of shrewd marriages and political coups, in part through wars, but primarily by encouraging the development of a commercial and industrial middle class. The kings began to bypass the feudal lines of authority by appointing their own governors, tax collectors, and judges, who administered laws uniformly throughout the realm. These improvements were appreciated by the people who heretofore had been subject to the caprice of local overlords who ruled, judged, and taxed without written rules or laws to restrain them. In the minds of the people, the monarchy was able to provide order, justice, and personal well-being precisely *because it was highly centralized;* and when, in the eighteenth century, the monarchy failed them, they chose to replace it with another government that was equally centralized.

The Capetians enlisted the support of the people in other subtle ways. Councils and parliaments were convened from time to time to deliberate on matters of public interest. A few even met without royal consent. Since these deliberative bodies sometimes included representatives of the nobility, the clergy, and the commoners, and differences of opinion and clashes of interests were inevitable, the kings shrewdly played one faction against the others. By appointing Colbert, a member of the *bourgeoisie,* or middle class, to be his chief minister, Louis XIV, the apotheosis of absolutist rule in France, was able to keep the various economic, political, and religious factions in balance. Nevertheless, the growing class of commercial, industrial, and professional people, supported in part by the individualistic tendencies in Calvinist Protestantism, ultimately insisted upon being heard. The rising *bourgeoisie* was not content with accumulating personal wealth, but was interested in the improvement of man himself. Descartes, Rabelais, Rousseau, Montaigne, Voltaire, and others over a period of two centuries helped define a new concept of the relationship of man to man and of man to his Maker. In the end Frenchmen committed themselves to the ideals derived from humanism rather than from Roman Catholic or Protestant theologies, a development which had profound educational consequences.

The crown finally fell victim to its own excesses. A succession of kings who recognized no limits to their authority other than their own whims and political expediency ultimately violated the dignity and rights of the people beyond endurance. French blood and treasure were wasted in foreign wars which had no purpose other than to satisfy the vanity of the kings. At home members of the opposing Jansenists, Huguenots, and ultimately Jesuits as well, fell before the royal might. Ultimately, the monarchy was destroyed by the people who ˌhad helped it to attain power.

When it fell, so did the nobility and higher clergy who had been its chief supporters in its last days. Only the Gallicanism of the lower clergy and the loyalty of the people to their local priests saved Roman Catholicism from a similar fate.

During the monarchy, the medieval cathedral, collegiate, cloister, court, and guild and burgh schools continued to operate under the supervision of the Church. In the twelfth century a university corporation had been formed at Paris. The University of Paris remained the stronghold of scholasticism long after other philosophical doctrines had taken over in other places. By the fourteenth century, however, prominent members of the clergy, as well as influential members of the nobility and the wealthier commoners had become strongly attracted to humanism. By the sixteenth and seventeenth centuries this trend had developed broad secular interests. The curricula of important schools were reorganized to include the works of the ancient Greeks and Romans.

Parallel with the literary and philosophical reforms there was also a new religious trend. Protestantism, primarily Calvinism, made extensive inroads among the strongly individualistic and self-reliant commercial classes. Like Protestants elsewhere, the French Huguenots established their own schools. Vernacular reading schools were set up for the younger children. Grammar schools, called *collèges,* provided a curriculum of humanistic studies together with others relating to Calvinist theological doctrines. Finally, an occasional *académie,* or academy, was established to prepare young men more specifically in the principles of Calvinist theology, although opportunities to pursue some secular studies were also provided.

Protestant schools, particularly the vernacular reading schools, proved so inviting that they aroused serious opposition as the crown and the Roman Catholic hierarchy drew closer together. Then the Church acquired authority to supervise all education, and under these conditions, Protestant schools were harassed and repressed. Education suffered and the Church did not venture to replace the schools it forced to close. However, a number of new religious orders were founded for the purpose of sponsoring educational activities. Some were inspired by humanistic ideals, and developed curricula and methods of instruction along the inductive lines of philosophical inquiry set forth by Descartes. Most important among these were the schools of the Port Royalists. Several other orders, notably the Brothers of the Christian Schools, the Sisters of Notre Dame, and the Congregation of St. Charles, instructed children of the lower classes in vernacular reading, writing, arithmetic, and other practical matters in addition to religion. The Jesuits, of course, were active in the education of upper-class boys until they fell into disfavor with the Church and crown. The teaching order known as the Oratory of France enjoyed more favorable treatment. The Order of Ursulines, founded at the end of the sixteenth century, gave its attention to the education of girls. Evidence of its activities can be inferred from the fact that it opened a school in Quebec in 1639 and another in New Orleans in 1727.[4] Even Madam de Maintenon, the second wife of Louis

XIV, established Saint Cyr, a boarding school for upper-class girls, and the Order of Saint Augustine to carry on its work.

In general, however, the official attitude toward education was not constructive. No measures were taken to spread learning among the people and no proposals were seriously entertained to institute a system of public schools. Illiteracy, as a consequence, was higher in France than in the Protestant German states, Scandinavia, or Switzerland. The lot of the common Frenchman was not a happy one, and his resentment was fed by indignities visited upon him by an irresponsible and unsympathetic officialdom. Even the new Catholic orders which operated schools for the benefit of the poor suffered from the lack of ecclesiastical and royal approval.

Toward the end the French hierarchy were accused of trying to make the monarchy subservient to the papacy. Humanism and a resurgence of Gallicanism among the people had come too far to permit this. The people aspired to self-determination. When Louis XVI was identified as the chief obstacle to the realization of their hopes, they arose to destroy him together with all his retinue of supporters in the nobility, in the Church, and in public office.

The revolutionary government

The French Revolution is sometimes pictured as a spontaneous uprising beginning with the storming of the Bastille and continuing as a bloody class war until the royal house and those loyal to it had been destroyed. This obviously is an oversimplification; but whatever the contributing causes the revolutionary parties turned rather quickly to the

[4] Frederick Eby and Charles Flinn Arrowood, *The Development of Modern Education,* Prentice-Hall, Englewood Cliffs, N.J., 1951, p. 359.

ancient practice of electing persons to positions of authority. While this practice had been kept alive in the local parishes and among the lower clergy, the royal house had preempted the functions of the traditional electors. Nevertheless, kings sometimes had been forced to enlist the help of the rising middle classes to gain supremacy over the nobles and the higher clergy. The commoners—actually wealthy merchants, traders, and manufacturers—had thus acquired some importance and had come to constitute a "third estate." It was from the third estate that the inductive philosophy of Descartes received the strongest following. Joined by the lesser clergy and some disillusioned nobles, this new class of intellectuals brought about a philosophical revolution in the eighteenth century which is known as the Enlightenment. The essence of its system was absolute dependence upon the methods of inductive logic in the search for knowledge of the good. Armed with theories which had been worked out inductively, the men of the Enlightenment were ready to combat authority based upon the intuition of kings, the dictates of revelation, or the dogmas of theology. Thus the Enlightenment, which started out as a revolution in philosophy, was not content until it had precipitated a revolution in government and religion as well. In May of 1789 the third estate forced the king to convene the ancient institution of popular government, the States-General. This was the first time it had been convened since 1614 [5] and it was in session a full two months before fighting broke out in the streets of Paris.

The third estate was represented in the States-General of 1789 by as many delegates as the other two "estates," the

[5] Guerard, *op. cit.*, pp. 231–232.

nobles and the higher clergy, combined. Even the parish priests were represented; and in true Gallic tradition their delegation tended to side with the people rather than with the hierarchy. In the struggle for power that followed, the third estate developed a unity of action that made it the master of the other two. It forced the action that transformed the States-General into the National Assembly, declared the old monarchy to be ended, and established a constitutional form of government in its place.

Two innovations of current educational significance were introduced by the National Constituent Assembly. The first was the organization of territorial France into *departments*. A department was defined as a geographic region of such size that its chief city, or capital, could be reached from any part in a day's journey. Acceptance of the department as the administrative unit signified that the old provincial loyalties had been supplanted by loyalty to a unified national ideal. The citizens were now Frenchmen first, and not Bretons or Alsatians. The departmental organization has been retained through numerous changes of government and is an important unit in the administration of public education today.

The second innovation also reflected the new national spirit. It called for the abolition of church control and the nationalization of education through the establishment of a system of public schools under civil control. This action stemmed in part from the revolutionists' philosophical rejection of religious authority, but also from the suspicion that the hierarchy wished to reinstate the monarchy and would use the schools to achieve this end. A third consideration, though not a direct cause, was the enormous wealth possessed by the Roman Catholic Church. The revolutionary government expropriated the property of the Church, including the schools. Nevertheless, it used this property to provide for the parish priests, and then diverted the surplus to other public purposes. The third estate was not ready to give up its spiritual ties to the parish chapel, although it was willing to dispense with the hierarchical controls originating in Rome and to end the special privileges enjoyed by the higher clergy.

The sweeping educational reforms proposed by the revolutionary government were not realized during its short life. Neighboring monarchies were fearful that the revolutionary spirit and dreams of popular government might be contagious. The new France was soon embroiled in war and torn by mob actions within her own borders. Unprepared to deal with crises of such magnitude, the Assembly, amid a liberal amount of bloodshed, allowed control to shift rapidly from faction to faction, ultimately to be usurped by a popular military hero, Napoleon Bonaparte.

From the Consulate to the Third Republic

The Napoleonic ascent to power was in some ways a political accident. Unable to control the confused political situation, the National Assembly was stampeded by a small faction into permitting the Provisional Consulate, with Napoleon as the First Consul, to take its place.[6] Napoleon moved quickly from First Consul to Emperor, and from popular leader of the people of France to illusions of being the invincible conqueror

[6] *Ibid.*, p. 265.

116

of the whole world. However, even as Emperor, he never claimed divine authority to rule, and from the outset made elaborate arrangements to give the impression that his regime was directed by the will of the people. It is true that he paid little attention to the popular will after he felt secure in his office, but Frenchmen followed him to the end because they believed he was leading them toward their own dreams of self-determination. His political reforms, represented in particular by a new code of civil law, were worked out by highly qualified experts and gave assurances that the rights of individuals would be fully respected. Unfortunately, Napoleon as Emperor was not always willing to be governed by his own laws. By 1815 a combination of forces shattered his empire and banished him from Continental Europe. The Congress of Vienna disposed of the pieces.

From 1815 to the establishment of the Third Republic, Frenchmen suffered one political crisis after another. Confirmed in their belief that they would someday be the masters of their own fate, and loyal to the principle of centralized control, they could not agree on the political institutions by which their goals were to be achieved. In every new crisis, however, the people looked to Paris, rather than to local governments, for solutions. All reforms were attempted on a national basis.

Although the monarchy was restored after the fall of Napoleon, the people of France rose again in 1830 and installed a constitutional monarchy. Modeled in many ways after that of England, the new monarchy, under Louis Philippe, brought the middle class to a position of major influence in French political life. But in the long run, Louis

Philippe and his wealthy supporters proved too conservative, and again the government was tumbled by a popular uprising in Paris. This time the working people were not to be denied a voice in public affairs. The Second Republic, installed in 1848, duly provided for manhood suffrage. But again the National Assembly, sobered by the realities of political responsibility, moved far too slowly to satisfy the masses calling for swift revolution. Consequently, "the Napoleonic legend" led the people to open doors which allowed Louis Napoleon to become Napoleon III and to establish the Second Empire. This promised to be a peaceful and prosperous reign but it was cut short by the Franco-Prussian War of 1870. France emerged from this disastrous defeat as the Third Republic, also a highly centralized government but one based on popular consent.

The beginnings of public education

As was noted earlier, republican sentiments before Napoleon's rise had favored a system of free education under state control. Indeed, proposals for such a system, though never acted upon, had been placed before the National Assembly by Talleyrand, Condorcet, and Lakanal. Meanwhile, the generally hostile attitude toward the schools of the Church and the religious orders had brought a virtual halt to formal education. Yet no agreement on a plan for schools under civil control was reached until 1795, when the National Assembly was persuaded to enact the Law of Daunou.

In contrast to earlier proposals to make education available to all children, the Daunou law called for primary schools in the larger centers of population only. At the same time secondary schools known as *écoles centrales,* or central schools, were introduced—one in each department. These new schools were conceived along remarkably progressive lines, inspired in part by the philosophical ideas of Descartes, Diderot, and Condorcet. Their curriculum and the methods of instruction stressed the development of rational powers, although scientific studies occupied a prominent place also. They differed sharply from the humanistic institutions which emphasized the classical languages and literature. There were also a number of higher schools where selected individuals might study astronomy, medicine, and other scientific and technical subjects. A National Institute of Arts and Science was set up to carry on a systematic search for knowledge useful to the people in the conduct of their government and other practical pursuits. In the same vein a polytechnical school, a Conservatory of Arts and Trades, and under the influence of Lakanal, a National Normal School were established. This last institution was sorely needed because the few primary and central schools that were established had almost no competent teachers. Indeed, disappointment with these public schools was so great that the religious orders were permitted to reopen their schools even before the rise of Napoleon brought an end to the revotionary regime.

Napoleon was fully aware of the influence a system of national schools could exert and he showed great interest in education from the outset. However, he had little respect for primary education and permitted instruction on this level to remain in the hands of the religious orders and other private agencies. On the other hand, he was exceedingly suspicious of educational ties with a "foreign head," as he regarded the pope, and he made the parish clergy and the teachers in the religious orders virtual civil servants by providing them financial support and supervising their instructional activities. Although he wished to inculcate national loyalties and provide the people with a common language and culture, he nevertheless seemed unwilling to develop a system of primary schools that would produce these results.

Napoleon gave extensive assistance and encouragement to secondary education, but was suspicious of the existing universities because of their associations with the Roman hierarchy and their history of independent thought and action. He did found the Université Impériale, more familiarly known as the University of France. This was an agency to administer a national system of secondary schools, however, and not an institution of higher education. In this sense it was an antecedent of the present Ministry of Education.

The Imperial University was headed by a grand master appointed by Napoleon. At the grand master's side was an advisory council of thirty members, ten appointed by the emperor for life, and the others by the grand master. The grand master exercised control over all education. Thus, no school could operate without his approval, and all such authorizations were subject to review every year. For purposes of secondary and higher education, territorial France was divided into twenty-seven administrative districts, or "academies." This development had no relation to the earlier arrangement by which France had

been divided into departments, since the latter had to do with internal government rather than education, although the departments later became the units for the administration of primary education. Meanwhile, Napoleon ordered the closing of the universities and the few remaining central schools, and incorporated all the secondary schools (*lycées* and *collèges*), as well as the remnants of the universities, within the administrative framework of the Imperial University. There was to be at least one *lycée* in each academy. At the head of each academy was a rector appointed by the grand master and responsible directly to him. Each academy also had an advisory council, appointed by the grand master, to assist the rector. Finally, the grand master appointed a corps of inspectors who made personal visits to the individual schools and reported directly to the central administrative staff of the Imperial University.

Napoleon had also intended to establish various faculties of higher education as integral parts of the Imperial University. He stipulated that there should be a faculty of letters and a faculty of science in each of the academies. These, together with the five central faculties and the several imperial *lycées*, were to constitute a single integrated agency serving the entire empire. Indeed, when Napoleon took possession of the northern portions of Italy, he incorporated the Italian universities and the *ginnasios* within the Imperial University as well. But he never was willing, or able, to provide the financial resources needed to implement his grandiose plans, particularly with respect to higher education; and the number and scope of the operating units never became sufficient to fill out the skeleton of the projected Imperial University.

In spite of almost constant warfare, the rapid shifting of the boundaries of the empire, and the obvious failures to achieve all that had been planned, the Napoleonic contribution to French public education was substantial. The Imperial University provided the foundation not merely for a system of public secondary schools and universities, but also for the administration of all public education. Teachers were made directly responsible to the central government through their appointment by the grand master and were paid from the imperial treasury. They were even required to take an oath of loyalty. The normal school at Paris was developed to train all teachers for the secondary schools. To supplement the limited number of imperial *lycées*, municipalities were permitted to establish somewhat comparable institutions called *collèges*. Both types have persisted, with some modifications, until modern times.

Perhaps because Napoleon had risen to power on the shoulders of the relatively prosperous middle class, he never seemed able to bring himself to provide education without cost to the recipients. Primary education therefore remained in private hands, and it was kept separate from secondary and higher education even under Louis Philippe when the law of 1833 established a national system of elementary schools.

Ignoring secondary education except to change the name of the imperial *lycées* to royal *collèges*, the law of 1833 was directed to primary education. It called for the establishment of a primary school in every commune, although in exceptional cases, two or three communes were permitted to join together

for this purpose. Provision was also made for the establishment of higher primary schools in all the capitals of the departments and in communes of more than 6,000 population. Finally, a normal school for the training of primary school teachers was to be established in each department. These were to be of a lower order than the national normal school in Paris which trained teachers for the secondary schools.

The department was now made the basic unit for the administration of primary education. However, it was subdivided to achieve more effective control. The *arrondissement* was the resulting subunit, and committees were appointed on this level by the central government to implement national legislation and directives. In addition to various public officials in the *arrondissement*, the committee membership usually included representatives of the Church and the local religious orders. As agents of the central government they could dismiss subordinate officials who failed to perform their duties and could operate the local schools until more tractable officials could be installed.

Thus it is apparent that a rather well-defined national program of education and an elaborate centralized agency for its administration had been developed before the Third Republic was born. There were two distinct systems of schools, one for elementary education and another for secondary or higher education, each of which had evolved separately. Both systems had been brought under the direct control of a national ministry of education by Napoleon III, although each was administered by a separate branch of the ministry. Further segregation was achieved by ordering separate schools for boys and girls in all communes of 500 or more inhabitants. The Third Republic inherited that system and enjoyed only partial success in redirecting it to serve more democratic ends.

French education

Modern France is said to date from the founding of the Third Republic. It was created by the republican elements of the population after the Prussian army under Bismarck destroyed the Second Empire in 1870. Two other governments in republican form preceded it. All three suffered opposition from the monarchists who have consistently adhered to the theory of divine appointment and drawn their strength from among those who claim noble ancestry and from the hierarchy of the Roman Catholic Church. These two groups have demonstrated strong reactionary tendencies which at times have succeeded in limiting the voice of the people; both have appeared to seek the return of the absolute monarchy. Needless to say, they have not favored a liberal form of popular education.

The strength of the republicans has been in the middle classes. Their economic ideal has been a system of small landholdings owned by the individuals who till them, supplemented by an extensive system of small manufacturing establishments and the commercial enterprises needed to exchange the products of shop and farm in a manner beneficial to all. This middle-class outlook on life has emphasized individual freedom; yet the preferred instrument of government has been a representative assembly, elected by the people, exercising sovereign powers for the people.

Republicans have been no less committed to the ideal of a strong centralized government than the monarchists. Only the philosophical bases of such government have separated the two and, of course, the agency by which social policy, once determined, is to be put into effect.

Social role

The philosophical foundations of the Third Republic were laid during the Enlightenment. Rejecting the twin doctrines of divine appointment and private revelations, the rationalists turned to the methods of inductive logic as the only valid basis upon which to build the good society and the proper state. They favored representative government and secular control of the church. Bent on subordinating government to rational processes, they did not believe that the ability to reason was equal in all men or that the process of right thinking could be engaged in successfully by all. Republicans, therefore, were not disposed to accept the working classes as equals and, prior to the Third Republic, had favored restricting the right to vote to those who paid taxes. The revolutionary slogan of "Liberty, Equality, and Fraternity" was not meant for all Frenchmen.

Under the Third Republic the state *lycées* and university faculties were taken over to form the core of a system of secondary schools to locate and produce future leaders. Although the theory of inherited class status was rejected, the educational system was highly selective. It segregated children into two classes from the day they first entered school. Ultimately, suffrage was made universal—even women became eligible to vote after World War II—but the tuition fees in the secondary schools perpetuated a form of class discrimination.

The French school system reflected the selectivity that was also found in government and other areas of social life. The French people rested the powers of government in a representative national assembly made up of two chambers. One, the Chamber of Deputies, was elected directly by the people; the other, the Senate, by an electoral college. Both houses, sitting as one, were empowered to elect a president. The office of the president receded in importance over the years, and the executive duties were taken over by the chief among the cabinet of ministers, all of whom owed their appointments and tenure of office to the two chambers of the national assembly. In effect, therefore, the people were not self-governing, for they had delegated their sovereignty to elected deputies and electors—persons better qualified, in theory, to exercise the rational powers than were the ordinary citizens.

The selective process also became operative within the several political parties. Candidates for public office even today are not nominated by those residing in the election district, but are submitted to the voters of the district by the central party leadership. Voters therefore do not elect their own representatives but merely approve or disapprove the party whose prepared platform and slate of candidates are preferred.[7] No split-ticket voting is permitted, a restriction that enables party leaders to exert extensive control not only over the members of their parties,

[7] Daniel Wit, *Comparative Public Institutions*, Holt, New York, 1953, p. 209.

but also over their delegations in the national assembly.

The theory that government must be exercised by a selected group whose powers of judgment have been disciplined by a rigorous course of formal studies has made a substantial impression upon the French system of education. Persons not in this selected group —and they constitute the vast majority —have had to be content not only with lesser stations in life, but also with an educational fare designed to fit them to follow rather than to lead.

Power structure and administrative organization

The Third Republic, like its predecessors, favored a highly centralized government. Indeed, French political history had taught the French to expect their natural rights and personal liberties to be better protected by national than by local agencies. They were—and still are—prepared to pay taxes to an agent of the government in Paris and to let the local governmental agencies get along with whatever the national government is willing to give back to them. In fact, most local government officials are employees of the Ministry of the Interior without specific local loyalties or responsibilities. Hence, when the average Frenchman becomes annoyed by some minor local malfunctioning he is more likely to call for a change in the national government than to take his complaint to the mayor or the council of his commune.

Educational administration was closely coordinated with the activities of the Ministry of the Interior. The previously developed organization for civil administration whereby all of France was divided into successive levels called departments, *arrondissements,* cantons, and communes, was retained, as shown in Figure 12, and still exists today. The Ministry of the Interior is headed by a minister who has cabinet rank. He has a substantial staff of administrative assistants and clerks, most of whom are civil servants with tenure. The Min-

istry is represented in each department by a prefect who is appointed by and is responsible to the Ministry rather than to the inhabitants of the department. However, there is an elected council in each department with which the prefect may consult. The departments are further subdivided into *arrondissements* within each of which there is a

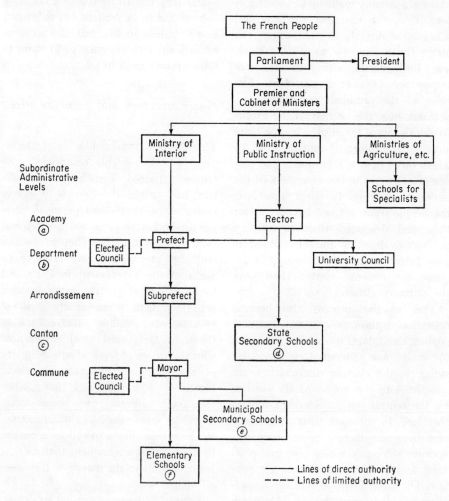

Figure 12. Lines of Educational Authority in France during the Third Republic
a. For university and secondary education only.
b. Elementary education primarily.
c. For consolidated elementary schools.
d. Lycées   *e. Collèges*   *f. Écoles primaires élémentaires*

subprefect. On the local level is the commune headed by the mayor. The mayor, too, is appointed by the Ministry and is an agent of the central government. That is, he carries out policies and executes directives made on the national rather than the local level. An elected council of the commune consults with the mayor to achieve some measure of accommodation of national policy to local wishes. Communes vary in size from small rural villages to large cities, but some of the largest, notably Paris, have special status. The canton, an administrative unit between the commune and *arrondissement,* is used chiefly for military purposes. Occasionally it serves as a centralized school district when the population is so small that effective schools cannot be maintained in the constituent communes. Cantons also serve as electoral districts in certain elections.

It can be seen from Figure 12 that during the Third Republic the lines of authority in civil matters ran from the people through the Parliament to the Ministry, and then down the administrative chain of command ending with the mayor of the commune. It may be inferred that the individual had little direct control over local government officials. The electorate could express its feelings only at the time of the national elections, but even then only to indicate which slate of candidates it preferred from among the slates offered by the leaders of the several political parties. The elected advisory committees on the commune and department levels have opened up more direct lines of communication in recent years, but neither mayor nor prefect is the agent of his council or responsible to it.

The lines of administrative authority

in education were made to run parallel to those of the Ministry of the Interior, and in the case of primary or elementary education, to be dependent on that Ministry for physical facilities and the enforcement of school laws. The Minister of Public Instruction has seldom been a professional educator and has remained in office only as long as the government of which he was a part continued to enjoy the confidence of Parliament. Until the formation of the de Gaulle government, such tenure of office had been brief, indeed, and the existence of a permanent staff under civil service appointments was all that kept the educational system from disintegrating.

The Ministry of Public Instruction was divided into separate administrative areas, each headed by a director. As shown in Figure 13, these areas were elementary education, secondary education, higher education, physical education, vocational education, fine arts, and accounts. The functions of the department of accounts recently have been broadened to include a variety of duties under the general label of administration. Each directorate was made responsible for implementing all aspects of educational policy in its area. This included the preparation and management of its budget; the preparation, certification, and appointment of the teachers; the location and inspection of the school buildings; the preparation of courses of study; the regular and detailed inspection of the work of each teacher; and the examination and promotion of each pupil, at least at the major points of transition from one level to the next.

Policy was to be formulated at the national level. Uniformity of administration of policy and quality of performance were to be guaranteed by staffs

123

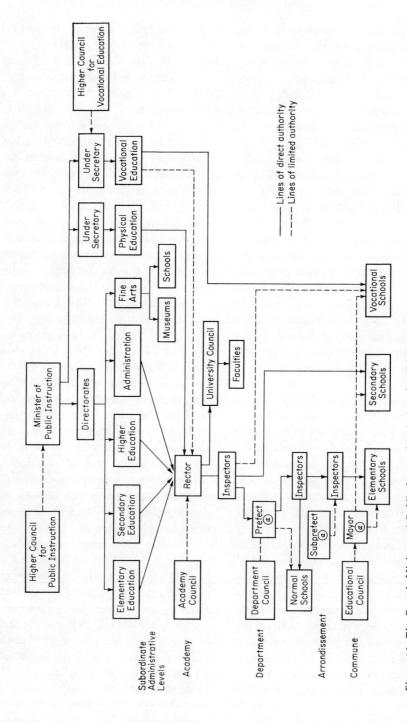

Figure 13. The French Ministry of Public Instruction during the Third Republic

a. Officials in the Department of Interior, but also responsible for administration of educational matters.

of inspectors responsible directly to the Ministry, and a system of external examinations administered nationally. Attached to the Ministry of Public Instruction was a Higher Council of Public Instruction made up of distinguished leaders and ambitious young politicians who were appointed either by the Minister or by a professional group. Thus the universities were represented by twenty-seven members, secondary schools by ten, and elementary schools by six. The Council had to be consulted on all policy matters affecting the curriculum, methods of instruction, examinations, textbooks, the supervision of private schools, and other matters relating directly to instruction. It also acted as a court of appeals in behalf of teachers, private groups, and others who felt themselves injured by actions of the Ministry or local officials. The Council was specifically created to place all education under the control of a highly intellectual leadership group.

The shadow of Napoleon's Imperial University remained over the secondary schools and higher faculties. Although separate directorates on the Ministry level were to look after secondary and higher education, their programs of study and manner of operation continued to be closely coordinated. The academy was retained as the administrative unit, immediately under the level of the Ministry, for both secondary and higher education, although the number of academies was reduced to seventeen. The rector remained as the key administrative officer for education in each academy. Not only was his office made responsible for the operation of the state *lycées,* but his staff of inspectors also supervised instruction in the municipal *collèges* and in all private secondary schools.

Higher education was left, for the greater part, to the separate and often geographically scattered faculties. However, the faculties in a given academy were directed to achieve coordination through a council of the faculties working with the rector. The Directorate of Higher Education within the Ministry was directed to develop a complete list of faculties, that is, a complete university structure, in each academy with the intention of providing a system of seventeen public universities to serve the nation as a whole. Generally, there already were one or more faculties in the academies, but each had operated independently. University councils were formed in sixteen of the academies as a result of this directive, and a movement to develop complete universities in each academy was started. This effort has not been completely successful.

The importance of the rector in the administration of secondary and higher education is apparent in Figures 12 and 13. But he gained greater importance when it became clear that the Directorate for Elementary Education also was required to operate through his office to reach the prefects and subordinate agents in the departments. A separate staff of elementary school inspectors, subordinate to both the rector and the prefect, was appointed to supervise instruction in the elementary schools. The inspectors, as officials of the Ministry of Public Instruction, were made responsible in all matters pertaining to the *instructional* aspects of national educational policy and law, and were empowered to force local officials to provide the physical facilities and equipment needed to carry out the national policies. But the prefects, subprefects, and mayors—all officials of the Ministry of the Interior—were made responsible for buildings, equipment, maintenance of physical facilities, and the enforcement of school laws and regulations. Beyond the minimum facilities prescribed by law, communes, either singly or in cooperation, could provide *collèges* and request vocational training in separate schools. Officials of both the departments and the communes were to be assisted by educational councils, but various reports state that their duties and authority sometimes have been so perfunctory and so routine that few citizens have been willing to serve. Such reluctance has been no handicap to the educational officials, however, because the authorities on the next higher level are fully empowered to act for them or to remove them from office should they insist upon action contrary to national policy.

After 1929 directorates for physical education and for vocational education were added. As indicated in Figure 13, each was headed by an undersecretary. It is significant that at the outset neither was required to operate through the office of the rector, but as the trend toward a unified system has progressed they too have been brought under the administrative control of the academies. Physical education was introduced to improve the health of the people through activities both in school and outside. In this sense it was imposed on top of the regular programs of instruction. Vocational education was introduced to provide training for pupils who had fulfilled school-attendance requirements but who were not qualified to enter a secondary school. The vocational schools

and programs, therefore, had no specific ties with either elementary or secondary education. This lack of coordination has become a matter of official concern in recent years.

Teacher education, certification, appointment, and promotion also were reserved to the Ministry of Public Instruction. National policy called for the maintenance of normal schools—one for men and a second for women—in each of the departments to train elementary school teachers. They were operated in connection with the department's office of elementary school inspection and thus provided the inspectors additional avenues for implementing national policy on the classroom level. Demonstration schools and experimental classes were also operated in connection with the normal schools. All these facilities and agencies located at the administrative center of the department provided conference and training centers, not merely for new teachers, but for experienced teachers as well. Secondary school teachers, of course, continued to be prepared in the universities, particularly after the Higher Normal School was incorporated into the University of Paris.

Private agencies, including religious orders, were permitted to operate schools which paralleled those operated by the Ministry of Public Instruction. However, private schools were required to comply with all laws and regulations relating to public education, including adherence to the prescribed curricula and courses of study. They were subject to inspection by the public school inspectors, and their graduates were required to pass the state examinations and to receive their diplomas, certificates, and degrees from the public officials. This also applied to private teacher training institutions, even those which prepared teachers for schools maintained by the religious orders only. French policy relating to financial support for private schools has vacillated between support equal to that given public schools and complete prohibition of any support. This issue was bitterly fought in the Third Republic. The present policy is to afford them support, but it is necessary to recall that the historic Gallic attitude does not consider such support a form of submission to authority originating outside the national boundaries.

Educational institutions

Each directorate in the Ministry of Public Instruction operated its own separate program of instruction. With the exception of physical education each program was housed in its own set of buildings, scattered throughout the nation, and was staffed by its own cadre of teachers. The pattern of the institutions and the individual school types has varied over the years; Figure 14 shows the pattern that existed shortly before World War II.

Elementary education received special attention when the Third Republic was formed. The primary concern was to establish a system of schools to teach the masses to become efficient and loyal followers. Leaders were to be supplied by the separate systems of secondary and higher education. The legal basis for elementary education was provided in the Primary Education Laws of 1881 and 1886. Among other provisions the laws specified that public elementary schools should be secular institutions and that they must be provided in such numbers that every child would have

convenient access to one. Although education was made a national responsibility and all children were required to attend school, parents could elect to provide for their instruction either privately or in an approved school other than a state school.

Several levels of instruction were available within the elementary school system. Influenced by the kindergarten movement initiated by Froebel in Germany, some of the larger communes introduced *écoles maternelles* for children between the ages of two and six. These were strictly voluntary schools and attendance was optional, but parents seem to have taken full advantage of them when they were available. In communes of less than 2,000 population a one-year *classe enfantine* sometimes was provided.

At the age of six, children entered the elementary school proper where they either continued to the end of the period of compulsory attendance or elected to transfer to an optional program. The period of compulsory attendance, which began at age six and ended at fourteen before World War II, was gradually extended as facilities and teachers became available. As the age for school leaving was raised, more optional programs were provided after the sixth and seventh school years. Several types of higher elementary schools were established to offer three-year programs that prepared for admission to normal schools or for clerical employment. As the Ministry of Public Instruction became interested in vocational education, pupils were given the opportunity to enter trade or vocational schools. Some of these offered programs of training only one year beyond the seventh year of the elementary school, while others provided two-,

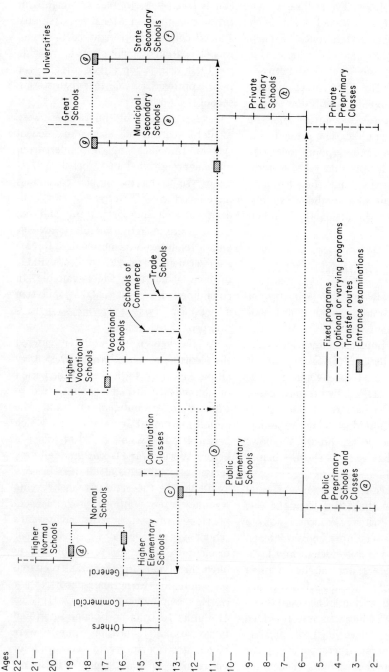

Figure 14. French Schools in the Third Republic

a. Communes of less than 2,000 sometimes had only a one-year *classe enfantine.*
b. This transfer route was open after 1925, and also is accessible from higher elementary schools by examination.
c. Pupils who passed this examination could either leave school or enter a higher elementary or a vocational school.
d. Competitive examination for certification as an elementary school teacher.
e. Collèges   f. Lycées   g. Baccalauréat   h. Classes préparatoires

three-, and even four-year programs. For the more gifted, special schools offered instruction in the arts and crafts, a few of which were of a high level, indeed.

Vocational training in limited forms had been available from the early days of the Third Republic. However, a department of vocational education was not established in the Ministry until 1929. Prior to this time various ministries had set up specialized schools in such fields as agriculture, forestry, and military science. Some of these are still maintained, but there has been a growing tendency to look to the schools under the Directorate of Vocational Education to supply specialized personnel for industry and many types of commercial employment. For this reason schools of arts and crafts, commerce, industry, and other specialized vocations, which may be entered after the seventh year of elementary education, are now generally regarded as forms of vocational education. Once terminal in nature, such programs are being extended to develop still higher levels of proficiency. A few are open on a part-time or evening basis.

Secondary education has traditionally been provided in state schools known as *lycées* and in municipal schools known as *collèges*. Historically, *lycées* were more selective, and had, therefore, a reputation for being more thorough. *Collèges* tended to accommodate modern tastes in education and to adapt more readily to popular demands arising from the inhabitants of the municipalities which supported them. However, both types prepared students for the *baccalauréat* examinations [8] and thus for admission to the universities.

[8] The French counterpart of the German maturity examinations.

As shown in Figure 14 secondary schools could be entered from the elementary schools, but the preferred route was by way of the *classes préparatoires*. These were private schools which frequently had a working arrangement with one or more *lycées* to assure the parents who patronized them that their sons would be admitted into a secondary school.

Higher education existed in several forms. University faculties of the conventional types were available in all academies but one. However, not all academies had a full complement of faculties. As science and technology developed, university offerings in these fields were expanded either by adding new chairs in the existing faculties or by adding new faculties. Also, a new type of institution known as *les Grandes Écoles,* or Great Schools, was strongly promoted. The name referred more to the level of instruction, of course, than to the size of the enrollments. They were technical and semiprofessional schools, and their graduates were in demand for attractive appointments both in industry and government. Both the Great Schools and the universities could be entered by way of the *baccalauréat* examinations, but admission to the former also was open to those who succeeded in a special competitive examination.

As the Third Republic progressed, the status and reputation of the normal schools also improved. The *école normale supérieure,* or higher normal school, which was established by Napoleon I to prepare secondary school teachers, was made a part of the University of Paris complex. But the normal schools preparing elementary teachers were looked upon as forms of secondary education. Now, however, higher normal schools, *écoles normales primaires supérieures,* were developed to prepare faculty for the normal schools, school inspectors, and other positions in educational administration which required training beyond that of a classroom teacher. The higher normal schools, therefore, stood on a par with the Great Schools; and from this connection with higher education a possible transition from the elementary system to the secondary and university system finally may have come into view.

Special schools of art, music, and drama were provided by the Directorate for Fine Arts. Individuals with unusual talent could enter these schools from any branch of the educational system, but there was no particular point at which the transfer had to occur. Both admission and the length of the period of study depended upon the promise of the student and the progress he made.

Educational opportunities

The dual or two-class structure of the educational system instituted by the leaders of the Third Republic is quite apparent in Figure 14. Children entered school either in an elementary school or a preparatory class, and continued in the track chosen for them until the opportunities provided therein had been exhausted. Because the opportunities in the two systems were far from equal the future status of the child—his social standing, economic situation, employment opportunities, and the level on which he later could participate in government—was to a large degree determined for him at the age of six.

French political theory held that all matters affecting the general welfare

130

should be settled by formal, inductive logic, a reasoning process which could only be perfected through rigorous schooling. As this philosophical attitude gained acceptance, secondary and higher education had been transformed into institutions providing that form of intellectual discipline; and the republicans of 1870 were disposed to leave social controls, as far as possible, in the hands of the graduates of these institutions. The Third Republic therefore looked upon secondary and higher education as training programs for an intellectual elite. It was thought necessary to separate the future leaders from the main body of the population as early as possible. Since the *lycées, collèges,* and universities had always had highly selected students, their character and programs were not changed significantly from what they had been under the monarchies; and as long as these institutions were kept filled, the nation's need for qualified leaders, it was felt, would be met.

And so matters stood through World War I. Among the soldiers, however, a more democratic attitude was gaining popularity. Coming from all strata of society and from all parts of France, forced to live as equals and to fight side by side, the soldiers concluded that the barriers which tended to keep them apart in civilian life were mostly artificial. The dual system of education was identified as a major cause of social disunity.

Under the leadership of a corps of public school teachers an organization was formed, known as the Compagnons de l'Université Nouvelle, to promote educational reforms. They published their views and promoted the idea of a unified school system. A form of elementary school, called the *école unique,* was proposed in which all children would enroll at age six. At the end of the basic elementary program, pupils would be classified according to ability rather than parental status, and all qualified pupils would have an opportunity to enter a secondary school. While no significant modifications were achieved in the basic primary education laws by this movement, a public sentiment was developed which has since had the effect of expanding the educational opportunities of the children enrolled in elementary schools. After 1925, for example, the programs of instruction in the five years preceding admission to *lycées* and *collèges* were made identical in both the elementary schools and the *classes préparatoires*. After 1930 the tuition fees charged by the *lycées* and *collèges* were gradually reduced in order to lower the economic barriers to secondary education. French policy generally, however, has favored scholarships for able but needy students rather than the elimination of tuition fees.

The development of trade, vocational, and technical schools was also a response to the demand for better educational opportunities for children in the elementary schools. Higher elementary schools were introduced which either duplicated or paralleled the offerings in the lower classes of the *lycées* and *collèges*. But as multiple programs of post-elementary schooling were made available, it became necessary to find a method for determining which was the proper school for each child.

The French have historically shown great confidence in formal examinations to evaluate both the potential and the academic achievement of students. Among their many types of selective examinations, the *baccalauréat* exami-

nation regulating admission to the universities, administered on a national basis, has enjoyed the highest reputation. Therefore, in keeping with established tradition the Ministry of Public Instruction now turned to a system of external examinations to determine which post-elementary program pupils should attend. A general examination was introduced to which elementary school children were admitted, generally around age twelve. This examination was not obligatory, but most parents elected to have their children take it, since those who passed could either leave school immediately or enter one of the higher elementary or vocational schools. Those who failed were required to remain in elementary school until they had passed a second examination or had reached the age at which compulsory attendance terminated. For such children there was little more in the way of educational opportunity except in the more populous places where courses of a practical nature were sometimes available on a continuing or evening basis.

Opportunities to transfer from the elementary to the secondary schools were provided, after 1925, both at the beginning of the secondary school programs and from the higher elementary schools. Children transferring into the *lycées* and *collèges* from elementary schools were required to pass rigorous entrance examinations. On the other hand, pupils in many of the *classes préparatoires* were admitted automatically, particularly by those schools with which they had a working arrangement. Even pupils transferring from higher elementary schools were admitted only on the basis of their performance in a highly selective examination. When it is recalled that great social as well as educational differences, including differences with respect to the languages studied, separated the two groups of students, it may be inferred that only the most resolute and gifted individuals ventured to make the transition at this late point.

Elementary school pupils who were attracted to academic pursuits and found attendance at school inviting usually elected to prepare for elementary school teaching. Admission to a normal school was open to those who had completed the program in a higher elementary school that offered the general program of studies. All applicants were required to take a competitive admissions examination, and only the number needed to fill the vacancies in the normal schools were given a passing mark. The basic training program was of three years' duration. Those who completed it were admitted to the examination qualifying for a teaching certificate and for appointment to a teaching position. Again, the number allowed to pass was determined by the number of vacant teaching positions. However, a few who distinguished themselves in this highly competitive examination became eligible to enter a higher normal school. Until very recently the higher normal schools were the only institutions in the elementary school system that could be regarded as institutions of higher education.

Although the Ministry of Public Instruction was late in accepting responsibility for vocational education, the commitment once made brought speedy results. The Directorate for Vocational Education was given its own budget and staff. The administrative staff on the national level proceeded to plan programs and to locate schools with minimum consultation with either the other

operating schools or the local civil and educational authorities. By their very nature, however, vocational schools soon needed to be articulated with the elementary school system. Such schools looked to the elementary schools for their students and expected them to come equipped with the necessary literary and mathematical skills. Admission usually came after the pupil had fulfilled his term of compulsory schooling— or a year earlier if he had passed the examination for the elementary certificate. Pupils entering vocational schools at age twelve or thirteen generally took short courses which emphasized the manual arts and manipulative skills useful in the factory or on the farm.

Soon, however, higher forms of vocational training were provided as preparation for more advanced industrial and commercial activities. Admission was usually restricted to pupils who had completed either the continuation or complementary course of the elementary school or who had attended one of the higher elementary schools. Only the very exceptional student in a lower vocational school could expect to qualify for admission to a higher vocational school. By World War I the system of vocational education had been sufficiently developed to provide progressively higher levels of instruction ranging from those preparing for semiskilled occupations to the skilled trades, general clerical posts, and even minor executive and supervisory positions.

As in the other branches of education, the selection process made extensive use of competitive examinations and permitted only a few students to continue to the next higher level. On the highest level in fields regarded as most worthy of special cultivation, there was a single national institution into which, it was assumed, the nation's most gifted young people would be gathered. Among such schools maintained by the Directorate for Vocational Education were the National School of Arts and Crafts, the Higher School of Commerce, and the National Agricultural Institutes. Similar schools, including some of the Great Schools, were operated by other directorates and ministries. Admission to every one of these was controlled by a competitive examination.

External examinations were also used to regulate progress in the secondary schools. Indeed, the rigorous *baccalauréat* examination acquired a worldwide reputation as a device for restricting admissions to higher studies; the *collèges* and, particularly, the *lycées* took pride in maintaining that reputation. The validity of this reputation came to be questioned, however, when it was seen that students from the private preparatory classes and from the socially more exclusive *lycées* and *collèges*, who were not required to pass examinations to stay in school, nevertheless showed an advantage in the *baccalauréat* and other examinations—possibly because the examinations had been deliberately designed to cover what their curricula had provided. Thus graduates of the *lycées* and *collèges* who failed the *baccalauréat* were still likely to make higher scores than graduates of higher elementary and vocational schools in the competitive examinations for admission to the Great Schools—or for appointments in the civil service, for that matter.

Such criticism of the discriminatory nature of the *baccalauréat* and other examinations suggests that more people were demanding opportunities to study on the university level. Indeed, the universities came under considerable pressure to expand their enrollments and offerings. The Directorate for Higher Education, working through the rectors, gradually achieved better coordination of the higher educational facilities in each academy. Uniform admissions standards were enforced and the Ministry of Public Instruction took over the exclusive right to award licenses and degrees. In return, the universities were given larger appropriations, and all professors were made civil servants. They are now appointed by the Ministry, promoted or removed by the Ministry, and receive their pay from the public treasury.

As the Ministry tightened its control, the universities gradually improved their services. New chairs and new faculties were added, particularly in the modern languages, mathematics, and social sciences. Nevertheless, their ancient reputation as the custodian of the French intellectual tradition and culture was not surrendered easily. Hence, when the cry for higher education in the technical and scientific areas no longer could be ignored, the Great Schools rather than the universities were developed to meet this demand. The function of the universities, it was said, is to supply leaders with broad cultural backgrounds and superior intellectual training. The Great Schools in spite of their name and their demanding technical and scientific curricula were, from this particular point of view, regarded as an inferior form of instruction.

A final word needs to be said about the education of women. French women acquired the right to vote after World War II. Prior to this they had played a subordinate role in public life and their opportunities in education were limited. Boys and girls were segregated

133

even in the public elementary schools wherever a sufficient population made this possible. A limited number of *collèges* and *lycées* for girls were established in time, and gradually some places were opened to them in the universities. However, girls were not generally encouraged to seek a higher education or to aspire to positions of responsibility in government or commerce. A girl with intellectual interests was most likely to be directed into the field of elementary school teaching, although even here she was likely to find men enjoying preferential treatment.

Subsequent developments

Two features of French education have elicited particular criticism in recent years: the two-track arrangement which has tended to keep the population separated into two social classes, and the extensive use of external examinations. The examinations have been attacked not only on the ground that they discriminate in favor of children enrolled in secondary schools, but also because they have been used deliberately to restrict opportunities for study on the upper levels.

The two-track system first came under heavy attack in World War I, after which the *école unique* was promoted as a remedy. Although the idea was well received by the people, the leaders in government who themselves were the products of the selective secondary school system, never permitted it to be enacted into law. Pressure for a unified system developed again during World War II, and resulted in the widely publicized Langevin Plan. But again the government buried the proposal under a mountain of parliamentary debate. Finally a

134

reform bill was enacted by the de Gaulle government in 1959 which proposed to deal with the problem along lines indicated in Figures 15 and 16.

Among important features of the 1959 reforms are the measures designed to eliminate discrimination in the secondary schools. Perhaps the most significant step is the consolidation of the directorates of elementary, secondary, and vocational education under "a single director general of the whole educational field, so establishing an indispensable link which formerly existed only at ministerial level." [9] The separate staffs of inspectors have also been consolidated under the office of the Director General. Similarly, administrative responsibility for the physical plants, payrolls, and other fiscal and managerial matters have been consolidated in a single Directorate for Administration. All these changes, indicated in Figure 15, are expected to bring greater coordination of elementary, secondary, and vocational education within the national system.

Other changes have expanded the opportunities of children of all classes to attend school beyond the basic elementary program. The extension of compulsory school attendance to age sixteen means that new schools and programs are needed. Thus, the traditional emphasis on classical studies is being broadened to include subjects useful to boys and girls who plan to find employment in industry or commerce. All programs on the postelementary level are coming to be regarded as secondary education, and simple economics demands that the several programs be housed together in the same buildings that formerly housed

[9] UNESCO, "Report from France," *Twenty-third International Conference on Public Education,* Paris, 1960, p. 58.

classical or modern programs only. In the transformation the name of the higher elementary schools has been changed to *collège,* an indication of the breadth which secondary education is acquiring.

Perhaps most revolutionary of all is the announcement that the general examination formerly administered to children in their last year of elementary school is to be abolished on an experimental basis. In its place will be a system of guidance under the direction of a special commission named from the elementary and secondary school inspectors in the district the commission serves. Eleven- and twelve-year-old children who have followed a normal elementary school program, and whose parents request their admission to the sixth form, the lowest class in a secondary school, are to be admitted to an "observation" class. Here they will be under observation for varying periods of time which, in some cases, may be as long as two years. All pupils will be enrolled in the regular program of studies. Their performance will be carefully observed and their aptitudes evaluated

to determine which specialized program of studies is most appropriate for each. After the guidance counselors have reached a decision, the child and his parents will be invited to a conference and told which program the child is to enter. In case of disagreement, however, the decision of the counselors is to prevail. If for some reason a child is not entered in an observation class, he will have an opportunity to enter a secondary school in the fourth form, that is to say, two years later than the others. Apparently the number expected to enter in this manner is substantial, because special reception and adaptation classes are to be provided them in the secondary schools.

Finally, even the *baccalauréat* examination is to be modified. The examination itself has been divided into two parts which are taken at separate times. Students may now write examinations in technical and scientific subjects as well as in the traditional languages, literature, mathematics, and philosophy. This change is said to introduce a new policy of admitting "to higher technical and scientific studies all who possess

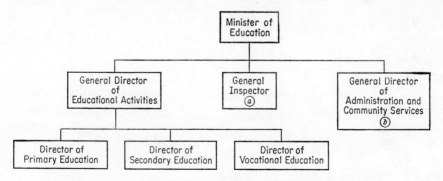

Figure 15. Reorganization in the Ministry of Public Instruction under de Gaulle
a. Responsible for coordinating the work of all inspectors.
b. "Controls documents, administration, general studies, judicial matters, financial affairs, manages personnel of all services, and is the authority for action in all directions." UNESCO, *Report from France,* Twenty-second International Conference on Public Education, 1960, p. 58.

at least average intelligence and good common sense." [10] In essence this means that the examination is to be used in the future to define the minimum preparation needed to gain admission to the upper levels and thereby to guarantee that all persons who meet those standards will be accepted. This is in sharp contrast to the former policy which restricted admissions to a predetermined number of candidates.

In all these changes there is evidence of a strong desire to develop a more democratic pattern. A single, unitary system is now anticipated, as shown in Figure 16, in which there are to be three levels or "degrees" of schooling, arranged vertically—elementary education, secondary education, and higher education. Progress from elementary to secondary education will be automatic for all children inasmuch as they now are required to remain in school to age sixteen. The fees formerly required by the secondary schools have been eliminated, and an extensive program of scholarships is expected to open the doors to the

[10] "The 'Baccalaureat' Degree," *Education in France No. 3,* French Embassy, New York, May, 1958, pp. 14–25.

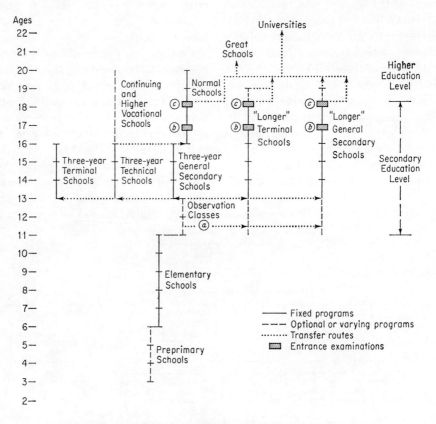

Figure 16. The de Gaulle Plan for Reorganizing the French School System

a. Pupils may be transferred from the observation classes after varying periods of time.

b. The first part of the *baccalauréat* examination.

c. The second part of the *baccalauréat* examination.

higher technical, professional, and even the classical studies to talented students from any stratum of society. Thus the French have accepted a new educational ideal, which may be defined as follows:

... every child should receive all the instruction that his aptitudes make him capable of receiving; that his education should not end with the acquisition of a few minimum essentials, but should continue until the age of eighteen; that the school should give him not only the common instruction that everyone can take, but also, and along with it, special instruction which he can choose in accordance with his tastes and abilities.[11]

If these words are indeed to point the way in French education, they mark the end of an excessive emphasis on what was once understood to be an intellectual education.

References

Books

Arnold, Mathew: *The Popular Education of France: With Notices of That of Holland and Switzerland,* Longmans, London, 1861.

Bougle, Celestin: *French Conception of Culture Generale and Its Influences upon Instruction,* Teachers College, Columbia University, New York, 1938.

Buisson, Ferdinand E., and Frederic E. Farrington: *French Educational Ideals of Today,* World, Tarrytown-on-Hudson, N.Y., 1919.

[11] Henri Wallon, "The Philosophy of Education in France," in Marvin Farber (ed.), *Philosophical Thought in France and the United States,* University of Buffalo Press, Buffalo, N.Y., 1950, p. 334.

Farber, Marvin (ed.): *The Philosophy of Education in France and the United States,* University of Buffalo, Buffalo, N.Y., 1950.

Furniss, Edgar S., *France, Troubled Ally: De Gaulle's Heritage and Prospects,* Harper & Row, New York, 1960.

Guerard, Albert L.: *France: A Modern History,* The University of Michigan Press, Ann Arbor, Mich., 1959.

————: *French Civilization: From Its Origins to the Close of the Middle Ages,* T. Fisher Unwin, London, 1920.

————: *The Life and Death of an Ideal: France in the Classical Age,* Ernest Benn, London, 1929.

Kandel, I. L.: *The Reform of Secondary Education in France,* Teachers College, Columbia University, New York, 1924.

Maurois, André: *A History of France,* translations by Henry L. Binsse and Gerard Hopkins, Straus and Cudahy, New York, 1956.

Miles, Donald W.: *Recent Reforms in French Secondary Education: With Implications for French and American Education,* Teachers College, Columbia University, New York, 1953.

Ministry of National Education: *Encyclopédie Pratique de l'Education en France,* Paris, 1960.

Wit, Daniel: *Comparative Political Institutions,* Holt, New York, 1955.

Pamphlets and periodicals

Bowles, Frank H.: "Contrasts in Opportunity: A View of European and American Education," *National Association of Secondary School Principals' Bulletin,* vol. 47, pp. 118–132, April, 1963.

Dobinson, Charles H.: "France and Technical Education Today," *Educational Forum,* vol. 21, pp. 159–166, January, 1957.

————: "French Educational Reform," *Comparative Educational Review,* vol. 3, pp. 5–14, June, 1959.

Eberhard, Paul: "School Controversy in France," *Christian Century,* vol. 77, pp. 969–970.

Ferrez, Jean: "Regional Inequalities in Educational Opportunities," *Ability and Educational Opportunity,* Organization for Economic Co-operation and Development, Paris, 1961, pp. 69–87.

French Cultural Service: *Education in France,* 972 Fifth Avenue, New York. Published quarterly.

————: *The French System of Education,* 972 Fifth Avenue, New York, 1962.

French Education, Yale French Studies, Yale University, New Haven, Conn., 1959.

Gal, Roger: "The Development of Education in France, 1945–1961," *Phi Delta Kappan,* vol. 43, no. 2, pp. 60–63, November, 1961.

Hotyat, Fernand, and Gaston Mialaret: "French-speaking Countries: Belgium, France, and Switzerland," *Review of Educational Research,* vol. 32, pp. 298–306, June, 1962.

International Bureau of Education Bulletin, International Bureau of Education, Geneva. See especially vol. 34, no. 134, pp. 7–8; no. 135, p. 67; no. 136, pp. 125–126; and no. 137, pp. 185–186, 1960.

CHAPTER 6

English Education: Encouraging Voluntary Schools

The people of the British Isles are of mixed stock and have a complex history. They had suffered successive invasions from the Continent even before the Romans planted a colony in the southern half of the main island in the first Christian century. The Roman institutions shortly were swept away by a new invasion, this time by the Angles, Saxons, and Jutes; and it was not until the seventh century that Christianity gained a sufficient foothold to justify the appointment of an archbishop and the establishment of the English branch of the Roman Catholic Church.

In A.D. 1066 still another invasion from Normandy imposed the continental brand of feudalism upon the Anglo-Saxon social pattern. Norman customs and institutions were transplanted wholesale. Castles and cathedrals dotted the countryside; and the Church, filled with Norman appointees, was granted privileges and land in great quantity. The Church was expected to subdue the restless natives for the foreign overlords. Monastery, chantry, and foundation schools, under the direction of the Norman clergy, multiplied rapidly. In spite of these elaborate measures, the English remained uneasy under Norman rule, and forced several restrictions upon the authority of the crown before the House of Tudor came to power in the fifteenth century.

Two unique traditions helped shape social institutions in England. First, the people had acquired confidence that England was capable of managing its own affairs without interference from abroad. Under the Tudors this conviction brought a complete break with the Roman Church, an end to dealings with the Holy Roman Empire even as an equal, and a turning away from the Norman provinces to which England had been subordinate. Second, the people had learned to expect government to be orderly and to rule with the consent of the governed. These beliefs led to the incident at Runnymede where King John was forced to sign the Magna Carta. By the time of Edward the people expected to be heard on certain matters, and a representative parliament had been brought into existence. That parliament included commoners as well as barons; and in return Englishmen of all ranks now expected to pay taxes and to render military service as required by the crown.

The outlines of a system of education, although still faint and incomplete, were also visible. The Roman Church, in England as on the Continent, was regarded as the custodian of truth and, therefore, as the proper agency for dispensing it. The relatively late arrival of Christianity in the islands, and the fact that some areas were spared the ravages visited upon other centers by the barbarians, permitted the English to escape in some measure the destruction of schools and libraries that marked the onset of the Dark Ages on the Continent.[1] In Ireland learning prospered in direct ratio to the interest taken in such

[1] Reginald Lane Poole, *Medieval Thought and Learning*, 2d rev. ed., Macmillan, New York, 1920, pp. 8–21.

matters by the cloistered clergy. In England the bishops took the lead in establishing schools and preserving learning. Theodore of Tarsus, Archbishop of Canterbury near the close of the seventh century, took great interest in teaching, and Canterbury and York became centers from which learning spread to other places. It was at York that Alcuin, the teacher imported by Charlemagne to establish schools in his empire, had received his training.[2]

Geographic as well as historical factors caused English schools to evolve along slightly different lines from those taken on the Continent. While English bishops took part in the teaching activities from the start, training the scholars to sing in the choir was soon turned over to the *precentor,* a member of the cathedral chapter who had charge of all musical portions of the religious services and festivals in which the clergy participated. This development gave rise to the "choir" schools. Choir schools sometimes also gave the boys instruction in the elements of Latin grammar. However, Latin studies were related more closely to theology than music, and when bishops relinquished the last of their teaching duties, both grammar and theology were delegated to a canon of the chapter who came to be known as the "chancellor." In due time the grammar studies were separated from the theological studies and made preparatory to the latter. This separation gave rise to the "grammar" schools which have dominated secondary education in England even into the present century. The schools of theology, on the other hand, quickly gave way to faculties of theology, and then to universities.

It should be noted that in England—but not on the Continent—chancellors acquired control over both the universities and the grammar schools. This brought about a degree of articulation between preparatory and higher studies in England, which was not matched on the Continent until the nineteenth century. The rest of English education developed around this nucleus of grammar schools and universities—sometimes, it has seemed, in spite of it.

The origin of the universities in England is a matter of some speculation and disagreement. Several schools of theology, which were not of university rank, had characteristics generally associated with a *studium generale,* the medieval name for a university, prior to A.D. 1200. However, the honor of being the first university is usually given to Oxford, which is said to have been founded early in the thirteenth century by a group of masters previously connected with the University of Paris. Since Cambridge University was founded a few years later by an exodus of dissident masters and students from Oxford, the Paris model of a corporation of masters, rather than the model that evolved at Bologna, became established in England.

Curtis has attached significance to two features of the early English universities that distinguished them from those on the Continent.[3] First was the absence of the "nations," the associations of masters and students from a given country or region. While it is true that a Northern nation and a Southern nation were formed in the beginning, both at Oxford and at Cambridge, they were soon made unnecessary by the development of the more typical English college. Colleges were founded as inde-

[2] S. J. Curtis, *History of Education in Great Britain,* 2d ed., University Tutorial Press, London, 1951, chap. I.

[3] *Ibid.,* pp. 59–60.

pendent corporations, usually managed by a chartered foundation and supported in part by gifts and endowments. They generally owned a hall which provided lodging as well as a place of instruction for the resident scholars and their tutors. Both of the older universities came to have a number of such colleges, each offering instruction parallel to that of the others. The university corporations then rendered general services, such as administering examinations, awarding degrees, and providing a library, which were shared by all the colleges.

The second difference related to the office of the chancellor. On the Continent the chancellor tended to be an ecclesiastic of influence who was not a member of the university corporation. He was the spokesman for the university when it ran into difficulties with the external authorities, particularly bishops. The official head of the continental university was—and still is—the rector. Thus, the rector and the chancellor of a continental university sometimes took opposite sides on issues. The situation developed along different lines in England, probably because neither Oxford nor Cambridge had evolved from cathedral schools. Indeed, they did not even arise in cathedral towns. Therefore, both developed independent status and freedom of action not enjoyed by the continental universities, even to the point of electing one of their own members as chancellor. Thus, English chancellors were members of their university communities, and as such they combined those privileges and duties belonging to both the rector and the chancellor on the Continent.[4]

English education by the fifteenth century differed from that on the Conti-

nent in other ways as well. Whereas many schools in northern Europe had been established in response to popular demand and were operated by guilds and municipalities, nearly all English schools were operated either by the Church or by foundations controlled by the Church. This had come about in large measure during the Norman Conquest. The Normans had regarded themselves as superior to the English, and so they had hoped to convert their new Anglo-Saxon subjects to the Norman way of life and build up a native elite disposed to support their rule. Ecclesiastical offices and grammar schools were prime instruments used to achieve this end. Not only did Norman appointees fill the high offices but they also replaced Anglo-Saxon teachers. Norman-French was made the status language and was substituted for English wherever the vernacular had been used in the schools. Generous endowments were set up to establish grammar schools in the right places; and the flow of funds, often provided by penitent nobles and wealthy landholders, increased their number substantially.

Parish priests seem to have had little interest in teaching the poor except to give them the elements of religious doctrine. However, the numerous monasteries and convents established in the Norman period acquired extensive funds to operate schools, particularly among the Irish and the Scots, although many such schools were opened in England, too. Nevertheless, instruction in reading and writing the vernacular was neglected to such an extent that the English people were less literate by the fifteenth century than were the people of northern Europe.

As noted earlier, the Church had served the Norman conquerors well and

---

[4] *Ibid.*, p. 60.

had been handsomely rewarded with lands, endowments, and privileges. It is estimated that the Church owned one-fifth of the revenue-producing lands by the fifteenth century. Of the 1,200 monasteries that had been established, approximately half were still in existence. However, many of the ecclesiastical estates now supported a mere handful of monks or clergy as compared with the large communities they had supported earlier. Charges of luxurious living and a general neglect of duties were leveled at the remaining religious communities, and the resentment of the land-hungry people grew increasingly bitter. Meanwhile, a continuing feud had evolved between the popes and the kings. The Vatican sent foreign clergy to England in disturbing numbers. Furthermore, appointees developed the practice of giving Rome the "first fruits," that is, all the revenues collected during the first year in office. Many Englishmen came to feel that the Church was intent upon draining away their resources without rendering a suitable compensating service. It was in this climate that the Tudors came to power.

From the fifteenth to the nineteenth century

The Tudors were more English in nature and outlook than any who had occupied the throne for some time. Henry VII, the first of the line, set about securing his country against military aggression. Next, he sided strongly with his people in resisting the abuses of the barons, many of whom had Norman antecedents. Finally, he resisted the Church in its drive to extend its power and increase its revenues. He encouraged commerce, avoided foreign wars, and

ruled with an even and frugal hand. Thus, he was able to bequeath to his son, Henry VIII, a realm that was vastly more prosperous, confident, and united than it had been when he assumed power in 1485; and Henry VIII could count upon the loyalty of the people to follow him even when he opposed the Parliament or the Roman Church.

Henry VIII was not one to yield easily to pressures or to accept distasteful advice, no matter how prudent. By respecting the feelings of his subjects he was able to execute policies that might have broken a less popular sovereign. Thus, when the pope and the Roman hierarchy infringed on what he considered the prerogatives of the crown, he countered by pressing with increased vigor a campaign, already in process, of closing the monasteries and expropriating the ecclesiastical estates and endowments. He then undertook to discredit the numerous religious shrines and "ecclesiastical frauds" and to expropriate the wealth that had been bestowed upon the high offices. Next, he took steps to limit the flow of ecclesiastical revenues out of the country.

The expropriation of ecclesiastical endowments had serious educational consequences. As Henry seized the endowments and closed the chantries—a campaign that was pushed with even greater enthusiasm by Edward VI—schools of all categories lost their financial support and were forced to close. It should be noted that the Church in England had neglected to support education out of current revenues.

The Tudors were not indifferent to the need for schools, however. Certain institutions which they felt could be made to serve the Tudor cause were reestablished. In general, these were favored grammar schools, particularly those few which, with two or three new ones, were to become the nine "great public schools" famous in later English history.[5] These schools, largely dependent on periodic grants from the royal treasury, have characteristically evidenced strong loyalties to the crown.

"Public" schools in England, beginning with the Tudors, came to refer to grammar schools that attracted students from outside the local region. Thus, they tended to become boarding schools. They resembled the more local grammar schools, however, in that they operated under royal charters and were governed by independent boards or agencies. They generally received grants or endowments from the crown and gifts from wealthy donors, given in honor of the king or some other member of the royal family, as indicated by the names of some of the schools. In the same sense, Oxford and Cambridge became "public" universities.

Individual colleges which refused to support the Tudors in their opposition to Rome were closed and their endowments used to found new ones more receptive to the royal will. Individual professors who opposed the crown were driven from their posts and replaced by persons of more congenial disposition. Thus, although the theological orientation of the universities changed during the Tudor quarrels with the Vatican, their corporate status remained uninterrupted.

[5] Frederick Eby and Charles Flinn Arrowood, *The Development of Modern Education*, Prentice-Hall, Englewood Cliffs, N.J., 1941, p. 151. These nine are Winchester, Eton, Westminster, St. Paul's, Merchant Taylor's, Shrewsbury, Charterhouse, Rugby, and Harrow.

The Anglican Reformation

But the Tudors did not quarrel with the Roman Church to promote the cause of religious freedom. Henry VIII retained strong religious commitments throughout his life, and it is said that he attended Mass every day even when on military campaigns and other extended journeys. His quarrel with Rome centered on whether the crown or the pope had final authority in England. It was on this issue of supremacy that he assumed the authority to purge the Church, the schools, and the government; and upon his assertion of the supremacy of the crown, he transformed the existing ecclesiastical system into the Church of England, with the English crown at its head. Under Elizabeth I this transformation was made official by Parliament in the Acts of Supremacy and of Uniformity.

The Church of England now inherited the educational privileges, duties, and responsibilities that had formerly belonged to the Roman Church. Anglican theology and Anglican clerics dominated the university scene. Anglican clergy exercised supervisory roles over the grammar schools and offered religious instruction in the parishes. There were, however, few places where people could acquire even the elements of reading, writing, and arithmetic, and the Tudors were not disposed to provide schools to instruct them in such matters.

Nevertheless, the Tudors are given credit for having laid the foundations of English education. Three guiding principles were operative from the fifteenth to the nineteenth century. The first, set forth in the Act of Supremacy, gave the crown supreme authority in ecclesiastical as well as civil affairs. The Act made it illegal for any school to exist which did not possess either a charter from the crown or a license from a bishop of the Church of England. However, the need to train persons for ecclesiastical as well as civil service made it necessary for the Tudors to reestablish some of the schools they had closed and to found new ones, mostly grammar schools or colleges.

The Act of Uniformity embodied the second principle, namely, that no schools would be authorized which refused to conform to the doctrines and practices of the Church of England. To this end all teachers were required to secure licenses from a bishop or his appointed agent, and the Anglican clergy were ordered to keep a watchful eye on any teaching activities conducted in their parishes to make certain that no unorthodox instruction was given. Under Elizabeth the Church of England became so strongly established, and so loyally supported by Parliament, that neither the Puritans nor the Roman Catholic Stuarts could set it aside for long. Nor were the dissenters able to gain the legal right to operate schools and to bring up their children in their own faiths until near the end of the eighteenth century.

The third principle identified the family as the agency financially responsible for education. In line with this principle, attendance at school was not made mandatory in England until long after compulsory school attendance legislation had been enacted in Protestant states on the Continent. Neither the Tudors nor any of their immediate successors created a national agency to look after education. Indeed, no direct tax

support was given to English schools until the nineteenth century; and when the government finally did accept some responsibility, great care was exercised to make certain that governmental agencies would not limit the freedom of action enjoyed by private schools.

Rise of parliamentary government

The reluctance of the government to enter the field of education in an official manner suggests that political control was held by a small segment of the people. Indeed, this was true until recent times, and was based on the makeup of the Model Parliament convened by Edward I in 1295. Edward had limited participation in the Parliament to three social classes: (1) the leading barons and highest-ranking clergy; (2) the Church, which was to be represented by members of the lesser clergy from each diocese, named by the presiding bishop; and (3) the commoners, who were to be represented by two delegates from each borough and each shire or county. Delegates from the three classes met as separate bodies from the very outset. And since the body representing the Church withdrew to form a separate "convocation" to deal with ecclesiastical matters primarily, only the "lords" and the "commoners" remained. From them have evolved the two chambers, or "houses," that make up the British Parliament today.

Membership in the House of Lords was limited to persons of noble birth, except for the prelates who took their seats on being elevated. But the commoners who sat in the Model Parliament also represented the landed gentry or other relatively privileged groups.

144

The summons calling for their appointment had been addressed by Edward, not to the people of the boroughs and shires, but to the royal sheriffs. Each sheriff proceeded to make the appointments in his own way. Some called together a handful of their closest friends and had them elect the delegates. Others consulted several of the leading landowners. In other cases the owners of certain properties, the occupants of a given house, the members of a given family, or the owners of a certain business or piece of equipment, such as a plow or stove, were the ones involved in the selection process. In some boroughs the mayor, the council, or the two acting jointly had been asked to name the delegates. But in nearly all cases *those who participated in the first election retained the right to elect representatives to future parliaments.* The privileges of serving as an elector, therefore, could be inherited or bought; and from this practice arose the "rotten borough" system. For centuries a relatively few wealthy or politically ambitious men were able to dominate English politics, even to control the House of Commons. Such men generally were members of the old landed aristocracy or of the new commercial and industrial classes. As a rule they were not interested in educating the lower classes, and considered the private schools already in existence quite well suited to teach their own children to follow in their footsteps. The rotten borough system was allowed to continue until the nineteenth century when a series of reform bills, sponsored by the Whigs against the opposition of the Tories, extended the franchise. Popular education progressed step by step with the extension of the franchise.

Private educational agencies

Education under the Tudors was not closely identified with either the civil or the ecclesiastical branch of government. Although the Anglican doctrine was made obligatory, the Church of England itself did not establish a system of schools. Elementary instruction was provided in the homes of the very rich by governesses and tutors. The less wealthy often joined forces to found "petty" schools. At about age ten, boys were expected to enter grammar school, and then to proceed to a college at one of the two universities. Some petty and grammar schools were operated as private profit-making ventures. However, many of the most famous schools were known as foundation schools largely because their income from permanent endowments supplemented the tuitions. Such income usually enabled them to provide more lavish premises and expensive instruction than other schools.

Many of the older foundations had been established by gifts of money or land to produce income to support a school for poor scholars. Management of the endowments usually was placed in the hands of self-perpetuating boards. Clergy usually were included as members of the board, thereby affording clerical influence in, if not actual control of, the school. In addition to supervising the endowment, the governing board usually employed the headmaster who, in turn, appointed the assistants and operated the school. Since each foundation received its charter from the crown or the Church, and since the charter, or statutes, usually stated how the endowment was to be used, foundation schools tended to be very inflexible. A notable exception was achieved in the matter of scholarships, for most soon found ways to circumvent the charter stipulations regarding the admission of poor boys, and adopted a scale of tuition which only the rich could afford. They proved less ingenious in matters relating to the curricula and methods of instruction.

The translation of the Bible into English and the introduction of the English forms of worship in the Church of England provided new impetus to vernacular education. This interest reached the level of a compulsion as Puritanism made its way through the ranks of the Church of England. Occasional rectors, particularly those who became fired by the Puritan zeal for reform, made it a matter of prime importance to offer reading instruction within their parishes. From such efforts parish schools emerged, many of which also were placed under the management of a school foundation endowed by gifts from local parishioners or other benefactors. These account for many of the foundation or independent primary schools found in England today.

At the outset, the Church of England had attempted to maintain a monopoly in all fields of education, but Puritans and Nonconformists operated clandestine schools. Their religious beliefs placed great emphasis upon Bible reading, and their schools reflected this interest by stressing instruction in reading. As members of the middle classes, the Nonconformists also developed numerous practical interests derived from their commercial activities. Thus their reading schools frequently offered instruction in writing and arithmetic, and their academies included modern languages, mathematics, and scientific studies to prepare older children for careers in trade and industry. Later, when Nonconformists were permitted to operate their schools openly, they established grammar schools to fulfill the needs of their future ministers. But Nonconformists continued to be discriminated against in the English universities until 1871, and many English boys found it preferable to complete their education at a Scottish university.

The Church of England was not indifferent, of course, to the needs of the common people for religious education. The local clergy had been directed to provide such instruction, and individual rectors dealt with the matter as their interests and the resources of the parishes dictated. Such limited activity satisfied the people for a time, but as economic and social changes brought an end to the feudal system and forced large numbers to congregate in cities the Church lost touch with the common people. At the same time, the development of the factory system caused a breakdown in the ancient pattern of apprenticeship training.

When it was realized that the rectors were no longer reaching the people by means of the catechetical classes, voluntary philanthropic societies were formed to operate charity schools among the poor. The largest and most prominent of these was the Society for Promoting Christian Knowledge which operated under the general sponsorship of the Church of England. While the Society's main function was to collect and allocate funds raised by private subscriptions—a service in which the Anglican clergy seem to have cooperated fully— it also provided encouragement and some direction to the local leaders. The leadership and the teachers generally were laymen. Although intended primarily to teach the elements of Anglican doctrine, the schools generally gave instruction in reading and writing and occasionally in arithmetic, spinning, and other arts and skills useful either in the home or the factory.[6]

Motivated by strong religious convictions, the Nonconformists were not inclined to let the Church of England operate alone in the field of charity education. Soon the charity school movement displayed a spirit of sectarian competition. The Anglicans founded two additional societies, namely, the National Society for Promoting the Education of the Poor in the Principles of the Established Church, and the Society for the Promotion of the Gospel in Foreign Parts. The latter became quite active in North America. Congregationalists and other "independents" organized the British and Foreign School Society and the Congregational Board of Education. Baptists created the Voluntary School Society. Quakers also became active, and the Methodists, though of later origin, assumed a leading role in operating Sunday schools. The charity school movement reached its peak with the introduction of the monitorial method of instruction at the close of the eighteenth century.

The beginnings of public education

As a teaching device, the monitorial method calls for the teacher or master to instruct a class of selected scholars, called monitors, in the lesson of the day, and then for each of the monitors to teach the same lesson to other pupils. Its virtue was not that it gave a superior education, but that it gave a little instruction to many children who otherwise would have had none. Two societies were formed specifically to exploit the monitorial principle, and they shortly dominated the field of elementary education. These were the National Society for Promoting the Education of the Poor in the Principles of the Established Church, organized by the Church of England in 1811, and the British and Foreign School Society organized by Nonconformists at about the same time. Both societies conducted vigorous campaigns to establish schools; and when in 1833 the government finally was persuaded to give financial support to education, it did so by making grants to these two societies.

The several societies also provided what little supervision their individual schools received, and furnished teaching aids and materials of instruction. In fact, the Society for Promoting Christian Knowledge had appointed an inspector to visit its schools in the London area as early as 1701.[7] More important, several of the societies had given some attention to the qualifications and training of teachers. Thus both the National Society and the British and Foreign School Society were operating "model" schools as training institutions in 1833; and when Parliament was persuaded that its original grants for the expansion of charity schools would be meaningless without qualified teachers, additional grants for training teachers were made to these two societies. The College of St. Mark's, Chelsea, and Borough Road College were the ultimate results of these subsidized activities.

[6] Curtis, *op. cit.,* p. 193.

[7] *Ibid.,* p. 193.

147

The first official step to create a government agency to supervise educational matters came in 1839 with the establishment of the Select Committee of the Privy Council. The Committee almost immediately appointed a physician, Dr. Kay, as secretary. Dr. Kay had previously served as an assistant commissioner in the administration of the 1834 Poor Law, where he had learned about the inadequate educational opportunities open to working-class children. Next, the Committee announced that henceforth any school receiving a government building grant would be subject to inspection. Three inspectors were appointed, one to visit the schools of the National Society, one for the British and Foreign School Society schools, and one for Scotland. Opposition from the church groups, however, made it necessary for the Committee to consult with the ecclesiastical authorities on the appointment of the inspectors and their duties.

Meanwhile the government had indirectly encouraged education among the poor through a series of poor laws and factory acts. The latter attempted to regulate the conditions of employment for children while the former introduced the principle of taxing the public to assist the indigent, particularly children. By the time the government was ready to assume more direct responsibility, the poor laws and the factory acts were already being written to require employers to provide instruction for employed children, aided by funds from the local taxes or "rates."

Dr. Kay's leadership as secretary to the Committee of Council was especially influential in the area of teacher training. Before his appointment he had

come upon what he called the teacher apprenticeship, or the pupil-teacher system of teacher training, which placed selected candidates with experienced teachers for a short training period. This direct experience was supplemented with formal instruction, preferably in a training school. Dr. Kay urged the Committee of Council to establish a government teacher training school, but this step was opposed by the charity school societies. Thereupon Dr. Kay, with the assistance of friends, established a private training school at Battersea in 1840. Although this enterprise demonstrated the value of the training program, financial difficulties persuaded the founders to turn the school over to the National Society, which immediately set up a number of similar institutions. This example was followed by other school societies, including the British and Foreign School Society.

Dr. Kay was more successful in introducing the apprenticeship aspects of his training scheme and in securing the upgrading of teachers through a schedule of salary supplements. Schools recommended by the Committee's inspectors were listed as eligible to participate in this program. The head teachers of such schools were required to give pupil-teacher trainees 1½ hours of instruction each day, a service for which they received salary supplements. The pupil-teachers also were given stipends while in training; and at the end of the five-year training program, some were invited to write a competitive examination for scholarships to attend a teacher training seminary or normal school. Regular teachers also were encouraged to earn increments in pay by further study at such institutions. The introduction of government supplements to teachers' salaries, together with the institution of a government-sponsored old-age pension plan, had the effect of making charity school teachers semi-public servants.

The Committee of Council carried on its program with such tact and diplomacy that its influence soon far exceeded its legal status. By using its powers to award or withhold grants, it brought about a substantial improvement in the quality of the school buildings and influenced the appointment of boards of managers for the local schools. This prepared the way for lay school boards which followed some years later. After 1852, all schools receiving grants were required to include a "conscience clause" in their statutes guaranteeing children whose parents objected that they would be excused from any sectarian religious instruction offered by the school.

English education

Nineteenth-century England presented a political picture substantially different from that of the Tudor period. Whereas the Act of Supremacy had established an absolute monarchy as extreme in its concentration of authority as any on the Continent, and the Act of Uniformity had attempted to prescribe a like-mindedness in the matter of religion not exceeded elsewhere with the possible exception of Spain, the enforcement of both measures had been somewhat modified by 1833. For the most part, the changes had been brought about by the rise of a powerful middle class.

The middle class had gained political strength as agriculture lost its relative

importance as the source of revenues for the crown. The merchants and industrialists built ships and employed seamen to carry goods to market, thus forming an array of sea power that could turn the tide in battle or even force the crown to lift restrictions on the conduct of private business. Middle-class political activities led to the formation of a party organization known as the Whigs. The royalists carried on countering activities under the label of Tories. It was largely Whig activity that turned out the Stuarts and placed William of Orange on the throne in 1689. The Whigs also forced Parliament to present William with a Declaration of Rights by which Parliament, and not the crown, was made the supreme authority in English government. From this achievement it had been but a short step to the appointment of the ministers by Parliament and the structuring of the executive branch of government in cabinet form responsible to Parliament and not to the crown. Only the wealthy merchants and industrialists were represented in the House of Commons, however, because of the continuation of the rotten borough system of elections, a defect that was gradually corrected in the nineteenth century.

Meanwhile the Tories with the aid of Nonconformists among the Whigs had defended the Church of England against the attempts of the Catholic Stuarts to return England to the Roman fold. Consequently, a policy of toleration toward the Puritans and Calvinists gained ground and was ultimately extended to Roman Catholics, Methodists, Quakers, and other dissenting sects. By the end of the eighteenth century all of them were permitted to carry on their religious activities openly and to operate schools in which they taught their sectarian doctrines.

Social role

Education was introduced in England by Christian missionaries. It continued under religious auspices, first under the Roman Church, and then under Anglican supervision, until well into the nineteenth century. Church-supported schools naturally placed emphasis upon transmitting their sectarian creeds and winning new members for their ecclesiastical bodies. While religious zeal marked the activities of the charity school societies, systematic religious instruction was also important in the schools operated by proprietors and private foundations. Indeed, English schools have continued to give religious instruction even to the present time.

Dependence upon private initiative and support in educational activities also contributed to the perpetuation of the social-class structure. The grammar schools and universities were regarded as the private preserves of the Tory ruling class well into the nineteenth century. But neither the Whigs nor the Nonconformists felt any compulsion to open the schools attended by their children to children whose parents could not pay a fair share of the costs. Charitable impulses among the Nonconformists and their Anglican contemporaries found expression in the support of separate charity schools for the poor.

Nor did the instruction offered in the several classes and types of schools foster criticism of the social stratification or the form of political control. In the spirit of the Act of Supremacy, the sovereign was still regarded as the agent of God and the interpreter of divine will. Charity education, whatever the source of its support, was expected to bring up obedient subjects instilled with a proper fear of the hereafter. Gentlemen's sons were carefully brought up to perpetuate the code of their class and to identify their personal well-being with the preservation of the existing class structure. Instruction in grammar school and college was oriented toward classical-humanistic studies. Not until the latter half of the nineteenth century did English schools accept any responsibility for upgrading the general welfare through the introduction of scientific and technical studies.

Power structure and administrative organization

As was previously stated, the English government first entered the field of education in 1833 by making small grants to two charity school societies. Prior to this the government had chartered private educational foundations and made sporadic contributions to their endowments and had delegated to the Church of England the authority to examine and license teachers and to inspect instruction. Official concern had not led to the establishment of a system of national schools, but merely to measures that would assure orthodoxy in matters of belief and loyalty to the established order.

The appropriation of public funds for educational purposes changed the government's policy rather quickly. From the beginning, grants were made only to schools specifically recommended by the National Society or the British and

Foreign School Society, and approved by the agency which distributed the funds. As the amount of the annual appropriation was raised, the previously mentioned Select Committee of the Privy Council was established—in 1839—to regulate and supervise the distribution of the grants. Under the enlightened leadership of Dr. Kay, the Committee defined standards for school buildings and the training and selection of teachers. In 1856 the Committee was changed to the Education Department, and was represented in the House of Commons by a vice-president appointed by the Prime Minister. Thereafter, education acquired more political significance and government appropriations fluctuated with the political complexion of Parliament. Pressures to expand educational facilities led to the appointment of several royal commissions, notably the Taunton and the Newcastle Commissions, to make inquiries on existing facilities and to report their findings and recommendations.

At mid-century the working classes still had no direct voice in government. The political control exercised by the upper classes over the Education Department perpetuated the stigma of charity which had always been attached to public funds for education. Nowhere was this made more apparent, or more odious, than in the Revised Code issued by the Department in 1861. In that year the Education Department, under the leadership of Robert Lowe, the vice-president, instituted the "payment by results" policy whereby the allotment to a school was based on (1) the attendance of pupils, and (2) the number who passed the Department's annual examinations in the basic skill subjects.

This policy continued until 1897 and was responsible for a generally hostile attitude toward "government" education during much of this time.

A second provision of the Revised Code was particularly distasteful to teachers in schools that received government assistance. Prior to 1861, a substantial part of the assistance had been paid directly to the teachers as salary supplements. The effect had been to give elementary teachers the status of civil servants, particularly since they also were made eligible for government pensions. Now, however, the grants went to the school managers and were not necessarily passed on to the teachers who earned them. At the same time new teachers were excluded from the retirement system. The new policy was so demoralizing that many schools did not request assistance, and the amount of the annual grants declined substantially.

Popular demand for government assistance to education under more favorable terms soon became irresistible. In 1870 Parliament laid the foundation for a system of government schools by enacting the Forster Bill. The Education Department was not materially changed by this legislation except that it was now instructed to establish and operate elementary schools *in places not adequately served by voluntary schools.* As a consequence, voluntary schools and the new government, or "board," schools came to exist side by side and to constitute what became known as "the dual system." The private or voluntary schools received preferential treatment, however, for no government school could be set up in a given place until private individuals or groups had been given an

151

opportunity to open a voluntary school first.

Prior to 1870 there were no local governmental agencies with which the Education Department might cooperate in setting up schools, except in the municipalities. Voluntary schools, on the other hand, had been required for some years to have boards of managers. The Education Act now provided for the creation of local school districts, each of which was to elect its local school board. The boards were given authority to establish and manage schools which were to be supported, in part, by government grants and, in part, by local taxes and fees. The administration of public education in England was thus decentralized from the beginning.

Secondary and higher education remained under private direction and dependent upon voluntary support (see Figure 17). The Department of Science and Art, which had been made a part of the Education Department, was an exception since it had authority to encourage, by means of supplementary grants, the teaching of technical and scientific subjects in higher elementary and secondary schools. However, the greater part of elementary as well as secondary and higher education remained free of supervision or direct control by the Department.

In spite of their economic and administrative independence, foundation grammar schools and the universities quickly achieved articulation that smoothed the student's progress from the former to the latter. This was brought about by the administrative relationship established in their early history by the university chancellors. Reference was made earlier to the fact that both Oxford and Cambridge elected

their chancellors and to the manner in which the university corporations came to include a number of colleges, each enjoying the status of a self-governing and self-supporting foundation with its own charter. Each college was presided over by its elected head. A university council, consisting of the heads of the several associated colleges, consulted with the chancellor on university matters—problems that concerned the associated colleges as a group. One such problem had to do with the preparation of applicants for admission, for as matters stood each college admitted its own students. The chancellor, with the support of the council, ultimately gained the right to appoint two masters to supervise the grammar schools in the vicinity of the university, and thereby to control preparatory instruction. Since other grammar schools also wished to have their pupils admitted to the universities, the programs developed under the direction of the university masters tended to set the pattern for the latter schools as well. English secondary education thus acquired a measure of uniformity even though there was no central agency of government specifically created to bring it about.

This is not to say that the self-regulating schools and universities were able to maintain a vital educational tradition on their own initiative. Indeed, scholarship deteriorated to such a degree that as the nineteenth century progressed the threat of government control and inspection was sounded. The universities were pressured to give greater attention to mathematics, and around 1800 they had instituted suitable examinations, at least for the honors degrees. Similar recognition was now given to science.

The grammar schools also found it

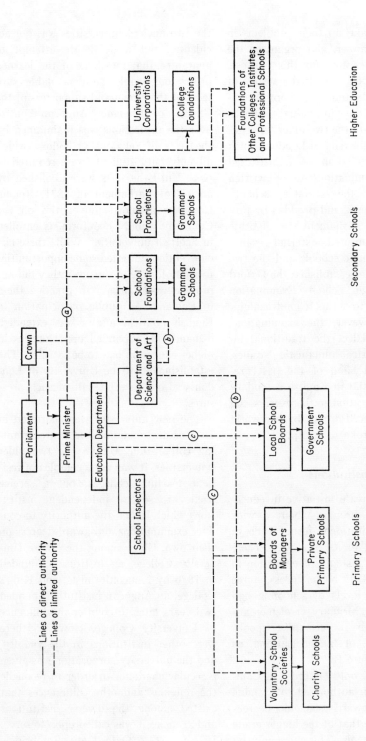

Figure 17. Lines of Educational Authority in England before 1870

a. Sources of charters and occasional grants.
b. Supplementary grants to encourage instruction in science and technology.
c. Supplementary grants for school buildings and operating expenses.

expedient to take up their problems in a collective manner, and organized the College of Preceptors for this purpose. In 1853 this body instituted a system of uniform examinations to improve instruction in the individual schools. Within five years the two older universities and the University of London, which had been chartered in 1836, instituted "external" examinations to be written by students in the secondary schools. From these efforts, and prodded by proposals before Parliament to institute government-sponsored external examinations, the public schools and the two older universities established the Oxford and Cambridge School Examination Board in 1873 to act as a joint examining body. However, the examinations continued to reflect the traditional interest in classical-humanistic studies, and the "dead hand of the past" remained influential in English secondary and higher education until severe social upheavals, induced in part by two world wars, finally broke its grasp.

Educational institutions

Reliance on private initiative in education inevitably brought about a wide variety of institutional forms, each of which operated in its own way. There was, then, no "system" of education in England in 1870. Nevertheless, three basic types or levels of schooling had become defined: primary or elementary schools, secondary or grammar schools, and institutions of higher learning, as indicated in Figure 18.

Prior to 1836 only Oxford and Cambridge had been authorized to examine candidates or award academic degrees on a level above that of the higher grade or grammar schools. This monopoly by

the two ancient universities was not accidental, but a deliberate attempt to guarantee that members of the learned professions would be dependable subjects of the crown and supporters of the Church of England. Anglican control over the professions was maintained by the tests of religious orthodoxy which all university students were required to pass. Until the tests were abolished by an act of Parliament in 1871, Roman Catholics attended universities on the Continent and Nonconformists enrolled in Scottish universities. While these circumventions afforded some opportunities to study for the professions, they did not provide ready access to practice them in England. As public participation in English political affairs was extended, demands for expanded opportunities in higher education had to be satisfied. The establishment of the University of London was one direct result of such pressures.

The new university was chartered in 1836 as an examining and degree-granting corporation. Unlike the two older universities, it was not a complex of resident teaching colleges, but a service agency to several independent institutions which lacked the authority to conduct examinations and award degrees on their own. Chief among these were University College, an institution founded in 1826 by Nonconformists, and King's College, an Anglican institution founded two years later to counter the influence of University College. However, there were other institutions in the vicinity, and the university corporation was given a secular character in order to reconcile the religious and other differences that existed among the diverse institutions and agencies it was called upon to serve. In contrast to Oxford and Cambridge,

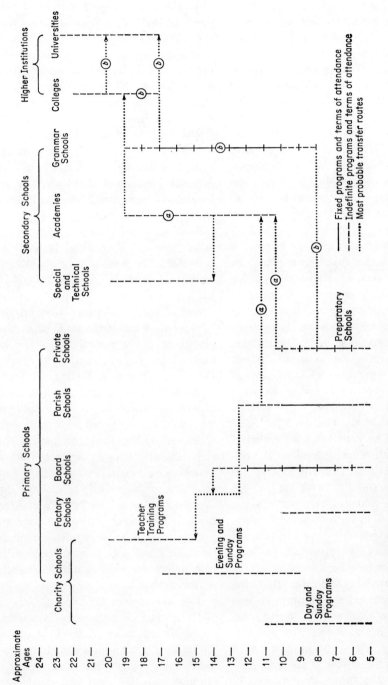

Figure 18. Educational Institutions in England before 1870

a. Most likely to be elected by Nonconformists.

b. Most likely to be elected by Anglicans.

155

both of which required candidates to be in residence while "reading for examinations," the University of London admitted candidates to examinations without residence. Thus a candidate could prepare for examinations either at an affiliated college or school or on his own. This arrangement invited the development of a variety of special courses of lectures, evening classes, and correspondence courses in addition to a number of more conventional institutes and colleges, some of which later became integral parts of this sprawling institution. The chartering of the University of London thus marked the beginning of a revolution in English higher education.

The existence of University College and King's College prior to the chartering of the University of London suggests that there were other institutions of higher education lacking examining and degree-granting powers. Indeed, there were several before 1870, most of which had been established to serve some specialized purpose. Thus the University of Durham, chartered in 1836,[8] was formed by combining the ecclesiastical foundation maintained by the collegiate church at Durham to offer instruction in theology with the College of Medicine that had been organized at Newcastle-on-Tyne in 1832. Furthermore, the existence of an independent medical school, as distinguished from the traditional medical faculties at the older universities, indicates that the training of physicians and surgeons was undergoing a change. Prior to this time, medical studies at universities had emphasized the theory of medicine as a philosophical discipline. Practicing physicians, on the other hand, generally were trained in a manner patterned

after the apprenticeship training developed by the medieval guilds. As scientific attitudes and systems of knowledge developed, a more sophisticated training was called for, and the development of specialized colleges of medicine, colleges of physicians, and colleges of surgeons had been the result. Both the Royal College of Physicians and the Royal College of Surgeons were in existence before the establishment of the Medical Faculty of the University of London. In time, they became associated with the Medical Faculty.

As science and technology progressed other types of specialized institutions appeared. The founding of the Royal Military Academy at Woolwich in 1741 had been followed by the opening of the Royal Military College at Sandhurst in 1799. This trend was continued in the nineteenth century with the establishment of the Royal Academy of Music, the Normal School of Design, the Government School of Mines, and a number of normal schools or training colleges for teachers, nearly all of which were sponsored by a philanthropic school society. Opportunities in higher education also became available to women at institutions such as Bedford College for Women and Queen's College. From these beginnings women ultimately were to gain admission to university examinations, although not on equal status with men before the close of the nineteenth century.

The founding of the Normal School of Design in 1837 made a special impact on higher education. After 1841 direct parliamentary grants were made to promote the establishment of similar institutions in the chief industrial and commercial centers. These developments were promoted by the Department of

[8] *Ibid.*, p. 418.

156

Science and Art which concerned itself mainly with the encouragement of scientific and technical instruction in the lower schools. However, the need for more advanced training, especially for teachers of science, could not be ignored, and special institutions, such as the College of Physical Science founded at Newcastle in 1871 and the Central Technical College founded thirteen years later, were the result.

Grammar schools provided virtually all that could be classed as secondary education in England from the time of the Tudors to the middle of the nineteenth century. The humanists had reformed the older Latin curriculum in the sixteenth century. Instruction in mathematics was added to the classical Latin and Greek studies early in the nineteenth, but the grammar schools, encouraged by Oxford and Cambridge, clung to the classical-humanistic curriculum with a tenacity that could not be shaken by the Industrial Revolution, the inroads of the Whigs in government, or the financial inducements offered by the Department of Science and Art.

Prior to 1799, when they were given freedom to operate schools, Nonconformists had found it necessary to educate their sons in a type of secondary school which became known as academies. They served sectarian ends, which called for vernacular reading instruction on a more elementary level, but they often boasted a rather broad range of studies. University openings were available in Scotland to those who desired to continue their studies, and instruction in Latin and Greek usually was available. However, the larger number of students had more immediate goals in view and found the offerings in modern foreign languages, mathematics, and the elemen-

tary sciences of greater interest. When Nonconformists received the right to teach, the academies disappeared rather quickly, and numerous Nonconformist foundations were formed to operate conventional grammar schools. Scientific and technical schools and colleges sprang up, around 1850, to accommodate those who planned to enter commercial and industrial fields.

Vernacular primary schools were the last level or segment of English education to be developed. They appeared late in part because the English language was not respected until long after the Roman Church had introduced Latin schools, and in part because economic and social conditions prior to the Protestant Reformation placed little practical value on the literary arts. By the nineteenth century, children of the highest social classes were receiving their elementary education in select private schools or were instructed by governesses and tutors. The Nonconformists looked after their own in parish reading schools. The complete dependence upon private effort, prior to 1833, had resulted in widespread neglect of the children of the agricultural and industrial workers, domestics, and other members of the underprivileged classes.

Because of the absence of governmental direction and the prominent role played by the voluntary agencies, particularly the philanthropic societies, vernacular primary schools came to be known by many different names. Charity schools, ragged schools, dame schools, monitorial schools, Sunday schools, petty schools, National Schools,[9] catechetical

[9] Schools maintained by the National Society for Promoting the Education of the Poor in the Principles of the Established Church.

schools, parish schools, circulating schools, and others, all of which were private and voluntary, provided children of the lower classes some form of sectarian religious education together with varying amounts of elementary reading instruction and, less frequently, a smattering of writing, arithmetic, and other useful skills. It should not be assumed, however, that these voluntary schools reached all the children. The introduction of child labor in the mines and factories and the demoralization of family and community life induced by the vicious labor practices associated with the early stages of the factory system defied even the most generous efforts by the voluntary agencies. Although the adoption of monitorial methods had increased the number to whom they were able to bring a little learning, a more effective system was clearly needed.

One way to a more adequate system of elementary education was explored by a few enlightened mill owners. By introducing "industrial" or "factory" schools, these pioneers instructed pauper children in salable skills, such as spinning, weaving, carpentry, gardening, printing, and sewing. The more enlightened of the schools also offered instruction in reading and writing. At New Lanark, Robert Owen even pointed the way to infant schools. While his factory schools offered part-time instruction to young workers, his infant schools sought to provide a wholesome environment for children too young to work in the mills.

At the outset the education of children employed in the factories had been left to the consciences of the individual mill owners; but as the working people became more aware of their rights and political power, Parliament set minimum

age and working standards. A series of factory acts required employees to provide at least part-time schooling for all workers below a specified age. Unfortunately, the enforcement of these laws was left to the local authorities, and in many cases ways were found to circumvent their more costly features.

As vernacular school facilities became available for children, adults who had been denied the opportunity to learn to read and write also began to seek ways to repair their loss. The work of Griffin Jones in Wales was particularly noteworthy. Building on efforts begun by Thomas Gouge in 1674, Jones promoted circulating schools in the poorer districts to instruct children in the daytime and adults in the evenings. Teachers moved from community to community for short terms of instruction, thereby making a limited amount of schooling avaliable to more people. This device was known as the "moving" school in the American colonies.

By mid-nineteenth century the ideas introduced by Pestalozzi and Froebel on the Continent were making their way to England. The Pestalozzian ideas on teacher education came in by way of Glasgow where they were introduced in the model schools developed by David Stow after 1826. The first English kindergarten was opened in 1854, and a Froebelian Society was organized in 1874. All these were activities of voluntary agencies, of course.

Educational opportunities

As indicated earlier, England was trailing far behind the Lutheran and Calvinist states at the close of the eighteenth century in providing educational opportunities to all her people. Informed estimates indicate that before the monitorial school movement was introduced around 1800, somewhere between 1 in 20 and 1 in 25 actually received some schooling. By 1820 the monitorial schools had increased this ratio to 1 in 14.[10] Meanwhile Prussia had achieved nearly 100 per cent school attendance and several other German states were doing as well, or nearly as well. Now, the rapid increase of Whig Party membership indicated that Englishmen were beginning to expect a better chance. The demand for increased educational opportunities was running far ahead of what the existing facilities could provide. The half measures adopted by the government in 1833—the supplementary grants—were far from sufficient to make education universally available.

But other factors besides the shortage of schools limited individual opportunity. Around 1850, thoughtful men began to realize that no effective program of education could be established as long as sectarian doctrines forced the agencies to work in separate directions and divided the school population into opposing religious groups. A movement to establish secular schools was started. An agency known as the National Public School Association opened a number of secular schools before 1870, and other groups, including several religious agencies, followed their lead. From these efforts the principle of public education without religious discrimination gradually spread.

The class structure also placed limitations on the availability of educational facilities. Schools catered to particular social strata, and corresponding social differences were evident in their courses of study. Select schools placed

[10] Curtis, *op. cit.*, p. 221.

first emphasis on the study of Latin. The grammar schools only reluctantly introduced mathematics and science before 1870, largely because the older universities also were clinging to the classical-humanistic studies. There was little opportunity to study in other fields until after the development of higher elementary schools and higher grade schools, the addition of an English curriculum by some of the more venturesome grammar schools, and the rise in status of new universities and scientific and technical institutes and colleges after 1870. Even then these limited opportunities were brought about primarily because the Great Exhibition of 1851 had revealed the shocking extent to which nations on the Continent surpassed England in science, technology, and industry.

Guided by studies her leading educators had made of the systems of education in other nations of Europe and America, England took the first long step in the development of a genuine national system by the passage of the Education Act of 1870.

Developments since 1870

The transition from a voluntary to a national system of education was led, step by step, by the extension of the franchise to the working people. The Reform Act of 1867, while falling far short of enfranchising even all adult males, nevertheless enabled the working class to control the balance of power between the Liberal and Conservative Parties in the House of Commons. Thereafter neither Liberal nor Conservative governments dared act without considering the wishes of the working people. In due time the working class decided to become politically independent by forming the Labor Party. The party's efforts to improve conditions through the agencies of government resulted first in a series of labor laws and educational reforms, and after World War II in the nationalization of transportation and certain basic industries and the introduction of socialized medicine, various insurance programs, and other welfare services.

The increase in the number of government services has inevitably called for an upgrading of the social education of all individuals to enable them to manage and use the new agencies wisely. Therefore, English schools no longer are permitted to limit their offerings to the elements of a sectarian creed and the literary skills needed to read and write the mother tongue. Nor is government or industry expected to thrive on the leadership of a hereditary ruling class. Educational programs must be given variety and depth adequate to prepare modern youth to meet the needs of the modern world. Similarly, talent is at a premium and must be recruited from every segment of the population. English education now recognizes that it has a social obligation to all the people. For a time after World War II even the famous public schools and the two ancient universities were incorporated in the national system of education and were expected to accept applicants on the basis of ability without regard for family connections or other social qualifications.

Administrative developments

The Education Act of 1870 left education to local initiative. As a result, the

least enlightened areas continued to have inadequate facilities. However, public sentiment began to favor free and compulsory schooling, and by 1902 Parliament was ready to take the necessary steps to bring this about. A few years earlier local government reform had eliminated the numerous overlapping local administrative units and placed their responsibilities in the hands of newly created county and borough governments. Every part of the country had thus come under the supervision of a duly elected and locally responsible county or borough-county council. Parliament then directed that the councils must also be responsible for education and that the local school districts, with their boards of education, created in 1870, would be eliminated. Furthermore, the Act of 1902 made it clear that the government accepted responsibility for providing education on all levels; and the county and borough councils were directed to take steps to implement this policy.

Meanwhile, the Education Department had been replaced, in 1899, by the Board of Education headed by a President who served as its chief administrative officer. Also a Consultative Committee was provided to which the Board might refer matters for study and advice. Secondary education had become the object of public concern after 1869 when the Endowed School Commissioners made numerous suggestions for improving the effectiveness with which the endowments were being used. Among other reforms, they suggested that girls be admitted to some schools and that some endowments be used to establish schools for girls exclusively. The powers of the Commissioners were transferred to a permanent agency known as the Charity Commissioners [11] in 1874. By 1902 the Charity Commissioners were made a division within the Board of Education, as was the Department of Science and Art, and England acquired thereby a central educational authority. Nevertheless, it was not until 1944 that this central agency was made a ministry and given a clear mandate to lead the public effort to establish a thoroughgoing national system of education open to all. At this time the Consultative Committee was replaced by two Advisory Councils, one for England and the other for Wales. Unlike the former Committee, these Councils are authorized to take up matters on their own initiative and make recommendations to the Ministry.

The administrative reforms initiated in 1902 were more drastic on the local than on the national level, however. Each county and borough council was to name certain of its members to constitute an education committee; other local citizens especially qualified to deal with educational matters should be added to the committee, but their number should not exceed the number of members from the council. The education committees acting on the authority of their respective councils were to constitute the Local Educational Authorities, or LEAs as they are commonly called. They soon became the most important link in the administrative chain of command and have remained so to this day.

While the 1902 legislation had merely given the LEAs *permission* to develop facilities and services, the 1944 legislation *directed* them to do so. Hence,

[11] *Ibid.,* p. 169.

government elementary and secondary schools, industrial and trade schools, teacher training colleges, and other institutions of special and higher education have been established by some or all of the 146 LEAs authorized in 1944. Government grants to voluntary schools are also now distributed from the county level, thereby bringing the voluntary schools which receive such aid under the jurisdiction of the LEAs. This development has made it logical for the LEAs to be responsible for school inspections as well as for the enforcement of school attendance, the systematic study of local needs, and the development of appropriate instructional materials and programs of study. In brief, the LEAs have gradually acquired the responsibility for providing a system of education fully adequate to meet the requirements of all persons residing within their respective jurisdictions. They have authority to levy taxes and to borrow money to provide the necessary facilities, and are assured rather generous supplementary funds from the national treasury.

The combined educational and financial responsibilities of the LEAs soon called for the employment of professional management. The Act of 1902 made the employment of such managers permissive; the Act of 1944 made it mandatory. Each LEA now employs not merely a highly trained specialist in educational administration as its director, but usually a rather extensive staff of assistants, inspectors, consultants, and other specialists as well. Together they carry on the administrative and supervisory work of the LEA, including the various health, counseling, and other supplementary welfare and social services now provided in connection with the schools. The present relationship between the Board of Education and the LEAs is indicated in Figure 19.

Institutional developments

An immediate and direct consequence of the Education Act of 1870 was a substantial increase in elementary schools. Not only were government schools established for the first time, but the private agencies operating voluntary schools were stimulated by this competition to multiply their efforts. However, because local communities were not required to elect school boards or compelled to provide instruction,

many places continued without schools. But where local school boards were formed, they enjoyed considerable freedom to set up elementary schools and to develop new programs of instruction. Some boards, particularly in the larger industrial and commercial centers, took up their work with enthusiasm and unexpected resourcefulness.

The Act of 1870 limited the powers of the local boards to elementary education but did not restrict their activities to the usual elements of reading, writing, arithmetic, and religion. Boards were authorized to formulate by-laws to regulate school attendance for children between the ages of five and thirteen yet were not restrained from pro-

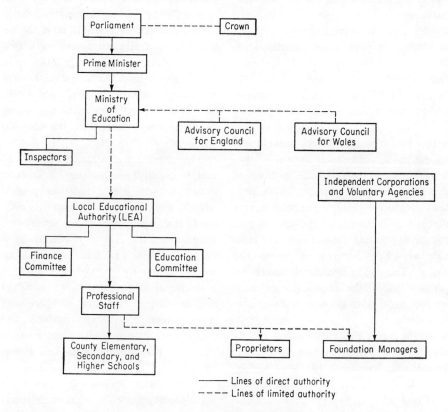

Figure 19. Lines of Educational Authority in England since 1944

viding for other age groups. As might be expected this permissive climate soon brought about extensive differences among the several districts. Some districts with ample resources and high expectations extended their offerings to serve the needs of persons not usually enrolled in elementary schools. The number of schools maintained in such districts and the number of pupils enrolled sometimes reached such proportions that boards were forced to find more efficient types of institutional organization. While the Education Department seems to have encouraged such efforts, it refused either to require boards and school managers to undertake reorganization or to prescribe new forms.

By 1870 a few voluntary schools had taken up the educational theories developed by Pestalozzi, Froebel, Herbart, and other reformers on the Continent. The popular response to these innovations persuaded some boards to introduce aspects of them in the government schools. One such practice led to the separation of children between the ages of five and seven from the older pupils in order to give them special instruction in separate rooms, departments, or even schools. Where separate schools were formed, the lower division became known as "infant" schools. Schools for the older pupils were then called "elementary" schools; their lower divisions were also separated later and were called "junior" schools. The program for children aged seven to thirteen then was divided into six grades or "standards." As child labor laws became more enlightened and employers were prohibited from employing children below the age of eleven, the completion of the first four standards was established as the absolute minimum of schooling to which every child was entitled. The goal of all boards and voluntary agencies, however, was to provide schools that boasted the full program of six standards.

Popular demand soon called for a voluntary seventh standard, and later several additional "ex-standards." The Education Department not only approved all these modifications and additions, but also provided supplementary grants to help support them. Schools which added one or more standards beyond the normal six came to be known as "higher elementary" schools. However, a district which boasted several elementary schools might prefer to bring all the pupils who had completed the basic six standards to a central place where a special school, a "higher grade" school, could be provided for them. Such schools soon standardized their offerings by adopting a three-year course as the minimum.

This upward extension of the elementary program was achieved, in large part, by the addition of science and technical instruction for which the Department of Science and Art provided both direction and financial support. Where higher grade schools offered a program heavily weighted in favor of science and technology they were authorized to be designated as "organized science" schools. This distinction seems to have been much sought after because it qualified the teachers of the science courses to receive supplements to their salaries based on the number of their pupils who passed the examinations conducted by the Department of Science and Art.[12]

Still another innovation in elementary education was introduced, not by the local boards, but by local civil au-

[12] *Ibid.*, p. 480.

thorities charged with the administration of the poor laws and factory acts. These officials were required to look after indigent and delinquent children with funds provided by local taxes and, sometimes, by the employers of children of school age. As the nineteenth century progressed such laws required the authorities to provide children who came under their jurisdiction a suitable education. As a rule the local officials did not take these responsibilities too seriously, but now and then an enlightened citizen or employer became instrumental in establishing an outstanding school in which underprivileged children were given instruction not merely in the usual elementary skills, but also in special skills useful in making a living. Such schools became known as "factory," "work," or "industrial" schools, and sometimes by the less flattering term of "ragged" schools. In 1902, when all educational responsibilities of the county councils were assigned to the LEAs, these schools were integrated with the other elementary and secondary schools to form unitary county systems.

The reluctance with which the government compelled local communities to provide schools or required individuals to attend them had allowed illiteracy to continue on a wide scale. Meanwhile, rapid social changes had created new educational needs, and the agencies operating schools, both government and voluntary, were pressed for help by persons far beyond the usual age of elementary school pupils. Thus, a substantial number of evening and other adult classes and schools were established. Indeed, after 1902, the LEAs were called upon to provide such facilities not merely to eliminate illiteracy, but primarily to extend the education

of adults into areas which the standard elementary programs did not reach. One might speculate on the possibility that the late entry of the government into the field of universal and free education may have contributed to the popular demand for further education and ultimately made England a world leader in adult education.

In contrast to the extensive developments in vernacular instruction enumerated above, secondary education continued for a time along the lines of the traditional grammar schools. Almost without exception secondary schools were either of the proprietary or the foundation type with respect to their sponsorship and control. The age range of their pupils paralleled that of the elementary and higher grade schools. Their programs of instruction differed from those in elementary schools primarily in that they offered instruction in foreign languages and prepared, or pretended to prepare, some of their students for admission to the older universities. To attract students, some of the weaker schools had added English curricula; to secure grants from the Department of Science and Art, they introduced instruction in mathematics, science, and technology. In such cases the distinction between the higher levels of elementary education and the English portions of the secondary schools became quite unclear. Conservative elements in government therefore came to look upon the higher forms of elementary education as unwarranted intrusions into a field reserved to the secondary schools.

Official expression of such feeling occurred in 1900 when the Cockerton judgment declared that tax money could not be used for educational purposes other than to support instruction on the elementary level. At the same time the Board of Education ruled that elementary schools would not be allowed to enroll pupils above the age of fifteen. That same year the Board ruled that elementary schools no longer could qualify for the grants they had been receiving from the Department of Science and Art. The combined effects of these adverse rulings would have restricted public support for elementary education to the infant schools and the six-standard elementary schools. It was too late, however, for the government to take such backward steps. A storm of protests precipitated the thoroughgoing educational reforms called for in the Education Act of 1902, the creation of the Local Educational Authorities, and the extension of public support to all levels.

The subordination of both elementary and secondary education under the same local administrative agency cleared the way for the development of a comprehensive, integrated system of education within each local district. The LEAs were authorized to raise money by taxation for secondary and higher as well as for elementary education. They were directed to establish and operate government secondary schools where needed to supplement the services of the private institutions. At the outset the LEAs were reluctant to do so and were disposed to encourage the private schools to expand their offerings and enrollments by giving them supplementary funds, but the existing foundations and school proprietors were not able to satisfy the demand. As a result some organized science and higher grade schools were taken over by the LEAs and operated as government secondary schools, and a number of new ones

were built. The curricula were made to include foreign languages and, in general, to provide a preparation for further study at a university or another institution of higher education.

This inclination to divert higher grade schools to the purposes of the traditional grammar schools threatened to leave pupils who wished to continue in school beyond the age of thirteen, but not in a highly academic program, without a suitable offering. Obviously a variety of postelementary school programs was needed, particularly when the compulsory school attendance age was raised to fifteen. In 1905–1906 the Board of Education approved the establishment of three-year higher elementary schools even in places where secondary schools of the more conventional type already were located. Such schools were to continue the type of instruction provided in the lower elementary schools so that pupils would be better prepared to enter employment in shops and mills. Furthermore, LEAs might provide specialized training "... bearing on the future occupations of the scholars, whether boys or girls." Such instruction would not be approved, however, unless it also provided a progressive course of study in the English language and literature, in elementary mathematics, and in history and geography. Drawing and manual work for boys and domestic subjects for girls had to be included as part of the general or special instruction.[13]

Admission to these special courses of instruction was limited to pupils who already had attended a regular elementary school for two years and had

[13] Hadow Commission, *The Education of the Adolescent*, H.M. Stationery Office, London, 1927, p. 29.

reached the age of twelve. No scholar might remain after completing three years, or beyond the end of the school year which would terminate before his sixteenth birthday. These provisions for a rather casual preparation for employment soon opened the doors to better-conceived training programs. Trade, industrial, and commercial schools were established by the LEAs, and sometimes operated side by side with higher elementary schools in populous regions.

The entrance of the government into specialized education on the postelementary level inevitably led to its extension to higher levels as well. Technical education, for example, was made available in "senior technical" schools for individuals beyond the age of fifteen, and in higher technical schools, institutes, and colleges for older students. New departments and faculties of science and technology were established by universities. Meanwhile, regional universities and colleges, reminiscent of the University of London with respect to their comprehensive offerings and special services, have extended opportunities in higher education to a large part of the population. These facilities can be utilized in residence, in extension, or even by correspondence. Whatever is lacking, the LEAs are authorized to supply.

Several new types of secondary institutions merit special notice. The first is the "secondary modern," or simply the "modern," school. It evolved from the higher grade and organized science schools to provide a general secondary education not heavily weighted with language instruction. Schools of this type are not so highly specialized as the technical schools. Thus grammar schools, secondary modern, and tech-

nical schools now operate side by side, serving the same age ranges, but dividing the secondary school population into three separate streams on the basis of postschool interests and to some degree on the basis of academic ability.

It is apparent that where communities are forced to maintain three parallel but separate schools, problems of social discrimination as well as of operational economy will arise. Hence, in some places experiments have been undertaken to combine the three types under one roof. These schools are called "comprehensive" schools and are currently receiving considerable attention both at home and abroad.

Finally, the LEAs have been directed to provide adequate educational opportunities to all persons beyond compulsory school age who need or desire such education. The Education Act of 1944 specifically stated that all young people below the age of eighteen, not in full-time attendance at some school, must receive part-time instruction.[14] At the same time the LEAs were made responsible for recruiting and training teachers, a task which had formerly been handled rather inadequately by the model schools and pupil-teacher centers, many of which were established by the voluntary societies prior to 1870. All these additional responsibilities gave rise to a new conception of that which the English now refer to as "further" education. Some of this is to be provided in *county* colleges under the sponsorship of the LEAs. While it appears that as yet only a very few institutions fitting this description have come into being, possibly because the technical institutes currently are proving more popular than

[14] British Information Services, *Education in Britain,* May, 1948, p. 16.

had been anticipated, county colleges ultimately might become a key section of the English educational pattern. They could, for example, carry the major responsibility for training teachers for the primary schools, and at the same time could offer a varied and extensive program of full- as well as part-time studies in other aspects of postsecondary education as well.

Extending and improving opportunities

This review of developments shows that educational opportunities have been extended both horizontally and vertically since 1870. There is now a wide range of general and special programs from which the individual may choose, according to his ability and interests, and he may rise through specialized training to a high level of competency in his chosen field. Meanwhile the compulsory school-attendance policy now requires that each child be sent to an approved and appropriate school for a specified number of years. While parents or guardians may still choose between government and voluntary schools on all levels, all elementary and secondary schools must submit to government inspection, meet minimum standards to protect the health and safety of the pupils, and provide curricula that conform with basic programs and standards of instruction set by the Ministry of Education. Voluntary schools may, of course, exceed the prescribed minima; but they are not free to set their own courses and standards except in the area of religious instruction.

Making the LEAs responsible for developing adequate educational facilities and services within their respective counties has brought about a high degree of coordination among both the government and the voluntary schools. While the dual system has been retained in principle, the LEAs provide support and direction to voluntary schools to enable them to make an acceptable contribution to the total national effort. In return, all schools receiving aid must accept on a scholarship basis substantial numbers of pupils who are unable to pay the tuition fees, but are otherwise qualified. Furthermore, the LEAs may assign children to voluntary schools if the special needs of such children can be better served there than in government schools.

So that pupils can transfer readily between government and voluntary schools, a standard program of instruction has been developed. All instruction to approximately age twelve is identified as "primary" education and is provided in nursery schools and kindergartens, infant schools, and junior schools. "Secondary" education covers the five-year span from age twelve to sixteen and is provided in grammar schools, modern schools, and technical schools or some combination of these. Since school attendance on either a full- or part-time basis is required to age eighteen, LEAs provide further education in technical schools and county colleges for the sixteen-to-eighteen-year age group; and to those who desire it and can use it, to age twenty and beyond. Semi-independent and independent universities and colleges provide a variety of opportunities in higher education.

Within this coordinated system of schools, colleges, and universities the individual may now move rather freely in whatever direction his interests and talent may determine. A program of

167

scholarships and stipends, including grants to the family to compensate for the loss of the student's earnings while attending school, encourage able but poor students to make the most of their intellectual endowments. To administer this scholarship program the English have borrowed the competitive examination system developed on the Continent. The qualifying, or selective, process is introduced at the completion of primary education in the form of the "eleven-plus" examinations. Prepared and administered on a national scale, these examinations are intended to help the LEAs determine which form of secondary education the child is qualified to enter. Since the grammar schools enjoy a preferred status, admission to them is highly desired but rather restricted. Similar selective examinations at the end of the secondary school programs regulate admission to specialized curricula and institutions on the level of higher education, including teacher education. The most selective of all are the matriculation or qualifying examinations administered by the universities.

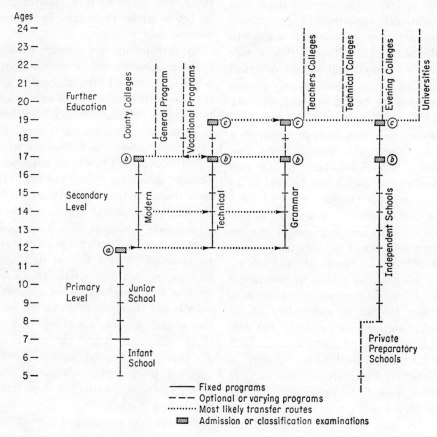

Figure 20. Educational Institutions in England since 1944

a. "Eleven-plus" examinations.

b. Ordinary certificate examinations.

c. Advanced certificate examinations.

These are of several forms, depending upon their specific use, and may be administered regionally as examinations for the school-leaving certificates, one part at age sixteen-plus, and the other at age eighteen-plus.

The new opportunities afforded by the English educational system include numerous auxiliary services which the LEAs are called upon to provide. Many of these are outgrowths of the emergency measures introduced during World War II when school children were evacuated from the major target areas. A government program for feeding school children was introduced at the close of the war when widespread malnutrition threatened. A similar program today seeks to assure each child at least the minimum diet needed for proper growth and good health. Medical and dental services also are provided, largely through periodic examinations. Treatment not available in the school clinics is provided, of course, under the National Health Service, England's form of socialized medicine. Clothing may also be provided to enable children to take full advantage of educational opportunities. An LEA might, for example, equip a young man or woman whom it is sending to a grammar school or university at county expense with a complete outfit of clothing. Finally, the LEAs are required to provide recreational programs and facilities, under suitable direction, to all young people between the ages of fifteen and twenty. This is known as the Youth Service. The Ministery of Education provides central direction, but the program itself is administered by the LEAs.

This extensive list of new educational programs, institutions, and auxiliary services indicates more clearly, perhaps, than any other facet of national life the extent of the social change England has experienced in the last one hundred years. The former rather rigid class structure has been replaced by arrangements that afford the individual substantial freedom of movement. The schools are expected to aid such movement, particularly that of gifted and ambitious young people in need of economic assistance. The national government now assumes full responsibility for placing adequate facilities and services at the disposal of every child, but it neither excludes private agencies from the field of education nor presumes to administer a national system of schools from a central office. English educational administration is highly decentralized. Each LEA has full responsibility and authority to provide the variety and quality of education deemed necessary in its jurisdiction. This unusual relationship between the Ministry and the LEAs makes the English system of education unique.

References

Books

Adams, George Burton: *Constitutional History of England*, Holt, New York, 1936.

Alexander, W. P.: *Education in England*, St Martin's, New York, 1954.

Armfelt, Roger: *The Structure of English Education*, Cohen & West, London, 1955.

Banks, Olive: *Party and Prestige in English Secondary Education*, Routledge, London, 1955.

Barker, Sir Ernest: *British Universities*, Longmans, London, 1949.

Barnard, H. C.: *A Short History of Eng-*

lish Education from 1760 to 1944, University of London Press, Ltd., London, 1947.

Baron, George: *A Bibliographical Guide to the English Educational System,* Athlone, London, 1951.

Brauer, George C.: *Education of a Gentleman: Theories of Gentlemanly Education,* Bookman Associates, New York, 1959.

Chester, D. N., and F. M. G. Wilson: *The Organization of British Central Government,* G. Allen, London, England, 1957.

Curtis, S. J.: *Education in Britain Since 1900,* Andrew Dakers, London, 1952.

————: *History of Education in Great Britain,* 2d ed., University Tutorial Press, London, 1951.

Dent, H. C.: *Change in English Education,* University of London Press, Ltd., London, 1952.

————: *The Educational System of England and Wales,* University of London Press, Ltd., London, 1961.

————: *Part-time Education in Great Britain: An Historical Outline,* Turnstile Press, London, 1949.

————: *Secondary Education for All: Origins and Development in England,* Routledge, London, 1949.

Elton, G. R.: *England under the Tudors,* Methuen, London, 1959.

Everett, Samuel: *Growing Up in English Secondary Schools,* The University of Pittsburgh Press, Pittsburgh, Pa., 1959.

Greenough, Alfred, and F. A. Crofts: *Theory and Practice in the New Secondary Schools,* University of London Press, Ltd., London, 1949.

Jacks, Maurice Leonard: *Modern Trends in Education,* rev. ed., Andrew Melrose, London, 1952.

Jackson, W. Eric: *Structure of Local Government in England and Wales,* Longmans, New York, 1949.

Kneller, George: *Higher Learning in Britain,* University of California Press, Berkeley, Calif., 1955.

Leach, A. F.: *English Schools at the Reformation,* Archibald Constable, London, 1860.

————: *The Schools of Medieval England,* Macmillan, New York, 1915.

Lowndes, G. A. N.: *The English Educational System,* Hutchinson, London, 1960.

Mack, E. C.: *Public Schools and British Opinion: 1780–1860,* Columbia, New York, 1939.

————: *Public Schools and British Opinion since 1860,* Columbia, New York, 1941.

Marriott, Sir John A. R.: *English Political Institutions,* The University Press, Oxford, 1938.

————: *Modern England 1885–1955,* Methuen, London, 1960.

Morrison, Herbert: *Government and Parliament,* Oxford, Fair Lawn, N.J., 1954.

Morton, A. L.: *A People's History of England,* Random House, New York, 1938.

Oglivie, Vivian: *The English Public School,* Macmillan, New York, 1957.

Passow, A. Harry: *Secondary Education for All: The English Approach,* Ohio State University Press, Columbus, Ohio, 1961.

Pedley, Robert: *Comprehensive Education: A New Approach,* Victor Gollancz, London, 1956.

Poole, Reginald Lane: *Medieval Thought and Learning,* 2d rev. ed., Society for Promoting Christian Knowledge, Macmillan, New York, 1920.

Richmond, William Kenneth: *Blue Print for a Common School,* Routledge, London, 1943.

Rickard, J. A.: *History of England,* Barnes & Noble, New York, 1961.

Trevelyan, George Macaulay: *History of England,* Longmans, London, 1926.

Pamphlets and periodicals

Board of Education: *The Education of the Adolescent* (Hadow Committee Report), H.M. Stationery Office, London, 1926.

———: *The Public Schools and the General Educational System* (Fleming Committee Report), H.M. Stationery Office, London, 1944.

———: *Secondary Education* (Spens Committee Report), H.M. Stationery Office, London, 1938.

British Information Services: *Books and Documents on Education in Great Britain*, Cox & Sharland, London, March, 1961.

———: *The British Parliament*, I.D. 952 (rev.), Cox & Sharland, London, November, 1955.

———: *Contemporary Britain*, New York.

———: *Education in Britain*, I.D. 606 (rev.), New York, May, 1948.

———: *Education in Great Britain*, I.D. 606 (rev.), New York, August, 1960.

———: *Government and Administration of the United Kingdom*, I.D. 1233, Cox & Sharland, London, November, 1957.

———: *Human Rights in the United Kingdom*, I.D. 1311, New York, October, 1958.

———: *Primary and Secondary Schools in Britain*, I.D. 1299 (rev.), New York, November, 1960.

———: *Social Services in Britain*, I.D. 780 (rev.), New York, November, 1959.

Department of External Affairs: *Report of the Commonwealth Education Conference*, Oxford, England, July, 1959.

Fisher, Norman: *Our Schools*, Bureau of Current Affairs, 117 Piccadilly, London, 1949.

Guterman, Simeon L.: "The 'Church-School Question' in England and France," *Comparative Education Review*, vol. 7, pp. 28–35, June, 1963.

Jessup, Frank: *Local Government in Outline: A Study of How the System Works in England and Wales*, Bureau of Current Affairs, 117 Piccadilly, London, 1948.

Ministry of Education: *Education: 1900–1950*, H.M. Stationery Office, London, 1951.

———: *The Future Development of Higher Technological Education*, H.M. Stationery Office, London, 1950.

———: *A Guide to the Educational System of England and Wales*, H.M. Stationery Office, London, 1945.

———: *School and Life*, H.M. Stationery Office, London, 1947.

———: *Special Educational Treatment*, H.M. Stationery Office, London, 1946.

Niblett, W. R.: "Trends in Education in England Today," *Educational Forum*, vol. 26, pp. 403–415, May, 1962.

Taylor, William S.: *Education in England*, Bulletin of the Bureau of School Service, vol. 11, no. 4, University of Kentucky, Lexington, Ky., 1939.

Webb, Robert K.: *The New Britain*, Headline Series, no. 114, Foreign Policy Association, New York, 1955.

Wilson, H. Martin: "Evaluation, Promotion and Grading in English Schools," *The Educational Forum*, vol. 18, pp. 187–195, January, 1954.

CHAPTER 7

Russian Education: Developing the Communist Man

One of the few radically new educational patterns to emerge in the twentieth century is that which has arisen under the direction of the Communist Party. It repeatedly has been labeled a "revolutionary" party, a term that describes very aptly its avowed purpose of establishing new political, economic, and social systems specifically designed to achieve its unique philosophical ends. The Communist revolution enjoyed its initial success in Russia during the period of turmoil created by World War I. World War II afforded further opportunity to topple governments in neighboring states. Through all these developments Russia has remained the mother country of the Communists, and it is there one must look for evidence of the basic pattern that is emerging in the satellite countries.

It is possible that in recent years students of comparative education have published more descriptive information on the Soviet Union than on all other national systems combined. There is ample information from which one may construct a picture of the operating schools and the activities carried on therein. What is lacking are accounts of why particular institutions and activities have been selected by the Party leadership to achieve their revolutionary ends. The following description will attempt to provide that type of information.

From the fifteenth to the twentieth century

Unlike Western Europe where ecclesiastical and civil authorities engaged in almost continuous struggles for supremacy, pre-Communist Russia presented an example of close cooperation between the two. By A.D. 1000 the Eastern Church, that is, the main body of the Christian (Catholic) Church which remained after the Roman branch withdrew, had taken firm root among the mixed peoples that inhabited the large area known as the land of the Rus, a Scandinavian word for northmen. Thereafter these peoples were subjected to a succession of invasions by Mongols, and it was not until the fifteenth century that the military exploits of Ivan III and Basil III stayed the Mongols and laid the foundations for national unity.

However, the church played the decisive role in bringing the Russian peoples together, because its ecclesiastical structure provided a religious basis for the absolute monarchy. When Constantinople, the seat of the Eastern Church, fell to the Turks in A.D. 1453, the Russian clergy put forth the claim that Moscow was now destined to become the capital of true (Orthodox) Christendom. Simultaneously, Archduke Ivan IV, better known as The Terrible, assumed the title of *Czar* (Caesar) and was pronounced the only true and faithful Christian prince. In freeing the Russians of Tartar despotism Ivan ruled like an Oriental potentate, but with the vigorous support of the clergy he was able to consolidate the powers of the crown so securely that they were never entirely relinquished until the monarchy was destroyed by the Communist Revolution in 1917.

Meanwhile the claims of the Russian clergy to independence from the Eastern Church were confirmed by Constantinople in 1589, and the Russian Orthodox Church became a reality. The church and the monarchy now established such close working arrangements that within two centuries the phrase "orthodoxy, autocracy, and nationalism," had become its distinguishing label. In return for the active support of the church, the ruling house used its civil powers to stamp out any signs of religious dissension. Wealth and power were gathered in by the civil administrators and the clergy. A feudal system was developed which rested on agriculture and hand labor and which reduced the peasants to a state of serfdom from which they were not released until 1861. Even as late as 1910, 84 per cent of the population was rural.

The beginnings of education

Early in the seventeenth century the Romanov family came to power; it ruled continuously until 1917, with absolute power for much of this extended period. While Russia did not share the Renaissance with Western Europe, the early Romanovs initiated cultural relationships with England, France, and Germany. As the seventeenth century drew to a close Peter the Great made a conscious effort to "Westernize" his vast empire. Western specialists were invited to help introduce new ideas and to develop more constructive forms of administrative control. A naval academy and several schools of engineering were founded. Lower schools were introduced, which came to be known as "cypher" schools because of the attention given to arithmetic. Children of the nobility

were ordered to attend them. In 1721 Peter called upon the Church to increase its efforts in education. Diocesan schools were then developed, and these gained such favor with the nobility that by mid-century the cypher schools had disappeared. The competition between cypher and diocesan schools, however, marked the beginning of a struggle between the crown and the Holy Synod for supremacy in education, which was joined shortly by other agencies, including local school councils.

Higher education also received its first significant support from the constructive efforts of Peter. Although a theological school had existed in Moscow from the end of the seventeenth century,[1] he resolved to foster a more practical trend in Russian intellectual circles by establishing an academy of science. He died before this was accomplished, but his widow founded the Academy of Science in St. Petersburg in 1726. The academy consisted of an association of learned men, who engaged in scholarly activities, and a teaching institution called the gymnasium which was designed along German lines and staffed with German teachers. The gymnasium later became the dominant type of secondary education in Russia. In 1755 Peter's daughter Elizabeth founded Moscow University. It, too, followed Western lines and boasted faculties of law, medicine, and philosophy. Significantly, provision was made to enable poor but able young men to acquire an education, but the proportion of such scholarship students probably never exceeded 5 per cent of the enrollments.[2]

[1] Vyacheslau Yelyutin, *Higher Education in the U.S.S.R.*, International Arts and Sciences Press, New York, 1959, p. 5.
[2] *Ibid.*, p. 7.

While Peter had been interested primarily in acquiring the benefits of Western science and technology, Catherine II, who ascended the throne in 1763, gave attention to a wide range of philosophical and educational ideas produced by Europe's eighteenth-century intelligentsia. She requested the French encyclopedist Diderot and the German-French Baron Friedrich Melchior von Grimm to present educational plans for her country. In keeping with the plan she ultimately accepted, the realm was divided into provinces for administrative purposes, with a "charity committee" in each province charged with responsibility for establishing schools in all cities and populous places. This was followed in 1782 by the appointment of a commission to develop a complete system of primary schools, including their organization and program, the preparation of instructional materials, and the training of teachers. When the commission presented its recommendation in 1786, she gave it imperial sanction. Although her grand plan to establish a network of schools was not realized, she did increase the number of technical schools and founded a school for girls at Smolny Monastery from which a limited program of education for women developed.

The establishment of charity committees was the beginning of an educational bureaucracy which soon came under the tight control of the central government and afforded channels for imperial domination of the state schools. From 1796 to 1863, especially, the central government worked to extend its control. Some of its efforts were motivated by benevolent impulses, as, for example, the establishment of the Ministry of Public Enlightenment by Alexander I in 1802. This was followed in 1803 by the di-

vision of the realm into administrative districts for educational purposes, each district headed by a curator appointed by the emperor. There was to be a university in each district, administered by its own university council. Primary and secondary education was to be provided by primary schools and gymnasiums with coordinated programs to provide a seven-year course. French and German influences were evident in these plans.

The Napoleonic Wars, and especially the burning of Moscow, were interpreted by many Russians as evidence of the untrustworthiness of the West. Consequently a reaction developed which brought on a resurgence of orthodoxy and the elevation of the Holy Synod to a position of domination over even the civil powers.[3] The church and the monarchy now combined to combat secularism; the university councils lost their autonomy and, together with the secondary schools, were placed under ecclesiastical scrutiny. All forms of private education were brought under supervision. The Jesuits, whose schools had become popular with the nobility, were banished. However, the opposition of the nobility and other influential families to these repressive actions soon won some exemptions for a few of their most favored institutions on condition that these would provide the monarchy with a flow of upper-class candidates for state service.

The repressive measures initiated under Alexander were intensified under his brother Nicholas I. The Ministry of Education increased its bureaucratic controls over all aspects of education and used its extensive powers to develop

[3] William H. E. Johnson, *Russia's Educational Heritage,* Carnegie Press, Pittsburgh, Pa., 1950, pp. 78ff.

174

stronger imperial authority, to enhance the status of the ruling clique, and to repress the masses. An official decree issued on December 8, 1828, ordered the breakup of the continuity that existed between primary schools and the gymnasiums. Primary school offerings were reduced to the bare elements in order that the masses might not be stirred to unrest. Secondary and higher education, on the other hand, were made to support the imperial ambitions by raising up a cadre of officials from the right families. But in spite of these strong measures, some liberal groups continued to resist, especially in the universities.

When Nicholas died in 1855, his successor Alexander II reversed the trend toward absolutism in a series of well-intended acts. Freeing the serfs in 1861 was most disruptive, for it brought social and economic consequences of almost catastrophic dimensions. For education, however, the authorization of elected county councils with power to establish schools with taxes raised locally was an act of significant consequence.[4] Known as *zemstvos,* these councils appear to have used their authority with enthusiasm. Although the formation of the councils was not mandatory and school attendance was not compulsory, *zemstvos* schools soon earned enough popular support to make the Holy Synod feel threatened. The Synod therefore set up a system of competing parochial schools in places where *zemstvos* schools existed; large areas of the country were left without schools of either type.

In the years that followed, various private agencies operated in the field of education either to provide children of

[4] Johnson, *op. cit.,* pp. 136–138.

the more affluent families a better education or to extend charity instruction to children of the extremely poor. But even the combined efforts of the Ministry of Education, the Holy Synod, and the *zemstvos* fell far short of what was needed to bring enlightenment to the millions of Russians who lived beyond the reach of the operating schools. As the nineteenth century drew to a close, the people became increasingly restless, and the crown and the Holy Synod seemed to draw together in an effort to consolidate their forces. The *zemstvos* schools as well as those of the private agencies came under stricter supervision. The curricula and materials of instruction were subjected to more exacting tests of religious and political orthodoxy. Popular demands for more schools and greater freedom of operation were suppressed. University students, inspired by the writings of a number of crusading liberal thinkers, demonstrated against these repressive measures while peasants repeatedly broke out in riots against specific abuses suffered at the hands of the imperial or provincial officials.

The beginnings of the revolution

That monstrous problems had been allowed to develop through the misguided policies of the monarchy was acknowledged in many quarters. But in seeking suitable solutions, the intellectuals split into two schools of thought. Some looked westward to the ideological goals directing the reform forces in Europe. The others extolled Russia's past and found therein the ingredients for building a great social system along Slavic lines. Herzen, representing the liberals, had written that the West alone could

175

enlighten the dark gulf of Russian life.[5] Gogol, an ardent spokesman for the Slavophiles, pictured Russia speeding toward world leadership in the opposite direction, as follows:

Russia of mine, are you not also speeding like a troika which nothing can overtake?—Whither are you speeding Russia of mine? Whither? Answer me! But no answer comes— only the weird sound of your collarbells. Rent into a thousand shreds, the air roars past you, as you are overtaking the whole world, and shall one day force all nations, all empires to stand aside to give way to you.[6]

However, poetic visions of the vast potential of their motherland were not enough to eliminate the hard facts of hunger, ignorance, and poverty with which the Russian people were forced to face the twentieth century. Restlessness continued among the peasants, the workers, the students, and the intellectuals. Much of the thinking of the reformers turned increasingly toward utilitarian ends. The developing technologies of Europe and America, together with their rich harvest of economic goods, became more and more attractive. The materialistic aspirations of this group were accompanied by a rejection of existing standards of excellence and conduct. The writings of Karl Marx and his disciples became attractive, and these materialistic leanings hardened into dogmas prophetic of the twentieth-century Communists.

It would be a great injustice to ignore the numerous courageous and enlightened leaders who risked economic and

[5] Hans Kohn, *Basic History of Modern Russia*, Van Nostrand, Princeton, N.J., 1957, p. 132.

[6] *Ibid.*, p. 129.

political ruin, exile, and even death to challenge the abuses of power of which the monarchy and the Holy Synod were guilty during the last century before the revolution. The fact remains, however, that whatever improvements these brave men were able to wring from the reluctant officials were far too few, too little, and too late to put off indefinitely the rising expectations of the underprivileged masses. Repeated revolts were put down with brutal force reminiscent of the practices of the ancient despots. The Holy Synod was given authority to supervise the content of the instructional programs to assure orthodoxy and loyalty to the crown. The ruling house was represented as having a divine mandate, and the imperial Ministry of Education was made responsible for education in all areas and on all levels. When the clergy could not quiet the outbreak of opposition by religious persuasion, the crown did not shrink from calling upon the ruthless Cossacks to put it down with the sword.

Thwarted by the united opposition of the church and the crown, the smoldering rebellion burst its restraints when the Russians found themselves hopelessly involved in World War I. In spite of the general state of ignorance— 70 per cent were illiterate even at this late date—the staggering losses of men and the breakdown of the machinery of control indicated the failures of the monarchy so clearly that the people were aroused to take direct action. This was a general uprising, however, and the Communists did not move to take advantage of the situation until the previously existing machinery of government had been destroyed and the people found they had no effective system to put in its place. This state of confusion was precisely what the Communists needed and wanted. Although they constituted a small minority, they had a plan and a well-organized and disciplined corps of adherents; and they succeeded in seizing power in a remarkably short time.

Russian education

The millions of Russians who revolted against the monarchy were neither acquainted with the philosophical foundations of communism nor dedicated to its materialism. But neither did they see clearly any prospect other than the leadership offered by the Communists for bringing order and prosperity to their confused land. Leadership obviously was not coming forward from their own ranks. The radical corps of social idealists, later known as the Bolsheviks, had been at work among them since 1903 teaching a doctrine of revolution by the workers and peasants. Under the leadership of Trotsky and Lenin this group, knit together by vigorous opposition, had grown to 200,000 fanatically loyal and disciplined members. After seizing power the Bolshevik political movement was transformed into the Communist Party, and the workers and peasants who the Bolsheviks had promised would rule their own world as a sort of workers' democracy were subordinated to its control. Real political power in the Soviet Union today is exercised not by the people, as promised in the constitution, but by those in control of the Communist Party, the membership of which includes a very small fraction of the total population.[7]

Philosophically speaking, communism

is the antithesis of absolute monarchy. Authority in the latter is said to be based on a divine mandate and is justified by theological arguments. A state church, protected and supported by the civil powers, invariably has been used to help keep the subjects under control. The functions of government are said to be guided by knowledge received from God. Therefore, to resist or merely to question the wisdom of royal commands or decrees is readily branded as sacrilege.

Within the Communist Party, however, dialectical materialism is the official philosophy and religion.[8] The Communist's religious position is that of atheism, that is, the assertion *as an act of faith* that there is no God or any reason for man to act as though there were a supernatural. The most direct contradiction to the monarchy offered by the Communists, therefore, was their rejection of the theological arguments on which the authority of the monarchy had rested. The slogan, "Religion is the opiate of the people," had a very specific reference for the Russians, and the violence with which the royal family was destroyed and the monarchy uprooted was matched by parallel actions against the Russian Orthodox Church and other forms of organized religion. The doctrine of divine guidance was scorned, and a militant atheism was made the official religious attitude.

Communism rapidly took on such orthodoxy that it has often been likened to a religious movement. Contemporary writers on Russian affairs have pointed out that the Soviet Union is a "theologi-

---

[7] Estimates since 1959 range from about 3 to 6 per cent.

[8] Religion here is defined as a positive assertion, as an act of faith, regarding the existence or nonexistence of God, and man's relationship to Him.

177

cal society" with its prophets, scriptures, martyrs, and dogmas. Communist dogma theoretically is infallible and deviationism or "revisionism" is considered rank heresy. This comparison between communistic doctrine and theology could be extended by referring to their definitions of morality and sin and to the sponsored programs of aggressive evangelism. But this easy analogy, while containing considerable validity, fails to explain satisfactorily the readily noticeable opportunism in Communist decisions of policy; nor does it identify the imputed source of their knowledge of the good.

The metaphysics of communism asserts a materialistic reality and, therefore, admits no source of knowledge by which men may guide their actions other than the material universe itself. Knowledge of the good is said to be acquired in the systematic study of the events of history, particularly the successive stages in the evolution of the social environment of man. The determining forces in this evolutionary process are said to be economic, and are evidenced in man's historic struggle for material goods. However, a comprehensive view of the evolving social scene is said to show a persistent trend to eliminate the class differences which have perpetuated the struggle throughout history. The conclusion is inevitable that evolution is on a course that eventually will eliminate class differences based on the possession of material goods, and thereby will bring an end to the class struggle and to the evolutionary process itself. The classless society therefore is taken to be the ultimate good, a state of excellence which man may neither contradict nor avoid. The victory of communism over all competing forms of

178

social direction and control is said to be assured. All that remains is for men to give intelligent assistance to the evolutionary processes in order that the maximum benefits of the classless society may be enjoyed by all within the shortest possible time. Any arrangement, regulation, or act that furthers this end is "good"; any resistance is destructive, inhuman, and immoral. The "communist ethics" must be regarded in these terms.

Social role

The Communist philosophy is so completely different from that which prevailed in Russia prior to the revolution that the Party found it necessary not merely to transform the social system, but the attitudes, loyalties, and emotional habits of the people as well. Indeed, the transformation must succeed in remaking the people before the new social order can be made to function as it should. This necessity the Party leadership recognized, and it is a matter of record that education was taken over within the first year as one of the chief instruments for establishing the new order.[9]

School attendance was made compulsory and free, conditions that had never been achieved under the monarchy. The policy of utilizing local school authorities, made popular by the *zemstvos,* was adopted, and all traces of a dual school system were eliminated. A basic program of instruction was prescribed to provide a common background and training for all, with opportunity for

[9] James Bowen, *Soviet Education: Anton Maharenko and the Years of Experiment,* The University of Wisconsin Press, Madison, Wis., 1962, p. 41.

each person to progress as far as ability and the available facilities would allow. Nevertheless, differentiated functions were recognized for those who ultimately might serve as leaders through the direction of the Party and those who would serve primarily as workers.

The Party leadership was expected to engage in a continuous search for ways in which the people, collectively, might render effective assistance to the forces of evolution in achieving the predetermined and ultimate goals. This is a process of discovery requiring intensive study, properly directed. Not only must those who engage in it be masters of the theoretical bases of communism, but they must also be able to observe in an objective and reliable way the forces of economic determinism at work and to identify accurately the existing status of society as the point at which assistance is to be provided. These functions, it is said, call for the employment of the instruments and procedures of objective science to study the social phenomena in both their historical and contemporary settings, and from such data to project by a process of extrapolation the trends that are indicated. One purpose of education, therefore, is to provide a continuous and adequate flow of leaders trained in these disciplines.

The need for leaders was regarded as especially acute following the revolution because of the "political immaturity" of the people. It was for this reason that the Communist Party, into which only trained and proven individuals were admitted as members, was declared the "vanguard of the people" [10] and established as the only political organization permitted to exist. The top eche-

[10] Article 126 of the Constitution of the U.S.S.R.

lons of the Party are said to be filled by those members best qualified by training and devotion to employ the Communist dialectic, the process of determining the next steps needed to move society nearer the ultimate goal. Schools obviously are expected to afford the necessary training, but the identification of leaders, and their ultimate specialized development, is left to the Party itself. For this purpose Communist youth organizations have been established parallel with the schools and operate cooperatively with them.

By far the largest part of the Russian educational effort, and the part which is most readily studied by outsiders, is directed to the training of the masses for their new role as members of the classless society. The schools seek to instill each child with the idea that he has a socially useful role to play. To do this he must acquire the usual literary skills. But the new order is to be built on productive labor. Therefore, technical skills and habits of work must also be acquired in order to produce the material goods needed to make society one of abundance for all. Lenin wrote:

It is impossible to conceive of the ideal future society without the younger generation combining schooling with productive work; neither schooling and upbringing without productive work, nor productive work without parallel schooling and upbringing could be raised to the heights demanded by the present state of technology and scientific knowledge.[11]

[11] As quoted by N. S. Khrushchev in his report to the Twenty-first Extraordinary Congress of the Communist Party of the Soviet Union, Jan. 27, 1959, in support of his reforms. Available from Foreign Languages Publishing House, Moscow, 1959, p. 68.

To this end the principle of "polytechnization" was proclaimed from the outset. Productive work was incorporated in the school programs not merely to develop desired skills, but in the expectation that in "the unification of the mental and manual" the bourgeois tradition would be destroyed.[12]

But the promotion of the new order through education was given a more direct task as well. The schools were to destroy the habits of thought and emotional attachments retained by the people from the preceding era and substitute for them the loyalties, expectations, and forms of security needed by the citizen of a communistic state. The nature of this task was forcefully stated by a leading educator as early as 1918 in the following passage:

> We must exempt children from the pernicious influence of the family. We have to take account of every child, we candidly say that we must nationalize them. From the first days of their life they will be under the beneficial influence of communistic kindergartens and schools. Here they shall grow up as real Communists. Our practical problem is to compel mothers to hand over their children to the Soviet Government.[13]

While the extreme measures suggested in the above passage were not attempted on any extensive scale, their intent was accepted. The making of Communists has been, and is today, the central role of the school in Russia. While only some students will be able to distinguish themselves so that they will be enlisted in the Party, all will be indoctrinated in Communist theories of the social good

[12] Bowen, *op. cit.*, p. 39.
[13] As quoted by Bowen, *op. cit.*, p. 36.

and trained in the practice of the "communist ethics."

Power structure and administrative organization

In the political sense, the name Russia should be used only when referring to the largest of the fifteen republics which constitute the present Soviet Union. However, this republic, the Russian Soviet Federated Socialist Republic (R.S.F.S.R.), includes three-fourths of the area of the Soviet Union and a majority of the people. Furthermore, it provided the nucleus around which the Union was built; and its institutions, including the constitution, have been closely imitated both by the Union and the sister republics. The Russian language is the standard medium of communication not merely in the higher levels of education throughout the Union, but among Communists generally.

Prior to 1936, political power resided with the workers inasmuch as the right to vote was restricted to persons engaged in productive labor and members of the armed forces. A worker's political residence—the place where he voted—was determined by where he worked. He and his fellow workers in the local factory or collective farm constituted a political unit which provided the basis for local government. Periodically, they elected delegates as members of the governing body called the "soviet." A soviet consisted of the main body of delegates, called the "plenum," who met from time to time to discuss matters of local concern, and an executive committee elected by the plenum. The executive committee constituted the administrative branch of government, and its various duties were assigned to its individual members. Thus, one or more members of the executive committee were designated to look after educational matters in the local district.

The local soviets were not autonomous political units, however, for those of a given area or major city were subordinated to a district soviet. Prior to 1936 the delegates to the district soviet were elected by the local soviets rather than by the workers, a method of indirect election which was applied to the higher levels of government as well. Like the local soviets, the district soviet also elected an executive committee to exercise its administrative functions, which were departmentalized in a manner similar to that on the local level. Thus, there was a district director of education to whom the local departments of education were subordinate. Indeed, the district director sometimes has been compared to an American superintendent of schools in a multiple-school district, and his departmental staff generally has included a substantial number of administrative assistants and inspectors. The district director has been a key person in the administration of primary and most secondary education. In addition to his many other duties, he may convene the educational directors or other groups of school personnel in his district in "congresses" to discuss educational policies handed down from the higher levels of government and to interpret such policies for implementation in the individual schools and classrooms.

Prior to 1936 the district soviets elected delegates to regional and provincial soviets. These, in turn, elected delegates to the soviet of the republic; and the all-union soviet was comprised of delegates elected by the soviets of

the republics and autonomous regions. Since 1936, this method of indirect elections has been abandoned and the members of the soviets are elected directly by all the voters of the unit of government involved. Also, local soviets are now based on geographic rather than industrial units, and the franchise has been extended to all citizens aged eighteen or older. Nevertheless, the hierarchical structure of control has been retained so that while the soviet on each administrative level elects its own executive officers, they have authority superior to that of the officers on lower levels. Administrative control in primary and in most aspects of secondary education, therefore, is said to reside with the director, or minister, of education for the republic; and authority extends downward through the successive subordinate levels of government to the directors of education in the local districts. These lines of authority are shown in Figure 21.

The fact that the minister of education of the republic is said to be the highest educational authority indicates that the administration of education is somewhat different from that of many other departments of government. Indeed, there is no all-union ministry of education except for the universities and other forms of higher education including teacher education. Periodically, however, the ministers of education in the several republics meet in a congress to work out uniform policies. When these have been submitted to the all-union executive committee, now known as the cabinet of ministers, and have received its approval, the policies must be followed by all. Thus ". . . although each republic of the Union has its own separate Commissariat [ministry] of

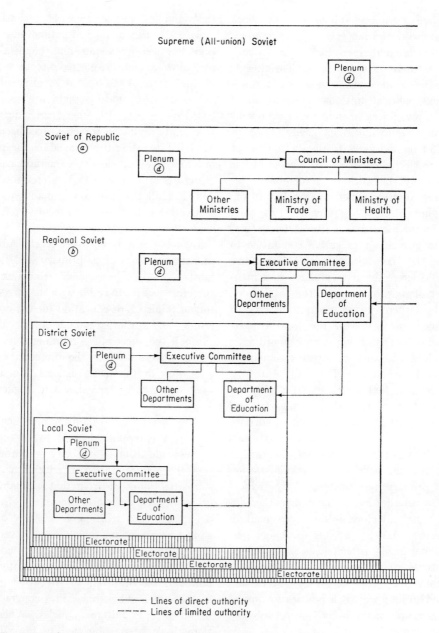

Supreme (All-union) Soviet

Plenum
d

Soviet of Republic
a

Plenum
d

Council of Ministers

Other
Ministries

Ministry of
Trade

Ministry of
Health

Regional Soviet
b

Plenum
d

Executive Committee

Other
Departments

Department
of
Education

District Soviet
c

Plenum
d

Executive Committee

Other
Departments

Department
of
Education

Local Soviet

Plenum
d

Executive Committee

Other
Departments

Department
of
Education

Electorate
Electorate
Electorate
Electorate

———— Lines of direct authority
– – – – Lines of limited authority

Figure 21. The Soviets in the Governmental Structure of the U.S.S.R.
a. Includes nationality and other autonomous groups.
b. Oblasts.   *c. Raions or gorods.*
d. An elected representative body.

182

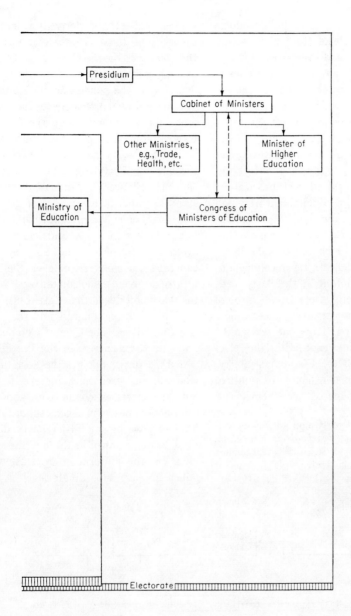

education, the system of public education in the whole of the Union is substantially the same everywhere." [14]

Figure 21 shows that each soviet is elected directly by the voters of the political unit over which it has authority. Theoretically, the soviets are legislative bodies and have control over their executive officers. Actually, however, the Communist philosophy does not permit such pluralism and all decisions leading to the formulation of administrative policy are made by the Central Committee of the Communist Party. Even the Supreme Soviet, which meets only infrequently, merely hears the recommendations placed before it by the Party leaders and transmits them down through the official administrative offices where they are enforced. Thus, the real political power resides not with the electorate, but with the Communist Party.

The Communist principle of political control is designated as "democratic

centralism." It is derived from the theory that there is only one form of the good society, the classless state, and that all government is good only to the degree that the policies adopted are deliberately directed to achieve that form. Since the Communists are the best informed on what is good, they must make policy for everyone. This is achieved through the Party organization, and as shown in Figure 22, a unit of the Party stands parallel to every unit of government. An official representative of the Party is assigned to "participate" in every meeting of a soviet, an executive committee, a congress, or even the faculty of a given school or university. At the all-union level there are both the All-Union Party Congress and the Central Committee. The Central Committee appoints the members of the Presidium which, in turn, appoints the Secretariat who are the executives for the Party. Similar congresses, committees, and secretariats appear on each subordinate level of government. Strict Party discipline locates control at the top and provides for the uniform interpretation of policy on each subordinate level.

[14] Paul Blonsky, "Union of Soviet Socialist Republics," *Yearbook of Education, 1927,* International Institute of Teachers College, Columbia University, Bureau of Publications, New York, 1928, p. 319.

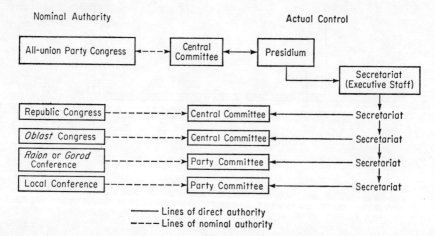

Nominal Authority   Actual Control

——— Lines of direct authority
- - - Lines of nominal authority

Figure 22. Lines of Control in the Communist Party of the U.S.S.R.

The locus of real power exists, then, in the Central Committee, and basic policies originating there are implemented by the secretariats of the lower Party echelons. The Party organization at each level serves as a sort of watchdog scrutinizing all governmental actions on that level. For example, candidates for election to the soviets, as well as for all other elective offices, are not chosen freely by the electorate, but are selected for them by the secretariats and submitted to the voters for approval as a single slate without opposition. At the local level multicandidate slates have now been introduced, but no information is available on how this experiment has been received. It might be observed that over the years candidates nominated by the Communist Party have enjoyed singular success at the polls. Not only are the key positions in the soviets filled by persons under Party discipline—as a consequence of the Party's control over elections—but also the programs of legislation desired by the Party are presented to the soviets in a form that leaves little for them to do but to vote approval. This limitation on legislative deliberation reaches to the Supreme Soviet of the U.S.S.R. itself.

Figure 23 shows the agencies responsible for education on the several administrative levels. The Ministry for Higher and Special Secondary Education is the only administrative agency specifically assigned to the field of education on the all-union level. Of late, however, even this Ministry has restricted its activities to the planning and policy-making areas and has worked with and through the ministries of education in the republics.

Other all-union ministries and agen-cies are operating agencies, but some have relations with the ministries of education and their subordinate departments. Among such is the Main Administration of Labor Reserves, which has a voice not merely in the operation of elementary vocational schools, but also in determining who may continue in school beyond the minimum levels and in what areas they may study. The Ministry of Health is concerned with medical education and the physical well-being of those enrolled in the schools. Other ministries operate specialized training schools to supply personnel for their departments, such as the Ministries of Railways and of Communication. The Ministry of Culture operates closely with the Communist Party to secure proper political indoctrination. Indeed, the Communist Party has two special secretariats operating from the central Committee level to make sure that the schools follow the proper line; and a separate agency, the All-Union Young Communist League, provides for the selection and training of the future Party members through its program of extracurricular activities carried on in close cooperation with the schools. The All-Union State Planning Committee exercises a measure of control over all ministries and agencies. This Committee is responsible for bringing the budgets and plans of all operating agencies on all levels into coordination and in line with the objectives laid down by the Party leadership.

In view of the high degree of control derived from the application of the principle of democratic centralism, it is evident that the republics and lesser divisions of government are concerned almost exclusively with the implementation of policy. Educational administrators must see to it that the prescribed programs in primary and secondary education are provided on the subordinate levels; but beyond this they must also coordinate the programs of the other ministries and departments with their own. The role of the educational administrator, therefore, is not only an important one, but a difficult and exceedingly complex one.

Departments of education on the republic, *oblast,* and *raion* levels generally are staffed by numerous specialists, each of whom is responsible for a different aspect of the program. Coordination is sought in collegium; that is, the minis-

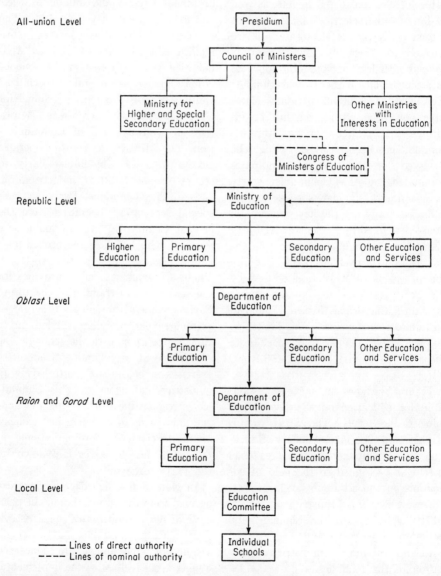

Figure 23. Lines of Educational Authority in the U.S.S.R.

ter or director calls his deputies into conference where they agree upon how best to implement the directives received from higher authorities. The minister, or director, then declares the decision to be an official directive, binding upon all subordinates.[15] Such collegiums make the necessary local adaptations in the prescribed curricula, materials of instruction, and methodologies, and appoint the needed operating personnel. Budget recommendations are determined locally and are passed upward through administrative channels. Appropriations then are transmitted downward through the same channels.

The Soviet administrative system is uniquely suited to meet the needs of the extremely diverse geographic and ethnic groups that live in its huge domain. While democratic centralism calls for a uniform educational program for all parts of the Union, the hierarchical structure of the administrative system provides for separate ministries and departments for minority groups and isolated regions. Thus the R.S.F.S.R. has several large nationality groups within its borders, each with its own language and traditions. Each of these has its own ministry of education and subdepartments responsible for adapting the basic program to its people. The prescribed textbooks are published in the local languages. Children are instructed in their mother tongue until they have progressed to the point that Russian can be introduced as a second language. Reading materials are based on local condi-

[15] William Kenneth Medlin, "The Union of Soviet Socialist Republics," in Theodore L. Reller and Edgar L. Morphet (eds.), *Comparative Educational Administration,* Prentice-Hall, Englewood Cliffs, N.J., 1962, p. 117.

tions and popular heroes, but are made to lead the young minds to a favorable attitude toward the Communist ideology, particularly the communist ethics. On the higher levels, the programs of study, including the use of the Russian language, become more uniform in all parts of the Union, a tendency that is fostered by the All-Union Ministry of Higher and Specialized Secondary Education.

The individual institutions are at the end of the administrative chain of command. As such, they receive their educational assignments from above and must fulfill them in the local situation in the most effective manner. Each school has a director or head teacher, who is assisted by a school council made up of the teachers and the school physician and a representative of the custodial staff, of the local organization of the Communist Party, of the Young Communist League, of the local soviet, of the local women's organization, of the parents, and finally a representative of each group of students with more than three years' standing, as long as their number does not exceed one-third of the council. Student representation is considered an important aspect of training in self-government according to the collectivist principle.

Universities and other higher institutions are administered in much the same way. Each institution is headed by an appointed rector or director who may have several assistants, depending upon the size of the institution. However, there also is an institutional council which includes representatives of the faculty, the students, and the "public organizations," meaning the Communist Party, industrial groups served by the institution, the soviet, and so forth. As a rule Russian institutions of higher education are not so diversified with respect to their teaching areas as are the larger universities in the United States, but each teaching area is presided over by a faculty or department. The administrative heads of faculties and departments are elected by the staff members concerned.

Educational institutions

The revolutionists lost little time in consolidating their rise to power in 1917. One of their first steps was to institute a comprehensive plan for schools on all levels. These were to be schools for workers, and of a type to erase illiteracy and impart the knowledge and skills necessary to transform the feudal agricultural economy into a highly productive industrial economy. All barriers that had formerly prohibited workers and peasants from entering the schools were banished. Private schools were closed. Coeducation was introduced on all levels, for sex discrimination was to be eliminated also. Education at all levels was directed to making the Marxist brand of collectivism work.

A nation without schools and with 70 per cent of the people illiterate obviously could not provide overnight the buildings and teachers needed to send everyone to school. The best that could be done was to project a comprehensive plan to place a minimum program of elementary instruction within reach of everyone, and to commit the national resources to extend and improve this nucleus as rapidly as possible. Further education was planned for all who had completed the basic elementary course; and higher education, particularly for workers who gave evidence of special

aptitude. The Communists were not interested, however, in educating a new class of exploiters. Proper indoctrination in communist ethics and the superiority of the collectivist society was called for at every stage.

The core of the new system of schools was the "uniform labor" school. This single institutional type was intended to provide a basic education for all children aged eight to seventeen. Figure 24 shows, however, that this nine-year program was broken into three levels or cycles. A number of nine-year schools were established, but schools offering only the first four years were far more common, particularly in places where no schools had existed before. Indeed, some reports indicate that remote rural regions sometimes were fortunate to have even the first two years. The uniform program made it possible, however, for pupils to transfer from an incomplete to a more complete school without difficulty, and the government stood ready to deal with the financial problems encountered in making the transfer.

The two cycles beyond the elementary cycle were referred to as secondary education. The first of these, a three-year cycle, was "permeated with elements of physics, chemistry, natural sciences, mechanics" and other matters relating to the technical development of local industry and agriculture. A form of general mathematics known as *physionism* was introduced which provided not merely an immediately usable body of mathematical understandings and skills, but also a basis for further specialized study. Political indoctrination also became crucial at this point, and included elements of sociology, political science, history, and literature. Pupils were also

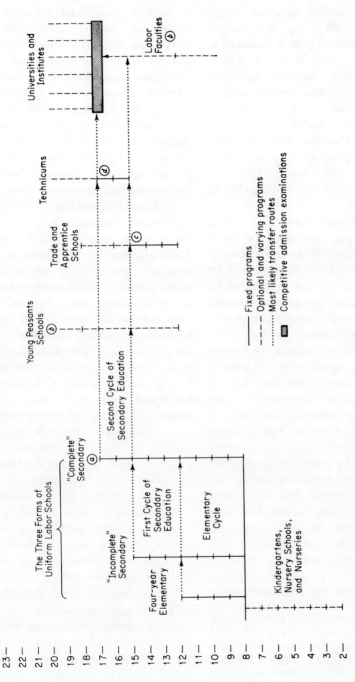

Figure 24. Educational Institutions in the U.S.S.R. after 1917.
a. Later was extended to ten-year secondary school.
b. Students of varying ages.
c. Must cover first cycle of secondary education.
d. Must cover second cycle of secondary education.

involved in collective activities, particularly those calling for direct physical participation. Through committees, councils, and other forms of student government the pupils performed clean-up chores, looked after the sanitation of the school premises, and engaged in other "socially useful" work. The schools were reminded that their purpose was to promote *labor* education, one aspect of which was to develop an intense interest in the political life of the community.

The second cycle of secondary education, a two-year program, was more specialized to provide a general basis for professional studies. The great need for teachers apparently was responsible for a program on this level which prepared teachers for the preschool and early elementary school levels.

Since school attendance was made compulsory to age seventeen, it appears that the planners intended that all schools would be "complete" [16] nine-year schools. However, the lack of schools and teachers, the high illiteracy rate, the enormous loss of resources and manpower in the war, and the pressing need for workers in the new government-sponsored industrial and agricultural projects forced large numbers of boys and girls to enter the labor ranks with no more than four years of elementary education, and frequently far less. Sup-

[16] According to Russian usage a "secondary" school is an "elementary" school which carries the pupil to levels higher than the basic elementary cycle. Thus the literature refers to "incomplete" and "complete" secondary schools; the former offered the first seven years of the program, and the second offered the full nine years. This usage has been retained by the educational planners as they have extended the basic program to ten and even eleven years, or reduced it to eight.

plementary educational activities were called for, and factories, collective farms, the Red Army, the educational sections of the local soviets and of the Communist Party were stirred to action. "Trade" schools were established by factories and farms which offered part-time instruction carrying the learner through at least the first cycle of the secondary school, with additional specialized training in the operations carried on by the sponsoring factory or farm. Parallel to the trade schools were "apprentice" schools for persons engaged in an organized trade or craft. These also enabled the learner to complete the first cycle of the secondary school program. The peasants presented a special problem since they had been neglected for so long that they had no local people qualified as leaders. "Peasant" schools were, therefore, established in the rural areas for pupils from twelve to eighteen years of age. Children of the lowest levels of the peasantry received preferential treatment with respect to admission. Although special attention was given to training leaders for rural areas, with due emphasis on the technology of agriculture, this program also included the instruction offered in the first cycle of secondary education. Graduates could then go on to further study on an equal basis with graduates of a seven-year secondary, trade, or apprentice school.

A third level of instruction, that of the *technicums,* was based upon the first cycle of secondary education, and the first two years of instruction, beginning at age fifteen or later, paralleled the second cycle of secondary education. Indeed, the technicums were required to include instruction encompassing the second cycle, although they trained operating specialists for a number of fields, such as agriculture, medicine, industrial-economic, education, and the arts.[17] Technicums for teacher education trained teachers for the elementary cycle of the uniform labor schools as well as for preschool and other educational services.

That persons enrolled in vocational schools, even as adults or on a part-time basis, were not separated from the general education program leading to higher studies is a matter of first importance. Indeed, the combination of work and study these programs required was highly desired, not merely because it prevented academic studies from becoming too theoretical, but also because it afforded workers and technicians the opportunity to become "politically enlightened." The Party leadership looked upon the working people as the foundation of the new order; and preferential treatment was accorded the workers, even on the highest levels of the educational structure. Admission to universities and other institutions of higher education, regulated by competitive examination, gave priority to those who had worked for at least two years. Even today approximately 80 per cent of the students have had such experience; only 20 per cent enter directly from the secondary schools.[18]

The number of workers who qualified for admission to university studies was extremely limited in the first years of the regime. Therefore, special "labor faculties" were established to function as preparatory schools for persons of "proletarian origin." Aside from at least three years' experience in some form of productive work, the applicants needed

to know only "the four rules of arithmetic," to be able to read and to express themselves clearly in speech and writing, and to have "a general political training," that is, be recommended by a proper Party official.[19]

Higher education was highly specialized in accordance with the Party slogan "Science for the Workers." Communist indoctrination was provided throughout in four prescribed subjects compulsory for everyone. Universities offered comprehensive programs of studies, although the number of faculties varied considerably and often reflected the needs of local industries. Technical institutes provided specialized training in one or more areas. Institutes of teacher education prepared for teaching in grades five or above, although more highly specialized personnel also were trained at the universities. Beyond the universities and institutes there were advanced research centers staffed by outstanding specialists, with additional staff drawn from universities, institutes, and industry on a part-time basis. Thus virtually every recognized field of productive labor, *including the propagation of communism,* came to be served by its special faculties, institutes, universities, and research centers.

The privileged status of the worker is more apparent in higher education than in any other area of education. Not only are workers accorded preferential treatment at the points of admission, but 80 per cent of the students receive living stipends and supplementary allowances while enrolled. Furthermore, the regular daytime instruction is duplicated in evening courses, in part-time programs, and by correspondence. Students assigned to work in a remote area are

[17] Blonsky, *op. cit.,* p. 330.
[18] Yelyutin, *op. cit.,* p. 26.

[19] Blonsky, *op. cit.,* p. 334.

granted vacations with full pay and travel allowances to visit their professors twice each year; and a full month's paid vacation with supplementary allowances is granted automatically when they must go to the home campus to write examinations.

Finally, the promise to free women from enslavement in the home and nursery led to the introduction of extensive preschool services and agencies. This program gained support, of course, from the need for workers, the presence of thousands of abandoned and homeless infants, and the desire to begin the formation of the Communist personality at the earliest age possible. Nurseries, playgrounds, and "children's corners" were provided to care for the small children of working mothers. These centers were run by trained personnel, and provided food and health services and a proper atmosphere of play and learning within which collectivist ideals could be inculcated. The homeless were gathered into orphanages where their education as well as their physical needs were provided for. Kindergartens were introduced and playgrounds provided, all under trained supervision. However, all preschool services were on an optional basis. They are not provided universally even today.

Educational opportunities

Officials of the Soviet Union often have boasted that their nation offers an educational program for all its people "from the cradle to the grave." This objective was evident from the outset, and has been steadily pursued during the intervening years. Including part-time and other on-the-job study, approximately 25 per cent of the Soviet population is

enrolled in some phase of the educational program today. This is equal to the enrollment level of the United States. The initial Soviet plans provided for such expansion and, indeed, could readily be extended to provide a place for everyone. Decentralization of the *operational* as distinguished from the *planning* aspects of school administration made it possible to set up operating branches and divisions of the master plan wherever there are people to be instructed. The development of a required elementary core of general studies, including vocational, provided for easy transfer from one place to another and for unlimited upward progress. The elimination of fees, the provisions for living stipends and supplementary grants, the extension of instruction in Russian as a second language, the elimination of sex discrimination, and the special encouragement given members of the former working and peasant classes—all contributed to the rapid development of a literate, skilled labor force. Education provided almost unlimited opportunities to advance in either industry or government. Nevertheless, the decision as to who would progress, and in what field, did not rest with the individual. In the final analysis, educational opportunities were distributed by the agents of the Communist Party operating on the levels where those decisions had to be made.

A second observation is closely related to the above. While all students are required to study the Communist philosophy, history, and economics and to take part in various activities designed to further their political enlightenment, leadership is regarded as a highly specialized skill requiring full-time study and attention. Thus the comprehensive system of schools extending from nursery school to university, which has attracted worldwide attention for its emphasis on science and technology, does not in itself provide the road to leadership in the Soviet Union. Future leaders may be recruited from that system, but they are trained in a separate system about which little seems to be known even in Russia except in the inner circles of the Communist Party.

Subsequent developments

The basic system of education introduced by the Communists during the first years of their reign now seems to extend rather uniformly throughout the entire Soviet Union. That the common program has been adapted to meet local conditions may be inferred from the fact that although there are but fifteen republics, there are more than thirty ministries of education operating at the republic level. The extra ministries accommodate different nationality groups residing within the republics or other groups which are treated separately for some reason. The special responsibility of these ministries is to interpret the prescribed doctrines to their constituencies, including the translation of the curricular materials into the local languages and cultural traditions, and to lead the people, step by step, to share a common language, to take pride in the workers' victory over capitalistic imperialism, and to aspire to the Communist goals of social development. The latter are prescribed, of course, by the Communist Party.

By 1958 the Soviet leadership complained that those who had enjoyed the most extensive educational opportunities showed a general reluctance to engage in productive labor. This unfortunate development, it was concluded, indicated that the program of studies had focused too narrowly upon the academic side of the curriculum. In the meantime, the nine-year program of the uniform labor school had been extended to ten years, the additional year having been added to the second cycle of secondary education. The desire to encourage students to achieve high-level specialization in science and technology had resulted in granting automatic admission to universities and institutes to students who had excelled in the secondary schools. This meant that such students did not need to engage in productive labor before they could be admitted, and the attraction of special privileges granted university graduates induced young people to enter by this shorter route.

To counteract the theoretical trend of education and the glorification of academic pursuits at the expense of productive labor, Nikita Khrushchev, Premier of the Soviet Union and head of the Communist Party, proclaimed the so-called "polytechnical reform" in an address to the Supreme Soviet in 1958. The Supreme Soviet adopted the proposed reforms in the Law for Strengthening the Ties between School and Life and the Further Development of the Public Education System. Khrushchev insisted that the proposed changes did not mark a shift in Party doctrine, but were in fact a return to the original goals for education defined by Marx and Lenin as "the combination of education with productive work." [20] To provide for more direct participation in productive work, the ten-year program of general education was reduced to eight years. At the same time, the seven-

[20] Khrushchev, *op. cit.*, p. 69.

year incomplete schools were extended to the eight-year level, thereby seeming to eliminate the many "incomplete" schools. Polytechnization was to be accomplished by relating school activities much more closely to local agriculture and industry, with a greater part of the pupil's time given over to developing related manual skills. In the later stages of the program, the pupils are expected to spend several hours each week in productive labor at a local factory or collective farm, in school gardens, or in the operation of an industrial machine loaned by industry to be operated by the pupils under the direction of the school as an integral part of a local factory. The requirement that persons admitted to higher education must first have experience in productive labor has been reasserted, although not with total success. The reappearance of the second three-year cycle of secondary education has initiated a trend toward eleven-year secondary schools with possible further direct admissions from these schools to university study.

Meanwhile, polytechnization of programs and schools has been promoted by the republic ministries of education and their subordinate divisions on every level. Even preschool services and educational programs have been affected. The master plan of the revised pattern of institutions, is shown in Figure 25. Crèches, or nurseries for infants, and kindergartens serve children under seven years of age. A few have been operated

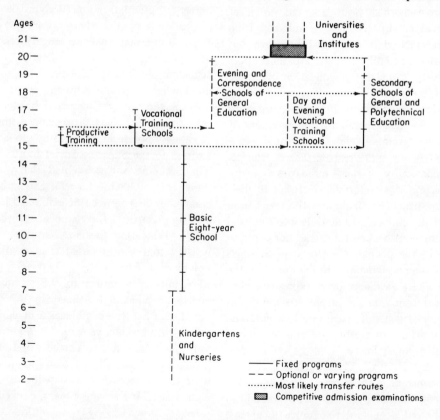

Figure 25. Educational Institutions in the U.S.S.R. Today

by departments or ministries of education, but the great majority have been, and still are, maintained by individual factories and collective farms to enable the mothers to work. Nurseries and kindergartens may be day schools or boarding institutions. They still serve only between 10 and 20 per cent of the eligible children and, surprisingly, charge fees scaled to the parents' ability to pay. The year 1965 was set in the current seven-year plan as the target date for making preschool facilities available to all children. If this goal is reached the Soviet Union will have the most extensive preschool program in the world.

The Soviet leaders are enthusiastic about preschool education, not merely because it frees mothers for productive work, but also because the children who have attended nurseries and kindergartens are said to do noticeably better in school. The attention given to physical health, language skills, disciplined behavior, and the development of a "collective sense" appears to pay educational dividends. As Soviet spokesmen point out, under the care of capable educators, nurses, and doctors, the children often receive better care than they would at home. As a result a move to merge nurseries and kindergartens has been started and the new unified institutions are being operated by the republic ministries of education. An Institute of Preschool Education has been created in the Academy of Pedagogical Sciences of the R.S.F.S.R. to direct the improvements in early childhood education. These changes are not only expected to provide preschool experiences which are pedagogically more sound but also to complete an articulated school system beginning literally in the cradle.

The eight-year school which replaced the ten-year school in the polytechnical reform is rapidly becoming the basic school throughout the Soviet Union. Central planning and control are clearly apparent in the program, which is offered in many languages and with numerous other adaptations to local conditions. The syllabi are prepared by the republic ministries and departments with the collaboration of the institutes of pedagogical science, as in the case of the Academy of Pedagogical Sciences in the R.S.F.S.R. A new syllabus for each subject is prepared each year to reflect new Party directives or changing educational views. The enforcement of educational policies is the responsibility of district school inspectors who make periodic checks to assure adherence to the prescribed curricula and to evaluate the quality of classroom instruction. The subjects receiving greatest emphasis are the native language, Russian language, arithmetic, with concepts of geometry beginning in the fourth grade, and music. Drawing, physical culture, natural science, history, and geography occupy less time; the last three gain prominence only during the fourth year. In addition, a lesson in "labor" is given once a week at each grade level; this may include learning how to use scissors, sewing, clay modeling, the construction of simple machines, and working in the school garden or doing "socially useful" work in the community. Although no specific instruction is given in politics at the elementary level, each subject is supposed to promote communist ethics.

Teaching methods tend to be quite formal. Lectures are used extensively; considerable drill is required when treating new knowledge or skills, and summary sessions are scheduled throughout to ensure mastery. Activities in physical education emphasize Swedish gymnastics and military marching and add

195

another formal note to the carefully planned schedules. Finally, the precise relationship between teachers and students, the manner in which students are required to respond, and the rigid rules of discipline which the students must memorize—all contribute to a semimilitary atmosphere. Elementary teachers are urged to take great care that their lessons inculcate scientific atheism. The study of nature is looked upon as a particularly effective means of dispelling religious and other types of superstitious beliefs. A leading Soviet teacher has suggested that in teaching about infectious diseases the teachers should explain the dangers of "indiscriminate kissing of church ikons and crosses." [21] The same author urged teachers to allow the children to grow seeds in order that they may observe the cycle of plant growth. Such observation it was said will "convince the children that harvests do not depend on God but on man, on man's knowledge and ability." [22]

The polytechnic reforms have been most strongly felt in the secondary school cycles. The new curriculum devotes 7,296 hours to general education and polytechnical subjects, compared with 6,256 hours in the seven-year school.[23] Moreover, "the various aspects of education and upbringing are more harmoniously represented. . . ." The subject matter allocations are as follows:

The humanities (Russian language and literature, history, the Constitution of the U.S.S.R., a foreign language) take up 39.5% of all school time (including 25.3% for the Russian language), the natural sciences and mathematics (mathematics, physics, chemistry, biology, geography)—32.5% manual training and socially useful work—15.3%, drawing, music and singing—6.2%, physical culture—6.5%.[24]

The basic shift in emphasis has reduced the amount of time devoted to the humanities by about 5 per cent, based on the 1955–1956 school year, and increased the hours spent at practical work by nearly threefold.

Some Western observers have viewed the development of the eight-year schools as an admission of Soviet failure to meet the earlier goal of "ten-year education for all." Soviet educators claim this is not so. Rather Soviet literature now refers to the eight-year school as "an incomplete labor-polytechnical school providing general education." It is not planned that the education of Soviet youth will terminate upon graduation from this school, but rather that it will be extended in one of the following ways: (1) by going directly into productive employment and studying part time at one of the various schools for young workers and peasants; (2) by going to a secondary polytechnical school which has factories, collective farms, repair shops, and the like located nearby and where rather intensive study may be combined with productive work; or (3) by attending a specialized secondary school or technicum which offers regular secondary education as well as work specialization. The first route is considered the usual path for Soviet youth, whereas the last is the preferred route to the universities. However, a

[21] N. Ia Potapsnko, "Atheistic Education in Elementary Schools," *Soviet Education*, vol. 3, no. 2, p. 3, December, 1960.

[22] *Ibid.*, p. 4.

[23] E. I. Monoszon, "Contents of Education in the Eight-year School," *Soviet Education*, January, 1961, p. 5.

[24] *Ibid.*, p. 5.

student in any of these programs can qualify for higher education.

A new development in Soviet education is the boarding school, first introduced in 1956. By 1959 there were 170,000 pupils enrolled, many of whom were from broken homes or underprivileged environments. On the other hand, Soviet leaders claim that the experiment has won such favorable acceptance that leading families request the privilege of enrolling their children. Khrushchev told the Supreme Soviet that by 1965 boarding schools would enroll 2,500,000 pupils, and "in future it is planned to afford all children the opportunity of attending boarding-schools, which will enable society to cope successfully with the Communist education of the younger generation and to draw fresh millions of women into the active building of Communism." [25]

To outsiders it is not clear whether the boarding school experiment is motivated more strongly by the need for workers or the desire to have children submitted to a more thoroughly collectivist environment than the family provides. In any event, the curriculum of the boarding schools is approximately the same as that in the regular schools, except that the former obviously have greater control over the pupils' activities.

Quite obviously the polytechnical reform has not as yet reached its zenith. Leaders, both in the Party and in education, are still seeking ways to bring about a closer relationship between the academic community and the social and industrial complex. The technicums with programs of study focused upon some particular field of specialization offer favorable conditions to pursue this end.

Technicums are often deliberately located where students may spend several hours a day working in an industry or social agency where their specialty is utilized. This interchange between work and study is said to be most beneficial in preparing students for advanced studies. The institutes, which specialize in only one or two technical fields, obviously also lend themselves to this type of coordination. But the more complex universities present a problem which has become a matter of concern to the state planners.

In writing of this problem, the Minister of Higher Education said in 1959 that a new type of institution is to be introduced which will be designated as a "factory" college. Theoretical studies will be supplemented with practical training in a factory. For this purpose

> A factory, or big shop is to be turned over entirely to the institute, for combining studies with work in production. The latter type [of institution] will be most suitable for the agricultural institutes which will in fact be converted into powerful state farm colleges.[26]

For similar reasons, evening courses, part-time study, and instruction by correspondence are to be greatly expanded. Indeed, it seems that in the future few if any students will complete their studies in an institute or university without having acquired the equivalent of at least two years of practical experience in the process.

The significant achievements discussed above could not have taken place without an adequately trained teaching staff. The history of teacher education in the Soviet Union, therefore, has been no

[25] Khrushchev, *op. cit.*, p. 70.

[26] Yelyutin, *op. cit.*, p. 43.

less dramatic than that of other social institutions. Beginning in 1917 with only 30 per cent of the population literate, the Communist leadership was forced to staff thousands of new schools with teachers who themselves had had little more than the elements of reading, writing, and arithmetic. Teacher training sections were often attached to the second cycle of secondary education. Even the pedagogical technicums, which supplied most of the preschool and elementary school teachers as late as 1954, were entered from incomplete seven-year secondary schools. Of late, however, most candidates have completed a ten-year school before entering a pedagogical technicum, and it appears likely that all teachers, preschool as well as elementary and secondary, will receive their professional education either in a pedagogical institute or a university in programs of at least five years' duration. It is the purpose of these changes to make teacher education equivalent to that for other professions.

On entering a pedagogical institute the student preparing to teach in grade five or above must enroll in a particular faculty, such as literature, history, geography, physics and mathematics, natural science, or languages. He is expected to develop considerable mastery of his specialty, but from 20 to 30 per cent of his program will consist of methodology, psychology, and practice teaching. New subjects and new adaptations of traditional subjects are now being introduced to meet the demands of polytechnical instruction.

Teacher education obviously lends itself quite readily to the combination of theory and practice which the principle of polytechnical education requires. Teacher education centers, operated in conjunction with the ministries and departments of education, long have maintained institutes for experimentation and for the demonstration of improved practices, both for the benefit of students and the teachers in service. This type of practical application of theory, combined with the search for new knowledge, is to be encouraged and extended. The Academy of Pedagogical Sciences of the R.S.F.S.R. may be regarded as the prototype of this kind of research and training center.

The Academy, founded in 1943, performs advanced educational research and experimentation in such areas as the theory and history of pedagogy, psychology, methods of teaching artistic education, physical education and school hygiene, and "defectology" or special education. Recently four new areas of research were added: preschool education, general and polytechnical education, production training, and evening courses for working youth.[27] Since there has been no equivalent in the other republics, the Academy through its activities and publications has greatly influenced instruction throughout the Soviet Union. Most textbooks, audio-visual aids, and equipment in use in Soviet schools are the products of the Academy's effort or show the influence of its recommendations. In 1960, the Academy was reported to be engaged in a total reexamination of Communist educational theory and practice. A feeling of the urgency of this task was expressed by a member of the Academy as follows:

> There was a time when the Communist society was a dream of the future. Now it is time to have a scientific description of this new society and to elaborate the theory of

[27] Gerald Read, "Trends and Problems in Soviet Education," *Phi Delta Kappan*, vol. 42, no. 2, p. 80, November, 1960.

education that will prepare our young people to live and work in such a society.[28]

With increased emphasis on work experience and participation in out-of-school activities that have social or industrial significance, the role of the Young Communist League, the Komsomol, and related Party organizations seem to have gained greater importance as supporting educational agencies. The early Bolsheviks were suspicious of the traditional social institutions and spoke hopefully of the withering away of the family as well as of the state. The youth groups, beginning with the Pioneers in 1922, were expected to provide peer pressures on young boys and girls between the ages of ten and sixteen to counteract the bourgeois influences of the home. Based on the prerevolution Boy Scout movement, the Pioneers provided uniforms, organized activities, political indoctrination in informal settings, and a code of communist ethics enforced by the members themselves. A year later a similar organization, known as the Little Octobrists, was formed for children aged eight to eleven. All children in the designated age groups are eligible for membership in these two organizations, and their activities are carried on in cooperation with the schools, with leaders and meeting rooms provided by the schools.

At age fourteen, boys and girls become eligible for membership in the Komsomol. This organization is in reality a junior division of the Communist Party, and membership is quite restricted. The social and political history of each prospective member is carefully scrutinized from the records of the Little Octobrists and Pioneers, and only those whose dedication to Communist prin-

[28] *Ibid.*, p. 80.

ciples is judged to be beyond question are invited to join. The direction of the Komsomols is regarded as an important Party function, and the organization is run along Party lines. Since 1959 the Party has appointed secretaries in each Komsomol region corresponding to the *oblasts* and larger *raions*. This permits the Young Communist League to participate more effectively in the new polytechnical education programs. As boarding schools increase in number, and the influence of the home becomes correspondingly weaker, the League may become even more influential in shaping the Communist personality of the future than the home and school combined.

At the beginning of this chapter, it was stated that the Soviet Union under Communist leadership had developed a radically different educational pattern. The Communists violently rejected their class-oriented educational heritage and pursued a new goal of equal educational opportunity for all "workers and peasants." Today the provocative question arises as to how successful the Party has been in destroying the remnants of class education and in preparing the people, through education, for the classless society. Since the revolution in 1917, succeeding generations of Soviet youth have been subjected to intensive Communist education. Marxist-Leninist doctrines have been widely disseminated and interpreted by the schools and the Party. Schools, factories, farms, youth and adult groups, and all mass media have been used as instruments in the education of the new Soviet citizen, and the "good books" of communism have been as widely read as the Bible in Christian nations.

During this period a new state has been created. In less than forty years, and in spite of massive destruction during World War II, the Soviet Union has been dramatically transformed from a backward, illiterate area to one of the world's great and powerful nations. In spite of linguistic problems and persisting poverty in some regions, illiteracy has been virtually eliminated, spectacular advances have been made in the natural sciences, and a new set of social and political values has been taught the people.

Persuasive arguments have sometimes been offered to prove that equal progress could have been made from the 1914 base in the normal course of change that occurred in all Western states during this same period. It would be useless to attempt to determine how much of the advance in science, industry, agriculture, education, and the general well-being of the people has been achieved solely as a result of the Communist principle operating through the agency of the Communist Party. That is to say, how much of this progress might have been achieved under equally vigorous leadership employing a different guiding principle. Nevertheless, the Communists have predicted from the outset that their effectiveness could be measured in quantitative terms, and in this respect their predictions have been sustained.

References

Books

Benjamin, Harold: *Under Their Own Command,* Macmillan, New York, 1947.

Bereday, George Z. F., William Brick-
man, and Gerald Read (eds.): *The Changing Soviet School,* Houghton Mifflin, Boston, 1960.

—— and Jaan Pennar (eds.): *The Politics of Soviet Education,* Frederick A. Praeger, Inc., New York, 1960.

Bowen, James: *Soviet Education: Anton Maharenko and the Years of Experiment,* The University of Wisconsin Press, Madison, Wis., 1962.

Bringing Soviet Schools Still Closer to Life, Soviet Booklets, London, 1958. Theses of the Central Committee of the Communist Party and the U.S.S.R. Council of Ministers on strengthening the ties of the school with life, and developing the system of public education.

Cohen, Carl: *Communism, Fascism and Democracy: The Theoretical Foundations,* Random House, New York, 1962.

Counts, George S.: *The Challenge of Soviet Education,* McGraw-Hill, New York, 1957.

——: *Education and the Foundations of Freedom,* The University of Pittsburgh Press, Pittsburgh, Pa., 1962.

——: *Khrushchev and the Central Committee Speak on Education,* The University of Pittsburgh Press, Pittsburgh, Pa., 1959.

Deineko, M.: *Forty Years of Public Education in the U.S.S.R.,* translated by D. Myshne, Foreign Languages Publishing House, Moscow, 1957.

DeWitt, Nicholas: *Soviet Professional Manpower,* National Science Foundation, Washington, D.C., 1955.

Grant, Douglas (ed.): *The Humanities in Soviet Higher Education,* University of Toronto Press, Toronto, 1960.

Heckinger, Fred M.: *The Big Red Schoolhouse,* Doubleday, New York, 1959.

Johnson, William H. E.: *Russia's Educational Heritage,* Carnegie Press, Pittsburgh, Pa., 1950.

King, E. J. (ed.): *Communist Educa-*

tion, Bobbs-Merrill, Indianapolis, 1963.

Kline, George Louis (ed.): *Soviet Education,* Columbia, New York, 1957.

Kluchevsky, V. O.: *A History of Russia,* translated by C. J. Hogarth, Dent, London, 1913.

Korol, Alexander G.: *Soviet Education for Science and Technology,* Technology Press, Cambridge, Mass., and Wiley, New York, 1957.

Levin, Deana: *Soviet Education Today,* John de Graff, New York, 1959.

Makarenko, A. S.: *The Road to Life: An Epic of Education,* translated by Ivy Litvinov and Tatiana Litvinov, 3 vols., Foreign Languages Publishing House, Moscow, 1955.

Marx, Karl: *Capital,* with an introduction by Max Eastman, Modern Library, New York, 1932.

Medynsky, Yevgeny N.: *Education in the USSR,* 2d ed. rev., Soviet News, London, 1953.

Moos, Elizabeth: *Soviet Education Today and Tomorrow,* National Council of American-Soviet Friendship, New York, 1959.

Pinkevitch, Albert P.: *The New Education in the Soviet Republic,* translated by Nucia Permutter and edited by George S. Counts, John Day, New York, 1929.

Rauch, Georg von: *A History of Soviet Russia,* 3d rev. ed., translated by Peter Jacobsohn and Annette Jacobsohn, Frederick A. Praeger, Inc., New York, 1962.

Shore, Maurice J.: *Soviet Education: Its Psychology and Philosophy,* Philosophical Library, New York, 1947.

Winn, R. B. (ed. and trans.): *Soviet Psychology: A Symposium,* Philosophical Library, New York, 1961.

Pamphlets and periodicals

DeWitt, Nicholas: "Soviet Student Profile and Prediction," *Teachers College Record,* vol. 64, pp. 91–98, November, 1962.

Khrushchev, N. S.: *Control Figures for the Economic Development of the U.S.S.R. for 1959–1965,* Foreign Languages Publishing House, Moscow, 1959.

Lindquist, C. B., and J. N. Rokitiansky: "Graduate Education in the Union of Soviet Socialist Republics: Contrasts with Advanced Study in the United States," *Journal of Higher Education,* vol. 34, pp. 73–84, February, 1963.

Read, Gerald: "Trends and Problems in Soviet Education," *Phi Delta Kappan,* vol. 42, pp. 49–51, November, 1960.

Soviet Education, International Arts and Sciences Press, New York. This periodical consists of translations of articles on education from Soviet journals.

U.S. Office of Education: *Education in the U.S.S.R.,* Bulletin 1957, no. 14, 1947.

————: *Soviet Commitment to Education,* Bulletin 1959, no. 16, 1959.

————: *Soviet Education Programs,* Bulletin 1960, no. 17, 1960.

Yelyutin, Vyacheslau: *Higher Education in the U.S.S.R.,* International Arts and Sciences Press, New York, 1959.

CHAPTER 8

Some Western Variations

Each of the patterns of education described in the preceding chapters evolved from a system of schools common to all parts of Western Europe in the fifteenth century. That system itself had borrowed extensively from the schools of ancient Greece and Rome. After the fifteenth century, the forces originating in Rome which made for unity and uniformity in education gradually weakened. Regional and local differences appeared with respect to matters of belief and forms of social organization and control. New power structures, new political institutions, and new ecclesiastical organizations emerged along lines determined, in part, by the particular time at which each abandoned the pattern inherited from Rome and, in part, by the specific forces which caused it to do so. Not the least of these forces were the national aspirations nurtured in the several divisions of what had been the ancient Roman Empire. The Reformation marked an early but important stage in this drive for political, ecclesiastical, and educational independence.

The splintering effects induced by endemic nationalism did not end with the Reformation. New groupings of peoples and new national governments continued to appear. Indeed, this trend seems not to have been fully spent even today. Contemporary European states, each one with its distinctive institutions, customs, and language, are for the most part offshoots of the political and social patterns that had evolved earlier. With particular reference to education, several national systems today, notably those of Austria,

202

Belgium, Italy, the Netherlands, the Scandinavian states, Switzerland, and the United States, combine elements borrowed from several of the earlier patterns.

Education in Italy

Historically, some of the most important elements out of which Western patterns of education were formed came by way of Italy. Italian cities, located as they were near the apex of the ecclesiastical hierarchy, were supplied with church schools relatively early. Nevertheless, their very proximity to Rome, together with a reviving commerce with Eastern Europe, seems to have encouraged Italian clergy to exercise a certain independence of thought and action not usually found in the more remote places. Furthermore, members of the local nobility, rich merchants, and a growing class of craftsmen and tradesmen fostered a disposition to support the rebellious clergy in acts of defiance. In educational matters this brought about a mixture of elements of the earlier Graeco-Roman culture with Christian theology, and from this mixture a more vigorous scholarly period emerged known as the Italian Renaissance. It preceded by two hundred years a corresponding revival of learning in Northern Europe. Similarly, humanism appeared in Italy long before it came to full fruition along the banks of the lower Rhine.

Italian cities were rather well supplied with schools for the elite before the end of the fourteenth century, each privately supported by its patron nobleman, merchant prince, municipal government, guild, abbot, bishop, or other dignitary. Each boasted its own intellectual fare made up of varying portions of the Graeco-Roman, Christian, and even humanistic elements in proportions that best suited the patron's tastes. A number of such schools became distinguished, and some attracted scholars in sufficient numbers to create a local university. Eleven Italian cities had been so distinguished by 1321.

Out of the court schools developed at Mantua by Vittorino da Feltre and at Ferrara by Guarino da Verona, both founded in the fifteenth century, German humanism received its first vital impulse. A century later these elements were amplified, combined with the Graeco-Roman and Christian traditions and reorganized to form the model for German secondary education by John Sturm at Strassburg. The subsequent infusion of this pattern of humanistic studies in the higher education of all Germanic peoples is indicated today by their use of the term "gymnasium" to designate their most respected form of secondary schools, institutions in which the study of classical Latin and Greek still holds a position of first importance. This Germanic development later was returned to Italy by way of Austria in the form of the classical *ginnasio,* traces of which are evident in Italian secondary education today.

While humanism was making its way through Italian schools, particularly those open to secular students, an educational reform along religious lines was being waged by the Jesuits. The Jesuits played a substantial role in Italian education, and as in Spain, their influence and the prestige of their schools helped deter the development of public educa-

tion until the Society was suppressed in the eighteenth century.

The development of a national system of schools was also retarded by Italy's turbulent political situation. Up to the nineteenth century, her territory had been divided among Spain, Austria, the Papal States, and a number of duchies and kingdoms, each claiming independent sovereignty and boasting its own ruling house or governing body, including the Vatican. Thus there was no central government capable of instituting a system of public education, and education remained a privilege of the few who could afford private instruction or who were satisfied to limit their educational opportunities to the instruction offered by the parish priests. The vast majority, perhaps 90 per cent of the population, remained illiterate.

The beginnings of public education

The first efforts to introduce public education were made in the latter half of the eighteenth century by the more enlightened sovereigns, and their extent and duration were related directly to the political fortunes of the states. Thus Prince Leopold I and a substantial number of his supporters decided that Tuscany could not prosper as long as education remained under the control of the Church. They promulgated a plan whereby elementary schools, open to the rich and poor alike, would be maintained in the cities and towns under public control. A few were opened, but the plan failed because there were not enough secular teachers, and instruction fell back into the hands of the parish priests. The republic of Venice, with a more secular tradition, enjoyed greater success, but its system was brought to an end by the conquering armies of Napoleon.

The Napoleonic conquest was not without some benefits, however. The short period of French rule introduced a pattern of centralized government and the principle of state support for education. More importantly, it united the Italian people in opposition to their common enemy, and from this feeling of unity a national movement ultimately emerged. Meanwhile, the French established secondary schools and universities under state support and control to train personnel for the state instead of the Church. Today the Italian *liceo* betrays this period of French domination just as the older *ginnasio* indicates Germanic antecedents. Lately the two have been combined serially to form the classical *ginnasio-liceo,* the most popular form of secondary education because it prepares for admission to the universities and the professions. Both the *ginnasio-liceos* and the universities now have become public institutions.

Elementary education was somewhat slower in getting started. This was due in large measure to the fact that Napoleon had no interest in promoting literacy among all the people. Indeed, when a "General Plan for Public Instruction" was announced in the Cisalpine Republic calling for free elementary instruction, the elimination of ecclesiastical influences, and the eradication of superstition through the teaching of natural sciences, Napoleon was fearful of its probable consequences. After five years, he called a halt to this experiment and turned the schools over to the parish priests.

A more successful beginning was made in the kingdom of Savoy where, from 1859 to 1870, King Victor Emmanuel

II led his people in shaking off both foreign and Vatican domination, and then in annexing, one after another, Lombardy, Parma, Modena, Romagna, Tuscany, the kingdom of Naples and Sicily, and the Papal States. On November 13, 1859, he promulgated the famous Casati Law named for his Minister of Public Instruction. Although originally intended for Savoy only, its enlightened form and popular reception brought about its gradual imitation or outright adoption in the annexed states as well. It has remained the foundation of Italian public education to this day.

The Casati Law did not propose either to replace the existing private schools or to ban religious instruction in the proposed public schools. The Ministry of Public Instruction, created to supervise its operation, was expected to promote public education in the interests of the state but not to monopolize or control all education. As in Napoleon's time, the secondary schools and universities were made the focal points of the government's interest. The crown assumed direct responsibility for the financial support of the universities as well as authority to name the rectors. Each rector was made directly responsible to the Minister of Public Instruction. A Royal Commissioner of Studies, also subordinated to the Minister of Public Instruction, was appointed in each province to administer secondary education. Royal inspectors, answerable to the Commissioners, were appointed to supervise primary schools.

As Figure 26 shows, four years of instruction in a primary school was projected as the minimum for all children. Indeed, four-year primary schools were made compulsory in all communities with a population over four thousand.

Smaller communities were urged to provide schools offering at least the first two years; but since the state gave no financial support to primary education, and official opinion frequently doubted the desirability of universal education, these provisions were not generally enforced. Indeed, illiteracy continued to be widespread until well into the present century.

It is significant, however, that state secondary schools, combining the older five-year *ginnasio* and the three-year *liceo,* opened the doors of the universities to pupils from the public primary schools. In this respect the Casati Law anticipated the breaking down of class barriers between primary and secondary education, a goal which was not achieved in most countries of the West prior to World War II.

The Casati Law also called for the establishment of technical schools and normal schools. However, none of these received full financial support from the state, but were established and maintained by the local governments. As in England, therefore, the development of these facilities depended upon the level of local interest and initiative, and those regions most lacking in education were the ones least likely to acquire the needed facilities.

The Gentile Plan

Lack of precedents, experience, trained teachers, and adequate financial resources meant that the development of a complete system of public schools proceeded very slowly until after World

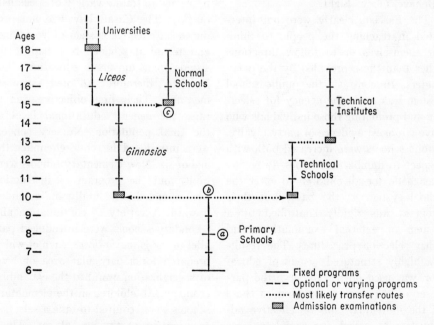

Figure 26. Italian Educational Institutions under the Casati Law of 1859
a. Two years required in all communes.
b. Four years required in communes over 4,000 population.
c. Normal schools might be entered by anyone who passed the admissions tests.

War I. Illiteracy was substantially reduced but not eliminated; and in many mountain villages in the south, children received at best merely the minimal two years of schooling. Nor did vocational and technical education receive support equal to that given classical education; Italy lagged far behind her neighbors to the north both economically and industrially.

Following the war, Italian social life was so disorganized that the people were ready to grasp any promise of direction and security. It was in this atmosphere that Benito Mussolini rose to power, and that Giovanni Gentile became the Minister of Public Instruction. Exponent of the doctrine that "all force is moral force," he willingly used compulsory education to achieve the social objectives implied in the Fascist slogan, "Believe, Obey, Fight."

The Fascists clearly were not interested in teaching the people to think for themselves or to follow directions other than those provided by the party leaders. In contrast, the public school system was made the agency for selecting and promoting those individuals who gave strongest evidence of party loyalty. Public schools were increased both with respect to number and types. Provision was made for all children to enter the school system at the base; but their progress was rigidly controlled by a system of external examinations and other selection procedures. The resulting highly structured system of education was used openly to serve the purposes of the state as opposed to those of the individual, and its effective administration called for complete state control. The Ministry of Public Instruction was given sweeping authority in 1929 when the Fascists made it their

prime agency for the control of the minds of the people.

Because the state was pictured by the Fascists as the best exemplification of the Graeco-Roman tradition, and the curriculum of the *ginnasio-liceo* was built upon that tradition, it was made the keystone in the Fascist system of education. The *ginnasio-liceo* was proclaimed the training school for the future leaders, and admissions were administered in such a way as to direct the most promising young Fascists into them. Since the personal qualities desired in political leaders did not necessarily assure academic proficiency, instructional practices were modified accordingly.

Like other totalitarian states bent on achieving rapid technological as well as social changes, Fascist Italy found it necessary to train a variety of specialists quickly. The Casati Law had not produced an effective system of vocational and technical schools. Nor had it insisted upon universal education. The Fascists therefore adopted stronger measures. Their first objective was to raise the general educational level of the total population. Nursery schools were introduced for children under the age of six. New elementary schools were built, and the program of instruction was expanded horizontally and extended upward. A variety of continuation and secondary schools were introduced parallel to the *ginnasio-liceos,* each of which prepared for a particular area or level of specialization useful to the expanding economy. All children in the elementary schools were required to take a selective examination at the age of ten. Those who passed were sent to the particular type of secondary school their test performance was thought to indicate. Those who failed were permitted to continue in one of the elongated elementary school programs to age fourteen, if they so desired.

Specialists were trained in a variety of postelementary school programs. Pupils diverted into one of the several streams of secondary education by the selective examinations were subjected to further screening at stipulated levels. Some differentiated programs of specialized training were introduced in 1922, but their number was greatly increased in 1939. Also, the age at which the major selection examination was to be taken was raised from ten to fourteen. These changes could not be carried out in their entirety, however, before Italy became involved in World War II.

The situation today

Since World War II, Italy has been a republic but the centralized administrative controls introduced under the monarchy and greatly extended by the Fascists have not been relaxed altogether. The people still look to Rome to deal with local problems, and except in some of the larger cities, the lower classes have not yet learned to accept responsibility for either government or social improvements. In education there has been an inclination to return to the system introduced under the Casati Law. This is quite apparent when one compares Figure 26 and Figure 27. The classical *ginnasio-liceo* has been retained and is still the only public school preparing for the examinations that admit to study in the university faculties of law and the liberal arts.[1] The *liceo-*

scientifico, a legacy from the Fascist period, is now acquiring considerable acceptance, and competes directly with the *ginnasio-liceo* in preparing for all other forms of higher education. However, it continues to suffer a considerable disadvantage because its students do not enjoy full privileges with respect to admission to the older faculties.

Teachers for the secondary schools are prepared at the universities, most of which have a faculty of education. The normal schools, formerly considered a form of secondary education and devoted exclusively to the preparation of teachers for the elementary schools, now provide access to these university faculties of education. This is a sign that greater coordination between elementary and secondary education may soon be achieved, but in the Ministry of Public Instruction, separate departments administer elementary, secondary, technical, and higher education, each with its jealously guarded prerogatives extending down to the individual schools. The Ministry of Public Instruction thereby tends to negate on the administrative level those principles of unity and freedom of choice which appear to be advocated in the education of teachers.

The Italian system is centralized in a manner reminiscent of the administrative pattern developed in France. Since 1929 the Ministry of Public Instruction has had extensive authority over all forms of education and types of instruction. All public school teachers are trained, employed, and paid by the central government. Each classroom is subject to inspection and is visited regularly by an official of the Ministry who is

[1] Faculties of theology also require this preparation, but since universities are public institutions, most of the faculties of theology have withdrawn to form private seminaries. This has occurred in other Roman Catholic countries as well.

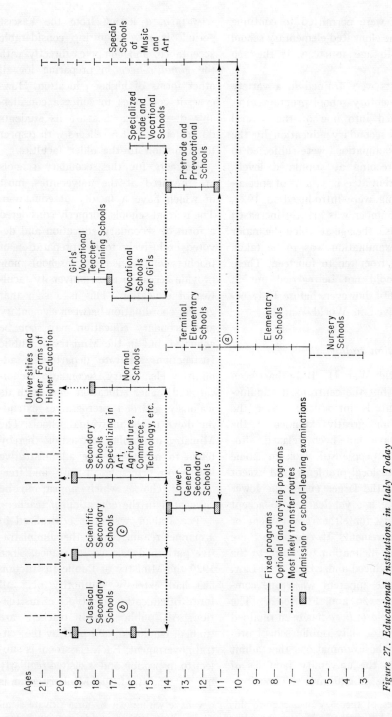

Ages
21 —
20 —
19 —
18 —
17 —
16 —
15 —
14 —
13 —
12 —
11 —
10 —
9 —
8 —
7 —
6 —
5 —
4 —
3 —

Universities and Other Forms of Higher Education

Normal Schools

Secondary Schools Specializing in Art, Agriculture, Commerce, Technology, etc.

Scientific Secondary Schools (c)

Classical Secondary Schools (b)

Lower General Secondary Schools

Special Schools of Music and Art

Specialized Trade and Vocational Schools

Pretrade and Prevocational Schools

Girl's Vocational Teacher Training Schools

Vocational Schools for Girls

Terminal Elementary Schools

Elementary Schools

Nursery Schools

——— Fixed programs
– – – Optional and varying programs
· · · · · Most likely transfer routes
▦ Admission or school-leaving examinations

Figure 27. Educational Institutions in Italy Today

a. Attendance is compulsory to age fourteen, but lax enforcement results in many leaving school after age eleven.

b. Ginnasio-liceo.   c. Liceo-scientifico.

responsible not merely for evaluating the work of the teacher, but also for enforcing the laws and regulations relating to teaching which, of course, are made in Rome. Nevertheless, the provinces and communes are expected to provide the physical facilities for elementary, trade, vocational, and some of the newer types of secondary schools. School attendance is compulsory to age fourteen, but reports indicate that adequate facilities are not yet available in all places.

Secondary education, particularly in the *ginnasio-liceos* and *liceo-scientificos,* enjoys state support. This is justified on the ground that the state must secure its future leaders from these schools. Tuition fees and the selective admissions procedures favor children from upper-class homes, although provision is made to waive fees in cases of extreme poverty. Standard curricula and courses of instruction are prescribed in all schools and on all levels. However, local committees of teachers appear to have some voice in the choice of textbooks.

Relations with the Roman Catholic Church are reminiscent of those in Spain. Except for a few years preceding the negotiation of a concordat between Mussolini and the Vatican, Italy has been officially a Roman Catholic state. As in Spain, the elementary schools are required to provide instruction in the Roman Catholic religion, and this is continued on a less rigorous basis into the secondary and even higher levels. Religious instruction is supervised directly by the Church, all materials of instruction used in the schools must be approved by the Church, and the instruction itself is given either by members of the clergy or by others licensed by the Church for this specific purpose.

Non-Catholics attending state schools may be excused from religious instruction, but the authorities sometimes have taken a dim view of the proposals of non-Catholic groups to maintain their own schools or to provide their own forms of religious instruction outside of school.

The Italians' traditional interest in the fine arts is evidenced by the number of state schools of art, drama, and music provided by the Ministry. Indeed, the fine arts appear to have the first choice of new talent, because these schools may admit pupils from the elementary schools one year ahead of the lower secondary and the pretrade and vocational schools. A pupil of great talent will be encouraged by the state without reference to the family's financial circumstances.

The nonacademic trade, vocational, and technical schools continue to occupy a less-favored status than the classical and scientific schools. The choice between vocational training and higher education is made for children at the age of eleven, and the choice is in effect irrevocable. Some steps are now being taken to provide opportunities for continuing education [2] for those who leave school early or who were required to elect one of the shorter, nonacademic programs. Opportunities in continuing education are provided in both part-time evening and full-time day programs, but neither is likely to establish a connection with schools that lead to study on the university level. Indi-

[2] The *scuola popolare* and other proposals to extend educational opportunities are discussed by Lamberto Borghi and Anthony Scarangello in "Italy's Ten-year Education Plan," *Comparative Education Review,* vol. 4, no. 1, pp. 26–30, June, 1960.

vidual opportunities, while they have expanded considerably since World War II, are still somewhat more restricted by the inherited social and economic status of the family than is the case in several of the countries to the north. There may be a connection between this fact and the strength of the Italian Communist Party; it is, numerically and proportionately, one of the strongest Communist parties west of the Iron Curtain.

Education in the Netherlands

The modern kingdom of the Netherlands dates only from 1831. However, a basis for political unity had been established by the legions of Rome, and had been extended by the armies of Charlemagne. The southern provinces, including those which now constitute Belgium, received the Christian religion from missionaries during the period of Roman domination, but the northern regions clung to their pagan ways until they were forced to the baptismal font by the rulers of the Frankish Empire. Utrecht was made the seat of a bishopric in A.D. 695 at the insistence of Pepin, the father of Charlemagne, and from the cathedral school that developed there the University of Utrecht ultimately emerged. The geography and social climate of the Low Countries seemed favorable to learning, and scholars from many parts of Europe congregated there in considerable numbers.

The drive for national status was impeded from many sides. Violent storms from the Atlantic tended to divide the land into isolated regions, in many of which forms of provincial government emerged around the leadership of local barons. Because the terrain was not

210

suited to agriculture and the usual types of defense based upon castle-fortresses and horse-mounted soldiers, the inhabitants were forced to take to the sea. Commerce became the basis of the economy and a strong middle-class society developed in the cities. Several of these became important units in the Hanseatic League. In brief, political life tended to remain decentralized. Each city or region developed its own leadership and local loyalties. As trade and manufacturing prospered these isolated cities became tempting prizes for the avaricious and more powerful neighbors and, beginning in the fourteenth century, the Low Countries, as they came to be known, paid dearly for their provincialism by losing their independence to Burgundy.

The harsh Burgundian rule was a sobering experience for the stolid inhabitants. Among other things they learned to work together in opposition to their common oppressor. In 1477 upon the death of Charles the Bold they forced his daughter Princess Mary to sign the "Great Privilege," a charter of rights and privileges which located the powers of government in a native legislative body, the Estates-General, and subordinate provincial governments. Although the crown was not yet to be retained by a native house—and was later worn by Austrians, Spaniards, and Frenchmen—the dream of one independent state within which the promised constitutional privileges could be enjoyed was kept alive until it was achieved by the Dutch provinces under the House of Orange.

Following the destruction of the Napoleonic empire, the Congress of Vienna in 1815 saw fit to include the present Belgian provinces with those of the

Dutch to form the kingdom of the Netherlands. Meanwhile, the Dutch had already accepted a constitution offered them by their sovereign in which individual liberties, including freedom of religion, were specifically guaranteed. When the Belgian provinces were added, the French-speaking Roman Catholic population strongly opposed the extension of this document to them, particularly since it specified that the crown should be worn by a Protestant. King William insisted that the matter be put to a vote, but when, under the conditions of privilege that prevailed among them, only a small fraction of the population were permitted to cast a ballot, he ordered the constitution ratified even though a majority of those balloting had opposed it. This and other points of dissatisfaction led to the withdrawal of the Belgian provinces in 1830. The present kingdom of the Netherlands dates from the settlement of the issues raised by the Belgian revolt.

The middle-class commercial peoples of the Low Countries had not always seen eye to eye on social and political matters with their more populous and aristocratic neighbors. Isolated geographically, their cities tended to harbor refugees from political and ecclesiastical persecution in other parts of Europe. The names of some of these refugees are among the most honored in the history of Western philosophy, literature, the arts, and education; and it is not surprising that the privilege of dissent came to be tolerated in these parts long before it was won elsewhere.

Roman Catholics had established the usual types of schools and universities in the Low Countries to serve their ecclesiastical purposes. Even before the Reformation, however, prosperous merchants and craftsmen had felt the need for more learning, and through their guilds and municipal councils had requested the Church to supply teachers for their sons. Latin schools under lay sponsorship were thus founded which duplicated the curricula of the church schools. Some of these burg and guild schools enjoyed such strong popular support that they became distinguished. Lay interests also encouraged vernacular instruction, sometimes as parallel programs in the Latin schools, but also as independent vernacular reading, writing, and elementary commercial schools. That is to say, schools tended to develop in the cities of the Low Countries as popular institutions responsive to the wishes and needs of the inhabitants. Instruction in the vernacular was developed to serve practical ends, and in time young men took up their studies in the traditional Latin as well as in the modern languages in the expectation that such studies could help promote a secular career.

The Low Countries therefore were relatively well supplied with a variety of schools under either ecclesiastical or secular control at the time of the Reformation. The population was mixed as a result of the successive infusions of exiles and voluntary immigrants. Therefore, the people had come to know a variety of theological and philosophical opinions and had developed an environment in which Reformation ideas quickly took root. The populations of the larger cities seldom had been homogeneous to the point that a single theological system could be uniformly established, although such efforts were made repeatedly. In the resulting atmosphere of mutual sufferance, Calvinists from France, Lutherans from Germany,

Puritans from England, and still other Reformation sects migrating to the Low Countries were able to perpetuate, for a time, their native languages and traditions. Each group brought its own educational ideas and set up its own schools. Each looked upon the education of its children as a natural right and a private responsibility. These views became so generally established that educational institutions are often identified with religious bodies even today, a feature that can be understood only in terms of these historical origins.

Some historians point out that unlike the northern provinces which lie on low lands easily defended from the sea against land attacks, the southern provinces are located on relatively high lands. This difference in terrain, it is said, enabled Catholic sovereigns of Spain and France to retain possession of these areas by the use of land forces while the northern, or Dutch, provinces were able to avoid defeat by taking to their boats. It is concluded that this difference accounts for the fact that the southern provinces, particularly those which now constitute Belgium, have remained almost uniformly Roman Catholic in religion and French in language and culture, while the people in the northern provinces became Protestant and now speak Dutch. Although this is true in a general sense, it should be noted that the northern provinces have nearly as many Roman Catholics as Protestants, and that neither group enjoys even a simple majority. The balance of power is held by approximately 20 per cent of the people who reject political domination by either Catholics or Protestants. But the struggle between Catholics and Protestants for control— or perhaps more properly, to prevent

domination by the other—has been a long and bitter one. It explains why even today there are three parallel systems of schools, each distinguished from the others on the basis of its religious commitment, and that each receives public support and is supervised by the state.

The beginnings of public education

Although municipal governments, guilds, and noblemen, as well as the usual ecclesiastical agencies, acted as patrons of schools even in medieval times, no attempt to introduce a coordinated and fully developed system of education to serve the general population of a given commune or region was successful before 1784. In that year John Nieuvenhuysen, a Protestant clergyman of the Mennonite faith, organized the Society of Public Good in Groningen. The purpose of the Society was to promote elementary instruction for all, and its activities, which included the publication of textbooks and the training of teachers as well as the establishment of schools, awakened widespread interest in mass education. So great was the interest that the republic of Batavia, the political unit under which Groningen and the several other Dutch provinces were governed at that time, appointed a special commissioner to develop a state plan. After some study a plan was proposed to introduce a system of primary education which was adopted as a law in 1806. Although the republic almost immediately thereafter was overrun by the armies of France and the separate provinces were incorporated in the Napoleonic empire in 1809, the educational project initiated by the law was allowed to continue under the direction of Van den Ende, the Dutch commissioner who had provided the leadership in securing its original enactment. Napoleon introduced the French type of centralized administrative control and provided for state inspection of all schools, regardless of their religious commitment or manner of support. Although the centralized educational administration was abandoned when Napoleon's empire collapsed, state inspection of schools was firmly established by royal decree in 1815. This decree also proclaimed the law of 1806 to be the legal basis for developing a system of primary schools throughout the newly created kingdom, including Belgium.

It is obvious that the law of 1806 had been influenced by revolutionary ideas similar to those in France, for it banned religious instruction in the schools and placed them under the control of the state. Roman Catholics understandably were furious at these violations of their traditions, but many Calvinists were equally agitated. These educational developments were a major cause of the Belgian revolt of 1830 and the withdrawal of the southern provinces from the kingdom. In the north, Calvinists and Catholics united, for once, in a bitter struggle against this secular trend. By 1848 they won a limited victory which allowed the clergy to inspect the materials of instruction, and the local school officials to select teachers on the basis of their religious affiliation to assure sectarian compatibility. More than this, all religious denominations acquired freedom to establish parochial schools without interference from municipal officials who, in general, were communicants of the Reformed Church. By 1857 parochial schools were granted limited state subsidies, and by 1920 they achieved complete equality with state schools in the matter of financial support.

Meanwhile the government's interest in education had been assigned to the Ministry of the Interior. A staff of school inspectors was appointed to make sure that the laws regarding curricula, instruction, and the maintenance of schools were being observed. Local authorities were given first responsibility in establishing schools and looking after their operation, with considerable freedom to initiate new forms and practices. This feature of decentralized administrative authority has survived to the present time. The law required that adequate primary education be made available to all children. Public schools were built and operated by the municipalities, with state assistance, to fulfill this requirement. Nevertheless, parochial schools, both Catholic and Protestant, were made available in almost equal numbers and parents enjoyed complete freedom of choice as to which type of school their children would enter.

The situation today

The Netherlands continues to have a three-track system of schools segregated on a religious basis. Public schools, Roman Catholic schools, and Protestant schools stand side by side in so many places that almost any child can receive an education beginning in the kindergarten and extending to the university without ever coming into contact with students who are being brought up in a religious faith different from his own. The establishment and management of schools is still left to private agencies or municipal authorities, usually a local school board. The complete freedom to

213

open and operate new schools has produced a variety of private and Protestant parochial schools other than those operated by the Reformed Church. Each is entitled to receive state funds for buildings, equipment, and operational expenses, including the salaries of teachers, on a basis equal to that of public schools. Even sectarian religious instruction is subsidized by the state except that no child can be required to receive instruction contrary to the wishes of his parents or guardian, and no such instruction is provided in the public schools during the regular school hours. However, public school facilities are made available to clergy and other agents of the religious bodies to offer religious instruction on a release-time basis to children whose parents request such instruction.

Today the state's participation in education is no longer administered by the Ministry of the Interior but by the Ministry of Education, Arts, and Sciences. As in most European countries, public education is treated as is any other branch of government; and the major business of the Ministry is transacted by a bureaucracy staffed by persons trained as professional administrators, usually lawyers, rather than as professional educators. However, a professional educator generally is appointed on a permanent basis to the office of Secretary-General. His duties are to advise the Minister and his staff. Also, a separate council consisting of distinguished citizens appointed by the crown advises the Ministry on matters relating to education. Among other things, the council investigates and decides upon complaints against individual schools reported to be falling short of the legal standards and therefore threatened with the loss of state financial aid.

The Ministry of Education is so organized that higher education, secondary education, primary education, and technical and vocational training are administered by separate departments. These department heads do not establish schools or operate them, but they do make certain that local authorities and private agencies fulfill their legal responsibilities in these matters. Educational administration in the Netherlands is decentralized, and the Ministry fulfills its duties through inspection and the distribution of state grants-in-aid rather than through the control of the teaching personnel or the issuance of official directives.

The institutional pattern reflects the various religious and cultural infusions that have occurred over the years. Thus, the early Latin schools were subjected to strong humanistic influences in the sixteenth and seventeenth centuries and were reorganized at that time along the lines of the German *Gymnasien*. Indeed, this name is still used for those secondary schools with curricula based largely on the classical language and literature. The universities of Leyden and Utrecht also came to reflect humanistic characteristics, as did the ancient faculties in the universities established later. The French influence is evident in the *lyceums*, and their relatively recent introduction accounts for their greater attention to the modern languages. Also, the *lyceums* delay until a later time than do the *Gymnasien* the choice between the traditional course, which prepares for the university entrance examinations, and a modern course, which leads either to further technical and scientific training or simply to the school-leaving examination. Teachers for these two types of secondary schools are usually prepared at a university.

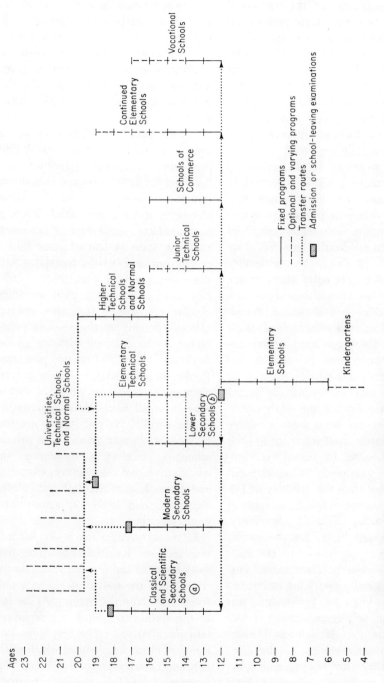

Figure 28. Educational Institutions in the Netherlands Today

a. Variously called *gymnasien, lyceums, höhere Bürgerschulen,* etc., depending upon their origins and purpose.

b. Also known as higher elementary schools.

215

Higher education has of late gone beyond the boundaries of the traditional faculty of arts and the three professional faculties. The number and types of institutions of higher education have also been extended. Admission to these newer institutions is not limited to the few students who have passed the conventional maturity or baccalaureat examinations, although some form of entrance examination is generally required.

Modern programs on the university level have made possible the development of a number of intermediate technical and vocational training programs which, though postelementary in character, are not necessarily terminal. Since they branch off the higher elementary schools, and pupils enter them at approximately age fifteen, they are coming to be looked upon as forms of secondary education. Commercial and trade schools, on the other hand receive pupils from the regular primary schools at age twelve, and do not connect directly with any institutions of higher education. Continuing and adult education programs are being made available to all persons without reference to their previous schooling. In general, such programs are sponsored by government agencies other than the Ministry of Education, Arts, and Sciences, however.

The primary, or basic elementary, schools evolved from the vernacular reading schools introduced by the Protestant religious sects. Their narrow curriculum, originally restricted to instruction in reading the vernacular, was almost completely remade under the influence of the Pestalozzian and Herbartian educational reforms of the nineteenth century. Arithmetic, geography, history, elements of science, a little handwork to develop coordination of

mind and body, and occasionally a modern foreign language were added at that time. Kindergartens were introduced by disciples of Froebel and have become very popular. Compulsory school attendance does not begin until age seven, although most children enter the first grade of an elementary school during their sixth year.

State support for elementary education is given on condition that all children enrolled receive instruction in a specified list of subjects and that the instruction comes up to stated minimal standards at the various grade levels. It is to enforce such legal requirements that the state system of inspection is maintained, and it is by complying with these requirements that private agencies qualify for government subsidies. Similar prescriptions, standards, and regulations prevail on the secondary and higher levels, although with far greater flexibility as to alternate programs. Public funds thereby enable private agencies to compete with the public schools on all levels. As a consequence of the parallel systems, pupils are free to transfer from a public to a private school, or vice versa, throughout the whole range of elementary education and through a substantial part of the secondary and higher education programs as well

Elementary education is divided into two sections longitudinally. The first section covers the first six years, during which time the course of study is uniform throughout the country. At the end of the sixth year, pupils are separated into three streams. The first leads into a higher elementary school which offers two additional years of schooling. The completion of this two-year program coincides with the end of compulsory school attendance for most children, and many go no farther. Some of these higher elementary schools now have a three-year course, a very popular form since it prepares for admission to the technical and higher vocational schools and institutes, including one which prepares for teaching these subjects on the secondary school level.

A second stream leaving the basic elementary schools at the end of the sixth year proceeds to lower vocational and trade schools. Each of these is highly specialized and offers a program of training of fixed length. Some, such as the school for fishing and inland navigation, have only a two-year program. Others, such as the schools of business, have programs covering as much as five years.

The third stream also leaves the basic elementary school at the end of the sixth year and, depending upon the type of entrance examination that is written and passed, proceeds to one of the more traditional secondary schools. The *Gymnasium* with its two parallel six-year curricula, one classical and the other mathematical-scientific, is the prestige institution. However, the *höhere Bürgerschule* also has an ancient tradition, for it is the direct descendant of the municipal Latin schools developed before the Renaissance. These duplicate the scientific curriculum of the *Gymnasium,* and offer a second, more modern curriculum as well. The *lyceums* represent a third type in some places and have appeal because, unlike the other two forms, their pupils are not required to make a choice between the two curricula they offer until the end of the second year. A general secondary school for girls, reminiscent of the German *höhere Töchterschule,* completes the list of schools in this category of postelementary education. It is not a preparatory school for the university, however, and generally is terminal.

The universities of Leyden, Utrecht, and Groningen are state institutions. They receive financial support from the state and the faculties, including the rectors, are appointed by the crown. Two municipal and two private universities also receive substantial state aid, but enjoy somewhat greater freedom in making appointments and developing their programs. The preparation of teachers for secondary schools has come to be recognized as a university responsibility, and some interest has been shown in providing further education to elementary school teachers. The six universities and a number of technical and professional schools and research centers are under the direction of the Department of Higher Education in the Ministry of Education, Arts, and Sciences.

Teachers for the elementary schools are prepared in normal schools under the Department of Primary Education. The training programs are entered from a three-year higher elementary school and continue for five years. Denominational interest is very much in evidence in the training of elementary school teachers, and Protestant and Roman Catholic normal schools operate parallel to the public normal schools. Also, each group maintains its separate research and information center, thereby extending the policy of religious segregation to the national level.

To the student of comparative education the religiously segregated schools of the Netherlands represent one of the most fascinating subjects for study in Western Europe. Two questions arise

217

immediately on which research is needed. First, it would be helpful to learn what effect the differentiated, and often hostile, programs of sectarian studies have upon the political and social life of the nation. Sectarian competition is known to be bitter, and religious hostility is said to be deliberately encouraged in the schools of the religious denominations. Perhaps the situation in the Netherlands should be compared with that in the canton of Soloturn, Switzerland, where similar religious strife recently led to the closing of all private schools and to a law which requires all children of elementary school age to attend public schools free of any sectarian influences.

The second question relates to the economics of supporting at public expense three parallel systems of schools. It is admitted that the density of the population in the Netherlands reduces the excessive duplication of costs which would occur elsewhere. But it has been noted [3] that the system places heavy burdens upon the teachers in the form of inadequate facilities, lack of division of responsibilities, large classes, inability to individualize instruction, and the loss of opportunity to enrich the program beyond the bare facts and fundamental operations specified in the state syllabi.

Education in Scandinavia

Three modern nations, Denmark, Norway, and Sweden, are elements of a geographic and ethnic complex frequently referred to as Scandinavia. Sometimes

[3] Norman H. Wilson, "Dutch Schools and Religious Segmentation," *Comparative Education Review*, vol. 3, no. 2, pp. 19–24, October, 1959.

Finland is also included, but present cultural differences induced in part by separate infusions of immigrant stock, foreign cultures, and social institutions warrant her exclusion in this account. The term Scandinavia is derived from Skane, or Scandia, the name of the southernmost province of present-day Sweden. Over the years, its strategic location overlooking the narrow waterway between the Baltic and the North Seas gave it considerable importance among the peoples of Scandinavia and Northern Europe.

The Scandinavians had achieved a rather advanced pagan culture before the coming of Christianity in the twelfth century. Their economy and mode of life were based upon the sea, and their longboats carried them in raiding expeditions against every vulnerable point in Europe. A few even reached North America. On their way they discovered Iceland and Greenland, countries where they subsequently established colonies. But more important, they developed a profitable commerce with Northern Europe. This flourishing trade, and the manufacturing required to support it, stimulated the development of coastal cities, a strong middle-class social system, and the potent Hanseatic League, which shortly was able to challenge the political power of the emerging absolute monarchies. As a consequence of these contacts with the mainland, various German innovations, including the Lutheran Reformation and its accompanying educational institutions, were transported northward. By 1550 all three countries had elected Lutheranism as the state religion and had established national churches over which each sovereign presided.

The usual forms of parish, cathedral,

and cloister schools had been introduced to Scandinavia by the Roman Catholic clergy. Even the University of Copenhagen had been founded in 1479. All these institutions, together with other properties of the Roman Church, were confiscated when the royal families joined the Reformation. However, many of the schools were reestablished under Lutheran auspices, and other properties seized were used to found new schools. Most of these were of the classical type and readily followed the pattern of the humanistic *Gymnasium* developed by Melanchthon among the German people. John Bugenhagen, another follower of Luther, devoted his life to the development of vernacular reading schools in the various parishes. He traveled in Scandinavia, and schools similar to those in the German states were introduced through his efforts. Eventually, the several Scandinavian authorities made the ability to read a requirement for confirmation, and thus indirectly for marriage—an early form of compulsory education.

As the heads of both the civil and the ecclesiastical branches of their governments, the sovereigns soon appointed ministers or directors to supervise ecclesiastical and educational affairs. The administrative organization in the ministries for religion and education generally developed along lines parallel to those in the ministries of the interior. The royal governments, of course, were most interested in the education of leaders, and financial support derived from public moneys was given almost exclusively to the gymnasiums and universities. Under these conditions of control and support, the nature of instruction and its availability were more directly affected by the social views of the royal

houses than by the wishes of the people. This was particularly apparent from 1648 to 1715, a period of royal absolutism.

The beginnings of public education

National systems of education did not develop until the nineteenth century. Influenced by liberal social ideas from France, the Scandinavian people by that time had begun to ask for more educational opportunities and a stronger voice in government. Meanwhile, curricular reforms and newer methodologies reflecting the development of a scientific attitude were attracting popular support on the Continent. The Scandinavian people, too, were becoming dissatisfied with the narrow literary and religious courses of instruction provided by the parish schools. In 1789 the government of Denmark was persuaded to undertake a thoroughgoing reorganization of the educational system. The report of the commission appointed to prepare a new plan resulted in the Education Act of 1814. Similar action was taken by Norway in 1827 and by Sweden in 1842. In each case the most significant change was to provide for a system of state-operated elementary schools.

The type of education that developed from these commitments to state schools is illustrated by the pattern existing in Sweden around 1850. There were two parallel sets of schools: the *folkskole* for the common people, and the gymnasiums and universities for the future leaders. The *folkskole* offered instruction in the mother tongue only, and boasted a course of study that included reading, writing, arithmetic, geography, history, religion, and sometimes a smattering of useful arts. The course of study was terminal. The second system introduced the study of classical Latin at an early age and included other humanistic studies designed to prepare for further study at a university. They were intended to prepare members of the clergy and the other learned professions, as well as the higher officers in the government bureaucracy.

This two-track system of education, segregated on the basis of social classes, persisted in all of Scandinavia into the twentieth century. Its replacement by a unified system is one of the major projects to which leaders in all three countries are committed today. The resulting developments merit the careful attention of students of comparative education. Further reference will be made to them in the latter part of this section.

The Peoples High Schools

The absence of educational opportunities beyond the elementary schools was a demoralizing influence among the Scandinavian peoples. Until the latter part of the nineteenth century, approximately 90 per cent of the boys and girls had no schooling after the age of twelve or thirteen. In rural areas and among the working classes in the cities the percentage was even higher. The situation had become particularly grave among the Danes, for they had experienced a series of political upheavals, somewhat similar to those in France and Germany before 1850, followed by a crushing military defeat at the hands of Bismarck as he moved to build the German Empire. It was in this period of deep gloom that Bishop Grundtvig developed the so-called Peoples High Schools among

the rural Danes, although the first school was founded in 1844.

Grundtvig believed that a proper education should awaken the individual's aspirations to live a meaningful and fruitful life. This could be accomplished, not by memorizing facts and acquiring vocational skills merely, but by cultivating a spiritual commitment through the study of man and his achievements both past and present. This cannot be undertaken with profit, Grundtvig believed, until the individual has reached late adolescence. Accordingly, his schools admitted young men and women, usually in separate semesters, at age eighteen or older. He believed that communication between teacher and student was a far more effective way to awaken the student's spiritual commitment than the usual lectures and formal exercises. Accordingly, his teachers engaged the students in informal discussions of historical and literary subjects. Examinations were not part of the program. Attendance was voluntary. Yet the results were so gratifying that the movement quickly spread throughout Scandinavia and a number of schools of this type were established abroad. The effect upon the morale of the Danish people was such that Grundtvig is honored today as one of Denmark's great heroes, and a magnificent church has been built in his memory in Copenhagen.

The original Peoples High Schools were opened for the benefit of rural youths, young people who ordinarily would not have had much education beyond the bare elements of reading and religion. However, as the quality of the state elementary schools improved and opportunities opened to their pupils to pursue studies in continuation, voca-

220

tional, and even in secondary schools preparing for the maturity examinations, interest in the Peoples High Schools dwindled. For a time young people from the cities and villages, particularly those from middle-class families, applied for admission. The curricula were changed accordingly and came to place a considerable emphasis upon art in its various forms and the development of creative talents.

The Agrarian Party reforms

Today, the Peoples High Schools have all but disappeared, their purpose and manner of operation having been taken over by schools under state control. This trend was initiated, in Denmark, when the Agrarian Party won power at the beginning of the twentieth century, and the government set as one of its goals the incorporation of the Peoples High Schools into the state system. However, the only place open for such a general cultural program in the vernacular was between the basic elementary school course and the lower classes of the gymnasiums preparing specifically for the matriculation examinations. Therefore, *Mellemskole,* or middle schools, were introduced in this space to accommodate children from ages eleven to fifteen. The new schools thus paralleled the upper classes of the elementary schools as well as the lower classes of the gymnasiums. They were joined to the gymnasiums by introducing a middle school examination which could be taken after four years of study. Those who passed were permitted to transfer into a gymnasium to take up intensive preparation for the maturity examination. Pupils continuing for a

fifth year in a middle school were admitted to the *Realeksam,* an examination that was particularly aimed at appraising proficiency in scientific and mathematical studies. Those who were successful in this examination were admitted to further studies in higher vocational and technical schools.

It had been expected that the middle school would function somewhat in the manner of a modern comprehensive school where the whole range of pupils' academic abilities and interests represented in the school's population might be accommodated. This failed to follow, however, possibly because Danish educators had not yet learned to use electives to adjust the instructional programs to the pupils' individual interests and needs. Instead, the middle schools increasingly came to be treated as progymnasiums; that is, they were made to duplicate the lower classes of the classical gymnasium, and pupils not qualified to pursue a university preparatory course were made very unhappy thereby. In the 1930s, the middle schools were divided into two parallel sections, one preparing for the middle school examination, the other offering a program with no terminal examination. Pupils were directed into one section or the other on the basis of a qualifying examination administered to all children in elementary schools just before the point of admission to the middle schools. Again, of course, the lack of status suffered by the nonexamination section simply created more unhappiness, and at an earlier age in the life of the pupil than before. Developments in the school systems of Norway and Sweden during this period were quite similar to those in Denmark.

221

The situation today

As late as 1950 pupils attending elementary schools in the Scandinavian countries were still being separated, at the end of their fourth or fifth school year, into two major streams. One led to a middle or secondary school program which terminated in an examination admitting those who passed it to higher studies. The other stream led to a program without an examination, and the program of studies terminated after two or at the most three years. The latter stream included as much as 80 per cent of the national school-age population, and almost 100 per cent in the rural areas. These were, of course, the children of the workers and the farmers. Quite recent studies have shown that only 1 out of 10 students in the gymnasiums has come from a home where the father makes his living in agriculture or works for wages. On the other hand 1 out of 4 comes from a home where the father is well educated and therefore a member of a profession or of the managerial and proprietor class. Other data show that even among those enrolled in a middle school, or *realskola,* various economic and social factors cause pupils of high promise to drop out before completing the course. As many as 50 per cent of the dropouts had IQs above the 90th percentile of those who stayed on to complete the course.[4]

Meanwhile, various social and political changes have occurred in the Scandinavian countries. The national econo-

mies, formerly heavily dependent upon agriculture, are becoming industrialized. Rural people are migrating to the cities. Labor has developed powerful political strength, frequently in cooperation with the farmers; and "liberal" governments reflecting the wishes of the common people have come into power. In this transition the weaknesses and inherent injustices of the traditional two-track school system have become apparent. Young people leaving school at age fourteen, particularly boys, have found that there is no place for them to go except on the streets. Formerly, they would have been absorbed into the never-ending activities on the farms or in the forests. At the same time school authorities have found that young people are tending to mature physically at a younger age. In 1959, for example, Swedish educational authorities spoke openly of the fact that girls were entering adolescence one year earlier, on the average, than had been the case only ten years before. Juvenile delinquency has been on the increase; action is called for; and educational reforms have been proposed and set in motion.

Reform movements have been making substantial progress since about 1957. While each government is dealing with its own problems in its own way, representatives from each country meet from time to time to exchange information and points of view. In these meetings the language of communication is English, reflecting the strong trend in each country to make this a required second language to be studied by all pupils.

Other indications that a common point of view is developing in the field of education are found in the general commitment to the extension of com-

[4] Thorsten Husen, "School Reform in Sweden: A Liberal Democracy Adopts the Comprehensive School System," *Phi Delta Kappan,* vol. 43, no. 2, p. 91, November, 1961.

pulsory school attendance to at least age sixteen. Norway and Sweden already have taken legislative action to accomplish this goal, whereas Denmark, for the moment at least, hopes to make education so attractive that young people will voluntarily stay in school to age sixteen and beyond.

The use of selective examinations to separate pupils into two or more streams is also being minimized in each country. This is made possible by the introduction of comprehensive schools in which all pupils are enrolled for nine years. Teachers are being trained to work with heterogeneous classes, and all pupils study the same subjects in the first six years. Beginning with the seventh year a limited number of elec- tive subjects are provided from among which the pupils are free to choose without pressure from their teachers. The list of electives grows longer each year, and is so constituted that individual pupils may explore such diverse areas as languages, science and mathematics, general business subjects, and the manual arts. The separation of the pupil population by schools does not occur until after the ninth school year, at which time standard admissions examinations come into limited use, particularly with respect to locating those who may wish to enter a program of study leading to the university.

The trend in Scandinavian educational reforms is illustrated in Figure 29 relating to Sweden. The Swedish plan was

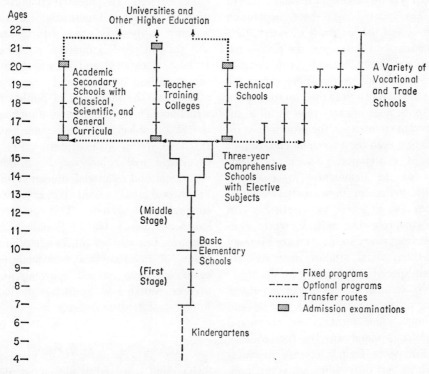

Figure 29. 1957 Plan for Reorganizing the Swedish School System
This plan calls for voluntary action by municipalities, with support from the national treasury.

recommended by a parliamentary committee in 1957, and it has influenced rather strongly the direction the reform is now taking. In keeping with her present democratic principles, Sweden refrained from seeking reform by legislating a specific plan on a national basis. She has chosen instead to let the municipalities and rural districts take the initiative. However, modest supplementary grants are made to those local communities which decide to reorganize their schools along lines recommended in the committee's report.

The reforms in Norway and Denmark differ from those in Sweden primarily with respect to the year in which the school population is divided into separate streams to be sent on to differentiated schools, the number and kinds of choices offered at these separation points, and the use made of external examinations to determine the pupil's educational future. Sweden seems to make less use of such examinations before the end of the ninth year than do the others.

Another significant trend in all Scandinavian countries is the growing awareness of a need for a common understanding of contemporary social problems and of the democratic processes by which action in these matters can be taken. On all levels, but particularly in the comprehensive schools, where children from every social class are gathered together, social studies programs are given special attention.

No account of Scandinavian education, no matter how brief, should end without some mention of vocational training. Finland was the first country in Europe to include courses in handwork as part of its educational program. These were introduced in 1858 by Uno Cygnaeus, a follower of Pestalozzi and

Froebel; and by 1866 the Finnish government had made some form of manual training compulsory for boys in rural schools and for young men preparing to become teachers. In 1872 Sweden, suffering an economic depression, decided that manual training might help restore prosperity, particularly in the rural districts. Influenced to some degree by the example of Finland, Sweden introduced a form of manual training known as "sloyd." The sloyd movement aroused the interest of educators and government officials in other countries, and before long some of them had introduced programs of vocational education.

Manual training of the sloyd type too often was looked upon merely as exercise to develop manual dexterity and moral strength. Its potential connection with vocational and industrial training was not easily recognized, with the result that, in the Scandinavian countries at least, vocational and industrial education had to be assumed by agencies other than the ministries of public instruction. This separation of functions is still a problem, and educational leaders have shown little concern over it. One might predict, however, that in time vocational and industrial education will be incorporated within the emerging comprehensive system. This prospect looms not merely for the Scandinavian countries but also for others where programs of intellectual and manual development have emerged separately and been perpetuated as completely distinct forms of instruction.

Education in Switzerland

Switzerland is a land of diverse peoples divided by language, cultural traditions, social institutions, customs, and a formidable cluster of beautiful mountains. The people are held together as a nation only by a universal, almost fanatical love for freedom and the right of self-determination. Once largely uninhabited, the isolated valleys and mountain meadows invited the oppressed from neighboring lands to find a haven from their enemies. Each group of refugees built its own way of life and educated its children in the manner it thought best. It is a significant fact that organized government was developed by the Swiss people on the local level first; and that cantonal governments (states) and the *Bund* (the nation) were created later by the delegation of power upward. Thus Switzerland, the nation, is essentially an association of many smaller governments, each enjoying a measure of independence and autonomy usually reserved to sovereign nations. This historic principle of local responsibility and local control is nowhere more evident in contemporary Swiss life than in the field of education.

The present Swiss nation was born out of the need for mutual assistance in resisting external tyranny. Early Swiss history is in large part the story of defensive military actions by the isolated settlements against invading troops and foreign political agents. Foremost among the hated oppressors were the Hapsburgs of Austria. Indeed, the confederation was born in A.D. 1291 when the leaders of three groups of natives residing around Lake Lucerne met on a small meadow known as the Rütli, which overlooks the lake. The meeting, immortalized in Schiller's "William Tell," produced a pledge of mutual assistance against Gessler, the current agent of Austrian imperialism. This event is still celebrated by the Swiss on the first day of August as their most significant national holiday.

The three groups, known as cantons, which formed the first confederation were soon joined by neighboring groups. By the sixteenth century there were thirteen cantons in the confederation. This growth was achieved not by military conquest, but by petition from peoples who had disassociated themselves from their previous political authorities. Today there are twenty-five cantons, although several are half cantons, two having been formed from a previous one.

The Swiss citizen today has three political loyalties. He is a citizen, first, of his local village or city, known as a *Gemeinde* or commune; then, of his *kanton,* or state; and finally, of the *Bund,* or nation. On each level, however, he insists upon participating directly in making many decisions which in other places are made by elected representatives or appointed agents. Indeed, several of the smaller cantons still do not have a representative legislative body but transact all their business in the *Landsgemeinde,* the assembly of all the male citizens meeting as a body in the public square of their principal city. Generally, however, an elected legislative body and an executive council transact the business of a given political unit. They also propose legislation and prepare budgets. But whether these are on the local, cantonal, or national level they must be submitted to the people for a direct vote. That is to say, the people vote their own laws and taxes in addition to electing their representatives in government. Significantly, an applicant for citizenship must first secure, by majority vote, his citizenship in a *Gemeinde.* Only then will his application be honored on the higher levels. And in nearly all *Gemeinden* even teachers are appointed by the direct vote of the people.

This long tradition of direct government has had its effect upon Swiss political institutions on all levels. The original confederation was formed as a mutual defense organization and therefore provided practically no facilities for dealing with other matters. By the nineteenth century revolutionary ideas originating in France were portraying government as the instrument of the people to be used by them to achieve their own ends. These ideas were favorably received in Switzerland and soon there arose a popular movement to replace the existing alliance with a stronger national government designed along liberal lines. A new constitution was drafted, similar in many ways to that of the United States, which provided for a federal form of government. This constitution was adopted in 1848 and, with substantial modifications in 1874, provides the basis for Swiss government to this day.

The first schools

Two factors contributed significantly in the development of public education in Switzerland. The first was the religious motive, and the second arose later with the recognition of a need to prepare children to become economically, politically, and socially self-sufficient. The first appeared in the early days of the Reformation. The second came in the nineteenth century and produced a variety of school reforms, some of which have been widely imitated.

As in other parts of Europe, schools were originally introduced in Switzer-
226

land by the Roman Catholic Church. Yet there were few large centers of population among the Swiss and therefore very few bishoprics to sponsor schools of the cathedral type. A notable exception was the Bishopric of Basle, and from this circumstance the University of Basle owes both its early founding and its valuable collection of ancient manuscripts and records. The Swiss countryside was better suited to the purposes of the monastic orders, and a number of cloisters were built at the northern end of mountain passes leading from Italy. These served as missionary outposts among the pagan peoples. Several cloister schools were introduced chiefly to train native youths to take up the work of the clergy. The monastery at St. Gall was one of these and is especially remembered for the literary treasures preserved there during the Dark Ages and fed into the Renaissance in later years. But the general population remained illiterate until the Reformation.

Because of their independent nature, the Swiss people had never been particularly receptive to an authoritarian form of ecclesiastical control. Their mountains and forests had sheltered followers of the Waldensian sect as early as the twelfth century. Later, Basle became the center of a movement to establish a council form of ecclesiastical control in the Roman Catholic Church. Other elements of dissent were introduced by missionaries and refugees. Inspired in part by the teaching of Luther, the Swiss produced two great religious reformers of their own, Ulrich Zwingli and John Calvin. Zwingli, the highest-ranking member of the clergy in Zurich, led the movement which resulted in the formation of the Reformed Church. It was speedily made the established church in several of the German-speaking cantons, and has remained so to this day. In Geneva, John Calvin led in the establishment of an ecclesiastical theocracy based upon his theological principles. His influence is apparent today not merely in the French cantons of Switzerland, but also among the French Huguenots, the Scotch, Irish, and English Presbyterians, some elements of Dutch Protestantism, and English Puritanism and Congregationalism.

Surrounded by sovereign states in which an established church was maintained as a necessary branch of government, the several Swiss cantons also adopted the principle of religious uniformity. Each canton declared for itself whether it would become a Calvinist, Reformed, or Roman Catholic state, decisions that usually were not made without much bitterness and some bloodshed. Nevertheless, the decisions gave direction to the types of schooling that emerged. Later, these commitments also served to increase resistance to interference in local educational matters on the part of any external authority including the emerging national government.

The beginnings of public education

The most extensive and complete system of education introduced by the reformers was established in Geneva by the Calvinists. John Calvin had been thoroughly dedicated to the principle of religious domination in the affairs of men. At his instigation the council of the theocratic government of Geneva was persuaded to establish and maintain at public expense four vernacular reading schools, one in each quarter of the city. Calvin was primarily in-

terested, however, in schools that would contribute more directly to the study of theology. Accordingly, a Latin grammar school was established, similar in many respects to the gymnasium developed earlier by Sturm at Strassburg. This and similar schools established by Calvinists in neighboring lands, were called *collèges*. An institution of higher studies, known as the academy, was also established. The University of Geneva developed from this academy. Similar developments in Lausanne and Neuchâtel produced the universities now located in these places.

It is significant that all the schools in Geneva were under the immediate control of the central council, a fact that may explain why the canton of Geneva today has a unified cantonal school system, centrally administered. This is in contrast to the other cantons which depend in varying degrees upon local schools, each locally administered. Generally speaking, however, the other two French-language cantons, Neuchâtel and Valais, also show a stronger interest in cantonal controls than do the German cantons. This probably is the result of their cultural ties with post-Napoleonic France where the principle of centralized government was strongly advocated.

The cantons which joined the Zwingli movement and made the Reformed Church their official ecclesiastical establishment followed the Lutheran practice of depending upon the local parishes to provide vernacular reading instruction. In Zurich the two Latin schools were reorganized and modernized along humanistic lines by the introduction of classical Latin as well as Greek and Hebraic studies. The name *Gymnasium* soon was adopted for these and similar

227

schools. Beyond this, Zwingli introduced regular "public" lectures in connection with the cathedral to instruct parish priests and other clergy in the reformed theology and ecclesiastical offices. Different portions of the lectures were given in Greek, Hebrew, and Latin; but at a later hour the same discussions were repeated in German for the benefit of anyone who wished to hear them.[5]

Zwingli was not indifferent to the educational needs of the common people. Indeed, he wrote a booklet on the subject of their instruction and generally showed exceptional interest, for his time, in teaching them scientific, technical, and even vocational subjects and skills. Unfortunately, he was killed in the prime of his life and therefore had no opportunity to carry out his ideas for popular education. As a consequence, vernacular instruction, although encouraged by the cantonal authorities, especially the ecclesiastical officials, was left to local initiative, support, and direction. In this manner the vernacular schools arose as local schools, literally schools of the people. A policy of decentralized educational responsibility thus became strongly entrenched. Dependence upon local initiative and direction dating from this early period has brought about a great variety of institutional forms and practices. In this atmosphere of freedom to act, a number of the educational experiments associated with the names of Pestalozzi, Froebel, and Fellenberg later took place. While each was a private enterprise, each also received some encouragement and support from a local governmental unit.

Several of the cantons, particularly those lying in the central and southern parts of the country, remained Catholic. These are largely mountainous regions and thinly settled. The people were—and have remained—strongly attached to their clergy and dependent upon the education the Church provided. Today none of them except Freiburg has a university and this was founded by external groups and is not strictly a cantonal institution. Several cantons have no secondary schools, but contract for the instruction of their youth with one or more religious orders that operate within their borders. Similar arrangements sometimes are made for the instruction of elementary pupils and for the training of teachers.

The historical factors reviewed above point to the fact that today no single educational pattern is followed in all parts of Switzerland. There is no central administrative agency for education and no uniform set of laws regulating the instruction of children. Variations in institutional forms, curricular content, school calendars, and even the language of instruction exist not merely within a given canton, but even within a single local school district. In spite of these differences education is one of the greatest concerns of the Swiss people and they enjoy one of the highest literacy rates in the world. The Swiss are quick to say that being one of the poorest nations on earth with respect to natural resources, their primary resource is people; and education is the only means by which they can utilize that resource to its fullest extent.

The situation today

The Constitution of 1848 did not delegate to the national government any authority in education already exercised

[5] Friedrich Paulsen, *Geschichte des gelehrten Unterrichts*, Verlag von Veit, Leipzig, 1919, vol. I, pp. 285–287.

by cantons and local communities. Article 22 did authorize the establishment of a national technical school, a national university, and such other institutions of higher education as might be needed to supplement the facilities of the cantons and communities. The Federal Technical Institute [6] at Zurich has resulted from the first of these constitutional provisions; the Commercial Institute at St. Gall from the last. But the cantons which already supported institutions of higher education [7] were not disposed to let a new university with national resources rise to overshadow their institutions. Accordingly, the provision in Article 22 for a national university never has been implemented, but small grants to support specified types of instruction are given to the cantonal universities.

The 1874 revision of the constitution was more direct in its assignment of educational responsibility. Article 27 made clear that education was a matter of national concern but left all administrative authority to the cantons and communities. Thus the cantons are directed "to provide sufficient elementary education," and warned that the national government has authority to take necessary action against any canton which fails to do so. It is further stipulated that elementary education shall be compulsory, free, and so structured that "adherents of all creeds may attend the schools without injury to freedom of faith or conscience." No official statement has ever been issued to define what constitutes "an adequate elementary education," yet no action has ever

been initiated by the federal government to make a reluctant canton comply. On the other hand individuals have brought their complaints to court "with significant consequences." [8]

The national government assumes some of the financial responsibility for elementary education. Each canton receives a modest subvention, based on population, which may be used for specified purposes only. Furthermore, each school is supplied with a wall map of Switzerland and other instructional materials that have similar widespread use.

Because the national economy depends on trade and manufacturing, these have been developed to high technical levels. The national government has been the leading agency in this effort, and federal funds are provided to support vocational and technical training. Here again the national government supports and encourages local initiative, neither competing with nor supplanting local or cantonal activities. By law no youth may enter apprenticeship training before age fifteen, but at that point unbelievably extensive and varied training courses and vocational schools are provided, and all apprentices and trainees are required to attend school on either a part-time or full-time basis.

Finally, Swiss military defenses are provided by a citizen army. Every Swiss man must render military service, beginning at age twenty, and must continue to do so on a reserve basis, with annual training periods of three weeks' duration, for approximately twenty-five years. The direction and support of this military effort is a major function of the national government. But the na-

---

[6] The *Eidgenossiche Technische Hochschule*, or the E.T.H., as the Swiss call it.

[7] Basel, Bern, Geneva, Lausanne, Neuchâtel, and Zurich. The university at Freiburg was not founded until 1889.

[8] Martin Simmen, *Die Schulen des Schweizervolkes*, Verlag von Huber, Frauenfeld, 1946, p. 16.

tional interest in the physical fitness of the citizen-soldier does not begin at age twenty. By law the military department provides compulsory physical education and physical fitness programs for all boys age seven to twenty. In addition to gymnastics and competitive games the program includes instruction in skiing, camping, hiking, map reading, mountain climbing, and other activities selected to develop boys for their future military duties. The instructors, employed by the military department, are trained in a school maintained by the national government for this purpose. A somewhat similar program now is available to girls on a voluntary basis. Because of these programs, the schools do not need to provide extensive physical education instruction, a fact which must be taken into account when Swiss schools are compared with those in other countries.

In the absence of any broad commitment to education on the part of the national government, the administration of education is a responsibility of the several cantons. Each of the twenty-five cantons has its own educational program, set of school laws, and some administrative agency, usually a director of education or an education department, to see that its children are properly instructed. By constitutional prescription all elementary education must be under the supervision of the cantons. However in only one canton, Geneva, is the canton the only agency responsible for providing public education. In all others, responsibility is divided between the cantons and the local communities. Indeed, local initiative and direction generally lead the way, particularly in elementary and vocational education, with the cantons contributing

230

supplementary support and setting minimal standards. The cantons assume a much larger responsibility in secondary education and teacher training, but local communities and even private agencies are not excluded from these areas.

The weight given local customs and wishes in educational matters is evident in the fact that in the canton of Ticino thirty communes protested the lengthening of the school year to nine months, "ten of which [protests] were accepted [approved] for 1959–60." [9] Similar variations within a given canton may govern the age range for which schooling is compulsory, the length of the school day, the hours of instruction, the beginning of the school year, the segregation of the sexes (except in the canton of Schaffhausen where coeducation is stipulated in all classes), the provisions for religious instruction, and attendance at private schools (except in the canton of Soloturn where all children must attend public elementary schools), and the arrangements for transition from basic elementary schools to schools of a higher order. The cantons usually employ professional school inspectors to see that minimal standards respecting curricula and instruction are met. The cantons also participate with the local communities in maintaining uniform salary schedules and suitable living quarters for teachers. Bonuses are generally paid to teachers who accept assignments in the more remote and less desirable places. But the cantons do not appoint teachers. They merely certify those who meet cantonal standards, leaving to the communities the privilege of selecting

[9] Henri Grandjean, "Educational Developments in Switzerland 1959–1960," *Twenty-third International Conference on Public Education*, Geneva, 1960, p. 34.

and appointing from the list of those certified the ones who are preferred locally. Appointment is usually by popular election.

Administrative leadership in the local communities is ordinarily provided jointly by the local teachers and a lay committee elected either by the voters directly or appointed by the local council. There are few specially trained full-time administrators, except on the cantonal level. In a multiple-teacher school on the elementary and secondary levels the faculty elects one of its own members as head teacher or rector. Budget proposals and curricular and other operational changes are drawn up by the teachers and submitted to the school committee. But neither the school committee nor the council can give final approval to such proposals, for they must be submitted to the people. Needless to say, Swiss teachers participate much more actively in public life—many serve in the cantonal and national legislative bodies—than do teachers in other lands.

Institutional variations are so numerous within the cantons, and even within the larger municipalities, that no single, completely descriptive diagram of the educational system of a given canton can be prepared, with the possible exception of the canton of Geneva. The variations are even greater and more numerous when one looks at the national situation. However, the following descriptive statements may be said to apply generally, with exceptions, some of which are noted:

1. Each local political unit (*Gemeinde* or commune) provides at least one public elementary school where children may receive instruction, without cost, for the minimum number of years required by cantonal law. *Exception:* Communities, decreasing in number, in which children attend private schools at public expense, usually schools operated by a religious body or order.

2. Each canton and many of the larger villages and cities provide one or more types of secondary schools, to which pupils who are scholastically able and whose families are willing to pay the fees may be admitted after attending an elementary school from three to six years. *Exceptions:* Several cantons which depend upon private or religious agencies to operate the schools. Zurich has taken the lead in abolishing secondary school fees; and most cantons provide tuition, living, and transportation grants to needy children, particularly those who must seek secondary school opportunities outside their home communities.

3. All children must be instructed for a period of eight years. *Exceptions:* Nidwalden, the lowest in this respect, requires only six years for girls, one-half year more for boys; Freiburg requires nine years for boys. Other cantons range somewhere between these two extremes.

4. All children attend a common, undifferentiated school for the first four years. *Exceptions:* Places where segregated schools are provided for boys and girls; where segregated schools are provided on a religious basis; children in sanitaria and other special schools; the canton of Waadt where differentiation may occur after three years; and in eastern Switzerland where differentiation generally does not occur until after the sixth year.

5. As a general rule, but with many ex-

231

ceptions, children enter school at age six in the French and Italian communities, and at age seven in the German sections.

6. Preelementary schooling is provided in many places on a voluntary basis.

7. Secondary education is differentiated from and, in its lower classes, runs parallel with the upper classes of the elementary schools. *Exception:* In Geneva, elementary schooling now ends with the sixth class, and the first year of secondary education (seventh class) is undifferentiated to provide an observation period from which pupils are directed into one of four streams of higher studies: literary, scientific, vocational, or preparation for manual trades.[10] This innovation is exciting much interest and may indicate a trend.

8. Teacher training and certification is a responsibility of the canton. *Exception:* Several of the smaller cantons maintain no teacher training institutions, but depend on neighboring cantons or on religious orders to supply their teachers.

9. Preparation for admission to university study is provided in a classical "maturity" school variously called a *Gymnasium, ginnasio, lycée,* or *collège,* depending upon which language is spoken locally. *Exceptions:* Classes that prepare for one or more of the several types of maturity examinations—the gateway to university study—now are available in some other types of secondary schools or through private study.

In spite of the highly decentralized systems of education and the countless variations from any standard pattern, two practices employed on a national scale provide a unifying influence: the examinations all young men must take on beginning their military service, and the maturity examinations all applicants for admission to university study must take. Recruits are examined on their ability to read and write their mother tongue and perform the fundamental operations in arithmetic, on their knowledge of history and geography, and on one or two additional accomplishments. Cantonal jealousies and competition have created intense interest in the comparative performances of the recruits from the different cantons and communities, with the result that considerable stress has been placed on teaching these subjects in the elementary schools.

A somewhat similar effect is exerted upon the secondary schools by the maturity examinations. The examinations—there are several types, each regulating admission to different segments of higher education—are administered by a national commission. However, there are differences in the way Swiss educators describe the purpose of these examinations and the manner in which they are used. Some, obviously influenced by the interpretation prevalent in Germany after 1850, regard the examinations as instruments by which only the most able students can gain admission to university study. Others, following a more liberal interpretation, insist that the examinations are intended to guarantee admission to anyone who meets the minimal requirements. The latter interpretation has special meaning when it is recalled that eighteen of the twenty-five cantons have no university of their own. Were there no minimal standard applied uniformly among the cantons, able students from

---

[10] *Ibid.,* p. 36.

those which have no university might find themselves barred by the cantonal authorities from the seven existing universities. Murmurs of discontent arising from this source have been heard.

Public interest in Swiss education today is centered upon the extension of educational opportunities for all classes of students in every geographic region. This is an aspiration that lies within the grasp of the people because they have the freedom to act and the experience in self-government to know what steps can be taken. Educational changes are occurring everywhere. Experimental procedures and arrangements of many descriptions are being tried. Because of these developments it is possible that Swiss education will be one of the most useful subjects for comparative studies in the next quarter century.

Education in the United States

Education in the United States cannot be understood apart from its historical antecedents. That it originated under conditions of English colonialism accounts for many features still in evidence today. French and Spanish colonies and social institutions established in what is now the United States have been either uprooted entirely or assimilated into the major stream of developments derived from English sources. The record shows that the English claimed territorial rights to all the area ceded to the thirteen original colonies following the War for Independence.

Under the Acts of Uniformity and Supremacy the English crown operated as the guardian of the true faith and assumed it had authority to suppress all teachings at variance with the Anglican creed. But the government did not operate schools of its own; nor did it provide regular and systematic support to any that were operating. Education was looked upon as a responsibility of the family, and individuals were free to operate in that field as they wished so long as their efforts presented no opposition to the crown or the established church.

The original English settlement at Jamestown and the early Virginia Colony were deliberate attempts to transplant the English civil and ecclesiastical systems to America. Education in Virginia thus began under the watchful eyes of the Anglican clergy. Private schools were preferred by the landed gentry as they tried to duplicate the ways of the English aristocracy. At best the formal schooling prepared young gentlemen to enter a university college back in England. Ultimately, of course, similar colleges were developed on this side, notably King's College in New York and William and Mary College in Virginia; but these came too late to duplicate the degree of Anglican uniformity maintained by the colleges at Oxford and Cambridge. As to elementary education, the Anglican settlers were not overly active in providing instruction for the common people except for some religious education offered by the local rectors or their assistants.

The situation in the Puritan settlements in New England was quite different. Though loyal to the crown, the Puritans nevertheless insisted on their right to teach their views to their children in schools free from the supervision of the Anglican clergy. The Stuart kings, anxious to find settlers to develop their overseas holdings and finding the dissenters uncomfortable subjects to have around, granted those Puritans willing

233

to settle in the New World certain exemptions from the Act of Uniformity. These exemptions, together with other agreements, were spelled out in the charter of the Massachusetts Bay Company.

The charter, it was believed, gave Puritan divines in the Colony the same privileges enjoyed by the Anglican clergy back home. The Puritans regarded education as a religious duty devolving both upon the individual, who must seek it, and upon ecclesiastical societies, who must provide it. Accordingly, the Colony in considered public actions almost immediately provided for a Latin school, then a college, and finally placed responsibility for establishing and maintaining vernacular reading schools upon the several congregations, each of which was organized as a separate ecclesiastical society.

At the outset, the ecclesiastical controls of the colonial government were accepted without complaint. Very quickly, however, individual ministers, sometimes supported by their congregations, and other individuals and groups began to take exception to various theological interpretations given by the colonial authorities. Such insubordination was met with official pressures, and when the circumstances became intolerable the insurgents gathered together their belongings and trekked through the wilderness looking for new locations free from colonial domination. The Connecticut Colony was established by three such groups which left Massachusetts in 1634–1635.

The Connecticut Colony differed substantially from the Virginia and the Massachusetts Bay Colonies in that it was established without the sanction of the crown or any other civil or ecclesi-

astical authority. The settlers had merely moved into a region they liked, made some sort of land purchase from the Indians, and set up housekeeping. Actually, the three groups which left the Bay Colony settled in different spots along the Connecticut River and remained more or less independent for several years. Each constituted itself an ecclesiastical society, arranged for the services of a minister, made the necessary regulations to govern community life, and gave some thought to the instruction of members who could not read. Only several years later did the need for mutual assistance against Indians and other hostile groups lead to the formation of a colonial government. When the government was established, the people very carefully spelled out its duties and the limits of its authority in a document known as the Fundamental Orders.

Some historians claim this is the first example of a government based upon a written constitution. The founders of the Connecticut Colony clearly presumed that sovereignty resided with the people and that governments are created by the people to serve the wishes and needs of the people. The Connecticut example set the pattern of decentralized government and of local responsibility and control in education which is today so deeply entrenched in the United States.

Clearly evident in the Connecticut Colony, and in other later colonies, was the principle that the schools belong to the people. Provisions for education were made within the ecclesiastical societies by the parents of the children who were to be served. Education, therefore, came to reflect local ideas and aspirations, and the quality and scope of instruction varied from place to place. The desire to guard against possible neglect in some places, and a resulting weakening of communal life, led the settlers to pass educational laws on the colonial level. The "Old Deluder Satan Act" passed by the Massachusetts Bay Colony in 1647 was one of these. It was hoped that such action would induce all local ecclesiastical societies to provide vernacular reading schools, and the larger ones to maintain Latin grammar schools. However, in the absence of colonial financial support, these expectations were not wholly met. On the other hand, Connecticut did contribute public funds to the support of Harvard College in Massachusetts until the liberal theological views emerging there led the religious leaders to work for a college of their own. Yale College, founded in New Haven in 1701, was the result.

The Puritan reform movement in England had been brought about in large part by Calvinist doctrines. Even Puritan educational activities had followed the basic pattern developed in Geneva. It was not surprising, then, that other Calvinists migrating to America also established vernacular reading schools and Latin grammar schools. The Dutch, in New York and New Jersey, and the Scotch-Irish Presbyterians, also in New Jersey but more prominently in western Pennsylvania and Virginia, soon were equipped with reading and grammar schools that resembled those in New England. Even some colleges were established, notably Princeton; and the character of Anglican William and Mary was altered by these influences. But the Puritan schools remained the dominant type, and since the New England inhabitants were very prolific and sent out many parties of young people to settle along the frontiers, their institutions became widely established.

The English pattern had tended to dominate colonial educational institutions as the War for Independence drew nearer. In addition to providing models for individual schools, this pattern also promulgated the policies of private effort, local control, and voluntary attendance. In consequence of these policies and the rapid expansion of the population, local communities soon found increasingly larger numbers of illiterates in their midst. It has been estimated that not more than two out of five children of school age were provided an opportunity to read before education was made a responsibility of the civil government sometime after the War for Independence had been won.

The beginnings of public education

The War for Independence marked a break in America's cultural as well as political ties with England. The war itself had been fed by liberal political ideas which shortly were to precipitate the French Revolution and incite the great liberal movements which reached their climax in Northern Europe in 1848. The temptation of cheap lands in North America and the uncertain political situations in both Europe and America caused a population movement westward of such proportions that a number of new states were added to the original thirteen in an incredibly short time.

From an educational point of view this westward movement was very significant. Its primary impact was the rise of the common man to a status of political equality with the traditional

235

landed aristocracy and members of the learned professions. The frontier farmers, small shopkeepers, craftsmen, and day laborers—persons who had not been credited with enough intelligence to take part in decisions of a public nature—found that under the conditions of necessity precipitated by pioneer life they could manage such matters very satisfactorily, indeed. This gave them courage to take local government in their own hands and in time to demand a voice in state and national affairs as well. Under the leadership of Andrew Jackson, they achieved a substantial extension of the right to vote. Thereafter, universal education, instead of remaining an impractical dream, became a matter of practical necessity.

After 1800 immigrants from Europe, particularly those from Germany, brought with them liberal political, educational, and even religious doctrines. Their theories of social equality, rational methods of philosophical inquiry, and even of the scientific method, posited new approaches to truth in opposition to the methods of revelation which had kept royal governments and established religions in control in Europe and the Colonies for so long. A secular outlook was encouraged, particularly in matters dealing with the affairs of this life. Knowledge was said to be derived from sensory data; and guides to the good life were to be sought by scientific inquiry.

It followed from such philosophical assumptions that individual man would seek good ends as he acquired the knowledge to do so. To provide such knowledge to all men, a form of universal education was called for. This, it was said, was a function that could be performed equitably and effectively only by government. Therefore, a popular movement arose to establish public schools, free to all, and teaching only those forms of knowledge useful and necessary to each. Finally, the financial means to establish and maintain such a system of free schools were believed to be available through the sale of public lands. Although such lands were held by the national government, the funds realized from their sale were distributed to the several states. States, in turn, distributed their receipts to the local communities to assist them in establishing schools under local control and direction. It was to supervise the distribution of such funds that Massachusetts appointed Horace Mann as its first state school official; Connecticut appointed Henry Barnard to a similar post. State departments of education have evolved from these and similar beginnings.

The battle to establish public schools was fought and largely won in the nineteenth century. At first widespread support for universal education at public expense was aroused and organized by voluntary groups which ventured to open schools in the manner of the English philanthropic societies. When these private efforts fell far short of what was desired, supplementary funds were requested from the local governments. Public funds were voted quite reluctantly at first, and in small amounts. At the outset they provided for scholarships to be made available on the basis of need, a precedent which incidentally later was followed in secondary education, and very recently in higher education. But this form of public support soon called for a public accounting, and ultimately for a special local branch of government, usually a school committee, to provide public control. Under public auspices and with control located in the local communities, the people were willing to support universal schooling as a public service.

Schools supported by all and open to all soon called for the severance of the ecclesiastical ties. The public schools were made secular agencies by public action. State legislatures enacted laws authorizing local governments to levy taxes on any property within their domains to raise money to operate their public schools. Other legislation provided for the organization of special school districts much smaller in size than municipalities, townships, or counties, but with similar authority to levy taxes and operate public schools. In an incredibly short time every inhabited part of the nation was included in a school district, and many states guaranteed each child a right to receive instruction at public expense even if it meant the employment of a special teacher to offer the instruction in the child's home. The drive for universal education was both rapid and thorough, and compulsory school attendance legislation followed in its wake.

The public school movement, beginning around 1820, focused upon developing a system of elementary schools. The name itself signified an interest in the elements of scientific knowledge as distinguished from the emphasis on reading and religion which had characterized the colonial schools. Similar scientific interests shortly came to be served by private secondary schools, known as academies, and even by a few private technical and scientific institutes. The

success of the public elementary schools gave rise to public demands for free secondary and higher education as well; and several states established public universities before the so-called Land-Grant Act of 1862 laid a foundation for a system of federally aided public institutions for higher education. Meanwhile, enterprising communities had taken steps to establish secondary schools under public control. The legality of supporting such schools by means of public taxes was established in 1870, and thereafter public high schools quickly replaced the private academies in most places.

By the end of the nineteenth century every state of the Union had taken at least the initial steps to provide a closely articulated system of tax-supported, free, and secular elementary, secondary, and higher schools under public control and available to all without prejudice to members of any faith or social class. The institutional models for that system were provided in large part by the pre-1850 Prussian system. The curricula and methods of instruction were adapted from those developed by Pestalozzi, Diesterweg, Froebel, and Herbart. The land-grant colleges and state universities borrowed heavily from the University of Berlin. In contrast, the private schools, few in number and located primarily in New England, were derived from the English pattern. However, both the public and the private schools have been substantially modified by a variety of later influences so that they have drawn closer together to form a unique American type. The two systems now parallel each other at every point, and it is possible to transfer from one system to the other at any level.

237

The situation today

Public education in the United States is still regarded as a responsibility of the people in the several states. There is no national school system or administrative authority. In some states, notably New York and California, the people have agreed that a substantial part of the responsibility for public education, both financial and administrative, rests with the state. Each, therefore, has developed a rather large, centralized administrative staff. Numerous laws and regulations prescribe minimum standards of health and safety, courses of instruction, and teaching standards. Substantial amounts of financial aid, usually distributed according to need and the economic ability of the local communities, help assure adequate opportunities to all children living within the state. In other states, responsibility and control have been retained in varying degrees within the local communities. The state educational agencies sometimes are very limited in size and have few duties beyond the certification of teachers and the distribution of school grants on the basis of a prescribed formula. Similarities among the individual schools on a given educational level throughout the nation have not occurred as a result of uniform administrative controls, but from voluntary actions by an informed public which has come· to common understandings through free and open discussion.

Local control and local responsibility have brought about good public schools, schools to which both rich and poor are glad to send their children. Furthermore, none of the schools is necessarily terminal. Freedom of movement exists

to such a degree that a child entering any elementary school has the opportunity to continue through elementary schools, secondary schools, and even higher education, in either public or private institutions, either in his own state or in any part of the country. If the facilities or programs are inadequate, the public is free to create new ones. Whenever existing institutions have become too selective, thereby denying educational opportunities to some who desire them, new schools have been established. It is expected that this process will continue.

The freedom of movement provided by the public school system of the United States is assured by its unitary character. All children enter an elementary school at approximately age six and study the same basic facts and skills for the first six years. The courses of study for the seventh and eighth years also show considerable uniformity, whether the students are enrolled in the upper two years of an eight-year elementary school or in the first two years of a junior high school. More extensive differentiation occurs at the ninth-year level; and the degree of separateness and specialization increases with each year thereafter.

It should be noted that the three types of secondary schools indicated in Figure 30 do not separate pupils into different but parallel tracks as is so often the case in other countries. Both the junior-senior high schools and the four-year high schools are comprehensive schools. The differences are administrative rather than curricular and, except in a very few places, only one form of these is available in a given community. That is to say, all secondary education in a given place is pro-

238

vided either in a comprehensive four-year high school program or in a six-year junior-senior high school program. The graduates of either type have equal status and enjoy identical opportunities to continue their studies. Vocational schools, on the other hand, are usually specialized and provide a parallel but somewhat different program of instruction. Admission to vocational schools is not compulsory, and those who study there are not necessarily excluded from transferring to an academic high school or from admission to an institution of higher education.

Comprehensive secondary schools are made practicable through the use of an ingenious elective system. Strangers to the system must be warned in the strongest terms that this does not mean

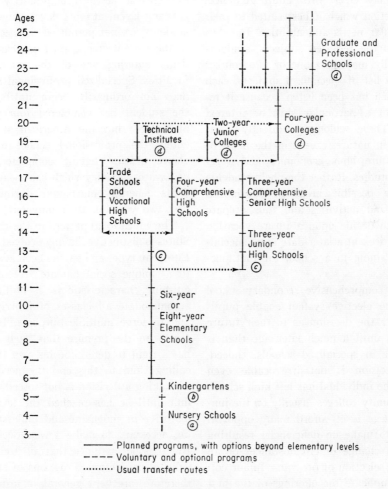

Ages

Graduate and Professional Schools *d*

Technical Institutes *d*

Two-year Junior Colleges *d*

Four-year Colleges *d*

Trade Schools and Vocational High Schools

Four-year Comprehensive High Schools

Three-year Comprehensive Senior High Schools

Three-year Junior High Schools *c*

c

Six-year or Eight-year Elementary Schools

Kindergartens *b*

Nursery Schools *a*

——— Planned programs, with options beyond elementary levels
– – – Voluntary and optional programs
·········· Usual transfer routes

Figure 30. Educational Institutions in the United States Today
a. Usually private.   *b.* Public or private.
c. Either type may exist in a given community, but usually not both.
d. Selective admissions based on applicant's previous scholastic achievement, special examinations, or a combination of these and other factors.

that pupils are free to elect any course or subject at any time. Indeed, the contrary is true, for all students are required to study certain basic courses at specified times or in a given sequence. However, a basic subject such as mathematics may be offered in several forms, each differing from the others with respect to the extent of coverage and the degree of difficulty. Individual pupils then may elect, with adult guidance, the section which is best suited to their particular needs and abilities. In addition to the required subjects, students generally may elect one or two courses from a list of specialized subjects, each of which has been listed because it relates to a particular skill or interest area. These seldom are directly vocational in nature, except in the fields of agriculture, home economics, and secretarial studies. Rather they help students explore possible areas of specialized study and activities and thus prepare them to decide upon a future vocation and to seek at a later date more specialized training in a school for that purpose.

The comprehensive secondary school and the elective system enable pupils to defer the decision as to their future careers until a much later age than is possible in specialized schools. Indeed, the decision is not irrevocable even after the individual has left high school. Community colleges, usually on the junior college level, afford many opportunities to make up deficiencies resulting from a change of circumstances or an unwise selection of program. Junior colleges duplicate the offerings of the first two years of four-year colleges, but they also offer additional, parallel programs that are more vocation-oriented and are generally terminal.

Persons wishing to compare education in the United States with European education should equate the completion of the academic program in a junior college, or the first two years of a four-year college, with the successful completion of a baccalaureat, maturity, or higher certificate examination. Concentrated study in a particular academic field—the American term is "majoring" —begins in the third, or junior, year of college. Even at this level, however, students are not permitted to specialize to the same degree as do European students entering one of the university faculties. Specialized professional study does not ordinarily begin until after the student has completed four years of college; but the American student enters the professional school of his choice already having completed the preparatory studies which European students generally must take during the first two years in their university.

The educational pattern in the United States is distinctive, having evolved from European types and having been adapted to a unique social climate. Its distinguishing characteristic is its ability to accommodate all classes of individuals and to serve multiple purposes. It operates on the premise that each child has a right to determine his own future calling; and to this end the necessity of making a decision is not forced upon him until he has reached the level of maturity in judgment and understanding necessary to make a wise decision. But it is not assumed that all decisions will be satisfactory. Programs of study, therefore, are kept general in order to permit ready transfer if a mistake is discovered. It is felt that these conditions are possible only in comprehensive institutions, schools that are designed to offer many programs and to accommodate all individuals of a given age, each with his unique abilities, interests, and aspirations.

References

Italy

Borghi, Lamberto, and Anthony Scarangello: "Italy's Ten-year Education Plan," *Comparative Education Review*, vol. 4, no. 1, pp. 26–30, June, 1960.

Hans, N.: "State and Church in Italy and France," *Comparative Education Review*, vol. 1, no. 3, pp. 10–12, February, 1958.

Justman, Joseph: *The Italian People and Their Schools*, Kappa Delta Pi Publication, 238 East Perry Street, Tiffin, Ohio, 1958.

King, Margaret L., and George A. Male: "Educational Data: Republic of Italy," *Information on Education around the World*, bulletin 18, U.S. Office of Education, July, 1959.

Scanlon, David G.: "Some Comparative Reflections on German and Italian School Reforms," *Comparative Education Review*, vol. 4, no. 1, pp. 31–34, June, 1960.

Scarangello, Anthony: "Church and State in Italian Education," *Comparative Education Review*, vol. 5, no. 3, pp. 199–207, February, 1962.

———: "Italian Universities Today," *Comparative Education Review*, vol. 1, pp. 10–12, June, 1957.

Visalberghi, Aldo: "La Scuola in Italia e in Europa," *Revista Pirelli*, Oct. 5, 1958; Dec. 6, 1958; and Feb. 1, 1959.

Netherlands

Barker, J. Ellis: *The Rise and Decline of the Netherlands*, Dutton, New York, 1906.

Barnouw, Adriaan J.: *The Dutch,* Columbia, New York, 1940.

Idenburg, Philip J.: *Education in the Netherlands,* Netherlands Information Office, The Hague, 1950.

MacLennan, A. M. (ed.): *The Netherlands,* Netherlands Information Service, New York; Holland, Mich.; San Francisco, etc., 1956.

Netherlands Information Service: *Holland: A Short Survey.* Available from Netherlands Information Service in New York; Holland, Mich.; San Francisco, and other offices located around the world.

Netherlands Ministry of Foreign Affairs: *Education and Cultural Aspects*, Digest of The Netherlands, no. 4, Netherlands Information Service, New York; Holland, Mich.; San Francisco, etc.

Netherlands Ministry of Social Affairs and Public Health: *Vocational Training for Adults in the Netherlands*, The Hague.

Verlinden, J. A. A.: "Public and Private Education in the Netherlands," *The Education Forum*, vol. 22, pp. 51–57, November, 1957.

Wilson, Norman H.: "Dutch Schools and Religious Segmentation," *Comparative Education Review*, vol. 3, no. 2, pp. 19–24, October, 1959.

Scandinavia

Bruun, Geoffrey, and Henry Steele Commager: *Europe and America since 1492*, Houghton Mifflin, Boston, 1954.

Chapman, Eunice: *Report of Scandinavian Study Tour*, American Association of Collegiate Registrars and Admissions Officers, Hastings College, Hastings, Neb., 1959.

Dahlmann-Hansen, J.: "The Transformation of Schools in Denmark," *Phi Delta Kappan*, vol. 43, pp. 54–59, November, 1961.

Dixon, Willis: *Education in Denmark*,

Centraltrykkeriet, Copenhagen, 1958.

Husen, Thorsten: "Loss of Talent in Selective School Systems: The Case of Sweden," *Comparative Education Review*, vol. 4, pp. 70–74, October, 1960.

———: "School Reform in Sweden: A Liberal Democracy Adopts the Comprehensive School System," *Phi Delta Kappan*, vol. 43, no. 2, pp. 86–91, November, 1961.

Huus, Helen: *The Education of Children and Youth in Norway*, The University of Pittsburgh Press, Pittsburgh, Pa., 1960.

Kyostio, O. K.: "Contemporary Finnish School Legislation," *Comparative Education Review*, vol. 5, pp. 130–135, October, 1961.

Swedish Royal Board of Education: *Survey of the School System in Sweden*, Norrkoping, 1958.

Switzerland

Archiv fur das Schweizerische Unterrichtswesen, 41 Jahrgang, Verlag Huber, Frauenfeld, 1955. (Selected articles in other issues of this publication also are useful. Available in French also.)

Arnold, Mathew: *The Popular Education of France: With Notices of That of Holland and Switzerland*, Longmans, London, 1861.

Barnard, Henry: *Public Education in Europe*, Case, Tiffany, Hartford, Conn., 1854, pp. 341–380.

Conference of Directors of Swiss Gymnasiums: *Wege Gymnasialer Bildung*, Verlag H. R. Sauerlander, Aarau, 1961.

"Die Organisation des schweizerischen Schulwesen," February, 1957. A mimeographed bulletin available from the Pro Helvetia Foundation, Zurich.

Guyer, Walter: *Erziehungsgedanke und Bildungswesen in der Schweiz*, Verlag von Huber, Frauenfeld, 1936.

Hawgood, John A.: *Modern Constitutions since 1787*, Macmillan, New York, 1939, chap. XV.

Lowell, A. Lawrence: *Governments and Parties in Continental Europe*, Houghton Mifflin, Boston, 1900, vol. II, pp. 180–336.

Simmen, Martin: *Die Schulen des Schweizervolkes*, Verlag von Huber, Frauenfeld, 1946.

Swiss Schools issued by the Pro Helvetia Foundation and available from Swiss embassy and consular offices.

Thut, I. N.: "Observations on Education in Switzerland," *Information on Education around the World*, Bulletin 49, U.S. Office of Education, December, 1960.

United States of America

Bidwell, C. A., and A. M. Kazamias: "Religion, Politics, and Popular Education: An Historical Comparison of England and America," *Comparative Education Review*, vol. 6, pp. 97–110, October, 1962.

Butts, R. Freeman, and Lawrence A. Cremin: *A History of Education in American Culture*, Holt, New York, 1953.

Cubberley, Ellwood P.: *Public Education in the United States*, Houghton Mifflin, Boston, 1919.

Downey, Lawrence W.: "The Task of the Public School in the United States and Canada," *Comparative Education Review*, vol. 4, pp. 118–120, October, 1960.

Good, H. G.: *A History of American Education*, rev. ed., Macmillan, New York, 1960.

Lloyd, John W.: "British and American Education in Cultural Perspective," *Comparative Education Review*, vol. 6, pp. 16–24, June, 1962.

Meyer, Adolphe: *An Educational History of the American People*, McGraw-Hill, New York, 1957.

National Council of Chief State School Officers: *Our System of Education*, 1201 16th St., N.W., Washington, D.C., 1950.

U.S. Office of Education: *Education in* *the United States of America*, 1960.

———: *Handbook: Office of Education*, 1960.

———: *Statistical Summary of State School Systems 1957–58*, 1960.

PART II

Representative
Oriental
Patterns

CHAPTER 9

The East Asian
Educational Tradition

Many of the dominating patterns of Asian ideological and social traditions have radiated from the three great cultural hubs of India, the Fertile Crescent area, and China. In recent decades Japan, formerly an ardent disciple of China, has begun to make an imprint of its own on Asian institutions, largely because of its technological advancement and military and economic aggressiveness. The culture and education of India are briefly described in a later chapter; this and the two following chapters examine the forces affecting education in China and Japan.

China, Japan, and Korea form what may be termed "East Asia." Historically, the ideologies and the political and educational institutions of the entire region emanated from China. From the nineteenth century to the advent of communism, however, China served less and less as a cultural spring. Industrialization, nationalism, democracy, and communism have created cleavages among the East Asian nations which in the future may obliterate much of the unity of the region.

Roots of East Asian traditions

Chinese history may be traced back for some five thousand years; thus China rivals India as the oldest highly developed civilization in the world. While much of early Chinese history is shrouded in myth, the last three millennia have been well documented. Archaeological discoveries have revealed the brilliance and the advanced state of Chinese cul-

ture as early as 1500 B.C. Indeed, the 1,500 years immediately preceding the Christian era proved to be one of the most creative periods in China for the arts, literature, and philosophy. Of particular importance in studying China's intellectual endowments is the fact that between the sixth and the third centuries B.C. four of the greatest Chinese thinkers of all times—Lao Tzu, Confucius (Latinized form of K'ung-fu-tzu), Mo Tzu, and Mencius (Latinized form of Mong-tzu)—lived and taught. The ideas attributed to these men, particularly Confucius and Mencius, were widely known and exceedingly influential throughout many nations in Asia.

Nearly two thousand years ago China began to share the fruits of its advanced culture with its less-developed neighbors, Korea and Japan. Directly to Korea and, by using Korea as a bridge, to Japan, China bequeathed two great and lasting contributions to East Asian culture. These were an all-inclusive ethical system, whose principles affected even the elements of daily living, and a means by which this system could be studied, a written language. China, acting as a transmitter rather than a creator, made a third significant contribution to East Asia through the introduction of Buddhism. This powerful and mystical religion made its way from India to China during the first century A.D.; its influence on Chinese life was striking, particularly in the arts and in literature. During the sixth century A.D., Buddhism, somewhat colored by its long period of adaptation to the Chinese environment, was carried to Japan where it enjoyed almost immediate success.

It was to Golden China, then, that Asian scholars throughout the centuries came to study, observe, and imitate. Confucius and Mencius and their disciples, particularly the distinguished scholars of the Sung period (A.D. 907–1279), initiated and perpetuated a scholastic tradition which grew to be the marvel of the Orient. In China learning was the mark of the well-bred man and prerequisite to admittance to the governing class. Chinese scholars were tutors and advisers in Japanese and other Asian courts. Quite understandably, the foreigners studying in China and the Chinese scholars abroad utilized the Chinese language, curriculum, and instructional methods in the pursuit of knowledge.

Yet it should not be implied that other East Asian nations were without traditions of their own. Japan, for example, traces its national identity to a descendant of the Sun-Goddess, thus making all its successive emperors Sons of Heaven. Japan blended other indigenous traditions with ideas imported from China to form a warrior's code of ethics, Bushido, and later a national religion, Shinto. More recently, particularly since the middle of the nineteenth century, Japan again showed its propensity for adapting foreign ideas by its large-scale importation of Western learning and technical skills. By the late nineteenth century, this amalgamation of Chinese, native, and Western ideas had produced two results. First, in the eyes of the Japanese, Japan's rapid industrialization was a real challenge to China's cultural superiority. And second, Japan had developed such a unique national character that at least one contemporary historian refers to the "Japanese

offshoot of the East Asian Civilization." [1]

The specific factors that promote unity and diversity in East Asian culture and education may best be understood in the light of some broad contrasts of Oriental and Western approaches to knowledge. F. S. C. Northrop in his masterful work, *The Meeting of East and West,* describes the basic differences between Eastern and Western civilization in the following terms: "The Orient [Northrop includes India, China, and Japan] for the most part has investigated things in their aesthetic component; the Occident has investigated these things in their theoretic component." [2] This aesthetic component involves, as Northrop further points out, two qualities which often appear contradictory to Westerners. First, there is a kind of realism, a passive acceptance of the cruelties, pains, and struggles of this world. Secondly, in seeming contrast, the Oriental appears to the Occidental to be exceedingly sensitive to the natural universe and yet at the same time otherworldly. This latter perception is confusing because the otherworldliness fundamentally is neither speculative nor theoretical in the Western sense. Rather it is a quality immediately experienced yet transcending the senses "due to the fact the senses deliver specific, limited, determinate data within it [Oriental view of universe] whereas it is indeterminate and all-embracing." [3]

That is, any mystical quality which

[1] Edward D. Myers, *Education in the Perspective of History,* Harper, New York, 1960, chap. 7.
[2] F. S. C. Northrop, *The Meeting of East and West,* Macmillan, New York, 1946, p. 375.
[3] *Ibid.,* p. 377.

makes the Oriental appear apart from or just uninterested in the natural world about him does not arise from reliance on an unseen God as in the Christian West. Passiveness, rather than lack of interest best describes the traditional Oriental attitude toward the daily world, and this stems less from a transcendant faith as in the Christian view than from the harsh realities of social conditioning and the rationalized cyclical view of history—with the future regarded as mere repetition of some portion of the past and not something to be altered by the actions of insignificant man.

Several Chinese authors have disagreed to a certain extent with some of Northrop's generalizations. One author, L. K. Hsu, analyzing Chinese character from a more anthropological view, takes partial exception to Northrop's interpretation of the positivistic component of East Asian culture as being aesthetic. His prime objection is that Northrop has identified aesthetic too strongly with emotion. Although he agrees that Oriental scholars have built few theoretical schemes in philosophy or science, Hsu identifies the distinguishing characteristic of the Orient as *humanism* or "the mutual dependence among man which makes attachment to the unseen needless and strong emotions out of place." [4]

A Japanese author has contrasted Eastern and Western thought in much the same terms as both Hsu and Northrup by emphasizing the Oriental's intuitive and unified approach to acquisition of knowledge.

Thinking and feeling, which in the West exist as separate entities, here operate as a single force. . . . The cen-

tre of gravity of spiritual activity in East Asia lies less in systematic comprehension of the universe and universal history than in real experience of totality through an intuitive perception of that essence in which all mental and sensuous functions combine.[5]

In this same work another Japanese is quoted in substantiation of this view:

The orientally viewed soul training is not usually included in the mental culture of the Occidental. Apparently the Westerners have three things, faith, morality, science-arts. These three things are severally secured in recognition of their different values and attributes, and so they are not combined to form one inclusive method of human learning, the comprehensive discipline of life. Herein can be perceived the special reason for the development of occidental culture as such.[6]

There is, then, a totalness in the approach of the cultured Oriental in seeking the Good Life. He is less apt than the Westerner to fragment his thinking into separate compartments labeled ethics, politics, religion, and science. The traditional Oriental scholar, for example, has often shown considerable amusement at the attempts of Europeans and Americans to separate emotion from intellect or religious views from scientific thinking. The results of this type of thinking have led one Chinese professor of the authors' acquaintance to coin the term "comprehensive harmony" to describe the traditional Chinese and Japa-

[4] L. K. Hsu, *Americans and Chinese,* Abelard-Schuman, New York, 1953, p. 374.

[5] Junyu Kitayama, *West-Ostliche Begegnung,* as quoted in Lily Abegg, *The Mind of East Asia,* Thames and Hudson, New York, 1952, p. 14.

[6] Yoshiro Nagayo, "Beauty in Contrast" (Contemporary Japan), as quoted in Lily Abegg, *ibid.,* p. 14.

nese view of the universe. This interpretation is demonstrated in the Oriental's view of his relation to his environment, as expressed in works of art which
show the essential harmoniousness of
the natural universe and avoid portraying the raucous world of change and
discord.

Thus by highlighting the peculiarities
of the Oriental approach to the Good
Life in most general terms, one finds an
aesthetic, intuitive East, humanistic in
interest and comprehensive in its method of seeking knowledge. Elaborate epistemological arguments, except in Buddhism, have not captured the fancy of
many Chinese and Japanese scholars.
The debate over whether the seen table
is real or illusory would not be taken
seriously or have significant meaning in
Oriental philosophy. Discussion of such
epistemological problems presupposes a
demarcation between the subject and
object, the knower and the known [7]—
a demarcation not present to the intuitive Oriental.

Influence of Confucianism

The main stream of East Asian thought
cannot be thoroughly understood without examining in detail the ideas and
teachings attributed to the Chinese sage,
Confucius. This man, the most famous
of Chinese scholars, lived and taught in
the latter part of the sixth and the early
part of the fifth century B.C. He and his
numerous distinguished disciples are
largely responsible for the picture of
the Good Life held by most Chinese,
indeed by most East Asians, at least
down to the influx of Western thought

and machines in the nineteenth century.
In many ways the doctrines of Confucius are only now being replaced in
China under the stark materialism of
communism. Unlike many Western philosophic schemes, Confucian ideas affected the actions of the man on the
street nearly as much as they did the
mind of the scholar. As Lin Yutang put
it:

The Chinese philosopher is like a
swimmer who dives but must soon
come up to the surface again; the
Western philosopher is like a swimmer
who dives into the water and is proud
that he never comes up to the surface
again and is happy in his profundity.[8]

The term Confucianism, actually
coined by European authors, is used to
indicate a school of philosophy or, more
precisely, a system of ethicopolitical
ideas attributed to Confucius and his followers. It has often been used rather indiscriminately, however, to denote the
influences of other schools of Chinese
thought as well as certain non-Chinese
philosophies. Because of its profound
influence on East Asian institutions and
its thorough delineation of man's proper
relationship to man, the impact of Confucianism on East Asian institutions
cannot be exaggerated. Though China
has felt many new forces in the two
millennia since Confucius, including
Buddhism and Christianity, the philosophy and religion of Taoism (which had
a lasting influence on the art and literature of Asia), and the ravages of invasion and subjugation to foreign peoples
such as the Mongols and the Manchus,
the basic roles of the ruled and ruling

[7] Fung Yu-Lan, *A Short History of Chinese Philosophy*, Macmillan, New York,
1948, p. 25.

[8] Lin Yutang (ed.), *The Wisdom of
China and India*, Modern Library, New
York, 1942, p. 468.

as defined by Confucianism remain unaltered.

Confucius never claimed to be a creator. In fact the Confucian tradition started many centuries before Confucius. Time and again he admonished his friends to study the writings of the ancients in order to find true wisdom. The ancients had discovered and had lived the Good Life, and all persons seeking the Good and the True should examine the nature of man and society in those ideal times. Thus the Good could be expected not through a flash of revelation or even through meditation, but rather, as in bygone days, through a more mundane route of discovery: "To hear much, select what is good, and follow it; to see much and remember it; these are the steps by which understanding is attained." [9]

Perhaps more than any other thinker of his stature Confucius divorced ethics from metaphysics. To him the major key to societal improvements was in the development—through education—of virtuous men. And virtue, somewhat like the Golden Mean of the Greek philosophers, consisted of establishing the proper middle path between excess and denial—thus following the Confucian "doctrine of the mean." Not all could discover the Way (Tao), however, for there were hereditary variations in the nature of men. But those favorably endowed and properly educated, the "superior" men, could find and pursue the Way illuminating the path that others might follow.

Because Confucius gave so much attention to the very practical problems

of man's relation to man, the terms utilitarian and rationalistic are often appropriately used in describing his beliefs. The sophisticated Confucians avoided the spiritual as well as the highly theoretical, but it should not be supposed that all ancient Chinese denied the existence of the supernatural. On the contrary, Chinese literature often refers to a supreme deity who took intense interest in the personal affairs of men. Furthermore, the common people believed in the existence of a variety of nature spirits and spirits of ancestors to whom sacrifices and services must be rendered. In the temporal world supreme authority was vested in the emperor, who was a "Son of Heaven"; but unlike the Japanese Mikado, he ruled not by divine right but by mandate from Heaven. This mandate was given to a ruler because of his wisdom and knowledge, and should he perform unwise deeds the mandate could be withdrawn. Thus, while both Japanese and Chinese might look to their emperors for final authority, the Chinese ruler was not guaranteed a permanent cloak of infallibility.

Role of the individual in society

The principal elements of the Confucian philosophy available to the West are found in the Confucian work, the *Analects*. These moral aphorisms, largely representing Confucius' answers to questions posed by his disciples, constitute the essence of Confucian teachings. Though deep in wisdom and abundant in homely charm, they hardly make exciting reading for young Western scholars intent on logical, theoretical schemes or schools of abstract philosophy. In the *Analects*, a good illustration of the Confucian temperament, as well as style,

[9] *Analects* 7. 27. as quoted in H. G. Creel, *Chinese Thought from Confucius to Mao Tse-tung*, Eyre and Spottiswoode, Publishers, Inc., London, 1954, p. 52.

is found in the Confucian concept of the five proper human relationships which constitute a good society. These relationships define the mutual responsibilities and respect to be shared between:

1. Ruler and subject
2. Father and son
3. Husband and wife
4. The elder and the younger brother
5. Friend and friend

It is noteworthy that three of these five relationships are involved in family life. In an era when the breakdown of the old form of government was causing dissension and civil war, Confucius was concerned with reestablishing the family pattern as the stabilizing basis of society. Time and again he emphasized that national well-being depended on proper filial relationships in the family. Even the basic requisite for being a capable monarch was found in examining family life. To set an example, the prospective ruler must learn to do the right thing at the right time, for as the ancient Chinese proverb stated: "The people are like grass, and the ruler like the wind."

And in keeping with Confucian ethics, the practice of proper conduct begins in the home. The relationship between ethical practices in the family and at a higher societal level have been described in typical Confucian manner as follows:

There is no one who fails in teaching the members of his own family and yet is capable of teaching others outside the family. Therefore, the superior man spreads his culture to the entire nation by merely remaining at home. The teaching of filial piety is a preparation for serving the ruler of the state; the teaching of respect to one's elder brothers is a preparation for serving all the elders of the country; and the teaching of kindness to parents is a training for ruling over the people.[10]

Here then is a description of Chinese political philosophy which has been aptly described as "government by example."

The vital significance of the societal role of the Chinese family cannot be overestimated. The tradition of arranged marriages, a system with more merit than most Westerners have accorded it, symbolized the individual's subordination to the family. To the family the first allegiance was given, and as was often true, the family formed the only limits for loyalty. In traditional China and Korea, for example, there was little interclan cooperation, and territorial allegiances, as found in the American and European communities, were much less pronounced. A case in point is the control of business in China; until the twentieth century, control tended to be located in the family. When the need arose to form large-scale industries, it was very difficult to get members of different families to cooperate. The primacy of family loyalty has been dramatically reflected in governmental organization. While nepotism certainly is not peculiar to Asia, rarely has it been practiced more intensely elsewhere. A person attaining a position of power in China or Korea, and to less extent in Japan, was expected to install members of his family in official posts under his jurisdiction. This situation gains added importance when it

[10] Lin Yutang (ed.), *The Wisdom of Confucius*, Modern Library, New York, 1938, p. 146.

is understood that the family usually includes the grandparents, the parents, the sons, the sons' wives, and their children.

While much of the above description of family responsibilities and loyalties applies to all East Asia, there was a feudal heritage in Japan and Korea which absorbed some of the loyalties commonly held within the Chinese family circle. In feudal as well as in modern Japan, the temporal lord or emperor could demand the first loyalty of his subject. Many stories of the conflicting loyalties of family and lords are found in Japanese classical literature. Korea, true to its traditional role of being a middle ground between China and Japan, did not have as many nearly autonomous feudal estates as did premodern Japan, but it did have a larger class of nobility and court favorites between the throne and the people than did China.

In all East Asia the implications of the unity of the family extended in both directions. Power or prestige awarded to one member of the family was reflected and shared by all members, and conversely, shame and failure by one member permeated the entire clan. Thus, when the student flunked his examinations, not only the individual failed but the entire family failed. Even today Asian students who are unsuccessful in their studies in the West show considerable trepidation about returning to their homeland because of the "loss of face" that will inevitably be shared by the other members of the family.

Significance of age and sex

Two additional characteristics of East Asian society affected the role of the individual. The first is the historic dominance of male over female. This life-long relationship becomes apparent to a student of East Asia in many ways, including the numerous ancient accounts of female infanticide, the preference for educating the male, and the genealogy of the family, which extends only in the male line. Further indication of the subordinate role of woman can be shown in the fact that the concepts "male" and "female" were viewed by ancient Chinese scholars as two complementary but contrasting elements. To the Confucian cosmologist the interaction of the two principles yang and yin produced the basic constituents of the universe. Yin was the attribute of all things passive, dark, weak, and female. Yang was the attribute of all things active, bright, strong, and male. Although the two elements were complementary, one was by nature subordinate and obedient to the other, and the strength of society lay upon the construction of the yang line.

Woman's lack of economic independence further limited the role of the woman in East Asian society. Her labor was in the home which, of course, brought her no income. The woman rarely owned property, being considered outside the family line for purposes of inheritance. Moreover, when divorced or widowed, the woman had little recourse but to depend on the succor of her relatives. Being subservient in her home not only to her husband but also to his sons and his parents, she was, at least theoretically, hardly more than a necessary appendage in a male hierarchy.

While all East Asian nations have been male-centered, a number of intracultural differences can be noted. With some justification, Korea claims that its women have been the most independent among the East Asian countries. Koreans say with pride that their girls never bound their feet, as did the Chinese, nor were they so submissive to the whims of men as were the Japanese girls. While these claims have a certain validity, there is evidence that the most highly educated East Asian women in earlier days were Japanese. Some of the finest works of history, prose, and poetry of early Japan were written by women. Even as recently as the Japanese "Middle Ages" (tenth to sixteenth century) male scholars imitated the stilted Chinese essays, while sophisticated and intuitive ladies produced in the vernacular the true belles-lettres of the period. Lady Murasaki's world classic, *The Tale of Genji*, written in the latter part of the tenth century, is a charming example. Interestingly enough, it appears to have been the Confucian (and also Buddhist) influences from China that curbed and restricted the position of women in the rest of East Asia.

A second important societal characteristic affecting the role of the individual is the dominance of the old over the young—the respect shown to elders and the increased power given to the old. Reverence for age and the natural extension of this view, "worship" of ancestors, were considered basic to maintaining the proper social order:

> When the sovereign behaves to his aged, as the aged should be behaved to, the people become filial; when the sovereign behaves to his elders, as the elders should be behaved to, the people learn brotherly submission; when the sovereign treats compassionately the young and helpless, the people do the

same. Thus, the ruler has a principle with which as with a measuring square, he may regulate his conduct.[11]

Theoretically then, the relationship of respect was two-directional. Not only should the son respect the father, but the reverse was also supposed to be true. In actuality, the relationship was usually one-directional; the young had little recourse but to obey the elders in all their wishes. The descriptive Chinese proverb, "No son shall build a house larger than his father's," was literally as well as figuratively true in East Asia prior to the twentieth century.

Orthodoxy in scholarship

The Confucian pattern, then, lends itself to those characteristics which have been long associated with Asia, such as the Golden Mean, conservatism, respect or reverence for ancestors, patience, and pacificism. Such a pattern further lends itself to paternalism at both the family and state levels. In fact, the state might be described with much accuracy as a family in macrocosm. The orthodoxy promoted by Confucianism, which, on the one hand, gave the past precedence over the present, thereby setting up obstacles to innovation, and on the other hand, delineated with great care the role of each societal member, provided a high degree of social stability. As Fairbank has noted:

> It has been the most successful of all systems of conservatism. For most of two thousand years, the Confucian ideology was made the chief subject

[11] James Legge (trans.), *The Philosophy of Confucius*, Peter Pauper Press, Mount Vernon, N.Y., n.d., p. 177.

of study in the world's largest state. Nowhere else have the sanctions of government power been based for so many centuries upon a singly consistent pattern of ideas attributed to one ancient sage.[12]

To further interpret the traditions in East Asian society the vital role of scholarship must be examined in greater detail. The extent to which scholarship is interwoven with family and national welfare is indicated in the following statement by a Confucian scholar:

> The achieving of true knowledge depended upon the investigation of things. When things are investigated, then true knowledge is achieved; when true knowledge is achieved, the will becomes sincere; when the will is sincere, then the heart is set right (or then the mind sees right); when the heart is set right, then the personal life is cultivated; when the personal life is cultivated, then the family life is regulated; when the family life is regulated, then the national life is orderly; and when the national life is orderly, then there is peace in this world.[13]

The phrase, "investigation of things," in this quotation may be misleading. It appears, rather clearly, to mean a study of human affairs. In no sense was the author speaking of man's attempt to probe empirically into natural phenomena. The human society always occupies the thoughts of the true Confucian scholar.

The importance of scholarship and the exalted role of the scholar were

transmitted by China to Japan and other parts of East Asia. From the arrival of the first Korean and Chinese scholars to the Japanese court in the third century until Japan sought fresh learning in the West during the nineteenth century, the writings of Chinese scholars formed the core of advanced studies. While it is true that Japanese law and certain national rituals were often included in a Japanese scholar's repertoire, these were of secondary importance. Even Buddhism, in spite of its wide acceptance in Japan between the eighth and nineteenth centuries, rarely challenged the primacy of Chinese learning among the upper classes in Japan.

The curriculum of orthodox scholarship consisted largely of the Five Classics and the Four Books which comprised the Confucian canon. All these bore the imprint of Confucius and his disciples. Portions of the Five Classics are believed to have been written by Confucius himself and all are said to have been subjected to his severe editing. The Four Books were written by later Confucians, including Mencius, who attempted to record or elaborate on the ideas of the sage. The content of this curriculum included the poetry, literature, customs and rituals, ethics, history and pseudo science consistent with the Confucian world view. In these works all the knowledge needed to become an educated man, or in Confucian terms, a "superior" man, could be discovered by the disciplined and diligent scholar.

Some attention must be given to the role of the Chinese written language in making possible the dissemination of ideas and institutions, for in East Asia as in the West the main human divi-

[12] John King Fairbank, *The United States and China*, Harvard, Cambridge, Mass., 1958, p. 52.
[13] Lin Yutang, *The Wisdom of Confucius, op. cit.*, pp. 139–140.

255

sions are linguistic rather than physical. During the third or fourth century the Chinese script, already known in Korea, was introduced to the Japanese court by a Korean scholar. The Chinese characters, largely pictographs and ideographs, were officially adopted and with subsequent modifications became the base of the written language still in use in Japan. Owing to the lack of a phonetic base, oral communication was not promoted, and the common Chinese script contributed greatly to communication among the East Asian nations. Korean and Japanese scholars proceeded to China for study and, in turn, Chinese and Korean scholars were invited to Japan to offer instruction. Nor was such intercourse limited to persons bent only on promoting a restricted form of scholarship. Trade was increased, craft and vocational skills were exchanged, and rules of government administration were borrowed. While some of this antedated the advent of a common written language, and while such exchanges of ideas and goods might well have been possible without this common medium of communication, the spread of Chinese culture was greatly expedited because of it.

Renaissance and decline of Confucianism in Japan

The transition of Japan from a feudal society, with power residing in the hands of local lords and with the Emperor hardly more than a spiritual head of state, to a unified state with responsible central leadership, took place during the Tokugawa period (1603–1868). Under a series of military dictators, or shoguns, local clans were forced to relinquish their power and declare themselves subservient to the central regime.

During the Tokugawa period Confucianism enjoyed high prestige in government circles and was a major unifying social and political force. The end of the Tokugawa regime, however, and the rise of modern industrial Japan saw the virtual elimination of Confucian concepts from Japanese thought and institutions.

Confucian doctrines, in the form of Neo-Confucianism, were disseminated through Tokugawa Japan by the *Jusha* or professional Confucian teachers. This new class of Confucians was composed of Japanese scholars, many of whom had been devout Buddhists but had despaired of finding in Buddhism solutions to the pressing political problems. As advisers or tutors of Tokugawa administrators, as faculty members and heads of colleges, and as government officials, the *Jusha* actively sought to build a Confucian society ruled by benevolent scholar-officials where learning was prized above all else. Just as Confucius had provided rational justification for the stratified society of ancient China so the Tokugawa Confucians gave moral foundation to the emerging hierarchy of Japanese social order. According to the *Jusha* the Emperor, shogun, and daimyo were leaders because of their wisdom and virtue; and the samurai, farmers, artisans, and merchants were willed to their respective roles by the natural order of things. All men irrespective of rank thus practiced the Confucian way.

The renaissance of Neo-Confucianism in Japan showed signs of waning by the mid-eighteenth century. New economic and political problems resisted Confucian solutions. Some Japanese scholars and officials advocated new interpretations of old Confucian truths, but a small, though increasingly vocal, group called for increased attention to Japanese and even Western studies. Young intellectuals questioned the validity of allotting so much of the students' academic preparation to the study of the Confucian Classics and Chinese language. By the early part of the nineteenth century it had become apparent that Western science with its demonstrated significance in medicine and the military crafts would soon eclipse the superstition-ridden Confucian theories. Further, a growing national consciousness among the Japanese was replacing the cosmopolitanism of Confucianism and thus completing the triumph of the new forces over the old.

Only in one important area did Confucian concepts persist in post-Tokugawa Japan. This was the most universally applicable aspect of Confucianism—its social ethics. Filial piety in the home and in public continued to guide personal and public actions. Respect for age and maleness, primacy of the family unit, acceptance of a rank-ordered society were incorporated into the Japanese world view. Not until after World War II did Japanese find it necessary to seek new guidelines for a social philosophy.

Scientific and technological lag

One last characteristic of East Asian culture should be considered. This is the historical lag in development of scientific and technical thinking. Early inventions in China and Korea included paper, the compass, gunpowder, the abacus, vaccination, and movable type, but between the fourteenth and nineteenth centuries scientific developments fell considerably behind the West. The reasons for this scientific lag in the Orient are undoubtedly complex. Some

of the factors involved can be understood, however, by reviewing certain cultural elements.

First, the theoretical foundation of scientific development was lacking in East Asia, for the scholars of this area built no conceptual schemes of thought, no ordered systems of logic. No great scholar in East Asia had split the universe into several fragments to search for specific causal relationships as Aristotle and others had done in the West. Even when probing into particulars (see the comment above about the "investigation of things"), the Oriental scholar looked only for the universal. The traditional thought of China and her neighbors could be described as aesthetic, humanistic, and even possibly positivistic, but certainly not theoretic or experimental, as in the West. The deficiency of East Asian thought in this regard can be further seen by an analysis of the writings of Chinese scholars which indicate their reluctance to interfere with the ways of nature or to transform natural processes in any way. The scorn with which the literary scholars viewed the followers of Mo Tzu, who two thousand years ago emphasized individualism and showed concern for scientific and technical matters, is a case in point. A disciple of Confucius, expressing the orthodox view held until the nineteenth century, condemned the Mohists by saying:

> You vainly seek the cause of things; why not simply appropriate and enjoy what they produce? Therefore, I say: To neglect man and speculate about nature is to misunderstand the facts of the Universe.[14]

The Chinese language further militated against both the theoretical de-

14 Quoted in Lily Abegg, *op. cit.*, p. 231.

velopment of science and its applications. The semi-ideographic script is not so precise or so adaptable to new terms and new ideas as a phonetic language. Furthermore, the prestige granted to a very limited form of literary and artistic scholarship through the centuries had given language an independent value and reduced its effectiveness as a tool. Civil examinations that tested only the style and technique of the literary classics placed further orthodoxy on learning. Finally, the total picture of the scholar as a person whose efforts were directed toward mental work and never toward handwork made impossible the artisan type of tinkering carried on extensively by the Western pioneers in science.

Especially during the periods when Confucianism dominated East Asian thought, all interests were subordinated to ethics and politics. The problems considered important enough to require scholarly attention were those involving man's relation to the state and to his fellow man. The ideal state could only be formed from a socially stable society in which the moral qualities of the ancients were pervasive. This combination of emphases on humanism and traditional values rendered unnecessary, or at least secondary, systematic analysis of causal relationships among elements of the universe. Confucian society demanded disciplined adjustment but neither required nor rewarded inventiveness, innovation, or imagination.

Yet these reasons are not sufficient to explain why Japan alone among the East Asian nations in the latter part of the nineteenth century began to foster an industrial and technical revolution. Several authors have suggested that the source of Japanese dynamism

lay in the values long held by the warriors or samurai but extended to wide segments of the population only during the Tokugawa shogunate. One author has further suggested that the amalgamation of the Buddhist, Confucian, and Shinto views produced in Japan during the seventeenth and eighteenth centuries an ethic that readily countenanced change.[15] This ethic, which has been described in terms somewhat analogous to the Protestant ethic in America, was characterized by diligence, frugality, and obligations to superiors—attributes favorable for economic development. Whether or not this analysis is true, certainly intense hierarchical loyalty and rigorous personal discipline, though not present in China, were living realities in all strata of post-Tokugawa Japanese society.

Continuity in change

A perceptive visitor to East Asia still sees many cultural similarities as he travels from nation to nation. The slowness of pace, the aesthetic—even ritualistic—characteristics of human intercourse, the gap in taste, action, and dress between the upper and lower classes, and the "unscientific" approach to daily problems. The same perceptive traveler will be impressed with the closeness of family ties and the resistance to any form of individualism which tends to breach the sanctity of the home. The remnants of a highly formal literary-linguistic scholarship are also apparent, though modern scientific and technical studies are acquiring a permanent place in the curriculum. This

[15] Robert N. Bellah, *Tokugawa Religion*, Free Press, New York, 1957, p. 197.

visitor will also be aware that forces are at work that will further break down the unity of East Asia. Some of the unity has always been more apparent than real, for deep religious and cultural cleavages have tended to give each nation's people a recognizable national character. Now, two more significant developments have become identifiable as a result of the restructuring of the Oriental economies under the pressures of industrialization and the redesign of national policies under the influences of nationalism, democracy, and communism. First, when there is a conflict, raising a nation's production and improving the standard of living are being given priority over maintenance of traditional ways. Secondly, the kindling or rekindling of nationalistic spirit has given new impetus to the desire to erase discernible foreign influences and build "peculiar" national images.

References

Abegg, Lily: *The Mind of East Asia,* Thames and Hudson, London, 1952.

Bellah, Robert N.: *Tokugawa Religion,* Free Press, New York, 1957.

Bereday, George Z. F., and J. A. Lauwerys (eds.): *The Year Book of Education, 1957: Education and Philosophy,* prepared under the auspices of the University of London Institute of Education and Columbia University Teachers College, World, Tarrytown-on-Hudson, N.Y., 1957.

Creel, H. G.: *Chinese Thought from Confucius to Mao Tse-tung,* Eyre and Spottiswoode (Publishers), Inc., London, 1954.

Fairbank, John King: *The United States and China,* Harvard, Cambridge, Mass., 1958.

Fung Yu-lan: *A Short History of Chinese Philosophy,* Macmillan, New York, 1948.

Latourrette, Kenneth Scott: *A Short History of the Far East,* 3d ed., Macmillan, New York, 1957.

Legge, James (trans.): *The Philosophy of Confucius,* Peter Pauper Press, Mount Vernon, N.Y., n.d.

Lin Yutang (ed.): *The Wisdom of China and India,* Modern Library, New York, 1942.

Myers, Edward D.: *Education in the Perspective of History,* Harper, New York, 1960.

Moore, Charles A. (ed.): *Philosophy: East and West,* Princeton, Princeton, N.J., 1944.

Northrop, F. S. C.: *The Meeting of East and West,* Macmillan, New York, 1946.

Reischauer, Edwin O., and John K. Fairbank: *East Asia: The Great Tradition,* Houghton Mifflin, Boston, 1958, vol. 1.

Thwing, Charles F.: *Education in the Far East,* Houghton Mifflin, Boston, 1909.

Wei, Francis C. M.: *The Spirit of Chinese Culture,* Scribner, New York, 1947.

From Confucianism to Communism

Confucius and his disciples did not claim to be the originators of a new social order in China. Yet a man of such insight and wisdom as Confucius could be no mere scribe of the past, and if he could not be called a creative thinker, he was at least a very creative interpreter. He and his followers, regardless of whether or not they were original, approved a content of traditional scholarship and shaped an image of the Chinese scholar which were to persist for over two thousand years.

Scholastic traditions

There developed in early China a well-defined body of writings which came to be known as "the Classics." The earliest and most significant were the Five Classics which included the *Book of Changes* or *Book of Divination* (descriptions of various methods of divination and interpretations of results); the *Book of History* (historical documents, proclamations of rulers, and the like); the *Book of Odes* or *Book of Songs* (anthology of poems, folk songs, hymns); the *Record of Rituals* or *Book of Rites* (a collection of texts covering various comprehensive and particular philosophic rules for self and universe); and the *Spring and Autumn Annals* (chronicle of historical events from 722–481 B.C.). Except for a portion of the *Spring and Autumn Annals,* whose editorship and partial authorship is ascribed to Confucius, all the Classics belong to pre-Confucian times; yet in each work Confucius

260

is said to have played at least the role of a commentator.

The scholar second to Confucius in shaping the Confucian tradition was Mencius (372–289 B.C.?). The words of this great teacher, whom the Chinese respectfully call their second sage, were recorded in a work that bears his name. In time the book of Mencius together with the *Analects* (or *Conversations*), in which Confucius' disciples tried to distill the master's most important thoughts, became the core of a new body of classics. The great scholar of the Sung period, Chu Hsi (A.D. 1130–1200) combined these two texts with two of the most popular essays found in the Five Classics, namely, *The Great Learning,* and *The Doctrine of the Mean,* and formed the Four Books. These four texts (*The Great Learning, The Mean, Analects,* and *Mencius*) were, in effect, the basic course of study for all aspiring young Chinese scholars down to the twentieth century.

For centuries after Confucius, Chinese scholars added their interpretation and commentaries to the Classics in attempts to explain the subtle points of these works. The sheer magnitude of this writing has often served to obscure rather than clarify many of the ideas of Confucius. Western students encounter further difficulty in attempting to construct an integrated picture of Confucian philosophy because of the form in which Confucian writings have reached us. Unfortunately the most common approach to a study of Confucian thought has been to read the *Analects* which presents a series of terse, epigrammatical sayings, largely out of context. As one author has suggested, analyzing the Confucian world view by reading the *Analects* is comparable to studying Western literature by reading *Bartlett's Familiar Quotations*.[1]

The true Confucian scholar was one who put learning above all else. Yet, although he was a lover of the ancients, he did not shirk his worldly duties. Rather, his acquired wisdom was used daily to guide his actions so that by his example he might influence men of lesser learning. This image of the Confucian scholar came to have a profound effect in succeeding centuries on Chinese teachers and government officials. During the periods when Confucianism had most prestige, even members of the hereditary nobility lost caste and position if they could not demonstrate scholarship, for the official was deemed superior not because of his family name but because of his learning.

Confucius consistently urged his followers to do original scholarship and to avoid imitation. Yet his advice went unheeded, and the followers of this great man enshrined his edited works and made canons of his teachings. Literary criticism sometimes reached a very high level, but little in the way of original literary effort was attempted. When Western scholars view the lack of creativity in Chinese literary scholarship, they often recall the formalization of humanistic learning during sixteenth-century Europe and aptly use the term Ciceronianism. The attention given to copying and memorizing and the prolonged quibbling over terminology indicate that study to the Confucians, as with those Europeans who slavishly imitated Cicero, was often little more than a hollow, pedantic exercise. The effects of limiting Chinese scholarship to a few "Great Books" were disastrous, as will be seen.

Education and schools in early China

In pre-Confucian times, but in good Confucian tradition, the paternal head of the nation, the emperor, was, in effect, the master teacher and all his subjects were students. The emperor instructed by example and through decree; he rewarded the good students with government posts and punished the recalcitrants by fines or banishment. Under imperial direction, a knowledge of certain prescribed ancient arts was required of all who sought the badge of the educated man. The ideal state was, in effect, an ideal school.[2]

It will be recalled that Confucius referred to the early part of the Chou period (1122?–221 B.C.) in the most glowing terms. In depicting this "golden age," Confucians wrote of the advanced refinement of Chou culture and the great economic prosperity of the people. Some

[1] For more insight into Confucian beliefs regarding scholars and scholarship and for illustrations of the terse style common to the Four Books, the student is referred to James Legge (trans.), *The Philosophy of Confucius,* Peter Pauper Press, Mount Vernon, N.Y., n.d., pp. 105–106, 138–139, 201.

[2] For a description of the paternalistic view of the educational obligations of the state and the specific duties of the government's chief education official, the student is referred to Howard S. Galt, *A History of Chinese Educational Institutions,* Arthur Probsthain, London, 1951, pp. 126–127.

popular education was said to have been offered as well as higher education, and while Confucian claims of a schoolroom in each home and a high school in each town may need to be discounted, there is evidence to show that education had reached an advanced state by the beginning of the period. The curriculum of the Chou period has been described by one author as including the six virtues, the six praiseworthy actions, and the six arts:

> The six virtues are wisdom, benevolence, goodness, righteousness, loyalty, and harmony. The six praiseworthy actions are honoring one's parents, being friendly to one's brothers, being neighborly, maintaining cordial relationships with relatives through marriages, being trustful, and being sympathetic. The six arts, which correspond to the Trivium and Quadrivium of the medieval schools, consist of rituals, music, archery, charioteering, writing, and mathematics.[3]

During the Han period (B.C. 206–222 A.D.) initial attempts were made to provide a nationally controlled educational system and a fixed curriculum, and it has been concluded that by the second century B.C. an able boy could matriculate along an articulated path from district school to university. New, sweeping edicts concerning education were issued by each succeeding emperor, and by the T'ang dynasty (A.D. 618–907) Confucians had established certain professional or specialized schools for calligraphy (brush writing and possibly some study of etymology), law (study of official rules, decrees, and prece-

[3] Ping Wen Kuo, *The Chinese System of Public Education,* Teachers College, Columbia University, New York, 1915, p. 18.

dents), and mathematics (the major purpose of which was to determine the annual calendar). Also during the T'ang period, an imperial order required every village to establish a school and appoint a teacher. Yet there is no evidence that any serious attempt was made to enforce this rule. Royal decrees in old China were not enough to give a very broad base to the educational enterprise. While Confucius and some of his followers urged that all men, irrespective of social status, should have opportunities for learning and advancement, sons of peasants had neither the leisure nor the expenses for schooling.

All discussions of formal instruction during the early history of China refer only to boys; little attention was given to the education of girls. Although women of noble birth might be taught the graces befitting their station, including the importance of virtue, duty, and social manners, girls of more humble birth were taught only the arts of preparing food and making clothing. It seems unlikely that girls spent much time on such formal studies as mathematics or even reading and writing. Woman's role in society dictated little formal education. After all, to the traditional Confucian, the ideal wife needed only to be inviolably chaste, completely obedient, and never "jealous of her husband's concubines."

Challenges and supplements to Confucianism

Confucian beliefs were the most pervasive intellectual influences in the history of China, but at no time did they completely usurp the intellectual field. Among the forces that challenged, at times with considerable success, the supremacy of Confucianism were Taoism, Legalism, and Buddhism. It must be borne in mind, however, that these schools of thought were not mutually exclusive or entirely competitive. For example, there can be said to be both a religion and a philosophy of Taoism. The former developed its own theology, literature, and pantheon, often in imitation of the richly variegated traditions of Buddhism. Attention here is largely directed to Taoism, the philosophy, for in this naturalistic world view are found supplementary and modifying influences to humanistic Confucianism. Thus it is apparent that one could accept many of the Confucian tenets and still worship at the Buddhist shrine or participate in Taoist festivals. Indeed, over the centuries Taoism and Buddhism became somewhat Confucian, while Confucianism was noticeably colored by these other movements. In the following paragraphs brief attention will be given to the contributions of Taoism, Legalism, and Buddhism to Chinese thought.

No less a perceptive student of China than Lin Yutang has claimed that to truly understand the Oriental mind one must study Taoism. For it is in Taoism that one finds the quiet, contemplative, even mystical, qualities that are ever present in Chinese culture. A clearer understanding of this school of thought may be obtained by seeing it in contrast with Confucianism.

In many ways the doctrines of Confucianism and Taoism complement each other, running side by side like two powerful streams through all later Chinese thought and literature, appealing simultaneously to two sides of the Chinese character. To the solemn, rather pompous gravity and burden of social responsibility of Confucianism, Taoism opposes a carefree flight from respectability and the conventional duties of society; in place of the stubborn Confucian concern for things human and mundane it holds out a vision of other, transcendental worlds of the spirit. Where the Confucian philosophers are often prosaic and dull, moralistic and commonsensical, the early Taoist writings are all wit and paradox, mysticism and poetic vision. As the two streams of thought developed in later ages, Confucianism has represented the mind of the Chinese scholar-gentleman in his office or study, being a good family man, a conscientious bureaucrat, and a sober, responsible citizen; Taoism has represented the same gentleman in his private chamber or mountain retreat, seeking surcease from the cares of official life, perhaps a little drunk but more likely intoxicated by the beauties of nature or of the world of the spirit.[4]

The father of Taoism (*Tao* usually is translated as "The Way" and is sometimes compared with the Greek word *logos*) was Lao Tzu, a contemporary of Confucius who, like him, believed that the knowledge of the Good Life was restricted to the very few—the superior man or sage. However, the Taoists downgraded the value of books, for in their opinion the truly superior man need only use reflection to acquire important knowledge. In the paradoxical words of Lao Tzu:

He who seeks learning may daily increase. He who seeks the way will

[4] William Theodore de Bary (ed.), *Sources of Chinese Tradition*, Columbia, New York, 1960, p. 50.

daily diminish: He will diminish and keep on diminishing until he does nothing. When he does nothing then he will accomplish all things.[5]

As the Taoists had little hope that all men could profit by education, they advocated that the common people would be much better off merely following their natural instincts rather than relying on formal education. At this juncture one is reminded of Rousseau's "natural man" theory, for in their dislike for the artificiality and corrupting qualities of society the Taoists and Rousseau had much in common. Thus, while to Confucius and his followers education was the foundation for individual and social improvement, the Taoists strongly repudiated formal schooling. Yet throughout the centuries, primarily because of the Confucian hold on officialdom and in spite of periodic strong resurgences of Taoism, the Confucian Classics were able to maintain their position of prestige with Chinese scholars.

The term Legalism is given to a third classic school of Chinese thought whose strongest advocates lived two centuries later than Confucius. The leading thinker from whom the Legalists drew inspiration was Hsün Tzu (300?–237 B.C.) who appears to have been well known as both a politician and a teacher. Hsün Tzu disagreed with Mencius' tenet that man was by nature good. On the contrary, he argued that men by nature were evil and could be improved only through education. He was a strong advocate of formal education, and in keeping with the budding Confucian tradition saw the Classics as the only appropriate content. Large portions of Hsün Tzu's writings

were incorporated into the *Record of Rituals*.[6]

The philosophy of Legalism, a sort of Chinese Leviathan doctrine, obtained its name from the emphasis its advocates placed on law as a means of gaining desired ends. The most prominent Legalists were government officials, so in a sense Legalism represented an attempt to justify strong central controls and give increased, even absolute, power to the ruler. The conflict between Legalism and traditional Confucianism becomes readily apparent. Both systems had deplored the chaotic conditions of the times and both sought better government as a means of rectification. However, the actions of the government advocated by the Confucians were subject to the approval of the people, while the government promoted by the Legalists was totalitarian.

The ideal state of the Legalists has sometimes been likened to the primitive society envisioned by the Taoists, since neither group believed in allowing the citizenry voice or power.[7] Yet in another sense the Legalists were at the opposite end of the spectrum from the Taoists. The latter suggested that the ills of state were largely the result of man's meddling and if rulers tampered less with natural processes, life would be easier. To the contrary, the Legalists argued for more elaborate governmental organization through which totalitarian control could be exercised.[8]

[5] Galt, *op. cit.*, p. 181.

[6] Edwin O. Reischauer and John K. Fairbank, *East Asia: The Great Tradition*, Houghton Mifflin, Boston, 1958, p. 81.

[7] *Ibid.*, p. 82.

[8] See the quotation by Han Fei Tzu, a leading Legalist theorizer, in Fung Yu-lan, *A Short History of Chinese Philosophy*, Macmillan, New York, 1949, p. 158.

The Legalists particularly turned their scorn on the Confucian idea that classical learning was the chief requisite for successful administration. Thus Legalism, like Taoism, gave a small role to the scholar who spent his life seeking truth from the works of the ancients. The Legalists were especially hostile toward the vain talk of the Confucian scholars and were adamant in their claim that frugality and diligence, rather than virtue, made the successful man.

In their concept of the state the Legalists were more modern than the earlier Confucians. The use of a system of law as a means of controlling governmental functions certainly is more equitable and efficient than considering a state merely as an extended family. But in final analysis the law of the Legalists represented little more than the desires of the hereditary rulers and thus, unlike Western law as derived from Roman law, could not transcend personality. This limitation was well understood by many Chinese scholars, with the result that Legalism was viewed with distaste throughout much of Chinese history.[9]

Buddhism entered China from India sometime during the first century by following trade routes across the vast central Asian desert. It was forced to fight an uphill battle against the rationalistic and worldly doctrines of Confucius, and centuries passed before it became firmly established. But Buddhism offered the Chinese something that had been missing in their existing schools of humanistic thought. In Buddhism, as in Taoism, man's spiritual and aesthetic sides were cared for; so the poor and

miserable found solace in the quietude and rituals common to this new faith. The rich and mighty, tiring of pedestrian Confucianism, also in time found it entertaining to become connoisseurs of Buddhist art and challenging to seek the sublime truths locked in the elaborate Buddhist metaphysics.

Buddhism stood unrivaled in its profound literary and philosophical traditions. Yet its diagnosis of the life on earth as sorrowful and its cure, rejection of this life through meditation, necessarily were at odds with the worldly traditions of the Confucians. Nevertheless, Buddhism, increasingly wedded with Taoist and even Confucian ideas, gained such strength that China from the third to the ninth centuries was often thought of as a Buddhist nation. During this period many of the best Chinese scholars devoted themselves to definition or elaboration of the various Buddhist sects. Buddhist temples became learning centers and Buddhist students from throughout Asia came to learn. Buddhist intellectual leadership in China was not permanent, however, for the great Confucian revival during the Sung period (A.D. 960–1279) was accompanied by a decline in the power of Buddhism. From that time forward, Buddhism never regained a preeminent position among Chinese schools of thought.

While Buddhism failed to remold basic Chinese institutions, it did make lasting cultural contributions. It added a new richness to Chinese literature and art and left new ideas about salvation, the soul, heaven, and hell. Much of its mythology and ritual became part of the religious lives of the Chinese people, and its metaphysics added fresh dimensions to Chinese philosophy.

[9] Reischauer and Fairbank, *op. cit.*, p. 84.

265

Renaissance in learning

The Sung dynasty saw great vitality in Chinese cultural advancement and the development of a literary and philosophical movement called Neo-Confucianism. Many of the leading scholars during the Sung period claimed to be seeking only a return to pure Confucian theory. However, it was at this time that elements of Buddhism, Taoism, and Legalism became inextricably woven into the main stock of Confucianism. Rulers, while advocating selection of Confucian "gentlemen" for official positions, demonstrated their Legalistic influence by giving increased attention to laws and institutions. Likewise the influence of Taoist cosmogony and Buddhist quietism was also apparent in the Neo-Confucian ideas. The intrusion of foreign ideas inevitably produced a richer Confucianism. While scholars of the Han and T'ang periods were largely content with memorizing the aphoristic principles of the ancients and imitating the style of the classic essays, the individualistic Sung scholars created new schools of philosophy.

The Neo-Confucianists, then, were at once traditionalists and reformers. The traditions they sought to preserve and the reforms they sought to promulgate are readily apparent in the prolific writings of the most profound thinker of this period, Chu Hsi (A.D. 1130–1200). In Chu Hsi's writings one again sees the greatness as well as the limitations of the Confucian doctrines. His commentaries on the Four Books were acclaimed as the most perceptive of all and have been so popular that in all subsequent Chinese history the teachings of Confucius have been primarily understood through

his interpretations. Yet with all his range of interests and scholarly activities, Chu Hsi never allowed his attention to go beyond the humanities to either the natural or the social sciences, boundaries of scholarship carefully observed by most Confucianists to the twentieth century.

With the exception of the languages and ideas introduced by the Christian missionaries and the slight changes made in the civil service examinations, the pattern of education existing at the close of the Sung dynasty continued almost unchanged for the next six centuries. An aspiring student in either the Ming (A.D. 1368–1644) or Ching (A.D. 1644–1912) dynasties received his beginning education in the Confucian Classics through a village reading and writing school or through the services of a private tutor. In like manner, the method of instruction which emphasized memorization of content and imitation of form remained essentially the same. Advanced education took place in academies which existed wherever large repositories of books were made available by private or public means. Buddhist temples, important centers for scholarship at the beginning of the Sung period, had permanently lost their place in the intellectual activities of China.

The typical chronology of instruction during the Sung and post-Sung periods began at the age of seven for the son of a wealthy or middle-class family. The first primer given to the child often was the *Three Character Classic,* so called because each sentence in the book contained but three characters. The characters were so arranged that when recited a rhythmic effect was produced which made memorization easier. The next reading books were likely to be the *Thousand Character Classic* and the *Three Thousand Character Classic*. These primers introduced the child immediately to Confucian principles of personal and family conduct, with the more advanced readers containing much of the information found in the Four Books.

As the boy's reading and writing skill increased he was required to master more difficult texts concerning the elaborate implications of filial piety. If several boys were taught concurrently by the same tutor, each student might be required to "back his book" in much the same manner as was done in early America and in Europe. Although the young boys were taught some arithmetic, the curriculum was rarely vulgarized by direct attention to the physical world. Nor were the young students allowed to develop individual academic interests, for the knowledge found in the classics was complete and its relevance universal.

Some elementary instruction was probably offered even in the smallest towns. Although there were no teachers available with special pedagogical training, there were, it seems, sufficient numbers of unsuccessful degree candidates who welcomed the opportunity to earn enough money to continue their studies. Some of the single-teacher schools could be considered public inasmuch as any child who could pay the required fee was allowed to attend. Moreover, in larger villages interested citizens banded together to support instruction; at times money was also forthcoming from the local government treasury. More advanced instruction could usually be acquired only in the larger cities and then at considerable expense to the student.

Civil service examinations

It has sometimes been said that before the nineteenth century China had no schools, only a system of examinations. Although this is an overstatement, as has already been shown, the civil service examinations have had long and profound influence on the goals and the content of all levels of education in China. Particularly for aspiring Chinese youth who had neither the benefits of high birth nor wealth, these examinations provided the only opportunity to attain government office. Acquiring the mantle of a government official was a prime objective of a true Confucian scholar and moreover was often the only route to wealth, prestige, and power.

The civil service examinations had their beginnings in pre-Confucian times, possibly as early as the Hsia (2205–1766 B.C.) and Shang (1766–1122 B.C.) periods. Little is known of the content of the early examinations, but it seems likely that they were used primarily for testing the ability of those already in office. The rulers of the Chou dynasty, unlike those of earlier periods, used examinations as a preliminary screening device in order that the national "university" (a body of scholars who, under the patronage of the emperor, gathered at the capital for advanced study) might have the most capable students. The actual selection of officials was made on the recommendations of the "university." During the Chou dynasty the system of examinations took permanent form and began to show a high degree of organization. An analysis of the uses to which the examinations were put during this period shows their great significance. First there was a remarkable democratic

267

quality involved, as in any system which rewards on the basis of ability and character. Next, the system during the Chou period demonstrated how the examinations could be used as a supplement to, rather than a substitute for, the schools. Finally the efficiency of centralization of the educational and governmental enterprise was discovered—a discovery which was to be exploited by subsequent rulers.

The civil service examinations were given varying emphases and included different content during their long history. At times they combined oral and written exercises and at times they were entirely written. Sometimes they were used in lieu of the educational system and sometimes they acted as a supplement to institutions of higher education. During periods when Confucianism was in disrepute, their role was reduced but never eliminated. During the T'ang dynasty some attention was given to better selection of candidates and more efficient administration of the examinations. It was during the Sung period, however, that the most important reevaluation of the whole process of examining took place, for the Sung scholars were trenchant in their criticism of what they considered a perversion of genuine Confucian scholarship. The examinations, it was argued, no longer measured creativity but only memory and imitative ability.

The Sung scholars were not suggesting that the examinations should test content other than the Confucian canons. On the contrary, although liberal thinkers asked for the inclusion of Taoist writings and even some contemporary works, they reemphasized that the Four Books and the Five Classics should be considered the core of a scholar's education. But the basic value of these works, the Sung scholars were eager to point out, lay in their content, not in their literary style. A student, if he were to profit by their study, must carefully seek the principles that their authors espoused and, as a final step, analyze the relation of these principles to current political and social problems. The Sung scholars further urged that a national school system be developed as a means of training for civil service. While this latter recommendation together with some of the other practical suggestions came to nought, the Four Books and the Five Classics remained the basis for the examinations until their abolishment in 1905.

The operation of the examination system is as difficult to describe as the content of the examinations. The various rungs to be climbed leading to official positions changed in number and form throughout Chinese history. The following steps indicate the typical route that was taken by the successful Chinese scholar from the seventeenth to the twentieth century. Only a handful of the many thousands attempting the first examination survived the competition to receive high positions in government service.

1. Matriculation examination at the local level.

2. Examination for the first degree, Hsiu T'sai (glowing talent), held in the chief city of the district. The Hsiu T'sai is sometimes referred to by Western students of China as the "bachelor of arts" degree. This admitted the successful to the honored class of literati.

3. Examination for the second degree, Chu Jen, held at the provincial capital.

One out of every one- to two-hundred candidates was likely to achieve this distinction.

4. National examination for the degree of Chin Shih held at the capital.

5. Examination by the emperor. Successful candidates received official rank and entered government service.[10]

The system of civil service examinations expressed as an ideal was a profound attempt at impartial selection of capable government leaders and, during certain periods, military leaders. Unquestionably, many successful and dedicated Chinese scholar-officials came through this route. In further praise, such a system gave a degree of stability to governmental office and to the political and social philosophy of the nation. Yet, inherent in the theory and the practice of the examination system were grave defects and serious limitations. Most apparent among the shortcomings was the extremely narrow concept of scholarship fostered by centuries of enshrining the ideas of a few authors. Since throughout the years the examinations tested the same content, an orthodoxy was produced that often lapsed into literary scholasticism. Scholarship became a vocation in itself and the saying, "once a scholar always a scholar," was a literal truth in China. The man of letters was the ideal, but all too often his only claim to scholarship was an intimate knowledge of the form and style of the old poems and essays.

Even when the system came under criticism, rarely were arguments raised over the narrow scope of the content

tested. Thus while the examinations at best made it possible to select men well founded in the wisdom of Chinese tradition, seldom was attention given to evaluating candidates in the professional requirements of specific governmental positions. The scholar-official, being completely lacking in a knowledge of any language, literature, history, or geography other than that of China, was understandably provincial in outlook. His lack of scientific training and subsequent reliance on astrology and superstition heavily affected his social policies as well as his personal rituals. The Confucian canons in a sense, then, were viewed as the traditional Seven Liberal Arts had been in early Europe. Both groups of studies were said by their proponents to provide certain academic discipline and instill general principles applicable in all problem situations. Both had some foundation in the practical needs of the early history of their respective cultures, but again, both became increasingly sterile in modern times.

Perhaps equally anachronistic in China was the narrow elitist principle involved in the examination system. Modern China needed, in growing number, persons skilled in a great many different vocational and professional skills. It further needed a broad educational base to provide a functionally literate population. The civil service examinations militated against the requisites of a modern nation and perpetuated the traditional Chinese reliance on moral principles for running a government to the exclusion of systems of law.

Christian and Western influences

China's first extensive contact with the spiritual and educational ideas of the

[10] S. Wells Williams, *The Middle Kingdom*, Scribner, New York, 1904, vol. I, pp. 546–560.

West came as the result of the work of European Catholic and Protestant missionaries. The story of Christian missionaries in China, from its humble beginnings to what may be its final chapter now being written by the Chinese Communists, makes for a fascinating tale, as yet neither well nor fully told. It is a story of extreme personal sacrifice and dedication. It is also a story of prejudice and fratricidal conflicts which pitted sect against sect and bewildered those Asians who had taken at face value the words "brotherly love." Some of the wisest leaders of the Christian church, such as the great Jesuits, Francis Xavier and Matthew Ricci, came to China. But the mediocre also came with their vague and pathetically naïve ideas of bringing the Good Life to the "benighted heathen." Although Christianity made some early and rather startling successes in both China and Japan, a total evaluation of its inroads on modern East Asian religious thought must show very limited progress. But as transmitters of Western education and culture the Christian missionaries were conspicuously successful.

The seventeenth century was perhaps the most rewarding century for the Catholic missionaries in China. The Jesuits, the first of whom had reached China by way of Macao in the sixteenth century, were particularly adept at making converts. Because of the prestige of the scholar class in China, the Jesuits sought to be students of Chinese learning as well as teachers of the Christian faith. They used their European academic training to good advantage, favorably impressing the Chinese court with their knowledge of mathematics, mechanics, astronomy, and architecture. On the other hand, the Jesuits were ardent students of Chinese language, philosophy,

270

and art, many even adopting the dress of the Confucian scholar. Their knowledge of the Chinese people not only served the missionaries well in China, but it also made the Jesuits the foremost interpreters of China to Europe.

The Catholic missionary effort was greatly impaired when in 1704 the Pope confirmed a statement by the Inquisition which forbade Christians to take part in Confucian or ancestral rites. The Chinese emperor's reaction was to impose an official ban—never fully enforced—on the proselytizing activities of the Catholics. Abolition of the Society of Jesus in 1773 added to the growing list of disasters for the Catholic Church in China. Yet in spite of the loss of the most successful mission sect and the intermittent but strong periods of persecution, Catholicism managed to survive in China, although by the middle of the nineteenth century there were far fewer converts than there had been 2½ centuries earlier.

The Protestant missionaries who began arriving early in the nineteenth century, like the Catholics, made proselytism their *raison d'être*. The first Protestant missionary to live in China was an Englishman; he was followed a few years later by several Americans. The political atmosphere of this period was hostile, however, and expansion of the Protestant mission movement awaited the conclusion of two successful wars (1839–1844 and 1856–1860) waged on China by European powers. By taking advantage of clauses in the treaties which provided for added protection of the missionaries, both Catholics and Protestants were in a position to expand their mission work during the second half of the nineteenth century.

Quite in keeping with their objectives,

Catholic missionaries had established but few schools in China. For several decades after their arrival, the Protestants likewise gave little attention to educational endeavors. It is likely that a large percentage of missionaries of all Christian faiths would have agreed with one of their rank who said:

> We are here, not to develop the resources of the country, not for the advancement of commerce, not for the mere promotion of civilization; but to do battle with the powers of darkness, to save men from sin and conquer China for Christ.[11]

The Catholics apparently continued to subscribe to this view until the twentieth century. Protestants, however, in spite of lingering opposition, gave increased attention to the development of schools as a means of winning converts and introducing Western culture. The objective of an early educational society founded by the combined efforts of American and English Protestants can be considered fairly typical. This organization proposed to:

> . . . establish and support schools in China in which native youth shall be taught in connection with their own, to read and write the English language; and, thru this medium, to bring within their reach all the varied learnings of the Western world. The Bible and books on Christianity shall be read in the schools.[12]

The early mission schools were usually elementary and secondary schools, though in due course, collegiate-level institutions were also introduced. Typically the curriculum, as described in the above quotation, involved both Western and Chinese subjects. However, no attempt was made to assist the students in the intensive study of the Classics so necessary to prepare for the civil service examinations. Indeed, under the Manchus, graduates of mission schools were barred from receiving government degrees, and hence, in effect, were not eligible for government employment. Here obviously was a situation subject to much criticism from the traditional Chinese scholars. The mission schools, the scholars pointed out, were foreign institutions which neither adequately met standards of scholarship nor prepared Chinese youth for employment in Chinese society.

A certain amount of such criticism was probably valid. The mission institutions were largely foreign importations with but cursory measures of adaptation taken to fit the Chinese situation. Moreover, many of the teachers of the mission schools were reported to be much higher on zeal than on academic qualifications. Facilities and finances were likewise often insufficient. Yet in spite of such shortcomings these schools provided a service not being offered in the pre-twentieth century national or private schools. Through language instruction and through the social and natural sciences, they provided a small number of Chinese youth with a window to Western culture and the opportunity to acquire some of the rudimentary skills necessary to enlarge this view.

A contribution of even more revolutionary proportions was the training given to women in the mission schools. In this area the Protestants were truly pioneers. The Chinese civil service ex-

[11] E. R. Hughes, *The Invasion of China by the Western World*, A. & C. Black Limited, London, W.1, 1937, p. 77.
[12] George H. Danton, *The Culture Contacts of the United States and China*, Columbia, New York, 1931, pp. 52–53.

amination had not been open to girls, nor had schools of any type. Although the Catholics had maintained schools where Chinese girls might learn the catechism, it was only in the Protestant mission schools that girls could receive instruction in the home arts and occasionally even in regular academic subjects such as Chinese literature and English. From these schools graduated many of the girls who became the leaders in church work, education, and women's rights in modern China.

Language and scholarship

The Chinese language played an important and unique role in scholarship and education. There are two major historical reasons for this. First, over a period of years literary Chinese, the written language used by scholars in modern as well as in ancient times, became a language in itself, much removed from the vernacular of the people. The extremely terse, formal literary style originally had developed, perhaps, for the sake of saving unnecessary labor; but even though scholarly diction became more relaxed and mechanical means of writing were introduced, the literary form persisted. The classics were so venerated that their style was copied by succeeding schools of scholars, and the divorce of the literary language from the common speech became permanent. A Chinese in order to prepare himself for both oral and written communication was required, in effect, to learn two separate languages.

The second reason why language has held such an important relationship to scholarship in China is its complexity. The Chinese language is partly ideographic and partly phonetic. Scholars believe that originally the Chinese char-

272

acters did represent spoken sounds; however, at present the whole body of Chinese characters must be viewed as pictograms, ideograms, and phonograms. The first are pictures of objects; the second are composite symbols, standing for ideas; and the third are compound characters, of which the more important elements simply represent the spoken sounds. Thus a page of Chinese characters is composed of independent units. Each unit may be thought of as a *word* since it stands for a particular sound and expresses an idea but, unlike words in the Indo-European languages, may not be further fragmented into letters.

The language situation becomes even more complicated when simple characters having only one meaning are combined with other characters to form an entirely new meaning. The difficulty in thoroughly mastering the language lies in the nearly unlimited possibilities of such new characters. As Fairbank has pointed out:

> Any part of the Chinese language is simple in itself. It becomes difficult because there is so much of it, so many meanings and allusions, to be remembered. When the lexicographers wanted to arrange thousands of Chinese characters in a dictionary, for instance, the best they could do in the absence of an alphabet was to work out a list of 214 classifiers, one of which was sure to be in each character in the language. These 214 classifiers, for dictionary purposes, correspond to the 26 letters of our alphabet but are more ambiguous and less efficient.[13]

Considering the complexity of the language and the high regard given to liter-

[13] John King Fairbank, *The United States and China,* Harvard, Cambridge, Mass., 1958, p. 39.

ary form, it is easy to see how mere knowledge of written language became equated with scholarship. It is also understandable that the language could become a revered institution and its mastery a symbol of prestige. The writing of the characters was considered one of the highest forms of art, and the brush strokes of scholars are still considered fitting *objets d'art* in the best of homes. Phrased in a different way, painting to the Chinese, Koreans, and Japanese was, at times, a branch of handwriting. The tools for both were brush and ink, and long arduous hours were required of all scholars in handling the brush and varying the strokes to obtain characters of beauty. Even today at social or political gatherings crowds collect to admire the brush signatures of visiting scholars.

Other problems posed by the nature of the Chinese language are inherent in its terseness and the lack of characters to represent modern concepts. The first problem becomes apparent when it is understood that two characters can often express a thought requiring a long sentence in English. Yet such brevity lends itself to vagueness and misinterpretation—a situation which accounts for some of the difficulties in effecting precise modern communication as well as for the obscurity of the Chinese Classics. This same terseness, together with the failure to adjust the vocabulary to modern demands, has demonstrated the inadequacy of the Chinese language for coping with ideas common to a modern society. By way of simple illustration, to express the word "elevator" three Chinese characters (meaning "rise," "descent," and "machine") are needed, and even then, obviously, the correct idea may not be conveyed.

It is estimated that a modern Chinese must know at least three thousand characters to attain bare literacy (an educated Japanese would need to know the same number), while a scholar would need to have ready grasp of about thirty thousand characters. Thus the complexity of language and its formal literary style, on the one hand, served to isolate China from scholars outside the country and, on the other hand, required so much of the Chinese student's time that he had little energy left for examining new tongues or other interests. Further, because of the long period needed to acquire language mastery, knowledge of the language was largely reserved for the wealthy. Only by herculean sacrifice could the peasant farmer allow his son the requisite years of leisure for language study. That some farmers made this sacrifice is a tribute to Chinese character. Yet, by and large, language through the centuries kept the majority of Chinese from a thorough understanding of their culture.

Education under the Republic

During the nineteenth century China reluctantly opened its doors to Westerners and, hence, to Western ideas. After a few disastrous brushes with Western soldiers on the battlefield all but the most recalcitrant Chinese officials realized that great changes must be wrought if China were to take its proper place in the family of nations. At first Chinese scholars claimed that Western science (the one area in which they admitted Western superiority) had really been understood by the early Chinese scholars and that students needed only to look deeply into the Classics to find all the important scientific concepts. Even those

Chinese who admitted that Western learning must be acquired directly from the West sought to borrow only those needed skills without altering the basic Chinese social and political institutions.

The naïveté of the official Chinese attitude is well expressed in an episode that took place in 1872. In that year, as the result of a persistent request made some years earlier by a young Chinese scholar, 120 Chinese students were sent to the United States to absorb American learning. It was the hope of the more progressive elements that these students would, upon return, spearhead a vast movement toward modernization. Yet, indicative of the official temper of the times, steps were taken to see that the students were not contaminated with too much Western learning. Official tutors went with the group to prepare them for the civil examinations which they would be forced to take upon return if they wished to enter government service; and by way of climax, a scholar of the Confucian Classics also accompanied the group to make certain that their morals were not undermined by American ideas.

The end of the nineteenth century found China still unwilling to take the drastic steps necessary to put its institutions on a scientific footing; but two events were straws in the wind and were to foretell a twentieth-century revolution. First, in 1895, to the great humiliation of all Chinese, China was decisively defeated in war by its former pupil, Japan. Secondly, in 1898, under the influence of a small but ardent group of reformers, the emperor was forced to make a series of sweeping edicts dealing with nearly every organized part of Chinese life, including the reorganization of the civil examination system and

274

the introduction of scientific applications into medicine, agriculture, and the military. These decisions were too drastic for the conservatives surrounding the emperor, however, and in order to resist further infiltration of Western ideas the colorful empress dowager, Tz'u Hsi, returned from retirement to lead a successful *coup d'état*.

The beginnings of a modern system

It was during this last conservative stand that China's modern educational system was established. In 1903, as the result of the findings of a national commission, a detailed plan for educational development was put into effect. This plan included provisions for a new organizational structure, new administrative channels, and changes in curriculum. The new school system was a multiple-track system in which the academic route included a five-year lower elementary school, a five-year middle school, a three-year higher school, and the university. Schools were controlled and supervised by a Ministry of Education which, after its establishment in 1905, removed educational affairs from the Ministry of Rites. The curriculum at all levels in the new system was still dominated by the Classics; however, some foreign languages and Western studies were introduced at each level.

The conservative rule of the empress dowager proved to be ephemeral, for the tides of change could not be stemmed. The growing dissatisfaction with the Chinese monarchy culminated in 1912 in the founding of the Republic. For the next decade and a half the revolutionary leaders tried with little success to identify for the people the principles underlying the new government and to make peace with the many rebellious factions. Gradually, however, the reorganized Kuomintang, the political party of Sun Yat-sen, father of the Chinese Republic, under the leadership of a young military clique headed by Chiang Kai-shek, began forcibly to bring a semblance of unity to China. With increased political stabilization came economic and industrial advancement, and China appeared to be undergoing something of a minor renaissance. Transportation and communication improvements were pushed forward rapidly, as was the expansion of medical and health facilities. To a certain extent teachers' working conditions and salaries were improved and new educational institutions experimented with. Long-range plans called for the thorough transformation of the traditional, agrarian nation into a modern, scientific state. Unfortunately, these plans were rudely interrupted by the outbreak of war with Japan in 1937.

The early goals of the Republic were national unity and military strength. Like Japan, years earlier, China looked abroad for institutions which might be adapted to the nation's new objectives. Also like Japan, China found attractive ideas in both Europe and America. Germany, because of its military power and efficient centralism, was admired and imitated; America, because of its use of mass education as a prime tool in national improvement, was also a model. An important immediate outgrowth of the extensive use of foreign ideas to implement national goals was the wedding of militarism and education. School-sponsored activities and even the classroom took on a semimilitary atmosphere, and military training was required in secondary and higher educational institutions. China was beginning to change from a land of scholar-officials to a nation of soldier-students.

Early progress and problems

Those who shaped the political and philosophical direction of the Republic saw no conflict between nationalistic and democratic goals. The *San Min Chu I* (Three People's Principles) plan, announced by Sun Yat-sen in 1924, included the objectives of nationalism, democracy, and people's livelihood.

Dr. Sun maintained that his three principles were the same as those enunciated by Abraham Lincoln when he referred to "government of the people, by the people, and for the people." However, in defining "people's livelihood" he used the terms socialism and communism and suggested that in order to apply the principle, equalization of landownership and regulation of capital were necessary.

Educators accepted these objectives and attempted to adjust the nation's educational aims accordingly. Textbooks were rewritten in light of the principles of "new education"—modern, scientific education—and to develop cultural and racial self-consciousness. Discipline and obedience to the laws of the republican government were stressed, scientific education was given official prestige, and a new respect for labor urged. In fulfillment of the aims of new education, Chinese educators frequently looked to America and its progressive educators. During the idealistic years immediately following World War I, John Dewey, in particular, stirred the imagination of young China through his analysis of the relationship between the school and a democratic society. Such slogans as individualism, freedom, progress, democ-

275

racy, and science became popular among the young scholars. The spirit of the times was forcefully expressed by a former student of Dewey, the distinguished Hu Shih, after his return to China.

> . . . I want to declare a revolution in literary studies with eight objects to be achieved; give up the use of classical quotations and allusions, of conventions of courtesy, of parallelisms both in prose and poetry; do not avoid common everyday words and expressions; set ourselves to the instruction of grammar; avoid unfelt exclamations; do not take the men of old as a pattern; in all expressions there should be an individual "I" present, there should be something in everything we say.[14]

The intricate problem of language proved to be an obstacle in extending educational opportunity and in fostering nationalism. There were significant sectional variations in the spoken language. Further, since the written language had been little influenced by the living dialects, it had not adapted to modern, scientific ideas. To overcome some of these difficulties the Chinese government fostered a movement to teach all courses in the schools in a standard language. The adoption of Mandarin, the most widely spoken language, as the language of instruction in the elementary grades was a major step toward developing a common tongue for the Chinese people. New characters and combinations of characters were invented to stand for the modern ideas being introduced in political, educational, and scientific circles. Steps to unify the written language also were partly successful, and a pho-

netic alphabet was developed under government sanction which was widely used in both schools and popular literature. This phonetic script was not to replace the thousands of Chinese characters but rather was a means to standardize their pronunciation. Finally, the prestige of the difficult and ornate literary language, no longer with strong official backing, began to decline sharply. These changes in language, initiated during the first two decades of the Republic, while not satisfying the radicals who called for a phonetic written language, were, perhaps, hardly less revolutionary than the substitution of Italian for Latin in Renaissance Italy.

Education for all classes had never been a goal of Confucianism or of the other ideological movements prominent in pre-Republic China. With the introduction of a modern educational system, attention naturally turned to the problem of universal education. The results of intense desire to expand educational opportunity are shown in the following figures: In 1910 there were in the Republic only 86,318 elementary schools, serving 2,793,633 pupils; 373 secondary schools for 52,100 students; and 4 universities with 481 students. Twenty years later there were 261,264 elementary schools with 11,667,888 pupils; 1,892 secondary schools with 403,134 students; and 111 higher educational institutions with 43,519 students.[15]

Most of the educational reforms described thus far were lacking in depth. Under the Republic constant internal struggle for power prohibited supervision and enforcement of educational

---

[14] Quoted in E. R. Hughes, *op. cit.*, p. 178.

[15] L'and Leang-Li (ed.), *Reconstruction in China*, China Today series, China United Press, Shanghai, 1935, pp. 69–72.

policy at the national level, and thus many of the forward-looking educational plans were never translated into action. Moreover, this was a period of rapid transition with many educational ideas being tried, found wanting, and discarded. There is no need to recount the many experiments which had no lasting influence on Chinese education. However, a look at the educational conditions at each level, the preparation of teachers, and the control and administration of education will serve as a basis for perspective in examining the changes wrought by post-World War II communism.

Elementary Education. Elementary education historically has received less attention in the plans of Chinese educators than have secondary and university education. In its haste to develop leaders, China, as early as 1870 established modern institutions of higher education; yet not until the twentieth century was the significant role of the elementary school recognized.[16] However, the revolutionary spirit which brought the Republic into being was favorable for the extension of educational opportunity, and successive ministers of education pledged themselves to increase the quantity and improve the quality of elementary education.

Beginning in 1920, under the leadership of the Ministry of Education, long-range plans were laid for extending opportunities in elementary education for every child in the nation. The date for the fulfillment of these plans was continually revised and by the outbreak of the Sino-Japanese War in 1937 com-

pulsory education was still far from becoming a reality. Although the elementary school enrollment doubled between 1915 and 1930, China still lagged far behind even the poorer European countries in the percentage of children attending school. For example, it has been estimated that in 1927–1928, Soviet Russia placed 82 per cent of its children between the ages of *eight and eleven* in school; in China, although accurate statistics are unavailable, one source indicates that during 1928–1929, only 21 per cent of the children between the ages of *six and nine* attended school.[17]

A summary of the weaknesses and problems besetting Chinese elementary education in the 1930s brings to light many shortcomings which were common to all levels of Chinese education and which still persist in many parts of Asia. First, the method of financing the elementary schools hampered achievement of universal instruction, for the money acquired through taxation, being insufficient to run the schools, had to be supplemented by the children's parents. Elementary education, then, typically was available only to the children from wealthier homes, a fact which colored the entire operation of the schools.

A second major weakness of the Chinese elementary schools lay in the area of curriculum and method. At the beginning of the Republic, steps had been taken to abolish the Classics and install a modern curriculum, but Chinese teachers did not have the professional understanding to make the new courses func-

[16] Chai-Hsuan Chuang, *Tendencies toward a Democratic System of Education in China,* Commercial Press, Shanghai, 1922, p. 69.

[17] C. H. Becker and Others, *The Reorganization of Education in China,* League of Nations, Institute of Intellectual Cooperation, Paris, 1932, p. 78.

tion as designed. Natural sciences and social sciences were incorporated into the school schedule; yet the pupils made little direct study of the natural or social environment. The method of instruction used was inevitably the formal lecture allowing little opportunity for discussion of independent work by pupils. There were few instructional aids or laboratory experiences to supplement the ordeal of memorization. "New education" was hardly more relevant to the children's lives than the ancient Classics had been.

A lingering prejudice against coeducation created additional economic pressures, since some villages insisted on separate schools for girls and boys. A continuing problem of organization frustrated articulation along the educational ladder. The division of elementary education into "upper" and "lower" schools (for some time a 4-3 system existed; later this became a 4-2) did not appear to be a permanent solution. To find a better terminal institution, urban areas began to experiment extensively with a six-year elementary school. A final important problem, the professional preparation of the elementary school teachers, will be discussed later.

In summary, the elementary schools under the Republic promoted, at best, a semifunctional literacy but hardly served as appropriate terminal education—which they were for the great majority of their pupils.

Secondary Education. Under the Republic the term secondary education came to include institutions designed for three different purposes. There were general or academic secondary schools which led to the university, and there were two categories of terminal secondary schools, the normal schools and

278

various vocational schools. Entrance to the variety of available secondary schools, more typically called middle schools, was possible only after the passing of an examination. The length of secondary education was dependent upon its function. Vocational schools ranged from two to six years in length, depending on the skill being taught. Normal schools prepared teachers for the elementary grades and were typically three to five years in length, drawing students directly from the elementary schools or from the lower secondary school. The general or academic secondary school, after revision in 1922, was organized somewhat like the 3-3 secondary school of the United States, with the first three years devoted to general education and the last three to specialization.

Many of the ills existing in the elementary schools were likewise present in the secondary schools. The formalism of instruction did more to develop memory than curiosity among the students. The docility and passiveness of the teaching-learning process kept secondary education from being a dynamic force in the social and economic development of China. The strong Chinese scholastic traditions which gave inferior status to practical and vocational subjects further prohibited the secondary schools from developing programs in the various industrial and commercial skills the modernizing nation needed. Even those secondary schools labeled "vocational" were usually hardly more than academic schools which had added a minimum of vocational subjects to a traditional college preparatory curriculum. In reality, then, not only the general secondary schools, but the normal and vocational schools as well, were strongly influenced by expectations of the universities.

Higher Education. After their reform in 1922, higher education institutions in China were typically four years in length, though some professional study such as law or medicine might take a longer period. What precisely constituted higher education was further clarified in 1929 when three categories of institutions—universities, independent colleges, and technical colleges—were defined. A university consisted of several colleges of arts, science, and professional studies while the independent college was defined as an institution with less than three colleges; technical colleges were two- or three-year institutions offering programs in agriculture, engineering, and other technical areas.[18]

In spite of their excessively humanistic orientation and lack of applied technical or scientific subjects, the universities and colleges were extremely important in the shaping of modern China. Not only were most of the leaders of government, industry, and education trained in these institutions, but it was in the universities that Western scientific and philosophic ideas were filtered and a synthesis formed of Chinese and Western thought. That the universities and colleges gave leadership to a growing China cannot be denied; however, the quality of that leadership is open to debate. The long heritage of expecting all important decisions to be made by the hierarchy of governmental officials had noticeable effect on the interests of university students. Well into the 1930s, legal, political, and literary

[18] China, Ministry of Education, *China Handbook, 1937–1943*, Macmillan, New York, 1943, p. 368.

subjects occupied the most exalted positions in the curriculum as students sought to prepare themselves for government employment. The natural sciences and technology did not attract large numbers of students, for these were callings not yet prized in conservative China.

Preparation of Teachers. The teaching profession in China has long been held in high esteem. The very Chinese word meaning teacher became a term used in addressing persons of seniority or in high position. Teachers in the secondary schools and most of all the professors in the universities were honored by all strata of society. The social status of teachers remained high throughout the years of the Republic. Yet in a China moving toward a modern economic footing, substantial financial advantage as well as prestige was needed to attract capable young people to a profession. This was an advantage that teachers were not offered during the Republic.

The beginning of professional preparation of teachers in China roughly coincided with the introduction of the modern educational system at the turn of the twentieth century. At that time institutions for the preparation of teachers began to appear. To prepare teachers for the middle schools, there developed four-year normal colleges and normal departments in universities. Courses in the latter ran from one to three years. The regular normal schools prepared teachers for the upper primary school, while the other institutions were designed to prepare teachers for kindergarten and lower primary schools. Only graduates of the junior middle school were eligible to enter the regular normal schools, while graduates of the upper primary school were admitted to the other training schools. In practice, however, many of the primary school teachers were young men and women who had attended a regular middle school for a year or two but had received no professional education.

The practice which calls for the preparation of secondary school teachers in colleges or universities and the preparation of primary school teachers in secondary level institutions is a pattern of teacher education common in China, indeed in much of the world, down to the present day. Although it is doubtful that secondary school graduates have either the academic, intellectual, or social maturity to carry out the demanding responsibilities of teaching children, the economic conditions in China for decades precluded extension of the professional preparation of primary school teachers. China under the Republic, like the economically underdeveloped countries of today seeking to utilize the schools in their plans for rapid growth, was faced with a quantity versus quality problem. Justifiably perhaps, a compromise was made on the quality of professional instruction in order that an increased number of children might receive some formal education.

Control and Administration. The long Chinese heritage of maintaining government leadership while allowing local freedom was reflected in the control and administration of the school system under the Republic. The Ministry of Education, with the assistance of its professional advisory council, established policies regarding curriculum, selection and certification of teachers, and standards for educational facilities. Direct control over the operation of the schools was exercised either at the na-

tional, provincial, or district level depending upon the nature of the institution. The Ministry provided direct control over those schools designated as national, which included certain of the universities, secondary schools, professional colleges, and institutes for adult education. Except for the national schools, the province assumed the responsibility for secondary education while the district provided for elementary schools.

The financing of the educational effort was likewise divided among the different administrative levels. Higher education was financed from the central budget, and the secondary and primary schools relied largely on support from provincial and district treasuries. The amount budgeted for education at each of these levels again demonstrates the privileged position of secondary and higher education. In European countries at this time the difference in expense to the state of a primary school pupil and one in the university was roughly in a ratio of 1: 8 or 1: 10 while in China the ratio was perhaps 1: 200.[19] These discrepancies in school budgets were also reflected in salaries, with the result that the primary teachers could hardly earn a living wage.

In spite of the considerable responsibility of the province and local unit in carrying out the educational effort, the amount of decentralization of control was relatively minor. The Commissioner of Education, the highest provincial educational officer, as well as the district educational officials were responsible to the Minister of Education on all important educational matters. Detailed accounts of each school's activity were

[19] Becker and Others, *op. cit.*, p. 51.

required for the Ministry's inspection. Furthermore, the schools used nationally approved textbooks and followed a national schedule. Although poor communication along with a variety of professional reasons often made the enforcement of national standards impossible, the goal of centralization gained increasing importance as the government of the Republic strove for unity through uniformity.

As the Republic matured, one of the many factors that proved distressing to Chinese educational leaders in their attempts to vitalize the Chinese school system was the variety of Japanese and Western (particularly American) educational institutions that had been transplanted to China. Many of these institutions were of questionable significance in China. First, they were imitations, usually rather cheap ones, of some well-known American or European school. They sought to attain the prestige and reputation of the institutions copied but had neither adequate facilities nor qualified staff. Secondly, these institutions, products as they were of highly literate and industrialized nations, had no cultural roots in agrarian China.

An educational mission from the League of Nations in a most outspoken report pointed out the danger of uncritically accepting Western educational institutions as models for China. The mission argued that "modern science and techniques" did not create modern Europe and America, but, on the contrary, it was the "European and American mind" which developed advanced science.[20] This report then went on to state: "The fundamental problem which arises in regard to education in China

is not a question of imitation but of creation and adaption."[21]

The "foreign" schools introduced by the Christian missionaries also received considerable criticism from both visiting educators and the Chinese. To improve their field schools the home organizations of the mission groups recommended limiting their number to a few institutions of high caliber. Chinese students, growing up in an iconoclastic period, accused the mission schools of fostering obscurantism rather than promoting the type of scientific training needed. Some of the students, moved by the arguments of Bertrand Russell and other Western philosophers, openly declared that religion had been ruled out by the sciences.

But more was involved in the criticism of the missionary activities than frustration over the curriculum of some mission schools. If education had been the only issue, then a few of the mission colleges and schools should have been rendered high praise, for they were fine institutions, as was demonstrated by the distinguished quality of their graduates. It must be concluded that basically the criticism was antiforeign rather than specifically anti-Christian. The tempo of the times was probably accurately expressed by the Young China Association, which in 1924 resolved:

That we strongly oppose Christian education which destroys the national spirit of our people and carries on a cultural program in order to undermine Chinese civilization.[22]

[20] *Ibid.*, p. 27.

[21] *Ibid.*, p. 28.
[22] Quoted in Kenneth Scott Latourette, *A History of Christian Missions in China*, Macmillan, New York, 1929, p. 697.

In this manner, the students expressed their intolerance for "foreign" ideologies and their passion for promoting an indigenous national character.

The anti-Christian attitude of large numbers of Chinese youth and scholars may have been related to a series of prohibitive measures taken by the Chinese government. In the two decades following the establishment of the Republic, the Ministry of Education ruled: (1) The curricula of the mission schools must be in conformity with those of the national schools; (2) the chief administrator and more than half of the board of directors of any private school must be Chinese; and (3) there should be no compulsory attendance in religious courses or at religious ceremonies. During the late 1920s the anti-Christian movement on several occasions erupted into violence. Several missionaries and many Chinese Christians were put to death by extremist groups. Attempts by the Chinese authorities to check such violence were largely ineffectual and by 1930 the majority of the Protestant missionaries had withdrawn from the interior areas to the safer urban centers.

Education as an agency for communism

The advent of communism in China did not mean a complete break with the social trends noticeable under the Republic. In the 1930s and 1940s when the Communists and the Kuomintang were vying for power, both groups often sought ideological justification in the same sources. For example, Sun Yat-sen was frequently quoted by members of the Kuomintang as well as by Communist Party spokesmen. To the Communists "people's livelihood" was interpreted as communism; "democracy" as dictatorship of the proletariat; and "nationalism" as anti-Westernism. Further, the nationalistic strand in Confucian thought could be viewed as foundational to the scientific ideas of both Communists and non-Communists. Nor were the positivistic, pragmatic, and materialistic ideas acquired by China from the West entirely antithetical to communistic thought. The denial of historical and humanistic methods of problem solving and the emphasis on scientific inquiry were quite in keeping with the tenets of a Marxist society.

Yet from the beginning the Communists showed a willingness to strike out in new directions. Their ready sanction of violence and extreme methods was certainly counter to the typical Chinese character. Moreover, the Communists were even less willing to compromise with the remaining elements of Confucianism than other political groups had been. In this regard in 1927, Mao Tse-tung, then an important local leader of the peasant rebellions in Hunan province, made a significant interpretation of the means by which a Marxist society might be acquired for China. Mao found that Confucianism had subjected the Chinese to three evil systems of authority:

1. The system of the state (political authority), ranging from the national, provincial, and county government to the township government.

2. The system of the clan (clan authority), ranging from the central and branch ancestral temples to the head of the household.

3. The system of gods and spirits (theocratic authority), including the system of the nether world ranging from the King of Hell to the city gods and local deities, and that of supernatural beings ranging from the Emperor of Heaven to all kinds of gods and spirits.[23]

Mao went on to say that women had been subjected to a fourth domination—the authority of the husband.

Since all four systems of authority were considered detrimental to the Communist plans, all must be destroyed. However, the task need not be so great as it might first appear, for again according to Mao, "The political authority of the landlords is the backbone of all other systems of authority."[24] The road to action then was clear; the landlord system must be broken. Even in the early days of communism, Mao had correctly argued that by eliminating the gentry and placing power in the hands of peasants—primarily the young peasants—the shattering of other traditions would quickly follow. Thus before 1930, the initial steps were being taken that would lead China to a "dictatorship of the people."

The new role

From the beginning of significant Communist activity, even when the peasant associations were still wresting power from the gentry class, education played a dominant part in Communist plans. As the geographic areas which in typically Communist phraseology were called "liberated areas" fell to Communist control, officials immediately bent their efforts to provide more schooling for the children and literacy programs for the adults. From 1949

to 1953 was a period of consolidation and experimentation. As Leo A. Orleans noted in *Professional Manpower and Education in Communist China* the Communist regime adopted Mao Tsetung's famous military principle "Enemy advances, we retreat; enemy halts, we harass; enemy tires, we attack; enemy retreats, we pursue." This flexibility of action made it possible to lessen the fear of "loss of face" and welcome experimentation. The 6-3-3 pattern inherited from the nationalists was suspect, and appropriate modifications were considered. In 1951 the Ministry of Education introduced plans designed to eliminate the dual-track primary system which had typically provided a full six-year school only in the urban areas. The establishment of a unified five-year school was attempted, but shortages of teachers and facilities forced a return to the dual-track system by 1954. At the secondary and higher levels short-term schools for workers and peasants were established in order to popularize advanced education.

Being of practical bent, the Communists took several specific steps to ensure that education could be used as a direct tool for accomplishing their social and material goals. First, the Communists sought to make wise use of reading materials to propagate the Marxist ideology. Further, as indicated by the popular Communist slogan of "People manage, public help" the people were given larger responsibility in carrying out cooperative community-development projects. Then, there was the critical need to reeducate the many Chinese who had fallen under the spell of "bourgeois" or traditional education. The Communists were quick to designate the humanistic Confucian Classics as sub-

[23] de Bary, *op. cit.*, p. 872.
[24] *Ibid.*

283

versive. All these planned steps pointed to the need for extended formal education.

The official Communist policy in China, as in the more mature Communist society, the U.S.S.R., was to make the school a more efficient tool for the economic development and the ideological orientation of the people. Official Communist documents castigating "bookworms" and education that amounted to a "monkist leaving of the world" brought a welcome response from liberal Chinese youth. Yet as perceptive Chinese soon discovered, practicality was never the highest aim, for the Communist view was that first and foremost all education should be class-oriented. In the words of a Communist spokesman:

> Our education is the education of the people, and it serves the people. But who are the people? They are the working class, the peasantry, the petty bourgeoisie, and the national bourgeoise. These four classes constitute the peasant people of China.
> Since it is so, why then, should we put serving the workers and peasants instead of serving the people in general, or serving the national bourgeoise or the petty bourgeoisie, as the essential policy in our present educational instruction?—In the first place, the People's Democratic Dictatorship is based on the alliance of the working class, the peasantry, and the urban bourgeoise, but principally on the alliance of the workers and the peasants, because these two classes comprise eighty to ninety per cent of China's population. The overthrowing of imperialism and the Kuomintang reactionary clique, depends chiefly on the forces of these two classes. The transition from New Democracy to

Socialism also depends primarily upon their alliance.[25]

In another important document, a government spokesman contrasted the reasons for workers acquiring an education in Communist and capitalist nations.

> In a capitalist country, the reason why laborers seek an education is only because they realize, under economic pressure, that their being unable to get better jobs and earn better wages is chiefly on account of their inadequate knowledge. Therefore, the objective of workers' education in such a country is to increase the workers' knowledge and technique so that they may be promoted from ordinary workers to skilled workers with better wages, positions and livelihood. Our objective is to educate the working class to contribute their efforts positively and efficiently toward the consolidation and development of the victory they have already achieved, toward the fortification and strengthening of their new position as the nation's master, and toward the ideal construction of their country.[26]

Two characteristically Communist elements became noticeable in Chinese educational policy during the decade after the mainland of China came under complete Communist control. One of these was the emphasis on relating school to "life," more exactly, a materialistic-productive-Communist life. Formal education was considered a national tool to be used in the most pragmatic way. As an example of functionalism in

[25] *Education for the Proletariat in Communist China,* Communist China Problems Research Series, The Union Research Institute, Hong Kong, Kowloon, 1956, p. 2.
[26] *Ibid.,* p. 4.

education, one of the first steps taken after the Communists assumed full control of China was a radical revision of the cumbersome Chinese script. While other parts of East Asia struggled with the complicated Chinese characters so ill-adapted for expression of modern ideas but which, due to pressure of scholastic tradition, could not be eliminated, the Chinese Communists promptly began to simplify their language to make it a direct, easy tool of communication. This was done, it should be recalled, in a nation where, until the twentieth century, language had been a highly esoteric medium of communication even, at times, a sort of artistic game used by scholars to bemuse each other.

A further and equally striking functional characteristic of the new educational curriculum was its marriage with industrial and agricultural production. Lu Ting-yi, Director of the Propaganda Department of the Central Committee of the Chinese Communist Party, outlined the dimensions for this trend in 1958.[27] Reiterating a view often expressed by Mao, Lu stated that academic endeavors unsupported by physical labor would not be tolerated. In keeping with this plan three types of schools were developed: full-time schools, part-time schools, and spare-time schools. The courses in all were pared of many of the "impractical" and "feudalistic" subjects in the social sciences and humanities, and factories or agricultural plots were located near the secondary schools and higher education institutions. Workshops for the construction of simple furniture and equipment were attached to primary schools.

[27] Lu Ting-yi, *Education Must Be Combined with Productive Labor,* Foreign Languages Press, Peking, 1958.

Students, particularly those in the universities and technical schools, in addition to doing manual labor were required to devote much of their time to technical projects for the benefit of the state. Geology students were used to find water supplies and minerals; medical schools produced drugs and medical apparatus; engineering students designed apartment houses, airplane plants, and bridges. Again it must be recalled that all this was taking place within a culture that for centuries had dictated: "The scholar should neither shoulder a carrying pole nor lift a basket."

The second characteristically Communist element found in Chinese educational policy was the consistent permeation of the schools with political ideology. Although the total curriculum was revised, the social science textbooks, in particular, underwent drastic changes. History was taught as the relentless process of the evolution of civilization from a slave system, through stages of feudalism and capitalism, to the final fruition of a classless society. Historical events and historical personages were reinterpreted so that all rebellions and revolutions were pictured as the people's struggles against oppression, and all former legal governments viewed as tools for the perpetuation of class divisions. But even after the textbooks were rewritten, major errors in interpretation could be expected, temporarily, because of the class origin of the writer or because of an invalid method of inquiry. Hence, to avoid mistakes and to develop "correct thinking" not only must class differences be eliminated but all youth as well as adults must study politics seriously. Students at all levels are expected to attend regular meetings and demonstrations which are wholly political, and are organized by Communist Party units. At periodic intervals students are tested on their ideological knowledge.

If anything, teachers have been forced to be more politically circumspect than students. Since teachers, at least those at the secondary and higher levels, were often persons with a higher education, they would fit into the category of intellectuals and therefore be suspect by definition. Except for the brief period in 1957 when Mao advocated letting "one hundred flowers bloom" the government has been rigorous in its attempts to break the spirit of the intellectuals. To promote full obedience to Communist doctrine among members of the teaching profession the Party has given attention to both the preservice and inservice programs of teachers. To the former have been added courses in political economy, history of the Chinese revolution, and dialectic and historical materialism. New inservice programs not only have exposed teachers to Marxist dogma but have required them to go through a period of self-criticism in order that they may purge themselves of bourgeois ideas. Special attention has been given to reforming college professors, who as a group seemed prone to rightist beliefs, particularly with regard to manual labor. At times, as two examples from Peking University illustrate, only extreme action could rectify the mistakes of the more recalcitrant.

A professor who had taught English in the university for many years, now found to have rightist tendencies, was immediately ordered to work as a typist so that he could rectify his thinking through labor. Another teacher was reduced to the position of a
janitor and made to sweep the floors so that he could learn the dignity of labor and re-establish his lost contact with reality.[28]

Thus, from the date that the Communists gained complete control of continental China, education has been politically oriented and integrated with labor. By 1958, the Central Committee of the Communist Party had agreed on four principles to guide the schools in their new roles. First, under Party leadership diverse educational opportunities should be fostered not only through regular schools but also through full-time or part-time schools run by factories, mines, agricultural cooperatives, and the like. The goal of all these schools must be the training of socialist-minded workers; thus the first principle is to "combine unity with diversity." Secondly, schooling must be improved in quality at the same time that it is popularized. In the many and variegated forms of instruction, constant effort should be made to improve standards; thus the second principle is to "combine the spreading of education widely with the raising of educational levels." Thirdly, the initiative of the central government, the local authorities and the masses should be utilized for increased educational efficiency. The third principle then is to "combine over-all planning with decentralization." Fourthly, administrators, teachers, and students should, under Party leadership, freely cooperate in the making of educational decisions. Old hierarchical relationships should be erased; for the fourth principle is to "apply the mass line in the

[28] Liu Shui Sheng, "Life in a Chinese University," *The Atlantic*, vol. 204, no. 6, p. 91, December, 1959.

political, administrative, pedagogic and research work in the schools."[29]

Changes in control

The initial national educational policy of the Communists had three distinct but obviously overlapping characteristics. It was, in official language, "nationalistic," "scientific," and "popular." "Nationalistic" meant adhering to the policies of the Chinese Communist Party. "Scientific" implied not only objective study of natural phenomena but also application of Marxian logic to all human problems. Education was "popular" inasmuch as it was primarily for the benefit of the peasants, the revolutionary class, although even the ardent Communist leaders did not expect immediate elimination of the middle and upper classes.

Article 94 of the Constitution of the People's Republic of China, adopted in 1954, proclaimed that all citizens had the right to education.[30] To ensure this right, as the article further explained, "the state establishes and gradually expands schools of various types and other cultured and educational institutions."[31] Educational power would thus seem to reside in the state. However, in reality the Party is of prime importance in the development and implementation of policy. At the national level the Party exerts its control through the Ministry of Education; and in Communist China the administration and organization, curricula, and financing of the schools

[29] Lu Ting-yi, *op. cit.*, pp. 25–26.
[30] *Constitution of the People's Republic of China,* Foreign Languages Press, Peking, 1961, p. 41.
[31] *Ibid.*

are governed by directives from the Ministry (see Figure 31). But the Communists have used even more direct methods to supervise the ideological training of Chinese youth. As in the Soviet Union, Party branches have been formed in the Chinese colleges and universities for the faculty members or older students, and Communist youth organizations have been organized for students in primary and secondary schools.

In 1952, a Ministry of Higher Education was created to control the training of advanced technical and scientific workers. While a majority of the institutions of higher education have remained administratively under the governments of lower administrative echelons, such as the provinces and municipalities, the important policies concerning finance, curriculum, personnel, and general planning have been made by the Ministry of Higher Education. Somewhat analogous to the situation in the Soviet Union, the control of specialized institutions has often been the responsibility of the Ministry of Higher Education and one or more other ministries. For example, the Institute of Petroleum Industry is jointly controlled by the Ministry of Higher Education, the Ministry of Fuel, and the Ministry of Geology.[32] In 1958 the Ministry of Higher Education was abolished and its responsibilities were assumed by the Ministry of Education.

Below the national level, in the provinces and municipalities, there exist educational bureaus. In the special districts and counties the basic educational

[32] C. T. Hu, "Higher Education in Mainland China," *Comparative Education Review,* vol. 4, no. 3, p. 161, February, 1961.

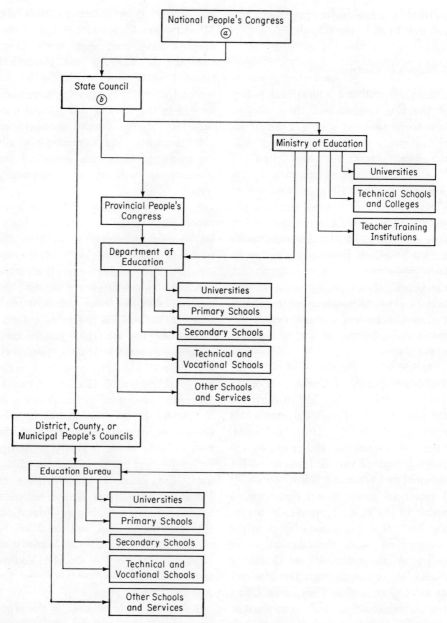

Figure 31. Lines of Educational Authority in Communist China

a. Theoretically, all governmental controls issue from the National People's Congress. It meets for two weeks each year at which time it decides upon the creation, continuation, or abolishment of all ministries and appoints members of the State Council who constitute the top government officials.

b. The Communist Party, as in the U.S.S.R., influences government at each level. Thus the Central Committee issues directives jointly with the State Council, etc., and scrutinizes educational operations at every level.

288

body is the educational and cultural office. The precise function of these lower echelons is not entirely clear although it is known that in most matters of policy they are subordinate both to the people's committees operating at their levels and to the national educational bodies. It is further known, however, that some "voluntary" schools and many institutions of higher education—probably more than half—are immediately responsible to the educational bureaus and to cultural offices for planning, financing, and maintenance. Nevertheless, with the exception of certain recent moves toward decentralization, to be mentioned later, China under communism has been consistent in its reliance on the Party for important educational leadership.

Beginning in 1958 there was a definite movement toward decentralization of many of the educational responsibilities hitherto reserved to the Ministry of Education. The movement to give increased educational control to the provinces, municipalities, or, in the case of vocational schools, often to the factory or related enterprise, was viewed by some in the West as a relaxation of Party discipline. Such was not the case, however. Decentralization was a planned

step in the master plan for communization. China's goal, expressed in 1958, of making the commune the basic social organization did not lessen the role of the Party in education. Although local leaders took on more management duties, policy making was largely reserved for the national authorities. The partial failure of the communes has made this doubly true.

Extension of opportunities

Table 1 shows the tremendous expansion of the educational enrollment which took place between 1950 and 1955. It will be recalled that in 1949, 80 per cent of the population was illiterate; the Communist aim was to reduce this to 5 per cent by the early 1960s. Most startling of all, however, have been the contents of the educational directive issued jointly in 1958 by the State Administration Council and the Central Committee of the Communist Party. This directive called for secondary schools in all communes and universal higher education in fifteen years. Reports from the Chinese press indicate that these as well as other educational goals are likely to be too ambitious. By 1959, for example, it was

Table 1 *Growth in School Enrollments in Communist China*

	1950	1955	1950	1955	1950	1955
Age groups	6–14		15–19		20–24	
Enrollment, thousands	16,180	53,126	1,567	4,437	133	2,552
Per cent of age group enrolled	17	43	3.6	8	0.4	5

NOTE: Data on size of the age groups were not found for 1950–1955. The size of these groups was estimated by use of 1950 and 1955 population figures given in the *United Nations Statistical Yearbook, 1952* and *The Statesman's Year-Book, 1956,* and 1953 percentages of age groups found in *Professional Manpower and Education in Communist China,* p. 157.

reported that from 30 to 40 per cent of youth were illiterate or semiliterate.[33] And while enrollments in colleges and universities between 1949 and 1959 were reported to have increased more than seven times, universal higher education was still a utopian goal.

Preprimary and primary schools

Following a large increase in work opportunities for mothers, kindergartens were introduced in China in large numbers. In 1958, thirty times more children were reported in kindergartens than in the previous year. By 1959 nearly 68 million children were enrolled in kindergartens.[34] This expansion becomes less impressive when it is realized that only a small percentage of these children received any professional guidance, many of them being cared for by girls too young or women too old for more strenuous work.

At the primary level, growth in enrollment was also significant. In 1950 fewer than 25 million were enrolled in primary schools while by 1960 there were 90 million. In terms of graduates, the number grew from less than 3 million in 1950 to over 16 million in 1960.[35] But the government was not committed to a policy of educational growth at all costs. Rather, the educational level should be adjusted in keeping with industrial needs; and when, as in the

early 1950s, production demands on labor were unusually great, the youth were discouraged from continued schooling.

As was described earlier, the six-year primary school (four years or less in rural areas) underwent modification and experimentation by the Communist regime. For a time it was reduced to five years and then returned to six years. Since 1958 attention has again been given to a five-year unified primary school as part of a 5-5 primary-secondary cycle. Or if the two cycles are merged to form a ten-year unified school, the primary cycle may lose its separate identity (see Figure 32).

Basic curricular changes in the primary schools have included incorporating labor into the weekly schedule (in 1959 generally four hours a week), rewriting and standardizing textbooks, and adding special political instruction. The learning of Chinese characters still occupies a dominant role in the curriculum, taking approximately one-half of the study time in grades 1 to 4 and one-third in grades 5 and 6.[36] Modifications in curriculum have been in keeping with the Communist concept of morality. The children must learn to be "valiant fighters" in the class struggle and develop the "Yenan spirit." Since a valid test for these attitudes can be found only in practice, increasing attention has been given to training the children for collective living. The popular slogan of "four collectivizations"—collective study, collective labor, collective residence, and collective board—has found concrete application in the establishment of a number of boarding schools.

[33] Leo A. Orleans, *Professional Manpower and Education in Communist China,* National Science Foundation, U.S. Government Printing Office, 1961, p. 49.
[34] *Ibid.,* pp. 29–30.
[35] For a more detailed account of growth in school enrollments and facilities, see *ibid.,* p. 32.

[36] *Ibid.,* p. 33. A sample curriculum for a six-year primary school is shown on p. 173 of this source.

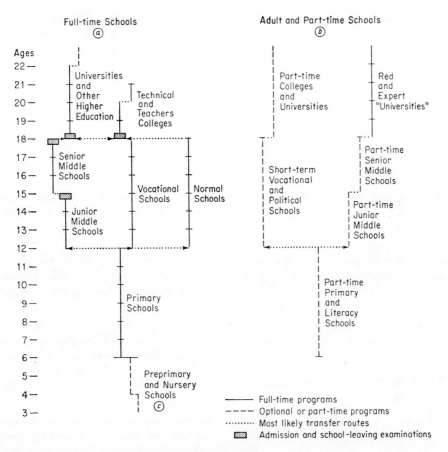

Figure 32. Educational Institutions in Communist China

a. In addition, there is some experimentation with nine- and ten-year unified institutions for basic programs.

b. Transfer to full-time school system is possible at any point.

c. Compulsory when schools are available.

Secondary schools

In spite of various attempts to shorten secondary instruction, the 3–3 pattern remains the standard for full-time, "general" secondary schools—those which supply most of the students who go to the universities and the ones which have shown the greatest expansion. In 1950 there were slightly more than 1 million students enrolled in the general secon- dary schools and in 1959 there were over 8.5 million. During this period the number of secondary school graduates had increased five times.[37]

In addition to general secondary schools there are two other major types of institutions which offer instruction on the secondary level: normal schools and vocational schools. The specialized sec-

[37] *Ibid.*, p. 35.

291

ondary schools do not have the prestige of general secondary schools and appear to have had difficulty in getting the caliber of students desired. Certainly this has been true of the normal schools and has caused concern about the quality of the future teachers. Moreover, because of the urgent need for teachers and other vocationally trained persons, students in the specialized secondary schools frequently are pressed into employment long before graduation.

Curricular changes in the secondary schools have largely paralleled those on the primary level. Six to eight hours of labor have been added to the weekly schedule. Work participated in by students includes both unskilled and semi-skilled endeavors. In 1958 it was reported that students from over 20,000 secondary schools were operating:

> ... 170,000 small factories, producing over 4,000 simple machines and 1,700,000 tons of organic and chemical fertilizer. They have more than 16,000 experimental farms and are getting good harvests.[38]

Without being too much of a cynic, perhaps, one may assume that most of the factories were indeed small and the machines produced simple.

Political instruction of one to two hours weekly has also been added to the secondary curriculum, as has increased emphasis on mathematics and science. Until 1959 few secondary schools offered foreign languages, but this gap is likely to be filled in the future.[39]

In 1960 important organizational reforms for primary and secondary education were announced. Statements from high Communist officials indicated that a combined primary-secondary institution, ten years or less in length, would become the basic institution for pre-university education. The reasons for the proposed changes were economic rather than pedagogical. Compressing and accelerating education would free youth at the age of sixteen or seventeen for full employment, for at these ages boys and girls could be considered, Communist authorities explained, "full manpower units."

The saving of two years from the primary-secondary cycle is not viewed as a reduction of standards. On the contrary, streamlining the curriculum—eliminating outdated content—and requiring more self-study from the students are expected to produce higher academic achievement. Communist spokesmen predict that ninth- and tenth-grade students will soon be studying subjects previously taught at the university level. Furthermore, throughout the ten years of schooling, more rather than less time will be devoted to productive labor.

Higher education

One of the earliest reforms made in higher education by the Communists was to reduce the typical four- to five-year curriculum of the universities to three to four years. This change proved to be premature, and in 1955 the earlier pattern was revived. Some special courses of study continued to require a shorter period of study. The implications for higher education of the reorganization of the primary-secondary cycle are not yet apparent. It might be hypothesized, however, that if the basic reason for the

[38] Quoted in *ibid.*, p. 39.
[39] A sample curriculum for a general secondary school can be found in *ibid.*, p. 174.

292

ten-year school is to free more youth for employment, higher education will increasingly be offered on a part-time basis.

Expansion of the availability of higher education is difficult to gauge because of the problem of defining which institutions legitimately fall into this category. Exempting the "Red-and-expert universities" described below, enrollment figures for higher education rose from 117,000 in 1950 to 810,000 in 1960.[40]

One plan designed by the Communists to extend the social base of higher education has resulted in the establishment of the "Red-and-expert universities." These institutions, which owe their origin to the rectification campaign of 1957–1958, seek, as their name implies, to promote technical competency and political orthodoxy. Although the impetus for the creation of "Red-and-expert universities" was derived from a Party slogan, support for these institutions seems to come primarily from the factories to which they are attached or from the communes in which they are located. Considering the academic background of the students, the qualifications of the teachers, and the level of instruction, the term "universities" is undoubtedly a misnomer. Entering students often have had only a junior high school education, or even less, while the teaching staff has been largely selected from skilled factory workers or farm employees and from the lower Party echelons. Considering the haste with which the "universities" were constructed, it probably would also be safe to conclude that their facilities for fostering higher education leave something to

be desired. According to the official Chinese accounts, for example, in one province forty-four "Red-and-expert universities" were established through the cooperative efforts of teachers and students in only two days.[41] With all their limitations, however, these institutions may well make important contributions in upgrading the technical level of agricultural and industrial workers and in reinforcing political discipline.

In addition to increasing the availability of higher education for peasants and workers other steps were taken in keeping with Communist economic and political goals. Increased specialization, particularly in the technical and scientific pursuits, was fostered and the proportional increase in the enrollments in engineering far outstripped that in any other area. In order to meet manpower needs and to reward those who had demonstrated appropriate political understanding, the state set institutional quotas and allowed "priority considerations" for loyal peasants and workers. Biasing educational opportunities in favor of the revolutionary classes means a concrete step toward intellectualization of the proletariat.

The haste to produce Red experts did not completely obscure to Communist leaders the need for advanced scientific research and experimentation. With the early assistance of Soviet scholars, but more recently under its own steam, the Chinese Academy of Sciences has steadily expanded its research activities. With a main responsibility for the training of high-level scientific manpower, the acad-

[40] *Ibid.*, p. 61.

[41] Referred to in Theodore Hsi-en Chen, "The Popularization of Higher Education in Communist China," *Information on Education around the World*, Bulletin 24, U.S. Office of Education, 1959, p. 8.

emy is able to remain somewhat aloof from the daily pressures of production and to concentrate on quality.

Problems and trends

During 1960 and 1961 the Communist Party made what might be termed an agonizing reappraisal of the progress and problems encountered in China's "great leap forward." Always willing to take "one step backward" in anticipation of "two steps forward," the Communists set about revising their social and educational practices in the cold light of experience. The communes, which earlier had been considered to have superlative productive powers and to be fundamental to a collectivistic society, were modified to include some provisions for family life and private ownership. Nor were the ambitious goals of industrialization satisfactorily reached, and so Communist leaders were forced to question the wisdom of the innumerable small shops and village blast furnaces. The realization that earlier agricultural and industrial goals were too ambitious led the official Party newspaper to note in terms more Confucian than Communistic: "If a person tries to catch ten flies with ten fingers at the same time, he may catch none."[42]

In education, dissatisfaction was voiced on several counts. The sacrifice of quality in instruction, facilities, and equipment was noticeable in all areas but perhaps felt most strongly in the technical field. The Communist policy of "walking on two legs," that is, using diverse approaches to accomplish goals,

[42] Quoted by Wolf Ladejinsky, "More than Mao Can Chew," *The Reporter,* vol. 23, no. 7, p. 38, Oct. 27, 1960.

while probably sound philosophy for a nation in China's stage of development, jeopardizes at times even reasonable standards of efficiency. In 1956, for example, 39 per cent of the primary school teachers had less than a junior secondary education. But the demand for numbers is great and the policy of substituting short-term courses and brief institutes for training previously received over a number of years is likely to continue for some time.

One way to reduce the length of educational programs is to carefully gauge manpower requirements and provide highly specialized training in the skills needed. The planning undertaken by the Communists was unprecise, allowing an overabundance of certain kinds of training courses and a shortage of others. Furthermore, overspecialization frequently prevented an interchange of specialists.

Nor did the twin goals of producing "Reds" and "experts" necessarily harmonize. Often those who were most expert—professionals and technical personnel educated in pre-Communist China or in the West—were least Red. Professors and scientists were among the leading "bloomers" and "contenders" during the brief political respite in 1958, and hence were subject to prolonged and intensive "rectification." As China moved into the 1960s there was some indication that occasional bourgeois ideas might be temporarily tolerated among the highly talented if the state was otherwise well served.

In spite of these and other important problems the basic Communist concept of a school-cum-factory is likely to retain official favor. Also entrenched is a curriculum which emphasizes science and vocational subjects. The contributions to economic development of a new curriculum in a new institution have thus far been significant but not so great as anticipated. Increased success in this great Asian experiment in Communist education would likely lead to its imitation in other parts of the world.

Tracing Chinese education from the long period of dominance by the Confucian Classics through the unsettled period of the Republic and into the Communist phase shows that the image of the educated person has changed from the scholar-official to the student-soldier to the "worker-intellectual." The change in educational philosophy represented in these transitions is obviously great. Yet the very swiftness with which the Communist pattern succeeded in ousting all preceding patterns forces the observer to question whether there are not elements in traditional Chinese thought that are conducive to such radical ideological change.

As mentioned previously, the Chinese Communists found much to their liking in the writings of Sun Yat-sen. Some Communist apologists, however, found friendly authors in a much earlier period. The totalitarian views of the Legalists were often favorably viewed as an indication of early Communist thinking. Both Lao Tzu and Confucius were said to have espoused Marxist theories—although the former received many more Communist admirers than the latter.

It is significant that under the Communists the glorious heritage of the Chinese past is still taught, but also taught are the great humiliations of the past when China's greatness was subverted by the capitalists from within and the imperialists from without. One source has identified four ties which communism has with traditional Chinese thought:

1. The possibility of achieving the ideal society

2. A kind of moral idealism and service to the state

3. Emphasis on what is right (orthodox) rather than what is profitable

4. Ideal of a ruling elite[43]

In spite of these attempts to link communism to past modes of thought, it is quite apparent that Chinese Communists were forced to look to non-Chinese thinkers, especially Marx, Lenin, and Stalin, to find the new tradition they sought. The new social order, in last analysis, had little place for the humanism of Confucius or the mysticism of Lao Tzu. Nor was there room for the quiet, esoteric scholarship so ardently fostered in traditional China. As with the Leninist schemes in Russia, education in China was conceived as a prime instrument in the material reconstruction of society and the building of a new social order.

References

Books

Becker, C. H., and Others: *The Reorganization of Education in China,* League of Nations, Institute of Intellectual Co-operation, Paris, 1952.

Bodde, G.: *China's Cultural Tradition,* Rinehart, New York, 1959.

Chi Tung-wei: *Education for the Proletariat in Communist China,* Communist China Problem Research Series,

[43] de Bary, *op. cit.,* pp. 944–945.

The Union Research Institute, Kowloon, Hong Kong, 1956.

China, Ministry of Education: *China Handbook, 1937–1943,* Macmillan, New York, 1943.

Chuang Chai-Hsuan: *Tendencies toward a Democratic System of Education in China,* Commercial Press, Shanghai, 1922.

Constitution of the People's Republic of China, Foreign Languages Press, Peking, 1961.

Danton, George H.: *The Culture Contacts of the United States and China,* Columbia, New York, 1931.

de Bary, William Theodore (ed.): *Sources of Chinese Tradition,* Columbia, New York, 1960.

Fairbank, John K. (ed.): *Chinese Thought and Institutions,* The University of Chicago Press, Chicago, 1957.

Fung Yu-lan: *A History of Chinese Philosophy,* 2 vols., translated by Derk Bodde, Princeton, Princeton, N.J., 1952.

Galt, Howard S.: *A History of Chinese Educational Institutions,* Arthur Probsthain, London, vol. I, 1951.

Hsiao, Theodore E.: *The History of Modern Education in China,* Peking University, Peking, 1932.

Hu Chang-Tu (ed.): *Chinese Education under Communism,* Teachers College, Columbia University, New York, 1962.

Hu Shih: *The Chinese Renaissance,* The University of Chicago Press, Chicago, 1934.

King, Edmund J. (ed.): *Communist Education,* Bobbs-Merrill, New York, 1963.

Kuo Ping Wen: *The Chinese System of Public Education,* Teachers College, Columbia University, New York, 1915.

Latourette, Kenneth Scott: *A History of*

Christian Missions in China, Macmillan, New York, 1929.

Legge, James: *The Philosophy of Confucius,* Peter Pauper Press, Mount Vernon, N.Y., n.d.

Lindsay, M.: *Notes on Educational Problems in Communist China, 1941–47,* Institute of Pacific Relations, New York, 1950.

Lu Ting-yi: *Education Must Be Combined with Productive Labor,* Foreign Languages Press, Peking, 1958.

Mao Tse-tung: *On the Correct Handling of Contradictions among the People,* Foreign Languages Press, Peking, 1960.

Orleans, Leo A.: *Professional Manpower and Education in Communist China,* National Science Foundation, U.S. Government Printing Office, 1961.

Snow, Edgar: *The Other Side of the River: Red China Today,* Random House, New York, 1961.

Sun Yat-sen: *San Min Chu I: The Three Principles of the People,* translated by Frank W. Price, Communist Press, Shanghai, 1928.

Tibor, Mende: *China and Her Shadow,* Coward-McCann, New York, 1960.

Williams, S. Wells: *The Middle Kingdom,* 2 vols., Scribner, New York, 1904.

Pamphlets and periodicals

The Annals of the American Academy of Political and Social Science, vol. 321, January, 1959.

The Atlantic, vol. 204, no. 6, December, 1959.

Barendsen, Robert D.: "Planned Reforms in the Primary and Secondary School System in Communist China," *Information on Education around the World,* Bulletin 45, U.S. Office of Education, 1960.

Chen, Theodore Hsi-en: "Education for

the Chinese Revolution," *Current History,* vol. 32, pp. 43–48, January, 1957.

————: "The Popularization of Higher Education in Communist China," *Information on Education around the World,* Bulletin 24, U.S. Office of Education, 1959.

Fraser, Stewart: "Recent Educational Reforms in Communist China," reprinted from *The School Review,* vol. 69, no. 3.

Hu, C. T.: "Higher Education in Mainland China," *Comparative Education Review,* vol. 4, no. 3, pp. 159–168, February, 1961.

CHAPTER 11

Japanese Education:

Imitation and Invention

Many of the forces that have shaped Japanese culture and education can be traced to the early centuries of the Christian era. While the oldest existing Japanese historical records, written early in the eighth century A.D., mention that the Japanese Empire[1] was founded in 660 B.C., there is sufficient evidence to believe that only tribal communities existed at this date. Even in the first Chinese accounts of Japan, written during the first century A.D., the authors pointed out the extreme barbaric state of the Japanese. These authors also noticed characteristics of the Japanese still found by modern visitors such as the love of nature, passion for cleanliness, honesty, politeness, gentleness in peace, and bravery in war.[2] Yet Japan learned much from these early contacts with China. Primitive tribes on the Japanese islands may have begun to mold a national character before extensive contacts were made with their more advanced neighbors; however, it was from China and Korea that social, political, and religious ideas were imported and then adopted to direct the people's destiny.

Roots of Japanese tradition

Among the early Chinese cultural exports that were carried over the Korean

bridge to Japan were Chinese writing, literature, arithmetic, and the Chinese calendar. The Chinese language, the story goes, was first introduced into the Japanese court by a Korean scholar, Wani, sometime between A.D. 285 and 405, with the latter date now generally accepted as more correct. The most immediate effect of the presence of Wani was to give official Japanese recognition to the Chinese culture. By the latter part of the sixth century there had developed a constant exchange of scholars among the East Asian nations, as Japanese went to learn in Korean or Chinese courts and the Chinese arrived to tutor their backward neighbors. The *Analects* of Confucius, called *Rongo* in Japan, · plus the other major Confucian Classics, as well as Buddhist writings introduced by Koreans during the sixth century, soon found their way to the Japanese court. Gradually these became the curriculum of a new class of Japanese court scholars, and the lasting effect of Chinese thought was indelibly written on Japanese institutions.

The Confucian doctrines are said to have interred themselves into Japanese life with a minimum of opposition. One reason for this lies in the relative underdevelopment of entrenched native religions or ideologies. Another reason can be found in the fact that in the Confucian Classics there are few ideas which could have been considered radical or subversive by the primitive cults of Japan. Moreover, the Confucian emphasis on man's proper relation to man and avoidance of rigid philosophical schemes

[1] The use of capitalized terms referring to the Japanese Empire deviates from the general rule of capitalizing only specific references in order to adopt the Japanese point of view.

[2] William Theodore de Bary (ed.), *Sources of Japanese Tradition*, Columbia, New York, 1958, p. 5.

or flights into religious ecstasy left little room for objection among the Japanese nobility.

The important chronicles, *Records of Ancient Matters (Kojiki)* and *Chronicles of Japan (Nihonshoki)*, are the earliest Japanese historical sources now available; but since these were not compiled until early in the eighth century it is understandable that the events and thoughts described should in part reflect Chinese traditions. Yet in these works also are found extensive descriptions of numerous non-Chinese gods at work or play in a rather chaotic supernatural world. The sun, moon, storms, mountains, and other elements of nature are involved in various anthropomorphic guises and functions. Japanese records give important historical roles to a variety of gods, but it was from the Sun-Goddess, Amaterasu-Omikami (Heaven-Shining-Great-August Deity) that Japan drew its imperial line. According to the legend, Prince Ninigi, a descendant of Amaterasu, was sent by her to rule Japan. A descendant of Prince Ninigi is said to have assumed the role of Emperor in 660 B.C. From this first Emperor, Jimmu Tenno, there has been an unbroken line of descent to Emperor Hirohito, who, at least until 1946 when under Allied insistence he shed his cloak of divinity, was considered, in colloquial phrasing, a Son of Heaven.

The Japanese traditions prohibited the Emperor from being merely a Confucian sage-king. The divine and mystical power attributed to the throne indicated that Japanese viewed their Emperor as closer to heaven than to earth. He symbolized and occasionally, if he was a strong personality, actualized permanence and truth. Japanese Emperors usually ruled in the paternal-

istic Confucian manner, even to the extent of making wide use of learned court advisers. Yet in final analysis, the judgment of the Japanese Emperor in carrying out his divine mission was infallible. He was, indeed, a God-Emperor and his position inviolable.

The significance of the divinity of Japanese rulers needs further explanation. First, because their nation had been created by divine will and their ruler was not only divine but also a descendant of the gods who created the world, the Japanese considered themselves divine children. They were, so to speak, a "chosen people." This element of divinity contributed to a sense of national superiority which was used by various Japanese leaders to emphasize, alternately, isolationism and imperialism. The former was promoted for centuries as the Japanese scorned foreign ideas and attempted to retain a "pure" national life. At other times attempts to establish an empire through military and economic means were justified because of Japan's divine mission.

Any discussion of the historical and religious tradition of Japan must give attention to Shintoism, the ancestral religion of the Japanese. The term Shinto (The Way of the Gods) did not actually appear in literature until sometime between the sixth and eighth centuries; however, the roots of this religion extend into the mythical past of Japan. The origins of Shinto are diverse—many of its rituals are not indigenous—and only in relatively recent Japanese history did it become a unified religion. Ancestor worship, nature worship, animism, fertility cults, and shamanism all became identified with early Shinto. The introduction and subsequent acceptance of Buddhism by the Japanese court ar-

299

rested the development of Shinto for several centuries. Although Buddhist and Shinto deities were not always easy to separate even during the greatest periods of Buddhism, the more indigenous cults were an important religion among the common people. Modern scholars sometimes discriminate between the earlier and less-developed Shinto and modern Shinto which, in later Japanese history, became a state faith. The term Sectarian Shinto is used for the former, while State Shinto is often used to describe the latter.

Since Amaterasu-Omikami was considered a chief Shinto deity, the Shinto religion is inextricably tied to the story of Japan's creation and the divinity of its Imperial house. The traditional Japanese home has a small altar at which offerings of rice and sake are made to this deity as the first Imperial ancestor. The household may also have a separate altar or "god-shelf" where tablets are kept bearing the names of the family ancestors. Similar offerings of food and drink are made before the second altar. In addition to these two forms of ancestor worship, respect and reverence are often paid to a variety of other spirits. As one Japanese scholar explained, anything that has served man's spiritual or material being can assume the nature of a godhead:

> There is a god of hearth and home, of fire and water, of thread and needles, of pots and pans, of brushes and brooms and what-not. Recently a god was created for typewriters, for pins. Whatever serves us is worthy of our reverence and affection.[3]

[3] Inazo Nitobe, *Lectures on Japan,* Kenkyusha, Tokyo, 1936, p. 150.

300

Shinto, then, with its easy acceptance of the facts of mortal life as divinely regulated, was from ancient times pervasive in its effects on daily life. In its more pure form and also after the infusion of ideas and rituals borrowed from Buddhism, Confucianism, and even Christianity, Shinto was important in shaping the early character of Japan. Important as Shinto was to older Japan, though, it was to become of far greater significance to modern Japan. When, in the nineteenth century, a few vigorous Japanese leaders envisioned a new, powerful Japan and sought a force to unify the people, they turned to Shinto and gave it a key role in their master plan.

Introduction of Buddhism

By the sixth century when Buddhism was introduced to Japan the forces of Confucianism, as well as many indigenous traditions, were already entrenched. Conservative Japanese elements, including the powerful Soga clan, fought the intrusion of Buddhism and warned the Emperor that the worship of foreign deities would anger national gods. This new faith, however, attracted favorable attention in the Japanese court and spread rapidly among the nobility. Buddhist priests from Korea came in numbers and proved to be qualified teachers of the Chinese Classics, skilled architects, and successful missionaries. So great was their success that during the seventh and eighth centuries most of the Japanese emperors and empresses were probably devout Buddhists, though this faith did not interfere with worship of the ancient Japanese gods.

Reasons for the rapid spread of Buddhism in Japan lie in the spiritual impoverishment of the country and in the flexibility and adaptability of this religion. Because Buddhism lacks the militant quality often found in other religions, its missionaries did not immediately demand that its converts disavow their traditional faiths. Moreover, the adaptations made by Buddhism during its long period in China rendered it more acceptable to the Japanese court members and scholars who were already bent on acquiring Chinese learning. Thus Buddhism was allowed to join the Japanese family of beliefs and was given a special role. During the later period some Japanese scholars rationalized a metaphor to show the interrelation of the existing faiths. The compromisers declared that there was really only one tree of life of which Shinto was the root, Confucianism the flower, and Buddhism the stem.

During recent centuries, the number of nominal Buddhists in Japan might seem to indicate that Japan has been essentially a Buddhist nation. However, statistics on Buddhism become less impressive when it is realized that the majority of Japanese profess adherence to at least two religions. Buddhism's great influence was not in creating a new way of life for the Japanese but in adding further mystical quality to a pattern already developed. Buddhism as a dynamic social and political force was greatly handicapped by its rapid fractionalization into many sects, most of which readily absorbed elements of the Shinto cult. The combination of the more joyous rituals attached to Shintoism with the somber Buddhist rites seemed to serve the needs of the Japanese. A popular anecdote tells that at birth it was common for the baby to be

taken to a Shinto shrine for blessing, but at death the funeral was presided over by a Buddhist priest.

Buddhism's greatest contribution to Japanese education was in literary, historical, and religious scholarship. Buddhist temples acted as a refuge for many scholars who sought a peaceful environment to carry on esoteric research of their own choosing. The first school in Japan is said to have been formed in a Buddhist temple and elementary instruction in language and religion was common at the temples; yet such efforts never constituted an organized school system. Although a few secondary schools and colleges were founded by Buddhist sects, they gained little prominence and the total number remained small. Except for the vital role of Buddhist monasteries in preserving learning during the troubled feudal times of Japan, Buddhism offered little in the way of lasting leadership in the development of educational institutions.

Early thought and institutions

There were two important attempts by early Japanese rulers to design a series of laws for the use of government officials in dealing with the people. The first of these, the Seventeen Article Constitution, was developed by Prince Shotoku, who acted as regent during much of the reign of Empress Suiko (A.D. 592–627). The second code of laws appeared in A.D. 701 and was known as the Taiho Code. The Confucian influence on both these documents is apparent;[4] however, the Taiho Code was far more

[4] For evidence of Confucian principles in the Constitution see de Bary, *op. cit.*, pp. 50–51.

than an imitation of the legal codes of China. In this code the Shinto priesthood was given recognition, as were other peculiarly Japanese institutions. The Taiho Code became increasingly important in Japanese thought, and with justifiable pride, a Japanese statesman once compared it with the Justinian Code of the West. The Taiho Code covered every phase of administration—civil, military, judicial, religious, and educational. It remained the basic law of Japan until after the Meiji restoration in 1868.[5]

Although a national university had been founded in A.D. 668, considerable enlargement of this institution and the creation of other facilities for advanced education waited the establishment of the Taiho Code. In A.D. 702 the university was reorganized, professors were appointed to teach calligraphy, medicine —the Chinese version, emphasizing acupuncture—almanac making, astronomy, music, and the sounds of Chinese characters.[6] By decree, one school was also founded in each province which offered approximately the same courses of study as the university, though undoubtedly studies were less advanced and instruction of a lower caliber. Capable students from among the noble families were selected to attend both provincial schools and the national universities. As in China, the goal of the students was government service.

The Taiho Code further enumerated specific laws regarding the duties of professors and the academic requirements of students. Students, sons of high-ranking government officials, were ad-

mitted to all branches of education between the ages of thirteen and sixteen. A maximum of nine years of study was allowed a student to complete a full course, and yearly examinations were given, the results of which determined the qualifications of the student for public office. It can be readily seen that this educational plan of the eighth century was meant to provide some classical education for those young men who, by virtue of birth, were destined to become government officials. For the common people there were paternalistic suggestions from the throne such as ". . . every house should preserve a copy of the Chinese book on Filial Piety and it should be read night and day"; but there were no schools.[7]

The limitations on schooling, and hence on persons qualified to attain government position, were in contrast to the Chinese system which, theoretically and actually, gave the poor but talented boy more opportunity for advancement. The Japanese nobility, larger proportionally than the aristocratic class of China, was jealous of its prerogatives and, much to the detriment of the vitality of Japanese leadership, continually thwarted any attempts to introduce a more democratic system of selection and promotion.

The movement of the capital from Nara to Kyoto led to the establishment of a new national university late in the eighth century. During the ninth, tenth, and eleventh centuries, however, private educational institutions made the most important contributions to scholarship. Powerful nobles in the provinces as well as in the capital established and subsidized private schools to educate the

[5] *Ibid.*, p. 81.
[6] Japan, Department of Education, *An Outline History of Japanese Education,* Appleton, New York, 1876, p. 38.
[7] *Ibid.*, p. 83.

youth of their clans. Arts and literature flourished under Buddhist and lay teachers, but concurrently, as private education gained in status, state schools lost significance.

It should be emphasized that the Japanese culture was undergoing many changes from the seventh to the twelfth century. Because of Japan's favorable geographic position, culture contact with China was relatively easy, and yet the stretch of water between the two nations was wide enough to minimize dangers of a Chinese invasion. Japanese students returning from Chinese embassies made important contributions to literary, legal, administrative, and architectural learning. Korean immigrants with their advanced knowledge of temple building likewise made a strong contribution in the field of architecture.

Chinese learning was put to good use but modified as the situation demanded. Learning from the Chinese the value of accurate historical records, Japanese scholars produced the *Kojiki* in A.D. 712 and the *Nihonshoki* in A.D. 720, which together with subsequent volumes comprised the official court histories. In poetry the *Manyoshu*, a collection of over 4,500 poems, has remained a classic to the present day. Such literary and historical efforts, while influenced by the Chinese style, gradually stimulated the Japanese to seek indigenous patterns. Japanese court society during the tenth and eleventh centuries exhibited high artistic and literary creativeness. As one source has noted:

. . . the higher culture of the Fujiwara demonstrated a complete and natural blend of now thoroughly assimilated Chinese elements and earlier native tendencies from which grew distinctive new trends in the fine arts and literature and a uniquely Japanese art of living.[8]

Bushido: Way of the warrior

The twelfth through the sixteenth centuries constitute what is often called the medieval period of Japan. Strong clans carved out huge estates and engaged in open conflict with one another and with the Imperial court. Even the great Buddhist temples formed their own armies for protection—or in some cases, for aggression. As power shifted from the cultivated Kyoto court to the rude feudal clans, scholarship and learning declined. By 1300 most of the great centers of learning had closed their doors for lack of students. And had it not been for the foresight and effort of interested Buddhist monks, the fruits of Japanese scholarship might have been completely lost.

During this turbulent period there developed a warrior class and a new kind of training in keeping with the needs of the changing times. Because success in the arts of war was necessary for individual as well as clan survival, fighting skills instead of literary or aesthetic pursuits came to be prized. For the fighting man a special education, in both the home and the school, and a special code of conduct gradually took form. Like the knights of medieval Europe, the Japanese warriors were required to go through a long and arduous training period and demonstrate devotion to their cause. Any further parallel drawn between these two historically important but overromanticized groups of fighting men would prove forced, however. The

[8] Edwin O. Reischauer and John K. Fairbank, *East Asia: The Great Tradition,* Houghton Mifflin, Boston, 1960, p. 506.

Japanese warrior, although possibly a devout Buddhist was never inspired to battle by religious fervor. And certainly any self-respecting Japanese warrior would have been amazed as well as embarrassed at the thought of doing battle to win a lady's favor.

The term now used to describe the chivalric code of the Japanese fighting men which developed during this period is Bushido (literally, military-knight-ways). The sources of Bushido were Confucianism, Shintoism, and Buddhism. Buddhism, more particularly the Zen sect, contributed:

> . . . a sense of calm trust in Fate, a quiet submission to the inevitable, that stoic composure in sight of dangers or calamity, that disdain of life and friendliness with death.[9]

From Shintoism came a sense of loyalty to the sovereign and reverence for ancestors. Confucianism, in addition to lending weight to the contributions of Shintoism, made its peculiar and very important contribution by furnishing the warrior with disciplined social ways and a sophisticated ethical system.

The members of the professional class of warriors were called "bushi" (fighting knights) or more commonly in recent literature, "samurai." The development of character, achievement of fighting skill, and acquisition of knowledge, in that order, were the educational goals of these fighting men. The virtues needed in molding character were courage, benevolence, politeness, truthfulness, honor, loyalty, and self control.[10] Consequently, the curriculum for train-

ing the samurai consisted of fencing, archery, jujitsu, horsemanship, the use of the spear, tactics, calligraphy, ethics, literature, and history. The samurai quite obviously was a man of action, and scholarship unrelated to personal conduct or the art of war was of little interest to him. He did, however, study the Confucian Classics, but he studied these for moral purposes rather than for their profundity of scholarship or fine literary style. The success of many samurai in attaining the high ethical standards of their code is attested to in numerous Japanese romances as well as in biographical accounts.

The lasting imprint of Bushido on the character of the Japanese people has been apparent to most students of Japan. One avowed apologist for Bushido wrote at the turn of the twentieth century:

> . . . Bushido, the maker and product of Old Japan, is still the guiding principle of the transition and will prove the formative force of the new era. . . . The great statesmen who steered the ship of our state through the hurricane of the Restoration and the whirlpool of national rejuvenation, were men who knew no other moral teaching than the Precepts of Knighthood.[11]

Shogunate to restoration

One author equates the establishment of the Tokugawa shogunate, A.D. 1603, with the beginning of the Japanese *universal state*, that is, the period of unification that some historians believe to typically follow the time of troubles and warfare in the development of civiliza-

[9] Inazo Nitobe, *Bushido: The Soul of Japan*, Shokwabo, Tokyo, 1901, p. 7.
[10] *Ibid.*, pp. 18–50.
[11] *Ibid.*, pp. 115–116.

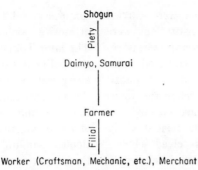

Figure 33. The Feudal Class Structure of Japan
The class structure of feudal Japan differed in one important respect from that of China. In China the scholar-officials traditionally formed the highest social class while in pre-Meiji Japan the shoguns, and to a lesser degree, daimyos (feudal lords) and samurai (warriors) held the upper positions. Certain scholars and moralists argued that in Japan more than in China the force of filial piety, theoretically two-directional, provided the unifying thread which could transcend class structure and reduce interclass conflicts.

tion.[12] The justification for this claim lies in the fact that it was the shoguns (military leaders) of the Tokugawa clan who brought peace and reunification to Japan after centuries of feudal strife. (See Figure 33 for an interpretation of the class structure in feudal Japan.) Tokugawa rule lasted for some two hundred and fifty relatively tranquil years, during which the arts of peace flourished as never before. It was a period which saw the creation of a new orthodoxy through the wide acceptance of the social and political ideas of Neo-Confucianism. Yet it was also a time when Japanese were intent on keeping out foreign peoples and foreign ideas. Failure to maintain this isolation coincided with the end of Tokugawa rule.

When the Tokugawa shoguns won the military elimination contest and found themselves ruling Japan, they immediately gave attention to ideological tools

[12] Edward D. Myers, *Education in the Perspective of History,* Harper, New York, 1960, p. 150.

to assist in strengthening their rule. Confucianism, because of its secular quality, seemed far more acceptable than the otherworldly Buddhist theology and once again Confucian studies became popular for the sons of Japanese aristocracy, and Confucian scholars played a leading role in shaping the laws and edicts promulgated by successive shoguns. During the medieval period students seeking Confucian learning usually had to do so under the Buddhist clergy. Now, with government support ensured, Confucian scholars began to discard their clerical robes and establish themselves as lay teachers. Ceremonies were initiated throughout Japan in honor of the sage and, as never before, a respect for Confucian learning was disseminated among all classes.

The period of the Tokugawa shogunate saw a great rebirth of Japanese literary and scientific studies as well as increased attention to the Chinese Classics. Under the patronage of successive shoguns monumental historical and genealogical studies were carried out and new literary institutions were established. Japanese literature was revived, ancient poetry collected, new forms experimented with, and painstaking efforts made to refine the Japanese language. The sciences of medicine and astronomy—and its related study "calendrical science"—received scholarly consideration and were developed to new heights. Yet in all these studies, both scientific and literary, restrictions of birth drastically limited educational opportunities to the upper classes.

Significant changes also took place in the education of the samurai. Feudal lords established and sometimes even made compulsory clan (han) schools open only to sons of samurai. Previously, to the samurai, acquisition of extensive book learning was considered only a fit pastime for the effete and was thought to be only slightly more honorable than seeking pecuniary reward for one's labor. During the eighteenth century, however, voices were raised urging the samurai to master the arts of peace as well as the arts of war. Many samurai heeded this call and devoted themselves to literary and historical scholarship with their customary vigor. As they became skillful in the "arts of peace" they took over teaching positions and civil administrative posts. The samurai turned scholars became a faction to be dealt with during the nineteenth-century Japanese political and social revolution.

But factors other than a new spirit of learning were giving the samurai incentive to enter into productive and peaceful pursuits. As the wealth shifted from the great feudal estates to the new class of town and city merchants, the

samurai found a variety of economically attractive opportunities open to them. The later Tokugawa shoguns recognized the political expedience of assisting in every way possible the establishment of the samurai as responsible members in the emerging society, and by the end of the Tokugawa period the once functionless samurai had become active in the government, army, and police and had formed a core of the rising business class.

The education of the samurai during the latter part of the shogunate strongly reflected Neo-Confucian influence. The formal instruction of a samurai boy was begun between the ages of six and nine. Like the young Chinese boy, he spent his first years of schooling copying Chinese characters and learning their pronunciation and meaning. By the age of nine he was expected to have memorized about one thousand characters and have some knowledge of the easier portions of the Chinese Classics. During these first few years of study, in keeping with the traditional Japanese view, emphasis was placed on morals and etiquette. Passages for reading were selected from such Chinese works as the *Book of Filial Piety* on the basis of the moral lessons described. At the age of nine, students entered more advanced study of the Chinese Classics and Chinese and Japanese history. This second stage of education might be prolonged indefinitely depending on the interest and obligations of the student.[13]

The shogunate government gave direct support to several important educational institutions. A famous school,

[13] Hugh Keenleyside and A. F. Thomas, *History of Japanese Education,* Hokuseido Press, Tokyo, 1937, pp. 52–53.

Shoheiko, for the advanced study of the Chinese Classics was founded in 1630 and restricted to the sons of high officials. The Shoheiko provided inspiration and served as a model for Confucian schools of lesser quality founded in other parts of the country.

Under the Tokugawa shogunate, in spite of restrictive laws, intercourse with the West did exist. The Dutch had established a small trading post at Nagasaki early in the seventeenth century and, though confined to this area, taught their language to a few curious Japanese. Thus a small breach was made in Japan's wall of isolation and the first Western learning began to seep in. Impetus to the spread of Western ideas was brought about by the arrival of Christian missionaries in the mid-sixteenth century.

After a series of early successes Christianity increasingly began to run afoul of the Japanese government. The refusal of the Christian missionaries to recognize value in the native faiths and their open contempt for the divine pretentions of the Imperial Family provoked anger from the increasingly nationalistic Japanese. Then, too, many of the Japanese leaders were highly suspicious of such Christian ideas as the brotherhood of man and equality of all people under the Fatherhood of God. Most of all, however, the ambitious Japanese leaders feared that Christian teaching and direct meddling on the part of missionaries might result in serious political opposition to their plans. Although Nobunaga and, for a time, Hideyoshi gave protection to the Christians, the later shoguns carried out a series of repressive measures which culminated in 1638 in the massacre of a group of some 37,000

Christians and various enemies of the Tokugawas who, for economic, political, or religious reasons, were in rebellion against the shogunate. Little overt expression of Christianity existed in Japan from this date until 1858 when the country was thrown open to foreign intercourse.

Unsuccessful though the missionaries had been in their evangelical attempts, they were successful in making a few Japanese scholars curious about Western learning. Indeed, some of the shoguns became so interested that they urged the Dutch to bring them the products of the scholarship from the different countries. During the eighteenth century, with the encouragement of the far-sighted eighth shogun, foreign books, except those dealing with religion, were permitted to enter Japan. An astronomical observatory was built in 1744 and three decades later two Japanese doctors succeeded in translating a Dutch anatomy book, a move which was destined to revolutionize Japanese medicine. The Japanese were particularly impressed with the Dutch works on medicine, physics, and other natural sciences. Yet the few that dared to study these did so at great personal danger, for in spite of support from an occasional leader, antiforeignism in Japan still had deep roots.

All the educational activities under the shogunate thus far described involved only the upper classes. As for the common people, there were some special provisions for education, largely through the facilities of numerous private schools called *terakoya*. Where there was sufficient wealth for support, and this was primarily among certain farmers, merchants, and town families, *terakoya* were founded to teach the reading and writing of a few Chinese ideographs. Other lessons consisted of rudimentary geography, history, and arithmetic—with the total curriculum having a decidedly moral flavor. When financial circumstances permitted, the sons and occasionally the daughters also were able to obtain this basic instruction. In addition to this elementary education there were two other important ways that the average Japanese learned something of his cultural heritage. There was the traditional custom of making frequent pilgrimages to national shrines under the guidance of an experienced leader and the popular institution of the professional storyteller, an itinerant entertainer who traveled about the country giving graphic accounts of historical deeds.[14]

A special word should be said about the education of girls during the shogunate rule. Daughters of the samurai families received some instruction in reading and writing, but the emphasis of their education, like that of all Japanese girls during this period, was to prepare "good wives and clever mothers." Instruction in sewing, flower arrangement, and the charmingly ritualistic tea ceremony were also popular for girls from families of means. The final educational goal for girls was, then, preparation for their rather circumscribed adult roles. In last analysis education was supposed to inculcate the virtues of chastity and obedience, for in Japanese tradition, every girl must obey her parents when she is young, her husband when she is married, and her son when she is old.

The most important educational de-

[14] Dairoku Kikuchi, *Japanese Education,* J. Murray, London, 1909, pp. 39–41.

velopments under the Tokugawa shogunate were two largely incompatible movements. The first was the renewed interest in Confucianism, actually Neo-Confucianism, which in time blossomed into a minor renaissance in learning. Neo-Confucianism was decidedly antiforeign in outlook and yet in its rationalism was laid the foundation for the later acceptance of Western scientific studies. The second movement, one which gained little momentum until the latter part of the period, was the expanding interest in Occidental scholarship—an interest which acted as a harbinger of a new era.

Modern education

The small breaches in Japan's isolation in the eighteenth century were forced wider in the nineteenth century. In 1808 a foreign language school offering English was opened, followed soon by schools for other languages.[15] In 1838 a medical school was established which gave instruction in the Dutch language and used Dutch textbooks. Meanwhile, a few bold young Japanese, by stowing away on European ships which had been trading through the port of Nagasaki, were able to make firsthand contact with foreign culture and bring home strange but appealing tales of the material advancement of the West. The timely arrival of Commodore Perry and his "Black Ships" in 1853 and 1854 proved to be the crucial blow in opening Japan's doors to the Western world.

[15] Yet even as late as 1835, the tutor of Yukichi Fukuzawa, who was to become one of Japan's most famous admirers of Western culture, was dismissed for daring to instruct his student in the multiplication tables.

The Tokugawa regime found itself being criticized, on the one hand, by those who felt that the Emperor's wishes were being subverted by allowing Western culture to gain a foothold and, on the other, by those who believed that the modernization of Japanese institutions was not taking place fast enough. In the face of heavy criticism Keiki Tokugawa, in 1867, relinquished his power to Emperor Meiji (then but fifteen years old). Thus, after some seven hundred years as titular rulers, the Imperial Family regained preeminence.

Goals of the Meiji regime

From the beginning of the Meiji era in 1868, there came, in rapid succession, a series of laws which were to set the goals and outline the functions of the modern Japanese state and its educational system. It is significant that in the very same year that the restoration began, a statement regarding education was included in the Imperial Oath of Five Articles, edicts which were established to guide the Emperor's reign. The Article on Education read: "Knowledge shall be sought throughout the world, so that the welfare of the empire may be promoted."[16] Yet even the word of the Emperor was not sufficient to completely eliminate the strong animosity toward things foreign. And as many vivid accounts tell, for years after the opening of the Meiji period Japanese scholars and statesmen who sought the promotion of Western learning and customs were constantly in danger of physical harm.

The fundamental objectives of the movement which saw the restoration of power to the Imperial throne have been summarized as ". . . national unification, unquestioning loyalty, an acquirement of modern scientific and economic techniques, and a perfection of national defense."[17] Japanese leaders sought to reinstill in the people a clear understanding of their divine origin and divinely inspired responsibilities. Since Japan was singularly blessed by its founder, the Sun-Goddess, its people must gracefully wear in peace or, if need be, in holy war the mantle which had been bestowed on them. To weld the Japanese people together and make them of singular purpose in carrying out these goals would be the task of the Emperor in whose person the political and legal, as well as the spiritual, leadership was focused.

Importation of Western ideas

Immediately after the restoration, three important educational institutions in Tokyo were reopened. These were the Shoheiko where Japanese and Chinese literature was studied, the Kaiseijo where European languages and sciences were taught, and the Igakujo where Western medicine was studied. Within the first five years of the Meiji period several other schools of significance, including a girls' school and a teacher training institution, were opened throughout the country. As further indication of the seriousness of the leaders in carrying out the proposed reforms, a distinct department in the national government, titled Department of Education (Mombusho), was created in 1871 and vested with all powers related to education. This new and powerful body was

16 Kikuchi, *op. cit.*, p. 45.

17 Keenleyside and Thomas, *op. cit.*, p. 72.

charged with full responsibility in all educational matters concerning public schooling.[18]

In keeping with the goal of seeking knowledge throughout the world the Japanese government sent numerous bright young Imperial princes and samurai to study in Europe and America and invited Western experts and teachers to Japan. Educational laws, textbooks, teaching methods, and even school plant designs were at first indiscriminately borrowed from Europe and America. The following account illustrates the degree to which foreign education was imitated:

> . . . The Minister of Education gave instruction to the American teacher that he was not to think of adapting his teaching to the Japanese, but was to teach just as he would at home. In consequence of this, spelling books, wall diagrams, etc., were made entirely after an American model, the only difference being the substitution of the Japanese alphabet for the American.[19]

Japanese and Western spokesmen have sometimes summarized Japan's imitation of foreign practices by stating that when Japan sought Western ideas she copied her navy from Great Britain, her army from France, and her educational system from America.[20] Like most historical generalizations, however, this statement needs considerable modification. In selecting a highly centralized organizational structure with a strong ministry of education, Japan had been influenced by the French tradition. The initial educational plan after the restora-

tion called for the division of the nation into 8 university districts, each district having 1 university. The university districts were further divided into 32 middle school districts, which in turn were subdivided into 210 primary school districts. This decidedly French arrangement was soon replaced by a more decentralized system which placed the financial as well as the moral obligations for education with the local communities. Since both local initiative and local control were foreign to the Japanese, this pattern likewise proved to be a failure and a process of partial recentralization of educational responsibilities was begun.

In addition to influencing the abortive plan for decentralized educational control, American educational ideas were strongly felt in the areas of curriculum, teacher education, and teaching methods. German influence on Japanese education was also felt, partly, in fact, in opposition to the American practices. During the second and third decades of the Meiji period some opposition was voiced against the individualism, pragmatism, and utilitarianism of American educational thought. German idealism and moralism seemed more in keeping with the Japanese character, and German professors increasingly were sought to replace the Americans lecturing at the honored Tokyo Imperial University, the university which set the pattern for higher education. Significantly, when the Japanese Constitution was being written in 1889, a model was sought in Germany rather than in America.

Preserving the Japanese Way

The Japanese government, while seeking to modernize its institutions, also sought to perpetuate the historic Japanese Way.

[18] Japan, Department of Education, *op. cit.*, p. 122.
[19] Kikuchi, *op. cit.*, p. 67.
[20] Keenleyside and Thomas, *op. cit.*, p. 84.

To this end, beginning during the latter part of the Tokugawa period, elaborate steps were taken for the revivification and purification of Shinto. Steps were also taken to delineate the boundaries between Shinto as a state faith and sect or Sectarian Shinto. State Shinto, officially instituted in 1868, representing in part a classical revival and in part a political necessity, did not countenance the wide variety of beliefs or the extensive folklore and magical rites found in Sectarian Shinto.

To promote State Shinto, and thereby strengthen the important policy of *Saisei itchi* (the unity of government and religion) certain shrines throughout the country were designated as state shrines. On official dates the Japanese people were expected to gather at these in worship of the Japanese deities, the spirits of loyal subjects, or the spirits of natural phenomena such as mountains, streams, forests, and the like. According to official government policy, however, worship at the shrines did not constitute a religious act. Rather, since the shrines were public sanctuaries—that is, they were administered and financed by the national government—visits to them could be considered equivalent to an American's visit to the Lincoln Memorial or a Frenchman's to l'Arc de Triomphe. Because of the depth of the religious experience at the shrine ceremonies and the widely accepted faith among the Japanese people in the divine beings of the shrines, most Western scholars consider this analogy a bit farfetched.

By distinguishing Shinto as a state cult from Shinto as a religion, Japanese authorities sought to convince the world and some of the more recalcitrant of the Japanese people that one's duty as a citizen requires submission and obliga-

tions to national traditions while personal religious beliefs may at the same time be retained. The installation of Shinto did prove a valuable weapon in promoting a unity of purpose among Japanese institutions; yet native religious groups and the recently returned Christian missionaries interpreted this action as a breach of religious freedom. Understandably, such rituals as worship of the Sun-Goddess at the national shrines and the belief in the divinity of the Emperor soon proved to be incompatible with the convictions of many Buddhists and Christians. With its penchant for rationalization, Buddhism was able to take advantage of its philosophical flexibility and continue its programs without extensive open conflict with Shinto. Catholicism, by accepting at face value the official statements of the Japanese government, could also make its peace with Shinto. Other Christian sects did not find compromise so easy, and to many Protestants, worship of Christ prohibited the obeisances required by Shinto ritual. Indeed, outstanding non-Christian Japanese scholars also pointed out the incompatibility of Christianity with the national policy of Japan. The unity, loyalty, and obedience which were the foundation of national well-being were being undermined, it was said, by the loyalties required by the Christian church. Inasmuch as modern Christianity places unusual emphasis on the individual, subjugating him in matters of faith only to God, conflict with Shinto was very real.

The 1890 Imperial Rescript

It has already been seen that the early years of the Meiji period were a time when old traditions and ideals were being rudely cast aside. Young iconoclasts

311

and liberal statesmen were forcing social and educational changes at such a rapid pace that for a time it appeared that Japan would lose its cultural identity. Some Japanese leaders, including the Emperor, sought measures to keep the true Japanese spirit alive and in practice by formulating a statement of the principles underlying the education of Japanese children and youth. In 1890 such a statement, the historic Imperial Rescript on Education, was issued by the Emperor. This document contained the educational principles which were to guide Japan until the end of World War II.

The Rescript on Education[21] set the goals for all Japanese school leaders to follow and, in parallel action, Mombusho decreed that increased emphasis should be placed on ethical instruction in the lower grades; indeed the basic purpose of the elementary school was defined as character building, and educational institutions of all levels were called on to give considerable attention to moral education. The moral principles contained in the Rescript are an interesting combination of Confucian teachings and Shinto theology. Reverence for ancestors, filial piety, loyalty to the state, and Emperor worship are all combined within an absolutist framework. As the basic statement of educational philosophy during the Meiji era, great homage was paid to the document by statesmen and scholars alike. Over the years commentaries in great number and volume were written on it, reminiscent of similar treatment of the early Chinese Classics. In schools throughout the Japanese Empire the Rescript was treated

[21] Several of the references found at the end of the chapter (e.g., Anderson, Kikuchi, etc.) contain translations of the brief Rescript.

as sacred and was read with considerable pomp and ritual by the school principals at all student assemblies. Stories are told of teachers losing their lives in attempting to rescue the Rescript from burning school buildings.

Growth in effort

The profundity of the change that took place in Japan during the last half of the nineteenth century must be emphasized. Perhaps never before in history had a few leaders of a nation built such a specific blueprint and then through unified, concentrated effort fulfilled the specifications. Yet as has been indicated, even during these times of great change perceptive leaders took dramatic and successful steps to preserve the national character of the people. Education was used as the key in both the modernization and Westernization of Japan as well as an important instrument in the preservation of the traditional spiritual and moral values. It is difficult to summarize the specific educational changes during this period because of the large number of ideas and procedures that were tested, found unworkable, and discarded. Generally however, Japan, through a system of centralized administration and control, attempted to promote free compulsory elementary schooling (four years before 1907 and six years after) for children of both sexes. Above the elementary grades, schooling was both intellectually and economically selective. At the secondary level students could select any of several tracks, only one of which could lead to university education, with all other routes leading to a terminal technical, normal, or general culture institution. At the pinnacle of the academic ladder stood a series of Imperial universities, including one each in Korea and Formosa. Entrance to any Imperial university was the prize most sought by erstwhile students, with acceptance to Tokyo Imperial University being the greatest reward of all.

The curriculum of the Japanese schools at all levels reflected the twin goals of modernization and unification. The elementary grades stressed the three R's, moral education, music, and Japanese history and offered an introduction to practical arts. In the academic middle school—provisions called for at least one in every province—boys received advanced general education as befitting those of "middle or higher social standing."[22] Studies offered in the middle schools included languages (Japanese and one foreign), Chinese literature, social sciences, natural sciences, mathematics, moral education, and physical education. The higher schools for girls, equivalent in grade level to the first four years of the boys' middle schools, offered approximately the same curriculum except that less stress was put on the natural sciences, and extensive time was devoted to domestic arts. At the highly select Imperial universities, entering students enrolled in one of the professional colleges, such as law, medicine, engineering, agriculture, or possibly literature or science.

A few statistics will show the truly tremendous educational effort made in the Meiji era. Even in the face of a rapidly growing population the percentage of children of school age receiving elementary education rose from 25 per cent in 1871 to 46 per cent in 1886 and to 95 per cent in 1906.[23] Secondary

education, well into the twentieth century, continued to be the privilege of a few; however, its growth was only slightly less dramatic. There were only 20 middle schools in 1873, while in 1901 there were 216 boys' middle schools and 70 girls' high schools. Similar expansion can be documented in higher education, vocational education, and adult and special education. Libraries, museums, and other institutions involved directly or indirectly with the education of youth and adults were likewise rapidly on the increase.

It should be emphasized that the Meiji era with all its educational growth and social effort represented primarily a modernization, not a democratization, of the Japanese nation. By the abolition of the Tokugawa shogunate a unified government was created to be led, theoretically, by the Emperor. Yet, in fact the authority of the Emperor was little changed; he again was hardly more than the titular head of the nation; the real power now lay with a small elite group of aggressive business, military, and government leaders.

Imperialism and education

Japan's modern military imperialism may be dated from the successful skirmishes with the Russian naval forces in 1905. During this same year Japan quietly assumed control of Korea and incorporated this nation into the Japanese Empire. Economically Japan was also on the march and it called on other Asiatic nations to join in a Greater East Asia Co-prosperity Sphere. Thus Japan embarked on a program of territorial and economic expansion which was to bring the nation into conflict with all major Asian powers and eventually nearly all of the major Western nations.

[22] Kikuchi, *op. cit.*, p. 205.
[23] G. B. Sansom, *The Western World and Japan*, Knopf, New York, 1950, p. 406. Some Japanese sources give the 1906 enrollment percentage a little higher.

The imperialistic venture was to last until its disastrous and humiliating finish in World War II.

Japan's march toward imperialism was interrupted only briefly by a flurry of liberalism immediately following World War I. For a few postwar years, especially at the universities, there was a demonstrated interest in the meaning of democracy and individualism. Translations of liberal European and American thinkers became popular among the intellectual circles. Dewey, Kilpatrick, and other progressive educators made visits to Japan and contributed to a new period of dynamic educational thought. Within a few years, however, Japan succumbed again to chauvinism and militarism. The brief liberal cure was all but ephemeral while the relapse seemed to have permanent qualities.

From 1931, when Japanese troops entered Manchuria, until the end of World War II, educational goals were increasingly subordinated to military interests. Only a decade after John Dewey had lectured to attentive Japanese audiences on the philosophic basis of democracy, Mombusho began to put into operation a tight plan of thought control. Japanese universities during the 1930s, caught as they were in a fervor of patriotism, ceased to subscribe to international journals—evidently afraid that the logic of Western criticism of Japanese militarism might prove a dangerous influence for Japanese students. As one author aptly put it, "Loyalty and patriotism were considered the highest virtues; individualism, internationalism and pacifism were allied with treason."[24] Nationalism was thus be-

[24] Ronald S. Anderson, *Japan: Three Epochs of Modern Education,* U.S. Office of Education, 1959, p. 18.

314

coming ultranationalism. The ultranationalists feared that Japan was becoming too Western in outlook, and although they urged expansion abroad they pressured for orthodoxy at home. In this setting State Shinto with its quasi-religious characteristics and its doctrine of racial superiority proved a powerful tool for promoting unity through patriotism. Still, however, the Japanese political and military leaders were not completely united in judging which political and social course was appropriate for their nation.

As on several previous occasions, the national government sought to enunciate the unique national polity of Japan in order that the people might better plan their part in the nation's destined future. In 1937 the Bureau of Thought Control of the Ministry of Education published a short work which was designed to clarify the ideological course of the people. Although now little known, this remarkable book, entitled *Kokutai no Hongi* (*Fundamentals of Our National Polity*), had an eventual sale of at least two million copies and was widely discussed throughout the nation. *Kokutai no Hongi* reiterated many of the themes expressed in proclamations issued during earlier periods of Meiji reign. The transcendant importance of the Japanese nation and state, the inviolateness of the Emperor, the vital significance of filial piety, and the responsibilities of patriotism were all analyzed once again for the Japanese people. Much attention was also given in this document to contrasting Western ideology with the Japanese Way, and many passages pointed out for the Japanese public the reasons why the rationalistic and positivistic ideas imported from Europe and America were incompatible with Japanese traditions. Suspect was the Western concept of individualism and the related doctrines of personal liberty and equality, for to the Japanese the role of the individual is inextricably tied to the intrinsic nature of the society.

With regard to education, *Kokutai no Hongi* again warned of the dangers of individualism.

> Education whose object is the cultivation of the creative faculties of individuals or the development of individual characteristics is liable to be biased toward individuals and to be led by individual inclinations, and in the long run to fall into an unplanned education, and so to run counter to the principles of the education of our country.[25]

However, no suggestions were made in *Kokutai no Hongi* to give less attention to the scientific and technical studies borrowed from the West. These should stay in the schools, but at the same time the traditional aesthetic and moral pursuits should not be avoided. Even the unnecessarily awkward Japanese language, although it might prove to be a handicap to the nation's rapid technical development, was justified on the basis that it was a reflection of the Japanese Way. In sum, the authors of *Kokutai no Hongi* admitted that the analytical and intellectual qualities of Western learning could continue to enrich Japanese culture. However, the group unity of the people and the aesthetic and intuitive qualities of Japanese life must be preserved at all costs—even at the price of exclusion of whole areas of Western knowledge.

[25] Robert King Hall (ed.), *Kokutai no Hongi,* translated by John O. Gauntlett, Harvard, Cambridge, Mass., 1949, p. 155.

Allied occupation

The military occupation of Japan after its defeat in World War II has sometimes been described as a happy experience for both the conqueror and the conquered. The Allies, primarily Americans, whose duty it was to establish a military government to rule Japan, were surprised at the docility of the Japanese. The Japanese, remembering years of virulent propaganda, expected only the harshest of treatment from their barbaric enemies and were pleased when their fears proved wrong. This peaceful but uneasy situation raised significant questions on both sides. Why did the Japanese prove to be so cooperative? Were they really sincere or merely acquiescing in face of the military might of the victor? How sincere were the Americans and how qualified were they to bring democracy and not merely Americanism to Japan? On the answers to such questions hinge any valid interpretation of the depth of postwar changes in Japan.

The Americans, at least officially, and one may suspect often individually, held the view that the Japanese people now freed from their military masters, who had "deceived" and "misled" them, were able to select their own way of life and eagerly were seeking democracy. Such an analysis, while containing some truth, is obviously too naïve to provide the basic answer. Undoubtedly multiple explanations are needed to fully understand the actions of the Japanese during the period of occupation, but perhaps the best single interpretation lies in what has been termed the "situational ethics" of the Japanese:

> Whereas Western civilization has developed a universalistic ethic which

regards all men as equal in the sight of God and before law, Eastern civilizations with their polytheistic concept of the divinity and their pluralistic concept of society regard human relationships as particularistic and specific. That is to say, while in the West all relations between individuals must ideally be reconciled with the universal principle of a common humanity, in the East what is proper in the relations between two individuals in a given situation is considered intrinsically different from what is proper in another situation or between other individuals.[26]

Thus the average Japanese, in spite of his divinely ordered life, had no valid guides for this new situation in which he found himself. In his uncertainty he welcomed the set of rules handed to him by the military government. That is, he welcomed them until the time when a new set of rules, less foreign, became available.

The new constitution and the fundamental law

The major action taken to ensure the individual liberties requisite to a democratic state was the establishment, in 1946, of a new constitution for the Japanese nation. The principles stated in the constitution and the manner in which the constitution came into being mark the most controversial event of the occupation period. Officially the new constitution was said to have been conceived and written by Japanese statesmen, approved by the Supreme Command Allied Powers (SCAP), and

[26] Kazuo Kawai, *Japan's American Interlude,* The University of Chicago Press, Chicago, 1960, p. 4.

adopted, after open debate, by the Japanese Diet. There is sufficient evidence now available, however, to indicate that the constitution was drafted by SCAP with little or no initial consultation with Japanese leaders. This action had a disastrous effect on the Japanese, who had assumed that in the spirit of democracy the modification of the old constitution or the drafting of a new one would be primarily the responsibility of the Japanese themselves. That foreigners whose cultural heritage was so different from their own and whose knowledge of Japan was extremely superficial should be so presumptuous as to interpret the principles by which they should live was inconceivable to Japanese intellectuals. This rather heavy-handed method of imposition caused many Japanese to question the integrity of SCAP, and in the postoccupation years voices were often raised which urged abolishment of the "MacArthur Constitution"—a symbol of foreign domination.

The most important provisions of the new constitution included the reduction of the role of the Emperor to a mere symbol of the state. Sovereign power henceforth was to reside in the people. Also included in the constitution were "inalienable" rights regarding civil liberties, provisions for local autonomy, permanent demilitarization, and an enhanced role for the judiciary as a guardian of the new freedoms. While many of these forward-looking concepts were readily acceptable to Japanese liberals, a basic difficulty thwarted both the understanding and the acceptance of the document. The new constitution, by placing sovereignty with the people rather than with the Emperor, had arbitrarily changed the historic character of Japan. Rarely had the Emperors actu-

Basic Educational Policy: Old and New

Imperial Rescript (1890)	Fundamental Law of Education (1947)
Nature of Society	
Society based on Confucian hierarchical relationships.	Society based on "mutual esteem and cooperation."
Nature of State	
Divine empire founded by imperial ancestors.	"A democratic and cultural State," built by the people.
Relation of Citizens to State	
Citizens have the *duty* to develop their intellectual and moral faculties, observe the laws, and offer themselves courageously to the State in order to guard and maintain the prosperity of the Imperial throne.	Citizens have the *right* to "equal opportunity of receiving education according to their ability"; freedom from "discrimination on account of race, creed, sex, social status, economic position, or family origin"; financial assistance to the able needy; "academic freedom"; and the *responsibility* to build a "peaceful State and society."
Aim of Education	
To promote loyalty to the Emperor and filial piety, thus to achieve unity of the people under father-Emperor.	To promote "full development of personality"; "esteem individual value"; and "be imbued with independent spirit."[27]

ally ruled Japan, yet in their persons sovereignty had been kept "unbroken for ages eternal." The Emperor had been the theoretical source of authority and had thus occupied the apex of a strict hierarchical system through which authority was disseminated downward and loyalty given upward. Many Japanese argued that Japan could democratize without doing damage to its historic Way.

Building on the general principles enunciated in the new constitution, basic laws were established governing the various institutions of the state. In 1947 the Fundamental Law of Education, embodying most of the progressive recommendations of American and Japanese educators, was passed by the Diet. In its spirit and stated philosophy this law

represented a chapter for "new education" in Japan. One author, recognizing that this law bore a significance to postwar Japan not unlike that held during the Meiji era by the Imperial Rescript on Education, has offered the above interesting contrasts in the two laws.

The most significant contrast between the 1947 educational law and that promulgated in 1890 has been correctly identified by Anderson as the goal of individual development. Clearly the individual, and not the family, was now perceived as the basic unit of society. Under the new constitution the individual was assigned new responsibilities and the Fundamental Law of Education spelled out the role of the schools

[27] Anderson, *op. cit.*, p. 26.

in preparing the young Japanese for them. Equal educational opportunity (limited only by ability), guarantee of academic freedom, and free public education for nine years were all seen as requisite to intelligent citizenship and were included in the new law.

Occupation and postoccupation policies

The basic concern of the Allied Powers with relation to Japanese education at the end of World War II was to erase the ultranationalistic and militaristic coloring from the educational goals and the curriculum. Concomitantly, SCAP was vitally concerned in assisting the Japanese in building an educational system appropriate for a democratic nation. In keeping with these purposes a series of educational reforms were initiated by Allied educational advisers, all of which, with an exception to be mentioned later, bore the official approval of the Japanese educational authorities. The changes, temporary though some of them were—lasting no longer than the time limit of the occupation (1945–1952)—have an important place in the pages of Japanese education history. For purposes of discussion the reforms initiated by SCAP can be classified into five categories: *demilitarization, individualization, decentralization, extension of educational opportunity,* and *language and other curricular reforms.* In helping the Japanese reformulate their educational goals, SCAP placed considerable reliance on the recommendations of the United States Education Mission, a group of highly distinguished American educators who had been invited by SCAP to study Japan's postwar educational needs. After spending only one month in Japan in early 1946 the Education Mission recommended many reforms, among which the most significant are the following:

1. Elimination of the multiple-track system and introduction of the single-track (6-3-3-4) system

2. Decentralization of control and administration of the schools

3. Encouragement of individual and creative instruction to replace the traditional pattern of memorization, drill, and recitation; the social studies program, guidance and extracurricular activities to replace the prewar courses in moral education

4. Extension of educational opportunity; establishment of coeducation at all levels and compulsory education through grade nine

5. Simplification of the Japanese language by the introduction of some form of Romaji.[28]

Although some of these recommendations had been made earlier by Japanese educators, and moreover, the members of the Education Mission did carry on extensive discussions with Japanese educators before making their final report, nevertheless, all these recommendations quite obviously bear the stamp of American educational commitments. The educational offices of SCAP referred the report to the Japanese Education Committee (later to become the Japanese Education Reform Council) which drew up a new but similar report to submit to Mombusho. All the suggestions of the Education Mission with the excep-

[28] *Report of the United States Education Mission to Japan,* U.S. Government Printing Office, 1946.

tion of those relating to language were incorporated into educational law and became a part of the postwar educational scene.

Responsibility for implementing these postwar educational changes was held by SCAP; but early in the occupation, channels were provided for cooperative planning with Japanese educators. Personnel from the Civil Information and Education Section of the Military Government usually were in contact with members of the Japanese Education Reform Council, a group of representative Japanese educators which, because of its successful work, had been raised to cabinet status. The Council became a powerful spokesman for "new education," and its advice to the Minister of Education carried considerable weight. After the first few months of the occupation, during which time most changes were made by Allied directive, many of the later and most far-reaching reforms were the result of recommendations from the Council. Although responsibility for policy and, hence, power of veto remained with SCAP, increasingly during the occupation educational change became Japanese-initiated if not entirely Japanese-conceived.

Demilitarization and individualization

The initial postwar policy as promulgated by SCAP said of education:

Militarism and ultra-nationalism, in doctrine and practice, including prior military training, shall be eliminated from the educational system. Former career military and naval officers, both commissioned and uncommissioned, and all other exponents of militarism and ultra-nationalism shall

be excluded from supervisory and teaching positions.[29]

In keeping with this policy, the Allies began the nearly impossible task of removing former militarists from the schools and reinstating liberals who had been dismissed during the immediate prewar period. As a result of this policy, during the first two years of the occupation nearly 120,000 Japanese teachers resigned or were dismissed. As the next step, State Shinto was banned from the schools and by way of implementation, textbooks were examined for the purpose of eliminating ideas concerning Japanese racial superiority, the divinity of the Emperor, and the like. History and geography courses were temporarily suspended from the curriculum and the formal course in Shushin, moral education, was eliminated. The Allied Command, as well as the American civilian educational advisers, saw these moves as fundamental in emphasizing the importance of human dignity and as protection of the individual against the omnipotence of the state.

Decentralization of control

An important educational policy not spelled out in the Fundamental Law of Education concerned the responsibility of control and administration of education. However, the principle of decentralization was accepted by SCAP officials early in the occupation and all that remained was the detailed planning for a workable scheme. The following statement of the United States Education

[29] Supreme Command Allied Powers, *Political Reorientation of Japan,* September, 1945–September, 1948, U.S. Government Printing Office, 1949, vol. II, p. 424.

Mission was indicative of the American view:

The principle is accepted that, for the purpose of democratic education, control of the schools should be widely dispersed rather than highly centralized as at present. The observance of ceremonies and the reading of the Imperial Rescript and obeisances to the Imperial Portrait in the schools are regarded as undesirable. The Ministry of Education, under the proposals of the Mission, would have important duties to perform in providing technical and professional counsel to the schools, but its direct control over local schools would be greatly curtailed.

In order to provide for greater participation by the people at local and prefectural levels, and to remove the schools from the administrative control by the representative of the Minister of Home Affairs at the local level, it is proposed to create educational agencies elected by popular vote, at both local and prefectural levels. Such agencies would be granted considerable power in the approval of the schools, the licensing of teachers, the selection of textbooks—power now centralized in the Ministry of Education.[30]

In 1950 the Second United States Education Mission, consisting of five members of the first mission, spent a month in Japan studying the results of the recommendations made by the original mission in 1946. This group reiterated its faith in decentralized educational control through elected school boards and urged that local boards be given fiscal independence. Again the role of the Ministry of Education was viewed as advisory and Ministry officials were counseled to assist in developing initiative and independence on the part of school boards, administrators, and teachers. These conditions were seen by the second mission as requisites to providing the type of education necessary in any democratic nation.[31]

In carrying out the principle of decentralization of educational control and administration, the Diet passed three laws: the Board of Education Law in 1948, the Ministry of Education Establishment Law in 1949, and the Private School Law, also in 1949. All three laws aimed at reducing the power of the Ministry of Education and increasing lay responsibility in the educational effort. The arguments by both Americans and Japanese for the necessity of these laws were essentially those expressed in the above quotation.

The Board of Education Law provided for prefectural boards of seven members and local boards of five members. One member in each case was appointed by the local legislative unit; all other members were elected by popular ballot. The prefectural boards, in addition to having full responsibility over the upper secondary schools and other prefectural schools, were in a position to indirectly influence the local schools. It was the prefectural board which had the responsibility for certifying and approving textbooks. All other matters related to the operation of the elementary schools and the lower secondary schools were under the jurisdiction of the local boards.

The new role of the Ministry of Education was not unlike that of the U.S. Office of Education. Since its fiscal powers were diminished and its other

[30] *Report of the United States Education Mission to Japan, op. cit.,* p. 59.

[31] *Report of the Second Education Mission to Japan,* U.S. Government Printing Office, 1950, pp. 3–4.

major controls given over to the prefectural boards, the Ministry was nearly reduced to a service and advisory agency. With the passage of the Private School Law much of the control formerly exercised by the Ministry with relation to private elementary and secondary education became a function of a private school council, a sort of private school board of education. The Ministry still retained the power to provide minimum standards, collect and disseminate educational information, and give general professional guidance, but it could no longer exert direct control over the instructional program.

The local boards of education did not live up to the expectations of the more optimistic American and Japanese educators. Almost immediately after their inception they came under criticism from government and lay sources. From the beginning the Ministry of Education had objected to popular election of board members and also to allowing the board to assume such broad educational responsibilities. The boards were further weakened by persisting financial problems, due at least partly to the inexperience of the school superintendents in such matters. Under the new laws the financing of the Japanese schools was defined as a cooperative effort by the local school boards and local assemblies. This dualism in responsibility proved quite unsatisfactory, however, and from 1953 to 1957 the national government passed a series of laws centralizing financial authority.

Neither the general public nor the Japanese educators understood the full significance of a lay policy-making body; they continued to look to Tokyo for important decisions. Moreover, the roots of local autonomy in Japan were so shallow that citizens failed to comprehend their new obligations and, even less, to appreciate the creative possibilities of their new position. An interesting public opinion survey on prevailing attitudes regarding boards of education was made by Tokyo University in 1952. In a town of 12,000 population and in a city of 73,000 population the question was asked, "Why did you vote for the person you did as a member of the board of education?" The results were as follows:

About 25 per cent of the people in the town and about 15 per cent in the city said they did so because of personal ties or a sense of obligation to the candidate. Some 10 per cent in each place said they did not know, or gave irrelevant answers. In the town, 45.9 per cent and in the city 54.1 per cent said they had voted as they had because of the qualities of the candidate, such as his personality, ability, education and teaching experience.[32]

This poll further indicated that about half of the persons interviewed had not heard of the board of education.

As a culmination of the pressing financial problems and the dissatisfaction of many of the government leaders and educational officials with the lack of sophistication of local voters, the Japanese government in 1956 passed the Law Concerning Organization and Function of Local Educational Administration. The reasons for replacing the old law and the purposes of the new law were explained by the Ministry of Education as follows:

The main criticisms of the board of education system were based on such points as the uncertainty of political neutrality of election, the unsatisfactory relationship of educational ad-

[32] Anderson, *op. cit.*, p. 87.

ministration and general administration, and the necessity of promoting the efficiency of local administration and of saving local expenditures.[33]

The new law provided that:

1. Members of boards of education shall be appointed by the chief of the local public body (Governor at the prefectural level, Mayor in the municicipalities, and head of town).
2. Education budgets shall be prepared by the local public bodies.
3. Appointment or dismissal of teachers shall be by the prefectural board of education.
4. The superintendent of the prefectural board of education shall be appointed by the board with approval of the Minister of Education. The superintendent of the municipality or town shall be appointed by the board with consent of the prefectural board.
5. The minister of education shall have the power to establish and enforce educational policies and standards.[34]

The channels of control under the new law are shown in Figure 34. By changing the method of selecting members of the boards of education, the national government took a major step toward the recentralization of control over the educational process. The people, under the new system, had only indirect control over educational policy by means of the elected officials, such as the mayor and governor, who now had the responsibility to appoint members of the board of education. The Japanese Ministry of Education, with questionable logic, defended this change

on the basis that the new system would necessarily produce better-qualified board members and was in fact more "democratic," for the people were provided protection from "ambitious persons," "those who are of wealth," and those who "represent some organization."[35]

The steps taken after the end of the occupation period by the Ministry of Education to regain its prewar power did not go unchallenged by many members of the Japanese teaching profession. The powerful Japanese Teachers Union expressed strong opposition to any movement of recentralization of educational power. The Japanese press often editorially expressed similar sentiments. These objections proved relatively ineffectual, however, and the Ministry, after acquiring fiscal and personnel control soon began to tighten its grasp on the curriculum.

Extension of opportunities

A major goal of Japanese educators and American advisers in the post-World War II years was to increase the educational opportunities for Japanese children and youth. The ideal of equal educational opportunity was incorporated into SCAP directives, the reports of both United States Education Missions and in the Japanese Constitution (1947). Under American leadership four basic steps were taken to assist in the realization of this ideal: (1) Reorganization of the multiple-track system into a single-track system with concurrent extension of compulsory education, (2) provisions for coeducation, (3) establishment of part-time and correspondence education, (4) restructure of higher

[33] Japanese Ministry of Education, *Education in 1956*, The Ministry, Tokyo, 1958, p. 82.
[34] *Ibid.*, pp. 83–88.
[35] *Ibid.*, p. 84.

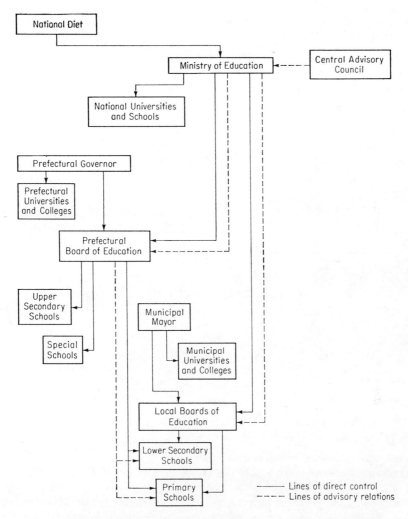

Figure 34. Lines of Educational Authority in Modern Japan

education including initiation of a system of junior colleges.

The Fundamental Law on Education adopted in 1947, the first inclusive educational law since the Imperial Rescript on Education in 1890, identified the single-track educational system as the system most in keeping with Japan's new democratic goals. The new system, like a common pattern in the United States, comprised a 6-3-3-4 ladder. The elementary grades and the lower secondary school were made compulsory, while examinations were required for those wishing entrance to the upper secondary schools and the colleges or universities. By 1960 over 60 per cent of the graduates of the ninth grade were continuing to the tenth grade. Extending free, compulsory education from six to nine years, while receiving popular support, did place a considerable finan-

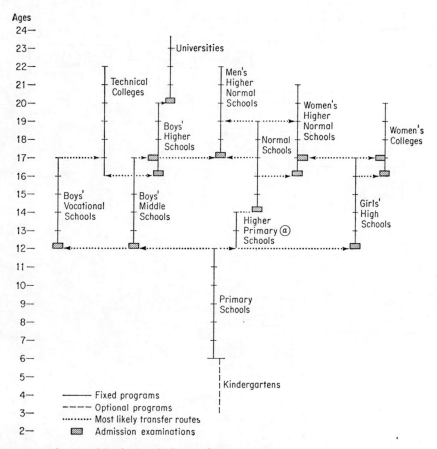

Figure 35. Educational Institutions in Prewar Japan
a. Graduates of higher primary schools were eligible to enter vocational schools.

cial burden on the Japanese people, and the success of this change was due in no small measure to the educational drive exhibited in the local communities.

Prior to World War II Japan had, in addition to the academic middle school, a variety of terminal vocational secondary schools. The basic change initiated by the new system, as shown in Figures 35 and 36, was the creation of a comprehensive upper secondary school which offered vocational courses as well as college preparatory work. The concept of the comprehensive or multipurpose school did not entirely meet

with favor among the Japanese population or the teaching profession. Although prefectures were urged to combine existing specialized schools or to broaden the curriculum of the existing school, in those communities which had only one upper secondary school such action was not always forthcoming. If professional opinion agreed that specialized secondary schools were capably meeting the needs of the people in certain areas, then the educational authorities did not require the building of comprehensive schools. Table 2 shows the expansion in school enrollment from 1950 to 1957.

324

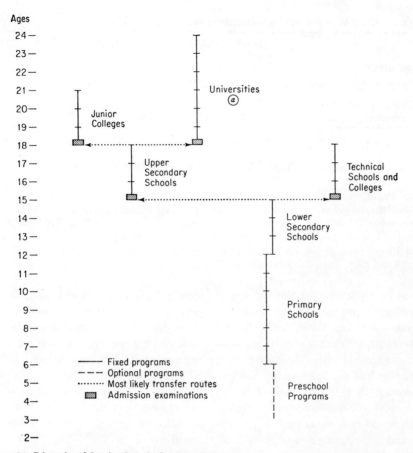

Ages

Figure 36. Educational Institutions in Postwar Japan
a. Universities award Bachelor's and graduate degrees. Lower schools award diplomas.

Another problem involved in winning converts to the idea of comprehensive upper secondary schools lay deep in the Japanese custom of ranking the schools. For example, in prewar years highest prestige was given to those middle schools which were consistently able to place a high percentage of their graduates in the Imperial universities. Alumni of the former "first-grade" schools objected to attempts to make these schools comprehensive in purpose, and thereby, they felt, no different in quality, from other upper secondary schools in the prefecture. Consternation among Japanese parents and educators was further increased when surveys of school achievement reportedly showed secondary school achievement during the occupation below the prewar level. Some Japanese intellectuals accused American authorities of introducing "mediocrity" rather than "democracy."

A plan to discourage boys of ambition or talent from trying to enroll in a few preferred schools was developed whereby each prefecture could divide itself into school districts. By 1949, thirty-six out of the forty-six prefectures had adopted the district system and the Ministry of

Table 2   *Growth in School Enrollments in Japan from 1950 to 1957*

	*1950**	*1957†*	*1950**	*1957†*	*1950**	*1957†*
Age group	5–14		15–19		20–24	
Enrollment, thousands	16,547	18,993	2,191	8,323	421	642
Per cent of age group enrolled	90.6	94	25.8	36	5.1	3

* Enrollment figures for 1950 taken from UNESCO, *World Survey of Education II*, p. 641.

† Enrollment figures for 1957 taken from UNESCO, *World Survey of Education III*, p. 58.

NOTE: Population by age group in 1950 reported in *UN Demographic Yearbook, 1955*, p. 248. Percentage of total population for age group calculated for 1950. More recent figures showed that by 1960 the enrollment in upper secondary schools had risen to 80 per cent of the 15–17 age group while the enrollment in higher education institutions constituted 10 per cent of the 18–21 age group. (See Japan, Ministry of Education, *Japan's Growth and Education*, Tokyo, 1963, p. 161.)

Education reported that the concept of hierarchy of prestige among secondary schools was losing favor.[36] The Second United States Education Mission, however, recognized that the problem of districting had not been solved and recommended that school districts be set up around natural community centers which would be large enough in population and tax resources to support quality schools.[37]

In prewar Japan, educational opportunity for girls had been drastically limited beyond the elementary grades. Furthermore, in keeping with Japanese traditions, above the first two grades of the primary school girls were taught in separate classes, and at the secondary level in separate schools. With the postwar emphasis on equalizing educational opportunity, coeducation became compulsory in the lower secondary schools and enrollment in the national universities became possible for women for the first time. In the upper secondary school

coeducation was optional, and, at this level and above, in spite of some protest from Japanese girls and women, education for a time often continued to be segregated on the basis of sex. Within a decade after the close of the war, however, coeducation was firmly entrenched in the public secondary schools, though still lagging in the national universities.

The third step taken to equalize educational opportunity in postwar Japan involved opening secondary and higher education to working youth. The old part-time continuation schools which offered a terminal postelementary instruction were eliminated. The newer educational policies called for evening and vacation courses to be offered in the regular secondary schools for those youth who found it impossible to attend regularly. In this manner credits could be acquired, if the student so desired, toward a graduation certificate. Correspondence courses at the secondary and university levels also proved a successful technique for bringing instruction to youth and adults who could not afford, or

36 Anderson, *op. cit.*, p. 51.

37 *Report of the Second United Education Mission to Japan, op. cit.*, p. 4.

were not physically able, to enroll as full-time students. The Ministry of Education and the Japan Teacher Education Association used correspondence study programs very successfully as a technique of inservice education for teachers. Later these services were turned over to departments of education in the national universities. Credit with prescribed limits could be received for studies completed by correspondence at either the secondary or higher level.

The prewar Japanese system of higher education was composed of many specialized and preparatory schools of advanced secondary or junior college level (*semmonygakko* and *kotoygakko*) and a few highly selected universities (*daigaku*). As a fourth step for extending educational opportunities, the First United States Education Mission recommended an increase in the number of colleges and universities. The preparatory schools and some of the normal schools and specialized colleges were transformed, at the recommendation of SCAP and in spite of the criticism of some Japanese scholars, into general four-year universities. The universities which in prewar years had been highly selective academically, with heavy emphasis on specialization and research, were now forced to assume functions formerly left to the preparatory schools and were thus changed to fit the American university pattern which typically leaves advanced specialization for the graduate school. All teacher education functions were placed with the universities. Attempts were further made, with only partial success, to establish prefectural universities after the pattern of state universities in America. Lastly, a system of two-year junior colleges was introduced to meet the expanding need

for semiprofessional persons. Many of the specialized institutes and preparatory schools unable to qualify as universities also become junior colleges. These institutions became particularly popular with Japanese girls who desired advanced education but disliked postponing marriage for four years beyond the upper secondary school.

The attempts to increase and equalize educational opportunities did not meet with easy success and were not without strong Japanese criticism. The most frequent and most valid complaint of Japanese citizens and educators was that academic standards had been lowered at both the secondary and university levels. The concept of nine years of compulsory schooling was readily accepted by Japanese—in fact some attempts to extend free, compulsory education had been made before 1945—and it appears that the basic 6-3-3-4 plan will remain. As Japanese educators have pointed out this has actually become a $6\text{-}3x3x4$ system, with x representing an unknown number of years spent preparing for entrance examinations to the next institution. The rapid expansion of opportunities at the upper secondary school and university levels greatly taxed available facilities and teachers. Not only did the average quality of instruction and the average intelligence of the student body become lower, but these institutions had neither the money nor the facilities to fulfill the new roles for which they had been designed. The upper secondary school was far from comprehensive in either curriculum or philosophy. Often very meager offerings were available in specialized or vocational courses, and most students concentrated on the higher prestige college preparatory subjects. By 1960 several

327

of the multipurpose upper secondary schools had been allowed to reassume the role of a one-course specialized institution. The belief that general or academic education should be separated from vocational education appeared to be on the increase.

Japanese criticism of the new system of higher education has stressed the expanded enrollments of the colleges and universities and the quality of the institutions raised to university status during the occupation. Japanese educators often point to the fact that many college graduates in the postwar years have not been able to find suitable employment. Complaints registered by university professors have agreed that present-day students are not so capable academically as those of the prewar period. Another important criticism, and seemingly a valid one, has to do with the introduction of "American-style" graduate schools with formal programming and series of prescribed courses. This move was particularly onerous to Japanese scholars who claimed that such requirements had bureaucratic but not scholastic significance and who preferred intimate work with a few selected students to such structured arrangements. While these criticisms appear to represent a majority of professional opinion, contrary views have been voiced by a few educators who place the blame for such problems on the inability of the university staffs to adjust their practices to meet the needs of (1) a more heterogeneous student body and (2) an expanding industrial economy which requires persons trained for a variety of positions other than the traditional professional pursuits.

In final analysis, however, with the exception of organizational form, Japanese higher education was only modestly influenced by American ideas. After the end of the occupation period the former Imperial universities regained much of their former prestige. Entrance to the older universities, particularly Tokyo University and Kyoto University, is still the prize most highly sought, and the graduates of these universities hold a virtual monopoly on desirable positions in industry, business, and government.

Curriculum reforms

During the immediate prewar years the Japanese curriculum at the elementary level and, to a certain extent, at the higher levels had been designed to make the individual a conforming citizen of the state and thereby a loyal subject of the Emperor. Regimented physical education and an authoritarian relationship between principals and teachers, and between teachers and students, added a militaristic atmosphere to the operation of the schools. The nationally prescribed textbooks and other teaching materials imposed further uniformity—the state was omnipotent and omnipresent.

In the postwar years an attempt was made to allow the elementary and secondary teachers more freedom in developing curricular materials adapted to the character of the individual student. American advisers together with those Japanese educators who had retained some of their professional competence in spite of two decades of militarism sought to insert a fresh human quality into the schools. The traditional freedom given by Japanese to their young children, coupled with the introduction of modern classroom methods, had re-

328

markable results in elementary education. At the secondary and higher levels attempts were made to break the formal lecture-recitation method so common in prewar Japanese schools by reeducating Japanese teachers in such techniques as the use of audio-visual aids and discussion methods. Nationwide workshops were held during which teachers analyzed ways of promoting responsible individuality among the students. These attempts met with more success at the elementary level than at the secondary level, with the conservative university the least affected. As might be expected, many excesses were promoted in the schools at all levels under the guise of individuality and freedom.

In a study designed to determine the attitude of Japanese elementary school teachers toward the progressive educational changes, Coledarci defined seven "reform-consistent" attitudes. These were:

. . . valuing pupil interests and purposes, emphasis upon inquiry, "permissiveness" in pupil-control, willingness to encourage pupil participation in education, viewing subject as having instrumental value (rather than disciplinary), willingness to recognize and provide for individual differences in ability, and optimism about pupil capacity for self-responsibility.[38]

This study showed that elementary teachers were at least able to satisfactorily verbalize "reform-consistent" attitudes. Moreover, although the younger teachers were somewhat more "reform-oriented" than their older colleagues the

[38] Arthur P. Coledarci, "The Professional Attitudes of Japanese Teachers," *Journal of Educational Research*, vol. 52, no. 9, pp. 323–324, May, 1959.

differences were not considered highly significant. In general, both the young and the old teachers, it seemed, favored the newer concepts of instruction.

The controversy over *shushin* (explicit instruction in moral education) in many ways typifies Japan's postwar curriculum dilemmas, and therefore will be discussed here at some length. This course had been used to instill in young Japanese an understanding of Japan's national spirit and a respect for its great heroes. Because of its militaristic flavor *shushin* was removed from the schools by an SCAP directive. As a substitute for *shushin* a new social studies curriculum was created during the Allied occupation to provide an opportunity for students to examine the changing Japanese society, review their ethical heritage, and develop worthwhile personal values. The school's role in moral education, as interpreted by the American advisers, was to develop in youth the ability to evaluate moral alternatives and possibly even to allow youth to share in creating new ethical directions. In the final analysis, morals, as in the common American tradition, were to be "caught" through the total school atmosphere and not taught through specific formal instruction.

The elimination of *shushin*, like many other changes which took place immediately following World War II, proved to be short-lived. From the beginning, a core of intellectuals and conservative bureaucrats fought to return to the traditional pattern. And from the early 1950s, each succeeding Minister of Education pledged ameliorative legislation. In the autumn of 1958 the Ministry of Education, knowing that there was both governmental and popular support for its action, directed that separate courses in moral instruction be reintroduced into the curricula of the schools.

The general temper of the Japanese postwar period must be adjudged in order to place the rebirth of explicit moral education and other postoccupation curriculum measures in proper perspective. In many respects the military defeat and subsequent breakdown of traditional Japanese institutions constituted a revolution fully as significant as the one nearly a century earlier that started Japan on the road toward modernization. Prewar Japan represented a divinely inspired social order in which the Good Life had been revealed through a God-Emperor. The alteration of the traditional power structure through the decentralization of control—Japanese writers critical of the changes initiated during the Allied occupation accuse Americans of confusing decentralization with democracy—and the substitution of horizontal loyalties for vertical ones represented fundamental societal changes, which necessitated an intense reexamination of basic values. Japanese intellectuals and social reformers searched diligently for a new social philosophy that would give stability and direction to the Japanese people. Some looked inward toward their nation's heritage of Buddhist and Confucian thought, seeking to find strength in the traditional Japanese Way. Others, particularly the university professors and university students, turned to Marxism and an extensive theoretical discussion of the benefits to be accrued in a materialistic, deterministic society. A third group, small in number, suggested that in Christianity both personal solace and social inspiration could be found. A final group urged a revitalization of

Japanese society by eliminating its intuitive, artistic, and imitative qualities and building in their stead an intellectual, scientific, and creative character. The sources of inspiration for this last group were many, not the least of which was the powerful American image.

While the debates among the reformers continued, situations were arising which called for immediate action. The extended freedom of youth and the general reduction of social discrimination on the basis of sex proved to be stimuli neither well understood by parents nor gracefully accepted or assimilated by youth. The unsettled conditions of the Japanese society proved an excellent breeding place for wanton practices which were often promoted under the name of individual freedom. Responsible citizens, concerned with maintaining a socially healthy society, unconsciously were allied with those who for personal aggrandizement urged a return to the *status quo*. Persons seeking easy answers to a complex question were quick to trace societal ills, real or imagined, to American-induced educational changes. The introduction of new social customs and the promotion of individualistic education were said by some to cause materialistic tendencies in youth and create a lack of interest in Japan's cultural and moral traditions. The startling increase in juvenile delinquency, a phenomenon practically unknown in Japan prior to Wor'd War II, caused many serious citizens to seek ways of restoring the values and stability of the past.

The Japanese Ministry of Education has been quick to point out that new attempts to strengthen the teaching of values in the schools differ fundamentally from the earlier methods of indoctrination in which the entire curriculum was permeated with militaristic and nationalistic propaganda. In the new courses in moral education, for example, the absence of the term "filial piety" would lend at least some credence to the official statement that no attempt is being made to promote subservience, as did prewar courses, to a lineally organized society under patriarchal and divine rule. A second significant difference lies in the failure of the new moral education, as well as the postwar social science courses, to emphasize explicitly the idea of national loyalty. How important these differences are is not yet apparent. Some progressive Japanese educators have expressed fears that only the words have been changed and that traditional forces are at work to rebuild a prewar school system.

When viewed with perspective the increased concern over the school's role in the teaching of values can be seen to be a manifestation of an uneasiness, felt not only by the Japanese officials but also by large numbers of the Japanese population. While many Americans might cast a jaundiced eye at the reintroduction of a formal morals course, there is much in Japanese tradition that would lead one to anticipate such a move. Since the beginning of the Meiji era in 1868, two parallel movements have shaped Japanese cultural development. One movement has been the all-out attempt to acquire the tools and skills of Western technology. The second, however, has been a continued and extensive effort to ensure national unity and preserve the national character of the people. Thus, the most accurate view of the steps to formalize certain parts of the instructional program would show this to be another step taken to reemphasize the traditional system of

ethics and values without lessening the attention paid to scientific and technical ideas.

There is room for criticism of many of the educational reforms sponsored by American occupation authorities. Democracy and democratic education cannot be proscribed by military order, nor can personal and academic freedoms be nurtured in an atmosphere of censorship. Valid criticism may also be registered against the scandalously low level of professional background and the complete lack of cultural and linguistic preparation of many of the American educational personnel under SCAP. Yet, with these things said, it must be reiterated that six years of military occupation, even under ideal circumstances, is not long enough to fundamentally alter the national institutions of a highly developed nation.

Following the occupation, the forces of liberalism lost several educational battles; the curriculum issues and the location of educational responsibility are cases in point. Some Japanese educators analyzing the conservative reactions to American-inspired changes found these to be inevitable in light of earlier American mistakes. One author, in viewing the educational changes which took place during the occupation period, states:

> The tragedies that ensued stem from the fact that these reforms were imposed without due regard for Japanese culture and social structure. It was as if a utopian dreamer forced a carpenter to build a house according to his dream blueprint.[39]

This same author and other Japanese

[39] Michiya Shimbori, "The Fate of Postwar Educational Reform in Japan," *The School Review*, vol. 68, no. 2, Summer, 1960, pp. 228–241.

331

have defended the return to centralism and elitism as being appropriate for the Japanese Way.

So, too, some conservative elements of Japan have refused to accept the idea that the crushing military defeat may also have been a defeat for the traditional Japanese value system. The increased freedom of choice by Japanese youth in moral conduct, caused by societal changes but stimulated by modern classroom methods and curriculum reorganization, led logically to an increase in moral mistakes. These moral lapses in turn were viewed, naïvely perhaps, by the Ministry of Education as justification for the reintroduction of moral instruction. Moreover the attempts to give the local community a larger role in determining educational policy were not entirely successful, owing to the general lack of experience in local government and to the political moves of the Communist-led Japanese Teachers Union. Because of such shortcomings the Ministry of Education felt justified in recentralizing the control of finances and supervision of the educational process.

While the total educational implications of these and parallel postoccupation actions can only lead to conjecture at present, Japanese education in the post occupation years, for better or for worse, was clearly moving away from the goals envisioned by many American and some Japanese educators at the close of World War II. The educational changes initiated during the occupation that will become a lasting part of the Japanese scene are those that are rooted in the Japanese society, not those artificially imposed from without. Extension of educational opportunities for children

332

of working classes is an example of a reform which has become a permanent part of the educational pattern of modern Japan. Increased educational and social privileges for Japanese women are another example of a lasting change. Yet the liberal ideas underlying both of these changes were visible in Japan before World War II. Increased availability of public schooling has been largely the product of the modernization and industrialization of the Japanese society which began during the Meiji restoration. And the changing attitude toward the role of Japanese women is an outgrowth of industrial needs as well as prewar liberal thought.

The reverse argument could be made regarding the future of local autonomy and the decentralization of educational control, for experiments in these directions have little foundation in Japanese educational history. This does not mean, however, as some Americans have suggested, that democratization is only "skin-deep" in Japan. Cultural traditions dictate that Japan cannot be immediately made over into the image of localized and individualized America. Yet judged in terms of its own past, Japan has made significant progress in providing increased freedom and opportunities for its citizens. The traditional Japanese state with its Emperor-God figure at the head is gone, as are many of the undesirable aspects of the patriarchal family system. If democracy means an opportunity for the people to have a voice in the type of government under which they will live and, in turn, be protected by that government from breaches of personal liberties, then the forces of democracy in Japan show signs of having a lasting quality.

References

Books

Anderson, Ronald S.: *Japan: Three Epochs of Modern Education,* U.S. Office of Education, 1959.

Beardsley, Richard K., John Hall, and Robert E. Ward: *Village Japan,* The University of Chicago Press, Chicago, 1959.

Bereday, George Z. F., and J. A. Lauwerys (eds.): *The Year Book of Education, 1958: The Secondary School Curriculum,* World, Tarrytown-on-Hudson, N.Y., 1958.

Burton, Margaret E.: *The Education of Women in Japan,* Revell, Westwood, N.J., 1914.

de Bary, William Theodore (ed.): *Sources of Japanese Tradition,* Columbia, New York, 1958.

Dilts, Marion May: *The Pageant of Japanese History,* Longmans, New York, 1947.

Dore, R. P.: *City Life in Japan: A Study of a Tokyo Ward,* University of California Press, Berkeley, Calif., 1958.

Hall, Robert King: *Education for a New Japan,* Yale, New Haven, Conn., 1949.

————— (ed.): *Kokutai no Hongi,* translated by John O. Gauntlett, Harvard, Cambridge, Mass., 1949.

—————: *Shushin: The Ethics of a Defeated Nation,* Teachers College, Columbia University, New York, 1949.

Hearn, Lafcadio: *Japan: An Attempt at Interpretation,* Macmillan, New York, 1919.

Japan, Ministry of Education: *Education in Japan: A Graphic Presentation,* Tokyo, 1959.

—————: *Education Reform in Japan,* Japanese Education Reform Council, Tokyo, 1950.

—————: *Japan's Growth and Education,* Tokyo, 1963.

—————: *Progress of Education Reform in Japan,* English ed., Tokyo, 1950.

Kawai, Kazuo: *Japan's American Interlude,* The University of Chicago Press, Chicago, 1960.

Keenleyside, Hugh, and A. F. Thomas: *History of Japanese Education,* Hokuseido Press, Tokyo, 1937.

Kikuchi, Dairoku: *Japanese Education,* J. Murray, London, 1909.

Nitobe, Inazo: *Bushido: The Soul of Japan,* Shokwabo, Tokyo, 1901.

Reischauer, Edwin O., and John K. Fairbank: *East Asia: The Great Tradition,* Houghton Mifflin, Boston, 1960.

Report of the United States Education Mission to Japan, U.S. Government Printing Office, 1946.

Report of the Second United States Education Mission to Japan, U.S. Government Printing Office, 1950.

Sansom, G. B.: *Japan: A Short Cultural History,* rev. ed., Appleton-Century-Crofts, New York, 1943.

Supreme Commander for the Allied Powers (SCAP): *Civil Information and Education in the New Japan,* 2 vols., Tokyo, May, 1948.

—————: *Post-war Developments in Japanese Education,* 2 vols., Tokyo, 1952.

Pamphlets and periodicals

Adams, Don: "Rebirth of Moral Education in Japan," *Comparative Education Review,* vol. 4, no. 1, pp. 61–64, June, 1960.

Cassidy, Velma Hastings: "The Program for Reeducation in Japan," *Documents and State Papers,* vol. 1, no. 1, U.S. Government Printing Office, April, 1948.

Coledarci, Arthur P.: "The Professional Attitudes of Japanese Teachers," *Journal of Educational Research,* vol. 52, no. 9, pp. 323–324, May, 1959.

Journal of Social and Political Ideas in

333

Japan: Education in Japan, 1945–1963, vol. 1, no. 3, December, 1963.

Oshiba, Mamoru: "Moral Education in Japan," *The School Review,* Summer, 1961, pp. 227–244.

Shimbori, Michiya: "A Historical and Social Note on Moral Education in Japan," *Comparative Education Review,* vol. 4, no. 2, pp. 97-101, October, 1960.

————: "The Fate of Postwar Educational Reform in Japan," *The School Review,* vol. 68, no. 2, pp. 223–241, Summer, 1960.

PART III

Newly Emerging Patterns

CHAPTER 12   *Education*
in Underdeveloped Nations

Two great wars in the twentieth century have dealt a death blow to colonialism and thereby freed millions of people to make their own economic, political, and educational decisions. Other millions of people, not touched by colonial rule, but long thwarted by rigid social traditions, few natural resources, and inept or corrupt leaders have also begun to find new freedoms and to express new wants. Vast improvements in communication and transportation have highlighted the inequalities in the world's wealth and have brought new hopes and desires to that two-thirds of the world's population which lives in the economically underdeveloped[1] areas of Asia, Africa, and Latin America. Today the whole world is concerned with what has been aptly termed "the revolution of rising expectations."

The nature of the problem

The underdeveloped areas vary widely in natural resources, climate, population, geography, and linguistic and cultural traditions. Such diversity makes it difficult to generalize about their physical, social, educational, and other needs.

Most underdeveloped nations, however, are rural, agricultural lands. (In fact one author in building models of underdeveloped and developed nations uses the terms "Agraria" and "Industria.")[2] Many of these nations are located in the warmer climates, and the enervating effects of the tropics have often been cited as a cause of low productivity and, hence, of poverty. Underdeveloped nations tend to have a high density of population, although some are sparsely populated. Some have little or no indigenous cultural heritage in literature, philosophy, and history; others can trace a rich cultural tradition to the very dawn of civilization.

Regardless of their differences, however, most underdeveloped nations have demonstrated that they share an abiding faith in education as a major key to future happiness and economic security. Developing nations have taken great pride in their programs of literacy, vocational education, and the general extension of educational opportunity. People living at subsistence levels, inspired by a dream of a better future, have made truly great educational efforts, a fact easily documented by an examination of the annual budget or the personal lives of the people of the underdeveloped countries.

To understand the role education can play in social and economic develop-

---

[1] The term "underdeveloped" is not a happy expression, for there is obvious difficulty in defining it. In a sense, all people, to the extent that they fail to marshal their physical and mental resources in building a better nation, are underdeveloped. Here, however, the term will be used in the way typically employed by the United Nations and the American agencies to refer to the nations whose standard of living and per capita real income are lower than those of the United States and Western Europe.

[2] Fred W. Riggs, "Agraria and Industria: Toward a Typology of Comparative Administration," in William J. Siffin (ed.), *Toward the Comparative Study of Public Administration*, Indiana University Press, Bloomington, Ind., 1959.

ment, one must first learn the causes or at least the factors which perpetuate the "poorness" of these nations. Traditionally when the economist has talked of factors contributing to the level of economy of a nation, he has spoken of the availability of land, labor, and capital. Modern economists who focus their attention on the underdeveloped areas tend to modify this classical list. For example, Brand has suggested that poverty in nations is caused by (1) low productivity of land, (2) lack of capital, (3) low level of education, and (4) lack of leadership to initiate economic development.[3] Other students of underdevelopment have suggested that population pressures (high birth rates tend to outstrip high mortality rates in the less-developed areas) and excessive orientation toward foreign trade, if not causes, are typical characteristics of poor nations.[4] It can be readily seen that these elements of economic backwardness may be linked together in cause and effect relationships to produce a series of vicious circles demonstrating how underdevelopment perpetuates itself. One such vicious circle, as seen by the economist, may be represented as follows:[5]

Thus, a host of elements, such as market imperfections, quality of labor, and the like, may lead to low productivity which eventually results in capital deficiency— a situation frustrating economic development and to a great extent social and educational development as well.

Similarly, other vicious circles of more direct concern to the student of comparative education might be sketched. A low educational level, for example, often leads to low productivity, which results in low income and prohibits educational advancement, etc. It becomes apparent that regardless of the vicious circle that is drawn, an educational factor is involved, although its significance and exact dimensions may be debatable.

But the picture is not so pessimistic as would appear at first glance. Obviously there must be ways of breaking the circles of poverty or nations will be doomed to remain perpetually underdeveloped. Forced saving, new techniques of production, foreign capital, and technical assistance may not only destroy vicious circles but create virtuous ones. Thus higher productivity can result in more income, increased savings, and a forward-moving economy.

Social and psychological variables in the development process may well be as crucial as the economic factors. Levy, for example, concludes that there are probably no societies totally devoid of industrial factors.[6] In analyzing the "internal" and "external" strategic factors for change, Levy emphasizes such

[3] W. Brand, *The Struggle for a Higher Standard of Living,* Free Press, New York, 1958, p. 9.

[4] Reprinted by permission from Gerald M. Meier and Robert E. Baldwin, *Economic Development,* Wiley, New York, 1961, p. 273.

[5] *Ibid.,* p. 319.

[6] Marion J. Levy, "Some Sources of the Vulnerability of the Structures of Relatively Non-Industrialized Societies to those of Highly Industrialized Societies," in Bert F. Hoselitz (ed.), *The Progress of Underdeveloped Areas,* The University of Chicago Press, Chicago, 1952, p. 115.

variables as (1) patterns of family organization, (2) patterns of production, and (3) patterns of authority and responsibility.[7]

A change in the first variable (family) is likely to be the result rather than the progenitor of economic change. However, the second and third variables may well bear an antecedent or causative relation to such change. Levy's suggestion that changes must be made in the location of authority and responsibility implies that in the underdeveloped nations there typically exist certain anti-development social rigidities.

The interpretations of other authors would bear out Levy in this regard. Hoselitz, drawing largely from the writings of Talcott Parsons, found certain patterns of social behavior directly related to economically relevant behavior (defined as production and distribution of goods and services). In the underdeveloped countries, Hoselitz points out, "ascription" and "particularism" tend to dictate societal roles. Status, occupation, privileges, and restrictions are the results of family, class, or caste rather than of achievement, as is more common in the highly developed nations. Moreover, the elite of the underdeveloped societies tend to be more self-oriented than those of developed nations —the latter assume a pattern described as "collectivity-orientation."[8]

A more detailed listing of the individual and social changes needed to transform a traditional society into one capable of self-sustained development has been provided in a UNESCO manual for field workers. The strategic kinds of changes are grouped under three headings:

[7] *Ibid.*, pp. 113–125.
[8] *Ibid.*

Changes in Individuals
(Their Information, Skills, Attitudes)

1. Increasing literacy, scientific knowledge, scientific and technological training and a scientific or engineering approach to problems.

2. Increasing dissatisfaction with traditional levels of living, traditional status relationships, traditional economic activities.

3. Increasing belief that economic and social advancement can be obtained through new techniques and new economic activities.

4. Increasing belief that economic and social advancement can be obtained through individual competence and effort (rather than through preference based on bribery, political favour, kinship, caste or social status, national origin, race, religion or sex).

5. Increasingly specific definition of economic privileges expected from society, and economic obligations to society (rather than the vague, open-ended security often expected from the village or family, and the indefinite but broad economic obligations often felt towards the village or family).

6. Increasing respect for honesty in business and government and for the use of contracts in economic relationships.

Changes in Social Relationships
and Institutions

1. Increasing interpersonal communication (through adoption of common language, growth of literacy, increased media of communication, social mobility, travel, etc.).

2. Increasing economic opportunity (through decreased monopoly, increased availability of credit and greater occupational mobility).

3. Increasing rewards for economic activity (through land reform, tax

339

changes, governmental aid of various kinds).

4. Increasing power of groups participating in these changes, and diminishing power of groups resisting change.

5. Increasing governmental activity in public service and in economic and social development.

Changes in Social Overhead Capital

1. Increasing investment in education, public health and sanitation, water supply.

2. Increasing investment in transportation, communications, power, irrigation.

3. Increasing competence (likely to involve investment) in public administration, civil police, and the military establishment.[9]

The complexity of the development process thus unfolds. Obviously, there is no easy mechanical formula for stimulating economic and social change. Human elements, ignorance, class or caste stratifications, extreme conservatism, and prejudice are involved and interlinked with such physical elements as mineral resources, land productivity, and power potential. This being the case, education must contribute not only to the acquisition of technical skills, in order that the people may learn to develop and utilize their resources, but must also help the people revise existing social traditions and accept new political responsibilities. Education that merely satisfies individual ambition or contributes to long-range cultural enhancement cannot suffice.

The strong desire for rapid change,

[9] Samuel P. Hayes, Jr., *Measuring the Results of Development Projects*, Monographs in the Applied Social Sciences, UNESCO, Paris, 1959, pp. 14–15.

the limited resources, and the exceeding faith in education make the task of educational institutions difficult indeed in a developing nation. Unfortunately there are very few sophisticated research studies which shed light on the precise contributions of education to economic or social development. What work has been done is largely the result of efforts by economists and, more rarely, sociologists. While such research has failed to uncover many specifics with regard to the interaction of education and other development variables, there has been a growing suspicion on the part of some scholars that educational transformation is often antecedent to economic change, and thus at certain phases of development, expenditures on human resources may be more productive than expenditures on material resources.

It may not be an overstatement to say that those responsible for educational planning in the underdeveloped nations are faced with a series of immediate decisions whose choices will profoundly affect the total development program. Such questions as the following must be raised:

1. Should concentration be placed initially on mass education or education of an elite? What should the educational "pyramid" look like at different stages of development?

2. What curriculum offers the best balance between the vocational education needed to produce the myriad of skills required by a developing nation and a general education needed for cultural sophistication?

3. What general education experiences contribute most to economic development?

4. What fraction of the available national budget should be spent on education in lieu of expenditures on industry, commerce, or agriculture at any particular stage of development?

5. Should the educational institutions prepare only those skilled and professional persons needed to satisfy existing national needs? Or should the schools be allowed to turn out more graduates than there are occupational openings on the premise that this excess of talent will create new possibilities for economic and social growth?

6. Should the educational institutions attempt to match the academic standards of the advanced nations of the world? Or would more but lesser-trained graduates better serve the cause of development?

7. How much direct leadership can the schools give in programs of community development? What is the role of the teacher as a community leader? How can the curriculum be streamlined to give attention to pressing community problems and at the same time not slight traditional areas of knowledge?

8. How much leadership should the schools be allowed in assisting such social changes as extension of the rights of women, elimination of social castes, promotion of political freedom, and the like?

9. How much of the educational planning must be done at the national level? At the local level?

10. What are the functions and limitations of bilateral and multilateral programs of technical assistance in education?

These questions spotlight the educational problems faced by the developing areas and will add meaning to the de-

scriptions presented below and in the following chapters.

The role of education

Education can contribute to the rapid development of a society, it can be used by a demagogue to warp the values of a people, or it can be an agent for the preservation of the *status quo.*

An education system could be designed that would assure neither progress nor retrogression. In it the same proportion of each generation would be enrolled. Students eligible for advanced education would be selected in the traditional way, whether eligibility is determined by social, economic, political, or intellectual status. Educating more or better qualified people would plant seeds of change. In no-progress education all the relationships between man and the body politic would be taught as conventional dogma. A spirit of inquiry among students about these affairs would be destabilizing. Scientific knowledge would be taught but not the scientific method for obtaining it. Research on education would be discouraged because the content and productivity of education might thereby be modified, causing unwanted change in the abilities of graduates. Such a system would satisfy the status quo seekers. But they are dwindling in number.[10]

To the extent that the underdeveloped countries have had long traditions of formal education, the "no-progress" education described in the above quotation has in the past been satisfactory to many of their leaders. As will be shown

[10] William J. Platt, *Toward Strategies of Education,* Stanford Research Institute, International Industrial Development Center, Menlo Park, Calif., 1961, p. 1.

341

in the next three chapters, however, educational institutions are being given an increasingly important developmental role, both in areas with little educational heritage (as in parts of tropical Africa) and in those with old educational traditions (as in India and much of Asia). Most leaders of these nations consider education a tool to be used deliberately to promote economic change. Many further expect educational institutions to take direct leadership in social change. Thus, what might be thought of as laboratory examples of educational systems designed to reconstruct the social and economic environment are emerging in several parts of the world. Unfortunately there are few, if any, appropriate models in the more developed societies for the underdeveloped nations to draw upon. Historically, educators and statesmen in the advanced Western nations have considered the schools a means to "perpetuate the cultural heritage" or transmit the "Good Life"; only rarely were schools considered instruments for direct social and economic change. Moreover, it was only after long centuries of development that the nations of Europe and America came to believe they could afford to give more than a minimum of education to any sizable proportion of their children. The peoples of the underdeveloped nations expect much more dynamic educational progress.

Some tentative generalizations

What hypotheses can be made about the educational problems of the underdeveloped nations? The problems are in some ways unique, but certain tentative generalizations regarding education and economic and social development can be suggested.

342

1. In economic-development plans, education may be considered an important form of investment. The belief among certain leaders of the underdeveloped nations that increased educational effort is rewarded by an improved national economy is illustrated by the opening paragraph of an article by Dean Rusk, Secretary of State for the United States under the Kennedy administration:

> The premier of a small nation questioned as to why a relatively large percentage of its budget was devoted to education is said to have replied: "It is because we are such a poor country."[11]

Yet in educational history, schooling has often been treated as a luxury item, something to improve an individual's taste, ennoble his spirit, and grace his leisure hours. Only recently has attention been focused on the direct relationship between the various levels and types of education and economic development. Professor Schultz, an economist, has studied the process of economic growth and suggested that increases in productivity are primarily due to improvement in the quality of human effort.

> Although it is obvious that people acquire useful skills and knowledge, it is not obvious that these skills and knowledge are a form of capital, that this capital is in substantial part a product of deliberate investment, that it has grown in western societies at a much faster rate than conventional (nonhuman) capital, and that its growth may well be the most distinctive feature of the economic system. It has been widely observed that in-

[11] Dean Rusk, "Education: Key to National Development," *Overseas*, vol. 1, no. 1, p. 6, September, 1961.

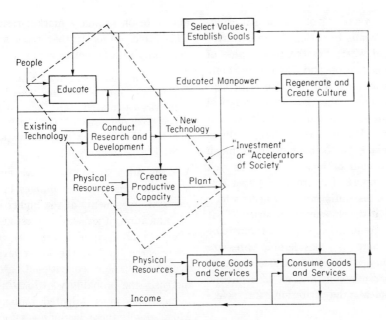

Figure 37. Education as a Contributor to Development
SOURCE: William J. Platt, *Toward Strategies of Education,* Stanford Research Institute, International Industrial Development Center, Menlo Park, Calif., 1961, p. 14.

creases in national output have been large compared with the increases of inputs of land, manhours, and physi-·cal reproducible capital. Investment in human capital is probably the major explanation for this difference.[12]

A model developed at the Stanford Research Institute by Platt demonstrates the manner in which education is related to other forms of investment in a nation's development. This model further relates the consumer and the investment aspects of education to each other and to the larger cultural goal.

While the Platt model may provide few new insights into the interrelationships of economic and educational variables it does emphasize rather dramatically the centrality of education. The

[12] Theodore W. Schultz, "Education and Economic Growth," *Social Forces Influencing American Education,* NSSE Yearbook, part 2, chap. 3, 1961, pp. 46–88.

model fails to take into consideration a major variable in the development process, however, and this is population. If more extensive education leads to lower birth rates, for example, then investment in an educational system takes on new dimensions of urgency. On the other hand, if education is unrelated to or, which is unlikely, negatively correlated with the population variable, then the priority of educational investment might be reduced.

Treating education as an investment as well as an item of consumption raises several provocative questions: What kinds of education may be thought of as an investment? Without much controversy the building of a technical school, which imparts skills and knowledge directly related to a nation's productivity, can be considered a capital investment. But where does one draw the line? Does literacy contribute primarily to a nation's output or is it essentially a means to enrich the individual's life? And where lies the basic value of general education and adult education? These questions are of more than academic interest; they have very practical implications in a nation's development program. When far-reaching educational plans are being built it is much easier to gain national support, as well as the support of international agencies, for those institutions and projects which have high developmental priority. That is, when educational choices must be made, there is considerable pressure in the underdeveloped nations to make the program's contribution to economic development the criterion for selection.

As yet, only minimal insight has been gained into the questions raised in the above paragraph. Initial investigations of the relationships between educational investments and growth of national income have been begun by both economists and specialists in education. A comparison of the "physical" and "intellectual" investment in selected countries has been made by Vaizey,[13] who also offers a few cautious interpretations of the implications of such investment for rate of economic growth.[14]

An increasing number of investigators, while admitting the crudeness of their measurement, are estimating that the rate of return on education exceeds that on many other investments. In the United States, according to one author, investment in education may pay itself off in only nine years—"a very favor-

able rate on ordinary market terms."[15] This same author further reports that, according to a Soviet scholar:

> . . . when universal four year education was introduced into the USSR, it was calculated that the benefit to the economy would be forty-three times greater than the sum expended on it.[16]

Various other economists have emphasized the long-term advantages of educational investment: at the higher levels of education, they say, investment is likely to produce high rates of return on research, and at the lower levels it provides a broader educational base and increases the probability of locating the population's more talented individuals. Most of all, these beginning efforts at treating education as investment point to the need for extensive research by students of economics and education.

2. Development plans must involve all educational levels. Social and economic development place enormous demands on educational facilities at all levels. More primary education is needed to extend the level of literacy, enhance the general development of citizens, and provide a foundation for further schooling. More secondary education is needed to prepare an increasing number of students for university work and to train the gamut of tradesmen and white-collar workers demanded by expanding economies. More university education is needed to prepare the professional, scientific, and administrative leaders—the elite that must perform the skills of the

[13] John Vaizey, "Education as Investment in Comparative Perspective," *Comparative Education Review,* vol. 5, no. 2, p. 101, October, 1961.
[14] *Ibid.*

[15] H. M. Phillips, "Education as a Basic Factor in Economic and Social Development," *Final Report,* United Nations Economic Commission for Africa, Addis Ababa, 1961, p. 100.
[16] *Ibid.*

highest level and give direction to national policy. In addition, adult education, with all its ramifications, requires careful attention in the underdeveloped nations. Quite obviously, many nations in Asia, Africa, and Latin America have neither the funds nor the talent to move ahead with equal rapidity in all these areas. The subtle and explosive problem of educational priorities therefore arises.

There appear to be two major factors impinging on any valid approach to the selection of educational priorities. The first has to do with the cultural goals and stage of development of the nation in question and the second is related to the pertinence of the experiences provided by the various educational institutions to the development process.

Rostow has suggested that developing nations go through five stages of economic growth: the traditional society, the preconditions for take-off, the take-off, the drive to maturity, and the age of high mass consumption.[17] Although no scholar has hypothesized the quantity and character of education at each stage in the Rostow model, some agreement has been reached concerning the changing educational needs of a nation as it moves toward modernization. As an educational precondition for take-off, for example, a nation needs an elite group of highly skilled persons for governmental, industrial, commercial, and professional positions. Yet some fairly substantial base of literacy (though not universal) is also required to open communication channels and provide a condition for self-help possibilities. As industrial and commercial activities multiply the demand for middle-level skills

greatly increases. In this regard it is interesting to note that at a UNESCO-sponsored conference in 1961 agreement was reached that secondary education should have highest priority in the immediate developmental plans for Africa.[18]

When education is viewed in terms of its immediate economic contribution, examples of misplaced educational emphasis can be found. While many countries in Africa were finding that they had too few secondary school graduates to satisfy their needs, India was finding that it had too many. In the Belgian Congo the colonial power had concentrated its efforts on providing opportunities for primary education and vocational education. The advent of independence found the Congolese nation with no elite native group to give leadership in governmental or professional affairs. On the other hand, in parts of Latin America a major problem has been to enlarge the number of persons trained vocationally by secondary level institutions.

The suggestion that it might be economically advantageous to lay initial emphasis on the training of an elite leadership group rests particularly hard with many American educators. These individuals, whose opinions are colored, perhaps, by an abiding faith in their own system of mass education, tend to argue from humanitarian and political points of view. The pleas calling for social justice, enhancement of the individual personality, and preparation for citizenship are well known and need not be repeated here. Less clear are the stages of development where particular

[17] W. W. Rostow, *The Stages of Economic Growth: A Non-Communist Manifesto*, Cambridge, New York, 1960.

[18] UNESCO, Conference of African States on the Development of Education in Africa, *Final Report*, Addis Ababa, May 15–25, 1961, p. 11.

amounts of literacy or primary enrollment become superfluous or uneconomic. There is much evidence to show that up to a certain point high per capita income, which is used as an index of economic development, and rates of literacy are closely correlated and that, conversely, low per capita income is accompanied by low rates of literacy. Exceptions to the rule, as in Venezuela and certain Near Eastern countries where the extreme wealth of a small elite distorts income averages, are usually explainable.

While literacy and per capita income appear to have a strong positive correlation, several examples can be noted where nations have relatively high postprimary school enrollment without a correspondingly high per capita income. Puerto Rico, Japan, and Yugoslavia, for example, rank among the top ten nations of the world in the percentage of their populations in secondary and higher education. The Philippines and the republic of Korea also have low per capita income but relatively high postprimary school enrollment.[19] With these deviates noted, it should be made clear, however, that *no economically advanced nation fails to rate at least moderately high in postprimary enrollment*. This condition leads Ginsburg to state:

> . . . one can reasonably conclude that those countries with high investments in post-primary education in particular (as measured by enrolment) are laying firm foundations for economic growth and cultural change, whereas those countries with low investments in this field will continue to be con-

[19] Norton Ginsburg, *Atlas of Economic Development*, The University of Chicago Press, Chicago, 1961, p. 44.

fronted with grave problems in the mobilization of their human resources.[20]

While it may be difficult to demonstrate a perfect correlation between expansion of educational opportunities and economic growth, the demand for a wide variety of skills and widespread innovative attitudes may justify a certain amount of "overeducation." Yet still another factor must be considered when expanding or limiting the opportunities at any particular level. This is the matter of cost. Typically, education becomes more expensive as one proceeds from the primary school to the university. Even with new and more imaginative ways of meeting educational costs there is a level where additional educational effort may actually be detrimental to development. For the Northern Region of Nigeria the so-called Ashby report has recommended as a first objective that 25 per cent of the children should complete primary education, 2.5 per cent should enter the secondary schools, and 002 to .003 per cent should enter a university.[21] Abhorrent as a system may be which excludes 75 per cent of the children from formal education, some underdeveloped areas may not immediately be able to support a more extensive program.

More optimistic than the recommendation of the Ashby report (which itself has been called utopian by some observers) were the targets proposed by the Conference of African States on the Development of Education. This confer-

[20] *Ibid.*
[21] *Investment in Education,* The Report of Post-school Certificate and Higher Education in Nigeria, Federal Ministry of Education, Nigeria, 1960, pp. 10–11.

	1960–1961	1965–1966	1970–1971	1980–1981
Primary level	40*	51	71	100
Secondary level	3	9	15	23
Higher level	0.2	0.2	0.4	2

* Numbers are percentages of appropriate age groups.

ence recommended a long-term plan for Africa as outlined above.[22]

It is not being suggested in this discussion of priorities that two underdeveloped countries at the same stage of development need have identical educational systems and educational philosophies. Each nation tries to preserve its peculiar cultural identity or, if it has no highly developed institutional heritage, to construct a new cultural synthesis. This national uniqueness will be reflected in formal and informal education, in language, history, literature, and art, and in out-of-school activities. The total atmosphere of the school is influenced by the culture's image of an educated person.

The second factor impinging on the establishment of priorities, the pertinence of the curriculum to national development, will be discussed in the next section.

3. The instructional programs of the underdeveloped countries should be development-oriented. Implied in this tautological statement is the thesis that curricular experiences which make maximum contribution to the growth of a nation must go beyond tradition and include any area in which the society needs trained intelligence. The accumulation of knowledge has rightly been an

[22] UNESCO, Conference of African States on the Development of Education in Africa, *op. cit.*, p. 19.

age-old function of schools, though unfortunately the application of knowledge to the achievement of national goals has received less attention. As has been pointed out by critics of colonialism in Africa and Asia, educational programs fostered by European rulers were largely limited to "saving souls and producing clerks." A development-oriented curriculum, however, must provide the technical and scientific skills needed by a developing nation and, in addition, foster certain personal drives and social attitudes.

Objectivity, rationality, and a favorable view toward change as a process are said to be attitudes conducive to economic and social change. This being the case, the peoples of the underdeveloped areas need new images, new values, new spirit, and new faith in the future. They need to envision a new culture and their place in that culture. Since new values and attitudes often will run into conflict with existing societal patterns, family structure, and various entrenched political and religious institutions, the reconstructive nature of a curricular experience becomes apparent. It may be expected that schools which seek to promote creativity, innovation, respect for entrepreneurship, and belief in the worth of hand skills will promote grave dissatisfaction with a nation's traditional values. To ease the divisive effects of a widening schism between school and

347

society, extensive communication and close interaction must be maintained between the two.

Rapid development, accompanied by a minimum of institutional conflict, therefore, requires careful planning at both national and local levels. At the national level, in the field of education, this means making studies of current and projected manpower needs and translating such needs into goals for national action. Leaders of a nation in dire need of technicians and agriculturists must see to it that the schools do more than prepare white-collar workers and leisure-oriented gentlemen. That balance has not been achieved in the past is seen in the overabundance of lawyers in Latin America and arts graduates in India and the dearth of technically trained persons in all underdeveloped nations. The image and the fact of incorruptible and competent educational leadership at the national level, a leadership capable of establishing educational priorities on a professional basis, is perhaps the first requisite for successful educational development.

To maximize the role of the school in directed economic and social change, instructional programs must be designed to provide grass-roots leadership. At the primary level, schools must not only develop literacy and prepare pupils for secondary schools but they also must take a direct part in solving the community's civic, health, and sanitation problems. Experiments that have been carried out in many countries in Latin America, Asia, and Africa under the titles of community education, fundamental education, and basic education, while varying in many respects, have all emphasized the extensive developmental role of the primary school and the pri-

348

mary school teacher. At the secondary level, the school can be drawn closer to the community by utilizing community resources within a problem-solving curriculum approach. Furthermore, as demonstrated in Taiwan, the Philippines, and elsewhere, students and their teachers can play an important role in directly teaching skills to the adult population and providing leadership for development projects. While universities usually conceive of their purpose in national terms, they too, through extension work, through research, and by institutionalizing the concept of service can assist local development.

The new streamlined curricula demanded in the underdeveloped countries must draw upon an international fund of knowledge and at the same time seek to maintain continuity with the past. The excess academic baggage imposed on former colonies—courses in the history, geography, literature, and possibly language of the colonial power—must be modified or deleted. Even the more technical experiences provided in programs for engineers, doctors, and teachers, designed as they often are to serve an industrial state, may need drastic modification. Indeed the native language itself may need to undergo revision in order that it may be a more efficient tool of communication.[23] Experience over the past two decades has shown most definitely that a single academic curriculum offered in primary and secondary schools is not sufficient to meet

[23] It is interesting to note that the development-minded Communists, immediately upon gaining power in North Korea and China, began to modify drastically the cumbersome script, while in the republic of Korea and on Taiwan language reform has been painfully slow.

the demands of development. Vocational courses must be given prestige in their own right. It must be anticipated that new knowledge and new ideas may be in conflict with traditional ways of thinking, and new syntheses must be attempted if the schools are going to ease the traumatic effect of social change.

Development-oriented curricula, as the foregoing has suggested, should be fostered at all levels and in all academic areas. The schools should take their tools of reading, language, mathematics, science, and technology into the communities in order that each individual may readily see the power of education. Both physical plants, often the best structures in the community, and teaching faculties, often among the best-educated persons in the community, should be utilized as fully as possible. Interchanges of students and faculty between school and factory, government, or business concern may well contribute to the virility of all institutions involved. In this regard, important lessons may be learned from the concept of poly-technization developed in the Communist nations.

Academic standards are an extremely controversial issue. The authors believe that, at least in the early stages of development, enforcement of high academic and professional standards may inhibit economic growth, although there is no easy way of demonstrating the validity of this hypothesis. Certainly many Asian, African, and Latin American educational leaders would not subscribe to this view. Indian educators, for example, frequently write of the need to strengthen standards at the secondary and higher education levels, while Nigerian and East African leaders are struggling valiantly, if vainly, to duplicate standards prescribed for English institutions.

Yet, bad as the psychological effects may be, the pressing need in most underdeveloped areas for large numbers of professional and skilled persons would seem to warrant a temporary lowering of standards. A midwife may be a useful temporary alternative to a professional nurse. Doctors and engineers who cannot pass the professional requirements of Western Europe or America may have a valuable role to play in a nation where medical and engineering skills are virtually nonexistent. And college-trained elementary teachers as an alternative for those prepared in seconary schools are a luxury most underdeveloped countries can ill afford.

4. Provisions should be made for extensive out-of-school education. The broadly conceived pattern of education necessary for developing countries must include part-time but articulated schooling for adults. Whether adult education is primarily a task for the regular schools or some other agency is debatable. Some successful attempts have been made to bring parents to existing schools. Children have at times become the teachers of their parents; a basic weakness in this approach, however, is that adult education, for a high degree of success, requires specially trained teachers and specially prepared instructional materials. On the other hand, some community-development schemes have brought about dramatic changes by utilizing multipurpose village workers, social education organizers, and agricultural extension specialists in cooperation with the teachers.

In any event, the developing countries must harness *all* their instruments of change to initiate general educational improvement. Every trained person should have a teaching function and every institution should in a sense be considered a school. The government itself, through its laws and decrees and through the actions of its personnel, is one of the most important educational institutions of a developing nation. The ministries of labor, health, and defense, as well as the ministries of education, have important educational functions. The national police, sometimes the only government employees to penetrate the most rural areas, can be used to promote local educational development. Mass media under either public or private control can, if used skillfully and objectively, become powerful tools for adult education. And to reinforce the progressive attitudes developed, provision must be made for a system of "life-long adaptation" whereby each individual in each nation can have continued access through at least one medium of communication to knowledge that will assist him in understanding his changing role in a developing society.

5. *An educational technology designed for developing nations should be created.* New, bold, and different instructional techniques and materials must be introduced into the schools and used by other agencies to communicate the content of development. Some of the educational technology used in the highly industrial countries may be adapted for use in the lesser-developed nations. Newspapers and radio certainly have important roles. Experimentation now being carried out with television suggests that under certain conditions this medium will be useful. UNESCO has expressed exceeding faith in the educational possibilities of all mass media

and has recommended that a minimum of five radio receivers and two television sets be provided for every 100 persons in each underdeveloped country. Inexpensive, individualized teaching machines offer another hope for reducing costs and possibly increasing the rate of learning. Sunlight and battery projectors make it possible to revitalize or even substitute for the traditional use of textbooks. Skilled use of drama, folk songs, and folk dances may in some rural areas be as rewarding as the use of mechanical and electronic devices. These and many other innovations require further testing and, when found applicable, need to be used on a scale not yet attempted in any of the underdeveloped countries.

The creation or innovation of devices and techniques that will influence key groups is a central development problem. An efficient educational technology will greatly assist the "multiplier" and "diffusion" effects of learning. There is as yet, however, too little research and accumulated experience to suggest the dimensions of the needed technology and the manner of its integration with the educational process. The need for an extensive, inexpensive, and rapid means of imparting skills and knowledge may well be met by a modern monitorial system of instruction.

For maximum efficiency national educational programs should be developed for the use of various media. Designated schools may be used as audio-visual centers or as outlets for national centers. Mobile training units carrying audio-visual equipment and operated by a team of educational and communication specialists are a necessity in the most rural areas. Such units have had considerable success in India, the Near

East, and Latin America. Visual demonstrations have been particularly effective in teaching the illiterates, because visual experience appears to be a most influential factor in their decision-making process. Many of the techniques mentioned here have yielded dramatic results in rural communities or small towns, but there have been discouragingly few nationwide attempts to use them. A conservative attitude toward experimentation seems to prevent their all-out use for a real educational breakthrough.

6. *A vital developmental role can be played by foreign assistance programs.* Underdeveloped countries need to draw upon an international fund of knowledge to hasten them along the path of social and economic growth. Two aspects of bilateral and multilateral educational exchange and assistance will be discussed here: (1) the participation of youth and young adults from the underdeveloped areas in the educational programs of the developed nations, and (2) the use of foreign technical advisers in the underdeveloped nations.

During the school year 1961–1962, 58,000 students from other countries, mostly the underdeveloped nations, attended educational institutions in the United States, and many others studied in Canada and Western Europe. In addition, nearly 14,000 professional persons came to the United States to study or observe our practices. There have been few attempts to conduct follow-up studies on the returned students in order to evaluate the efficiency of their academic or training programs,[24]

although some general hypotheses based on experience have been offered.

The main advantage of studying in a highly developed nation is that the student comes into contact with modern institutions and equipment and with instructors who make decisions from an advanced fund of knowledge. The main disadvantage of advanced foreign study, especially for the less mature student, is the possibility that such study may actually be dysfunctional for the student. Unless the institution attended is willing to build an individualized program consonant with the peculiar needs of the student, the training received may better prepare the student for living and working in the host country than for carrying out developmental tasks at home. To take an example, a Tanganyikan returning home to practice medicine after completing his medical studies in Western Europe or America would need to make tremendous technical, as well as social, adaptations to successfully practice his profession.

It is quite widely accepted that a nation's educational policy must be developed by the native leaders of that country. The choice of basic values to be promoted and the selection of educational priorities do not fall within the prerogatives of a foreign adviser. Yet there remains a role for the outside specialist, a sensitive but important role. A foreign educational adviser presum-

---

[24] One survey of American programs for foreign students reported three conclusions of wide-reaching significance: (1) A high percentage of participants had a change in attitude toward the United States after they left; (2) about 63 per cent felt that their training was being utilized in the home country; (3) some 23 per cent felt that the training period should be longer than one year in order to be more effective. See *Government Programs in International Education: A Survey and Handbook,* Forty-second Report by the Committee on Government Operations, U.S. Government Printing Office, 1959.

ably holds certain knowledge and skills not found among the native educators; furthermore, he has a professional detachment which increases his objectivity. Thus technical assistance should be able to help in the clarification of existing problems and in the identification of possible alternative solutions. For example, the concepts, as well as the skills, of educational research are practically unknown in the developing nations; this vacuum can be easily filled with the assistance of scholars from advanced nations. One of the imperative educational needs in the underdeveloped countries is the application of a more scientific and experimental approach to such problems as the writing of textbooks and other instructional materials, the design and utilization of school buildings, the operation of libraries and laboratories, the improvement of methodology, and the construction of a truly professional program of teacher education.

Utilization of foreign advisers in educational development is fraught with sundry and subtle dangers. Not only must the adviser be of high professional caliber, but he must be a careful student of culture as well. The presence of cultural pitfalls in advisory work has been described elsewhere in these metaphorical terms:

There is an old Oriental story that accurately depicts the plight of an unwary foreign educational adviser: Once upon a time there was a great flood, and involved in this flood were two creatures, a monkey and a fish. The monkey, being agile and experienced, was lucky enough to scramble up a tree and escape the raging waters. As he looked down from his safe perch, he saw the poor fish strug-

gling against the swift current. With the very best of intentions he reached down and lifted the fish from the water. The result was inevitable.[25]

Avoiding mistakes requires preparation not usually received by the foreign adviser. Ideally this person should be well versed in the general educational conditions of underdevelopment and specifically trained in the language and culture of the area in which he carries out his work.[26] He should, for example, understand the educational implications of such principles of cultural change as:

1. . . . people do not vary their customary behavior unless they feel some need which existing ways do not satisfy.
2. Needs cannot be established by fiat.
3. Devising means for participation in the light of knowledge of culture and social organization would seem to be a fundamental procedure in the process of directing cultural change.[27]

Continued study of the educational problems of the underdeveloped countries offers a great challenge and opportunity to students of comparative education. A variety of studies must be undertaken ranging from the broadly descriptive, as in the case of general sociohistorical educational surveys in

[25] Don Adams, "The Monkey and the Fish," *International Development Review,* vol. 2, no. 2, p. 22, October, 1960.
[26] For a more complete discussion of the principles of innovation applied successfully to community-development work, the student's attention is called to George Foster, "Guidelines to Community Development Programs," *Public Health Reports,* vol. 70, no. 1, January, 1955.
[27] Edward H. Spicer (ed.), *Human Problems in Technological Change,* Russell Sage, New York, 1952, pp. 292–293.

particular countries, to more definitive research on particular problems. The latter category would involve testing a plethora of hypotheses regarding education and social and economic growth. Better measures of the investment value of education need to be found. Clearer enunciations need be made of the indirect returns of education, such as changed values, attitudes, and behavioral patterns. Admittedly there will be methodological difficulty in undertaking such studies. Yet the moral urgency of the educational problems involved in the underdeveloped countries certainly warrants giving them increased attention. Education, it has been said, may be a nation's best asset or its worst liability depending on its use. The conditions under which it is the former are yet to be fully explored.

References

Books

Adams, Don: "Education and Nation Building," in Clarence W. Hunnicutt (ed.), *America's Emerging Role in Overseas Education,* Syracuse University School of Education, Syracuse, N.Y., 1962, pp. 51–69.

Agarwala, A. N., and S. P. Singh (eds.): *The Economics of Underdevelopment,* Oxford, Fair Lawn, N.J., 1963.

Bowman, Mary Jean, and C. Arnold Anderson: "The Role of Education in Development," *Development of the Emerging Countries,* Brookings, Washington, 1962, pp. 153–180.

Brand, W.: *The Struggle for a Higher Standard of Living,* Free Press, New York, 1958.

Burns, Hobert W. (ed.): *Education and the Development of Nations,* Center for Development Education, All-University School of Education, Syracuse University Press, Syracuse, N.Y., 1963.

Curle, Adam: *Educational Strategy for Developing Societies: A Study of Educational & Social Factors in Relation to Economic Growth,* Tavistock Publications, London, 1963.

Frankel, Sally Herbert: *The Economic Impact on Underdeveloped Societies: Essays on International Investment and Social Change,* Harvard, Cambridge, Mass., 1955.

Ginsburg, Norton: *Atlas of Economic Development,* The University of Chicago Press, Chicago, 1961.

Government Programs in International Education: A Survey and Handbook, Forty-second Report by the Committee on Government Operations, U.S. Government Printing Office, 1959.

Hagen, Everett E.: *On the Theory of Social Change: How Economic Growth Begins,* Dorsey Press, Homewood, Ill., 1962.

Halsey, A. H., Jean Floud, and C. Arnold Anderson (eds.): *Education, Economy, and Society: A Reader in the Sociology of Education,* Free Press, New York, 1961.

Hayes, Samuel P., Jr.: *Measuring the Results of Development Projects,* Monographs in the Applied Social Sciences, UNESCO, Paris, 1959.

Hoselitz, Bert F. (ed.): *The Progress of Underdeveloped Areas,* The University of Chicago Press, Chicago, 1952.

——: *Sociological Aspects of Economic Growth,* Free Press, New York, 1960.

—— and Wilbert E. Moore (eds.): *Industrialization and Society,* UNESCO, Mouton, 1963.

Investment in Education, The Report of Post-school Certificate and Higher Education in Nigeria, Federal Ministry of Education, Nigeria, 1960.

Lerner, Daniel: *The Passing of Traditional Society,* Free Press, New York, 1958.

Lewis, W. Arthur: *The Theory of Economic Growth,* Irwin, Homewood, Ill., 1955.

McClelland, David: *The Achieving Society,* Van Nostrand, Princeton, N.J., 1961.

Meier, Gerald M., and Robert E. Baldwin: *Economic Development,* Wiley, New York, 1961.

Neff, Kenneth L.: *National Development through Social Progress: The Role of Education,* U.S. Office of Education, 1963.

Parnes, Herbert S.: *Forecasting Educational Needs for Economic and Social Development,* Organization for Economic Co-operation and Development, 1963.

Platt, William J.: *Toward Strategies of Education,* Stanford Research Institute, International Industrial Development Center, Menlo Park, Calif., 1961.

Rostow, W. W.: *The Stages of Economic Growth: A Non-Communist Manifesto,* Cambridge, New York, 1960.

Samper, Armando: *A Case Study of Co-operation in Secondary Education in Chile,* National Planning Association, Washington, D.C., 1957.

Schultz, Theodore W.: "Education and Economic Growth," *Social Forces Influencing American Education,* NSSE Yearbook, 1961, part 2, chap. 3, pp. 46–88.

Spicer, Edward H. (ed.): *Human Problems in Technological Change,* Russell Sage, New York, 1952.

United Nations Department of Economic Affairs: *Measures for the Economic Development of Under-developed Nations,* New York, 1951.

UNESCO: Conference of African States on the Development of Education in Africa, *Final Report,* United Nations Economic Commission for Africa, Addis Ababa, 1961.

Ward, W. E.: *Educating Young Nations,* G. Allen, London, 1959.

Pamphlets and periodicals

Adams, Don: "The Monkey and the Fish," *International Development Review,* vol. 2, no. 2, pp. 22–24, October, 1960.

Foster, George: "Guidelines to Community Development Programs," *Public Health Reports,* vol. 70, no. 1, January, 1955.

Lewis, Oscar: "Some of My Best Friends Are Peasants," *Human Organization,* vol. 19, no. 4, pp. 179–80, Winter, 1960–1961.

Nielsen, Waldemar A.: "The Newest Frontier," a guest editorial in *Saturday Review,* Apr. 1, 1961, p. 22.

Ruffner, Ralph W.: "American Educational Aid for National Development," *Teachers College Record,* vol. 62, no. 5, pp. 348–55, February, 1961.

Rusk, Dean: "Education: Key to National Development," *Overseas,* vol. 1, no. 1, pp. 6–7, September, 1961.

Vaizey, John: "Comparative Notes on Economic Growth, and Social Change in Education," *Comparative Education Review,* vol. 5, no. 1, pp. 7–12, June, 1961.

———: "Education as Investment in Comparative Perspective," *Comparative Education Review,* vol. 5, no. 2, pp. 97–104, October, 1961.

CHAPTER 13

Latin American Education:
From Colonialism to Nationalism

This chapter and the next two will explore not only the cultural bases of existing educational ideas and institutions but also the various educational factors retarding social and economic progress. The most obvious difficulty in such a task is to identify the inner logic or cohesive forces significant to decision making in each of the areas discussed. Latin America, Africa, and even India comprise vast areas; each envelops diverse religious, political, and social traditions and is subject to a variety of topographical and climatic influences. Such diversity imposes limitations on the student. The student of comparative education, with his customary penchant for painting on a broad canvas, must accept the limitations, however, and seek valid generalizations pertinent to contemporary educational policies and programs.

Evolution of the republics

The term "Latin America" is used here to include Mexico and Central and South America, a total of twenty independent countries inhabited by over 200 million people. This region comprises an area approximately 2½ times that of the United States and stretches from 35 degrees North Latitude to 55 degrees South Latitude. While some regions of southeastern Brazil, Uruguay, and much of Argentina have well-developed industrial and educational programs, most of the Latin American nations, when judged by per capita income, degree of literacy, or standard of living, fall into the underdeveloped category. Unlike many of the economically underdeveloped areas, however, Latin America is blessed with rich forests, minerals, good fishing grounds, and other resources.

The main racial strains in Latin America have derived from Indian, European (Spanish and Portuguese), and African stock. These groups have mixed rather freely, but three relatively distinct racial regions are sometimes identified. The racial combination of Europeans and Indians has taken place primarily along the western side of the mountain chain that extends from Mexico through Central America, Colombia, Ecuador, Peru, Bolivia, and Chile. In the mountain areas of these countries, however, large pockets of Indians continue to live in traditional ways. Four nations, Ecuador, Bolivia, Peru, and Guatemala, are sometimes referred to as the Indian countries, since over 40 per cent of their total population is Indian. A second region, including portions of Brazil, Venezuela, and Colombia, is represented primarily by an African-European racial combination. The third region, which covers southern Brazil, Uruguay, Argentina, and much of Chile, is predominantly European in racial and cultural heritage.[1]

Further generalizations show Latin America with a long background of political instability, illiteracy, and social

[1] Vera Micheles Dean, *The Nature of the Non-Western World*, Mentor Books, New American Library of World Literature, Inc., New York, 1957, pp. 178, 179.

355

elitism which have combined to thwart exploitation of the vast economic potential. Historically, extreme centralization of power has undermined local and individual initiative, and a long period of minority rule has corrupted popular expression. A multiple-track system of education whose prestige route offered a sterile conception of traditional European literary and professional curricula has served to harden the boundaries of highly segmented societies.

On the brighter side, there has been no paucity of great Latin American thinkers in the political, artistic, social, and educational fields. Moreover, the early colonial policies of Spain and, to a greater degree, of Portugal, set a course that prevented the development of flagrant racial and ethnic discrimination in Latin America. Nevertheless, reform has been slow. Poverty, economic underdevelopment, political instability, social frustration, and real or imaginary fears of the various forms of imperialism still persist in the 1960s. A brief historical sketch of the development of Latin America may assist in giving perspective to the gap between desires and fulfillment and between potential and realization.

Colonial policies

Shortly after the initial explorations of the New World, Spanish conquistadors established their rule over the Caribbean area, Mexico, Peru, and much of the remainder of what has come to be known as "Spanish" America. In 1500 the vast territory of Brazil became a colony of Portugal. Iberian institutions made rapid inroads in spite of the advanced culture of the Aztecs, Mayas, Incas, and other Indian groups in Mexico, Central America, and Peru. Native

rule was destroyed, native religions were officially displaced by Catholicism, and for governmental and commercial purposes, native languages were supplanted by Spanish and Portuguese.

By mid-seventeenth century the Spanish and Portuguese were militarily and culturally entrenched in Latin America. The viceroyalties of New Spain (Mexico) and Peru had celebrated their centennials, and colonial governmental arrangements were taking on a permanent form. From the very beginning the conquistadors and their clerical companions had claimed each new area and its population for the crown and the Roman Catholic Church, thus establishing in Spanish America the Iberian tradition of strong, centralized, church-state control. Indeed the fact that the Spanish crown was specifically charged by Rome with the responsibility of establishing the Church and conducting education had very specific influences on educational development in Latin America.

In the Spanish colonies, a highly centralized hierarchy, headed by a viceroy, was created in each of the four viceroyalties: New Spain, Peru, New Granada, and La Plata. Holders of high administrative posts were of Spanish birth and were appointed directly by the king; no man born of Spanish parents in the colonies, regardless of education, wealth, or lineage, could hope for a governmental position higher than that of head of the *cabildo* or local government. The large majority of the population — mestizos (white-Indian), Indians, mulattoes (white-Negro), Negroes, and zambosi (Indian-Negro) — had little opportunity to demonstrate responsible leadership.

Economic opportunities and social prestige likewise were related to race and Old World cultural values. Spanish colonists and homelanders controlled all highly productive economic enterprises, while the mestizos occupied an upper-lower-class role as farmers or small entrepreneurs. Indians and Negroes furnished the agricultural, mining, and domestic workers. They were often without individual rights and freedom, being considered slaves during the early colonial period and later tied in a feudal type of relationship to the large land-owner or commercial concern.

The Portuguese pattern of colonization was of somewhat different design. Although the first Portuguese claims on Brazil were made in 1500, the area attracted little immediate attention from the Portuguese crown, absorbed as it was in acquiring the riches of its colonies in Africa and the East Indies. Consequently, colonization and local control were largely left to the initiative of private groups. (Even the brief period of Spanish control over Brazil, 1580–1640, did little to alter this pattern.) Although a viceroyalty was eventually established in Brazil, colonial government was never so centralized or, in fact, so well organized as in the Spanish colonies. Indeed, the owners of the great northern sugar plantations which flourished in the seventeenth century and the pioneerlike Paulistas, advancing inland in the south during the same period, scarcely felt the hand of the central government at all. Moreover, the Catholic Church in Brazil was neither so strong nor so politically active as was the Spanish Church; the Brazilian clergy tended to concentrate its effort on promoting education in the "civilized" areas and on protecting the Indians from the inhuman conditions imposed on them by settlers.

In Portuguese Brazil societal and cultural institutions were made as much akin to those of the Old World as feasible. However, culture was less highly developed than in the Spanish colonies, and ties with the homeland were less pronounced—as evidenced, for example, by the fact that few legal or social distinctions were made between Brazilian and peninsular Portuguese. Yet there was, to an even greater extent than in the Spanish colonies, a paternalistic, feudal relationship between the privileged elite and the less fortunate elements of the population.

In both Spanish and Portuguese America, political and economic power as well as social prestige resided with those of European lineage. One source offers dramatic statistical evidence of the Iberian aristocracy that came to be established in Latin America. Stokes has estimated that in 1823 the following racial groups existed:[2]

	Thousands	Per cent
Whites (*peninsulares* and *crillos* combined)	3,276	19.4
Mixed	5,328	31.5
Indians	7,530	44.5
Negroes	776	4.6

As Stokes further comments, the Spanish-born whites (*peninsulares*) had the most prestige.

The "whites" constituted a social aristocracy during the colonial period with a dominant position in the Church, army, economic system and government. The *peninsulares* made up the elite of the aristocracy. Out of 166 viceroys and 588 captains-general, governors, and presidents who held office during the colonial period (754

[2] William S. Stokes, *Latin American Politics,* Crowell, New York, 1959, p. 5.

posts in all), *peninsulares* held 736. *Peninsulares* held 357 of the 369 bishoprics up to 1637. Of the 706 bishops in America prior to 1812, 601 were *peninsulares*. When the intendant system was established late in the eighteenth century it was provided that only *peninsulares* would be eligible to hold the new posts.[3]

In the absence of any sizable dissenting religious sects the Catholic Church enjoyed great prestige in colonial Latin America. The Church at once represented a new faith, a protector of the Indians, and a progenitor of European culture. To spread Christian light, a Church hierarchy was established, extending from the lowly parish priest who cared for the spiritual needs of the village folk to the mighty archbishop who, as a key member of the aristocracy, represented the crown first and the papacy second. Proselytism was made easier by the remarkable similarities between Christian beliefs and the beliefs held in many of the Indian religions. Peculiarly enough the Church often considered these resemblances the subversive work of Satan.

In seeking to protect the Indians from the more avaricious landowners and officials, the Church occasionally found itself in conflict with secular authority. On the whole, however, the efforts of the Church and crown were supplementary. The Church performed proselyting and charitable work no other institution could perform and in turn grew rich and powerful as the commercial, agricultural, and mining ventures of the colonists proved successful.

The educational function of the Church led to the introduction of European language and customs to the Indians and to the establishment of various types of educational institutions. Catholic priests of the Benedictine, Franciscan, and Jesuit orders were active in establishing schools for both natives and colonials by the end of the sixteenth century. A few Catholic educational leaders were exceedingly progressive in their philosophy, urging, for example, the founding of schools to serve all people irrespective of class or race, the introduction of scientific subjects and methods, and closer ties between school and community life.

The most significant educational efforts were carried out by the indefatigable Society of Jesus. By mid-eighteenth century, the Jesuits had established eighty-nine colleges and thirty-two seminaries in Latin America. Scattered primary schools were also founded to teach religion and arts and crafts to the Indian groups, but it was in secondary and higher education that the Jesuits made their strongest educational impact. The *colegios,* which offered a curriculum of the traditional liberal arts to the Spanish, Portuguese, and creole elite, became the models for much still found in Latin American secondary education.

The most important seats of higher learning were also in the hands of the Jesuits. The University of Mexico (1551),[4] the University of San Marcos in Lima (1551), the University of Santiago (1624), the University of Chuquisaca (1624), and many other leading institutions were founded by the Society of Jesus. The expulsion of the Jesuits from Spanish America in 1767, and earlier from Brazil, was temporarily ob-

[4] The institution founded in Santo Domingo in 1539 is usually credited with being the first university in Latin America.

[3] *Ibid.,* pp. 5–6.

structive to advanced learning and permanently disastrous for the Jesuit educational monopoly. Although after the reestablishment of their order, the Jesuits again became involved in Latin American education, new revolutionary and secular forces, some frankly anti-clerical, were arising to limit their influence.

The universities, strongly scholastic in character and influenced by the Bologna, Padua, and Salamanca traditions, offered preparatory courses for the traditional "learned" professions, work in Spanish literature, and often study of Indian languages. Owing to the lack of a system of lower schools, some universities conducted their own elementary and secondary instruction. As in the universities of the mother countries, successful students at the universities might receive any of four degrees: bachelor, licentiate, master, and doctor. In spite of strict Church censorship, during the latter part of the colonial period the writings of Locke, Descartes, and Newton leaked into the universities and challenged the Aristotelian-Thomistic monopoly in philosophy and science. Although the immediate effect of this new learning on the university curriculum was far from dramatic, an attitude of questioning authority was nurtured, the fruition of which was seen in the revolutionary role of some of the university graduates.

In addition to the colleges and universities which served only the elite groups, other schools were founded by local priests for the lower social classes. Schools emphasizing various trade skills, the three R's, and Christian religion were established for the mestizo and mulatto. Programs for Indians were largely limited to instruction in religion,

Spanish, and certain crafts. For the vast majority, the rudiments of religion were considered sufficient.

The strengths and weaknesses in Latin American education during the colonial period were, then, the educational strengths and weaknesses of Spain and Portugal. The emphasis was on higher education, and several universities were to gain distinction. These institutions, in the tradition of the University of Salamanca, were autonomous and extended many protections and privileges to faculty and students. A certain amount of intellectual liberalism flourished among faculty members. Yet, in final analysis, the curricula were designed to fit the tastes of only a small cultured class. The youth of the rich continued to matriculate in European institutions where it was felt the best education could be procured.

Implications of independence

The tradition of elitism and Old World values in general were strongly in evidence at the beginning of the Latin American colonists' struggle for independence, a struggle which spanned the first third of the nineteenth century. In Portuguese America, independence was won by peaceful proclamation, with the Brazilian-raised son of the Portuguese King, Pedro I, becoming the constitutional emperor. In Spanish America, most of the leaders of the struggle for independence were creoles and many were intellectual liberals; all sought a greater voice in government.

Professor Thomas cites six general causes for the wars for independence in Spanish America: the usurpation of official positions by the Spanish, prejudicial trade arrangements, heavy taxa-

359

tion, tradition of revolt, new social philosophies, and the examples of the French and American Revolutions.[5]

The ideas that led to the struggle for Latin American independence were those of the Enlightenment in Europe. The institution of Freemasonry, whose lodges spread from France and England to Spain, Portugal, and Latin America, aided greatly in the spread of radical political, social, and even pedagogical theories. A Masonic lodge in London brought together Bolívar, San Martín, O'Higgins, and other great revolutionary leaders who laid plans for Spanish America's separation from Spain. In London also Latin American leaders came under the influence of Jeremy Bentham and other proponents of utilitarianism. These ideological influences, the writings of the French philosophers and encyclopedists, the Benthamic principle of "greatest happiness of the greatest number," and the expressed goals of the French and American Revolutions formed the principles for Latin America's struggle for independence. Many diverse ethnic and occupational groups found inspiration in such ideas as representative government, freedom of speech and press, and other principles of individual protection.

Initially the leaders of the independence struggle favored the authority of the Spanish crown and opposed the liberal Spanish Cortes which defied Napoleon and attempted to limit the authority of their absent monarch. Later, the conflict broadened into a struggle for complete independence, individual liberty, and a republican form of government. The Church leaders had cus-

tomarily supported the crown, and even in time of revolution continued to support the *status quo*; for this action the Church drew not only scathing reproof from the intellectuals but also popular criticism and distrust. Nevertheless, the Church was deeply embedded in Latin American life, and it remained a social and religious power even after the overthrow of the colonial control.

As royalist forces were defeated, idealistic constitutions were penned, and humanitarian reforms were proclaimed. The new liberal social philosophy was well understood by only a few of the new leaders, however, and had practically no roots in the great masses of people. Indeed, the separatist movements changed the ruling oligarchies but had little effect on the social role or the living conditions of the lower classes.

The unstable postcolonial period was the beginning of the age of the caudillo, the strong man, backed usually by a relatively small band of loyal followers who pledged allegiance to the most appealing banner; but in effect, the caudillo fought only to substitute his authority for that emanating from the homeland or from a previously successful caudillo. To the caudillos went the fruits of independence, while the great leaders in the battle for freedom died in exile or in chains. Although with few exceptions the Latin American states were freed from foreign rule, they did not follow the path toward political democracy and social justice. As the disillusioned champion of social democracy, Simón Bolívar, finally was forced to conclude, "We who have worked for the cause of Latin-American freedom have ploughed the sea."

The period of conflict in the decades immediately following independ-

[5] Alfred Barnaby Thomas, *Latin America: A History with Maps,* Macmillan, New York, 1956, pp. 219–222.

ence meant social instability and educational retardation for most of the Latin American nations. New concepts of individual rights and human liberties continued to have popular appeal and were used by aspiring politicians, but they were not gracefully assimilated into cultures where great social cleavages existed, and primary authority was likely to rest with a single individual. If political and social reforms were slow, so too were educational changes. Empirical and pragmatic methods of inquiry, while certainly not unknown among the intellectual classes, never gained extensive popularity. The neglect of mass education by colonial rulers, the hostility of the Church toward secular instruction, indeed, the total use of education as an instrument to build and perpetuate a rank-ordered society all caused delay in applying revolutionary educational principles. The economic and political chaos immediately following the independence struggle had to be resolved, and a new commercial, industrial, and social era had to evolve before common secular education could secure a foothold.

Independence had little effect on the prevailing social philosophy. The Latin American nations, like the Iberian nations, failed to assimilate the bold, new philosophic ideas that swept England and Western Europe in the seventeenth and eighteenth centuries. The assumption persisted that men were by nature unequal, and social and economic institutions reflected this assumption. Of equal importance and directly related to its contemporary underdevelopment, Latin America also missed to a large degree the new concepts of production dramatized by the term "Industrial Revolution," which were introduced in

Northern Europe in the late eighteenth and early nineteenth centuries. As one author has summarized:

> No Spanish lords had ever gathered at a Spanish Runnymede to impose checks on the absolute power of their king. No emerging middle class or industrial revolution during the long centuries of Spanish rule in America worked to enforce a modification of the traditional authoritarian forms of Spain. No *habeas corpus* or English common law provided any check on, or appeal from, the acts of the Inquisition.[6]

Contemporary societal problems and educational policies

Two facts stand out in any attempt to analyze the cultural and educational problems of Latin America. First, the nations of Latin America have not been able to take full advantage of their economic potential. Second, the political, economic, and educational advances that have been made have not been evenly distributed (see Table 3 for ranking of countries on selected demographic data). Thus, some of the most modern cities of the world are surrounded by areas where life is primitive and poverty cruel; and while Argentina and portions of Uruguay and Chile have virtually eliminated illiteracy, Honduras, Venezuela, Guatemala, Bolivia, and large areas of Brazil are still plagued by an illiteracy rate of at least 50 per cent.

As in other developing areas, urbanization, specialization, and division of labor have all accompanied the early stages of development in Latin America; but certain expected social changes have come about slowly. Only recently, for

[6] Dean, *op. cit.*, p. 180.

Table 3 *Demographic Data on Latin America*

Country	Literacy rate	Per capita gross national product	Per cent of population in cities over 20,000	Per cent of active population in agriculture, lowest to highest	Infant mortality, lowest to highest
Argentina	1	3	1	1	3
Bolivia	18	20	9	18	12
Brazil	12.5	8	8	12.5	18
Chile	4	14	2	2	17
Colombia	10.5	6	6.5	8.5	15
Costa Rica	4	7	11	10	11
Cuba	4	4	3	5	
Dominican Republic	14	11	17	11	6
Ecuador	9	12	10	7	16
El Salvador	16	10	15	15	8
Guatemala	19	15	16	17	14
Haiti	20	19	19	19.5	
Honduras	16	17	18	19.5	2
Mexico	8	13	5	12.5	10
Nicaragua	16	9	12.5	8.5	5
Panama	6.5	5	6.5	6	1
Paraguay	6.5	18	12.5	8.5	5
Peru	12.5	16	14	14	13
Uruguay	2	2		3	9
Venezuela	10.5	1	4	4	4

NOTE: All data translated into ranks.

SOURCE: Data were taken from tables in Norton Ginsburg, *Atlas of Economic Development,* The University of Chicago Press, Chicago, 1961. For a discussion of reliability, definitions, and comparability of data, see this source and the primary sources noted by Ginsburg. Most data are for the period 1950–1955.

example, has a numerous and morally responsible middle class been visible:

> . . . to fill the void that long has existed between a small elite at the apex of the social pyramid and the impoverished, servile, uneducated, and underprivileged masses that constitute its base.[7]

[7] Lynn T. Smith, *Current Social Trends and Problems in Latin America,* Latin-American Monograph, University of Florida Press, Gainesville, Fla., 1957, p. 9.

The absence of a strong middle class has been viewed by many North American observers as one of Latin America's most crucial problems. Moreover, the failure of technical advancement to keep pace with the economic and social desires of the people has not provided a setting for continued political security. Nor has the centralized and authoritarian structure of society with its hierarchy of classes provided the framework within which a citizenry can readily foster change through evolutionary or democratic means. Inequitable tax systems and unfair land-tenure policies further hinder development and add to the distrust among societal groups. Finally, the Latin American schools, formal in method, narrow in curriculum offerings, and providing sharply limited educational opportunities, have not yet made their maximum contribution either to economic or social development.

Economic problems

It must be emphasized that there are vast differences in economic viability and economic potential among the Latin American nations. In Argentina, for example, the gross national product per capita in 1961 was the equivalent of $799 (United States dollars) while in Bolivia this figure was only $122.[8] The annual rate of population growth likewise shows great variance, ranging for the period 1950–1960 from a high of 3.9 per cent in Venezuela to a low of 1.3 in Honduras.[9] Equally significant variances could be cited with regard to financial stability, dependence on agriculture as a means of livelihood, availability of particular raw materials, and the size of the pool of trained manpower.

Three factors have special relevance to the contemporary economic problems of Latin America. First, a population growth rate which has averaged 2.5 per

[8] Pan American Union, Organization of American States, *Perspectivas de Desarrollo de la Educacion en 19 Paises Latinoamericanos (1960–1970)*, Washington, D.C., 1963, p. 36.
[9] Pan American Union, Organization of American States, *La Educacion en America Latina (Presentacion Estadistica)*, Washington. D.C., 1963, p. 2.

cent annually since World War II has placed great strain on production capacity. Second, Latin Americans, like the people of other underdeveloped areas, have been affected by what economists have colorfully dubbed the "demonstration effect"; that is, the desires of the people have been stimulated by continued exposure through various means of communication to the higher standard of living in the more developed nations. Third, Latin American economies rely heavily on the sale of primary products which are subject to wide price fluctuations on the world market. A further structural difficulty involves the important agricultural sector which remains technologically underdeveloped and, therefore, productively inefficient.[10]

Low agricultural productivity is often traced to the *latifundismo*, or system of land tenure in big holdings. The *latifundios* (also called *haciendas, estancias, fazendas,* and *fundos*) are usually privately owned by members of the upper classes. Since little competition exists among the *latifundios*, their owners feel little urgency for technological improvement of their methods of operation, and thus the system tends to be monopolistic, rendering small landholding very difficult and placing farm labor at the mercy of the owner class. Even under the arrangements whereby the land is community-owned, as under the *ejido* system of Mexico, poor management has thwarted higher productivity, and the farmer still has no plot of land to call his own.

Most Latin American countries have

[10] Reynold E. Carlson, "The Economic Picture," in Herbert L. Matthews (ed.), *The United States and Latin America*, The American Assembly, Columbia, New York, 1959, pp. 115–141.

put into action, or are considering, methods for breaking up the huge estates. At best—and not infrequently—the *latifundismo* presented a happy, gently paternalistic community where the relationship between owner and workers was as father to children. Yet even the best paternalistic arrangements are not in the best interests of economic development, which requires continuous technical improvements, and social development, which demands social justice and responsible individualism.

Most Latin American intellectuals and government leaders appear to be committed to centralized economic planning or at least to systems of "mixed economy." Economists often speak of "bypassing the capitalist stage" or an "anticapitalistic revolution" and are relentless in their criticism of economic practices in the United States, in general, and of North American private investments in Latin America in particular. As a final castigation, capitalism, inasmuch as it is said to take from the weak and reward the powerful, is equated by some reformers with imperialism. A so-called "third force" has been developing in Latin American economic theory with strong Catholic backing which advocates a system somewhat between capitalism and socialism.[11]

The emphasis on centralized planning partly reflects Latin America's long authoritarian heritage and partly results from new nationalistic movements. Fortunately, inter-American economic cooperation has been possible and regional trade and economic associations have been functioning for several years. The Act of Bogotá, proclaimed in 1960, outlined in broad terms social and economic goals for all of Latin America. The formation of the Alliance for Progress in 1961 at the urging of the United States was a further step in getting down to hard planning for regional attacks on problems of illiteracy, land tenure, taxes, housing, health, agricultural and industrial productivity, trade, and domestic savings.

The factors affecting the economies of the Latin American nations are closely interrelated with social and political facts. The lack of capital, which prohibits technical and industrial expansion, is related to the lack of a tradition (as well as ability) of saving and investment on the part of the Latin American peoples. The absence of a spirit of cooperation in enterprise can be traced in part to the paternalistic ties which historically have bound the people to their superiors and to the pattern of the extended kinship responsibilities which have thwarted true community spirit. Moreover, the tax structure in much of Latin America is prejudiced in favor of the wealthy classes; large landowners and other independently employed groups pay little or no income tax. In Brazil in 1959, for example, only 340,000 of the nation's 4 million independently employed lawyers, doctors, farmers, etc., filed a tax return.[12]

Political and social problems

A fact often forgotten but of vital importance in considering the political and social characteristics of Latin America is its long colonial history. Latin Ameri-

[11] Stokes, *op. cit.*, p. 5.

[12] Walter V. Kaulfers, "Latin-American Education in Transition," *The Educational Record*, vol. 42, p. 97, April, 1961.

ca had the longest experience with colonialism of any world area; and its underdevelopment has a "direct lineal relation to idealized Iberian feudalism."[13] Like other former colonial regions, Latin America has resisted large-scale industrialization but, somewhat uniquely, she has internalized many European social customs and values. In this manner, both colonialism and the long struggle for independence (first from the European powers and more recently, according to some Latin Americans, from the North American imperialists) have given political and social identity to the area.

The forces contributing to political and social similarity and diversity or, when viewed in another perspective, affecting progress and retardation, may be grouped under three interrelated categories: class, church, and other pressure groups. These categories are not mutually exclusive, as has been shown by the fact that the latter two cut across the social-class structure.

Societal structure in urban areas may differ markedly from that in rural areas; thus, in effect, there are often two social systems in one nation. Further, in some parts of Latin America there is a historical dichotomy between the nature of traditional social cleavages and the social arrangement evolving during the recent movement toward industrialization and modernization. Perhaps the most significant social change pertinent to political and economic development in the past decades has been the emergence of new middle-status groups which, while not self-consciously representing a class, have some resemblance to the

Western European and North American middle class.[14]

Within these social systems at least two lower classes and two upper classes can be identified. The lower classes are composed of peasants or agricultural workers in the rural areas and of industrial workers in the urban centers. These classes harbor the seeds of much real and potential unrest. In the past the peasant, tied socially and economically to the *latifundio*, may have been content with paternalistic arrangements; but now, as a result of his own enlightenment or, more likely, under the stimulation of the local political party, he is demanding land of his own. In like manner, the urban lower class, which is often largely composed of displaced rural elements, has, through organized labor movements, become aggressively assertive in its fight for a higher standard of living.

The two upper classes include members of the landed aristocracy and the new business and political elite. For the traditional upper class, purity of family stock is the main criterion for membership, while wealth has usually provided the main key to recognition for the new upper class. Both groups covet wealth and power, but in ways that are often in conflict. Although the new upper class is less homogeneous in its ideologies, in general it exerts influence through the industrial, commercial, and govenmental organizations that constitute the power structure of modern nations. Historically, the traditional upper class has been

[13] K. H. Silvert, "Political Change in Latin America," in *The United States and Latin America, op. cit.,* p. 60.

[14] John T. Gillin, "Some Signposts for Policy," in Richard N. Adams et al., *Social Change in Latin America Today,* Council on Foreign Relations, Harper & Row, New York, 1960, p. 25.

strongly allied with the Church, forming a powerful entente for the preservation of the *status quo.*

The expanding middle class is characterized by high aspirations, instability, growing articulateness, and disdain for manual labor. As might be expected, it is from this class that nearly all the women are drawn who are active in public and professional work. This phenomenon of expanding middle-level social groups, stimulated not a little by immigration of skilled labor from Europe, is particularly apparent in Argentina, Brazil, Chile, Mexico, Uruguay, and Venezuela, nations which have relatively well-developed programs of industrialization.[15]

One author groups the controlling values of the Latin American middle class under the following rubrics:

. . . personalism, kinship, hierarchy and stratification, materialism of a special kind, transcendentalism or interest in spiritual values, the high worth of *inner states* and emotional expression, and fatalism.[16] [Italics supplied.]

Some of these values contrast markedly with those of the middle classes in the United States and Western Europe. Many of them, such as extended family commitments, reliance on personal confidence as a basis for business transactions, and an underlying theme of resignation (particularly in those nations with a Spanish heritage), are not regarded as conducive to economic development.

[15] John J. Johnson, "The Political Role of the Latin-American Middle Sectors," *The Annals of the American Academy of Political and Social Science,* vol. 334, p. 21, March, 1961.

[16] Gillin, *op. cit.,* p. 25.

Race, culture, and economic position are the strongest determinants of social-class position in Latin America.[17] Although Latin American nations appear to be relatively free from racial prejudice, certain facts are obvious even to a casual observer. In some areas there may be more discrimination against the Indian than the Negro, yet typically the persons lighter in color occupy the higher range of the social hierarchy. The upper classes tend to be lighter than the middle classes, which in turn are lighter than the lower classes. Men struggling for position and prestige, it has been noted, frequently marry women lighter than themselves.

The relationship between color and employment is also clear. Whites are dominant in such positions as: bank employees, priests, businessmen, cabaret entertainers, professors, lawyers, teachers, politicians, physicians, commercial employees, and government functionaries. Mulattoes appear to be predominant over blacks in these positions: barbers, musicians, street sweepers, streetcar conductors, firemen, taxi drivers, bus drivers, and soldiers. The relatively unmixed blacks are concentrated in low-pay, low-status employment; they are seldom found in the upper levels. Blacks appear to be predominant among *carregadores* (porters and baggagemen at the ports), laundresses, *carroceiros* (men with mules and two-wheel carts who transport goods), masons, stevedores, truck helpers, domestics, street laborers, candy peddlers, cobblers, venders, newsboys, shoe-shiners, streetcar motormen and truck drivers.[18]

The other two determinants of class,

[17] Stokes, *op. cit.,* p. 13.
[18] *Ibid.,* p. 14.

culture and economic position, take on those characteristics common to most class-divided peoples and need not be examined in detail. Family background, wealth, occupation, education, religion, language, and personal manners are all influential factors. Thus, a family that (1) has a respected cultural and racial heritage, (2) has acquired or inherited wealth, (3) avoids manual or mechanical labor and enjoys much leisure, (4) prepares the sons for work in the professions or arts, (5) speaks Spanish or Portuguese, and (6) is a member of the Catholic Church will be considered with the upper class in Latin America.

Considering the traditional influence of the Church among all groups but perhaps especially among the lower classes and women, its role in the social and political revolutions now under way becomes significant, if not of prime importance. The Church, although remaining virtually unchallenged as a provider of religious experiences, has lost many of its large landholdings and much of its monopoly over education, marriage, and public welfare. Nor can it now, as it was once able to do, efficiently censor media of communication. While it can no longer be said that "the Church rules," the historic involvement of the Church in politics continues; it even manages political parties in some countries, as in Colombia and Ecuador, and its opposition can be a vital component in the overthrow of governments, as in Argentina and Venezuela during the 1950s. Moreover, although the Church has been criticized for being unaware of the full dimensions of the social upheaval taking place in Latin America and for refusing to lend its full support to liberal democratic movements, the Church in Latin America has itself been embroiled in ferment in recent years. The outcome of this ferment will determine the role the Church will play in the future. In any case, the image of a monolithic institution with its leaders united in a commitment to preserve the *status quo* is no longer a valid picture of the Catholic Church in Latin America.

A third group which has shared power with the upper social classes and the Catholic Church is the professional military class, the "primary protector" of the nation's honor and dignity. Typically before World War II the military branches supported the ruling oligarchs and staunchly resisted popular pressures for social and political change. Beginning in the mid-1940s, a series of revolutions, primarily of social rather than political character, were led by younger military officers. The new alignment often saw some civilian middle-class leaders linked with younger members of officer cadres, fighting for popular causes against the entrenched upper classes, including the senior military officers. More recently, however, the military, in somewhat counterrevolutionary manner, has acted in some cases to restrain excessive measures. Thus, the military has moved from the role of protector of the conservative elite to a radical revolutionary force to a moderator of its own revolutions. And since the ranks of the military are increasingly being filled by the lower classes, any political party which seeks its support must stand for social reform.

Needs and objectives

The American Declaration of the Rights and Duties of Man, endorsed by all Latin American nations, states in its preamble:

Inasmuch as spiritual development is the supreme end of human existence and the highest expression thereof, it is the duty of man to serve that end with all his strength and resources.

Since culture is the highest social and historical expression of that spiritual development, it is the duty of man to preserve, practice and foster culture by every means within his power.[19]

The acquisition of culture (*la cultura*) is frequently referred to in Latin America as a major educational goal. In this sense, culture implies intellectual and artistic development. A cultured person is urbane, exhibits personal refinement, and demonstrates a high degree of verbal skill. The definition, it can be seen, has certain upper-class overtones.

Article XII of the Declaration, quoted from above, describes further the right of every Latin American to an education:

Every person has the right to an education, which should be based on the principles of liberty, morality and human solidarity.

Likewise every person has the right to an education that will prepare him to attain a decent life, to raise his standard of living, and to be a useful member of society.

The right to an education includes the right to equality of opportunity in every case, in accordance with natural talents, merit and the desire to utilize the resources that the state or the community is in a position to provide.

Every person has the right to re-

ceive, free, at least a primary education.[20]

A brief but comprehensive list of educational needs was included in the Act of Bogotá, 1960, and serves admirably as a statement of specific objectives. To improve education, the act suggested that special attention be given to:

a. The development of modern methods of mass education for the eradication of illiteracy;

b. The adequacy of training in the industrial arts and sciences with due emphasis on laboratory and work experience and on the practical application of knowledge for the solution of social and economic problems;

c. The need to provide instruction in rural schools not only in basic subjects but also in agriculture, health, sanitation, nutrition, and in methods of home and community improvement;

d. The broadening of courses of study in secondary schools to provide the training necessary for clerical and executive personnel in industry, commerce, public administration, and community service;

e. Specialized trade and industrial education related to the commercial and industrial needs of the community;

f. Vocational agricultural instruction;

g. Advanced education of administrators, engineers, economists, and other professional personnel of key importance to economic development.[21]

Recent statements of educational goals have indicated some shift in emphasis from primary to secondary education. For example, an Organization of Ameri-

[19] Pan American Union, *The Americas and Illiteracy,* Washington, D.C., 1951, p. 21. Appendix H of this document contains educational provisions of the Charter of the Organization of American States and of the American Declaration of the Rights and Duties of Man.

[20] *Ibid.,* p. 21.

[21] *Special Study Mission to Latin America: Venezuela, Brazil, Argentina, Chile, Bolivia and Panama,* Appendix A, U.S. Government Printing Office, 1961, p. 43.

can States (OAS) task force reporting to a meeting of the Latin American Ministers of Education in 1963 recommended that primary education expenditures be reduced temporarily while expenditures for secondary and technical education be substantially increased. Although this recommendation remains controversial in educational circles, economic planners have tended to give it their support.

Administration

Latin America has a long heritage of centralism in the administration and control of education. This pattern has usually meant that primary and secondary schools are maintained and supervised, courses of study written, and teachers appointed and paid by the ministry of education of the national government. Mexico, Argentina, Venezuela, and Brazil, which offer modified patterns of decentralized administration, are exceptions to this pattern, and several of the other Latin American nations are now experimenting with a mixed administrative arrangement which provides for semiautonomous educational control at the provincial level.

The need for a national plan, national goals, and a certain degree of national financing may justify a considerable degree of centralization. Scarcity of professional talent may also justify concentration of control and supervision. Yet the bureaucratic arrangement in Latin America runs the danger of reflecting the shortcomings in the political scene. Political instability has produced frequent changes in the top personnel of the ministries of education, and has thus prohibited long-range planning. Likewise, the propensity which many Latin American countries have shown toward totalitarianism has meant restrictions on academic freedom at the upper educational rungs and the introduction of extensive propaganda into the curriculum at all levels. Another weakness of educational bureaucracy in Latin America is the separation of the central authorities in ideology, as well as in distance, from the problems of education in the more rural areas. Plans formulated at the central level have only recently begun to reflect the educational needs and potentials of the poorer areas; moreover, centralized control of education has often meant a concentration of educational institutions and opportunities in the capital city and other politically powerful urban centers. In sum, since Latin American schools have nearly always been created or established by national laws, there has been the problem of what some Latin Americans have termed the "social authenticity" of the schools.

Although space does not permit examination of the organization and functions of the central educational organs of each Latin American country, it is possible to select one more or less typical centralized pattern for scrutiny. In this regard, Colombia will serve our purpose.

Article 41 of the Colombian Constitution locates educational authority:

> Freedom of education is guaranteed. The state shall exercise, however, overall supervision of institutions of learning, both public and private, in order to ensure that the social aims of culture and the best intellectual, moral, and physical development of the students are achieved.

General responsibility for control and administration of education in Colombia, though legally residing with the President, actually is located in the Ministry of Public Education. Within the Ministry a body of national inspectors ensures that national policies and programs with regard to primary education are put into operation. Administration of secondary and higher education is shared by the federal, provincial, and municipal educational authorities. Administration of vocational and technical education does not fall within the jurisdiction of the Ministry of Education but rather is the responsibility of the Ministry of Industries.

The central government of Colombia is also deeply involved in the financing of education. In 1954, for example, 44 per cent of all public expenditures for education came from the central government.[22] At the primary level, slightly less than 7 per cent of the total expenditure was furnished by the central government; the remainder came from departmental (provincial) and local authorities. A different picture is presented at the secondary level. Here, nearly half of the funds come from the central government. Vocational schools and higher educational institutions receive over 80 per cent of their funds from the national government.

Educational aspirations and opportunities

Although the similarity of educational and cultural conditions among Latin American nations is striking, there are important national differences in available resources, composition of the popu-

[22] UNESCO, *World Survey of Education: Primary Education*, Paris, 1958, p. 265.

370

lation, religious, political, and social traditions, and educational systems. Tables 4, 5, and 6 represent indices of educational opportunities and illustrate further the educational diversity within Latin America.

Table 4 *1961 Primary Enrollment Ratios in Latin American Countries*

Country	Percentage	Rank order
Argentina	91	3
Bolivia	65	13.5
Brazil	65	13.5
Chile	78	9
Colombia	56	17
Costa Rica	89	4
Cuba	127	1
Dominican Republic	81	8
Ecuador	70	11.5
El Salvador	64	15
Guatemala	38	19
Haiti	33	20
Honduras	61	16
Mexico	72	10
Nicaragua	54	18
Panama	82	7
Paraguay	94	2
Peru	70	11.5
Uruguay	87	5.5
Venezuela	87	5.5

NOTE: The primary enrollment ratio is defined here as the proportion of children in the seven- to fourteen-year age group attending primary school. Percentages taken from UNESCO, America Latina, *Proyecto Principal de Educacion*, Boletin Trimestral, no. 14, p. 191, April–June, 1962. These percentages are derived from population figures (school-age population and students enrolled in primary schools) that were provided UNESCO by each Latin American nation. Some of the percentages are highly questionable and in at least one case (Cuba) obviously false.

Table 5 *Literacy Rates in Latin American Countries*

Country	Percentage	Rank order
Argentina	85–90	1
Bolivia	30–35	18
Brazil	45–50	12.5
Chile	75–80	4
Colombia	50–55	10.5
Costa Rica	75–80	4
Cuba	75–80	4
Dominican Republic	40–45	14
Ecuador	55–60	9
El Salvador	35–40	16
Guatemala	25–30	19
Haiti	10–15	20
Honduras	35–40	16
Mexico	60–65	8
Nicaragua	35–40	16
Panama	65–70	6.5
Paraguay	65–70	6.5
Peru	45–54	12.5
Uruguay	80–85	2
Venezuela	50–55	10.5

SOURCE: UNESCO, *World Illiteracy at Mid-Century,* Monographs on Fundamental Education, XI, Paris, 1957.

Primary education

Primary education in Latin American nations varies from four to seven years in length (the trend being six years) and represents terminal education for most children. The percentage of children in the seven- to fourteen-year age group attending primary schools in 1961 varied from over 90 per cent in Argentina (possibly higher in Cuba) to a low of 33 per cent in Haiti.[23] Further light is shed on primary school attendance by the high dropout rate. In 1956 it was

[23] UNESCO, America Latina, *Proyecto Principal de Educacion,* Boletin Trimestral, no. 14, p. 191, April–June, 1962.

estimated that less than 20 per cent of the children then enrolled in school would complete their primary education. The dramatic effect of the year-end examinations and other causes of dropout can be seen in Brazil, where in 1958:

. . . 52.3 per cent of all elementary school children were in the first grade, 22.1 per cent in the second grade, 15.5 per cent in the third grade and only 1.3 per cent in the fourth grade.[24]

Thus, low initial attendance and rapid dropouts have combined to produce an average level of education in Latin America only slightly above the first grade.

Primary education is further affected by the discrepancy in standards, facilities, and motivation between the urban and rural areas. The rural primary schools in particular have shortages of books and equipment and, because of poor pay and poor living conditions, are not popular working sites for teachers.[25] The rural areas often have large Indian populations for whom formal education may hold little attraction or, in any event, be an economic impossibility. The vernacular spoken in the Indian homes adds a further burden on both the child, for whom the language of instruction is foreign, and the teacher, whose success is related to his bilingual ability. By

[24] Adams et al., *op. cit.,* p. 203.
[25] The average for fourteen Latin American countries in 1956–1959 showed 77.7 per cent of the rural primary school teachers officially unqualified to teach while only 35 per cent of the urban teachers fell into this category. See Pan American Union, Organization of American States, *Perspectivas de Desarrollo de la Educacion en 19 Paises Latinoamericanos (1960–1970): Anexos,* Washington, D.C., 1963, p. 57.

Table 6   *1960 Secondary and Higher Education Enrollments in Latin American Countries*

Country	Secondary		Higher	
	Percentage	Rank order	Percentage	Rank order
Argentina	31	2	10.0	1
Bolivia	12	13.5	1.3	15
Brazil	12	13.5	1.6	14
Chile	23	5	4.5	3.5
Colombia	15	9	1.8	12.5
Costa Rica	28	4	3.7	6
Cuba	17	7.5	3.2	7
Dominican Republic	5	19	1.8	12.5
Ecuador	12	13.5	2.5	10
El Salvador	13	10.5	1.1	16
Guatemala	6	17.5	0.8	19
Haiti	3	20	0.3	20
Honduras	8	16	0.9	18
Mexico	12	13.5	3.1	8
Nicaragua	6	17.5	1.0	17
Panama	30	3	4.5	3.5
Paraguay	13	10.5	2.3	11
Peru	17	7.5	2.8	9
Uruguay	32	1	7.6	2
Venezuela	20	6	4.3	5

SOURCE: Percentages taken from UNESCO, America Latina, *Proyecto Principal de Educacion,* Boletin Trimestral, no. 14, p. 146, April–June, 1962. As in the previous tables, statistics may be subject to question.

contrast, educational opportunities in the cities are more numerous. The case of the urban Federal District in Mexico, which in 1955 registered twice the nation's average enrollment, is duplicated in most Latin American nations.

One of the major problems of development and hence a goal of primary education is the incorporation of large population groups into national civic and political life.

In Latin America the population bulge (the proportion of school-age children to adults in Latin America is twice what it is in Europe) demands supreme national and local efforts if educational opportunities are to be improved. If

primary education is to be extended to all children, about 500,000 teachers, thousands of school buildings, and huge supplies of equipment, books, and other instructional materials—all expensive items—must be provided. Such needs can only be fulfilled by sacrificing other necessary items in a development program.

In terms of qualitative defects, the rural schools often have not made adaptations that would win the support of the rural adult population. Farm parents see little relationship between the program of study in the schools and the daily problems of life; they have demonstrated apathy, indifference, and even hostility to attempts at compulsory education. Moreover, as a terminal institution, the primary school often fails to provide the prevocational experiences and the motivations necessary for self-sufficiency. Yet only part of the difficulty can be traced to educational theory and practice. The shortcomings basically stem from the relatively low priority given to the rural sector by national governments in comparison with other development demands.

Teaching methods in the primary schools, while currently representing an important point of controversy, tend to differ from those found in the schools of North America and, to less extent, from those of Europe. The influence of the educational philosophy of the United States was felt early in Argentina, owing to Sarmiento's friendship with Horace Mann, and more recently in Uruguay, Chile, Cuba, and Mexico; but no deep inroads have been made into the formalism of most Latin American instruction. Though significant variances exist in methodology throughout Latin America, the following generalizations can be made: (1) Accumulation of factual knowledge is a major educational goal; therefore the teacher lectures or dictates, and the pupils are expected to take careful notes. Pupils do not read extensively in supplementary books; in fact, the lack of appropriate reading materials contributes to a recurrence of illiteracy among school dropouts. (2) There are few pupil discussions or other forms of pupil participation. (3) There is little recognition of differences in pupils' interests and abilities. (4) The social skills and attitudes emphasized so much in North American schools receive little attention. As in most underdeveloped areas where teachers are ill-trained and facilities poor, traditional teaching techniques involve excessive memorization and verbalism.

Schools in Latin America are not institutions which spring from an expression of interest and aspiration of the local community. Although all nations are officially committed to the principle of compulsory education and recognize the need for an "enlightened citizenry," social traditions perpetuate elitism. Because of the social class structure, "the masses are conditioned to relinquish claims to education."[26] Moreover, the paternalistic relationship between *patron* and *peones* has often placed the choice of going or not going to school in the hands of the former. And undoubtedly many *patrones* still conclude: "We need peons, not degrees or diplomas."[27]

Secondary education

Most nations in Latin America have systems of primary-secondary education of eleven or twelve years. The highly esteemed academic secondary schools, usually called *liceos, institutos,* or *colegios,* are five to seven years in length and act in varying degrees as preparatory schools for the universities and as steppingstones to social distinction. The course of study in the secondary school, whether public or private, is prescribed by the central ministry of education and emphasizes languages, literature, mathematics, science (rarely is the experimental approach stressed), physical education, and possibly manual training (particularly in the *institutos*). The schools for girls (few secondary schools are coeducational) also include home

[26] Stokes, *op. cit.*, p. 49.
[27] *Ibid.*

economics, needlework, and the like. Philosophy and ethics are considered important for the moral education of the advanced secondary student. Although well over 80 per cent of those who enter secondary schools do not go on to the university, attempts to broaden the secondary school curriculum to include vocational and prevocational skills, or to provide large numbers of vocational secondary schools, have just begun.

Students in Latin America usually attend secondary schools to maintain or improve social status or to prepare for an occupation. Probably the secondary school is most successful in helping the middle and upper classes maintain their position and somewhat less efficient in promoting social mobility. One source estimated that only 5 to 15 per cent of working-class children were entering the secondary schools in 1960.[28] Graduates of vocational and academic secondary schools have little difficulty finding employment. Much criticism, however, has been leveled at the secondary schools for their failure to provide citizenship preparation through a critical study of contemporary social problems.

The curriculum is characterized by fragmentation and an encyclopedic approach to learning. Often the student must take twelve or more courses at one time. This arrangement, based on questionable education theory, means that most courses meet but once or twice weekly, thus posing a variety of instructional problems. Latin American educators justify the requirement by saying

that the students need all the content offered. Yet it is certain to be a major issue as Latin American leaders continue to struggle to streamline their educational institutions.

Considering the limited availability of primary instruction, the historically elite role of secondary schools, and economic impoverishment, educational opportunity at the secondary level is highly restricted (see Table 8). Yet as shown in Table 7 the expansion of the secondary school population since 1940 has uniformly outstripped population growth.

Secondary schools, like institutions at the primary and higher levels, suffer from the usual shortages of buildings, equipment, and teachers. In Brazil, for example, many urban secondary schools operate on three shifts, and in the rural areas secondary educational opportunity is virtually nonexistent. This condition not only produces a bottleneck in the middle-level skills needed in the developing economies but also, because of the frustration to aspiring youth, creates a dangerous political situation. Inadequate teaching staffs not only reflect the inability of the teacher education facilities to keep abreast of needs but also produce the phenomenon of the part-time teacher whose main interests may lie outside the school.

Concern for the quality of instruction in the public secondary schools, enrollment pressures, and certain historical class prejudices have perpetuated a strong tradition of private secondary education in Latin America. The majority of the private schools are controlled by the Catholic Church, although Protestant schools and lay, private-venture institutions are on the increase. In Brazil during the school year 1954–

---

[28] Robert J. Havighurst and Jayme Abreu, "The Problem of Secondary Education in Latin America," *Comparative Education Review,* vol. 5, no. 3, p. 170, February, 1962.

Table 7 *Secondary School Enrollments Related to Population Increases in Selected Latin American Countries*

Country	Date	Per cent of increase in secondary schools	Per cent of increase in total population
Brazil	1940–1960	380	60
Costa Rica	1941–1954	265	48
Chile	1940–1953	104	22
El Salvador	1935–1954	868*	39
Mexico	1940–1954	266	46
Panama	1948–1953	53	14
Paraguay	1951–1954	26	7
Dominican Republic	1930–1955	580*	87
Uruguay	1949–1954	47	7

* From an initial number that was very small (about 1,200).

SOURCE: Robert J. Havighurst and Jayme Abreu, "The Problem of Secondary Education in Latin America," *Comparative Education Review*, vol. 5, no. 3, p. 168, February, 1962. Original source: Gustave Zakrzewski, Centro Regional de La UNESCO en el Hemisferio Occidental, Havana, Cuba.

1955 more than twice as many youth received instruction in private secondary schools (predominantly Catholic) as in public secondary schools.[29] In Spanish America the percentage of students attending private schools runs somewhat smaller. For example, in 1960 Colombia had 64 per cent of its secondary school population in private institutions while Peru reported only 35 per cent.[30]

Although the private secondary schools, generally the recipients of public funds, often set somewhat higher academic standards than the public schools, they, too, largely limit their purpose to preparation for the university and also cater to the wealthier children. Private secondary schools for some

[29] Pan American Union, Organization of American States, *Perspectivas de Desarrollo de la Educacion en 19 Paises Latinoamericanos (1960–1970): Anexos, op. cit.,* p. 48.
[30] *Ibid.*

time to come will play an important and constructive role in the extension and improvement of secondary education; yet their elitism and class orientation (except possibly for a few mission-sponsored secondary schools) do not make them an appropriate permanent substitute for public instruction.

The preparation of teachers for the primary schools, with rare exceptions, as in Costa Rica, takes place in normal schools. These secondary-level institutions offer both general education and professional experiences. In the urban areas the training programs are equal to or longer than the academic secondary course, but in the more rural areas the normal schools, which often are the only available secondary schools, may offer a program of only two or three years. Indeed primary school teachers with no postprimary education can often be found in the rural areas.

375

University education

Traditionally the university in Latin America has been essentially a confederation of individual schools, faculties, and, more recently, research institutes. Lately a few specialized agricultural and technical institutions have also assumed the title "university." Students graduating from secondary schools and receiving the baccalaurate degree compete for entrance to a faculty of their choice and take few if any of their studies in the other faculties. (Some of the newer universities, such as the one at Concepción, Chile, are exceptions to the rule and follow the curriculum pattern common in the United States.) The administration of the universities is centralized largely in the office of the rector, whose power is limited only by the university council and the minister of education who hold certain purse strings. With few exceptions the universities are nonresidential and are located in large urban areas.

The proud Latin American universities have undergone two revolutions in this century. The first was initiated at Córdoba in 1918, and its effects, which still linger, were largely political and social while the effects of the second and more directly academic are yet to be fully felt. One author, speaking of the first revolution, states:

> The revolution of aspirations that has provided so much of the driving force behind Latin America's urge for social change and economic development has had, perhaps, its longest continuous expression through a university-centered movement, the *Reforma Universitaria* that took shape

376

in Argentina and Uruguay during the second decade of this century.[31]

This reform, then, was not designed to revise standards or curricula but rather to integrate the university with economic, social, and political change. Actions taken by the students were designed to ensure their voice on directive councils or other university administrative bodies. Thus, as in the tradition of the ancient University of Bologna, students were to be in a position to influence greatly the operation of their institution. In this aspect and in the emphasis on complete institutional autonomy, the reform movement was reactionary. Yet to the extent that the movement conceived of a university graduate, as Ortega y Gassett suggested, "as a man in his circumstances," it represented a break with the traditional Spanish university which had sought to wall itself off from the societal forces about it.

Since 1945 a steady, though not dramatic, trend has become increasingly discernible toward a university different from both the student-controlled, politically and socially oriented reform university and its colonial predecessor. This trend, while perhaps not so clearly defined philosophically as the reform movement, nevertheless is a distinct expression of the demands for the higher technical education and professional skills demanded by industrializing and modernizing societies. In contrast to earlier movements, changes now sought are directed:

[31] John P. Harrison, "The Confrontation with the Political University," *The Annals of the American Academy of Political and Social Science,* vol. 334, p. 75, March, 1961.

. . . almost solely to improving the quality of academic training within specific disciplines to the end that Latin American universities will produce graduates who are professional equals of those trained in the best universities of the United States and Europe and who are technically competent to resolve their own social, economic, and cultural problems.[32]

The increasing focus on contemporary economic and industrial demands indicates a new service function for the Latin American university and draws it closer to its counterpart in North America. Not that the Latin American university has had little influence on society in the past; on the contrary, because of its unique level of advancement as compared with other institutions, its role was of paramount importance. But its contribution was ideological and political rather than economic or social. As Professor Quesada has perceived: ". . . [Latin American] society sees it as the crucible in which the political ideas that will orient and guide its future are formed and refined."[33] And, again:

> The social group that creates and maintains the university considers it perfectly natural that the university should be capable of determining the highest aims and final goals of society.[34]

The Latin American university reflects the exclusive and aristocratic pattern of Latin American culture to an even greater degree than the secondary schools. Few students from the lower classes attend the universities since neither tradition nor cultural environment nor financial requisites have worked toward this end. For similar reasons, proportionately few women enter Latin American universities. Both these factors contribute to the shortage of trained personnel. Table 8 indicates the elite character of Latin American education; if figures had been included on female enrollments[35] the educational prejudice against women would also have been apparent.

The status of the university in Latin America is well demonstrated by what has been called "the cult of the doctor."[36] The prestige of the title of "doctor" illustrates the symbolic value placed on higher education. The graduate in the professions, for example, who obtains this degree often does not practice in his field; indeed his training probably has been so theoretical that he is not equipped to do so. Rather, the title is a necessary qualification for obtaining a government post. Stokes has pointed out: "In politics, the *doctor* and the *general* compete with each other for control of government. Happy is the politician who is both *doctor and general*."[37]

The percentage of university students enrolled in law and medicine in Latin America is considerably larger than in most economically advanced areas. Comparatively few Latin American students

[32] *Ibid.*, p. 80.
[33] F. M. Quesada and R. J. Havighurst, *The University South and North,* Education in the Americas, Information Series Bulletin 1961, no. 1, Pan American Union, Washington, D.C., 1961, p. 2. (Reprinted from *Americas*, vol. 12, no. 12.)
[34] *Ibid.*, p. 3.
[35] See, for example, UNESCO, *World Survey of Education: Primary Education, op. cit.*, table 15, pp. 58–59.
[36] Stokes, *op. cit.*, p. 72.
[37] *Ibid.*

Table 8   *1960 School Enrollments in Latin American Countries*
(Figures in thousands)

Country	Primary	Secondary	Higher
Argentina	2,902	606	166.1
Bolivia	424	57*	4.0*
Brazil	8,014*	1,177*	93.2
Chile	1,108	230	26.9
Colombia	1,674*	286*	22.9*
Costa Rica	198	35	3.8
Cuba	1,368	122	19.2
Dominican Republic	499	22	5.0*
Ecuador	595*	67	9.0*
El Salvador	290	34	2.4
Guatemala	297	27	3.0*
Haiti	238	19	0.9
Honduras	205	15	1.5
Mexico	4,807	487†	87.0*
Nicaragua	153*	10*	1.3
Panama	162	39	3.9
Paraguay	305	28	3.3
Peru	1,433	202	26.6‡
Uruguay	322	87	16.0*
Venezuela	1,095	148	24.9

* Estimate
† Agricultural education not included
‡ 1959

SOURCE: Data taken from UNESCO, America Latina, *Proyecto Principal de Educacion,* Boletin Trimestral, no. 14, p. 145, April–June, 1962.

prepare themselves for work in technology, business administration, or the agricultural sciences. Little training is offered in either the applied social or natural sciences, and students wishing advanced training in these areas must go abroad.

In Latin American universities changes in academic standards and curricula have not been rapid. University autonomy has been a two-edged sword, at times protecting students and professors from government coercion and at other times thwarting enlightened policies initiated by the government. Student power has often been irresponsible to the

extent of making a mockery of academic standards. A corps of "professional" students, many well over thirty years of age, provides continuing leadership to the various political clubs and, in fact, uses the universities as political proving grounds. This situation has caused one analyst of Latin American education to quip: ". . . in spring when United States students turn lightly to thoughts of love, Latin American students turn lightly to thoughts of revolution."[38]

The universities' lack of progress in

[38] Kaulfers, *op. cit.*, p. 96.

making serious curriculum and teaching changes has resulted in severe criticism from both North American and Latin American scholars. A North American observer notes that:

> The outsider . . . gains the impression that the universities are sometimes more concerned with defending traditions of the past than with meeting the new needs of the present.[39]

The rector of the University of Buenos Aires is even more outspoken in his condemnation:

> . . . The Argentine university has wasted much of its energies in the search for ingenious solutions to administrative questions, without becoming aware that the problems of the university are of a pedagogical nature . . . that instruction should be scarce or nonexistent has seemed of little importance. Nor does it matter that the university does no research, that one turns one's back on the necessities of the country, that there are no professors fit to teach many courses, that the students still keep on repeating by memory the used-up notes of previous years, that the professors themselves repeat those same notes and demand them back in the examinations, that there is no university life, that the degree is the principal goal . . . and . . . the examination the immediate objective.[40]

This dark picture of the universities of one Latin American country, while

[39] Harold E. Davis, "The University in Latin America," *Panorama*, Winter, 1960–1961, p. 11.
[40] Quoted in William Benton, *The Voice of Latin America*, reprinted from the 1961 *Britannica, Book of the Year*, Encyclopaedia Britannica, Inc., Chicago, 1961, p. 50.

not an appropriate description of the more forward-looking institutions, particularly the newer private universities, nevertheless summarizes the persisting ills. The passive classroom with lack of discussion or laboratory experience; the emphasis on and popularity of law and the other ancient professions to the slighting of such areas as the natural and social sciences, applied engineering, and public administration; the inattention to pertinent and continued research; the part-time professorial staffs whose main interests lie in other occupations; the low professorial salaries; the inadequate library and laboratory facilities—these are problems which must be overcome if the Latin American universities are to adapt to the requisites for trained manpower in dynamic industrializing societies.

Innovation and experimentation

Before identifying some of the specific educational changes that have taken place in recent years, mention should be made of the spread of national educational planning throughout Latin America. Since 1956, when the idea of educational planning was presented at the Inter-American Meeting of Ministers of Education at Lima, several countries have developed national plans, and every country has given some attention to the forecasting of educational needs and the establishment of educational priorities. Success in national educational planning has been limited by lack of adequate data, shortages of skilled personnel, long-standing educational and cultural traditions that are resistant to change, and the penchant for a *projectismo* approach (the construction of plans as an intellectual exercise with little attention to the realities of the situation or the problems of implementation). Assistance from US-AID, UNESCO, and OAS and the establishment of educational planning courses at the Institute for Economic and Social Development Planning at Santiago, Chile, are expected to increase the sophistication of national educational planning efforts.

The growing interest in educational planning as a means for realizing the goals of social justice and economic development is another indication of the importance now being placed on education by Latin American leaders. In light of this understanding, significant educational innovations are being attempted from the rural primary school through the prestigious universities.

Improvement and extension of rural education

Many attempts have been made in Latin America in the decades following World War II to increase rural educational opportunities and, in general, to give education in the rural areas a community orientation. One of the early efforts of rural vitalization took place in Mexico during the latter stages of the revolution. The promises by the revolutionary leaders of *tierra y escuelas* (land and schools) and *educar es redimir* (to educate is to redeem) led to a rural school movement and the establishment of so-called "cultural missions." Competent persons, usually experienced teachers, were appointed by the federal government as secular missionaries and charged with the responsibility of ascertaining the social, political, economic,

and educational needs of the rural villages. Since the key to expansion and improvement of rural education was availability of teachers, the cultural missions became in effect rural normal schools. The titles of the faculty members of the first cultural mission tell the functional orientation of the curriculum. There were teachers of soapmaking and perfumery, rural education, tanning, agriculture, music, physical education, and nursing.[41]

By 1961 eighty cultural missions, rural and urban, were operating in Mexico and the concept had spread to other Latin American countries. While it is not possible to evaluate precisely the contributions of the cultural missions to rural development in Mexico, it can be noted that during the period since their establishment illiteracy has been reduced from 80 to 40 per cent and, owing to improved standards of living and opportunities for social contact, the rural village has become integrated into the nation. Most of all, though, the cultural missions stimulated a variety of schemes which sought to give the school a more dynamic role in community development.

Another significant experiment, initiated in the early 1930s but gaining particular strength in recent years, has been the *nucleos escuelas* of Bolivia, Guatemala, and Peru. These "nuclear schools" attempt to enrich and extend rural education within the very limited financial means of rural Latin America. The Bolivian and Peruvian governments saw the nuclear school primarily as a means of solving the "Indian problem,"

[41] Lloyd H. Hughes, *The Mexican Cultural Mission Programme*, UNESCO, Paris, 1950, p. 11.

that is, providing Indians with the motivation, knowledge, and skills to improve their standard of living.

Under the nuclear school arrangements, each geographic region has a designated nucleus where a central school is located and from which a number of subsidiary schools (usually fifteen to thirty) draw equipment, supplies, and professional supervision. Each area with its complement of schools may thus be considered a social and cultural region. The curricula of the nuclear schools typically include health education, instruction in the national language, arithmetic, moral and social education, prevocational instruction, domestic arts, crafts, and farm management. In the subsidiary schools the course of studies is generally more simple and of shorter duration.

Various regional training efforts which transcend national boundaries have also been initiated. A regional project of note is the Inter-American Rural Education Center in Venezuela, one of the many educational institutions created and supported by the Organization of American States. The purpose of this center is to provide training for rural teachers and supervisors, and in the long run it is hoped that from this school will come a nucleus of faculties for rural normal schools throughout Latin America.

The Fundamental Education Center at Patzcuaro, Mexico, founded through the cooperation of various agencies of the United Nations and supported by the United Nations and the Mexican government has, since its inception in 1951, turned out leaders in literacy and fundamental education for several parts of Latin America. Students at the center have a chance to combine field work in

rural and impoverished communities with theoretical studies. By graduation time, students have acquired some competency in community development, education, health, agriculture, home economics, and recreation.

Many dynamic educational reforms have been attempted in postrevolution Cuba. From 1959 to 1963 illiteracy was reduced, a volunteer teacher corps created to fill temporarily primary teaching vacancies, vocational schools established, the public universites reopened and expanded, and textbooks rewritten to include the "revolutionary point of view." Although the precise details of many of the changes are difficult to obtain, quite obviously the government plans to make the Cuban schools politically orthodox and closely attuned to manpower needs. The creation of an educational planning unit under the Ministry of Education (an important trend in much of Latin America) was a significant move to adjust all preuniversity education to national economic needs.

Other innovations are fostered by private national and international agencies. Increased services in agricultural and home economics extension and in developing a more wholesome home life are having a significant grass-roots effect. Mobile training units, modernized versions of the Mexican cultural missions, made up of specially trained teachers and provided with audio-visual equipment, conduct literacy campaigns and community development projects in remote areas. The "radio-phonic" schools of Colombia have had some success in literacy and community education. Government-sponsored production of low-cost instructional and supplementary reading materials is having a significant effect in maintaining and improving literacy among those who have had but little schooling. Experiments in low-cost school buildings may produce a partial answer to the enormous school-building needs existing in most rural areas. While all these innovations and experiments are making contributions to educational development, the need for large-scale comprehensive efforts persists.

New programs in secondary education

Recent changes in secondary education have, in large part, been concerned with providing increased vocational opportunities and night schools and other arrangements for out-of-school youth and adults. In effect attempts are being made to see that secondary education reflects more than the ideals of the upper class.

Vocational secondary schools, excepting normal schools for the preparation of primary school teachers, are a relatively recent phenomenon in Latin America, the great majority having come into existence since 1940. Although international specialists from such organizations as the International Labor Organization (ILO) have lent assistance in planning, the problem of gauging manpower needs has proved difficult, owing to inadequate statistics and a number of other factors. Interest in and facilities for some of the newer trades for men have not yet developed. Vocational education for girls still runs heavily toward the traditional feminine pursuits of embroidery, dressmaking, and the like. Vocational guidance programs already in effect or being planned should assist greatly in identifying for young

382

people the vocational needs and opportunities of their nations.

Establishment of agencies at the national level in cooperation with business and industrial concerns demonstrates the priority that the upgrading of the skill of vocational workers is receiving. In Brazil, for example, two programs have been instituted, National Service of Industrial Apprenticeship (SENAI) and National Service of Commercial Apprenticeship (SENAC), to assist in meeting growing needs for trained manpower.[42] Yet even these national efforts are estimated to be producing only one-fourth of the number of skilled workers required to keep pace with Brazil's industrial growth. Technical assistance from the United States and United Nations agencies and numerous philanthropic foundations has further spurred recent expansion in secondary vocational education. Unfortunately, perhaps, the schools have been tardy in providing leadership to shape the vocational programs.

Possibly the most revolutionary experiment in academic secondary education in Latin America has taken place in Chile. In 1945, Chilean educators formed the Commission for the Gradual Renovation of Secondary Education. Later they attempted to redesign the education in the *liceo* on the premise that more dynamic methods of instruction and a less classical curriculum would better contribute to national development efforts. A greater emphasis would be placed on education for citizenship, family life, and economic life.

[42] Augustus F. Faust, *Brazil: Education in an Expanding Economy,* U.S. Office of Education Bulletin 1959, no. 13, 1959, pp. 73–82.

The Commission recommended that all school life be organized into six areas: health education; economic and vocational education; esthetic education and use of leisure time; language, communication, and expression; scientific education; and philosophic education.[43]

The "renovation" plan was introduced into chosen *liceos* in 1946. Yet in spite of careful planning and the involvement of distinguished educators from both Chile and the United States, the experiment did not prosper. Conflicting educational philosophies among Chilean educators, criticism from certain lay groups, and opinions expressed by certain vested political interests spelled its doom. Yet even in failure the experiment was important, for it may be considered the forerunner of the educational experimentation and research found in Chile today.[44]

By 1960 the industrially more advanced Latin American countries had begun to introduce more comprehensive offerings in the lower stages of the secondary schools. It appears likely that these schools will in the future draw a large majority of youth. If so, then only the upper stages of the secondary schools will offer specialized—vocational or academic—education.

Changing functions for universities

At the university level certain organizational experiments are being made to limit student power and to provide more responsible administrative leadership. In

[43] Armando Samper, *A Case Study in Cooperation in Secondary Education in Chile*, National Planning Association, Washington, D.C., 1957, p. 24.

[44] *Ibid.*, p. 83.

Mexico, Uruguay, Chile, and Brazil, university cities are being founded in suburban areas which on first analysis appear to be rather grandiose but which, by virtue of their location, may give more stability to the operation of the institutions. Newer private universities under religious or nonsectarian auspices, lacking entrenched traditions, are providing some of the needed leadership.

One innovation being tried at the university level is the addition of programs in general education traditionally left to the secondary schools. North American observers have tended to hail this as an important progressive step, believing that these programs will counterbalance the excessive specialization. To the extent that this occurs, the change may be justified; but as some Latin American educators have noted, the programs may merely transfer a defect of secondary education to the university level. Another innovation involves attempts to incorporate normal schools into the university. Advocates of this move argue that it will raise professional standards. Historically, graduates of Latin American universities frequently had become secondary school teachers; yet the universities and the normal schools were worlds apart in philosophy, prestige, and program, and while new universities might make the adjustment fairly easily, it would be unbearably painful for others.

Although Latin American universities still lead the world in proportion of law students, new faculties are being added in the social sciences, natural sciences, agriculture, nursing, humanities, fine arts, architecture, and public administration. Moreover, laboratory and empirical research is being introduced for the first time through the regular faculties or through attached research institutes. In some universities, attention is being given to the peculiar technical and professional problems caused by underdevelopment. And, although technicians and professional people form a small percentage of the economically active population, the trend toward the establishment of junior colleges with a technical bias may help alleviate shortages in one level of technically trained personnel.

Regional and national efforts in higher education are being supplemented by various contractual arrangements with private religious or philanthropic organizations, United States agencies, and international organizations. Assistance from such agencies provides expert advice; fellowships for study abroad; student and faculty exchange; loans for library, laboratory, or other improvements; translation and publication; and aid in carrying out adaptive and basic research. It is likely that the next decade will see a vast increase in bilateral and multilateral agreements affecting universities.

References

Books

Adams, Richard N., et al.: *Social Change in Latin America Today,* Council on Foreign Relations, Harper & Row, New York, 1960.

Azvedo, Fernando de: *Brazilian Culture,* translated by William Res Crawford, Macmillan, New York, 1950.

Bailey, Helen Miller, and Abraham P. Nasatir: *Latin America: The Development of Its Civilization,* Prentice-Hall, Englewood Cliffs, N.J., 1960.

Beltran, G. A.: *Organization and Structure of Latin American Universities,* Pan American Union, Organization of American States, Washington, D.C., 1956.

Booth, George C.: *Mexico's School-made Society,* Stanford, Stanford, Calif., 1941.

Dean, Vera Micheles: *The Nature of the Non-Western World,* Mentor Books, New American Library of World Literature, Inc., New York, 1957.

Faust, Augustus F.: *Brazil: Education in an Expanding Economy,* U.S. Office of Education Bulletin 1959, no. 13, 1959.

Filho, M. B. L.: *Primary School Curricula in Latin America,* Educational Studies and Documents, no. 24, UNESCO, Paris, 1957.

Gillin, John T.: "Some Signposts for Policy," in Richard N. Adams et al., *Social Change in Latin America Today,* Council on Foreign Relations, Harper & Row, New York, 1960.

Ginsburg, Norton: *Atlas of Economic Development,* The University of Chicago Press, Chicago, 1961.

Hall, Robert King: *La Educacion in Crises,* Universidad Nacional de Tacuman, Tacuman, Argentina, 1950.

Hanke, Lewis: *Modern Latin America: Continent in Ferment,* Van Nostrand, Princeton, N.J., 1959.

Hjelm, Howard F.: *Alliance for Progress and Education in Latin America,* Pan American Union, Organization of American States, Washington, D.C., 1962.

Krumwiede, Grace I., and Charles C. Hauch: *Educational Data: Cuba,* U.S. Office of Education, Division of International Education, 1962.

Linke, Lilo: *Ecuador: A Country of Contrasts,* 2d ed., Royal, New York, 1955.

Mac-Lean y Estenos, Roberto: *La Crisis Universitaria en Hispano-America,*

Universidad Nacional, Instituto de Investigaciones Sociales, Mexico, 1956.

Matthews, Herbert L. (ed.): *The United States and Latin America*, The American Assembly, Columbia, New York, 1959.

National Conference on International Economic and Social Development: *The Alliance for Progress*, Report of the Ninth Annual Meeting of the Conference, Chicago, 1962.

Organizacion de los Estados Americanos: *Acta Final de la Tercera Reunion Interamericana de Ministros de Educacion*, ser. K/V.3.1, Bogotá, Colombia, 1963.

Pan American Union, Organization of American States: Comision Especial para Promover la Programacion y el Desarrollo de la Educacion, la Ciencia y la Cultura en America Latina, Comision Especial de Educacion, Alianza Para el Progreso, *La Educacion En America Latina: (Presentacion Estadistica)*, Washington, D.C., 1963.

————: *Perspectivas de Desarrollo de la Educacion en 19 Paises Latinoamericanos: (1960–1970)*, Washington, D.C., 1963.

————: *Second Inter-American Meeting of Ministers of Education: Documents*, Washington, D.C., 1956.

Pike, Frederick B. (ed.): *Freedom and Reform in Latin America*, University of Notre Dame Press, Notre Dame, Ind., 1959.

Quesada, F. M., and R. J. Havighurst: *The University South and North*, Education in the Americas, Information Series Bulletin 1961, no. 1, Pan American Union, Washington, D.C., 1961. (Reprinted from *Americas*, vol. 12, no. 12.)

Raine, Philip: *Paraguay*, Scarecrow Press, New Brunswick, N.J., 1956.

Rio, Angel de (ed.): *Responsible Freedom in the Americas*, Doubleday, Garden City, N.Y., 1955.

Samper, Armando: *A Case Study of Cooperation in Secondary Education in Chile*, National Planning Association, Washington, D.C., 1957.

Schutter, Charles H.: *The Development of Education in Argentina, Chile, and Uruguay*, The University of Chicago Press, Chicago, 1957.

Science in the Americas, prepared by the National Academy of Sciences National Research Council for the United States National Commission for UNESCO, Denver, Col., 1959.

Smith, T. Lynn: *Current Social Trends and Problems in Latin America*, University of Florida Press, Gainesville, Fla., 1957.

Some Educational and Anthropological Aspects of Latin America, Latin-American Studies V, University of Texas Press, Austin, Tex., 1948.

Stokes, William S.: *Latin American Politics*, Crowell, New York, 1959.

Thomas, Alfred Barnaby: *Latin America: A History with Maps*, Macmillan, New York, 1956.

UNESCO: *La Situacion Educativa en America Latina: La Ensenanza Primaria: estados, problemas, perspectivas*, UNESCO, New York, 1960.

————, America Latina: *Proyecto Principal de Educacion*, Boletin Trimestral, no. 14, April–June, 1962.

U.S. Office of Education: *Present Situation in Latin American Education*, 1962.

Vocational Training in Latin America, International Labor Office, Geneva, 1951.

Pamphlets and periodicals

The Annals of the American Academy of Political and Social Science, "Latin America's Nationalistic Revolutions," vol. 334, pp. 1–147, March, 1961.

Arriagada, Guillerma Sanhueza: "Education in Latin America," *Interna-*

tional Review of Education, vol. 6, pp. 471–474, 1960.

Benton, William: *The Voice of Latin America,* reprinted from 1961 *Britannica, Book of the Year,* Encyclopaedia Britannica, Inc., Chicago, 1961.

Cook, Mercer: "Recent Developments in Haitian Education," *Education,* vol. 76, no. 10, pp. 611–617, June, 1956.

Hans, Nicholas: "Comparative Study of Latin America," *Comparative Education Review,* vol. 5, no. 1, June, 1961.

Henry, Nelson B. (ed.): "Community Education," *The Fifty-eighth Year Book of the National Society for the Study of Education,* part I, The University of Chicago Press, Chicago, 1959.

Journal of Inter-American Studies, School of Inter-American Studies, University of Florida, Gainesville, Fla.

Kandel, I. L. (ed.): "Education in Latin America," *Educational Year Book,* Columbia University, Teachers College International Institute, New York, 1942.

Kaulfers, Walter V.: "Latin-American Education in Transition," *The Educational Record,* vol. 42, pp. 91–98, April, 1961.

Moreira, J. Roberto: "Some Social Aspects of Brazilian Education," *Comparative Education Review,* vol. 4, no. 2, pp. 93–96, October, 1960.

Olson, Arthur R.: "The Status and Role of Public Secondary Education in Latin America," *High School Journal,* vol. 44, pp. 26–32, October, 1960.

Sanchez, Luis Alberto: "The University in Latin America," *Americas,* part I: "The Colonial Period," vol. 13, no. 11, pp. 21–23, November, 1961; part II: "Cradle of Republican Thought," vol. 13, no. 12, pp. 20–23, December, 1961; part III: "The University Reform Movement," vol. 14, no. 1, pp. 13–16, January, 1962; part IV: "As It Looks Today," vol. 14, no. 2, pp. 14–17, February, 1962.

Soto, Joaquin Mena: "Education in Ecuador and Its Problems," *International Review of Education,* vol. 6, 1960.

Villages, Abel Narajo: "The Paradox of Feudal Education in a Democratic Nation," *Panorama,* Winter, 1960–1961.

CHAPTER 14

Indian Education:
Search for Economic and Political Independence

Since 1947, when the Indian subcontinent emerged from British colonial rule, Indians have optimistically referred to their nation as the New India (Bharat). And the republic of India is new in the sense that for the first time in its history India has become a politically unified nation. India is new also in its increasing influence in world affairs and in the democratic political pattern on which its government is structured. Moreover, the introduction, on a larger scale, of modern techniques and institutions designed to promote social and economic changes portend a permanency for such "newness." Yet dramatic changes notwithstanding, the progressive label, New India, should not be understood to mean that India has sloughed off her past and is an entirely new cultural creation. Modern India is deeply marked by her past, both ancient and recent.

Historical development

Long before Europeans came under the spell of the variegated riches of India, Indian culture had developed to an advanced stage in every field except the technological. In seeking to understand contemporary India, then, one must come to know ancient India—its religious and literary traditions, its scholastic contributions, and the ethnic and other factors that have made for social diversity and unity in modern India.

Ancient historical traditions

Indian civilization is usually traced to 4000 B.C., at which date it is believed

to have been on a par with the culture of the Chinese. By 2000 B.C., this civilization had experienced considerable decline and become relatively easy prey for the tall, fair-skinned Indo-Aryans who were pressing into India through the mountain passes of central Asia. The Aryans, culturally inferior to the indigenous groups (the largest of which were called Dravidians), nevertheless were able to succeed in their plan of conquest. It was during the period of settlement and fusion of the Aryans with the Dravidians and other indigenous peoples that the great Indian traditions were put into print and thus preserved for the future. The result of this fusion of people and ideas under Aryan leadership has been called the Indic civilization.[1]

During the "period of growth" of the Indic civilization, roughly 1300–700 B.C., the great philosophic-religious Vedic literature of India was born. The four main collections of writings which make up the Vedas are (1) the Rigveda—"a collection of hymns that were chanted or recited by the priests at the sacrifices"; (2) the Samaveda—"a collection of melodies for the chants"; (3) the Yajurveda—"a series of prescriptions or directions for performing the sacrifices"; and (4) the Atharvaveda—"less sacerdotal than the other three, being a prayer book for the simple folk."[2]

Vedic hymnals gave rise to ritualistic interpretations termed "Brahamanas" and "Aranyakas" which later led to

[1] Edward F. Myers, *Education in the Perspective of History*, Harper & Row, New York, 1960, p. 49.
[2] *Ibid.*

387

symbolic and philosophic interpretations called "Upanishads." The speculative treatises of the Upanishads are concerned mainly with a "mystical interpretation of the Vedic ritual and its relation to man and the universe."[3] In addition to the Vedas and the Upanishads, two epics of gigantic scope and dimension should be mentioned, the *Mahabharata,* called the longest poem in the world, and the *Ramayana.* These epics, which often are compared to the *Iliad* and *Odyssey* of ancient Greece, embody the essential Vedic philosophy in a form which has had great popularity among the Indian people through the centuries. For people denied the knowledge of the written word the *Mahabharata* and *Ramayana* contributed greatly to the development of a rich oral heritage.

Since scholars are in fair agreement that the basic ethos of the Indic and the later Hindu civilization was religious, a clearer picture is needed of the pervasive principles found in the Vedas and their expository supplements. Perhaps most basic to Vedic philosophy is the belief that beyond the experiential world, beyond the pantheon of naturalistic gods, lies a unifying principle or spirit, Brahma. The individual self, the Atman, is related to Brahma for "the Universe is Brahma, but the Brahma is the Atman." This identity (Brahma = Atman) indicates a unity among all living things—a view that is reminiscent of certain Chinese philosophies but contrasts sharply with the dualistic views of the West. The need to experience this identity—this quest for a unity of the individual and the Universal—

remains a significant motivating force for Indians today.

These literary works are important to an understanding of modern India not merely as chronicles of history but primarily because in them, particularly in the Upanishads, are given the basic precepts of what is now known as Hinduism. Hindus historically have regarded the Vedas as a body of revealed and absolute truths; and the authority of these revelations is still recognized by a great majority of Hindus today. Without a knowledge of Hinduism one cannot find the key to an understanding of the modern Indian, his relationship to God and to his fellow beings, and his image of himself. More than a religious dogma, in fact it has no canon, Hinduism for over two millennia has been a way of life, with social, economic, and political as well as religious implications for the majority of the Indian people.

Although it is the all-encompassing director of life, Hinduism[4] has viewed worldly existence and its entrappings as unimportant in the soul's journey to its ultimate goal of nirvana (the term originated with Buddha), in which individuality is lost in a mystical union with Brahma. A Hindu who is to achieve nirvana, or nonbeing, must perform the secular duties and religious rituals appropriate to him in his station of life, but even more important, he must engage in meditation so that his thought may be purified of worldly concerns. The soul must carry on its quest through aeons of time, finding rewards through

[3] Wm. Theodore de Bary (ed.), *Sources of Indian Tradition,* Columbia, New York, 1958, p. 5.

[4] The term Hinduism apparently did not come into use until the time of Moslem invasions during the eleventh or twelfth centuries. "Hindu" is the Persian term for "Indian" and hence Hinduism—the belief of the Indians.

successive reincarnation in the bodies of persons in higher societal positions as it progresses toward its ultimate goal. Thus Hinduism has tended to produce a society tinged with fatalism in which the status of the individual is considered the result of his behavior in previous lives, and any attempts on his part to achieve higher status are looked upon as deterrents to his soul's progress. The importance of meditation and the ultimate goal of achieving a state in which human and material concerns are of no consequence have tended to produce a people characterized by many observers as being otherworldly rather than materialistic and as being more contemplative than active.

Closely associated with the Hindu concept of life, yet also rooted in the desire to maintain racial and cultural differences in the face of continued onslaughts from invaders, is the caste system, one of the major divisive forces in Indian society. Although scholars disagree to a certain extent on its precise origins, caste appears to have been related to both occupation and color. Within the Indo-Aryan tribes caste cleavages were defined occupationally, while a color prejudice was practiced between the Indo-Aryan and other peoples. Out of the societal divisions emerged four major castes. Traditionally the Brahmans, the spiritual leaders, were the most revered, and following them in descending order were the Kshatriyas, men of war and politics; the Vaisyas, tradesmen; and the Sudras, or serfs. Within these four major castes there developed numerous smaller castes and subcastes created by the continued incorporation of successive invaders, trade guilds, religious groups, interracial groups, and even groups of dissenters

against the system. Each caste was hereditary and endogamous, and responsible for its internal affairs as well as the contacts of its members with other castes.[5]

The definition of caste has become so complicated that the original fourfold classification has had little meaning in modern times. Instead, Wallbank suggests that all castes may be placed in three broad categories: The first group includes the Brahmans; the Rajput clans, the declared representatives of the ancient Kshatriyas; and the traders who claim descent from the Vaisyas, all of whom constitute the twice-born.[6] The second group embraces the traditional Sudra castes that are now all lumped together as being *not* twice-born. At the bottom are the untouchables, also known as the "depressed classes" or "scheduled castes."[7]

The castes have varied in composition throughout Indian history, and indeed the concept was rejected by Buddha and later by certain of the Moslem conquerors. During the period of *Pax Britannica* (ca. 1850–1910) the British belief in "equal justice" came into direct conflict with caste traditions. The most decisive action to curb the inequities of caste, however, awaited the advent of national independence.

As a means of maintaining the individuality of a multitude of cultures within one stable society, the caste system has been referred to as the "supreme

[5] J. H. Hutton, *Caste in India: Its Nature, Function, and Origins,* Cambridge, New York, 1946, chaps. 5–12.

[6] Traditionally, in contradiction to the Wallbank classification, only the Brahmans were called *Daija* or twice-born.

[7] T. Walter Wallbank, *A Short History of India and Pakistan,* New American Library, New York, 1958, p. 26.

expression of the genius of Indian Civilization"; [8] however, at the same time it must be considered an extremely powerful deterrent to both individual aspirations of mobility and national goals of development.

Along with the caste system, the extended or patrilocal family and the village community have been looked upon as supporting pillars of Indian society. The extended family included father, sons, grandsons, and their respective womenfolk who historically shared estate, income, food, and worship. Daughters and granddaughters were also members of the extended family until they became married. Whether the family actually lived together in one household, or whether, as is more common in modern times, the sons established new households shortly after their marriage, the major individual or group decisions were made by a council of the family's elder men presided over by the eldest male member. The entire family also functioned as a united group in the religious observances of its caste, in large economic enterprises, and in protecting and regulating the social affairs of its members.

The village, which forms the third pillar of Indian society, likewise developed in ancient India and combined families of the several castes into semi-independent and self-sufficient units which are still the center of the lives of the rural population of contemporary India. Traditionally the affairs of the village unit were directed by a council composed of the heads of families, the local headmen of the castes, and other particularly influential men of the community. Major decisions involving the entire village were made and implemented through this council, and frequently it acted along with the family or caste to regulate undesirable behavior of individuals or groups within the community. The villages of India have frequently been characterized as essentially democratic units because of the representative nature of the village council and its reliance on persuasion rather than force whenever possible. Furthermore the villages provided India with another effective structure of societal stability. Considering its long heritage of invasions and religious and social divisions, such stability was a requisite for the formation and continuance of the Indian nation; however, such arrangements were also to India's disadvantage since the tightly structured rural village historically resisted political, economic, and social change even to the point of prohibiting the settlement of families from other villages within its domain.

Although a definite cultural unity had existed, ancient India had never been united into a political whole and for this as well as other reasons had developed no program of state education. However, a type of formal education designed to develop moral character through the study of the Vedic literature and other religious writings did evolve for boys of the three upper castes. The most common pattern of education was a private tutorial type of arrangement under the direction of gurus (masters), men who originally had performed all the prescribed religious rites and were usually, though not always, members of the Brahman caste. A guru would accept a certain number of students into his household where they would serve him,

[8] Amaury de Riencourt, *The Soul of India*, Harper & Row, New York, 1960, p. 97.

beg alms (as a form of moral training), and engage in academic studies in which great stress was put on oral work and memorization. The close bond between student and teacher was the key to successful education:

> The pupil found his teacher; he lived with him as a member of his family and was treated as a son. . . . Thus the pupil learned and imbibed the inner method of the teacher and was in touch with the spirit of his work.[9]

A quiet, preferably wooded, setting for instruction was considered of utmost importance.

> . . . the school was the home of the teacher, a hermitage amid sylvan surroundings away from the hubbub of town life, amidst silence and in a calm atmosphere, a place of solitude, an ideal place for contemplation and meditation on Truth or Reality.[10]

The education which a boy received in these "sylvan surroundings" was a combination of ritualistic and academic learning and was considered complete at any time that the master pronounced it so.

The acceptance of a boy by a guru was part of a religioeducational ritual and took place after the boy had participated in simple religious ceremonies, learned the alphabet, and perhaps acquired the rudiments of arithmetic and, by the fourth century B.C. when a script had been developed, writing. Education, being governed by a Hindu ideal, concentrated on the development of self-

discipline and religious knowledge which would aid in attaining the spiritual goal and, in effect, amounted to a spiritual birth—in contrast to physical birth. Although a highly literary flavor permeated the curriculum, specific attention was given to the role which the student as a caste member would play in society. Thus military science and economics, the arts of war and commerce, might be taught for those who would have future need for them. This latter, more practical consideration of the curriculum was also based on Hindu philosophy which dictated that man could only achieve his spiritual goal by performing his task in the present life to the best of his ability.

In addition to the home-school another type of educational institution arose to satisfy the needs of advanced students. Bands of students in ancient India, much like those of medieval Europe, wandered through the countryside to sit at the feet of learned scholars to listen and to debate. Such arrangements, as they became more institutionalized, were called academies, debating circles, or sometimes "universities."[11] Although education was private, the large universities were open to all scholars, and studies were not assigned according to caste. By the fourth century B.C. these universities, particularly at Taxila and Benares, had gained renown as great centers of learning and were attended by students from all over Asia. In addition to advanced religious studies, there were sports activities, military and medical institutes, and departments in economics, botany, philosophy, and possibly astronomy.

In India, then, several centuries before Christ a rather extensive system of

[9] Sobharani Basu, "Forest Universities in Ancient India," *The Year Book of Education*, World, Tarrytown-on-Hudson, N. Y., p. 319, 1957.

[10] *Ibid.*

[11] de Bary, *op. cit.*, p. 331.

education was in operation at least for a few members of the upper castes. It should be noted that women had not been entirely barred from intellectual activities as is attested by the prestige of such philosophers as Gargi and Maitrey whose conversations are preserved in the Upanishads. While largely limited in its concern to the moral side of man's nature, this education did spread a common language (Sanskrit) and a common culture. Moreover at the advanced stages a wide range of secular learning was available. Thus education, in effect, supplemented military prowess to ensure Aryan domination over the various non-Aryan peoples.

Impact of Buddhism and Islam

Gautama Sakyamuni, who later became known as the Buddha, lived in a time of intellectual ferment and growing discontent with the excessively aristocratic and ritualistic temperament of Hinduism. Buddha was especially distressed at the ostentatious opulence of the merchants and the Brahmans, for he believed that man's troubles stem from his inability to discipline himself against the desire for material things. The interpretation of the route to nirvana given by Buddha and his followers is summarized in the "Four Noble Truths" of Buddhism.

1. . . . all life is inevitably sorrowful;

2. . . . sorrow is due to craving;

3. . . . it can only be stopped by the stopping of craving;

4. . . . this can only be done by a course of carefully disciplined and moral conduct, culminating in the life of concentration and meditation led by the Buddhist monk.[12]

[12] *Ibid.*, p. 95.

In time the teachings of Buddha spread throughout India and remained a vital religious force for ten centuries. They exerted a democratizing influence on society, as evidenced, for example, by the acceptance of all castes into Buddhist centers of learning. Although such things as the *ahimsa,* or love and nonviolence toward all living things, can be traced to Buddhism, the full influence of Buddhism in India can scarcely be determined, since by the twelfth century it was once again absorbed into the main stream of Hinduism. In much of the rest of Asia it was a different story, however, and Buddhism as a separate religion lives on as a force in the lives of millions of people.

Neither the military conquests of the Aryans and other less powerful invading groups nor the successful penetrations of Buddhism could completely unite the Indian subcontinent. One empire after another was established in northern India, but these affected only slightly the various kingdoms in the south.

The Moslems began their vigorous invasions of India in the tenth century A.D., but not until the end of the seventeenth century did the sword of Islam succeed in uniting briefly the entire subcontinent under one ruler. Owing largely to the influence of Islam, which was as much an all-encompassing way of life as was Hinduism, the Moslems, in contrast to previous invaders of India, refused to be absorbed by the Hindu-dominated society. However, although these societies remained separate, they exerted a great deal of influence on each other. Certain democratic elements found in Islam led to reform and liberalizing movements in Hinduism, while Hindi, a common Indian vernacular combined with some Arabic, formed Urdu which became a kind of lingua franca among the Moslems. Hindu women, who had been losing status since the time of the great women scholars of the early Vedic period, were given a final push toward seclusion by the Moslem influence.[13] While attempts by Hindu and Moslem leaders to create a synthesis of these two great religions met with little success, they did serve to enrich greatly the native vernacular literature.[14] An aesthetic synthesis of the two cultures created profoundly beautiful works of art, particularly of architecture.[15]

During the later Moslem period, especially during the Mogul empire (1526–1707), India became once again a center of scholarship and literary creativity. Although the early Moslem rulers lacked a consistent educational policy the great Mogul leaders—Babar, Akbar, Aurangzib, and others—while not always friendly toward Hindu education, expended great efforts toward the furthering of Moslem scholarship. The Moslem education that was introduced followed the same pattern as that which had been established in the Arab lands and formed a second educational stream flowing side by side with the relatively unchanging Hindu inheritance from ancient India. The centers of Moslem educational, as well as civil and ecclesiastical, activities were the mosques. Here in the *maktabs* (primary schools) and *madrasas* (high schools or colleges) children learned to memorize and recite the revealed truths of the Koran, acquired some grammatical skills, and achieved some knowledge of arithmetic. Lectures on literary and religious topics were held at the mosques,

and great collections of books were stored in them. In addition, certain academies or universities, which it is said some Hindus attended, were established in all Moslem lands to promote advanced learning. At these institutions again the Koran and Arab literature formed the backbone of the curriculum, with law (largely theocratic), mathematics, and history also receiving emphasis.

Although neither Moslem nor Hindu rulers had established a state educational system, both groups considered the support of education a religious obligation. Royal patrons supported scholarship through direct donations to institutions and by providing patronage to distinguished poets, artists, and musicians. Both Moslems and Hindus gave social prestige to the art of teaching, and stories are told of mighty military and political leaders paying homage to humble teachers.

Yet in India, as in China, a great scholarly tradition hardened into a system of orthodoxy which resisted societal change. The movements of religious heterodoxy and the powerful secular force of rationalism which successfully destroyed European ideological conformity and ushered in a modern age were not present in precolonial India. The goals of Indian education as of life itself were sacral rather than secular and offered few visions of new philosophical or material frontiers to challenge man's efforts.

Anglicization of education

The riches of India, luxuriant spices and beautiful textiles, acted as a dazzling magnet to attract adventurous European traders. From the end of the fif-

[13] T. Walter Wallbank, *India in the New Era*, Scott, Foresman, Chicago, 1951, p. 39.
[14] Riencourt, *op. cit.*, pp. 173–174.
[15] *Ibid.*, p. 175.

teenth century, however, the perilous ventures of enterprising individuals gave way to large-scale operations conducted by trading companies of the Portuguese, Dutch, French, and British. By the middle of the eighteenth century, the British East India Company, founded in 1600, had succeeded in eliminating its rivals from the subcontinent and thus paved the way for the acquisition of the richest jewel in the British colonial empire. By mid-nineteenth century when India passed from the authority of the East India Company into the control of the British government the entire subcontinent was administered either directly by British representatives or indirectly through subsidiary treaties with the rulers of the protected princely states. The British were cautious about interfering with the social customs of the Indians, as demonstrated by their reluctant abolition of suttee—the burning of widows on their husbands' funeral pyres—but British ideas and ideals nevertheless reigned supreme in economic and political affairs.

To develop India as a source for raw materials and a market for England's growing industrial economy, the British initiated several far-reaching policies. Modern communication and transportation systems were introduced which to some extent provided the formerly isolated villages with wider markets and in the process made them more dependent on a money economy. The concern of the British with civil order and stability resulted in the establishment of a legal system based largely, though not exclusively, on Western concepts. The underlying principle of equality before the law, regardless of caste, had revolutionary implications in the traditionally ascriptive Indian society.

Another facet of British policy was the development of India's first effective and impartial administrative system. After some experimentation the British established the policy of allowing various geographic areas which were under the stable rule of hereditary princes to manage their own internal affairs. Thus vast regions of the Indian subcontinent were never administered directly by the British but remained under the control of indigenous autocrats. All external affairs were under the control of the colonial government, which also reserved the right to intervene in local affairs if the conduct of the prince was particularly detrimental to the welfare of the people. The result of this permissiveness was that some of the princely states remained extraordinarily backward and virtually isolated from the change taking place in India throughout the colonial period. Furthermore, the vested interests of the princes as well as the lack of a national feeling on the part of the people created obstacles to unification when India later emerged as a new nation.

The core of the administrative system[16] was the Indian Civil Service, a select group of hard-working capable men who justifiably took pride in their efficiency and immunity from corruption. The group was amazingly small, because it delegated considerable responsibility to large numbers of Indian employees. The Indian Civil Service was originally made up entirely of British; it was with some reluctance opened to Indians, although until the latter part of the colonial period they were virtually excluded from higher positions. In 1892

[16] For a diagram of the complete British administrative system see Wallbank, *India in the New Era, op. cit.*, p. 62.

only 21 of the 939 members were Indians. In spite of its many strengths, the officialdom of the British colonial government and administration has been generally criticized for its machinelike impersonality and aloofness from the people it controlled.

The changes which the British made in the social structure of Indian society were based primarily on the need for an efficient administrative system. This goal eventually prompted the establishment of an educational system which used English as the language of instruction and followed the curriculum of the British schools. The transplanting of English schools into India, it was felt, would produce clerks and other government servants who had the language skills and character traits necessary to operate British governmental offices.

The policy of the British East India Company did not originally allow it to become involved extensively in the development of Indian institutions; therefore, with certain exceptions to be noted later, Western educational ideas were introduced by European missionaries. Although Catholic missionaries, particularly Portuguese Jesuits, were active in early educational work, Protestant missionary societies largely usurped the educational field in India. During the eighteenth century the Bible and other Christian literature were translated into Indian vernaculars. Some employees of the East India Company gave at least moral support to the missionaries, but the company directors voiced frequent opposition. Moreover, a hostility from Hindu and Moslem believers, bred of mutual distrust, further hampered missionary efforts in education. And, in spite of the lack of discretion and a certain amount of bigotry not unknown

to missionary activities,[17] the mission schools though small in number became an important wedge for the introduction of Western learning.

The English Protestant missionaries, who were active in establishing vernacular schools from Ceylon to Bengal, were not without support in Parliament for their educational and religious cause. Demands were made that the English government fulfill its obligation to bring light, through Christian teachings, to the darkness of India. In 1793 attempts were made by a member of Parliament to introduce into the charter of the East India Company specific provisions for the encouragement of the work of missionaries and schoolmasters in India. Opposing this proposal the directors of the company argued for a hands-off policy and suggested that the Hindus:

. . . had as good a system of faith and of morals as most people and that it would be madness to attempt their conversion or to give them any more learning or any other description of learning than what they already possessed.[18]

Moreover, one member of Parliament is said to have remarked, "We . . . lost our colonies in America by importing our education there, we need not do so in India, too."[19]

In this manner one of the most fascinating and significant battles in the

[17] A Baptist society in 1807 is said to have published a pamphlet titled *Addresses to Hindus and Mohamedans* in which "Mohamed was referred to as a false prophet and Hinduism was denounced as a mass of idolatry, superstition and ignorance." S. N. Mukerji, *History of Education in India*, Acharya Book Depot, Baroda, 1951, p. 29.
[18] Quoted in Mukerji, *ibid.*, p. 32.
[19] *Ibid.*

educational history of India began to take shape. By the early part of the nineteenth century the following controversial issues were debated:

1. Should the basic educational objective in India be that of promoting oriental learning, or the introduction of Western languages and culture?

2. Should the language of instruction be English, Persian and Sanskrit, the modern Indian vernaculars, or some appropriate combination? Other issues involved the location of educational responsibility, and the relative emphasis that should be placed on elementary and higher education.[20]

Advocates of increased involvement in Indian education succeeded in getting a clause written into the East India Act of 1813 which provided that a minimum of £10,000 be spent yearly for (1) the revival and improvement of literature and the encouragement of the learned natives of India; and (2) the introduction and promotion of a knowledge of the sciences among the inhabitants of the British territories in India.[21] With the East India Company now officially committed to promotion of education in India, decisions needed to be made regarding the relative emphasis the various parts of the curriculum should have. In this manner the famous Orientalist-Anglicist controversy was brought to a head, the outcome of which would decide the direction of Indian education until independence. There were Englishmen and Indians on both sides of the argument.

The Orientalists, or Classicists as they were sometimes called, held that education should emphasize India's cultural heritage through the medium of Sanskrit for Hindus and Arabic for Moslems. Otherwise, the group argued, although it was not entirely unified in its views, India would be cut off from its glorious past. Such Western learning as was of value could be taught through the classical languages; thus a synthesis of Western and Eastern cultures could be effected.

The Anglicists advocated the use of English as a medium of instruction and Western learning in general as the best route for Indian progress. Both sides agreed that the great mass of people should be educated in the vernacular, and although one group urged that the vernacular be used at all levels of education, the main point of debate centered on the content and language of instruction in higher education. Rammohum Roy, who has been called the father of modern India, represented an articulate but minority group of Indians who strongly supported English education. He set forth his position most effectively in his "Letter on Education" (1823). In this letter he protested against further government support of Hindu education which:

> . . . can only be expected to load the minds of youth with grammatical niceties and metaphysical distinctions of little or no practical use to the possessors or to society. The pupils will there acquire what was known 2000 years ago with the addition of vain and empty subtleties since then produced by speculative men such as is already commonly taught in all parts of India.[22]

It was Roy's belief that through Eng-

[20] *Ibid.*, p. 34.

[21] Sir Philip Hartog, *Some Aspects of Indian Education Past and Present,* Oxford, Fair Lawn, N.J., 1939, p. 9.

[22] de Bary, *op. cit.*, pp. 471–474, 593.

lish education and its concern with science and rational thought India could enter into a new period of enlightenment.

The decisive blow to the Orientalists' hopes was struck by Thomas Babington Macaulay when in 1834, as president of the General Committee of Public Instruction, he composed his famous "Minute on Education." Macaulay, totally ignorant of Sanskrit and Arabic learning, easily dismissed these as unimportant and argued instead for a Western education which would:

> . . . form a class of persons, Indian in blood and color, but English in taste, in opinions, in morals and in intellect. To that class we may leave it to refine the vernacular dialects of the country, to enrich those dialects with terms of science borrowed from the Western nomenclature, and to render them by degrees fit vehicles for conveying knowledge to the great mass of the population.[23]

In fairness to Macaulay it should be added that he believed that an Anglicized program of advanced education would not only acquaint Indian students with the wonderful achievements of the West but would also offer them more extensive political and leadership opportunities.

Thus the third stream of education that entered India was in some respects similar to the other two: it had its own special language, its special concern with the education of one class, and its highly literary character. It differed from the others in its secular outlook and its concern with science and Western thought. Neither Hindu nor Moslem education was suppressed; however, lack of government support plus the

[23] *Ibid.*, p. 601.

material advantages to be gained from Western education resulted in the gradual narrowing of the older streams.

In 1854 a document of great educational importance was produced by the East India Company. Coming at the end of a series of documents which included the Charter Act of 1813 and minutes by a long list of distinguished Englishmen, the Educational Despatch of 1854 was the most comprehensive and significant of all. Sometimes called the Magna Charta of Indian education, the Despatch included provisions for an education department in each province; universities in Calcutta, Madras, and Bombay; a network of graded schools throughout India; increased use of vernacular languages as media of instruction; and grants-in-aid to lower schools and scholarships to able but needy students. The Despatch further concerned itself with such problems as the education of women, the training of teachers, and the employment opportunities of educated Indians.

Since the political power of the East India Company ended in 1858 when India came to be placed directly under the crown, implementation now fell to the British government. In spite of its ambitious program, the new education provided instruction for a class rather than for a total population. The English schools drew students primarily from the middle classes who looked to them for professional preparation or as the pathway to government jobs—which indeed they were. Under these circumstances English education in India concentrated most heavily on higher education. As one critic noted:

> Education was to permeate the masses from above. Drop by drop from the Himalayas of Indian life useful information was to trickle

downwards, forming in time a broad and stately stream to irrigate the thirsty plains.[24]

The Despatch of 1854 dominated educational thinking and policy in British India until the turn of the twentieth century, although Indian leaders criticized it and sought more dynamic educational progress. Agitation for a larger voice in the national policy decisions led to the Government of India Act in 1919, which brought partial control of the central Education Department to the Indians. In the two decades prior to World War II educational facilities and enrollment steadily increased at all levels, various forms of vocational education were introduced, and there were several, mostly abortive, local attempts at compulsory education. Still the transferral of educational power into native hands raised an expectation of rapid educational improvement that was only partly fulfilled.

Perhaps the most dramatic of the changes in the preindependence period was the progress in Moslem school enrollments. Between 1921 and 1936 primary school attendance grew from 1.5 million to 3 million, secondary enrollments grew by 25 per cent, and college enrollments increased threefold. It has been estimated that by 1936 the percentage of Moslem pupils in schools was greater than the average of India as a whole.[25]

Some Indians had complained that British educational policy stressed quality at the expense of quantity. Yet even after the Indians assumed increased re-

sponsibility in making educational decisions, expansion of educational opportunity, particularly at the lower levels, was disappointing. In 1921, for example, the percentage of literacy in British India was estimated at 7.2.[26] By 1941 the percentage had been raised to only 12.2.[27] More striking, however, is the fact that the actual number of illiterates was greater in 1941 than in 1931.

Repeated plans for extending the lower levels of the educational pyramid never seemed to get off the paper on which they were written, but the institutions of higher education found expansion relatively easy, thus creating:

. . . a new caste or class in India, the English educated class, which lived in a world of its own, cut off from the mass of the population, and looked always, even when protesting, toward their rulers.[28]

The Anglicized Indians were unified not by heredity but by a common language, which for the first time permitted communication between educated men from all parts of India, and by the great ideological and social influence which their Western education exerted upon them. Like the other privileged castes throughout India's history, this group was separated from the masses; however, unlike many other castes, it was to some extent concerned with the welfare of the masses.

Although English statesmen had called for the creation of an elite group of Indians who in taste and loyalty would be oriented toward England, it was from

[24] A. Mayhew, *The Education of India*, Faber and Gwyer, London, 1928, p. 92.

[25] Syed Nurallah and J. P. Naik, *A History of Education in India*, Macmillan, New York, 1951, p. 718.

[26] *Ibid.*, p. 545.

[27] *Ibid.*, p. 780.

[28] J. Nehru, *The Discovery of India*, John Day, New York, 1946, p. 412.

this very elite class that the most ardent nationalists came. Indians had reacted favorably to the peace and stability brought by British rule. But multiple factors, not the least of which was the intellectual contact with virile European thought, in time turned faith and gratitude into distrust and hostility. Indian students through their Anglicized curriculum had read the history of Europe sprinkled with its many nationalistic movements, studied the philosophies of men such as Locke and J. S. Mill, quoted English poets exulting in freedom and love for country; and nationalism was born in India. The Indian National Congress, established in 1885, became the center of organization for nationalism as it grew into a movement for independence. With time, nationalism fused with religion and led to a Hindu revival, and although the leaders of this growing movement continued to be Western-educated men, they were men who also had a deep appreciation for "Mother India."

As nationalism grew, reflecting a strong religious influence, the gap between Hindus and Moslems widened in spite of several attempts at conciliation. The story of India's progress toward independence in the first half of the twentieth century is a story of conflict between the Hindus and Moslems, a conflict at times encouraged by the British, and a story of flux due to the two world wars and their effects. In this period two men stand above all other dedicated leaders, Rabindranath Tagore and Mahatma Gandhi. Widely different in views, these men were nevertheless both representative of India. Tagore wanted freedom for India, but freedom from poverty, the growing Moslem-Hindu conflict, the caste system, and other social and religious as well as political restraints. His greatest expression was his spiritually charged poetry which opened the heart of India to the world. Seeing India's spiritualism as complementary to the materialism of the West, Tagore established a college at Shankinketan dedicated to the rebirth of Indian culture and world brotherhood. This school, which emphasized learning through contact and communion with nature, became a model for later Hindu educational institutions.

In contrast to Tagore, Gandhi's great drive was toward political independence. In answer to a description of him as ". . . a saint trying to be a politician" he described himself as "a politician trying my hardest to be a saint."[29] But his method included great social reforms which for the first time brought the masses into active participation in the movement. Nationalism and independence had previously been primarily the concern of the small group of Western-educated intellectuals. Through Gandhi's personality, example, and doctrine of passive resistance they became the concern of India. Gandhi showed the people their power and urged them to return to their crafts in order to help themselves overcome their many problems rather than waiting for some outside force to bring them relief. The success which he had in influencing the people of India plus the untiring work of the Indian Congress and the Moslem League, and the increasing unpopularity of colonialism in the world resulted finally in independence and partition for India. On midnight, August 14, 1947, Pakistan and the Union of India became two free nations.

[29] de Bary, *op. cit.*, p. 802.

•

A new nation and new educational policies

The Union of India was designed as a republic dedicated to the concept of progress through democracy. While free from the shackles of foreign rule, India still had many chains to loosen before the goals envisioned by such leaders as Tagore and Gandhi would be achieved. The new India emerged with a doctrine of universal suffrage extended to a population nearly 90 per cent illiterate. There was little industry, and agricultural efficiency was low. There were conflicts and distrust between urbanites and villagers, educated and noneducated. Poverty, disease, and a passive view of life loomed as monstrous obstacles to the Gandhian vision of self-initiated change; yet there was some room for optimism. Great physical resources remained untapped, and educated, honest, and experienced leaders were available in numbers unknown in most developing areas.

Economic problems

The most serious economic problem facing independent India and one with which the nation has traditionally been plagued was the inability of the agricultural sector to provide sufficient food for the population. The low fertility of the soil, irregular monsoon rains, marketing defects, and antiquated farming methods resulted in one of the lowest agricultural yields per acre in the world. With the assistance of exceptionally favorable weather conditions, India has succeeded during the last few years in raising rice production nearly to the level of need. However, large quantities of other basic foodstuffs still have to be imported. The

drain on foreign reserves, brought about by such importations, restricts India's efforts to purchase the tools and equipment necessary to develop its industrial sector. Because of the Hindu principle of *ahimsa*, or nonviolence, which prevents the slaughter or eating of cattle, efforts to improve the diet of the Indian population have not been widely successful. The vast number of cattle and other nonproductive animals that are kept consume large quantities of food yearly. The cattle may be used in plowing the land and transporting the produce, but their puniness makes for low efficiency even in such functions. Moreover, owing to poor breeding and improper feeding, the cows give little milk; the cow dung, which is burned for fuel, is perhaps the most useful contribution these animals make to the economy.

The problem of producing sufficient foodstuffs is compounded by India's rapidly growing population, which by 1961 had reached approximately 400 million. Medical improvements and humanitarian reforms have reduced famine and disease, but these factors combined with a high birth rate have resulted in a population growth rate of 2 per cent per annum. To counteract the perpetuation of starvation conditions brought on by population pressures a national program of planned parenthood has been initiated. Fortunately neither the Hindus nor the Moslems have religious strictures regarding birth control; but the tradition of large families and the importance of male lineage have proved to be formidable obstacles. Because of increasing concern over the population problem and the necessity for dramatic action, Nehru had suggested that Indian women consider voluntary sterilization after having borne three children.

Landownership and distribution form an Indian problem of both economic and social dimensions. Land in India has traditionally been a main source of wealth and status; and in recognition of this fact, the states in India after 1947 began a land-reform movement. As outlined in the third five-year plan the overall land-reform objectives are to "reduce disparities in the ownership of land," create a condition where "the vast majority of cultivators . . . would consist of peasant-proprietors" who would be encouraged and interested in organizing themselves in voluntary co-operative bodies for credit, marketing, processing, and distribution and, with their consent, progressively also for production.[30] Even with the unofficial assistance of the Gandhian disciple, Vinoba Brave, who traveled about the countryside urging landlords to voluntarily give up portions of their land, the Indian government admits only partial success. The land problem is more than one of maldistribution, for simple arithmetic shows that there is less than 1 tillable acre per capita. Indian leaders of the reform movement fully realize that overfragmentation of the larger estates may result in landholdings of uneconomic size. The goals, therefore, have a more moderate ring about them than might be expected in the case of such an explosive issue.

The combination of private responsibility within the framework of group planning, backstopped when necessary by direct government action, typifies India's approach to improvement of its agricultural sector and to economic development in general. Perpetual indebt-

edness to moneylenders and landlords has sapped the spirit of the Indian farmer, for as a popular Indian saying goes, "the bania (moneylender) goes in like a needle and comes out like a sword."[31] Direct government action to help states and local communities make credit available at reasonable rates of interest has been a helpful stopgap measure, while community-development projects and cottage industries may be a long-term solution for making the underemployed farmer more self-sufficient. (It is estimated that the average farmer is productively employed only 150 days of the year.) One of the greatest boons to reducing the indebtedness of rural and city folk alike, however, has been the enactment of the so-called "dowry law," prohibiting the traditional lavish gifts of money and land by the bride's family.

Economic development in a nation the size of India also demands a rapid program of industrialization, balanced with light, medium, and heavy industries and designed to meet immediate consumer needs while not neglecting capital goods industries. Finding and training the skilled manpower needed for such an undertaking requires enlargement of Indian educational facilities and extensive utilization of foreign institutions. Financing large-scale industrial operations requires close cooperation between government and private enterprise and since the government is the biggest holder of capital, it has become responsible for the establishment of most of the major industries, as well as the infrastructures of power and transportation that make their operation

[30] India, Government Planning Commission, *The Third Five-Year Plan: Draft Outline,* Manager of Publications, New Delhi, 1960, p. 93.

[31] E. Blunt (ed.), *Social Service in India,* H. M. Stationery Office, 1939, p. 109, quoted in Wallbank, *A Short History of India and Pakistan, op. cit.,* p. 263.

possible. Yet in spite of its socialist philosophy, the government by 1961 had allowed private ownership of 90 per cent of industry.

During India's first and second five-year plans, covering the period 1951–1961, progress could be recorded in agricultural and industrial production, including the production of consumer goods. Per capita income increased 11.1 per cent during the first five-year plan and by approximately the same percentage during the second five-year plan. Aggregate real income was increasing at the yearly rate of nearly 4 per cent. India's productive efforts are receiving well-deserved plaudits throughout the world, with industrial production in particular causing surprise among the mature countries and envy in the under-developed ones.

Yet all is far from well with India's economic-development plan. Certain rural groups, particularly in the mountainous and desert sections of the country, have been little affected. India's industries are producing far below their capacities, owing in no small part, according to foreign observers, to inefficient management. Moreover, when the growth of national income is adjusted by the increase in population, the rate of real growth becomes nearly 1.5 per cent. Substantial as the progress under the first two five-year plans has been, it is still not dramatic enough to produce the level of development expressed in India's goals.

Social and political problems

At least five major social and political problems face India in its struggle for development. The first of these concerns the very existence of a unified India.

Independence has not merely meant substitution of Indian rule over the territories formerly ruled by the British, but has also meant the establishment of a federation which includes 561 of the 562 princely states. These states had not been subject to British control, but rather had been ruled in an authoritarian manner by hereditary princes. The amalgamation of all these states but one (Kashmir) was a masterpiece of statesmanship on the part of the new central government.

But the process of unification had other more formidable obstacles. The Moslem minority, long uneasy about the prospect of Hindu majority rule, took steps through its own political party, the Moslem League, to form a separate nation; "the Indian Moslems felt themselves to be Moslems before they were Indians."[32]

A second problem which thwarted rapid unity was the lack of a national language. English was well known to the educated elite who occupied high governmental, professional, and commercial positions, but it was practically unknown among the masses where the regional vernaculars remained strong. Acknowledging the need for a national language for political as well as economic and social reasons, the national government considered its alternatives. Since English was unacceptable for cultural as well as nationalistic reasons, the most popular vernacular, Hindi, became the logical choice, and 1965 was set by the government as a target date for making it the national language.

The language problem, however, is far from being solved, for Hindi was the language of only half of the Indian

[32] *Ibid.*, p. 169.

402

population. Nine other major languages are each spoken by at least 1 million Indians. Opposition to Hindi has been particularly strong in the southern part of the nation where fears were voiced that language would be used as a weapon to assist the northern region in perpetuating its traditional dominance in Indian affairs. The specific educational implications of the language problem are analyzed in a later section.

Social cleavages in the new nation resulting from traditions of caste posed a third problem which had economic and social dimensions. Caste hindered mobility of labor, for traditionally children were expected to take up the occupation of the parent. This situation had unfortunate implications for both the dying skills, for which there tended to be an oversupply of labor, and the expanding of new occupations, for which there tended to be labor shortages. Financial and other rewards assisted in removing the economic defects of the caste society but the inherent social evils remain.

Social mobility while on the increase was still limited in the highly divisive Indian society. The untouchables, the caste outside the caste system, were given official recognition; but since custom often transcended law, they still moved only on the fringe of civilized society in many regions. Although the national Constitution promises no discrimination on the basis of color, race, caste, or sex, the age-old prejudices are dying slowly. Repugnant and irrational though discrimination is to most Indian leaders, they feel its disappearance will necessarily be slow. It is their hope that the closer contact of people required in a modern industrial and urban society will be more effective than official proclamations.

A fourth condition affecting social and political development, one which does not lend itself to easy or brief description, has been the attitude of the Indian people toward the process of change. While some students of India have been favorably impressed with the ability of the Indian villagers to adopt new methods of crop cultivation, sanitation, and health care, other observers have emphasized the resistance to new ideas and methods. As in countries all over the world, the villages and rural areas in India are much less susceptible to change than are the urban centers. Recognizing that the villager often lives a precarious existence would lead one to hypothesize that a mixture of hope and apprehension may be rather widespread among the poverty-stricken masses. Villagers often suspect the government of ulterior motives when officials offer help; moreover, the traditional paternalistic role of the government militates against a cooperative approach by government and governed to the solution of problems. And living as they often do on the borderline of starvation, the Indian villagers well understand that any change in living or working habits literally becomes a gamble with life and death.

But attitudes implicit in Indian culture, not conducive to economic and social development, can be traced to other than rural influences. The extended family which has afforded security has discouraged initiative, enterprise, and risk taking on the part of the individual. A traditional hierarchical society, with power closely correlated with position, has made vertical cooperation difficult with all organizations. The multiplication of new occupational caste groups has hindered communication and promoted new separateness. The traditionally subordinate role of women has frustrated the optimum use of this part of the population in carrying out development plans. Moslem groups in particular have been slow to accept public education, especially coeducation, for their girls. And acting as a cloak sheltering the Indian youth from new ideas is the illiterate adult population.

A final problem, related to the foregoing, is concerned with defining the political character of the new nation and giving leadership to it. During the turbulent struggle for independence and in the uneasy years of nation building, India has been guided by persons of unusual intellectual and moral strength. Mahatma Gandhi and Jawaharlal Nehru provided charismatic but responsible leadership in their efforts to bring unity out of diversity and stimulate greater national effort. These men, so unlike in many respects, were in agreement that the New India should be both socialistic and democratic. Gandhi and Nehru, however, gave special qualifications to these terms, for each had found grave limitations in the practice of the political philosophies in other nations bearing such names. Gandhi distrusted concentration of wealth and power in the state as much as he did their concentration in the hands of a few individuals. Nehru did not share Gandhi's fear of industrialization or his great preoccupation with the spiritual aspects of development. While Nehru had shown a certain approval of the theoretical concepts of Marxism and admiration for the material progress in the Soviet Union, his actions and his words made it clear that his goal was a mixed economy, involving both government and private participation.

Nehru's "liberal democratic socialism" has been generally accepted as the guiding philosophy for India's social, economic, and political development. Its wide acceptance has lent stability to India and provided a fundamental requisite for development and growth. However, healthily perhaps, other political philosophies exist and have articulate proponents. As many as five other schools of political thought are significant in India today: Hindu nationalism, dictatorial national socialism, revolutionary international communism, evolutionary national communism, and Gandhian decentralism.[33] Should any of these groups gain political control of India, the direction of change is certain to be altered; but for the time being India, in spite of its lengthy period of rule by a single party, resembles a welfare democracy.

The administration of education

Although education in India since 1921 has been under state (provincial) control, independent India has developed important educational responsibility at both the national and the local levels. With the important exception of higher and advanced technical education which are under the central government, the Constitution of India now provides for a continuation of the decentralized pattern of educational control. The states are still the responsible units for educational administration. However, Indian commitment to national planning means that the central government must be more than a disinterested spectator. The image of the New India is being shaped at the national level, and the aims, di-

[33] de Bary, *op. cit.*, p. 878.

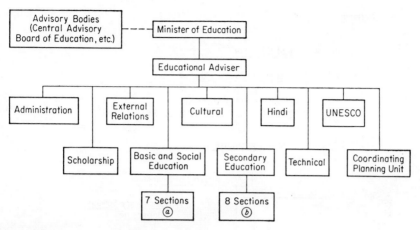

Figure 38. The Indian National Ministry of Education

A more detailed diagram of the Central Ministry can be found in *World Survey of Education II: Primary Education,* UNESCO and Evans Brothers, London, 1958, p. 539.

a. National book trust; folk literature; social and adult education; preprimary, primary, and basic education; central education library; audio-visual aids; national centers for research.

b. Secondary education and multipurpose schools; education of handicapped and juvenile delinquency; rural higher education; public schools and education in Part C [nationally controlled] states; Central Bureau of Vocational and Educational Guidance; Central Bureau of Textbook Research; sports, scouts, etc.; youth welfare, festivals, and camps, etc.

rection, and dimensions of the educational endeavor are regarded as foundational to success. Lacking specific constitutional rights, the central government has been assisted by three important factors in extending its educational influence: (1) the large-scale educational expansion or improvement requires the states to seek financial grants from the central government; (2) the states are dependent for statistical and other educational information on the central government which acts both as a repository and a clearinghouse; (3) lastly, the fact that the same political party has dominated both state and national politics since independence has reduced political conflict between the two levels which otherwise might have frustrated educational cooperation.[34]

[34] Hamayan Kabir, *Education in New India,* G. Allen, London, 1956, p. 5.

The official national body charged with planning, guiding, and coordinating educational reconstruction is the National Ministry of Education (see Figure 38). In addition to carrying out general policies of development the Ministry is charged with such specific functions as:

1. Providing exclusive educational direction in the centrally administered areas (the new Indian Union formed in 1956 includes fourteen states and six centrally administered territories)

2. Directly administering to the eighteen *public schools,* four central universities and a variety of research and training centers

3. Granting scholarships for scheduled castes,[35] backward tribes

4. Giving grants-in-aid to the states and,

[35] The Harijan or "untouchables."

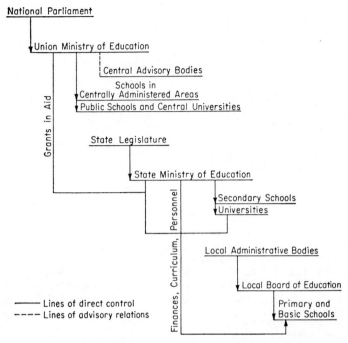

Figure 39. Lines of Educational Authority in India

under certain conditions, directly to institutions of higher education[36]

The National Ministry is directly responsible to the Indian Parliament, and the Minister of Education is appointed by the Prime Minister (see Figure 39). The chief administrative officer of the Ministry is the Educational Adviser who advises the Minister on all matters of administration and policy (see Figure 38).

To promote a degree of uniformity and coordination among the states, various central advisory bodies have been created, the most important of which is the Central Advisory Board of Education. The members of this body include a number of specialists, all of the state ministers of education, and the national Minister of Education who acts as the

chairman. By the very nature of its composition, recommendations of the Central Advisory Board carry considerable weight. In the fields of secondary and university education, the All-India Council for Secondary Education and the University Grant Commission provide similar advisory services. Uniformity of goals and standards gets additional impetus from India's commitment to central planning, and the National Planning Commission has included specific targets for educational progress in the first three five-year plans.

In addition to the Ministry of Education other central ministries, such as those of defense and railways, through various training programs are deeply involved in educational matters. Moreover, the relatively new Ministry of Scientific Research and Cultural Affairs whose functions until 1958 had been combined with those of the Ministry of

[36] UNESCO, *World Survey of Education II: Primary Education,* UNESCO and Evans Brothers, London, 1958, p. 537.

Education is responsible for cultural activities, scientific research and survey, and technical and scientific education.[37] The establishment of this separate body for scientific and technical matters demonstrates the government's expectations of the contributions by these fields to development.

State governments have full autonomy for the administration of their educational programs except those for which they receive grants-in-aid from the central government. The administrative hierarchy of the state is topped by an elected minister of education who is responsible to the state legislature of which he is a member. The director of public instruction, in some states called director of education, is the executive head of the department and is in charge of the inspecting and teaching staffs of government and recognized private schools. With respect to higher education, the state governments share their power with the universities; with respect to primary education, they share power with local government bodies (panchayats). The trend in India has been for the local bodies or councils to assume more and more control over local affairs, including primary education. Typically the councils operate through the school boards to formulate policies for the financing, managing, and expanding of primary schooling. In some states the local boards even maintain their own supervisory and administrative staff.[38]

Educational institutions

Article 45 of the Indian Constitution charged the states with responsibility for providing compulsory education up to fourteen years of age for all Indian children by the year 1960. Although this goal was far too ambitious, in the period between 1950 and 1962 the percentage of the six- to eleven-year age group in school grew from 42 to 66 and the percentage of the eleven- to fourteen-year age group climbed from 13.4 to 27.0.[39] However, India still ranked well below the world mean with respect to primary enrollment ratio. (Table 9 shows the enrollment by school levels in 1962.) Most states, temporarily disregarding higher aspirations, were attempting to provide four to six years of education. Moreover, it should be emphasized that educational conditions vary widely throughout India. One Indian state, Kerala, as early as 1956–1957 could boast that nearly all children of primary school age were attending school, while during the same year in the North East Frontier Agency, a centrally controlled territory, less than 7 per cent of the children were in school.[40]

Although there is a propensity to describe elementary education as that which is provided children in the six- to fourteen-year age span, this structure is not uniform throughout the country. Most typically the initial stage of primary education, covering ages six to eleven years, approximately, takes place in what is called a primary school or junior basic school. For a simplified view of the school pyramid, see Figure

[37] S. N. Mukerji, *Education in India: Today and Tomorrow*, 4th ed., Acharya Book Depot, Baroda, 1960, p. 22.
[38] *Ibid.*, p. 24.

[39] India, Government Planning Commission, *The Third Five-Year Plan: Draft Outline, op. cit.*, p. 99; India, Ministry of Education, *Provisional Educational Statistics: (As on 31st March 1962)*, New Delhi, 1962, pp. 1–2.
[40] India, Ministry of Education, *Education in India: A Graphic Presentation*, Ministry of Publications, New Delhi, 1959, p. 29.

Table 9   *Number of Students by Stage of Education in India*

Stage of education	Boys	Girls	Total
1. University stage:			
a. Ph.D./D.Sc./D.Phil./etc., arts and science only	4,233	681	4,924
b. M.A., arts and science only	27,059	7,701	34,760
c. M.Sc., arts and science only	10,392	1,670	12,062
d. M.Com., arts and science only	5,333	48	5,381
e. M.Ed., arts and science only	972	424	1,396
f. B.A., pass and hons	139,034	52,841	191,875
g. B.Sc., pass and hons	111,638	19,027	130,665
h. B.Com., pass and hons	51,181	697	51,878
i. Teacher training, B.T/B.Ed. and equivalent diplomas:			
(1) Basic	3,238	1,550	4,788
(2) Nonbasic	10,442	4,954	15,396
j. B.P.E., bachelor of physical education and equivalent diplomas	613	120	733
k. Teacher training, undergraduate level:			
(1) Basic	14,603	4,696	19,299
(2) Nonbasic	6,430	5,687	12,117
l. Institutes of arts	177,603	33,942	211,545
m. Institutes of science	23,818	3,071	26,889
n. Preuniversity:			
(1) Arts	105,504	36,023	141,527
(2) Science	82,671	8,965	91,636
(3) Commerce	23,034	561	23,595
2. School stage:			
a. Classes IX and above	2,469,165	581,773	3,050,938
b. Classes VI–VIII	5,680,711	1,878,681	7,559,392
c. Classes I–V	25,748,556	12,683,341	38,431,897
d. Preprimary	133,359	98,432	231,791
e. Teacher training, primary:			
(1) Basic	85,477	29,124	114,601
(2) Nonbasic	10,830	5,167	15,997
f. Teacher training, preprimary	178	1,661	1,839
g. Commerce	78,271	14,897	93,168
h. Physical education	2,885	438	3,323
i. In schools for the handicapped	6,723	1,885	8,608
j. In schools for social workers, Janta colleges	3,243	507	3,750
k. In schools/centers for adults	1,497,389	801,156	2,298,545

SOURCE: India, Ministry of Education, *Provisional Educational Statistics: (As on 31st March 1962)*, New Delhi, 1962, p. 2.

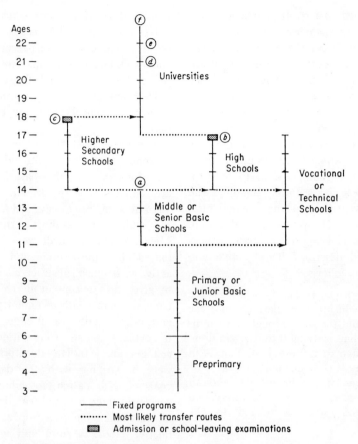

Figure caption: Ages scale with institutions

- Fixed programs
- ·········· Most likely transfer routes
- ▨ Admission or school-leaving examinations

Figure 40. Educational Institutions in India Today

a. Diploma.
b. High school certificate.
c. Higher school certificate.
d. Bachelor of arts degree.
e. Bachelor of teaching degree.
f. Advanced degrees.

40. Three-year higher primary schools or vernacular middle schools have been established in a few states. This second stage usually is divided into two sections, the first of which covers ages eleven to fourteen, approximately, and is termed the senior basic or middle secondary school. In some cases a senior division extends from age fourteen for an additional three years. However, some of these have been made into four-year higher secondary schools by adding what has hitherto been the first year of the university preparatory stage. The first degree course at the university requires a minimum of three or four years, depending on whether or not the student has attended a regular or higher secondary school.

Educational aspirations and opportunities

Primary and basic education

Social reformers, particularly Mahatma Gandhi and his followers, have long been concerned with the character of

409

primary education. In particular, the emphasis on memorization, the divorce of contents from the environment, the overwhelming costs, and the general impracticality of the curriculum of the primary school have come under criticism. As a cure for these ills, Gandhi, at a famous educational conference at Wardha in 1937, recommended a new concept of primary education, a concept he considered fundamental to his program of social reform. Gandhi, who believed that the teaching of handicrafts was essential to purposeful education, called his new approach "basic education" and described its objective and method as follows:

> The principal idea is to impart the whole education of the body and the mind and the soul through the handicraft that is taught to the children. You have to draw out all that is in the child through teaching all the processes of the handicraft, and all your lessons in history, geography, and arithmetic will be related to the craft.[41]

In the basic schools the study of crafts, theoretically at least, consumes 20 to 25 per cent of the week's schedule. Typical subjects and the hours of instruction per week in each are as follows: mother tongue (regional vernacular), 8; mathematics, 5; social studies, 5; general science, 4; Hindi, 3; physical education, 5; arts and crafts, 12 (9 or 10 hours per craft); and extracurricular, 2. Crafts include: spinning and weaving; gardening leading to agriculture; book crafts, including paper and cardboard work, leading to wood and metal work; leatherwork; clay work and pottery; fisheries; housecraft.[42] Since the

reorientation of primary education involves this complex of changes, it might be expected to be a long-term process. Indian statistics bear this out, and by the end of the second five-year plan (1961) only about 24 per cent of the elementary schools were of the basic pattern.[43]

The terms used by Indian educators in condemning the traditional primary school and in justifying basic education are reminiscent of the arguments of the advocates of progressive education in the United States during the 1930s. Memorization and drill were to be replaced by purposeful and creative activity. Bookish, abstract content was to give way to content derived partly from the immediate community. Cooperation in socially useful endeavors was to replace harsh competition. Such changes, many Indian educators argued, were in keeping with the democratic goals of their nation, for education so conceived could help to break down class barriers and promote a respect for productive labor. A rural and vocational bias favoring primary education would slow the exodus to the already-overcrowded urban areas. Moreover, other advocates added, primary education built on functional experiences and the interest of the child was in keeping with the best learning theory.

In addition to the educational considerations, there was also an important economic reason for the expansion of basic education. Progress toward the goal of universal primary education placed a tremendous burden on the limited financial means of India, and any expensive system would be auto-

[41] Quoted in Kabir, *op. cit.*, p. 23.
[42] UNESCO, *op. cit.*, p. 538.

[43] India, Government Planning Commission, *The Third Five-Year Plan: Draft Outline, op. cit.*, p. 100.

matically ruled out. Under a system of basic education the items produced by the children had an economic value which could help meet schooling costs. Food, clothing, and the products of handwork could be utilized by the teachers and children within the school; and when the children became further skilled, the surpluses could be sold on the market.

As conceived by Gandhi and his followers the long-range goal of basic education was no less than a spiritual reconstruction of society. Gandhi, while concerned with the material poverty about him, was most disturbed by what he considered a prevailing spiritual poverty. Western culture and education inasmuch as they had divorced Indians from their own cultural heritage were, he felt, a major contributor to this latter problem. Indians had become strangers in their own land, a view often expressed by Nehru also, and political and social disunity were the result. Gandhi further deplored the lack of respect for manual labor in the imported English pattern of education.

Evaluations of the success of basic education in contributing to the new society envisioned by Gandhi have been mixed. While the basic education concept at the primary level has found general support, there appears to be more than a little lingering confusion about its precise purpose and content. Some Indians emphasize the contributions of basic education to rural reconstruction. Others claim the concept is equally valid in urban development. Primary schools which offer little or no handicraft classify their programs as basic education. Certainly a sizable group of social scientists and educators view basic education as hardly more

than a romantic experiment with little relationship to social development, economic growth, or even sound education. Then, the increased centralization of Indian economy has not been conducive to a craft-centered education;[44] nor, in fact, has the suspicion of material wealth, fostered by some of the advocates of basic education, supported the developmental goals of entrepreneurship and industrialization. It is probably fair to conclude that the contributions thus far of basic education toward producing the Gandhian ideal, a classless, nonviolent society, have been modest.

Although top priority is being given to creating basic schools through a reorientation of the primary curriculum, by 1960 three-fourths of the Indian primary schools were still of the nonbasic variety. These schools in general were faced with even greater shortages in financial and human resources than the basic schools. Merely keeping the children in school long enough to acquire a functional literacy was a major task. Obstacles to extension of the length of schooling included costs to pupils (noonday meal and clothing); ill health; and, most of all, parents unsympathetic to the values of education. A dearth of women teachers was particularly detrimental to any prolongation of the education of girls.

Indian leaders hope that increased financial support from national, state, and local levels will help make compulsory education a reality. Historically much of the expense for education has been borne by the community, and new laws enabling local authorities to levy a special tax for education should increase community responsibility and, hopefully, community initiative. Other

[44] Mukerji, *Education in India: Today and Tomorrow, op. cit.*, p. 59.

steps taken by some communities under the five-year plans to extend opportunities in elementary education include initiation of a double-shift system to make maximum use of school facilities; extension of out-of-doors classes; experimentation with cheap building materials; and the establishment of short-term, streamlined teacher preparation programs. Finally, a continuing scheme of social education—programs in literacy, use of libraries, citizenship, group community development, etc.—is expected to assist adults in making more positive contributions to the education of their children.

The expansion and transformation of Indian primary schooling has brought new demands on the teacher training institutions. Teachers for the primary schools normally are prepared in middle schools and may or may not receive professional training. There is a strong movement to make high school graduation a requirement for primary teaching; yet by 1957, one-third of the primary school teachers were still without any professional preparation.

Since there are two types of primary school in India, basic and nonbasic, there are two kinds of institutions for the preparation of primary school teachers. By 1956 there were 520 schools specifically designed to prepare teachers for basic schools and 403 for nonbasic schools.[45] These schools, over one-third of which were private, might admit either primary school graduates or secondary school graduates. The former group of students could expect to receive a junior teacher's certificate, while the matriculates could qualify for a senior teacher's certificate.[46] The main

difference in the curricula of the two kinds of training institutions is that those candidates preparing to teach in basic schools receive lengthy instruction in craft skills and intensive community observation and participation.

Secondary education

Under the British, secondary education in India served to introduce European culture and, less frequently, to teach certain vocational skills to a few selected Indian youths; in addition, it prepared young men for clerical positions in British administrative offices. English was the language of instruction, and the curriculum was dominated by university requirements. Although the Hunter Commission of 1882 and several later commissions recommended a dual-track system of secondary education, "one [track] leading to the Entrance Examination of the Universities, the other of a more practical character,"[47] no action in this latter direction was taken. Products of the secondary schools, together with the microscopic number of university graduates, formed an Indian elite whose cultural ties with the great proportion of the population were often very limited.

Independent India has attempted to Indianize and extend secondary schooling. Again, however, as with the primary schools, the exact role and structure of secondary education are still to emerge. Some Indians have been advocating a three- or four-year multipurpose secondary school, following eight years of primary (basic) education. This pattern appears to be gaining favor, but by 1961 few attempts had been made at

[45] *Ibid.*, p. 300.
[46] *Ibid.*, p. 301.

[47] Quoted in Mukerji, *Education in India: Today and Tomorrow, op. cit.*, p. 116.

actual implementation, and some differentiation of instruction before the age of fourteen is likely to persist for some time. Further, multiple institutions at the secondary level probably will continue, with certain curricular and administrative safeguards to ensure that no capable student in any stream is kept out of higher education.

A comparison of the analyses of the weaknesses of Indian secondary education shows considerable agreement. An examination of the publications of an Indian educator, a visiting American specialist, and the Indian Secondary Education Commission, revealed the following common recommendations:

1. The curriculum should be vitalized by supplementing verbal learning with practical and "lifelike" activities through utilization of community resources and by bringing about a closer relation to community life.

2. More attention should be given to identifying and providing for individual differences through increased personal and vocational guidance.

3. Opportunities should be provided for the students to develop skills in group discussion and practice in planning, researching, and arriving at independent judgments.[48]

The trends in Indian secondary education in the period since independence have been in the direction of meeting many of the needs recognized by these

educators. As summarized by one Indian educator these trends are:

1. A strong movement for the diversification of the courses and introduction of vocational bias

2. Enrichment of the curricula by introducing new subjects, such as civics, crafts, and agriculture

3. Emergence of new types of postprimary schools, viz., the postbasic school and the higher secondary school

4. Greater emphasis on the regional and the national languages

5. Increasing recognition of the importance of physical education[49]

As suggested by this list the commitment to basic education at the primary level has had implications for the direction of secondary education. Indian leaders are reconciled to the fact that for many years secondary education, because of financial restrictions, must remain the prerogative of a few. Nevertheless, a secondary school whose curriculum is restricted to those subjects traditionally regarded as the best preparation for the university does not set well on an institution that stresses activities and socially useful labor. The role of crafts, the relationship between knowledge and work, and the importance of cooperative activity in Indian secondary schools are issues raised by the philosophy of basic education and are yet to be resolved.

The multiplicity of Indian languages (the Constitution has recognized fourteen) is a major problem for secondary education. The trend for several decades has been toward the use of the regional vernaculars as the languages of instruc-

[48] Chaube, S. P., *Secondary Education for India,* Atma Ram & Sons, New Delhi, 1956, p. 112; Henry Harap, *Improvement of Curriculum in Indian Schools,* Government of India Press, New Delhi, 1959; India, Ministry of Education, *Report of the Secondary Education Commission,* October, 1952–June, 1953, Hindi Union Press, New Delhi, 1953.

[49] Mukerji, *Education in India: Today and Tomorrow, op. cit.,* p. 125.

tion in the secondary schools. In no region has the customary language of instruction been English, the language used in the universities.

The Indian solution to the language problem appears gradually to be taking shape, although dissenting opinions are still heard. The use of the mother tongue at the elementary and secondary levels now appears to be well accepted. Opinion continues to be split on the language of instruction at the university level, with the adoption of a regional language gaining support. These trends would place a heavy, but not impossible, language burden upon the secondary school students, since, at least for students for whom Hindi is not the mother tongue, two additional languages, Hindi and English, would need to be mastered. The former, because it is destined to be the national language, must be mastered by at least those students who extend their education beyond the elementary school, and the latter dare not be neglected because of its peculiar historical significance in India and its importance as a vehicle for modern scientific thought.

An even more fundamental problem facing Indian secondary education is related to its nonfunctional qualities in a developing democratic society. One Indian educator sees two conflicting philosophies operating in Indian secondary schools:

> One is represented by the traditional school which stands for authoritarianism, strict external discipline, a predetermined curriculum, and an attempt to discipline the mind for a remote future without paying due attention to the needs of the present. . . .
> The other is the democratic philosophy represented by the modernists

who advocate cooperative planning and recognition of the present needs and problems of the learner. The modernists also assert that the teacher is not a dictator; he is merely a sympathetic guide. . . .[50]

Attempts to broaden the scope of secondary education have led to the introduction of multipurpose high schools which provide instruction for several alternative courses. The proponents of these schools argue that such institutions would reduce class distinctions, allow greater adaptation of the school to community needs, and perform an important guidance function by helping the student find a course to fit his aptitude. With the absence of an educational heritage friendly to the educational philosophy underlying multipurpose schools and the lack of teachers trained in the applied subjects, recognition of the potential value of these schools has been slow in coming. However, future years are likely to see increasing experimentation in this direction.

Although the first two five-year plans proposed to emphasize expansion of primary education, the period covered by the two plans saw greatest expansion in secondary and higher education. Since many Indian educators have long considered the secondary schools the weakest educational link, this level received heavy emphasis throughout these two plans. Efforts were made to improve science instruction, extend facilities in vocational education, and as mentioned above, experiment with multipurpose schools. Before the first plan, only 5 per cent of the youth between the ages of fourteen and seventeen were in sec-

[50] Chaube, *op. cit.*, p. 112.

414

ondary schools. By 1961 this percentage had been raised to 12, and the 1965 target was set at 15 per cent. In the first two plans considerable attention was also given to developing higher secondary schools, increasing teachers' salaries, and improving their working conditions.

The expansion and redesign of Indian secondary education have made heavy demands on the teacher training institutions. Teachers in the high schools typically are prepared through one of two routes. They may attend a secondary teacher training institution whose course of study is two years for the holder of a high school or higher secondary school certificate. A second route for the prospective secondary teacher is to take a one-year course in a graduate teacher training institute after graduation from a university. Such a course leads to the degree of bachelor of teaching, bachelor of education, or licentiate in teaching. In spite of sizable expansion of both basic types of teacher training institutions, by 1962 nearly one-third of Indian secondary teachers still lacked minimum professional training.

A third and subtle problem encountered by Indian secondary schools as they attempt to orient themselves toward the demands of democracy, nationalism, and economic development is concerned with the selection of students. Admittedly in the past the most important single requisite for secondary schooling was wealth, not talent. The cost of attending secondary schools was prohibitive to lower-class families. Moreover, the cultural deprivation of the poorer Indian homes, as in other parts of the world, hindered the success of the poor children in the academic requirements. While the problem is well recog-

nized, steps for its cure have only begun. New selection procedures have been developed that will ensure more objectivity in selecting students; and as a necessarily parallel step, scholarships are being provided for some able but poor students.

Higher education

The first modern universities in India were established in 1857 at Calcutta, Bombay, and Madras and were modeled after the University of London. The function of the universities, then, like that of the University of London, was to establish courses of study for the affiliated colleges, examine the candidates prepared by the colleges, and grant degrees to the successful candidates. This pattern has been modified in recent years, and most modern Indian universities are either classified as "teaching and affiliating" or "teaching and residential."

The course for most of India's forty-five universities traditionally has been four years beyond high school graduation. At the end of two years there is an intermediate examination. The successful candidate then proceeds for two more years and, if successful in his degree examination, is awarded the bachelor's degree. For some time there has been criticism of the two separate and essentially unrelated stages of university education, and there has been a long-standing argument for an integrated three-year university course leading to the bachelor's degree. By 1962 well over half of the universities had agreed to introduce a three-year course, and it is likely that the remainder will follow suit.

Beyond the bachelor's degree a master's degree is awarded after one or two years of additional study and completion of an examination. In some universities honor graduates—under one arrangement the honors' degree is awarded for three years' study after the intermediate examination—automatically receive their master's degree after the lapse of a prescribed period of time. A Ph.D. degree requires a thesis but no course work beyond the master's degree.

The changes recommended in a postwar report of the Central Advisory Board of Education, together with the report cited below, set the course for university education in independent India. Among the recommendations were: (1) the conditions for admission should be revised with the object of ensuring that students admitted to a university course would benefit by it; (2) the intermediate course should be abolished, one year being added to the high school and the other to the university, thereby making three years the length of the university degree course; (3) the tutorial system should be widely extended; (4) high standards and postgraduate courses and research should be maintained; and (5) an Indian university-grant committee should be constituted to exercise general supervision over the allocation of grants to universities from public funds.[51]

A more definitive report on university education was presented in 1949 by the University Education Commission. This respected and influential report called upon the universities to prepare educated men and women for the leadership positions required by a modernizing

nation. Higher education should be at once scientific, technical, and liberal. As stated in the report:

> Democracy depends for its very life on a high standard of general, vocational, and professional education. Dissemination of learning, incessant search for new knowledge, unceasing effort to plumb the meaning of life, provision for professional education to satisfy the occupational needs of our society are the vital tasks of higher education.[52]

Committing itself to scientific progress, the report nevertheless warned against overspecialization and the dangers of

> . . . scientists without conscience, technicians without taste who find a void within themselves, a moral vacuum and desperate need to substitute something, anything, for their lost endeavor and purpose.[53]

Indian universities, in their attempt to teach the myriad of cultural and vocational goals charged to them, have been beset with a host of problems, many of which are common to most underdeveloped countries but some of which are peculiar to India. Those university problems shared with other poor nations include the need for adjusting enrollments to fit manpower demands;[54] the modernization of an outmoded cur-

---

[51] India, Estimates Committee, *Seventeenth Report, 1957–1958,* Ministry of Education and Scientific Research, Lok Sabha Secretariat, New Delhi, 1958, p. 3.

[52] *Ibid.,* p. 67.

[53] *Ibid.*

[54] Enrollments in medical, engineering, and certain technical courses have been somewhat adjusted in terms of manpower needs through the cooperation of the government and the professional organizations. However, enrollments for the arts degree continue to soar while the market for B.A. degree holders shows little expansion.

riculum, especially in the natural and social sciences; further development of native languages which have potential as effective vehicles for higher learning; provisions for increased opportunities for women's education; finding and keeping competent staffs; preventing urbanization of the country student; improvement of plant and equipment; and objectifying means by which students are selected. In India, as in most former colonial nations, higher education is often viewed as a route to secure and profitable government employment. Adjustments in the labor market are being considered to ease the pecuniary attraction of Indian higher education, for it is hoped that elimination of degree requirements for recruitment into public services will slow the rush of students to the arts colleges. Among the more or less peculiar problems facing Indian universities are those related to the process of synthesizing India's cultural traditions with the newer knowledge from the West.

Indian leaders realize that the task of deliberately planning a nation's future without utilizing Draconian measures is fraught with obstacles. They further realize that the first requisite to the infusion of knowledge is a group of leaders who have a vision of India's future as an extension of the past. Indian universities thus far have not been able to integrate past modes of thought with modern European thought to form a new social philosophy that promotes development without forsaking cultural identity. In this regard Kabir points out:

> Even today European, Indian and Islamic philosophies are treated as isolated and self-contained subjects. What is worse, Indian philosophy is

often treated as an alternative to Arab thought. A national system of education would require systematic and connected study of the three systems —Indian, Saracenic and European— which have influenced modern Indian consciousness.[55]

The most concrete step taken to remedy this ill has been the introduction of experimental programs of general education at the university level.

Innovations and problems

Many Indian educators would undoubtedly agree with Prof. S. N. Mukerji that "an educational apparatus which even after a hundred years has left 80 per cent of the people unable to read and write stands self-condemned."[56] Yet since independence Indian educators have learned the hard fact that limitations of funds and trained personnel are at times as big an obstacle to progress as lack of vision.

In considering the priorities of development, Indian leaders, have given much attention, too much in the view of some economists, to grass-roots change. A nationwide program of community development was instituted within the provisions of the first and second five-year plans and received support not only from the Indian government but also from many foreign sources. To remold village life rural India is being divided into blocks of approximately one hundred villages and further subdivided for the sake of operational efficiency. Teams of specialists in such areas as agriculture, public health, cooperatives, small industries, village government, and so-

[55] Kabir, *op. cit.*, p. 114.
[56] Mukerji, *Education in India: Today and Tomorrow, op. cit.*, p. 397.

417

cial education, professionally supported by a national research center, are assigned to coordinate schemes of reconstruction. By 1961 impressive statistics had been compiled on the accomplishments. For example, under the technical assistance of the specialists and with the self-help of villages, millions of farming demonstrations were held, over 100,000 miles of roads constructed, and 3.7 million men and women taught to read through new adult literacy centers.[57] The precise contributions of these activities for national development are yet to be measured.

Unfortunately, extension of educational opportunities in the villages and the establishment of governmental controls over the schools has brought about a reduction in the prestige of the teacher. In the past there were mostly single-teacher schools in the villages, and the schoolmaster was an important and respected figure. The contemporary system, which has eliminated student fees and holds the teacher responsible to the headmaster, inspectors, and local authorities, has made the teacher's economic position more precarious and reduced his independence. With his needs no longer met in a well-defined traditional procedure and with the ineffectiveness of teachers' associations in collective bargaining, the teacher can hardly be considered a leader in community development.

For a larger role in economic-development plans, education must be more attuned to manpower requirements.[58]

Secondary education, finding it difficult to free itself from a literary curriculum and white-collar vocational goals, has still been unable fully to adjust its program to the wide variety of needs of the terminal student; thus, large numbers of secondary school graduates are unemployed. The limited experiments in differentiating the curriculum at the upper secondary level hold promise, but first must win professional and public confidence. Also of possible far-reaching significance are experiments in newer methods of instruction, other techniques in student evaluation for the traditional year-end examination, establishment of guidance services, formation of academic clubs, and extension of the activities of the parent-teacher association. These attempts to increase the efficiency and broaden the concept of schooling may serve to modify the mechanical teaching procedures and reduce the preoccupation of Indian secondary schools with the meeting of diploma requirements. Empirical research is badly needed to judge the result of these and other innovations.

In higher education the number of graduates in arts, teaching, and commerce has been rising steeply, but the increase in medicine, science, and engineering has been disturbingly low, and in recent years no gain at all has been registered in forestry and agriculture. Moreover, universities remain predominantly urban; in 1957 only 4.4 per cent of the enrollment in universities came from rural areas, and university graduates show a strong preference for city

---

[57] Ford Foundation, *Roots of Change,* Office of Reports, Ford Foundation in India, New York, 1961.

[58] A welcome trend which is certain to pay economic and social dividends is the increasing educational opportunities for

girls—opportunities which the girls have shown themselves capable of taking advantage of by consistently having a higher percentage of "passes" on the university matriculation exam than the boys.

life. Two types of experiments initiated under the first two five-year plans hold some promise for establishing closer ties between higher education and rural life. One experiment involves the development of people's colleges inspired by the famous Danish folk schools. A second experiment involves the creation of a number of rural higher institutes whose purpose will be to carry out rural extension programs and conduct research pertinent to rural problems. The people's colleges and rural higher institutes exist only in small number and their potential cannot be anticipated at this time.

Under the first two five-year plans investment in education lagged behind that in irrigation, power, agriculture, industry, and railways. Moreover the proportion spent on education was less for the second plan than for the first. Of further significance is the shift in emphasis in expenditures under the two plans, as shown in Table 10. The increased attention to secondary, vocational, and higher education under the second plan drew criticism from some Indian educators who pointed to the large number of unemployed graduates of secondary and higher educational institutions and argued that the most important immediate task was to promote mass education. The planners argued that, considering India's economic needs, the highest educational priority should be given to the development of technical and administrative skills which are attainable only through postprimary instruction.

The requirements for involving Indian educational institutions more deeply in social change are at least as subtle as gearing them more efficiently for economic growth. Indian leaders have shown admirable reticence in resisting

Table 10 *Proposed Expenditures for Education in India (Rs. in crores[*])*

	First plan	Second plan
Elementary education	93	89
Secondary education	22	51
University education	15	57
Technical and vocational education	23	48
Social education	5	5
Administration and miscellaneous	11	57
Total	169	307

* At the official exchange rate 1 rupee = U.S. $0.21. A crore = 10 million rupees.

SOURCE: India, Government Planning Commission, *The Second Five-Year Plan*, Ministry of Publications, New Delhi, 1956, p. 500.

what they have considered the dangers of dehumanization in the development process. Yet, protection of the human element need not mean reluctance to allow Indian institutions to give dynamic leadership to social change. One author has pointed out that the Indic-Hindu societal pattern has been "emotional, mystic, aesthetic, collectivistic, aristocratic, easygoing and conservative."[59] These characteristics obviously conflict with the scientific, materialistic, aggressive pattern which is usually associated with rapid economic and social growth.

If, for example, India is to be a secular, democratic, industrial nation then the schools, as Indian educators have pointed out, need to assist the people in acquiring a new social philosophy. The implications of representative government, urbanism, and technological

[59] O. K. Ghush, *Problems of Economic Planning in India*, Kitabistan Allahabad, 1957, p. 21.

change must be made understandable at the popular level. To Gandhi this task meant preservation of the Indian spiritual strength through the perpetuation of the traditional crafts. Other Indians have argued that the Gandhian idealized society is not the image of future India and that his approach essentially negates development. Success in more clearly identifying the social pattern and value system consonant with the goals of New India and then communicating these through an advanced educational technology is fundamental to more dynamic educational planning.

References

Books

Chaube, S. P.: *Secondary Education for India*, Atma Ram & Sons, New Delhi, 1956.

Datta, Dhirendra Mohan: *The Philosophy of Mahatma Gandhi*, The University of Wisconsin Press, Madison, Wis., 1953.

Dean, Vera Micheles: *New Patterns of Democracy in India*, Harvard, Cambridge, Mass., 1959.

de Bary, Wm. Theodore (ed.): *Sources of Indian Tradition*, Columbia, New York, 1958.

Despai, A. R.: *Recent Trends in Indian Nationalism*, Popular Book Depot, Bombay, 1960.

Dube, S. C.: *Indian Village*, Routledge, London, 1955.

———: *India's Changing Village*, Routledge, London, 1958.

Gandhi, Mahatma: *All Men are Brothers*, UNESCO and Columbia, New York, 1958.

Ghush, O. K.: *Problems of Economic Planning in India*, Kitabistan Allahabad, 1957.

Ginsburg, Norton: *Atlas of Economic Development*, The University of Chicago Press, Chicago, 1961.

Harap, Henry: *Improvement of Curriculum in Indian Schools*, Government of India Press, New Delhi, 1959.

Hartog, Sir Philip: *Some Aspects of Indian Education Past and Present*, Oxford, Fair Lawn, N.J., 1939.

Hutton, J. H.: *Caste in India: Its Nature, Function, and Origins*, Cambridge, New York, 1946.

India: *Review of the Third Five-Year Plan*, Ministry of Publications, New Delhi, n.d.

———, Estimates Committee: *Seventeenth Report, 1957–1958*, Ministry of Education and Scientific Research, Lok Sabha Secretariat, New Delhi, 1958.

———, Government Planning Commission: *The Second Five-Year Plan*, Ministry of Publications, New Delhi, 1956.

———, Government Planning Commission: *The Third Five-Year Plan: Draft Outline*, Ministry of Publications, New Delhi, 1960.

———, Ministry of Education: *Education in India: A Graphic Presentation*, New Delhi, 1959.

———, Ministry of Education: *Provisional Educational Statistics: (As on 31st March 1962)*, New Delhi, 1962.

———, Ministry of Education: *Report of the Secondary Education Commission*, October, 1952–June, 1953, Hindu Union Press, New Delhi, 1953.

Kabir, Hamayan: *Education in New India*, G. Allen, London, 1956.

McCully, Bruce T.: *English Education and the Origins of Indian Nationalism*, Columbia, New York, 1940.

Mayhew, A.: *The Education of India*, Faber and Gwyer, London, 1928.

Mudaliar, A. L.: *Education in India*, Asia Publishing House, Bombay, 1960.

Mukerji, Shridhar Nath: *Education in India: Today and Tomorrow*, 4th ed., Acharya Book Depot, Baroda, 1960.

————: *History of Education in India,* Acharya Book Depot, Baroda, 1951.

Myers, Edward F.: *Education in the Perspective of History,* Harper & Row, New York, 1960.

Nehru, Jawaharlal: *The Discovery of India,* John Day, New York, 1946.

Nurallah, Syed, and J. P. Naik: *A History of Education in India,* Macmillan, New York, 1951.

Panikar, K. M.: *A Survey of Indian History,* Meridian Books, Ltd., London, 1948.

Philips, C. H.: *India,* Hutchison's University Library, London, 1948.

Rawlinson, H. G.: *India: A Short Cultural History,* Frederick A. Praeger, Inc., New York, 1937.

Riencourt, Amaury de: *The Soul of India,* Harper & Row, New York, 1960.

Saiyidain, K. G.: *Education, Culture and the Social Order,* Asia Publishing House, Bombay and Calcutta, 1952.

UNESCO: *World Survey of Education II: Primary Education,* UNESCO and Evans Brothers, London, 1958.

————: *World Survey of Education III: Secondary Education,* UNESCO and Evans Brothers, London, 1961.

Wallbank, T. Walter: *India in the New Era,* Scott, Foresman, Chicago, 1951.

————: *A Short History of India and Pakistan,* New American Library, New York, 1958.

Pamphlets and periodicals

Basu, Sobharani: "Forest Universities in Ancient India," *The Year Book of Education,* World, Tarrytown-on-Hudson, N.Y., 1957.

Deshpande, A. R.: "Education for Social Change," *Journal of Education,* vol. 89, pp. 378–381, London, September, 1957.

Fowlkes, J. G.: "Where India Is Going," *Phi Delta Kappan,* vol. 38, no. 2, p. 64, November, 1956.

Hingorani, D. K.: "Education in India before and after Independence," *Educational Forum,* vol. 19, pp. 217–225, January, 1955.

————: "Higher Education in India: Recent Developments," *Higher Education,* vol. 11, pp. 77–86, February, 1955.

Journal of Educational Sociology, vol. 28, January, 1955.

Kabir, Hamayan: "Basic Education: Indian Experiment," *Journal of General Education,* vol. 8, pp. 93–99, January, 1955.

————: "Indian Education since Independence," *Phi Delta Kappan,* vol. 39, no. 3, pp. 107–117, December, 1957.

Maw, E. W.: "Impressions of Education in India," *Educational Outlook,* vol. 30, pp. 55–62, January, 1956.

Rice, T. C., and B. Roy: "Some Aspects for Youth in India," *Journal of Educational Sociology,* vol. 28, pp. 194–236, January, 1955.

Ward, F. F.: "Some Polarities in Indian Educational Thought," *Phi Delta Kappan,* vol. 39, pp. 108–111, December, 1957.

CHAPTER 15

Education in Middle Africa:
Search for National Identity

Of the estimated 240 million people in Africa, 180 million live in the thirty-two countries of middle Africa. Over 99 per cent of the total population is African, that is, "persons whose forebears were domiciled in the region before the coming of the Europeans, Arabs, and Asians."[1]

Topographical varieties are great. The thick, damp jungles, extended desert land, and open dry velds, which have served as popular stereotypes, can certainly be found. However, there are also hilly and mountainous regions which in East Africa achieve heights greater than the Rocky Mountains of America. Forests, including highly valuable hardwood trees such as mahogany, are abundant, as is the bush country (mixed grassland and forest) where most of the livestock and field crops are located.

The natural environment strongly influenced patterns of colonial settlement, and hence colonial policy. From the point of view of outside influences at least four African regions are identifiable: (1) the Mediterranean belt which has felt strong influences from Europe and the Arab world; (2) the western "bulge," extending through the Congo, which has received relatively few permanent white settlers; (3) the highlands of eastern and central Africa where Europeans and Asians settled in larger number; and (4) the Republic of South

Africa where the white man is deeply entrenched.[2]

Parts of the Mediterranean coastal region and the Republic of South Africa, by virtue of their contact with European cultures and subsequent development of industry and commerce, do not fit into the underdeveloped category. This chapter, therefore, is essentially concerned with the second and third of these areas, that huge, geographically amorphous region stretching from the great Sahara Desert in the north to the Republic of South Africa in the south—an area increasingly being referred to as "middle Africa." More particularly, the discussion is limited to the independent nations and those areas which are now or were in the past under the control of France, Belgium, or Great Britain. The cultural diversities and contrasts within this region are great; yet there are also underlying similarities among many of the institutions, problems, and goals of the African peoples living there.

Middle Africa by any common index of development would rate as one of the poorest areas of the world. Yet because of rising levels of aspiration, enlightened colonial policies, and various forms of international assistance, the area is also among the world's most rapidly changing regions. Between the end of World War II and 1964 twenty-six nations had

[1] George H. T. Kimble, *Tropical Africa: Problems and Promises,* Headline Series no. 147, Foreign Policy Association, New York, 1961, p. 14.

[2] Vera Micheles Dean, *The Nature of the Non-Western World,* Mentor Books, New American Library, New York, 1957, p. 55.

received their independence. The spirit of nationalism, or perhaps Africanization, was the rallying cause and considered prerequisite to all other desired change; but if freedom and nationhood were the ideas that fostered cohesion, education was the magic to be practiced in making the dreams of personal and national material advancement come true. Education was seen by most African leaders as the basic tool needed to tap natural resources, improve agriculture, and initiate programs of industrialization. To many Africans education was considered the key to better jobs, better homes, indeed, to the comfortable world of the European.

It is the purpose of this chapter to survey the educational and cultural background of the peoples of middle Africa, to describe the forces and problems of cultural continuity and change, and to identify contemporary educational innovations and experiments.

Historical development

Lack of a written history has greatly hindered the piecing together of Africa's long past; but anthropologists, through extensive field studies, have found evidence of remarkable cultures flourishing 800 to 1,000 years ago. Ghana, an empire which stretched from Timbuktu to Senegal, lasted for several hundred years before falling to Moslem invaders in the eleventh century. Later, during the fourteenth, fifteenth, and sixteenth centuries the Mali and Songhai empires dominated much of West Africa while the Bornu state extended over the area encompassed by modern Ghana and northern Nigeria. There is some evidence that present-day Rhodesia was also the site of an ancient empire which was well developed in political organization and advanced in cultural attainments.

However, there is no contemporary African culture which has not felt the impact of centuries of contact with European and Near Eastern peoples. Overland caravans and sea traders brought new foods, weapons, and clothing, and thus altered the living habits of the Africans. Moslem and Christian proselytizers modified the traditional beliefs of many Africans and caused a few to view the religion of their forefathers as nothing but superstition. Finally, the example of European institutions and successive waves of European colonists had such an effect on the legal and political philosophy of African leaders that each new African nation has inaugurated some form of constitutional government reminiscent of the European parliamentary pattern.

Powerful elements for continuity as well as for change struggle continuously in tropical Africa. In spite of the inroads of Near Eastern religions, native religions retain their vitality and strength. Western education and Western cultural institutions are recasting the world view of many young Africans; yet the converts may still be outnumbered by their illiterate fellows who prefer to follow the path of their ancestors. An understanding of the direction of educational and social change in Africa and an interpretation of the nature of such change demand an analysis of indigenous institutions and colonial policies and practices.

Indigenous culture

Many of the tribal societies and states of tropical Africa to this day have not developed a written language, and even

Swahili, a relatively advanced language, has not been used for the faithful recording of a people's history. The most that can be done, then, in trying to understand African peoples is to seek out those important characteristics of life and culture which predated European immigration, admitting that a full understanding of their origin may be impossible.

Historically, the basic social and economic unit of African society has been the family. In Africa, as in Asia, the concept of family often includes not only the immediate family but also a wide range of more distant relatives. The *elementary* family of most African societies consists of the father, the mother, and the children, regardless of the lineage or the clan organization. However, in many parts of Africa the *extended* family—a grouping of two or more families of several generations who are united by consanguinal kinship ties and a common place of residence—is the more important domestic unit. The extended family is the grouping within which most of the relationships of daily living take place. It is a closely knit organization under the leadership of a single recognized head, usually the senior member in the dominant line of descent. This group shares the same living compound, the same economy, and the same system of values. Loyalty to the family tends to supersede loyalty to any other institution; indeed, the family is a working social unit, complete in itself. An entire village may be a single kinship group or, if the village is large, it may be made up of several extended families which have banded together for fulfillment of mutual interests.

Both the patrilineal and the matrilineal family patterns can be found in tropical Africa, although the patrilineal structure is more common. Under the patrilineal arrangement the relationships between individuals are identified through the male line. Associated with the patrilineal family is the patrilocal system in which the woman upon marriage is required to join the household of her husband or that of his parents. Thus, with several generations under one roof, the traditional criteria for power—age and maleness—are easily perpetuated.

In addition to the influence of family on the values, conduct, and responsibilities of the individual, kinship and family pattern play a very important role in the political systems of Africa. Lineages and clans often contribute to the creation of different types of political structures. Through marriages and alliances with other powerful families, an extended family may control many villages or even a whole nation.

Although several types of government have been classified by scholars specializing in African studies, the most prevalent indigenous political control system in tropical Africa has been termed "primitive democracy."[3] Leadership and decision making under this governmental arrangement have been described as follows:

> Leadership and a measure of prestige, but not authority, are vested typically in a head man and a council of elders or family heads with perhaps a few other semi-specialized functionaries to direct hunting or conduct particular rituals. The head man, though often hereditary, is merely *primus inter pares*. Neither he nor any other

[3] George P. Murdock, *Africa: Its Peoples and Their Culture History*, McGraw-Hill, New York, 1959, p. 33.

424

leader has the power or the right to compel compliance. He can only advise or persuade.[4]

Typically, then, the chief or headman of the clan functions as a protector rather than an executive authority, an arbiter rather than a judge, and a distributor rather than a collector. His power usually lies in the good will of his fellow tribesmen rather than in any use of force.

The political system may, as in parts of East Africa, rest upon a structure of age grades and not on kinship.[5] At different age levels new sets of responsibilities and privileges arise and terminate. In the Galla tribe, for example, members can successively occupy five well-defined age periods. The next to last period is the one occupied by the politically powerful. Occupants of the fifth period constitute a senior set of advisers and elders who wield little political weight but are shown considerable respect. As described by Murdock:

> Where the system is highly developed, political authority is vested in the holders of a diverse series of offices, including a tribal chief, a speaker of the tribal assembly, head men of local communities, judges, legal advisers, and religious functionaries, all chosen from the age set occupying the semi-final age grade, and all retiring together at the termination of this period to become honored but politically powerless elders.[6]

Age sets usually refer to groupings of men, but in some cases, such as certain of the Ibo of Nigeria, women are also thus organized.

Although the chief or headman in

[4] *Ibid.*, p. 33.
[5] *Ibid.*, p. 35.
[6] *Ibid.*

African society rarely rules by fiat, the importance of his position must not be underestimated. The chief is often the embodiment of power, a mighty force for or against change, a fact realized and capitalized upon by colonial nations. In some tribes the chief is considered a descendant of the Creator, and in most he is at least the hereditary custodian of highly revered tradition. He may be both lawgiver and judge. Not only the chiefs but counselors and other office-holders may form a hereditary caste or class.

As will be seen in later discussion, colonial powers, upon annexation of African territories, were faced with the dilemma of destroying or utilizing the indigenous power structure. Either choice was to pose great difficulties. Destroying the traditional role of the chief in some societies was tantamount to undermining the whole way of life. Yet attempting to use the chief to bridge the gap between colonial government and the people at times frustrated rapid realization of colonial goals. Moreover, with the coming of independence and the evolution of modern power structures the new African elites were to view a chief-centered society as a disdainful anachronism.

Pre-European Values. Tropical Africa, like the less-developed regions of Asia and Latin America, until recently was outside the main stream of rationalistic and scientific tradition common to Europe and North America. While it is not easy to generalize about the world view of Africans, the absence of such traditions and the lack of specialized and technical knowledge have often blurred the distinction between natural and supernatural. To the traditional African, death, disease, crop successes and failures, human fertility, and the like are the result of the work of the spirits. From the African vantage point the explanation that the anger of an ancestor or the wrath of a spirit caused an illness or a misfortune is eminently more logical than the germ theory of the Europeans.

The several types of beliefs held in varying degrees by Africans have been grouped into the following categories: ancestral and nonancestral spirits; magic; witchcraft and sorcery; and nonnative religions, such as Christianity and Islam.[7] The role of ancestral spirits in many African societies is reminiscent of the East Asian practice of ancestor worship. Respect for age and seniority is extended to ancestors and fostered by the belief that communication does not cease with death but that all acts of the living are under the continuous scrutiny of the departed ones. Thus the relationship between the living and the dead is not too different from that among the living. Indeed, the sharp dichotomy between life and death as known in Western societies does not exist. "The living and the dead compose a close, interdependent community, and anything which disturbs the harmony between them is regarded as a crime."[8] This type of relationship obviously promotes continuing stability of the kinship system, yet has evil overtones inasmuch as the authority of the dead acts to thwart progressive acts of the living. The intimate relationship between persons of

the Uuluba tribe of the Congo and their ancestors has been described as follows:

> The Uuluba lives intimately with the dead. He encounters them; he venerates them; he fears them. He does not flee from them. This is impossible. He is dependent on them, and at the same time he keeps them alive.[9]

The dire consequence of failure to keep trust with the dead is suggested by a member of the Ba-ila tribe of Rhodesia.

> We must not fail in our duty to the dead, for they have the power and the disposition to call us back to loyal obedience by sending sickness and misfortune upon us.[10]

Nonancestral spirits control the actions of such natural phenomena as earth, water, thunder, and lightning; they are frequently associated with fertility of the soil and human reproduction and can act as guardian spirits.[11] The particular environmental conditions and concepts of the Good Life may determine the number and type of nonancestral spirits at work in a particular society. Agricultural groups tend to revere spirits concerned with productivity of the soil. Groups living in areas frequently beset by flood, electrical storms, and the like give greater attention to the spirits which control these events.

Both ancestral and nonancestral spirits work to maintain the stability of the social order, punish the evildoers, and reward the good. Both contribute to the

---

[7] Simon Ottenberg and Phoebe Ottenberg (eds.), *Cultures and Societies of Africa*, Random House, New York, 1960, p. 61.

[8] Edwin W. Smith, *Golden Stool*, Edinburgh House Press, London, edition 1957, p. 191, copyright Epworth Press, London.

[9] Translated from T. Theeuws, *"Natir et Mourir dans le Ritual Luba," Zaire*, vol. 45, nos. 2, 3, p. 116, 1960.

[10] Smith, *op. cit.*, p. 105.

[11] Ottenberg and Ottenberg, *op. cit.*, p. 62.

Good Life by helping people "cope with the undependability of nature and fallibility of man."[12] One important distinction between the ancestral and nonancestral spirits should be noted, however. While the decisions of the former were sometimes known to be colored by human frailties as in the case of "renegade ancestors," the decisions of the latter were consistent and irrevocable.

The interrelations between the spirits of African religious systems vary, as do the types of influences of deities. In some African societies the number of deities is small and their functions are clearly defined, while in others there are "complex pantheons of gods, headed by a high god who is often the creator, with a number of gods, godlins, and sometimes minor spirits."[13] The particular organization of the gods and spirits may parallel the political structure of the society. Moreover, the people may have many spirits to choose from as their interests and needs dictate.

> The spirit world can thus be an "empire" with a formalized power structure or a "democracy" in which the people, to some extent at least, choose their own supernatural authorities.[14]

Knowledge of the Good Life may be transmitted from the spiritual world in various ways, depending on the type of relationship between people and spirits. Priests and diviners may be present to serve the people in their own specialized capacities. There is an important difference in the function of these two groups, however; priests act as intermediaries

12 *Ibid.*
13 *Ibid.*
14 *Ibid.*

between a particular god or spirit and a person or group of persons; diviners employ magic to determine the cause of a particular illness, misfortune, and such. As has often been pointed out by students of African culture, divination may be a highly complex practice, the successful knowledge of which requires skill in intricate rituals, dances, use of magical potions, cures, etc. As might be expected, the diviner is often a master of applied psychology. It has even been suggested that the rigorous preparation necessary for this profession is comparable to that for the Ph.D. degree in Western society.

As for the two major nonnative religions, both Islam and Christianity have been actively represented by mission groups and both can boast large numbers of converts.[15] Yet, although Islam is still suspect in parts of East Africa because of the former slave trading carried on by Moslems, it is generally considered less "foreign" than Christianity. Islam is untainted by association with colonial rule and skin color prejudices; it has shown less propensity for conflict with common African customs related to *rites de passage*, tribal rituals and sacrifices, and the practice of polygamy.

On the other hand, Christianity has gained some popularity because of its association with the Western or modern way of life. Among many young African intellectuals Christianity, in spite of its harboring of color prejudice, is con-

15 Owing to inadequate statistics and the problem of definition, the exact number of Moslems and Christians cannot be given; a rough estimate gives each faith between one-fourth and one-fifth of the sub-Saharan population.

sidered more in keeping with African developmental goals. The extensive efforts of the Christian missions to introduce modern education and protect the rights of women have left profound impressions, as have their records in medical work. The future of Christianity in Africa will be greatly aided or retarded by the effectiveness of the African Christian church.

The close link between living and dead, the numerous spirits that structure human relationships and evoke communion between nature and man, and the prevalence of the priests and other technicians to interpret and enforce the will of the unseen have contributed to stable but relatively static societies. In societies where political decisions could not be divorced from religious considerations, indeed where all customs and rules of life, work, and religion were dependent on one another, the African was a prisoner sheltered from the vicissitudes of change. Under these conditions, the disintegrative forces of European ideology and technology become apparent. Less apparent, however, is where and how the old and new world come to terms and the nature of a meaningful integration of the two.

Ethnic and Racial Groupings. The problem of classifying Africans into subspecies of the species Homo sapiens has caused modern anthropologists considerable difficulty. In the past many inaccuracies and misconceptions regarding African physical types have been fostered by observers who confused linguistic and racial groups. The frequent references still found to the Bantu "race" are a case in point.

One classification scheme lists the following "races or stocks":

The Negritos or Pygmies, the Bushmen and Hottentots or Khoisan peoples, the Negroes, the Hamites (from whose miscegenation with the Negroes and others arose the Nilotes, Nilo-Hamites and Bantu) and the Semites or Arabs.[16]

Kimble, using physical characteristics such as stature, head form, skin color, etc., found ten identifiable categories: Bushmen, Pygmies, Hottentots, Negroes, Hamites, Half Hamites, Nilotes, Bantu Negroes, Semites, and Malgachers. Under Kimble's classification the Negroes, Bantu Negroes, and Hamites are the major racial groups in tropical Africa. The combined numbers of these peoples comprise all but a few million of the population. The well-publicized Bushmen, Pygmies, and Hottentots are less developed culturally and exist in relatively insignificant numbers, probably totaling less than 200,000.[17]

Language. Linguistically Africa is considered one of the most complex regions of the world. Most of the more than eight hundred languages spoken on the continent can be found in the tropical belt. The reason for such linguistic diversity, while concluded to be related to the pattern of settlement, still has not been successfully explained by historians. On the contrary, it may well be that further scientific study of African languages may be an important route to the writing of a more definitive African history.

As with ethnic and racial groupings,

[16] "Africa," *Encyclopaedia Britannica,* 27th ed., Encyclopaedia Britannica, Chicago, 1959, vol. I, p. 309.

[17] George H. T. Kimble, *Tropical Africa,* Twentieth Century Fund, New York, 1960, vol. I, pp. 83–87.

some difficulty has been experienced in the classification of African languages. Although the linguistic differences are great, certain similarities exist in structure, and many common features of semantics and idiom can be found.[18] Some of the African languages are spoken by millions, others by mere hundreds. The more widely used languages include Hausa in Nigeria and other parts of West Africa; Swahili in Tanganyika, Kenya, and other parts of East Africa and the Congo; Nyanja, Mdepele, and Shona in the Federation of Rhodesia and Nyasaland; and Lingala in the Congo.

In tropical Africa, most of the languages remained unwritten until the coming of the Christian missionaries from Europe. An important exception to this is Swahili, which has a considerable literature. The fostering of educational programs by missions and colonial governments in indigenous tongues has given further impetus to the development of literary languages. Much is left to be done, however, in the technical refinement of languages and the development of printed materials for increasing numbers of literates.

Indigenous Education. Education in the more remote areas of Africa today, as in former times, is a family and tribal affair. The child learns from his parents, from his peer group and age set, and through participation in the life of the community. A specialized role in society for girls and boys is taught respectively by mother and father. From the mother the children typically acquire habits of cleanliness, respect for relatives, and approved modes of dress. By

imitation of her mother, the girl learns to cook, to care for younger children, to carry water and other supplies on her head and back, and when older to conduct herself appropriately in her relationships with men. By imitation of or apprenticeship to his father the boy learns to hunt and fish, to plant crops and care for domesticated animals, to use craft skills, and to perform the duties of the husband. Through the observation and imitation of accepted community activities, the children learn dances, rituals, and proverbs.

Although the specific rituals and customs vary from state to state and from tribe to tribe, all African children are taught to be intimate students of their physical, social, and spiritual environments. The child must know the possible values and dangers that lie in the streams, forests, and pasture. The nature and uses of plants, fruits, insects, reptiles, and small animals must be learned. Because his community includes the living and the dead he must not only learn the speech, customs, laws, and taboos of his people, but he must also learn his ritualistic obligations and relationships to his ancestors.

African children do not usually have a prolonged, dependent childhood.

By the age of three or four they can tell their kinsfolk from others—a difficult task when the kinsfolk run to a hundred or more. By the age of six they are likely to know the precise terms in which they should address each one of them and behave toward them. They will also know their food, taboos, and the penalties of infringement.[19]

[18] *Encyclopaedia Britannica, op. cit.*, p. 334.

[19] Kimble, *Tropical Africa, op. cit.*, vol. II, p. 15.

Since African children are rarely isolated from adult members of the society, maturity and responsibility come quickly. Children graduate fully into the adult world during the years of puberty, usually by undergoing rigorous, even dangerous, initiation rites or attending initiation schools. Boys may be subject to floggings, trials of survival in the forest, strenuous dances, and the like. Girls may be tested on their ability to bring food from the jungle and may be required to undergo a crude and dangerous clitoridectomy. The brave and resourceful are, after the successful passing of these tests, men and women.

The possible conflicts between this informal education and school-centered education become apparent. Formal schooling may mean a new scale of values, leading to disrespect for old ways, affinity for urban life, and postponement of marriage. Rifts between mother and daughter and father and son are almost sure to arise. Increased social and economic independence of girls conflicts with the traditional restrictive roles. The son's new knowledge and skills may not be appreciated by a father who lives in a more restricted world, for the degree of receptivity varies greatly among family and cultural groups.[20]

Colonization

Intercourse between African and non-African peoples probably began many centuries before the Europeans made initial attempts to form settlements. Evidence of a substantial borrowing of ideas, tools, and language from the Near East can be traced to the pre-Christian era. Probably by the time of Christ, Arab and Asian peoples in some numbers had settled in parts of East Africa. By A.D. 1000 Moslem Arabs had spread across much of North Africa and, by following old trade routes and establishing new ones, had soon penetrated the Sahara southward. It is also likely that early culture contact was made between southwest Africa and south Asia.

Of most significance to a study of contemporary education in middle Africa, however, are the modern historical period and the policies of the colonial powers which were involved in shaping much of this history. Four major periods of contact with Europe have been identified. The first, 1600 to 1850, was the period of European exploration of the African coastal areas and the development of extensive trade in slaves. During the second period, 1850 to 1900, tropical Africa was partitioned into colonies for major European powers, and exploration of the interior followed. The third period, 1900 to 1945, saw the further evolvement of colonial policies, the beginning of a drive to develop the continent's natural resources, and a recognition of their importance to the world market. The fourth period, the post-World War II years, has been characterized by growing nationalism and political independence.[21]

Although schools in tropical Africa had been established before the twelfth century by the Coptic Christian sect in Ethiopia and by Moslems along caravan

[20] See Simon Ottenberg, "Ibo Receptivity to Change," and Harold K. Schneider, "Pakot Resistance to Change," in William R. Bascom and Melville J. Herskovits (eds.), *Continuity and Change in African Cultures*, The University of Chicago Press, Chicago, 1959.

[21] Ottenberg and Ottenberg, *op. cit.*, p. 75.

routes, extensive formal schooling of a lasting nature awaited the penetration of Europeans. The remainder of this section therefore will be concerned primarily with the pattern of French, English, and Belgian colonial policies, particularly with reference to education, as they developed during the second and third historical periods.

During the latter part of the nineteenth century Africa underwent a thorough political transformation. Territorial dependencies had been carved out earlier by Portugal, England, and France, but rules for a more orderly process of imperialism were the result of the Berlin Conference of 1884–1885. The pact resulting from this conference established —in tempered, idealistic wording—certain principles regarding commerce, elimination of slave trade, regulations governing any new occupation by European nations, and improvement of the physical and spiritual lot of the natives. By the beginning of the twentieth century all of tropical Africa, with the exception of Liberia and Ethiopia, was controlled by some European power. When the land race terminated and inventory was taken, the major colonizers were found to be Great Britain, France, and Belgium. Great Britain controlled sections of coastal West Africa and the region which came to be called East Africa. France emerged with the large section of mostly inland territory in West Africa, and Belgium became responsible for the heart or central region of tropical Africa.

The general pattern of colonization had an economic basis, and profit was the key to the policies and practices of the traders and settlers. The African was of little interest to the colonizing powers except as a force to be controlled and perhaps made useful for economic enterprises. Only the Christian missionaries were concerned with the African as an individual. These missionaries accompanied the advance of European influence in Africa almost from the beginning, and as they spread throughout the continent, they offered to the Africans new services in health and education as well as a new concept which held that the Good Life was to be found only in following the Christian way. For educational development it was a happy decision that the missions exerted their efforts beyond those activities of the purely spiritual realm; or put in another way, it was fortunate that the missions sought societal reform as a step toward Christian conversion.

The colonial policies followed by the ruling powers reflected the different political, social, and economic attitudes of the several European countries. Yet certain important similarities in educational policies are discernible. First, for convenience or for principle, each colonial power encouraged the educational efforts of the Christian missions. Secondly, each colonial power regarded education as essentially the handmaid of administration. Educated Africans were needed to occupy the lower administrative and teaching positions. And, thirdly, at the secondary level and above each attempted to preserve high academic standards.

British. In the early stages of colonialism, Britain, like other European nations, viewed the African colonies only as a source of income and a place for settlers. During the latter part of the nineteenth century, however, a more humane, though strongly paternalistic, view developed in keeping with the British tradition of democracy and political freedom. Increasingly, the purpose of colonial policy was declared to be that of preparing the native for self-government within the Commonwealth.

The term "indirect rule" is used to describe the colonial policy of the British, implying that rule was administered through the existing indigenous institutions.[22] While this is reasonably accurate, British policy varied in degree-depending upon the level of development of the natives, the type of political organization already in existence, and the number of white settlers in the area. Where the indigenous political and judicial organizations bore some relationship to those of the colonial power, as in those areas which are now known as Ghana, Nigeria, Sierra Leone, Northern Rhodesia, and Tanganyika, attempts were made to make as much use of them as possible.[23] Schools were set up for training tribal chiefs, or those boys who, because of birth were destined to become tribal chiefs, in order that bridges might be formed between the colonial authority and the people.[24] In areas where traditional organizations seemed unadaptable or the people were at a relatively primitive stage by European ideas of society, greater external control was established. Those areas, such as Southern Rhodesia and Kenya, in which white settlers formed a stable and fairly numerous population, were soon allowed a great degree of self-rule, with the white minority usurping political power and work advantages.

[22] Sir Andrew Cohen, *British Policy in Changing Africa*, Routledge, London, 1959, p. 22.

[23] *Ibid.*, pp. 22–25.

[24] Lord Hailey, *An African Survey*, rev. ed., Oxford, Fair Lawn, N.J., 1957, p. 1187.

The utilization of chiefs and councils of elders greatly assisted the evolution of democratic self-government in the British areas of influence. Where this system was successful, the responsibilities of the native authorities were increased to include not only judicial and executive matters but also the levying and expending of tax moneys. In this manner the chief and his council became an important interim arrangement on the path to local government and, eventually, national self-rule.

Within this policy of indirect rule there developed the doctrine of differentiation. This doctrine, applied in varying degrees throughout the British territories, rested on the idea of evolving separate institutions appropriate to African needs and thus differing from European institutions. In regions where Asian, European, and African populations existed, three separate systems of primary and secondary schools evolved. Differentiation as a principle and as an educational practice was carried to its extreme in the white-controlled Union of South Africa, with the resulting policy of apartheid (apartness).

Southern Rhodesia and Kenya, the two other areas of British influence in which there is a relatively large, stable white population, followed the doctrine of differentiation to a lesser degree than did the Union of South Africa. This was due to many factors, among which the principal ones appear to be the continuing control exercised by the British government, the proportionately smaller number of whites, and the realization of the inevitable coming of a society in which Africans could not only become equal but possibly even dominant. Thus, those settlers who wished to continue calling Africa their home increasingly acquiesced to African demands for a greater share in the total life of the society. In areas where there were few, if any, white settlers, as in much of West Africa, the policy of differentiation was carried on at a level more closely reflecting the original theory behind the principle.

Beginning with the famous report of the Phelps-Stokes Commission in 1922, the British government began to take a more active interest in colonial education in Africa. This report and a series of memoranda to follow over the succeeding two decades emphasized that mission-sponsored education, which should continue to be encouraged, was not enough to meet the needs of nations that one day would be independent or at least full-fledged members of the Commonwealth. British authorities were careful to point out that increased government leadership in establishment of general principles and policies did not mean uniformity:

> The territorial differences in racial composition (e.g., between the largely monoracial west African territories and the multiracial east and central African territories), religious affiliations (e.g., between the Mohammedan northern region and the Christianized eastern and western regions of Nigeria), economic development (e.g., between comparatively advanced Uganda and comparatively backward Tanganyika), and inclination (e.g., between the Kikuyu, who eagerly embraced the chance for schooling, and the Masai, who didn't), ruled out any such possibility.[25]

The policy of differentiation meant that from the time of the earliest mis-

[25] Kimble, *Tropical Africa, op. cit.,* vol. II, p. 119.

sion schools, much of the teaching at the primary level was in the vernacular. As the colonial government, through its educational officers, became more directly concerned with native education, it fully endorsed this method, at least for the early primary grades. Not only was it expedient to teach in the vernacular, but it was the stated belief that:

> . . . only through the wise use of the Mother tongue can clearness of thought, independence of judgment and sense of individual responsibility be developed at the start.[26]

Thus primary education, at least the first three to four years of which are taught in the vernacular, is a characteristic peculiar to those areas which were under British influence. The advantages derived from this policy are extensive, according to the advocates of the differentiation principle, because most of the African children who attend school do not go beyond the first few years of the primary level. Therefore, by the simple medium of the vernacular, subjects useful to the child in his everyday life can be more easily and quickly taught.

Criticisms of the use of the vernacular and the establishment of racially segregated schools are a criticism of the whole idea of differentiation; at least a vocal number of Africans did not want to be given a separate place in the society; they wanted, instead, an education identical to that of the European. Special problems in using the vernacular as the language of instruction are derived from the fact that in some areas so many languages are current that the

[26] *Report of the Calcutta University Commission, 1919,* quoted in Hailey, *op. cit.,* p. 92.

433

dominant vernacular is difficult to determine. Moreover, the use of the vernaculars serves to strengthen language barriers between tribes and makes national unity an even more difficult goal to achieve.

Paradoxically, the concept of differentiation, which was designed to educate the child within his environment, was negated to a great extent by the use of British external examinations. According to this practice the exams which were administered to the children in Great Britain as a graduation requirement were, with minor local modifications, also given to African children. At the close of six to eight years of primary schooling, children took the locally administered primary leaving examination. Those who passed could proceed to secondary grammar school where, after completing four to six years of study and certain intermediate examinations, they were eligible to take the Cambridge Overseas School Leaving Certificate Examination. Where available two additional years of study (sixth form) led to the higher school certificate. The aura of prestige and the real economic advantage which accompanied the passing of these exams led not only to an acceptance of, or a preference for, a Europeanized curriculum with heavy literary flavor, but also to a resistance on the part of Africans to the transfer of certification powers from British to African bodies. Many Africans, for example, feared that the establishment of the West African Examination Council with the authority to award the school certificate would lower the value of this prized academic symbol. At the higher educational levels a degree of standardization was acquired by the affiliation of colonial colleges with the University of London or other British universities.

434

The British policy with respect to educational control and administration was to establish in each territory a Department of Education with a Director as its executive head. Authority was delegated from the territorial level to provincial and district educational officers. Where feasible much of the authority for primary education was transferred to the local African governments—the "native authorities." The reliance on the initiative of the colonial administration and the traditional reluctance of the British to subject education to state control led to a lack of system among the British colonial educational enterprises. However, although some differences in structure and curriculum are noticeable in British West Africa and British East and Central Africa, above the first few years of schooling standardized curricula and standardized examinations have made for considerable uniformity.

During World War II Great Britain announced a policy for her colonies which provided for greatly increased expenditure and represented decades of examination of colonial principles:

> We are pledged to guide Colonial peoples along the road to self-government within the framework of the British Empire . . . to build up the social and economic institutions . . . to develop their natural resources.[27]

The scope of these improvements was enunciated in the postwar development and welfare acts and ten-year development programs. After World War II, Britain expended a yearly average of 40 million dollars on her colonies, and a large proportion of this went for edu-

[27] Quoted in T. Walter Wallbank, *Contemporary Africa: Continent in Transition*, Van Nostrand, Princeton, N.J., 1956, pp. 42–43.

cation. In Ghana, for example, the first British colony to become independent (1957), 15 per cent of the total development expenditure from 1950 to 1960 went for education. This financial outlay was sufficient to double primary and secondary school enrollments and increase vocational school enrollments by fivefold. Further details of postwar educational expansion will be described later in the chapter.

The policy of indirect rule, with increasing responsibility being placed on the African to make his own decisions, worked more successfully in some areas than in others; it received both plaudits and criticism from outside observers. In East Africa where nationalism got a later start and the African political structure lent itself to chief-rule, the British policy provided an intermediate step toward self-government. In West Africa where few British settlers migrated, nationalism gained strength so rapidly that a system of indirect rule was never fully developed. Criticism has sometimes also been leveled at the British for their failure to recognize the strength of African aspirations and to better prepare the Africans for development and independence. The direction in which a policy of indirect rule was supposed to lead and the final goal of "native administration" were too little analyzed or discussed with African leaders. Valid as this criticism may be, the British did leave a small but valuable legacy in the form of modern judicial, political, and educational institutions, all European in character but each adaptable after a fashion to Africa.

French. The stated desire of French colonial policy from its formulation in the nineteenth century until 1958 was to create in Africa a civilization that was essentially non-African. Thus the French developed the doctrine of "assimilation." The ultimate objective was ". . . to integrate the overseas possessions with France, to assimilate the colonial people into the body of French political, social and cultural thought and practice. . . ." This goal ". . . stemmed from economic and political considerations but also from the faith of the French in their superior culture."[28]

The French believed, for example, that the strong uniting and disciplinary force which continued to emanate from ancient African beliefs stressed within the family unit, even in groups converted to Christianity or Islam, should be utilized for goals beyond those of individual or family units. That is, the Western concept of group society or nation should take the place of the African familial society. Likewise, the animistic religions which concentrated on the relationship between man and the natural forces which he saw or felt about him should give way to a more sophisticated religion of change and progress, preferably Christianity, which was concerned with man as a social being.[29] The French soon realized that assimilation would be a long and difficult process; therefore, "association"—the education of a small group of Africans, an elite, who could occupy a leadership role—became the immediate aim. This elite group would be granted the full rights and privileges of French citizenship.

Following this policy France, rather than utilizing indigenous institutions as the British sometimes attempted, set up characteristically French institutions closely tied to the metropolitan govern-

[28] *Ibid.*, pp. 93–94.
[29] Lucien Paye, "France's Hope for Instruction and Education of the African Citizen," *Phi Delta Kappan,* vol. 41, no. 4, p. 186, January, 1960.

ment. These institutions were staffed by French officials, although the educated African elite increasingly came to act as administrative and economic auxiliaries. Indeed, it has sometimes been argued that France gave the African more opportunities to occupy leadership roles than any other colonial power.

An examination of French educational policy serves to clarify the role designed for the African under French colonial rule. The first general educational plan for France's African colonies was drawn up in 1903. This plan with no major modifications remained in effect until World War I when new social, political, and economic forces caused a sweeping review of colonial policy. Unlike the flexible British educational policy, French policy called for an educational system in the colonies closely modeled after that in metropolitan France. Reflecting long-standing liberal traditions as well as the policy of separation of church and state (in effect in France since 1903), African education was to be free and nonreligious. The French did not, however, prohibit the educational activities of missions; up until 1945 at least one-third of all Africans seeking primary education attended mission schools. Indeed, in spite of anticlericalism at home, the French government not only subsidized the mission schools but appeared to view them as vital instruments for the extension of national policy.

Following the policy of assimilation, both mission and state schools used French as the language of instruction from the earliest grades. This not only promoted an interest in and a knowledge of French culture, but was also intended as a means of unifying the many separate communities within the indigenous society. Criticisms of the practice stated

that, since the majority of the children enrolled attended school for only two years, the time spent in this acculturation process was wasted. Another approach to the goal of imparting French civilization was the policy of common schools and free education for all ethnic and racial groups within an area. It was believed that association between French and African children would have a positive effect on the outlook of the African child toward the French way of life.[30]

A further word needs to be said about the education of the African elite who were to function as intermediaries between the French and the less-acculturated indigenous population. This elite consisted of those Africans who showed greatest promise in the primary level and who survived through the progressively select levels of secondary and higher education. As part of official policy, chiefs and their sons were also usually included in the elite and given training in special schools.

Because of lack of sufficient funds and, possibly, reluctance to face the danger of an "educated unemployed," the French limited their courses in both secondary and higher education to those which would train students for positions in which a particular need existed. A counterpart of this policy at the upper primary levels stressed rudimentary agricultural and vocational education on the premise that most Africans needed skills immediately salable. This emphasis on terminal vocational education has come under increasing criticism from contemporary Africans who have sought to improve their social and economic positions through advanced education.

Before World War II, France, like

[30] Hailey, *op. cit.*, p. 225.

Britain, followed a policy of colonial self-support. As a result, although the purposes and policies of education remained essentially the same in each of a nation's colonial territories, educational opportunities varied greatly among the territories. For example, French West Africa, a relatively wealthy area, was able to adopt a secular system of education in which agricultural schools operated in rural areas and other types of vocational schools were available in urban areas. Furthermore, evening classes for adults were initiated early, and attempts were made to provide greater educational opportunities for girls. On the other hand, in French Equatorial Africa the relative lack of resources resulted in heavy reliance on mission schools, and programs of adult education were not undertaken until 1951.

After World War II France sought to develop the concept of a union of French states in which the African areas would be classified as overseas territories. As a result, full French citizenship was granted to all Africans living in French areas. Along with this concept came greater emphasis on aid and development; under the Fund for Economic and Social Development to the Overseas Territories (FIDES), in 1959 renamed Fund for Aid and Cooperation (FAC), the metropolitan government expended about 240 million dollars a year on the colonies.[31] A large proportion of this expenditure was devoted to education, especially secondary education.

Prior to 1946, French educational

policy had been attuned to the principle that only a few Africans could acquire full French citizenship. The new policy demanded new educational practices. Attention was given to creating a primary school that would be functional in the African environment, and French officials discussed the need to respect African culture. Educational services were extended not only in the area of formal education, but in areas of technical assistance, fundamental education, literacy campaigns, and resource development. The vernacular was used in much of the adult education.

As Table 11 shows, the expansion of school enrollments was sizable after World War II. Yet by 1962, still only 25 to 30 per cent of school-age children were enrolled in school in the French-speaking areas. Moreover, although the

Table 11 *Comparison of Number of African Students in Public and Private Schools in 1946 and 1957*

Territory	Total number	Per cent girls
French West Africa:		
1946*	107,470	19
1957*	379,186	24
French Equatorial Africa:		
1946	34,150	9
1957	175,956	22
French Cameroons:		
1946	114,722	14
1957	278,889	27
French Togo:		
1946	17,230	18
1957	67,950	23

* Figures are as of Jan. 1.
SOURCE: Data taken from *African Affairs*, Service de Presse et d'Information, French Embassy, New York, May, 1958, pp. 8–9.

[31] Barbara Ward, "The Emerging Africa," *The Atlantic*, vol. 203, no. 4, p. 31, April, 1959.

French point with pride to the number of African poets and writers trained in their colonies, the system was dangerously unbalanced in favor of primary education, for only approximately 5 per cent of those attending schools were in secondary and higher educational institutions. Until 1958 only one institution in the whole French region of Africa, the University of Dakar, offered training at the university level. In spite of financial and other problems the numbers enrolled could have been further increased if the French had been more willing to sacrifice academic standards.

With the creation of the Fifth Republic, in 1958, the concept of the French Union was replaced by the Franco-African Community. The new political arrangement provided technical equality for the former territories and gave each the choice of remaining in the union or becoming independent from France. Guinea was the only territory to vote immediately for independence; but by 1961 the other eight French territories had followed suit. Economic and cultural intercourse between France and her former colonies has continued but the "Frenchness" of the African institutions, including the schools, is likely to diminish progressively.

Belgian.[32] In 1908 the Belgian government took on the "national duty and international necessity" of directing the administration of the Congo Free State. Belgian colonial policy, to the extent that an explicit policy existed, followed a path more or less midway between

[32] Discussion in this section is limited to the Congo although most comments would also apply to the former trusteeship territory Ruanda-Urundi. In 1962 the two independent states of Rwanda and Burundi were formed from this territory.

that of the British and French—a pattern of modified differentiation. Unlike the French, the Belgians were less concerned with promoting strong European associations than with development within the existing range of social and economic institutions, and thus, at least until World War II, they promoted practices of indirect rule. Unlike the British, however, the Belgians entirely divorced local political institutions and administration from the concern of the African or European population; the inhabitants were allowed little participation in any political bodies.

In the Congo, effort was concentrated on developing physical resources and raising the productivity of the people. The great mineral deposits in particular invited exploration and exploitation. To take full advantage of the potential wealth of the Congo, an efficient work force was needed, a fact that led the Belgians to stress primary and vocational education. Indeed, because of this educational policy and the ready availability of skilled work, the Congolese under Belgian control could boast the highest standard of living of any African population in tropical Africa.

Professing to develop the African within his own environment, the Belgians provided differentiated schooling on the basis of race and emphasized the vernacular language in the early years of African schooling. That advanced education for the African had little place in this scheme is seen by the fact that not until after World War II was it possible for a Congolese to obtain a full secondary education leading to a university.

Kimble, impressed perhaps by this latter fact, in rather bold language suggests that there were two assumptions underlying Belgian educational policy, the first paternalistic and the second religious:

> First, it is better to have 90 percent of the population capable of understanding what the government is trying to do for them and competent to help the government in doing it than to have 10 percent of the population so full of learning that it spends its time telling the government what to do.[33]

The second assumption according to Kimble is "that all education is the better for being in the hands of men of faith."[34]

To an even greater extent than the British and French, the Belgians relied on mission support to carry out educational plans. Inititially the Catholic missions and later Protestant missions were eligible for government subsidies. The missionaries reduced the vernacular to writing and printed textbooks; however, until well into the twentieth century, schools above the primary level were for the training of the clergy.

Schools in the Congo could be classified under four categories. Listed in the order of their historical appearance, these were nonsubsidized parochial schools, subsidized parochial schools, "congreganist" government schools, and secular (official) government schools. The only difference between the first two groups was that the subsidized parochial schools conformed to government standards and received government support. The congreganist government schools were established by the government but turned over to mission groups for operation. The last

type of school, the most recent to appear, was established by the government and operated by civil servants.[35]

By 1959 all schools able to meet official standards with regard to qualified personnel, curriculum, textbooks, facilities, and size of enrollment could receive government subsidies and were subject to government inspection. This action led to improved instruction and considerable standardization.

A few secular or official government schools, schools directly under the control of the state, established in the Congo prior to 1954 were staffed by Roman Catholic clergy. After 1954 many new schools were opened under lay personnel. In addition to the mission and official schools a number of commercial firms provided opportunities in both primary and vocational education for the children of their employees. Moreover, adult education in the form of literacy, health, and vocational training was almost entirely in the hands of industrial and commercial concerns and was part of an effort to develop more efficient employees.

The school system introduced by the Belgians consisted of a five-year primary course divided into lower and upper divisions followed by a three-year post-primary course. Instead of attending the upper stage of the primary school, a highly selected few African children were allowed to enter a special preparatory course for secondary education. The secondary schools, in addition to those specially designed to offer a variety of terminal vocational courses, were six years in length and bore a strong resemblance to the French secondary schools.

[33] Kimble, *Tropical Africa, op. cit.*, vol. II, p. 115.
[34] *Ibid.*, p. 115.
[35] *Belgian Congo*, Information and Public Relations Office, Brussels, 1959, vol. I, pp. 443–444.

In the "modern" secondary school, the lower three years offered a common curriculum while the upper three years offered specialization in any of four fields: administrative and commercial; survey; science (as a preparation for agricultural, veterinary, or medical work); and teacher training.[36] The other type of secondary school, more academic in nature, offered the traditional program of arts and sciences; the language of instruction beyond the primary school was French.

A Catholic order in 1954 founded the first Congo university, Lovanium, near Leopoldville. This university is affiliated with the Catholic University of Louvain in much the same way that colleges in British colonial areas are related to the University of London. Belgium founded the second Congo university in 1956, the State University (Université de l'Etat, later Université Officielle du Congo) at Elizabethville. The late establishment of higher education facilities in the Congo was unfortunate in light of the rather substantial educational progress that had been made at the lower levels. For example, the Belgian Congo in 1957 could boast a primary enrollment ratio higher than all but one of the other thirty-two countries of middle Africa. The secondary enrollment ratio also compared favorably with other African areas; however, statistics here are somewhat biased by the Belgian definition of certain vocational institutes as secondary schools. Yet at the time of independence the Congo had but sixteen university graduates.

In final analysis the Belgian educational policy in the Congo was characterized by "too little too late." Like the British and French, the Belgians

had brought bits of the modern world to Africa—new modes of communication, improved transportation, scientific methods in health, a beginning technology, and a European school system. Although the Belgians were not so anxious as the French to Europeanize the African, neither were they so willing to accept the educated African as an equal. The tools with which a livelihood could be earned were distributed with generosity. But the realities of national affairs, the intricacies of finance and the art of administration were not taught. And perhaps most fundamental of all, little spirit or concept of national unity was fostered.

Economic and social development in emerging Africa

As Margaret Mead has described so graphically in *New Lives for Old*, a people with the right personal and social attitudes, values, and skills can move from primitiveness to membership in the modern world in one generation. There is no doubt that many Africans are favorably inclined toward change and are being rapidly and dramatically transformed. Even today few African families live as they did a generation ago. And, of course, it may well be that only those African groups which accept and practice the hygienic, technical, and economic methods of modern societies will be able to survive in the coming years.

But the problems of Africa are not merely those of absorbing and utilizing Western knowledge. There are the complex problems of maintaining and reactivating nations whose territorial boundaries do not coincide with cultural boundaries. People whose traditions and language are not closely akin must learn

[36] Hailey, *op. cit.*, p. 1210.

to live and work together. New loyalties and commitments based less on kinship and community must be developed. The new African states must not only adjust their economies to world markets but must also maintain political integrity in a world split ideologically and militarily into two camps.

Economic problems

Until the last few decades the means of livelihood were few for most Africans. An African might be a food gatherer (hunter, fisherman, or gatherer of wild fruits, berries, etc.), like the Pygmies in the upper Congo basin or the Bushmen of the Kalahari; an animal herder like the Masai in East Africa who owned cattle and the Somali of the Somali Republic and French Somaliland who owned camels; a crop cultivator like the Kikuyu and other peoples whose land conditions and rainfall were favorable; or he could be involved in a combination of these activities.[37]

In parts of tropical Africa a subsistence and barter economy still prevails. In every area, however, European influence has fostered a money economy and increased the range of money-earning activities. Many Africans have left agriculture and gone into manufacturing, mining, or commercial enterprises. Nevertheless it is still probable that the proportion of the population that makes its living directly from the land is higher in tropical Africa than on any other continent. Many of the most pressing economic problems, then, will continue for some time to center around the African's ability to carve out an existence directly from the soil.

[37] Kimble, *Tropical Africa: Problems and Promises*, Headline Series No. 147, Foreign Policy Association, New York, 1961, p. 51.

The problems of the pastoralist and farmer are many. The incidence of disease, the problems of preserving meat, milk, and other foodstuffs in the tropics, the finding of edible fodder, the difficulties of marketing, etc., plague the cattle herder. The seasonal rains, a soil not tolerant to man's abuse, the uneconomic technique of bush fallowing, and the practice of one farmer working several small landholdings are among the difficulties faced by the crop cultivator. The African himself represents both strength and weakness in the economic situation. His ignorance, poverty, and fear thwart changes which might result in increased productivity, better marketing arrangements, and the like. On the other hand, the African has often shown himself to be a much better student of his environment than the European has given him credit for. In the past his very livelihood depended on his understanding of the conditions in which he worked. In the future the realization of his minimum aspirations will depend on his ability to develop greater skill and insight.

In recognition of the importance of agriculture, the colonial powers and, more recently, the national governments have instituted many reform programs and experimental schemes. Governments have urged crop rotation, a mixed agricultural economy of cattle and crops, and large-scale schemes of resettlement to provide fresh opportunities. Model and experimental farms are being developed and agricultural schools built. Rather surprisingly, in spite of the importance of agriculture, relatively little attention has been given to agricultural education. In The Report of the Commission on Post-school Certificate and Higher Education in Nigeria, for example, the following comment is found:

441

Investment in agricultural improvement and agricultural education could double Nigeria's wealth. Yet investment in agriculture is inadequate and is rarely in the public eye. Publicity goes to industrialization, construction and the like.[38]

In this report, the agricultural expert is considered one of Nigeria's most urgent high-level manpower needs. The report goes on to suggest not only more agricultural schools at the secondary and higher levels and more research at the graduate level, but also more flexibility in programs so that young farmers could take "refresher courses."[39]

The new university colleges in the British areas of influence offer both diploma and degree work in the agricultural sciences. The French practice has been to establish apprenticeship centers and agricultural technical colleges which offer courses to the standard of a *lycée premier cycle*. In the Congo a series of centers for agricultural extension work which also conduct training programs has been established and, more recently, advanced agricultural study has become available at the University of Lovanium. Though facilities have become increasingly available, the study of agriculture lacks prestige; African youth strongly prefer administrative, professional, or technical pursuits.

Because of the magnitude of the experiments, a further word should be said about the various resettlement schemes attempted since World War II. Some of the larger but unsuccessful

schemes have been at Damongo in the Gold Coast, initiated in 1949; the Mokwa Settlement in Nigeria in 1949; and the well-known Groundnut Plan in Tanganyika. The reasons for failure of these attempts are complex; but, in general, social as well as technical factors were involved. The Tanganyika groundnut scheme, the most spectacular failure of all, apparently was begun with too little advanced technical information and planning. The project called for the opening up of giant farms for peanut raising. From the beginning, the exorbitant cost of land clearing, unsuitability of soil, inadequate rainfall, and other problems doomed the scheme to failure.

Other resettlement schemes in former French and British colonies designed to open new farming regions and reduce population pressures in certain overcrowded areas proved more successful, however, than those noted above. Perhaps the boldest attempt, one which has achieved reasonable success, was initiated by the French in the Niger Valley. By 1958 about 35,000 people had been resettled on irrigated land, and 100,000 new acres had been put under cultivation.[40] Complete villages, houses, wells, etc., were built, and medical, administrative, and teaching personnel were provided free to the settlers. Each village was settled by Africans of the same cultural origin. By 1964 the full impact of this outstanding project was yet to be felt; however, the net personal income of the "immigrants" was several times that of the farmers in nearby areas.

Other natural and human factors of economic significance relate to the retardation of mining, commerce, and in-

---

[38] *Investment in Education,* The Report of the Commission on Post-school Certificate and Higher Education, Federal Ministry of Education, Lagos, Nigeria, 1960, p. 21.

[39] *Ibid.*

[40] Kimble, *Tropical Africa, op. cit.,* vol. I, p. 176.

dustry. In tropical Africa there are a number of large, soundly financed, well-managed, profitable mines, businesses, and factories. In a much larger number, however, there exist uneconomic enterprises, characterized by low output per man hour. The advantages of mechanization available to some of the European farmers and entrepreneurs are only now becoming available to the Africans. Shortages of capital and technical skill have forced the Africans to operate mines, cottage factories, and other enterprises on a small scale only.

The presence or lack of incentives on the part of the African with respect to a money economy has caused considerable speculation and has stimulated a few empirical studies. Some observers have held that traditional African values prohibit response to money incentives. It has also been argued that the African, after becoming aware of the opportunities possible through contact with the money economy, would automatically make an effort "to maximize the real income of his family."[41] Another thesis suggests that it is not that the Africans lack acquisitiveness ". . . but their ability to make use of their resources acquisitively was limited by institutional structures, both indigenous and colonial."[42] The proponent of this thesis offers, by way of illustration, descriptions of tribal groups which, because of institutional patterns, either succeeded or failed in their attempt to move to a wage economy.

It has been further pointed out that economic incentives frequently take the form of a "target demand" and the African becomes a "target laborer."

[41] *African Studies Bulletin*, vol. 3, no. 1, p. 21, March, 1960.
[42] *Ibid.*, p. 24.

Thus the worker remains employed only until he has earned enough money to purchase certain specific articles. As population becomes stabilized, this condition is likely to be ameliorated.[43]

Problems of labor shortages and inadequacy persist in spite of the large increase in semiskilled labor during the last few years. Occupational opportunities have grown significantly in those nations with a large European population as well as in those without. Yet few Africans hold managerial and supervisory positions. It is notable that in Ghana, one of the most advanced of the middle African countries, the number of foreigners occupying high positions in government, industry, etc., increased rather than decreased immediately after independence.

The shortages in both capital and high-level manpower suggest that large-scale external assistance is a prerequisite to African development. Significantly, in a five-year plan of educational development proposed at the UNESCO conference at Addis Ababa in May, 1961, over 30 per cent of the costs and many of the personnel needed to implement the plan were expected to come from non-African sources.[44]

Political and social problems

The bursting forth of nationalism in the post-World War II era has been one of

[43] Frank R. LaMacchia, "African Economics: Basic Characteristics and Prospects," *The Annals of the American Academy of Political and Social Science*, vol. 298, p. 42, March, 1955.
[44] UNESCO, Conference of African States on the Development of Education in Africa, *Final Report*, United Nations Economic Commission for Africa, Addis Ababa, 1961, p. 14.

the most dramatic characteristics of contemporary Africa. In 1945 nearly all administrative, executive, and judicial positions in tropical Africa were held by Europeans. Contemporary African leaders, such as Kwame Nkrumah, Tom Mboya, Julius Nyerere, and Sekou Toure, were able to gain regional and even international stature in a period of ten years or less. At the beginning of World War II, Liberia was the only self-governing territory in middle Africa (Ethiopia, long independent, had been overrun by Italy). By 1964, twenty-nine countries were self-governing, and those remaining under foreign rule anticipated independence soon.

The route to political leadership, even after the elimination of colonial obstacles, has not been an easy one. In fact, the unity promoted by colonial rule often ceased to exist under independence. Separatist movements in the Congo and the less violent but serious regional conflicts in Nigeria are a good example of this. Cultural and ethnic diversity at times thwarted national unity. Great distances, poor transportation, and low levels of literacy usually slowed communication. At least four problems have affected the acquisition and maintenance of capable political leadership: (1) real or potential conflict between the modernist and traditional leaders (as in Nigeria and Ghana); (2) power struggle between those who had attained leadership in an earlier period and the younger, usually more radical, university leaders; (3) political leaders who have often become prisoners of nationalism and continue flogging "the dead horse of colonialism" rather than facing real problems; and (4) the better educated who tend to prefer the civil serv-
444

ice or other employment to politics.[45]

Colonialism, in spite of its many shortcomings, appears to have left a legacy of democratic inclination among young African leaders. Each individual nation, as noted above, has built a government along constitutional lines. It is true, however, that politics have often been dominated by a single political party and led by a charismatic personality. Dangers of dictatorship emerging from such a situation seem more obvious to the outsider than to the Africans, who tend to argue with Julius Nyerere, Prime Minister of Tanganyika, that " . . . a country's struggle for freedom from foreign domination is a patriotic struggle. It leaves no room for differences."[46] Yet already in some of the older independent nations, such as Ghana, opposition groups are demanding more freedom of expression and more power in national decision making while the party in power speaks of using force if necessary against dissident minority groups.

Three terms—urbanization, detribalization, and acculturation—may be used to identify the most significant social changes now taking place in tropical Africa. Urbanization has meant the movement of large numbers of Africans from rural areas and rural societies to urban settings. These moves have forced on the African new modes of living never dreamt of in tribal societies. For the African in his traditional setting there were no assembly lines, factories, hospitals, banks, or schools, and the

[45] The American Assembly, *The United States and Africa,* 1st ed., Background Papers prepared for the Thirteenth American Assembly, New York, 1958, p. 43.
[46] "Will Democracy Work in Africa?" *Africa Report,* February, 1960.

depth of transformation necessary for the urbanizing African cannot be over-estimated. In the new urban areas, unlike in the old village, the person's status, at least when not decided on a racial basis, is more likely to be achieved through individual competence than ascribed through lineage. Political power and commercial enterprises are largely divorced from kinship. The ethnic heterogeneity and mobility of population add to the anonymity of the individual, and the regularity and discipline of industrial work require habits unknown in rural areas. Social and business contacts tend to become more casual and impersonal. Since the younger men and, less frequently, women sever their family ties when they go to the cities, the influence of the tightly knit African family no longer serves as a mooring. Such independence frequently leads to alcoholism and other forms of excess on the part of men and loose living or even prostitution on the part of girls.

The process of urbanization appears to go through several stages. For a time the villager looks to the town or city merely as a source of temporary employment to fulfill an immediate material need. He may spend only his working time in the urban area and return frequently to his village home. The semirural character of numerous Africans provides extensive interaction between city and village, resulting especially in the modification of the latter. As industry expands and the need for labor increases, the urban population becomes more permanent.

Traditionally only two classes existed in urban areas of tropical Africa, and discrimination and rationalization perpetuated them. Stabilization of urban centers is fostering class stratification which, though only in the incipient stage, is becoming increasingly significant. The top stratum of urban society is still reserved for the powerful and wealthy European minorities. However, with independence and top governmental, industrial, and commercial positions opening to the Africans, a tiny African elite and a growing middle class are becoming identifiable. Growth of social classes, as well as the association of the urban African with educational, trade union, religious, and political groups, forecasts the doom of tribal ties which may have initially been carried over into the urban environment.

Urbanization acts as a representative of Westernization, or perhaps industrialization, in promoting "detribalization." To the extent that there are educational solutions to the problems of adjusting to the urban societies, the schools have a significant function to perform. If the schools are attuned to the changing manpower needs, technical and vocational training can assist the African in occupational adjustment and mobility. In the areas where juvenile delinquency is on the increase, where there are seasonal or migrant labor conditions, or where families are trying to build a new home life more in keeping with urban conditions, the school can, if it conceives its function in broad terms, ease the trauma of change.

The process of modifying traditional cultural patterns to include new goals and values, new behavioral modes, can be called "acculturation." The significance of this process is suggested by Ottenberg, who describes the dramatic effect of a new cash crop on the lives of Afrikpo women, members of the Ibo

445

group in Nigeria. The introduction of cassava, considered a woman's crop and not cultivated by Afrikpo men, made the women less dependent on the charity of men. As one Afrikpo woman suggested, a money income from a cash crop, if not eliminating the need for a man, at least reduces his importance.[47]

The dilemma caused by the introduction of new values is illustrated in the case of a Sebei man from Uganda, described by Goldsmitt:

> Cattle and wives, the two major symbols of success for Sebei men, are interchangeable. But now a new value intervenes. It was another young official, an educated Sebei and a self-made man, who placed the dilemma in values before me. A handsome girl was throwing herself at him—not to his displeasure—and I asked if he were planning to take her to be his fourth wife. There was no doubt about his ambivalence, but he was truly in a quandary. His sons were growing up and he wanted them to have an education. He wanted the girl, but perhaps he should keep his cows to provide money later for his boys' schooling.[48]

Various terms have been used to describe the rapid social and political change taking place in Africa. Probably the most common are "magnitude," "speed," "unevenness," and "superficiality." Certainly examples of all these characteristics can be documented in the towns and cities of tropical Africa. Changes in living habits wrought by urban environment, availability of new material comforts, and improved communication are striking indeed. With slavery dead only a little more than half a century, hundreds of Africans now hold university degrees and have demonstrated capability to compete scholastically with students throughout the world. The unevenness is shown in the contrast between the polished urban society and the rude tribal ways still found in the more remote areas. The question of superficiality is perhaps the most provocative. Many observers suggest that the African only accepts those European habits and tools that are temporarily expedient in meeting his needs and that reversion to the old ways is the norm rather than the exception.[49] However, to the extent that industrialization and modern institutions are permanent in tropical Africa so also is the death of traditional society. This does not mean that African leaders believe in the desirability or inevitability of thorough Westernization.[50] Political and ideological eclecticism are at least the temporary goals.

Educational opportunities

Lack of space prohibits an analysis of contemporary education in each of the nations in tropical Africa. The quantitative problems and the progress of the whole region, however, can be shown by presenting pertinent educational data in

[47] Phoebe Ottenberg, "The Changing Economic Position of Women among the Afrikpo Ibo," in William R. Bascom and Melville J. Herskovits (eds.), *op. cit.*, p. 215.

[48] The American Assembly, *op. cit.*, p. 175.

[49] In *The Lonely African*, Simon and Schuster, New York, 1962, Colin Turnbull describes an African who on the upper floor of his home lives a thoroughly Westernized life while on the lower floor lives as the head of a traditional extended family.

[50] James S. Coleman, "Current Political Movements in Africa," *The Annals of the American Academy of Political and Social Science, op. cit.*, p. 101.

tabular form. Since statistical information on population and school enrollments is highly unreliable in much of Africa, all figures regardless of source should be viewed as estimations.

The primary and secondary school enrollment ratios are shown in Table 12. The figures in the third column were obtained by dividing the primary enrollment ratio by the secondary enrollment ratio. The term "index of emphasis" was coined to describe the quotient.

Relating enrollment ratios to present or former colonial status uncovers certain interesting facts. The two nations of tropical Africa which have enjoyed independence during most of their histories, Liberia and Ethiopia, do not rank particularly high in either primary or secondary enrollment ratios. Ethiopia ranks thirtieth among the thirty-two tropical African nations in primary enrollment ratio while Liberia ranks fifteenth. With regard to secondary enrollment ratio Ethiopia is tied for thirty-first and Liberia ranks ninth.

If the primary and secondary enrollment ratios are suitable indexes, British rule was more educationally beneficial to African peoples than the French. The means of the enrollment ratios are higher in the group of present or former British colonies than in the French areas of influence. However, easy conclusions about the superiority of the educational rewards from having been colonized by the British are dangerous, for the range in enrollment ratios is great among countries falling into either the British or French group. In addition to the educational policy of the colonizing power, other important factors must be considered, such as the level of economic development, the presence of settlers, and the activities of the missionaries.

The indexes of emphasis seem to show that several of the tropical African countries have promoted primary education at the expense of secondary education. Probably this is a natural result of colonial policies designed to ensure that positions of responsibility were reserved for citizens of colonial powers. The situation also reflects the rising educational expectations of the people, for it often has become politically imperative to expand primary school opportunities. Regardless of the cause of the imbalance, targets being proposed call for rectification of the situation. The long-range plan for African educational expansion resulting from the UNESCO-sponsored Addis Ababa conference in 1961 calls for a much more rapid increase in the secondary enrollment ratios than in the primary enrollment ratios.[51] Under this plan the goal by 1980 would be universal primary education, 23 per cent of the appropriate age group enrolled in secondary institutions, and 2 per cent of the university-age students in higher education.[52] (By way of comparison, the Education Task Force for the Organization of the American States recommended that by 1975 Latin America should enroll 35 per cent of the youth in secondary

[51] UNESCO, Conference of African States on the Development of Education in Africa, *op. cit.*, p. 11.

[52] Later projections suggest that the goal with regard to higher education was too optimistic. In 1962 a new enrollment target called for 274,000 or 1.51 per cent of the population aged twenty through twenty-four years in attendance in colleges and universities by 1980. *The Development of Higher Education in Africa*, Report of the Conference on the Development of Higher Education in Africa, Tananarive, September 3–12, 1962, UNESCO, Paris, 1963, p. 22.

Table 12   Comparison of Estimated Age 5–19 Population by Country, and School Enrollments in Middle Africa for 1957–1958

Country	Estimated total population 1957, thousands	Pupil enrollment, thousands			Estimated enrollment ratio		
		Primary	Secondary	Primary plus secondary	Primary, 5–14 age group	Secondary, 15–19 age group	Index of Emphasis
Belgian Congo*	13,124	1,572.8	61.3	1,634.1	49.5	4.5	11
British Somaliland	650	2.1	0.2	2.3	1.3	0.3	4.3
Cameroon	3,187	294.0	10.3	304.3	38.1	3.1	12.3
Central African Republic	1,140	45.8	1.5	47.3	16.6	1.3	12.8
Chad	2,580	32.6	0.7	33.3	5.2	0.3	17.7
Congo (Brazzaville)	762	79.0	3.4	82.4	42.7	4.3	9.9
Dahomey	1,715	75.4	2.8	78.2	18.2	1.6	11.4
Ethiopia	20,000	173.8	6.8	180.6	3.6	0.3	12.0
Gabon	410	39.8	1.2	41.0	4.0	2.8	14.3
Gambia	290	5.9	0.7	6.6	8.4	2.3	3.7
Ghana	4,763	468.0	146.9	614.9	40.6	29.7	1.4
Guinea	2,498	42.5	2.8	45.3	7.0	1.1	6.4
Ivory Coast	2,607	90.9	4.8	95.7	14.4	1.8	8.0
Kenya	6,254	548.0	16.5	564.5	36.2	2.5	14.5
Liberia	1,250	46.1	4.6	50.7	15.2	3.5	4.4
Malagasy Republic	4,930	321.5	20.4	341.9	26.9	4.0	6.7
Mauritania	630	6.5	0.3	6.8	4.3	0.5	8.6

Niger	2,450	11.8	0.4	12.2	2.0	0.2	10.0
Nigeria, Fed. of	33,995	2,498.5	96.2	2,594.7	30.4	2.7	11.3
Rhodesia and Nyasaland, Fed. of:†							
Northern Rhodesia	2,240	245.0	7.7	252.7	45.2	3.3	13.7
Nyasaland	2,650	266.1	2.3	268.4	41.5	0.8	51.9
Southern Rhodesia	2,560	439.2	19.2	458.4	70.8	7.2	9.8
Ruanda-Urundi‡	4,568	237.5	5.0	242.5	21.5	1.1	19.6
Senegal	2,280	80.5	6.1	86.6	14.6	2.6	5.6
Sierra Leone	2,120	61.9	7.4	69.3	12.1	3.4	3.6
Somaliland (It.)§	1,310	14.4	0.9	15.3	4.5	0.7	6.4
Sudan (Mali)	3,730	42.1	2.7	44.8	4.7	0.7	6.7
Tanganyika	8,760	374.3	48.7	423.0	17.7	5.3	3.3
Togo	1,093	70.6	2.1	72.7	26.7	1.8	14.8
Uganda	5,680	434.1	33.4	467.5	31.6	5.7	5.5
Upper Volta	3,380	40.5	2.4	42.9	5.0	0.7	7.1
Zanzibar and Pemba¶	285	16.2	1.2	17.4	23.5	4.0	5.9
Total	143,891	8,677.4	520.9	9,198.3	24.9	3.5	

* The Belgian Congo became the Congo Republic in 1960 (with its capital at Leopoldville).
† After seceding from the Federation, Nyasaland became independent and took the name Malawi in 1964.
‡ This former Belgian trust territory became independent in 1962 and split into two nations, Burundi and Rwanda.
§ In 1960 the Republic of Somalia was formed from the former British Somaliland and Italian Somalia.
¶ A union was formed between Zanzibar and Tanganyika in 1964.

SOURCE: Data taken from UNESCO, *World Trends in Secondary Education*, Paris, 1962, p. 37.
Reprinted from *World Survey of Education III: Secondary Education*.

schools and 8.6 per cent in higher education.)

In 1961 there were probably less than ten million of the fifty million African children and youth between the ages of five and nineteen enrolled in school. The great preponderance of those in school, possibly two-thirds, were boys. Not only do fewer girls than boys start school, but the dropout rate during the upper years of the primary and secondary school is greater for girls. In 1957, for example, based on data from twenty-nine tropical African countries, it was estimated that only one-fifth of the secondary school enrollment was girls.[53] Colonial policy, as in the Congo, which emphasized the education of boys because of their usefulness in industrial and commercial enterprises, lingering conservatism, and the inability to develop a concept of woman's new role in the changing African societies continue to thwart expansion of education for girls. Both the educational bias in favor of boys and the high dropout and failure rate indicate the pressing need for adequate programs of guidance and counseling—programs which would involve parents as well as students.

Because the problem of dropouts or "wastage" is unusually severe in the schools of tropical Africa, further comment on this phenomenon is in order. The general problem is pointed up by the great disparity in primary and secondary enrollment, as shown in Table 12. UNESCO data on education in tropical Africa further show that while "the enrollment of pupils in the first and second years of primary school is gen-

Table 13 *Kenya School Enrollments*

	Number of pupils, 1962
Standard I	159,800
Standard IV	148,200
Standard VI	61,000
Form I	2,700
Form IV	1,300

SOURCE: International Bank for Reconstruction and Development, *The Economic Development of Kenya,* Johns Hopkins Press, Baltimore, 1963.

erally 40 to 50 percent of the total enrollment" by the final grade of middle school (eighth school year) only 1.6 to 8.6 per cent of the total enrollment was still in attendance.[54] More detailed data are available on Kenya (4-4-4 school structure) and are presented in Table 13. The data in Table 13 somewhat exaggerate the dropout rate since more children begin school each year. Nevertheless, Kenya, one of the most educationally advanced countries of middle Africa, in 1962 enrolled only approximately 38 per cent as many pupils in Standard VI as in Standard I and less than 1 per cent as many in Form IV as in Standard I.[55]

It has been argued with respect to other tropical African countries as well as Uganda that only the poor students are eliminated and that all capable ones can find places in the secondary schools. Yet if this is true, one must conclude that either (1) educational or cultural deprivation is leaving African children ill-prepared for secondary or higher education or (2) the African is intellectually

[53] UNESCO, *World Trends in Secondary Education,* reprinted from *World Survey of Education III: Secondary Education,* Paris, 1962, p. 39.

[54] *Ibid.,* p. 40.

[55] International Bank for Reconstruction and Development, *The Economic Development of Kenya,* Johns Hopkins Press, Baltimore, 1963.

below the European. Since there is considerable evidence of the former and little of the latter,[56] it is safe to conclude that the problem of dropouts will lessen as the quality of primary instruction and the total cultural environment of the African are improved. Furthermore, one could, of course, question the validity of any educational system which set standards that would eliminate 90 per cent of the pupils between grade one and the junior secondary school.

All thirty-one of the institutions of higher education found in middle Africa in 1964 achieved their present status after 1945. These colleges and universities, many of which were outgrowths of lower-level missionary institutions, usually were modeled after the universities of the metropolitan powers. This is hardy surprising since most of the African universities were founded by colonial governments or missions; many have a "special relationship" to a metropolitan university, and Europeans outnumber Africans on the teaching staffs.[57]

Four basic weaknesses in African higher education have been identified as: (1) the lack of emphasis on African studies, (2) the minor attention given to the education of women, (3) the underutilization of existing university resources and equipment, and (4) the concentration of students in liberal arts.[58] By way of further explanation: Only recently have African universities given serious attention to the study of African history and culture; females constitute less than 10 per cent of university enrollment; the teacher-student ratio frequently is as low as 1:4 or 1:5, well below that of the wealthier American universities; and as Table 14 shows, considering technical manpower needs there is perhaps an overpreference among the students for "liberal" studies.

In addition to the African students studying in African universities, at least an equal number attend institutions of higher education in Europe, Asia, or North America. Since complete data on these students are unavailable, any analysis of the distribution of students by courses of study is impossible. However, if the distribution in Table 14 is roughly proportional to the total distribution, then at least two countries, the Malagasy Republic and Senegal, are plagued with a problem common to many underdeveloped areas, namely, an excessive number of law students. (At least one of the newly independent countries, Tanganyika, has a serious short-

---

[56] There appears to have been little serious study of the mental aptitudes of the African people. One study has been reported where use was made of the Culture Free Intelligence Test by R. B. Cattell. The results of this test showed a considerable gap in the mental aptitude of young African and American children, but this gap lessened and nearly disappeared among older school children. The high correlation between the test results and literacy forced the user to conclude that the test is not "culture free." See the International African Institute, London, *Social Implications of Industrialization and Urbanization in Africa South of the Sahara,* UNESCO, Paris, 1956, pp. 333–336.

[57] In five university colleges in British areas of influence there were 655 expatriate teachers in 1960 to 96 Africans. In all of middle Africa for the same year 1,572 of the 2,166 university teachers were ex-

patriates. See *Africa and the United States: Images and Realities,* United States National Commission for UNESCO, Eighth National Conference, Boston, 1961, p. 67; and A. M. Carr-Saunders, *Staffing African Universities,* The Overseas Development Institute, London, 1962.

[58] *Ibid.,* p. 70.

Table 14 *Higher Education Enrollments, by Study Areas, in Ten Middle African Countries*

Country	Total enrollment	Human- ities	Educa- tion	Fine arts	Law	Social sciences	Natural sciences	Engi- neering	Med- icine	Agri- culture
Belgian Congo§	398	41	58	—	41	91	54	37	61	15
Ghana	1,255	215	66†	75	93	323	116	226	56	85
Kenya	797	30	442‡	43	—	65	37	78	40	62
Malagasy Republic	424	30	—	—	282	—	112	—	—	—
Nigeria, Fed. of	1,984	529	117	91	—	272	631	146	176	22
Rhodesia and Nyasaland, Fed. of§	125	—	28	53	—	—	37	—	—	**7**
Senegal	1,458	317	5	—	576	21	312	14	178	35
Sierra Leone	371	108	91	—	—	105	57	10	—	—
Somaliland (It.)§	245	—	—	—	—	245	—	—	—	—
Uganda	837	282	78	22	—	7	246	14	101	87
Total*	7,894	1,552	885	284	992	1,129	1,602	525	612	313
Percentage	(100)	(20)	(11)	(4)	(12)	(14)	(20)	(7)	(8)	(4)

* The total number of students shown in each branch of study includes students from other countries and, in certain cases, students studying abroad.

† Students in faculties or schools attached to university in 1957. Excluding separately established teacher training colleges with some 3,900 students in 1957.

‡ Students in higher teacher training courses.

§ See Table 12 for information on changes in political status.

SOURCE: UNESCO, *World Trends in Secondary Education*, reprinted from *World Survey of Education III: Secondary Education.* Paris, 1962. p. 42.

age of lawyers.) Striking also is the small number of students in agriculture, considering the importance of this field of study.

Grim as the school enrollment figures may be in terms of the developmental plans and expectations of the people, the growth of enrollment over the past few years offers a more optimistic picture. From 1953 to 1957, enrollment in the primary schools of tropical Africa increased by 63 per cent while enrollment in secondary schools increased 72 per cent.[59] These rates of increase are considerably higher than the world averages and represent an accurate index of the educational drive of the African people.

Educational innovation and experimentation

African educators see their main goal as twofold. First, through a process of creating or borrowing and adapting, new educational patterns must be developed consistent with the ambitious economic goals. Secondly, the content of education and the attitudes, values, and moral purposes must be redirected in keeping with the cultural or social features common to the African nations.

In light of these two guidelines three areas were given immediate priority by African educators and international advisers at a UNESCO-sponsored conference in 1961: secondary education, curriculum reform, and teacher training.[60] Secondary education, as pointed out earlier, in most tropical African

[59] UNESCO, *World Trends in Secondary Education, op. cit.*, pp. 37–38.
[60] UNESCO, Conference of African States on the Development of Education in Africa, *op. cit.*, p. 11.

countries has not kept pace with the expansion of primary education, nor is it yet designed to meet current manpower needs. The curriculum reform envisaged, in keeping with the basic goal mentioned above, includes more attention to technical and agricultural education, taking care that changes should be within the context of "African social and cultural conditions." Fundamental to all expansion of enrollments or curriculum reform is an adequate supply of teachers; thus a "massive expansion of teacher training facilities" is required.[61]

In attempting to meet both the earlier educational priorities which tended to stress primary education and literacy and the newer ones outlined above, several experiments of note have begun to take shape. In one category are those attempts to hasten communication of ideas among both the school-going and the vast non-school-going segments of the population. A second category includes regional and international attempts to meet manpower needs. And a third category includes numerous and fascinating efforts of African and foreign scholars to identify and to a certain degree evaluate African cultural attainments in order to promote cultural revitalization.

One highly successful experiment which might fit into the first category has been the extension programs of colleges in certain of the English-speaking sections of Africa. These programs or "extramural work" are designed to offer general education to interested adults. Offerings include courses in African history, English literature, economics, local government, and the British constitution. Neither credit nor certificates are

[61] *Ibid.*

given for enrollment in these courses but attendance in general has been quite gratifying. Perhaps the extramural programs in Ghana serve as the best single national illustration.

An experiment utilizing adult education as a means of community development carried on by the Jeannes School near Nairobi, Kenya, has received international publicity. This institution, operated by the Kenya government, offers courses in "labor relations, village management, the running of recreational clubs, and shop-keeping, hygiene and homecrafts."[62] Women leaving the courses have been instrumental in establishing Women's Progress Clubs throughout the country. These clubs, which had a reported membership of 50,000 in 1961,[63] are dedicated to the improvement of family life, the betterment of community hygiene, and the advancement of civic interest and responsibilities. It is said that communities in which the clubs exist can be recognized by their cleanliness and attractiveness.

Other innovations used as multipliers of ideas include the radio, television, and programed learning. As early as 1948 the "saucepan" radio—a sturdy, cheap, shortwave radio set resembling a saucepan in shape—was put on the market in east and central Africa. The reaction of the initial purchasers was so favorable that soon a firm began mass production of the radio, thus making it available to tens of thousands of persons and causing one observer to liken the effect of the radio in Africa to the invention of printing in Europe. All the modern radio networks rapidly being established across middle Africa offer some educational programs. Television has been introduced and used experi-

mentally for educational purposes in Nigeria, Ghana, Mali, and elsewhere. Initial experimentation with programed learning in Nigeria may prove to be a forerunner of larger-scale testing of the utility of "teaching machines."

Quite obviously the traditional bush school and initiation ceremonies cannot satisfy the educational needs of developing Africa. Yet these institutions did perform a socializing role not accomplished in the imported European school. Interestingly, an experiment with residential colleges for adult education in West Africa in a sense provides a recreation of the bush school. But whereas the bush school taught about the tribe and fostered the *status quo*, the residential college deals with local problems in a national and international context and seeks to produce *les animateurs*.[64]

The enlarged role expected of colleges and universities in contemporary Africa can be seen in a report of the Conference on the Development of Higher Education in Africa held in Tananarive, Malagasy Republic, in September, 1962. In addition to the traditional functions of teaching and promoting scholarship, African institutions of higher education are expected:

1. To maintain adherence and loyalty to world academic standards;

2. To ensure the unification of Africa;

3. To encourage elucidation of and appreciation for African culture and heritage and to dispel misconceptions of Africa, through research and teaching of African studies;

4. To develop completely the human resources for meeting manpower needs;

[62] *Ibid.*
[63] *Ibid.*

[64] P. H. Bertelsen, "Folk Schools for West Africa," *International Development Review*, vol. 3, no. 3, p. 28, October, 1961.

5. To train the "whole man" for nation building;

6. To evolve over the years a truly African pattern of higher learning dedicated to Africa and its people yet promoting a bond of kinship to the larger human society.[65]

It obviously is no mean task to solve the problems of staffing, financing, and adapting a curriculum for higher education in order that these developmental functions may be performed. For example, the need for foreign college teachers is expected to rise to 7,000 by 1980, and by the same date expenditures are expected to amount to 357 million dollars over resources.[66] Analyses of these problems and some suggested solutions can be found in the source referred to above.

While most African nations have continued, with certain modifications, the higher education pattern most familiar —that of the colonial power—some attention has been given to universites in other parts of the world, such as the American land-grant university. The responsiveness of many American state universities to public needs and also, perhaps, their easy combination of teaching and research functions have impressed some African educational and political leaders. These qualities were influential, for example, in the decision of the Nigerian government to seek the assistance of Michigan State University in the establishment of a University of Nigeria. The influence of American higher education is likely to grow as the educational contact between Africa and the United States increases; yet any lasting African pattern of higher educa-

tion is certain to be of eclectic composition.

For political reasons, and since from the point of view of economic development it is perhaps the last major frontier in the world, Africa has received considerable attention from national and international technical assistance agencies. In addition to the cultural, scientific, economic, and educational work of the United Nations, scholarships are being offered to worthy Africans by dozens of private groups and by all major nations of the world. In 1963, for example, nearly eleven thousand Africans were studying in universities abroad. Furthermore, more than any other underdeveloped area, tropical Africa has sought foreign teachers and administrators—not only in advisory capacities but in the actual operation of the schools.

Among the more novel of the arrangements to fill the grave shortage of classroom teachers that exists in most of tropical Africa have been the Peace Corps projects sponsored by the American government and the Teachers for East Africa Project operated by Teachers College, Columbia University, but largely financed by the Agency for International Development. The Peace Corps, created in 1961, had by 1963 sent several hundred young people to Africa to work in a wide variety of technical and teaching jobs. The possible impact of these volunteers can be seen from the fact that in one nation, Nyasaland, the arrival of Peace Corps groups in 1963 increased the number of secondary school teachers available by 100 per cent. The Teachers College program is likewise of a size to make itself felt, having sent 270 American teachers to East Africa by 1963.

The first step in planning for eco-

[65] *The Development of Higher Education in Africa, op. cit.,* p. 19.

[66] *Ibid.,* pp. 32, 47.

nomic and social change is a thorough knowledge of a people's culture and personality. For this reason and for the somewhat less rational purposes often imposed by nationalistic or supranationalistic movements, there has recently been an upsurge of interest in African culture among African educators. Not only is the search on for the imprecise and somewhat romantic idea of "Negritude" or "the African personality" but more orthodox inquiry is being undertaken by African and foreign scholars who are probing into Africa's past and present to learn its contributions to philosophy, law, history, geography, art, and languages. The knowledge resulting from this research will contribute to a more Africanized curriculum and to the elimination of much of the meaningless imitation of European curricula.

But the search for identity has implications beyond alteration of the factual content of the school programs. A study of African culture may reveal an ideological base for Pan-Africanism which itself would provide emotional stimulus to cooperative planning and rapid development. More than this, however, Africans must be able to measure themselves —particularly their familial and temporal values—against the personal and social requisites of modernization. Only when the necessary new styles of living and new modes of thinking become definable can legitimate aims of education be formulated.

References

Books

Africa and the United States: Images and Realities, United States National Commission for UNESCO, Eighth National Conference, Boston, 1961.

The American Assembly: *The United States and Africa,* 1st ed., Background Papers Prepared for the Thirteenth American Assembly, New York, 1958.

Bascom, William R., and Melville J. Herskovits (eds.): *Continuity and Change in African Cultures,* The University of Chicago Press, Chicago, 1959.

Belgian Congo, 2 vols., Belgian Congo and Ruanda-Urundi Information and Public Relations Office, Brussels, 1959, 1960.

Busia, K. A.: *The Position of the Chief in the Modern Political System of Ashanti,* Oxford, Fair Lawn, N.J., 1951.

Cohen, Sir Andrew: *British Policy in Changing Africa,* Routledge, London, 1959.

Gluckman, Max: *Custom and Conflict in Africa,* Blackwell, Oxford, 1953.

Hailey, Lord William M.: *An African Survey,* rev. ed., Oxford, Fair Lawn, N.J., 1957.

Hall, Robert King, N. Hans, and J. A. Lauwerys (eds.): *The Year Book of Education: Technological Development,* prepared under the auspices of the University of London Institute of Education and Columbia University Teachers College, World, Tarrytown-on-Hudson, N.Y., 1954.

Hilliard, F. H.: *Short History of Education in British West Africa,* Thomas Nelson, London, 1957.

International African Institute: *Social Implications of Industrialization and Urbanization in Africa South of the Sahara,* UNESCO, Paris, 1956.

Investment in Education, The Report of the Commission on Post-school Certificate and Higher Education in Nigeria, Federal Ministry of Education, Lagos, Nigeria, 1960.

Kimble, George H. T.: *Tropical Africa,* 2 vols., Twentieth Century Fund, New York, 1960.

———: *Tropical Africa: Problems and Promises,* Headline Series no. 147,

Foreign Policy Association, New York, 1961.

Mason, R. J.: *British Education in Africa,* Oxford, Fair Lawn, N.J., 1959.

Ottenberg, Simon, and Phoebe Ottenberg (eds.): *Cultures and Societies of Africa,* Random House, New York, 1960.

Parker, Franklin: *African Development and Education in Southern Rhodesia,* Kappa Delta Pi International Education Monograph, Ohio State University Press, Columbus, Ohio, 1960.

Read, Margaret: *Africans and Their Schools,* Longmans, London, 1953.

————: *Children of Their Fathers,* Methuen, London, 1959.

Smythe, Hugh H., and Mabel M. Smythe: *The New Nigerian Elite,* Stanford, Stanford, Calif., 1960.

Southall, Aidan (ed.): *Social Change in Modern Africa,* Oxford, London, 1961.

A Study of Educational Policy and Practices in British West Africa, a report prepared on behalf of the Nuffield Foundation and the Colonial Office, Oxford, London, 1953.

Thompson, Virginia, and Richard Adloff: *The Emerging States of French Equatorial Africa,* Stanford, Stanford, Calif., 1960.

UNESCO: Conference of African States on the Development of Education in Africa, *Final Report,* United Nations Economic Commission for Africa, Addis Ababa, 1961.

————: *The Development of Higher Education in Africa,* Report of the Conference on the Development of Higher Education in Africa, Tananarive, Sept. 3–12, 1962, Paris, 1963.

————: *World Trends in Secondary Education,* Reprinted from *World Survey of Education III: Secondary Education,* Paris, 1962.

Wallbank, T. Walter: *Contemporary Africa: Continent in Transition,* Van Nostrand, Princeton, N.J., 1956.

Pamphlets and periodicals

African Abstracts, Bulletin Analytique Africaniste, International African Institute with Assistance of UNESCO, London, January, 1950.

African Affairs, French Embassy, Service de Press et d'Information, New York, May, 1958.

African Studies Bulletin, African Studies Association, New York, April, 1958 —.

The Annals of the American Academy of Political and Social Science, vol. 298, pp. 1–248, March, 1955.

Hodgkin, Thomas: "The Idea of an African University," *Universities Quarterly,* June, 1961, pp. 229–237.

Kimble, George H. T.: "Compelling Need: Education for Africans," *The New York Times Magazine,* Mar. 5, 1961, pp. 31ff.

Macintosh, D. H.: "Thoughts on the Education of Africans in a Senior Secondary School in Uganda," *International Review of Education,* vol. 4, no. 4, pp. 460–467, 1958.

Oversea Education, A Journal of Educational Experimentation and Research in Tropical and Subtropical Areas, London, 1929—.

Phi Delta Kappan, vol. 41, no. 4, pp. 137–200, January, 1960.

Seck, Assane: "Education in French West Africa," *Institute of International Education News Bulletin,* November, 1960, pp. 47–57.

Ward, Barbara: "The Emerging Africa," *The Atlantic,* vol. 203, no. 4, pp. 29–32, April, 1959.

The preceding accounts of representative educational patterns have provided an introduction to the comparative study of education. Hopefully, the reader now feels rewarded for his time and effort by having gained broader perspectives on various educational matters of concern to him. To some readers, however, this first look at education on an international basis may be a stepping-stone to further studies of a more specialized and penetrating nature, studies that are characteristic of specialists in this new but rapidly developing area of scholarly inquiry.

Comparative education has not as yet attained the status of a neatly defined discipline. The activities of those who declare themselves specialists in this field are not of one kind. Some indication of how widely they range may be found by glancing through a few issues of *Comparative Education Review,* a leading journal in the field. Titles of papers published recently have ranged from "The Education of Don Quixote"[1] and "School Psychology in Germany"[2] to "The Rise of Soviet Athletics."[3] Apparently each has been accepted as a legitimate contribution to the growing body of literature. One may assume,

therefore, that a decision as to where a new study should begin or what study procedures should be employed need not as yet be narrowly restricted.[4]

The wide range of interests and the variety of methods of study currently encountered in comparative education were referred to in Chapter 1. We may conclude that the historical-descriptive studies, although they no longer overwhelmingly dominate the field, are still popular and highly useful. Indeed, an account of the origins and present status of education in a given nation or among a given people is virtually indispensable to the projection of plans for its improvement or even to the investigation of a special facet of its cultural or social significance. An inventory of the literature will show that little is known of education in countries other than the major Western powers; yet many other nations, even some such as Albania and Portugal, which have a long history, today are emerging as forces to be reckoned with on the international scene. Knowledge of their cultures and present social commitments is sorely needed, and any historical-descriptive studies, particularly by qualified persons who may have ethnic ties to such countries, could become highly valuable contributions.

A second category of studies requires a problems approach. By focusing upon a specific need, such as the elimination

[1] Juan Estarella, "The Education of Don Quixote," *Comparative Education Review,* vol. 6, no. 1, pp. 25–33, June, 1962.

[2] Helmut Hoffmann, "School Psychology in Germany," *Comparative Education Review,* vol. 3, no. 1, pp. 23–26, June, 1959.

[3] Joseph A. Marchiony, "The Rise of Soviet Athletics," *Comparative Education Review,* vol. 7, no. 1, pp. 17–27, June, 1963.

[4] Pedro Rosselló, "Concerning the Structure of Comparative Education," *Comparative Education Review,* vol. 7, no. 2, pp. 103–107, October, 1963.

of illiteracy or the conversion of the working force from tribal agriculture to technical industry, cross-national comparisons may be made of the educational methods by which such transformations are attempted. Entire national systems need not be examined, but only the aspects which have direct bearing on the problem at hand. Since the circumstances under which the problem arises and the practices that are employed to cope with it have an impact upon society as a whole, cross-national studies should be firmly grounded in the research methodologies developed by the social scientists. The disciplines of anthropology and sociology, as well as of economics, appear to be especially valuable for these purposes.

Sociological interest is evident in studies that seek to discover causal relationships or functional correlations between educational and social variables. Since individuals, whether members of a highly sophisticated or of a newly developing group, ordinarily are reluctant to serve as subjects in an experimental study, the social scientist must often make his observations in situations where the variables are operative without his intervention or are beyond his control. In many cases the significance of the variables can only be estimated by making cross-national or cross-cultural comparisons. In other cases comparisons may be made of different stages in the development of a single culture or group. By employing the latter technique, anthropologists have studied how values are transmitted from one generation to the next and what happens to value patterns as social groups undergo transition. Educational sociologists, on the other hand, have been interested in studying the relation-

ships between education and social mobility, vocational aspirations and attitudes of teachers and those of students, causes of school dropouts and what encourages school retention, and the like. Economists are likely to look for relationships between general educational level of the population and productive capacity of their economy, or how changes in educational level will affect economic development.

Studies of these types obviously can be very useful in predicting the impact of improved educational facilities and services in newly developing areas. Political leaders planning for such development need to know what the potentialities of education are as an agent of development; what the educational pyramid—the proportions of the population receiving formal schooling at the various levels—should look like at successive stages of development; and how the educational programs may, or even must, be altered in the light of changing manpower requirements. As previously stated, the successful investigation of these and similar problems calls for specialized training in the research methodologies of the contributing disciplines.

Yet this field of study has to do first and foremost with education, and every educational activity is in essence a deliberate effort to change the behavior of people. Such efforts now generally are complex operations that have as their constituent elements philosophically derived goals or commitments, structured curricula and practices, and administrative controls. In bringing about improvements the educator must ultimately deal with politicians and government officials, and he will be expected to speak with authority on questions relating to the formulation of educational policies and to have at hand reliable information to guide decisions on how much and what kinds of education a particular policy will require. Professional educators are called upon to provide information of this kind in comparative studies of educational theories, systems, structures and organizations, curricula, and methods.[5] And when such topics are studied cross-nationally and cross-culturally, the needed information is likely to become available in its most illuminating form.

It would appear from the foregoing that an invitation to further study in comparative education is almost a *carte blanche* invitation to investigate any aspect or problem of education as long as at some stage it is viewed in a foreign cultural setting. A comparative dimension is provided in such studies even when no overt comparisons are made, since the data are seen to be similar or different from those with which the researcher or reader is already familiar. Indeed, some very illuminating comparisons are made between two different periods in the evolution of the same system.[6] Nevertheless, a student wishing to proceed further in his study will need direction in selecting the systems, topics, or problems which promise to yield rewarding results.

An initial step in identifying worthwhile studies might be to look for classification arrangements that provide significant categories for cross-national or cross-cultural comparisons. Since no single classification system has been established to the exclusion of others, a choice is also available in this matter.

Anderson[7] has suggested that societies might be classified as:

1. Peasant or industrial
2. Democratic or authoritarian
3. Rural or urban

He did not imply that these six categories are mutually exclusive, but rather that an investigator could select one of the three pairs of categories depending upon whether his primary interest lay in economics, philosophy, or sociology.

By way of illustration, a philosophically oriented student might conclude that the most illuminating information is derived from comparing democratic systems with authoritarian systems. He would then classify systems with respect to how the individual is regarded in the social structure. Stated in a somewhat oversimplified manner, the question would be whether the individual were looked upon as a "citizen" or as a "subject." In systems of the first type the educative process could be expected to interpret social conventions and institutional arrangements as resources by which the people could attain their individual expectations. In the second case, education would be an agency of the existing power structure by which the new members of society were informed of their appointed places and prepared to play their assigned roles. In the first category would be placed the societies whose institutions and arrangements were subordinate to the will of the people; in the other category would be societies whose peoples were subordinate to the established order and were expected to be satisfied only as the system

---

[5] *Ibid.*, pp. 104–106.
[6] Rosselló refers to these as "dynamic" studies as contrasted with "static" studies. *Ibid.*, p. 107.

[7] C. Arnold Anderson, "The Utility of Societal Typologies in Comparative Education," *Comparative Education Review*, vol. 3, no. 1, pp. 20–22, June, 1959.

itself first attained a high level of order and prosperity. The student might note for further study that either type of education could function effectively when its social climate was consistent with its goals, but that neither existed for long in a climate committed to opposite goals or values.

After having identified representative members of each of the two opposing categories, the student might then proceed to make comparisons with respect to specific features according to his interests. For example, would economic goals play a more prominent role in determining group policy in one category than in the other? Would a centralized system of educational administration, as opposed to a decentralized system, more likely be encountered in one group than in the other? What about the prescription of a particular system of theological or political beliefs as a part of the required programs of study? Would there be differences with respect to the controls exercised over private schools or even the freedom of parents to visit the schools attended by their children?

Assuming that the democratic-authoritarian dichotomy were still employed, the student might note that the Comparative Education Society in Europe, meeting in Amsterdam in June, 1963, identified equality of educational opportunity and reorganization of secondary education, particularly the junior-senior cycle, as the two aspects of education calling most urgently for study;[8] that the persistence of social class differences was the one most important remaining

barrier to equal educational opportunities; and that much new information was needed with respect to both the means presently employed and the results achieved by the various individuals and groups engaged in seeking reforms. In view of the importance attached to the elimination of class differences, studies should be made of the possible relationships between the persistence of such differences and the existence of language-dominated curricula, external examinations, segregated schools,[9] tuition fees, and centralized administrative controls. The apparent roles of an established religion, of compulsory religious instruction, or of a prescribed political doctrine might also be studied in this connection.

Using the peasant-industrial dichotomy suggested by Anderson would lead to other considerations. Educational planners in newly emerging nations need to know whether economic development progresses more rapidly in social systems where rigid controls are exercised over the training opportunities afforded the potential labor force, usually by means of competitive admission examinations and fixed quotas, than in those which permit free choices and merely seek to provide opportunities in response to popular demands. Information is also needed on what value changes have occurred in societies where substantial progress in the transformation to industrial status has already been made and how the changes have been brought about. Comparative studies are needed to determine the relative importance of universal elementary instruction as opposed to some comprehensive even

[8] Denis Kallen, "The Present Status of Comparative Education in Europe," *Comparative Education Review*, vol. 7, no. 2, pp. 108–112, October, 1963.

[9] Children may be segregated in schools on a variety of bases, such as religion, sex, social class, race, and vocational objective.

though selective secondary education, as agencies for development where economic limitations require that a choice must be made. The relative merits of sending native youths abroad to study for future leadership responsibilities as opposed to accepting foreign aid in establishing training schools on native soil perhaps also needs to be studied in a comparative manner.

The dynamic study, which to date seems to have been used very little, might also yield new knowledge of considerable value to educational planners. This is the method of comparing two separate periods in the development of a given system, particularly a system that has achieved a substantial transformation under circumstances not unlike those faced by social groups contemplating such a transition. A study of one of the Southern states in the United States in the transition from pre-World War II to the postwar period might be quite useful. Studies of Canton Bern in Switzerland, or of Pakistan, in the same periods should also be illuminating. Perhaps the most promising study of this type would be one on Japan because of the "induced" educational and economic changes achieved there during the latter half of the nineteenth century. Studies of this type might provide answers to the perplexing questions of what kinds of education are needed at various stages of development and, equally important, in what ways and to what extent the introduction of modern education may be disruptive. The problems of a transitional education seem to arise, in part, from the fact that the normal socialization process which is operative in any stable society, even a preliterate one, wherein cognitive, affective, and instrumental learnings remain well integrated,

is disrupted by the transition. Dynamic studies might show whether it is possible for societies facing modernization pressures to develop an educational process which will retain the advantages of the existing processes of socialization throughout the period of transition.

The classification dichotomies suggested by Anderson as bases for grouping societies for the purpose of making comparative studies are only three of many that have been suggested in recent years. Another proposal is that instead of grouping societies, a more useful arrangement would be to group educational systems or even educational processes. A group of European experts has proposed that educational data be grouped for descriptive as well as comparative purposes according to whether they pertain to (1) regulatory factors, (2) school factors, or (3) out-of-school activities.[10] Other classification arrangements, employing categories borrowed rather directly from sociology, have been proposed to facilitate cross-cultural analyses of educational institutions or processes. Such systems range from the simple categories suggested by Bone[11] to the detailed groupings of Henry.[12] Obviously, many different frameworks could be established. The specific classification system employed, if indeed one is employed at all, should depend upon

[10] Bryan Holmes and S. B. Robinsohn, *Relevant Data in Comparative Education,* UNESCO, Institute of Education, Hamburg, 1963, p. 25.

[11] Louis W. Bone, "Sociological Framework for Comparative Study of Educational Systems," *Comparative Education Review,* vol. 4, no. 2, pp. 121–126, October, 1960.

[12] Jules Henry, "A Cross-cultural Outline of Education," *Current Anthropology,* vol. 1, no. 4, pp. 267–305, July, 1960.

the nature of the problem and the purpose for which it is studied.

This very brief and fragmentary account of the interests and activities of specialists in comparative education should indicate that much work remains to be done and that a long list of questions remains to be answered. The search must continue for new patterns of education that will more adequately meet the rising expectations of peoples as individuals and the requirements of the various systems for effecting social controls to which they give their support. Efforts to describe more accurately and in greater detail the effects of educational investments upon the individual, the economy, and the state must be pressed with increasing vigor. It is reassuring to know that research techniques and other tools of inquiry, though still imperfect, are being improved. Even the present lack of precise delimitations of the field of study should challenge, rather than discourage, those who are willing to accept the invitation to further study.

Index

Beauchamp, George, 109
Beck, Robert, 75
Becker, Carl, 107
Becker, H., 107
Bedford College for Women, 156
Belgian colonial policies, 431, 438–440
  in Africa, 431, 438–440
  modified differentiation, 438
Belgian educational policies in Africa, 438–440
  curriculum, 439–440
  influence of Christian missionaries, 439
  organization of school system, 439
  primary education, 438
Belgium, 27, 202, 210–213
Benedict, Ruth, 6
Benjamin, Harold, 22, 200
Bentham, Jeremy, 360
Bereday, George Z. F., 200
Berlin, educational innovations in, 84
  University of, 88, 94, 96, 229, 237
Berlin Conference of 1884–1885, 431
Bertrand, Louis, 74
Bharat (the New India), 387
Bible reading, importance of, for Protestants, 79
Bidwell, C. A., 242
Bishop's schools, 30
Bismarck, Otto von, 79, 83–84, 87, 99, 120, 220
Blonsky, Paul, 184
Board of education, in England, 160–161, 163, 165
  in Japan, 318–323
Board schools in England, 151
Boarding schools, in China, 290
  in Germany, 88
  in Soviet Union, 195, 197
Boards, of education in Spain, 65
  of managers in English voluntary schools, 152–153
Bodenman, Paul, 108
Bohemia, 37, 78
Bolívar, Simón, 360

Bolivia, 355, 361–363, 380–381
Bologna, University of, 34, 40, 140
Bolsheviks, 177, 199
Bonaparte, Joseph, 60
Bone, Louis W., 462
Book of Filial Piety, 302–306
Books of Moses, 11
Borghi, Lamberto, 209, 241
Borough-county councils in England, 160
Borough Road College, 147
Bougle, Celestin, 137
Bowen, James, 178, 200
Bowles, Frank H., 137
Brahma, 388
Brandenburg, Reformation in, 78
Brauer, George C., 170
Brave, Vinoba, 401
Brazil, 355–362, 364, 366, 369, 374, 382–383
Brenan, Gerald, 61, 74
Brickman, William, 200
Brinton, Clarence Crane, 47
British colonial policies, 431–435
  in Africa, 431–435
  doctrine of differentiation, 432, 433
  "indirect rule," 432, 435
British East India Company, 394–397
  educational policies of, 395–397
  and mission education, 395
British educational policies in Africa, administration and control, 434
  curriculum, 434
  evaluation of, 447
  expenditure and finance, 434–435, 437
  external examination, 434
  use of vernacular, 433–434
British and Foreign School Society, 147–148, 150–151
Brothers of the Christian Schools, 114
Browne, George Stephenson, 7, 22
Bruun, Geoffrey, 241
Buddhism, 247–248, 250, 255, 258, 262

Buddhism, in China, 265
  compared with Confucianism, 265
  Four Noble Truths, 392
  in India, 392
  in Japan, 298–301, 311
Bugenhagen, John, 219
Buisson, Ferdinand E., 137
Bulgaria, 37
Burckhardt, Jakob, 29, 47
Bureaucracy in Prussia, 83–84
Burgherschule, 90, 92
Burgundy, 210
Bushi (*see* Bushido)
Bushido (Way of the warrior), 248, 303–308
  education and training, 304
Butts, R. Freeman, 242

Calatrava, Order of, 50
Calvin, John, 46, 78, 226–227
Calvinists, in American colonies, 235
  in England, 149
  in France, 113
  in Low Countries, 211
  in Switzerland, 227
Cambridge University, 40, 140–141, 143, 152–153
Canterbury, Archbishop of, 140
Canton, in French government, 122–123
  in Swiss government, 225, 230
Capetian dynasty in France, 110–112
Carlson, Marjorie, 75
Carolingian revival of learning, 30
Casati Law, 204–207
Cassidy, Francis P., 74
Caste in India, 389
  and education, 390, 392
  and social change, 403
Castiglione, Count Baldassare, 47
Castile, Kingdom of, 49, 51, 53
Castillejo, Jose, 74
Catalans, 65
Catechetical schools, 157

DATE DUE